A HISTORY OF SOVIET RUSSIA

A HISTORY OF SOVIET RUSSIA

by E. H. Carr

in fourteen volumes

*with R. W. Davies

SOCIALISM IN ONE COUNTRY

1924-1926

BY

E. H. CARR

Fellow of Trinity College, Cambridge

VOLUME TWO

First published 1959
Reprinted 1965, 1978

Published by
THE MACMILLAN PRESS LTD
London and Basingstoke
Associated companies in Delhi
Dublin Hong Kong Johannesburg Lagos
Melbourne New York Singapore Tokyo

Printed in Hong Kong by
CHINA TRANSLATION AND PRINTING SERVICES

British Library Cataloguing in Publication Data

Carr, Edward Hallett
    Socialism in one country, 1924–1926
    Vol. 2. — (Carr, Edward Hallett. History of Soviet
    Russia; 6)
    1. Russia — Social conditions — 1917–
    I. Title
    309.1′47′0842   HN523

ISBN 0–333–07161–1
ISBN 0–333–24216–5   Boxed set

PREFACE

THE general arrangement of the three volumes to be published
under the title *Socialism in One Country, 1924-1926*, of which the
present is the second, was explained in the preface to the first of
these volumes published last year. Since I worked on the first
and second volumes more or less simultaneously, the record in
that preface of the names of friends and scholars to whom I had
been especially indebted for advice, assistance and encouragement,
and of the libraries and institutions which had supplied me with
much of my material, applies equally to the present volume ; and
I need only here reiterate the very warm thanks which I continue
to owe to all of them.

I should, however, like to take this opportunity of adding
some further names. Professor Yuzuru Taniuchi, Professor of
Political Science and Public Administration in the University of
Nagoya, who is engaged in a detailed study of Soviet local govern-
ment, has given me valuable assistance in the chapters on
Regionalization and on the Revitalization of the Soviets. Dr.
J. M. Meijer, head of the Russian division of the International
Instituut voor Sociale Geschiedenis at Amsterdam, helped me
with important material for the chapter on the Red Army, and
Dr. R. M. Slusser of the Hoover Library, Stanford, for the
chapter on Order and Security ; in the section on party education,
I have drawn on an unpublished thesis on the subject written by
Mr. Zev Katz in the London School of Economics. To all of
these I express my sincere thanks. I am also particularly grateful
to Professor Merle Fainsod for having allowed me, while I was at
Harvard early in 1957, to inspect the "Smolensk archives" on
which he was working. The magnitude of the archives would in
any event have prevented my investigating them in detail ; and
what I saw confirmed the impression that their major value is for
periods later than 1926. But I was able to dip into a few files of
special interest to me, and found some points which are recorded
in footnotes in the present volume. Professor Fainsod's book,

Smolensk under Soviet Rule, which contains a description of the archives, unfortunately came out too late for me to use.

Certain technical points should be noted here. References in the footnotes to "Vol. 1" relate to Vol. 1 of *Socialism in One Country, 1924–1926* ; the two previous instalments of the History, *The Bolshevik Revolution, 1917–1923*, and *The Interregnum, 1923–1924*, are quoted by their titles. To save space, I have not repeated the list of abbreviations which appeared at the end of Vol. 1 : I have merely listed a few abbreviations which appear for the first time in Vol. 2. Dr. I. Neustadt has once again supplied the index. A bibliography will appear at the end of Vol. 3 ; progress on this volume has been somewhat delayed by illness, but I hope to complete it next year.

The main burden of typing this volume has been most efficiently borne by Miss Jean Fyfe.

E. H. CARR

May 4, 1959

CONTENTS

PART III

THE STRUGGLE IN THE PARTY

PART IV

THE SOVIET ORDER

PART III

THE STRUGGLE IN THE PARTY

LESSONS OF OCTOBER

T HE summer months of 1924 were marked by the usual seasonal respite in political strife, while both sides prepared for a renewal of the struggle in the autumn. The thirteenth party congress in May had not only confirmed and registered the defeat of Trotsky and of the opposition of 1923, but had added its quota of encouragement to the cult of Lenin spontaneously initiated after the leader's death. The word " Leninism " crept unnoticed into the party vocabulary, together with the honorific epithet " Leninist " as applied to the " Lenin enrolment " and " Leninist pioneers ".[1] In June 1924, when the fifth congress of Comintern assembled in Moscow, the delegates marched in solemn procession to the newly constructed Lenin mausoleum in the Red Square, and listened to commemorative addresses by Kalinin, Ruth Fischer and Roy, whose speech ended with the words " Long live Leninism ! "[2] A month later the Russian Communist League of Youth (Komsomol) held its sixth regular congress, and decided to change its name to " Russian Leninist Communist League of Youth ". The decision was unanimous, though Krupskaya in her speech at the congress recalled that Lenin had often used the word *ikon* in a derogatory sense, saying of a revolutionary who was honoured, but no longer had any influence : " Well, he is already an *ikon* ".[3] The Lenin mausoleum containing Lenin's embalmed body was opened to visitors on August 1, 1924.[4] Petrograd had been renamed Leningrad

---

[1] See *The Interregnum, 1923–1924*, pp. 354, 361.

[2] *Protokoll : Fünfter Kongress der Kommunistischen Internationale* (n.d.), i, 30-39.

[3] *Shestoi S"ezd Rossiiskogo Leninskogo Kommunisticheskogo Soyuza Molodezhi* (1924), p. 13.

[4] *Leningradskaya Pravda*, August 1, 1924. In the outlying regions of the USSR the cult spontaneously assumed exotic forms. Legends of Lenin in prose and verse current in Central Asia are collected in *Krasnaya Nov'*, No. 7,

immediately after Lenin's death; in May 1924, before the party congress, Simbirsk, Lenin's birth-place, was renamed Ulyanovsk.[1] These tributes to the dead leader had a surprising sequel, which seems to have been little noticed at the time. In June 1924 Yuzovka, an iron and steel town in the Ukraine, originally named after a British ironmaster who had no doubt founded the works, was renamed Stalinsk; the neighbouring railway station, known as Yuzovo, became Stalino.[2] It was not till September 1924 that Elizavetgrad, also in the Ukraine, was named Zinovievsk; and in the same month two other towns, Bakhmut and Ekaterinburg, were renamed, in honour of dead party leaders, Artemovsk and Sverdlovsk respectively.[3] The conversion of Tsaritsyn, the scene of a famous civil war clash between Trotsky and Stalin, into Stalingrad came only in April 1925.[4]

Two minor episodes occurred during the summer of 1924. In a speech to a party meeting in Moscow, after the thirteenth party congress, Stalin went out of his way to join issue with both his fellow triumvirs on points of party orthodoxy. He good-humouredly derided Kamenev by name for having at the congress misquoted Lenin's famous remark about the transformation of NEP Russia into socialist Russia. Kamenev had represented Lenin as speaking of " nepman Russia "; and this slip Stalin pompously attributed to " habitual carelessness in regard to questions of theory ". He went on to dissociate himself more sharply, though without mentioning Zinoviev's name, from the doctrine enunciated by Zinoviev with some emphasis a year earlier of " the dictatorship of the party " : this he bluntly called " nonsense ".[5] The motives of this deliberately provocative gesture are

September 1925, pp. 306-309, No. 6, June 1926, pp. 188-201 ; the favourite theme was to depict him as a liberator sent by Allah to make people happy. The Transcaucasian SFSR issued a decree in February 1925 prohibiting the sale and distribution of representations of Lenin in painting or sculpture except with the approval of the Narkompros of the republic concerned (*Sobranie Uzakonenii Zakavkazskoi SFSR, 1925*, No. 2, art. 359) ; a year later a further decree required the submission to the presidium of TsIK of the Transcaucasian SFSR of all projects to erect monuments to " revolutionary leaders or other persons " on the territory of the republic (*id. 1926*, No. 5, art. 651).

[1] *Sistematicheskoe Sobranie Deistvuyushchikh Zakonov SSSR*, i (1926), 278-279.   [2] *Ibid.* i, 280.

[3] *Sobranie Zakonov, 1924*, No. 8, art. 83 ; No. 11, art. 108 ; No. 25, art. 209.

[4] *Sobranie Zakonov, 1925*, No. 25, art. 171.

[5] Stalin, *Sochineniya*, vi, 257-258 ; for the history of the phrase " dictatorship of the party " see *The Bolshevik Revolution, 1917-1923*, Vol. 1, pp. 230-232.

difficult to assess. Discussion of minor differences between party members was still at this time relatively free. Stalin's criticism of his colleagues was less significant than it would have been at a later date. He was feeling his ground, and was ready to retreat when he found that he had gone too far. Nobody minded the baiting of Kamenev. But Zinoviev, whose vanity was more vulnerable, succeeded, apparently after some delay, in arraigning Stalin before an informal meeting of leading party members and securing a disavowal of his heresy. Stalin submitted; and a full-page anonymous article written by Zinoviev was published in the press reaffirming the true doctrine of the dictatorship of the proletariat and the dictatorship of the party. It was headed with the three passages in which Lenin had used the phrase, and concluded that " the doctrine of the rôle of the party " was " the most important constituent part of Leninism ".[1] The dispute had no sequel. It was by this time more urgent to close the ranks against an expected new offensive by Trotsky than to pay off scores between members of the triumvirate.

The other event which followed hard on the thirteenth party congress was the publication of Trotsky's commemorative pamphlet On Lenin. It was distasteful to the other party leaders in two respects. In the first place, it was not a biography of Lenin, but rather a sketch of Trotsky's personal relations with him, which inevitably created, and was consciously or unconsciously designed to create, an impression of the nearness of Lenin to Trotsky and of a distance between him and the other leading Bolsheviks.[2] Secondly, while it treated Lenin in terms of affectionate respect, the writer and the subject of the sketch were clearly placed on terms of equality incompatible with the attitude of veneration of the dead leader which was rapidly becoming the rule in party circles; Zinoviev in a speech delivered a few days after publication of the pamphlet referred indignantly to the way

[1] The article was published in Pravda, August 23, 1924. Zinoviev's account of the condemnation and submission of Stalin, who at one point is said to have tendered his resignation, was given to the fourteenth party congress in December 1925 (XIV S"ezd Vsesoyuznoi Kommunisticheskoi Partii (B), pp. 454-455), and not contradicted; the meeting which passed the verdict, and was attended, according to Zinoviev, by " 15 or 17 " party members, was probably identical with the meeting of August 17-19, 1924, described p. 6 below.

[2] This point was emphasized in an enthusiastic review by one of Trotsky's supporters in Krasnaya Nov', No. 4 (21), June-July 1924, pp. 341-343.

in which Trotsky had equated his own error at Brest-Litovsk with Lenin's error in supporting the advance on Warsaw two years later.[1] At a later date the pamphlet became a minor target in the party controversy, and attacks were also directed against a speech in which Trotsky had somewhat rhetorically contrasted Lenin the man of action with Marx the theorist.[2] But the gravamen of the charge was that Trotsky, in purporting to glorify Lenin, had glorified himself by representing himself as the equal partner and coadjutor of the great leader. In particular, he had depicted himself as playing a decisive rôle in the organization of the October *coup*, and Lenin as turning readily to him for advice : even the title of People's Commissar and the name of Sovnarkom had issued from Trotsky's fertile brain.[3]

After Trotsky's declaration of submission at the thirteenth party congress in May 1924,[4] he remained silent throughout the summer on the issues which divided him from the other leaders. When in June he was specifically invited by the presidium of the fifth congress of Comintern to open a debate on the differences in the Russian party, he declined on the ground that the discussion had been closed by the decision of the party congress.[5] But, in spite of this discretion, fear of what Trotsky might do still haunted the triumvirate. In the middle of August, nineteen members of the party central committee (if Zinoviev's count is correct) met in a three-day session to discuss tactics.[6] The only decision known to have been taken was to set up a septemvirate

---

[1] *Leningradskaya Pravda*, June 13, 1924.

[2] The speech, delivered on April 21, 1924, is in L. Trotsky, *Zapad i Vostok* (1924), pp. 30-41 ; this and other more abstruse points were taken up in an article in *Bol'shevik*, No. 2, January 31, 1925, pp. 9-23.

[3] Vardin, a Leningrad party official and follower of Zinoviev (see p. 80, note 3 below), reviewed the pamphlet with ironical politeness in *Bol'shevik*, No. 10, September 5, 1924, pp. 80-85, accusing Trotsky of concealing his past differences with Lenin and with Bolshevism, hinting at self-glorification, and convicting him of various errors : Trotsky replied at length *ibid.*, No. 12-13, October 20, 1924, pp. 92-104, and was answered editorially, *ibid.* pp. 105-109.

[4] See *The Interregnum, 1923-1924*, pp. 363-364.

[5] *Protokoll : Fünfter Kongress der Kommunistischen Internationale* (n.d.), ii, 583, 619.

[6] Information about this meeting is contained in a statement of Zinoviev to the party central committee of July 1926 preserved in the Trotsky archives. Leaders of first or second rank absent from Zinoviev's list of those present were Kalinin, Molotov, Yaroslavsky, Dzerzhinsky and Frunze·; these may have been on holiday, or the list may well be incomplete.

consisting of the six members of the Politburo, excluding Trotsky, and Kuibyshev, together with Molotov, Yaroslavsky, Rudzutak, Dzerzhinsky and Frunze as candidate members of the group.[1] This septemvirate effectively replaced the Politburo, which was hamstrung so long as Trotsky belonged to it, for the next two years, and formed the general staff of the anti-Trotsky campaign. Throughout the summer pinpricks against Trotsky were the order of the day among party leaders,[2] but no concerted action was undertaken. The isolation of Trotsky was carried some steps further. In April Frunze, a staunch supporter of the triumvirate and an antagonist of Trotsky in military doctrine, had succeeded Sklyansky as Deputy People's Commissar for War.[3] In September Trotsky's private secretary Glazman, persecuted or threatened by the party authorities for his association with Trotsky, committed suicide.[4]

From this point the struggle moved forward to a climax which neither side foresaw or deliberately planned. In the battle between Trotsky and the triumvirate, provocation from each side in turn incited the other to fresh extravagances, and both were responsible for a growing intransigence and bitterness which was inherent in the situation from the start. But most of the calculation was done by the triumvirs, who were fully conscious of their aim and consistent in their pursuit of it. Trotsky's behaviour, on the other hand, was often governed by an intellectual passion for debate and, later, by the blindness of anger and desperation. After the Bolshevik victory had been won, current preoccupations caused the disputes which had preceded it to be forgotten or ignored in the party. When in 1922 Trotsky republished a collection of his earlier articles under the title *1905*, and added a note referring to the " ideological re-equipment " of Bolshevism undertaken by Lenin in the spring of 1917, he plainly implied that Lenin had rallied in the " April theses " to Trotsky's original standpoint,

[1] Trotsky refers to the group as a " secret politburo " of seven (L. Trotsky, *Moya Zhizn'* (Berlin, 1930), ii, 240).

[2] See, for example, L. Kamenev, *Stat'i i Rechi*, x (1927), 256 ; A. I. Rykov, *Sochineniya*, iii (1929), 110 ; Semashko in *Izvestiya*, August 21, 1924.

[3] For the place of military questions in the campaign against Trotsky see pp. 382-391, 394-398 below.

[4] His suicide is referred to in L. Trotsky, *Moya Zhizn'* (Berlin, 1930), ii, 149, 295 ; *id. Stalin* (N.Y., 1946), p. 390 ; no details are on record.

and hinted at the reluctance of other Bolsheviks to follow Lenin
at that time.[1] But the publication excited no interest among the
other leaders, and passed without comment or reply. Nobody
but Trotsky cared to rake over these ashes of dead controversies.
In the winter of 1923–1924 a new stage began when Stalin contested Trotsky's credentials as " an old Bolshevik ", and Zinoviev
referred to " Trotskyism " as " a definite tendency in the Russian
workers' movement "; the reference to the significance of
Trotsky's " non-Bolshevism " in Lenin's testament, even with
the proviso that it should not be " used against " him, inevitably
seemed to legitimize the process of delving into Trotsky's past.
But, if the skeletons in Trotsky's cupboard were to be exposed,
he could hardly be expected not to retaliate. " If the question
is to be put on the plane of biographical investigations ", he had
written ominously in December 1923, " then it must be done
properly." [2] In the pamphlet of June 1924 *On Lenin*, some con-
ventions of forbearance were still observed. " The dissensions
which came to an open break in the October days ", as well as
the disputes over the April theses, were mentioned. But none
of those implicated was named. In the autumn, provoked by the
further pinpricks of the past few months, Trotsky cast aside all
restraint and launched an open attack on his persecutors.

The year 1924 had seen a beginning of the publication of the
collected works of Zinoviev and of Trotsky.[3] The third volume
of Trotsky's writings, which was devoted to articles and speeches
of 1917, was due for publication in October 1924. In September
Trotsky, then on holiday in Kislovodsk, wrote a lengthy article
with the title *Lessons of October*, which was published by way of an
afterthought as a preface to the volume.[4] The tone was set, for
those in the know, by the appearance on the first page of two

---

[1] See *The Bolshevik Revolution, 1917–1923*, Vol. 1, p. 59, note 3.
[2] See *The Interregnum, 1923–1924*, p. 331.
[3] Six volumes of Zinoviev's works (G. Zinoviev, *Sobranie Sochinenii*, i-iii,
v, xv-xvi) appeared in 1924 ; the preface to the first was dated October 1923.
Three volumes of Trotsky's works appeared in the same year ; according to
an undated letter to Ryazanov in the Trotsky archives, Trotsky's contract with
Gosizdat provided that Gosizdat should pay the editors and copyists, but that
he should receive nothing himself.
[4] *Lessons of October*, dated " Kislovodsk, September 15, 1924 ", was printed
with separate pagination (Trotsky, *Sochineniya*, iii, i, pp. xi-lxvii) ; the body
of the volume had evidently been set up first.

phrases borrowed almost textually from Lenin's testament. The differences which had arisen in October 1917 were described as " profound and not at all accidental " ; but " it would be too petty to attempt to use them now, several years later, as a weapon against those who then went astray ". The defeats of the past year in Bulgaria and in Germany showed the disastrous result of neglecting the lessons that could have been learned from the Russian October. " For studying the laws and methods of proletarian revolution there is up to the present no more important or profound source than our October experience " ; in 1923 all conditions for successful revolution had been available in Germany except this understanding among the leaders of the lessons of October. In his account of the Russian revolution, Trotsky guardedly returned to his criticism of Lenin's formula of " a democratic dictatorship of the proletariat and the peasantry ", which made sense only as " a stage on the way to the socialist dictatorship of the proletariat supported by the peasantry " (his own formula [1]), and repeated the substance of his footnote of 1922. Lenin's formula had led in practice to misinterpretation in a Menshevik sense :

> In certain circles in our party the emphasis in Lenin's formula was placed not on the *dictatorship* of the proletariat and the peasantry, but on its *democratic* character, which contrasted with a socialist character. This in turn meant : in backward Russia only a democratic revolution is conceivable. The socialist revolution must begin in the west. . . . But to put the question in that way inevitably ended in Menshevism, and this was fully demonstrated in 1917.

Had not Lenin himself in his controversy with Kamenev in April 1917 described the famous formula as " outdated " and " dead " ? The essence of the argument was to turn back on Kamenev's head the imputation of Menshevism covertly levelled against Trotsky by the triumvirate.

From this point Trotsky launched into a biting attack on the attitude of the " old Bolsheviks " from April to October 1917. Kamenev was pilloried as Lenin's principal antagonist throughout this period. Other names appeared sparingly. Nogin, now dead, was mentioned once. Rykov's sceptical utterance at the April

---

[1] See *The Bolshevik Revolution, 1917–1923*, Vol. 1, pp. 60-61.

conference [1] was quoted at length, though without naming him. When Trotsky reached the events of October, he twice indicted Zinoviev and Kamenev by name for their opposition on the eve of the insurrection, and recorded their resignation from the party central committee ten days after the victory. The article contained no allusion to Stalin. This restraint may be attributed partly, perhaps, to a scrupulous desire to be fair — Stalin had been only a mild and occasional offender in this period — but mainly to a refusal even now to recognize in Stalin a serious adversary. In the concluding sections of the article Trotsky returned to his comparison of the German with the Russian October. Victory had been won in 1917 because Lenin forced action at the right moment on his wavering opponents ; in 1923 no leader was at hand to force similar action on the German party. In a postscript Trotsky reverted to his own record. From the moment of his arrival in Petrograd in May 1917 he had supported Lenin's policy of the seizure of power by the proletariat " fully and wholly ". As regards his view of the peasantry, " there was no shadow of any disagreement with Lenin, who at that time carried out the first step of the struggle against the Right Bolsheviks with their slogan ' a democratic dictatorship of the proletariat and peasantry ' ".. Once more Trotsky's adhesion to Lenin and the Bolsheviks in the summer of 1917 seemed to be qualified by the implied claim that Lenin, in abandoning his formula of 1905 to the " Right Bolsheviks " of 1917, had come over more than half-way to Trotsky. Meanwhile Trotsky's campaign gave fresh encouragement to the efforts of his supporters. Lentsner, the editor of his collected works, in a preface to the volume in which *Lessons of October* appeared, quoted Trotsky's American letters of March 1917, remarking that they " fully anticipated " Lenin's famous *Letters from Afar* written in Switzerland in the same month : the claim of Trotsky to be the co-author, if not the main author, of the policy inaugurated by the April theses was once more substantiated. An obscure follower of Trotsky named Syrkin published a pamphlet reviving an apocryphal story of the behaviour of the leading Bolsheviks which had originally appeared in 1919 in John Reed's *Ten Days that Shook the World*. In October 1917, according to this version,

[1] For this see *The Bolshevik Revolution, 1917–1923*, Vol. 1, p. 84.

Lenin and Trotsky " alone of the intellectuals " had stood for an immediate rising ; a majority of the central committee of the party had voted against it ; and it was only after the intervention of " a rough workman, his face convulsed with rage ", that the vote was reversed. The unfortunate feature about this story was that Reed's book had been praised by Lenin, in a preface to a recently published Russian translation, as " a truthful and unusually vivid " account of the revolution.[1]

The official publication date of the volume containing *Lessons of October* was November 6, 1924.[2] But it was apparently available to the members of the party central committee when they met in session from October 25 to 27. It created a considerable stir in party circles. Mutual sniping had been increasingly practised during the past year ; but no attack yet launched in the party controversy was anything like so closely reasoned or so far-reaching in its impact as Trotsky's broadside. Few members of the party now remembered exactly what had happened when Lenin returned to Petrograd in April 1917 ; fewer still knew the details of the dissensions in the central committee before and after the seizure of power in October. Trotsky's article recalled much that many would willingly have continued to forget. The major weight of his blows fell on Kamenev, and to a lesser degree on Zinoviev. But few of the leaders could feel themselves wholly immune : even Lenin emerged from this searching examination of party history as something less than infallible. The first recorded comment came from Kamenev. At a meeting of the Moscow party committee on October 29, 1924, he observed that " many members of the central committee, of whom I am one, refused to bring before the plenum of the central committee the question of the meaning of Trotsky's outburst "; that " we " — meaning the " many members " whom he did not name — none

[1] John Reed, *Ten Days that Shook the World* (N.Y., 1919), p. 38 ; Lenin, *Sochineniya*, xxiv, 661. Lenin's preface was written at the end of 1919 when he first read the book, but first appeared in print in a Russian translation published in 1923 (*ibid.* xxiv, 831, note 205).
[2] The edition of 5000 copies was quickly sold out and, when the discussion was at its height, was virtually unobtainable ; this led to rumours that it was officially banned (M. Eastman, *Since Lenin Died* (1925), p. 123).

the less regarded it as " a falsification of the history of the Bolshevik party in the October days ", and proposed to reply " on the literary plane " ; but that Trotsky would not be allowed to " stir up out of this an extensive discussion ".[1]   The official party retort to Trotsky's offensive was contained in an article in *Pravda* on November 2, 1924, entitled *How not to Write the History of October*, which, though unsigned, was recognized as the work of the editor, Bukharin.   Trotsky's essay, it declared, had evidently been written largely for the benefit of foreign comrades ; and, since its inaccuracies were likely to spread confusion in foreign communist parties, a reply was necessary.   Trotsky had distorted the perspective by leaving out of account everything that had happened in the party before 1917 (this was a delicate hint at Trotsky's own record) ; he had misrepresented Lenin's position in 1917 by depicting him as constantly at loggerheads with the majority of the central committee and in close agreement with Trotsky.   In Trotsky's story of the events of October the rank and file of the party had been entirely effaced :

> It does not exist, its temper cannot be discerned, it has dis-appeared.   Only comrade Trotsky stands out clearly, Lenin is visible in the background, and we discern a dull-witted, anonymous central committee.   The Petrograd organization, the real collective organizer of the workers' insurrection, is altogether absent. . . . Is it permissible for Marxists to write history in this style ?   This is a caricature of Marxism.

The analogy of the German with the Russian October was totally false :   none of the conditions had been similar.   The article ended with the usual appeal for party unity :

> The party will know how to judge fairly and promptly this stealthy undermining operation.   The party wants work and not fresh discussion.   The party desires real Bolshevik unity.

Izvestiya waited till November 16, 1924, to come out with an inconspicuous review on a back page.   It referred to the article which had already appeared in *Pravda*, and declared that an otherwise unexceptionable volume had been " spoiled " by Trotsky's introductory article and by " some remarks " of his editor.   The party journal printed an article by Sokolnikov entitled *How to Approach the History of October*, which corrected

[1] L. Kamenev, *Stat'i i Rechi*, xi (1929), 209-210.

Trotsky's account of the events of 1917 on several points, and accused him of seeking to diminish Lenin's rôle and to exaggerate the difference between Lenin and other members of the central committee.[1]

But the rudeness of Trotsky's assault left no hope that the controversy would be allowed to remain on this relatively calm and restrained and " literary " level. The triumvirate decided that the time had come to unmask all its guns. The discussions which took place at this time among the triumvirs and their supporters were partly revealed two years later when the triumvirate had broken asunder. Kamenev then declared that " the Trotskyite danger was invented for the purpose of our organized struggle against Trotsky " ; Lashevich admitted that " we invented this ' Trotskyism ' at the time of our struggle against Trotsky " ; and Zinoviev added that " the whole art consisted in connecting old disagreements with new issues ".[2] Trotsky had set the example in raking up the discreditable episodes of the past ; an unsparing broadside against Trotsky's whole party record could now be made to seem a legitimate act of retaliation. The major reply was appropriately entrusted to Kamenev who had borne the brunt of Trotsky's attack. While the reply was evidently the concerted work of the triumvirate, Kamenev's position as editor of the official collection of Lenin's writings gave him special authority as an expositor of Lenin's teaching and opportunity for copious quotation. His speech was delivered no less than three times : at the Moscow party committee on November 18, 1924, at the party fraction of the trade union central council on the next day, and at a meeting of the party military organization two days later.[3]

---

[1] *Bol'shevik*, No. 14, November 5, 1924, pp. 105-113.

[2] *Byulleten' Oppozitsii* (Paris), No. 9, February-March 1930, pp. 31-34 ; similar testimony by Radek and others is quoted in *Stalinskaya Shkola Falsifikatsii* (Berlin, 1932), pp. 101-108.

[3] The text printed in *Pravda* and *Izvestiya* on November 26, 1924, under the title *Leninism or Trotskyism ?* was described as a " stylistic elaboration " of the speech delivered on the first occasion ; how far it accurately represented what Kamenev said, cannot be discovered. The audience on the third occasion consisted of some 200 representatives of political commissars, central organs and staff of the Red Army (*Izvestiya*, November 23, 1924) ; the desire to appeal to a circle where Trotsky might be presumed to enjoy some influence is obvious. The speech was several times reprinted in pamphlets, and is in L. Kamenev, *Stat'i i Rechi*, i (1925), 188-243.

Kamenev's speech was long and exhaustive. The issue, he explained, could not be treated as a personal dispute : the danger was that *Lessons of October*, emanating from a leading member of the party central committee, might be " taken as a textbook, not only for members of our party, for our youth organization, but for the whole of Comintern ". From time to time in his speech Kamenev turned aside to pay formal tribute to Trotsky's services : when Trotsky entered the party, he had " passed the examination and passed it brilliantly " and had " written glorious pages into his own personal history and into that of the party ". But these passages merely threw into relief the bitterness of an attack which was carried back to the earliest period of Trotsky's career. " From the moment of the birth of Menshevism down to its final collapse in 1917 ", Trotsky had played the rôle of " the agent of Menshevism in the working class ". In 1905 Trotsky made an attempt to escape from " Menshevik negation ", and " expounded in his own words Parvus's idea of ' permanent revolution ' " ; but the adoption of this " Leftist phrase " did not hinder his continued collaboration with the Mensheviks. The *clou* of Kamenev's speech was the systematic quotation of a wealth of phrases from Lenin's writings, from 1904 onwards, which reflected unfavourably on Trotsky. Scarcely a year before 1914 failed to yield its contribution.[1] During the war, when Trotsky collaborated with Martov and the Left wing of the Mensheviks, the shafts flew still thicker. Trotsky "is in fact helping the Liberal-Labour politicians of Russia whose ' denial ' of the rôle of the peasantry implies a *lack of will* to incite the peasants to revolution ". Martov and Trotsky, like Kautsky in Germany and Longuet in France, " are doing the greatest harm to the workers' movement by defending the *fiction* of unity and thus *hindering* the mature and real unification of the *oppositions* of all countries, and the creation of a Third International ". As late as February 1917 Lenin summed up Trotsky's position as " Leftist phrases and a bloc with the Rights against the aim of the Lefts " ; and it was after his return to Petrograd in April 1917 that he fathered on Trotsky Parvus's phrase of 1905 " without a Tsar, and a workers' government ", and described it as the essence of " Trotskyism " (apparently

[1] Some of these passages have been quoted in *The Bolshevik Revolution, 1917–1923*, Vol. 1, p. 63.

Lenin's only use of the term) — neglect of the peasant and desire to " skip " the bourgeois phase of the revolution.[1]

Equipped with this formidable armoury of quotations, Kamenev now set to work to drive a wedge between Trotsky and Lenin, between Trotskyism and Bolshevism. He poked ironical fun at Trotsky's phrase of a year earlier : " I came to Lenin fighting ".[2] What Trotsky really meant, as *Lessons of October* showed, was that " I, Trotsky, came to Lenin because, in the fundamental questions of the character of the Russian revolution, Lenin had brought the party to Trotskyism ". The Trotsky who entered the party in 1917 did not change his spots : the fundamental hostility to Leninism, to Bolshevism, remained. Kamenev enumerated Trotsky's four errors of the post-1917 period, the four issues on which he had been at variance with the majority of the party, and by strangely contorted arguments forced them all into the basic category of " under-estimating the peasantry ". Trotsky's policy at Brest-Litovsk had been " an underestimate of the rôle of the peasantry, masked by revolutionary phraseology "; Trotsky's line in the trade union controversy had been an attempt to tighten the screws of war communism in the face of peasant resistance ; Trotsky's insistence on planning was inspired by a desire to establish " the dictatorship of industry "; and Trotsky's attack in the autumn of 1923 on " the fundamental framework of the dictatorship " through his denunciation of the party leadership and the party bureaucracy had been due to " an underestimate of the conditions in which we have to realize the dictatorship in a peasant country ". Kamenev now confessed his own " impermissible hesitations " of 1917 — Trotsky's " trump card in his struggle against Bolshevism " — but quickly returned to the unbridgeable gulf between Trotsky and Lenin. In conclusion, he briefly denied rumours which were current " that Trotsky's book has been prohibited, that Trotsky is about to be expelled from the party, that Trotsky has left Moscow ". Repressions of that kind would be pointless : it was for the party to make its choice between the incompatibles of Leninism and Trotskyism. But it was necessary to " strengthen all kinds of explanations about the incorrect attitude of comrade Trotsky ".

[1] The passages quoted are in Lenin, *Sochineniya*, xviii, 318, xix, 22, xx, 104, 182.   [2] See *The Interregnum, 1923-1924*, p. 331.

Of the other interventions in the debate the most important was that of Stalin. He had not himself been directly attacked. But, as at the twelfth party congress eighteen months earlier he had displayed dutiful zeal to defend Zinoviev,[1] so now he hastened to the support of Kamenev, speaking immediately after him in the party fraction of the trade union central council on November 19, 1924. Stalin's speech was briefer, more concentrated and more pungent than Kamenev's diffuse oration. He began by attempting to take the edge off Trotsky's attack on the defection of Kamenev and Zinoviev in October 1917. This had been exaggerated. Had the dissension been profound, a split in the party could not have been avoided. " There was no split, because, and only because, we had in the person of comrades Kamenev and Zinoviev Leninists, Bolsheviks." Stalin then passed on to Trotsky's own record. Like Kamenev, he did not wish " to deny comrade Trotsky's undoubtedly important rôle in the insurrection ". But it had not been a " special " rôle. Stalin here embarked on his first essay in the re-making of history. He quoted from the still unpublished minutes of the meeting of the party central committee of October 16, 1917, the decision to appoint a " centre " — what Stalin now described as " a practical centre for the organizational direction of the rising " — consisting of himself, Sverdlov, Dzerzhinsky, Bubnov and Uritsky ; and he commented ironically on the absence from the list of the man whom popular legend described as the " inspirer ", the " sole leader ", the " chief figure " of the insurrection. It is reasonably clear that this party centre was appointed for the purpose of establishing liaison with the military-revolutionary committee of the Petrograd Soviet which was in charge of all military preparations : it was for this reason that neither Trotsky nor any of the other prominent members of the committee was included in it. Nor is there any trace in the party records of any meeting of the centre or of anything done or proposed by it.[2] But in 1924 it was

---

[1] See *The Interregnum, 1923–1924*, p. 284.

[2] For the " centre ", described in the minutes of the central committee as a " military-revolutionary centre ", see *The Bolshevik Revolution, 1917–1923*, Vol. 1, p. 96 : it is nowhere mentioned again in any document earlier than 1924, when Stalin rediscovered it in order to belittle Trotsky's rôle. The account of the episode given in the "opposition platform" of 1927 (L. Trotsky, *The Real Situation in Russia* (n.d.), pp. 221-223), supplemented by further details in *id. Stalin* (N.Y., 1946), pp. 232-235, is plausible.

taken as a matter of course that any party organ, however in-
formally constituted, was supreme over any Soviet organ ; and
it was difficult to remember how things had really been done in
the hurly-burly of October 1917.   Stalin's protest against the
legendary inflation of Trotsky's rôle seemed moderate and reasonable.   Trotsky, Stalin conceded, had " fought well in October ".
But so had others — including the Left SR's.   And it was a pity
that, later on, " his courage had failed him in the period of
Brest-Litovsk ".[1]   Stalin at this point intercalated a brief confession of his own error, so much less grave than that of Kamenev
or *a fortiori* that of Trotsky.   He, too, had hesitated before Lenin's
return to Petrograd in April 1917, and for some days after it, to
come out against the Provisional Government :

> This mistaken position I then shared with other comrades
> and completely abandoned it only in the middle of April when
> I adhered to Lenin's theses. A new orientation was necessary.
> This new orientation was given to the party by Lenin in his
> famous April theses.

In conclusion, more briefly but more dramatically than
Kamenev, Stalin juxtaposed " Trotskyism " with " Leninism ".
He introduced here his most telling novelty — two quotations
from Trotsky's still unpublished letter of 1913 to Chkheidze,
intercepted by the Tsarist police, and discovered in the archives
in 1921 by the commission on party history.   " The whole
foundation of Leninism at the present time is built on lying and
falsification ", Trotsky had written, adding that Lenin was " a
professional exploiter of everything that is backward in the
Russian workers' movement ".[2]   Here, Stalin triumphantly proclaimed, was irrefutable evidence of Trotsky's desire to " dethrone " Lenin.   He proceeded to define the three main ingredients

---

[1] In the published version of Stalin's speech the passage referring to
Trotsky's attitude in 1917 carried a long footnote applying a similar critique
to his record in the civil war.   While " far from denying the important rôle of
comrade Trotsky in the civil war ", Stalin rejected the legend of Trotsky as
" the ' chief organizer ' of the victories at the front " ; the victories over both
Kolchak and Denikin were achieved " in opposition to comrade Trotsky's
plans ".

[2] *Lenin o Trotskom i o Trotskizme*, ed. M. Olminsky (2nd ed. 1925), pp. 217-
219 ; the letter has already been quoted in *The Bolshevik Revolution, 1917–1923*,
Vol. 1, p. 63.   For the publication of Trotsky's letter of 1921 to Olminsky
see p. 27 below.

of " Trotskyism ". The first was " permanent revolution ",
which meant " revolution without taking into account the poor
peasantry as a revolutionary force ". The second was " lack of
faith in the party essence of Bolshevism, in its monolithic character " : to this Trotsky's whole career before 1917 bore ample
witness. The third was " lack of faith in the leaders of Bolshevism ", and especially in Lenin : the " new Trotskyism " was
just as much concerned as the old to " dethrone " Lenin, but
worked more subtly. Stalin ended with some quotations from
Trotsky's pamphlet *On Lenin*, in which the dead leader was
depicted in intimate, half-serious, half-flippant moods : was not
this, too, " an attempt ' ever so little ' to dethrone Lenin " ? [1]
The conclusion reads lamely. But Stalin knew his audience.
The time had come when it was no longer possible, without giving offence, to treat Lenin with the easy familiarity
of an equal. The moral was plain. Trotsky was a stranger
to the party, a stranger to the cult of Lenin as well as to his
teachings.

While Kamenev and Stalin appeared in the forefront of the
battle, Zinoviev remained for the moment relatively inconspicuous : it was the first occasion on which he had been content to
figure as the third member of the triumvirate. On November
24, 1924, a few days after his colleagues had spoken, he addressed
a Komsomol meeting in Moscow in celebration of the fifth
anniversary of the Communist Youth International. But this was
not the occasion for taking up Trotsky's challenge and he confined
himself to one sally in his peroration :

> For one thing we should be grateful to comrade Trotsky,
> that by his struggle against Leninism he will help us to instruct
> the young generation in the true history of the party and in
> genuine Leninism.[2]

Zinoviev's major contribution to the controversy was an article
which appeared in *Pravda* and *Izvestiya* on November 30, 1924,
under the title *Bolshevism or Trotskyism ?* A great deal of it was

---

[1] Stalin, *Sochineniya*, vi, 324-357 ; the speech was first printed (with
Kamenev's speech) in *Pravda* and *Izvestiya* of November 26, 1924, and both
were several times reprinted in the next few weeks.

[2] *Leningradskaya Pravda*, November 25, 1924 ; *Pravda* and *Izvestiya*,
December 12, 1924.

devoted not to the attack on Trotsky, but to a defence of Zinoviev's own record. He did not seek to " minimize " the " grievous error " which he had shared in October 1917 with Kamenev, and which he had more than once publicly confessed. But he was careful to dissociate himself from Kamenev's shortcomings before that date, and took pains to rehabilitate himself in the character of Lenin's favourite disciple. After making some play with the familiar quotations from Lenin and Trotsky, he plunged into a theoretical enquiry whether a Right wing could make its appearance in the party. Between 1903 and 1910, when relations between Bolsheviks and Mensheviks had not yet been clarified, such a phenomenon was possible and had in fact occurred. Between 1910 and 1917 such a thing had been impossible (this in reply to the suggestion that Zinoviev and Kamenev had formed a " Right wing " in October 1917). After the seizure of power, when other parties had been destroyed, and some of their former members had joined the Bolsheviks, when the country and the régime were passing through a period of transition, the danger was once more present : the logical outcome of Trotskyism was a " Right deviation ", against which the only safeguard was to close the party ranks. Zinoviev took refuge in one of his favourite purple passages :

> Where then in these conditions is the way out ? What then is to be done ? A split ? Folly ! There can be no thought of it ! Our party is more united than ever.
>
> A break-away ? Folly ! There is practically nobody to break away, and the party does not wish to carry things to that point.
>
> Party reprisals ? That too is folly ! Nobody needs that : something else is needed.
>
> What then is needed ?
>
> What is needed is that the party should *guarantee itself* against the repetition of " assaults " on Leninism. Serious party guarantees are needed that the decisions of the party shall be binding on comrade Trotsky. The party is no discussion club, but a *party* — and a party operating in the complicated environment in which ours finds itself. The watchword of the day is :

> *Bolshevization of all strata of the party !*
> *Ideological struggle against Trotskyism !*

B *

Above all, enlightenment, enlightenment and once more enlightenment !

Trotsky's other assailants in the debate made up in numbers for what they lacked in weight and originality. Safarov, a prominent Leningrad Bolshevik and author of a popular anti-Trotskyite pamphlet, *Foundations of Leninism*, wrote a monster article under the title *Trotskyism or Leninism ?* which ran through seven consecutive numbers of *Leningradskaya Pravda*, and was also published in pamphlet form. It specialized in the exposure of Trotsky's " Menshevik hesitations " before 1917, and concluded that " the party cannot live under the sword of Damocles of endless discussions ".[1] Kviring, the secretary of the central committee of the Ukrainian party, published an article in the Ukrainian party journal *Kommunist* under the title *The Party does not Want Discussions*.[2] Molotov attacked Trotsky's pamphlet *On Lenin* as part of a campaign for the glorification of Trotsky at the expense of Lenin's memory and for " the revision of Leninism under the flag of Lenin ".[3] Krupskaya, deeply distressed at this recrudescence of dissensions in the party, and angry with Trotsky for having so recklessly provoked it, published an article which bore obvious signs of prompting by the triumvirate. While she expressed doubt whether Trotsky had " really committed all the mortal sins of which he is accused ", the tone of *Lessons of October* had inevitably led to " controversial exaggerations ". " Marxist analysis ", she remarked severely, " was never comrade Trotsky's strong point " ; and " this is the reason why he so much underestimates the rôle played by the peasantry ". One purpose of the article was to condemn " the very foolish interpretation " put by Syrkin on John Reed's book, which contained " legends and inaccuracies ", and had been commended by Lenin only because it gave an admirable picture of the spirit of the revolution.[4] On the following day Gusev began the process of sapping Trotsky's military reputation in an article which, no doubt ironically, borrowed the title of Trotsky's own collection of articles on the

[1] *Leningradskaya Pravda*, November 13-20, 1924.
[2] It also appeared *ibid.* November 22, 1924, and was quoted in *Izvestiya*, November 23, 1924.
[3] *Pravda*, December 9, 1924 ; *Leningradskaya Pravda*, December 10, 11, 1924.
[4] Krupskaya's article was published in *Pravda*, December 16, 1924.

civil war — *How the Revolution Armed* — and gave examples of
Trotsky's high-handed behaviour in the civil war.[1] Finally these
and other speeches and articles were collected in a small volume
entitled *For Leninism*, with an introduction by Rykov, which was
published in time for the meeting of the party central committee
in the middle of January 1925.[2] Nor did this collection exhaust
the flow of articles. On December 12, *Pravda* published a long
theoretical article by Bukharin (followed by a further article
in *Bol'shevik*[3]) entitled *A New Discovery in Soviet Economics, or
How to Ruin the Worker-Peasant Bloc* — an attempt to identify
Trotsky with Preobrazhensky's theory of primitive socialist
accumulation and industrialization at the expense of the peasant ;
and on the next day Bukharin read a report to a meeting of party
propagandists in Moscow on " The Theory of Permanent Revolution ", which later appeared in the press.[4] Finally, on December
20, 1924, *Pravda* and *Izvestiya* carried an important article by
Stalin on *October and Comrade Trotsky's Theory of Permanent
Revolution*, which was designed as an introduction to a collection
of his speeches and confirmed the growing impression of Stalin's
desire to enter the arena of party doctrine.[5] It contained Stalin's
first formulation of the new doctrine of " socialism in one
country ".

The campaign of denunciation was not confined to pronouncements by the leaders. The rank and file of the party was called
on to play its part. An important operation had just been carried

[1] *Ibid.* December 17, 1924 ; this article served as the introduction to a
pamphlet entitled *Our Differences in Military Affairs*, which was an attack on
Trotsky's refusal to recognize a Marxist military science (for this controversy
see pp. 383-392 below) and was originally published in the form of two articles
in *Bol'shevik*, No. 15-16, December 10, 1924, pp. 34-49 ; No. 1 (17), January
15, 1925, pp. 58-70.

[2] *Za Leninizm* (1925) ; a German version appeared under the title *Um den
Oktober* (1925), and an English version containing only the principal items
under the title *The Errors of Trotskyism* (CPGB, 1925). Rykov's introduction, which first appeared in *Izvestiya*, December 23, 1924, is in A. I. Rykov,
Sochineniya, iii (1929), 376-382 ; the volume was reviewed in *Izvestiya*, January
22, 1925.

[3] For these articles see Vol. 1, p. 207, note 1 ; Bukharin's article was preceded in *Bol'shevik* by a particularly bitter unsigned attack on Trotskyism —
perhaps from the pen of Yaroslavsky, who had recently joined the editorial
board.   [4] *Izvestiya*, December 28, 1924.

[5] For the substance of this article, which made no great impact at the time,
see pp. 40-42 below.

out in the Moscow organization. In the previous winter Moscow had been the principal focus of Trotskyism — a breach in party unity which reflected no credit on Kamenev, the president of the Moscow provincial party committee, or on Zelensky, its secretary. The triumvirate appears to have been agreed that no risk should be taken of a repetition of this outbreak of dissent in the capital ; and in September 1924, at the instance of Zinoviev and Kamenev, Uglanov, the secretary of the provincial committee in Nizhny-Novgorod for the past three years, was transferred to Moscow to replace Zelensky, with a mandate to clean up the party organization.[1] This task he appears to have discharged ruthlessly, but efficiently.[2] The Moscow party now went into action with exemplary unanimity. The party meeting in Moscow at which Kamenev had first delivered his broadside on November 18, 1924, passed a resolution expressing " indignation at comrade Trotsky's distortions regarding the real relations between Lenin on the one side and the central committee and the party on the other ", condemning Trotsky's action as " a breach of the promises made by Trotsky at the thirteenth party congress ", and urging the central committee to take " decisive and exhaustive measures " to prevent further distortions of party history and of the " fundamental ideas of the party ". This resolution was also adopted at the next day's meeting, addressed by Kamenev and Stalin, of the party group in the trade union central council and at the military meeting of November 21.[3] Other local party organizations followed suit. The central committees of the Ukrainian and White Russian parties hastened to pass resolutions dissociating themselves from Trotsky's attacks.[4] Lower party organs were mobilized to express their detestation of Trotsky's heresies and their confidence in the party leadership. On November 22, 1924, even before

[1] For the appointment see *XIV S"ezd Vsesoyuznoi Kommunisticheskoi Partii (B)* (1926), pp. 192-193 ; the appointment was specifically said to have been made at the instance of Zinoviev and Kamenev, though Uglanov had apparently been transferred from Leningrad in 1921 after friction with Zinoviev, the circumstances of which were a matter of controversy (*ibid.* pp. 510-512, 954-955). The date of the appointment is fixed by the biographies of Zelensky and Uglanov in *Entsiklopedicheskii Slovar' Russkogo Bibliograficheskogo Instituta Granat*, xli, i (n.d. [1927]), Prilozhenie, col. 143 ; xli, iii (n.d. [1928]), Prilozhenie, cols. 175-176. [2] See p. 223, note 4 below.

[3] *Pravda*, November 19, 23, 1924 ; *Internationale Presse-Korrespondenz*, No. 152, November 25, 1924, pp. 2065-2066.

[4] *Izvestiya*, November 23, 1924.

Kamenev's and Stalin's speeches had been published, *Pravda* carried a resolution by the Kharkov provincial party committee denouncing Trotsky ; and this was only the first of a flood of such resolutions appearing in *Pravda* in the following days and weeks. The Leningrad city and the Leningrad provincial party committees in turn passed resolutions urging that Trotsky's action should be placed on the agenda of the next session of the party central committee ; according to some accounts his expulsion from the party was explicitly demanded.[1]

The mobilization of the party press for the struggle was equally intensive and was described in the quarterly report of the head of the press section of the central committee :

> In connexion with the last campaign of comrade Trotsky, the newspaper political section undertook supplementary work by way of elaboration of the questions of Leninism and Trotskyism, the study of the treatment of these questions in the most important central and local newspapers, the examination of the character of articles, notes and resolutions, and the distribution through the press bureau of special articles on this question.[2]

An instruction from the central committee on the programmes of party schools ordered special attention to be paid to exposing " the opportunism of all groupings, both outside and inside the party " and " the negative rôle of such groupings, and of Trotskyism in particular ".[3] The Komsomol central committee issued a detailed instruction to its subordinate organs on propaganda against Trotskyism. The subject was to be dealt with under three heads — " Trotskyism before October ", " Trotskyism after October " and " Trotskyism or Leninism ". Emphasis was laid on the need for a " cautious approach " to the question in Komsomol cells and careful preparation of those chosen to make reports on it. A list of suitable literature was provided.[4] In the controversy of November and December 1923 some appearance of calm and

---

[1] *Leningradskaya Pravda*, November 21, 29, 1924 ; Stalin, *Sochineniya*, vii, 379 ; *Leningradskaya Organizatsiya i Chetyrnadtsatyi S"ezd* (1926), p. 70.

[2] *Izvestiya Tsentral'nogo Komiteta Rossiiskoi Kommunisticheskoi Partii (Bol'shevikov)*, No. 11-12 (86-87), March 23, 1925, p. 1.

[3] *Spravochnik Partiinogo Rabotnika*, v, 1925 (1926), 319.

[4] *Izvestiya Tsentral'nogo Komiteta Rossiiskoi Kommunisticheskoi Partii (Bol'shevikov)*, No. 1 (76), January 5, 1925, pp. 2-4 ; for the attitude of the Komsomol, see pp. 95-96 below.

rational argument had been maintained. Conflicting opinions had found expression in the press, and a battle of wits had been waged. A year later the sole public manifestation of the struggle was a boiling torrent of denunciation in which no adverse voice was, or could have been, heard. The impression thus created of overwhelming unanimity against Trotsky certainly did not correspond with the facts : one of the most popular charges against Trotsky was that of spreading dissension in the party. A rather embarrassed leading article in *Izvestiya* on November 28 expressed apprehension about the effect of the discussion on non-party people and on those who had recently joined the party, especially on the youth, and protested that it was not the party which had provoked this controversy. Yet it seems clear that, as in the previous year, support for Trotsky came rather from the higher party intellectuals and from groups of young students than from the rank and file of the party, and that it was everywhere weaker than it had been a year earlier. This weakening was due mainly to improved organization by the leadership and to increasingly real fears of the victimization of dissenters, but partly also to disillusionment with Trotsky's own attitude. It was impossible to follow a man who intermittently raised his voice in protest against the policies and methods of the party leadership, but himself refused to lead or organize an opposition.

No risk was this time to be taken of foreign communist parties intervening on Trotsky's side, as the Polish party had done in December 1923.[1] Kuusinen, Zinoviev's faithful henchman in Comintern, published an article simultaneously with Zinoviev's own exposing errors in Trotsky's account of the " German October ", and drawing attention to his endorsement of the very different verdict in the theses presented by Radek to IKKI in the previous January.[2] Two other foreign stalwarts of Comintern, Bela Kun and Kolarov, wrote articles exposing the fallacies of *Lessons of October* ; Kolarov, whose article appeared in *Pravda*, December 20, 1924, pointed out the errors of Trotsky's diagnosis of the Bulgarian crisis of 1923. The principal foreign parties were

[1] See *The Interregnum, 1923–1924*, pp. 234–235.
[2] For these theses see *ibid.* p. 237 ; Kuusinen's article was published in *Pravda*, November 30, 1924, and *Leningradskaya Pravda*, December 2, 1924, and included in the collective volume *Za Leninizm* and in the foreign versions of it (see p. 21 above).

promptly mobilized to play their part in the campaign. In Germany the response appears to have been spontaneous. The present " Left " leaders of the KPD had an axe of their own to grind, and hastened to use the divisions in the Russian party to strengthen their own hand against the remnants of the Right wing in their own party. In October 1924 the theoretical journal of the KPD had contained an ironical notice of Trotsky's pamphlet on Lenin headed *Belles Lettres or Material for a Biography ?* and signed "A. M." (Maslow), and a detailed, but equally hostile, review apparently from the same hand.[1] On November 10, 1924, a few days after the publication of *Lessons of October*, the Zentrale of the KPD addressed a letter to the central committee of the Russian party declaring against " a renewal of the debates " in the party and proclaiming its solidarity with the party leadership.[2] The motive of the gesture was made transparently clear in an article in the *Rote Fahne* of November 13, 1924, under the heading *What is Trotskyism ?*, which reached the conclusion that " all adherents of Brandler are Trotskyites ". Brandler and Thal-heimer, who had remained in Moscow since the fifth congress of Comintern, drew up a brief statement in reply. The argument was complicated by the ambiguities of Trotsky's position in the autumn of 1923, when he had been an unconditional supporter of revolutionary action in Germany, but had at the same time main-tained his long-standing friendship for Brandler and his personal antipathy to the Left group in the KPD.[3] Brandler now sought to show that he had always been in the opposite camp to Trotsky. He had opposed him in the old controversies of 1909–1913, in the discussions on the militarization of labour preceding the introduc-tion of NEP, and in the analysis of revolutionary possibilities in Germany in October 1923. He had consistently dissented from the conclusions which Trotsky had drawn from the October fiasco, beginning with the Radek-Trotsky-Pyatakov resolution submitted to the presidium of IKKI in January 1924 [4] and ending with *Lessons of October*. The statement included a reminder that the present Left leaders of the KPD (Ruth Fischer, Scholem and Maslow were named) had been formerly associated with the

---

[1] *Die Internationale*, vii, No. 19-20, October 1, 1924, pp. 614-615, 618-621.
[2] *Pravda*, November 21, 1924 ; *Internationale Presse-Korrespondenz*, No. 154, November 28, 1924, p. 2106.
[3] See *The Interregnum, 1923–1924*, p. 229.   [4] See *ibid.* p. 237.

Russian workers' opposition [1] and had " only become Leninists in 1924 ". It ended with an appeal to all communist parties to support the Russian party in " liquidating the opposition ". Bearing the date " Moscow, November 20, 1924 ", it was published in *Pravda* on November 29 with an acid editorial note which praised Brandler and Thalheimer for dissociating themselves so decisively from Trotsky's " present action ", but censured them for their opposition to the present KPD leadership and to the line of the fifth congress of Comintern. The statement was not published in the *Rote Fahne*. The distinction was subtle : an attack on the Left leadership of the KPD could still be printed in *Pravda*, provided that it also contributed to the campaign against Trotsky, but not in the paper of the German party.[2] While both wings of the KPD thus vied with each other in turning their back on Trotsky, *Lessons of October* appeared in a German translation from a SPD press with a preface by the renegade Paul Levi.[3] Meanwhile the example of the KPD was followed in the next few weeks by the French, Polish and Czech parties and by the federation of Balkan communist parties.[4] Even the Workers' Party of America produced a resolution recording its support of the central committee of the Russian party against Trotsky.[5] It was the first occasion on which the Comintern machine had exercised so smooth and automatic a control over the foreign parties. Only the German party still possessed some slight measure of independence.

The most crushing blow of the whole campaign was, however, the publication of the full text of Trotsky's letter to Chkheidze of 1913 with its crude denunciation of Lenin which had been briefly quoted by Stalin in his speech of November 19, 1924. Trotsky himself in his autobiography later described " the use made by the epigones of my letter to Chkheidze " as " one of the greatest

---

[1] See *The Bolshevik Revolution, 1917–1923*, Vol. 3, p. 413, note 2.

[2] It was, however, published in *Internationale Presse-Korrespondenz*, No. 164, December 19, 1924, pp. 2254-2255, together with a long article replying to it on behalf of the Left.

[3] Another German translation appeared belatedly *ibid.* No. 18, January 29, 1925, pp. 222-238 — the same issue which also published Trotsky's letter of January 15, 1925, and the decision of the party central committee condemning him (see pp. 30-33 below).

[4] *Ibid.* No. 157, December 5, 1924, pp. 2130-2131 ; No. 163, December 16, 1924, p. 2240 ; No. 166, December 22, 1924, pp. 2283-2284.

[5] *Izvestiya*, December 13, 1924.

frauds in the world's history ", but admitted that masses of
people " read Trotsky's hostile remarks about Lenin " and were
" stunned ".[1] The effect of the letter was redoubled by the
simultaneous publication of another Trotsky letter. A man more
sensitive than Trotsky to the feelings of others might have had a
moment of embarrassment and apprehension when, towards the
end of 1921, the commission on party history (Istpart) unearthed
from the police archives his long-forgotten letter to Chkheidze,
and Olminsky, the president of the commission, wrote to him —
not, surely, without a touch of malice — enquiring whether he
wished it to be published. On December 6, 1921, Trotsky, then
at the height of his self-confidence and power, returned a reply
which, in the light of later events, seems complacent to the point
of foolhardiness. He thought publication inopportune ; for " the
reader of today will not understand, will not apply the necessary
historical correctives, and will simply be confused ". The letter
would have to be accompanied by explanations, and Trotsky saw
no reason to revive his old differences with the party. " For, I
frankly admit, I do not at all consider that, in my disagreements
with the Bolsheviks, I was wrong on all points." In his analysis
of the underlying forces and prospects of the revolution, he had
been justified by the event ; only in his attitude to the two factions
in the party he had been in error. To publish now would be
pointless. " Let someone else publish in ten years, if anyone is
still interested by that time." [2] He offered no word of regret or
remorse for his insulting remarks about the leader, and failed
altogether to realize how his refusal to admit that he had been
wrong in his " disagreements with the Bolsheviks " would jar on
the ordinary party member. His arrogant letter to Olminsky
remained in the files of Istpart. Three years less one day later,
on December 5, 1924, when Lenin was dead and the cult of Lenin
in full swing, Kamenev read the letter to a meeting of the Moscow
party committee as convincing evidence that Trotsky still believed
himself right and the party wrong.[3] The texts of the letter to
Chkheidze and the letter to Olminsky were published in *Pravda*
on December 9, 1924, and in *Izvestiya* on the following day.

[1] L. Trotsky, *Moya Zhizn'* (Berlin, 1930), ii, 259.
[2] *Lenin o Trotskom i o Trotskizme*, ed. M. Olminsky (2nd ed. 1925), pp. 219-
220.   [3] L. Kamenev, *Stat'i i Rechi*, xi (1929), 285.

Kamenev devoted a special article in *Pravda* to these revelations. Trotsky's letter to Olminsky spoke for itself :

> May the doubters and hesitators read comrade Trotsky's letter again and again ! We are convinced that it will finally free them from their doubts and hesitations.

After the publication of Trotsky's letter, the issue was really " not worth arguing about ". The letter demonstrated beyond the possibility of contradiction that Trotsky " deliberately chose, and chooses for the future, a different path from that of Lenin ".[1]

The reaction of Trotsky to these savage assaults proved, once more, baffling to friend and foe alike. At the height of the controversy he wrote or dictated a 54-page typewritten memorandum which remained among his papers. It was headed *The Purpose of This Explanation*, with a sub-title added by hand, *Our Differences*. He rebutted the charges that he was revising Leninism under the " secret banner " of Trotskyism ; that *Lessons of October* was written from a special Trotskyist angle or was designed to disparage Leninism ; and that it was intended as a platform for a new " Right wing " in the party. Trotsky repeated previous admissions of the points on which he had been wrong against Lenin, and accused Kamenev of unfair selection of quotations and of the improper practice of mixing up quotations from different periods and contexts. He reiterated his criticism of Kamenev's errors in 1917. He defended himself against the charge of ignoring the peasantry, and argued that the danger of a rift between the proletariat and peasantry was twofold. It might result from an attempt to put too great a burden on the peasant. But there was also an opposite danger : " If the working class came to the conclusion over a series of years that it had been drawn, in the name of the maintenance of its political dictatorship, to excessive sacrifice of its class interest, this would undermine the Soviet state from the other side ". The tempo of industrialization was subject to objective limitations which must be observed. But equal danger would result from " a lagging of industry

---

[1] *Pravda*, December 10, 1924 ; the article was reprinted in L. Kamenev, *Stat'i i Rechi*, i (1925), 244-249.

behind the economic recovery of the country, inevitably begetting a goods famine and high retail prices which in turn inevitably lead to the enrichment of private capital ". That the memorandum was written for publication is shown by a passage near the beginning, partially underlined for emphasis :

> If I thought that my explanations might bring oil to the flames of discussion, or if the comrades on whom the printing of this essay depends were to tell me so directly and openly, I would not print it, however hard it may be to rest under the charge of liquidating Leninism.

These words may provide a clue to the eventual decision not to publish.[1] A brief editorial note appeared in *Pravda* on December 13, 1924, stating " in response to questions from a number of comrades " that no articles had been received from Trotsky or his closest associates in reply to the published criticisms of Trotskyism.

Trotsky's silence seems, however, to have been due not so much to calculated discretion as to shocked bewilderment. When he wrote and published *Lessons of October*, he had evidently expected no such violent outburst in response to it. Earlier in the year he propounded his views on the German revolution and on the situation in the party without provoking any particular sign of official resentment. For a year he had been subject to incessant personal attacks. It did not occur to him that, by personally attacking Zinoviev and Kamenev, he would bring the quarrel to breaking-point in conditions least favourable to himself. The suddenness of the shock made it all the more severe. His own isolation and the fierceness of the storms which he had called down on his head played on his nerves, and produced the same physical symptoms as had made their appearance exactly a year earlier. On November 24, 1924, the Kremlin doctors, including Semashko and Guétier, reported that he had been suffering from " fever due to influenza " for the past ten days. On December 5 they re-examined him, found continued fever and " inflammation of the bronchial glands " — a condition " precisely similar to his

---

[1] The copy in the Trotsky archives (T 2969) carries a MS. note " Only Copy. Was not Printed " and the date " End of November 1924 ", obviously added later; the only precise internal evidence of date is the reference in a footnote to Kuusinen's article, which was published in *Pravda*, November 30, 1924.

illness in the previous year " — and advised his removal to " a
warm, mild climate ".[1] This time Trotsky made no haste to
follow the advice of the doctors and move southwards. In
January 1924 he had left Moscow just before the party conference
assembled. Now he remained, a sick man, alone and silent, in
the Kremlin awaiting the meeting of the central committee called
for January 20, 1925. His mood was one of apathy shot through
with occasional gleams of hope. He would not attend the meeting
of the committee. But perhaps something would happen to
mitigate the fury of his persecutors, some shame would be felt,
and he would be invited to offer explanations, to argue his case.
On January 15, 1925, breaking silence for the first time since the
publication of *Lessons of October*, he addressed a letter to the
central committee in preparation for its forthcoming session which
is sometimes referred to as Trotsky's " letter of resignation ".
The description is not formally incorrect. It was, like his
declaration at the thirteenth party congress,[2] an act of formal submission to the party which, however, carried with it no recognition
that he had been in the wrong. His silence in face of " many
untrue and even monstrous charges " had been, he said, " correct
from the standpoint of the general interests of the party ". For
the past eight years he had never approached any question " from
the standpoint of ' Trotskyism ', which I have considered, and
consider now, to have been politically liquidated long ago " : the
word itself had made its appearance only in the recent controversy. " Permanent revolution " was a matter of party history
and had no relation to current issues. He had not since the
thirteenth party congress made any attempt to challenge or reopen
party decisions ; and he firmly repudiated the charge, now or in
the past, of " revising Leninism ". Denying that he aimed at
" some special position " in the party, he firmly professed his
willingness to undertake any work entrusted to him by the central
committee, and added — almost, it seemed, as an afterthought —
that, " after the recent discussion, the interest of our cause
demands my speedy release from the duties of president of the
Revolutionary Military Council ". He concluded by saying that
he had " remained in Moscow until the session in order, if it

[1] *Ekonomicheskaya Zhizn'*, December 10, 1924.
[2] See *The Interregnum, 1923–1924*, pp. 303-304, 331.

should be desired, to answer this or that question or give any necessary explanations ".[1]

As had happened before in this paradoxical struggle for power, Trotsky's submission, combined with refusal to admit error, eased the path of his adversaries and seemed to invite the verdict against him. Stalin, emphasizing his rôle as the spokesman of the secretariat and thus appearing to disclaim any personal animus, made a brief statement to the committee on the many resolutions against Trotsky received from local party organizations. He divided these into three groups : those which demanded Trotsky's expulsion from the party, those which demanded his expulsion from the Politburo and from his office as president of the Revolutionary Military Council, and those which merely demanded his expulsion from the last-named office. As between these three disciplinary measures, Stalin refrained from expressing any opinion, leaving the decision to the committee. Behind the scenes a keen struggle ensued. The Leningrad organization, primed no doubt by Zinoviev, had come out for a proposal to expel Trotsky from the party, or at any rate from the central committee : Zalutsky, one of the Leningrad party publicists, had published a pamphlet in this sense. This proposal received no support in the central committee. Kamenev, supported by Zinoviev, then put forward a compromise proposal to expel Trotsky from the Politburo. This was opposed by Kalinin, Voroshilov, Orjonikidze, Stalin, and " in part " Bukharin, and was defeated by a large majority. Trotsky's resignation from his military office was unanimously accepted. No decision was reached about his future employment.[2]

[1] Trotsky's letter was published in *Izvestiya Tsentral'nogo Komiteta Rossiiskoi Kommunisticheskoi Partii (Bol'shevikov)*, No. 3 (78), January 19, 1925, pp. 2-3, and in *Pravda*, January 20, 1925 ; an English translation, with one omission, appeared in M. Eastman, *Since Lenin Died* (1925), pp. 155-158.

[2] No record of these discussions was published, and information is derived from the recollections of participants almost a year later (Stalin, *Sochineniya*, vii, 379-380 ; *XIV S"ezd Vsesoyuznoi Kommunisticheskoi Partii (B)* (1926), pp. 276 (Tomsky), 318 (Kalinin), 458-459 (Zinoviev); *Leningradskaya Organizatsiya i Chetyrnadtsatyi S"ezd* (1926), p. 70 (Andreev)). Stalin's unctuous explanation of his attitude was significant of his determination to avoid extremes : " We knew that a policy of expulsion was fraught with great dangers for the party, that the method of expulsion, of blood-letting — for they demanded blood — was dangerous and infectious : today one is excluded, tomorrow another, the next day another — and what will remain of our party ? "

The long resolution which was adopted at the close of the proceedings attempted a reasoned analysis of Trotsky's short-comings. " The fundamental premiss of all the successes of the Bolshevik party ", it began, " has always been its steel-like unity and iron discipline, a genuine unity of opinions on a basis of Leninism." Trotsky had assailed this unity, both at home and abroad, by encouraging dissent. Trotskyism was " a falsification of communism in the spirit of an approximation to ' European ' patterns of pseudo-Marxism, i.e. in the last resort, in the spirit of ' European ' social-democracy ". This was the fourth major occasion on which Trotsky had been responsible for splitting the party. The first had been the debate on Brest-Litovsk, the second on the trade unions, and the third on the scissors crisis. The present occasion was the most serious of all, since he had denied the Leninist doctrine on " the motive forces of the revolu-tion ", opposing his theory of " permanent revolution " to the party line in the past and in the present. The resolution noted that Trotsky in his letter of January 15 had made no confession of error, failed to renounce his " anti-Bolshevik platform ", and limited himself to " formal loyalty ". It proposed to relieve him, in accordance with his own request, of the office of president of the Revolutionary Military Council, and declared him unfitted for further military work. It postponed till the next party congress the question of his further employment, and warned him that any fresh violation or non-fulfilment by him of party decisions would make it impossible for him to remain a member of the Politburo and would raise the question of his exclusion from the central committee. (The ultimate sanction of exclusion from the party was not mentioned.) Finally it was decided to undertake propa-ganda to explain throughout the party, as well as to the " non-party masses of workers and peasants ", the anti-Bolshevik character of Trotskyism. The resolution was carried at a joint meeting of the central committee and the central control com-mission, two members of the former voting against it and one member of the latter abstaining.[1] The two dissentient members of

---

[1] *VKP(B) v Rezolyutsiyakh* (1941), i, 636-641. According to Stalin, *Sochineniya*, viii, 295, the resolution was drafted by Zinoviev. The reference in the resolution to the " European " character of Trotsky's heresies was a favourite idea of Zinoviev at the time ; in an article on *Proletariat and Peasantry*

the central committee were Rakovsky and Pyatakov; the abstaining member of the central control commission was one Pravdin, who had a previous record of dissent from the party line.[1]

The meeting had ended on the eve of the first anniversary of Lenin's death, which was celebrated as a day of mourning and commemoration. Immediately afterwards the official Soviet machinery was set in motion. A record of the decisions appeared in *Pravda* on January 24, 1925. Two days later the presidium of VTsIK announced Trotsky's resignation from the position of president of the Revolutionary Military Council and People's Commissar for War, and appointed Frunze in his place.[2] Kamenev had proposed Stalin for the post, apparently in the hope of removing him from the secretariat. But nobody — least of all Stalin — took the proposal seriously.[3] On February 6 Unshlikht was appointed deputy commissar — the post held since the previous April by Frunze.[4] Trotsky, who left Moscow after the meeting of the committee and was in the Caucasus by the time these decisions were published, made in his autobiography a belated comment on his resignation :

> I yielded up the military post without a fight, even with a sense of relief, since I was thereby wresting from my opponents' hands their weapon of insinuations about my military intentions.[5]

The rationalization was far-fetched, but significant. Trotsky failed to the last to understand that the issue of the struggle was

published in *Izvestiya*, January 13, 1925, he had spoken of " the ' European ' theories of Trotskyism ".

[1] The names of the dissentients were not officially recorded, but were divulged by Kamenev at the Moscow provincial party conference on January 27, 1925 (L. Kamenev, *Stat'i i Rechi*, xii (1926), 58) : Krupskaya was a member of the central control commission and evidently voted for the resolution. Pravdin was one of the 22 who appealed to Comintern after the expulsion of Myasnikov from the party in 1922 (*Odinnadtsatyi S"ezd RKP(B)* (1936), p. 732 ; for the appeal see *The Bolshevik Revolution, 1917–1923*, Vol. 1, pp. 209-210) ; he escaped specific censure on that occasion, presumably as a minor participant.

[2] *Pravda*, January 31, 1925, accompanied the announcement with a full biography of Frunze ; on January 21, 1925, immediately after the resolution of the central committee, *Pravda* had published a long article by Frunze entitled *How the Red Army is fulfilling Lenin's Behests*.

[3] *XIV S"ezd Vsesoyuznoi Kommunisticheskoi Partii (B)* (1926), p. 484.

[4] The announcement, with a biography of Unshlikht, appeared in *Pravda*, February 7, 1925.

[5] L. Trotsky, *Moya Zhizn'* (Berlin, 1930), ii, 261.

determined not by the availability of arguments but by the control and manipulation of the levers of political power. He had no stomach for a fight whose character bewildered and eluded him. When attacked, he retreated from the arena because he instinctively felt that retreat offered him the best chance of survival.

What, however, most fatally paralysed Trotsky's capacity for action at critical moments, and hampered him even in formulating a case against his opponents, was his unqualified acceptance of the supremacy of the party and of the claims of party discipline. Something of his attitude may be explained by the fervour of the belated convert compelled to demonstrate, among men whose party records were longer and less sullied, that none was a better Bolshevik than he. He had voted without qualms for the resolution of the tenth party congress of March 1921 which outlawed " fractions " and " groupings " in the party.[1] He continued to insist with greater fervour than any other leader that " one cannot be right against the party ".[2] When many years later he wrote in an obituary of Krupskaya that " her revolutionary feeling struggled with the spirit of discipline ",[3] he was diagnosing the plight of his own conscience. Conscious of the moral dilemma which would confront him once his views were condemned by a party vote, he struggled by every means to postpone the crucial issue. Again and again he compromised on what could be made to seem secondary points ; again and again he disappointed and abandoned those who were ready and eager to support him ; again and again he refused to join battle, till at length battle was forced on him in conditions most unfavourable to himself and when he had already lost most of his potential allies. Morally unable to face the consequences of excommunication, he lacked the courage to take in time the only measures which, by appearing to court it, might yet have averted it.[4]

---

[1] See *The Bolshevik Revolution, 1917–1923*, Vol. 1, pp. 200-201.
[2] See *The Interregnum, 1923–1924*, p. 363.
[3] *Byulleten' Oppozitsii* (Paris), No. 75-76 (March–April, 1939), p. 32.
[4] The irresolution of the " liberal " Catholic bishops who were opposed to the proclamation of papal infallibility in 1871 has been described in terms which could be applied to Trotsky's attitude without changing a word : " The bishops, even those of the minority, had so long cultivated the habit of blind obedience that they had become constitutionally incapable of effective opposition. . . . Each time they were tempted to reject a decree they decided instead to save their strength for the main battle, but, by the time that battle had

One curious detail remains to be noted. In spite of what had happened, Stalin continued to speak of " comrade Trotsky ". In speeches delivered at the Moscow and Leningrad provincial party conferences after the central committee's decision, Kamenev intermittently, and Zinoviev consistently, omitted the prefix.[1] Stalin's attitude to Trotsky remained, throughout, formally correct. Kamenev, and still more firmly Zinoviev, had by implication read him out of the party. Kamenev made it clear that in his view Trotsky's expulsion from the Politburo had been merely postponed through the unwillingness of the central committee to take a decision " in advance of the party ". He expressed the hope that the next party congress would " draw the political and organizational conclusions from the discussion which has now ended ".[2] Eleven months later the fourteenth party congress was to provide an ironical commentary on this ambition.

arrived, they had dissipated both their strength and their will-power " (G. Himmelfarb, *Lord Acton* (1952), p. 107). Trotsky was in exactly the position taken up on that occasion by Acton, who wrote of his submission : " The act was one of pure obedience, and was not grounded on the removal of my motives of opposition to the decrees " (unpublished note quoted *ibid.* pp. xxvi-xxvii). Trotsky, as Zinoviev correctly said, " attempts to deny everything, to admit nothing, to confine himself to a formal, loyal, ' I obey ' " (*Leningradskaya Pravda*, February 5, 1925).

[1] Kamenev's speech is in *Izvestiya*, January 30, 1925, and in L. Kamenev, *Stat'i i Rechi*, xii (1926), 7-59 ; Zinoviev's in *Izvestiya*, February 6, 1925.
[2] L. Kamenev, *Stat'i i Rechi*, xii (1926), 44, 59.

CHAPTER 12

SOCIALISM IN ONE COUNTRY

THE doctrine of socialism in one country was, in its origin, a blow struck in the struggle against Trotsky. Stalin first propounded it in his article of December 1924[1] as a counterblast to Trotsky's " permanent revolution ", and in a conscious attempt to provide a positive alternative. Trotsky himself accepted the antithesis :

> The theory of socialism in one country . . . is the only theory that consistently, and to the end, is opposed to the theory of permanent revolution.[2]

Like every doctrinal argument advanced in the campaign against Trotsky, socialism in one country conformed to the tactical pattern, later described by Zinoviev,[3] of assimilating " old disagreements " to " new issues ". It revolved round a distinction — or rather a confusion — between the process of making a socialist revolution and the process of building a socialist economy once the revolution had been achieved. As regards the first question, Russian Marxists before 1905 had in general been content to accept the view that a socialist revolution could not be made in an economically backward country like Russia, i.e. in a country where the proletariat was in a small minority and where the bourgeois revolution had not yet occurred. The coming revolution in Russia could therefore only be a bourgeois revolution ; and the rôle of Russian Social-Democrats could only be to support the bourgeoisie, not to attempt to make a revolution on their own. After 1905, only the Mensheviks stuck to this view. Both Lenin and Trotsky assigned a positive revolutionary rôle to the Russian

---

[1] See p. 21 above.
[2] L. Trotsky, *Permanentnaya Revolyutsiya* (Berlin, 1930), p. 168.
[3] See p. 13 above.

Social-Democrats, though they defined it differently. Lenin held that the party, acting on behalf of the proletariat, should place itself at the head of a worker-peasant revolutionary coalition under proletarian leadership. The revolution achieved by this coalition would, owing to peasant predominance, still necessarily be a bourgeois revolution. It would result in the setting up of a bourgeois-democratic dictatorship of workers and peasants ; and this dictatorship would prepare the conditions in which the socialist revolution would become possible. Trotsky argued, like Lenin, that the Russian proletariat, supported by the peasantry, should take the lead in bringing the bourgeois revolution to fruition. But he believed that it would not be possible, even if it was desirable, to stop at this point. The proletariat, in completing the bourgeois revolution, would inevitably be impelled in the course of the same process to begin the socialist revolution. One revolution would lead into the other. This was the doctrine to which Trotsky gave the name, borrowed from Marx, of " permanent revolution ". Lenin expressed disbelief in the doctrine.[1] But when in April 1917 he declared that the revolution which had broken out in Russia could not remain a bourgeois revolution, and incited his Bolshevik followers to a direct seizure of power in the name of the proletariat, he adopted a position distinguished only by the finest of differences from that of Trotsky.

These discussions before 1917 did not touch on the question what would happen after the achievement of a proletarian revolution, i.e. whether and in what conditions it would be possible to build a socialist economy. Neither Lenin nor Trotsky contemplated the possibility of building a socialist economy in backward Russia alone, for the simple reason (if for no other) that for some time after October 1917 they continued to assume, in common with all other Bolsheviks, that the régime would be unable to maintain itself in Russia at all unless a proletarian revolution occurred in the more advanced European countries ; and the Bolsheviks had therefore the strongest possible interest in working to extend the revolution to those countries. In this sense both Lenin and Trotsky believed in " permanent revolution ". This was not the sense in which Trotsky had originally used the term.

[1] For these discussions see *The Bolshevik Revolution, 1917-1923*, Vol. 1, pp. 56-62.

But it was the only sense which had any relevance to the situation after 1917.

In 1924 the triumvirs, eager to discredit Trotsky by raking over every point on which Lenin had formerly differed from him, turned their attention to the issue of " permanent revolution ", and reprinted every passage in which Lenin had expressed his dissent from the doctrine. Trotsky protested in vain that the argument about " permanent revolution ", whatever its merits, belonged to history and was irrelevant to any of the issues now confronting the party or the Soviet Government.[1] The very irrelevance of the argument had the curious effect of causing it to be assumed that it turned in fact, not on the now obsolete question of the conditions in which a socialist revolution could be brought about, but on the still crucial question of the conditions in which a socialist economy could be built. It began to be said, and was sincerely believed by many, if not by the leaders themselves, that what Trotsky had meant by " permanent revolution " was the view that a socialist economy could not be created in Soviet Russia except with the aid of a proletarian revolution elsewhere, and that this was the view from which Lenin had dissented. The misunderstanding was furthered by the fact that, in the autumn of 1923, with Lenin dying and out of action, Trotsky, unlike Stalin (though not unlike Zinoviev), had been a fervent advocate of stimulating the revolution in Germany. It came to be assumed, without evidence and indeed without argument, that Lenin would on that occasion have occupied a position opposite to that of Trotsky, and that Stalin represented the line which Lenin would have taken.[2]

By a flash of originality of a quality so rare in Stalin's career that it has sometimes been described as an accident, Stalin perceived that this was a real and burning issue which called for a new elaboration of doctrine. Every Bolshevik believed that the revolution which had proved victorious in October 1917 was a

---

[1] In his letter of January 15, 1925, to the party central committee (see p. 30 above) Trotsky wrote that " the formula ' Permanent Revolution ' . . . belongs wholly to the past " and that, if he had mentioned it on any recent occasion, this was " a reversion to the past and not in the sphere of present political problems ".

[2] For the positions adopted by the various leaders on the German question in the autumn of 1923 see *The Interregnum, 1923-1924*, pp. 201-203.

socialist revolution ; nobody dreamed of returning to the old
controversies about the character of the revolution. Yet, according to party doctrine, it was impossible to build a socialist economy
in a single backward country, if the revolution was confined to
that country alone. So long as confidence was felt in the early
consummation of the socialist revolution in Europe, no need was
seen to readjust party doctrine on this point. But now, after the
fiasco in Germany in the autumn of 1923, this confidence had
vanished, and the party found itself suspended in mid-air. It
could not be expected to admit that, through the failure of the
proletariat of other countries, the Russian enterprise, after its
brilliant initial victory, was doomed to peter out. In practice, the
foundations of a socialist economy were now being laid. Something must be done to revise the theory of the conditions in
which the building of socialism was possible. This was the task
to which Stalin now addressed himself. None of the leaders had
hitherto faced this problem. Kamenev and Bukharin ignored it ;
Zinoviev took refuge in meaningless eloquence about world revolution ; Trotsky, who was conscious of the dilemma, could find no
way out except to insist on the urgency and importance of a
proletarian revolution in Europe. Fortunately Lenin, though he
had never attempted to argue the point, had been led from time to
time by the practical exigencies of laying the socialist foundations
of the economy to imply that the building of socialism even in
backward Russia was not a hopeless undertaking ; and Stalin
now avidly seized on these few scattered passages in an attempt
to prove that Lenin had indeed believed in the possibility of
building " socialism in one country ". The material was slender.
But constant reiteration would suffice to create the impression
that Lenin had believed that a socialist economy could be brought
into being even in backward Russia, that Trotsky held the dia-
metrically opposite view that this was impossible in the absence
of proletarian revolution elsewhere, and that Stalin, in resuscitat-
ing the doctrine of " socialism in one country ", was Lenin's true
and faithful disciple.

The stages by which the new conception took shape in Stalin's
mind can be clearly charted. In April 1924 he had been content
to repeat the conventional view that " for the final victory of
socialism, for the organization of socialist production, the efforts

of one country, particularly of a peasant country like Russia, are insufficient ".[1] In the elaboration of the campaign against Trotsky in November 1924 he argued, quoting Lenin, that Trotsky's theory of permanent revolution meant to " jump over " the peasantry, thus failing to recognize their essential place in the revolutionary process. The danger of Trotskyism was that it would " divorce from the Russian proletariat its ally, i.e. the poor peasantry ".[2] Stalin at this moment propounded no alternative view. But in the next few weeks a great deal of thinking was done. Stalin took the momentous decision to pit himself against Trotsky as the upholder and interpreter of Leninism. He was, however, anxious to assume a positive and independent rôle. The essay which had appeared in the newspapers on December 20, 1924, as *October and Comrade Trotsky's Theory of Permanent Revolution* was given a new title. Renamed *The October Revolution and the Tactics of the Russian Communists*, it reappeared as the introduction to a collection of Stalin's speeches and articles published under the title *On the Way to October* in January 1925.[3]

The major theme of the essay was an analysis of " the two peculiar characteristics of the October revolution " — the fact that the dictatorship of the proletariat had been established in Russia " in the form of a power arising on the basis of an alliance between the proletariat and the working masses of the peasantry ", and the fact that it had been established " as a result of the victory of socialism in one country ". Lenin had repeatedly dwelt on the implications of the first of these peculiarities. It remained to prove that he had equally recognized the implications of the second. Like Trotsky and like all the other leading Bolsheviks, Lenin had said again and again that the final victory of socialism could not be achieved in one country — least of all in a country that was economically backward. This, of course, remained true. But, in an article of 1915, he had offered, though without special reference to Russia, a more detailed analysis of the prospective course of events.

The unevenness of political and economic development [Lenin had written] is an unconditional law of capitalism. Hence it follows that the victory of socialism is possible in the first

[1] See *The Interregnum, 1923–1924*, pp. 358-359.
[2] Stalin, *Sochineniya*, vi, 349.   [3] *Ibid*. vi, 358-401.

instance in a few capitalist countries or even in one single capitalist country. The victorious proletariat of such a country, having expropriated the capitalists and organized socialist production at home, would stand up against the capitalist rest of the world, attracting to itself the oppressed classes of other countries, causing revolts among them against the capitalists, acting in case of necessity even with armed force against the exploiting classes and their states.

Stalin produced two further passages from Lenin in support of his new thesis of " socialism in one country ". In the peroration of the last speech he ever delivered, Lenin had described socialism as " not a question of the distant future " and expressed the hope (in the phrase carelessly misquoted by Kamenev [1]) that " not to-morrow, but in a few years . . . NEP Russia will become socialist Russia ". And in one of his last articles on the co-operatives he had asked, and answered in the affirmative, the rhetorical question whether the control by the proletarian state of the means of production, coupled with the alliance between the proletariat and millions of small peasants, did not provide " all that is essential for the construction of a full socialist society ".[2]

[1] See p. 4 above.

[2] The three passages quoted by Stalin are in Lenin, *Sochineniya*, xviii, 232-233 ; xxvii, 366, 392. The question whether these passages can legitimately be made to bear the interpretation placed on them by Stalin is, perhaps, academic. The passage of 1915, from which the famous phrase was derived, related primarily to the seizure of power, not to the building of a socialist economy ; nor can it be shown that Lenin had Russia in mind at all. The context suggests that Lenin was trying to counter a possible argument of, say, the German workers, that they could not start a revolution because the French workers could not be counted on to rise simultaneously. Zinoviev later deprived himself of an argument by his apparent unwillingness to admit that the passage did not refer to Russia (G. Zinoviev, *Leninizm* (1925), pp. 297-298) ; but Kamenev argued cogently that it applied, and could only apply, to western Europe (*XV Konferentsiya Vsesoyuznoi Kommunisticheskoi Partii (B)* (1927), p. 475). In Trotsky's view this passage from Lenin had been " turned upside down and interpreted in an illiterate manner " (L. Trotsky, *Permanentnaya Revolyutsiya* (Berlin, 1930), p. 125). The two later passages seemed at first sight more convincing. But Lenin in 1918 had already described Bolshevik strategy as being " to carry out the maximum that can be achieved in one country in order to develop, support and encourage revolution in all countries " (Lenin, *Sochineniya*, xxiii, 385 ; the context, both in the original and in a quotation of this passage in March 1923 in Stalin, *Sochineniya*, v, 179, strongly stressed the international aims of Bolshevism). It is not clear that Lenin, if challenged, would have considered himself to have gone beyond this in the two later passages. But it is idle to speculate on the view which Lenin would have taken of a contingency which had not arisen in his lifetime.

That was all. But, isolated from the context of Lenin's other writings and sharply opposed to Trotsky's far more clear-cut pronouncements, it was enough. Trotsky with his doctrine of permanent revolution both played down the need for the alliance with the peasantry and maintained that " the real rise of a socialist economy in Russia will become possible only after the victory of the proletariat in the most important countries of Europe ". Trotsky's theory of permanent revolution was the antithesis of Lenin's theory of socialism in one country. It was " a variant of Menshevism ". Having thus established " socialism in one country " as a fundamental item of Leninist doctrine, Stalin ended by redressing the balance in favour of its international function. " The victory of socialism in one country is not a self-sufficient task " ; it is " the beginning and the premiss of world revolution ". He summed up in a formula designed to saddle Trotskyism with the odium of a passive and negative (i.e. a Menshevik) rôle :

> Wrong are those who, forgetting the international character of the October revolution, declare the victory of the revolution in one country to be a purely and exclusively national phenomenon. But wrong also are those who, remembering the international character of the revolution, are inclined to think of this revolution as something passive, destined only to receive support from without.

Outside aid was no doubt necessary for the *final* victory of socialism in Russia ; but Russia was a dispenser, as well as a recipient, of aid. Stalin ended on a note which stressed Russia's positive rôle. The argument was conducted throughout on a theoretical plane, and no element of personal animosity was allowed to appear. It was among the most carefully pondered of all Stalin's writings.

It is probable that when Stalin first propounded this doctrine, in the winter of 1924–1925, he only dimly realized the importance which it would presently assume. His partners in the triumvirate certainly had no inkling of it : they shared with Trotsky the common assumption of Stalin's insignificance in matters of theory. At the best, socialism in one country was one more nail driven into the coffin of Trotskyism. At the worst, it was a harmless personal fad of Stalin. No serious attention was paid to it. It did not figure in the resolution drafted by Zinoviev which condemned Trotsky in January 1925. Stalin did not mention it in his short speech on that occasion ; and nobody thought of invoking it in the difficult discussions of agrarian policy which went on throughout the winter. Its original appearance in the article of December 1924 was followed by a three months' silence, during which the theory of socialism in one country seems to have been ignored by party leaders and publicists, including its author.[1] But it soon derived adventitious aid from current discussions of relations of the Soviet Union with the capitalist world. The fiasco of the projected German revolutionary *coup* in the autumn of 1923 had led to a reassessment of the powers of resistance inherent in capitalism and of the interval likely to elapse before its final overthrow. The session of IKKI in March 1925 was much occupied with the problem of the " stabilization of capitalism ".[2] This could be met only by the increased strength of the Soviet Union. In a speech delivered to the Moscow party committee early in April 1925, which was issued as a pamphlet, Bukharin enquired " how far this turn in the process of the struggle for the strengthening of the Soviet state is enriching the science of the Soviet state with new ideas " ; and the non-committal answer showed that Stalin's formula had started a train of thought in Bukharin's ingenious and speculative mind :

Can we build socialism in one country so long as there is no victory of the western European proletariat ? When we began to work on this question, it turned out that the question itself was not so simple as it appeared earlier, when we thought little about it. It proved much more complicated than it had seemed on first examination.[3]

It was in this context that it emerged, later in the same month, in the debates of the Politburo on the eve of the fourteenth party conference. The occasion was the preparation of the resolution which Zinoviev was to submit to the conference on the report of

[1] Stalin's collected works contain a short letter of January 25, 1925, to an unnamed correspondent explaining and defending the theory (*Sochineniya*, viii, 16-18) ; but this was published for the first time in 1947.

[2] This question will be discussed in Part V in the following volume.

[3] N. Bukharin, *Tekushchii Moment i Osnovy Nashei Politiki* (1925), pp. 7-9 ; a reference, in an article in *Sotsialisticheskoe Khozyaistvo*, No. 3, 1925, p. 6 (published in May 1925), to "the question put by Bukharin about the possibility of building socialism in only one country " shows that the question was still unfamiliar, and not specifically associated with Stalin.

the party delegation to IKKI. The initiative clearly came from Stalin — or perhaps from Bukharin acting at his instigation. If the " stabilization of capitalism " meant that the capitalist régimes in other countries had momentarily achieved some measure of stabilization, so also — and more significantly — had the régime in the Soviet Union, which, if it had not yet achieved socialism, was advancing at an increasingly rapid rate towards it. The counterpart of the recognition of the stabilization of capitalism was recognition of the possibility of "ˎsocialism in one country ". This should, it was argued, find its place in the resolution.

The evidence does not suggest that the debate in the Politburo on this question was anything like so sharp as was afterwards pretended. About the time it took place Kamenev addressed the Moscow provincial congress of Soviets in language which, though he did not introduce the word " socialism ", was substantially the same as that used later by Bukharin :

> Better by the exertion of our own forces and our own labour to obtain the results which we need, not with the help of the capitalists, but with the help of the use of our own energy, by travelling our own road. Better to travel this road more slowly, but it will be sure ; better let Russia develop more slowly, but remain ours, rather than more rapidly, but become alien, become foreign.[1]

In the recriminations which preceded the fourteenth party congress eight months later, it was alleged that Kamenev and Zinoviev had " defended in the Politburo the point of view that we shall not be able to overcome our internal difficulties owing to our technical and economic backwardness if we are not saved by international revolution ".[2] In fact, the argument turned not on the possibility of the process of building socialism in the Soviet Union, or on the impossibility of finally completing that process (on both these points everyone was in agreement), but on the far more esoteric question why the final achievement of socialism was pronounced impossible in the absence of a proletarian revolution in other countries. Kamenev and Zinoviev thought that this was due in part to the backwardness of the Soviet economy ; Stalin

---

[1] L. Kamenev, *Stat'i i Rechi*, xii (1926), 141.
[2] For the letter of the Moscow party committee from which this quotation is taken see pp. 126-127 below.

and Bukharin insisted that it was due exclusively to the external
threat of a capitalist environment.   The issue was clearly explained
by Bukharin in December 1925 to the fourteenth party congress :

> On this question a dispute broke out at one of the sessions of
> the Politburo, about the time of the fourteenth party confer-
> ence. . . . Comrade Kamenev, and after him Comrade Zino-
> viev, maintained at this session the position that we shall not
> be able to complete the building of socialism owing to our
> *technical backwardness.* It was *on this point* that we disputed
> with them, *for this* that we broke lances.   We agreed with them
> that the only guarantee against intervention, against a fresh
> war, against restoration imposed by the bayonets of capitalist
> armies, would be an international socialist revolution.   But we
> denied with passion the proposition advanced by them that
> we were doomed to perish on account of our technical back-
> wardness.[1]

This fine-spun distinction was afterwards to become the starting-
point for far-reaching conclusions.   But at the moment it may
well have seemed trivial and not worth fighting about.   According
to Stalin, " the point of view of Zinoviev was rejected by the
Politburo " ; [2] Voroshilov, more naïvely, but perhaps more
accurately, reported that, " after comrades Stalin and Bukharin
had spoken, the decision was unanimous ".[3]   Zinoviev's easy
acquiescence may have been part of a tacit bargain, Stalin's support
on other questions being the *quid pro quo* ; it is perhaps more
likely that Zinoviev made what seemed a harmless, or perhaps
pointless, concession to Stalin's importunities.   It was agreed to
include " socialism in one country " in the text of the resolution.

The resolution, which was adopted by the conference on a
report by Zinoviev without discussion, dealt with the existing
" stabilization " in the capitalist world.   IKKI at its recent
session had recognized that no " immediately revolutionary

---

[1] *XIV S"ezd Vsesoyuznoi Kommunisticheskoi Partii (B)* (1926), pp. 135-136.
[2] Stalin, *Sochineniya*, viii, 73.
[3] *XIV S"ezd Vsesoyuznoi Kommunisticheskoi Partii (B)* (1926), pp. 397-398.
Confirmation of the impression that the issue was not seriously contested in the
Politburo in April 1925 comes from statements made at the fourteenth party
congress by Bukharin and Molotov ; when Kamenev called the April resolution a " compromise " (*ibid.* p. 471), Bukharin retorted that " we have learned
this only today " and Molotov that " until yesterday Kamenev and Zinoviev
nowhere mentioned their disagreement with the resolution " (*ibid.* pp. 602,
662).   Tomsky (*ibid.* p. 277) also referred to the dispute in a quite casual way.

situation " existed in Europe or, by implication, anywhere else.[1]
But, besides the temporary stabilization of capitalism, the resolution
also drew attention to the corresponding stabilization produced
by " the growth of state industry and the strengthening of the
socialist elements of the economy of the USSR ". It then quoted
the Lenin article of 1915 on the victory of socialism in one country.
Lenin had, of course, taught that " the *final* victory of socialism
in the sense of a complete guarantee against the restoration of
bourgeois relations is possible only on an international scale "
(this point was illustrated by copious quotations). But a new,
though somewhat ambiguous, quotation was found to add to
Stalin's previous discoveries. " 10-20 years of correct relations
with the peasantry ", Lenin had written in 1921, in some notes
for his pamphlet *On the Food Tax* which were now hastily dis-
interred and published, " and victory on a world scale is assured
(even given a delay in the proletarian revolutions which are
growing)." [2] This seemed to put socialism in one country well
in line with the NEP tradition. The distinction between the two
alleged obstacles to the *final* victory of socialism — the technical
backwardness of the country and the threat from the capitalist
world — was drawn in a roundabout way, which concealed the
embarrassment of divided opinions.[3] And the resolution proclaimed that " in general the victory of socialism (*not* in the sense
of *final* victory) is unconditionally possible in one country ".[4]
The resolution excited no particular interest. Stalin's description
of it eighteen months later as " one of the most important party
documents in the history of our party " [5] would certainly have
startled the participants at the conference. It was, nevertheless,

[1] The proceedings of IKKI will be discussed in Part V in the following
volume.
[2] Lenin, *Sochineniya*, xxvi, 313 ; the notes were first published in *Bol'shevik*,
No. 7, April 15, 1925, pp. 72-80, and in *Leninskii Sbornik*, iv (1925), 371-378.
[3] Zinoviev's account of the matter in his report to the conference was characteristically wordy and confused : " For all the technical backwardness of our
country, *we can and must go on building, we must and shall build, socialism, notwithstanding the retarded tempo of the international revolution.* We have said clearly
that the *final* victory is in the international arena, but that the retarded tempo
of the revolution puts back not the victory itself, but the moment of its realization " (*Chetyrnadtsataya Konferentsiya Rossiiskoi Kommunisticheskoi Partii
(Bol'shevikov)* (1925), p. 244). For Stalin's elaboration of the distinction see
pp. 164-165 below.   [4] *VKP(B) v Rezolyutsiyakh* (1941), ii, 26-31.
[5] Stalin, *Sochineniya*, viii, 266.

a notable, though unperceived, victory for Stalin. He celebrated it by giving socialism in one country for the first time a modest place in a speech which he delivered a few days after the conference to a party meeting in Moscow.[1] By this time another quotation had come to light. Lenin had told the eighth All-Russian Congress of Soviets in December 1920 :

> Only when the country is electrified, only when industry, agriculture and transport have been put on the technical basis of modern large-scale industry, only then shall we be finally victorious.[2]

It was the first coupling of the new doctrine with the drive for intensive industrialization.

The first and immediate impression of " socialism in one country ", when it began to make its impact in the summer of 1925, was of a not very novel or important contribution to party doctrine which provided a counter-weight to the " stabilization of capitalism ", and suitably carried on the work of NEP in adapting party policy to the peculiar conditions of the Russian environment. It offered a fresh antidote to Trotsky's alleged under-estimate of the peasant, and revealed NEP as the road of advance to socialism in a predominantly peasant economy. In this interpretation NEP was the specifically Russian form of the great revolutionary design. By giving a national colour to the revolution, it had helped to reconcile to it many of those Russians, both at home and abroad, who had originally rejected it as non-Russian and anti-national. Socialism in one country made a far stronger emotional appeal of the same character. It reawakened a vague sentiment of national pride or patriotism which had been temporarily silenced, but not destroyed, by the resounding international appeal of the revolution. As the régime stabilized itself at home, and became the mouthpiece of the interests of the Russian state abroad, this sentiment revived with unexpected force, and lent an exceptional strength and vitality to the doctrine which seemed to embody it. It was no accident that Stalin's article which launched the doctrine had begun with a discussion of the " peculiarities " of the October revolution. It would be misleading to speak at this time of chauvinism, or even of nationalism

---

[1] *Ibid.* vii, 109-121.   [2] Lenin, *Sochineniya*, xxvi, 47.

as commonly understood. The sentiment wás one of pride in
the achievement of the revolution, but also of pride that this was
a Russian achievement, that Russia had been first in a field where
other allegedly more advanced countries had hitherto failed to
follow. It was immensely gratifying to this new-found national
revolutionary pride to have the assurance that Russia would lead
the world not only in carrying out a socialist revolution, but
in building a socialist economy. Kamenev, in his indictment
of Trotskyism in November 1924, had complained that " the
theory of ' permanent revolution ' places the workers' government in Russia in exclusive and complete dependence on an
immediate proletarian revolution in the west ".[1] Socialism in
one country was a declaration of independence of the west. " A
fig for Europe — we shall manage by ourselves " was the description of the new doctrine in the Menshevik journal published in
Berlin.[2] Socialism in one country was no mere piece of economic
analysis and no mere announcement of policy. It was a declaration of faith in the capacities and in the destiny of the Russian
people.

The initial emphasis of those who propagated or welcomed
the new doctrine seemed, therefore, to rest on the words " in one
country " and on its national aspect. In 1921 the urgent need
had been to appease the peasant with concessions which would
induce him to produce food for the towns and factories and put
the whole economy back into gear. The national appeal of NEP
was associated with the traditional faith in the Russian peasant
and even had Slavophil affiliations. Socialism in one country
seemed at first sight to have the same appeal and the same affiliations : it was the legitimate successor of NEP. It was on these
grounds that it was welcomed by the *smenovekhovtsy*,[3] and by
those innumerable Russians who stood outside the ranks of
Bolshevism, but whom NEP had reconciled to the régime. It was
on these grounds that it was assailed by Zinoviev and Trotsky
as the embodiment of " national narrow-mindedness " and

---

[1] L. Kamenev, *Stat'i i Rechi*, i (1925), 229.
[2] *Sotsialisticheskii Vestnik* (Berlin), No. 11-12 (105-106), June 20, 1925,
p. 21.
[3] Ustryalov, for instance, hailed it in an article of November 7, 1925, as
" the nationalization of October " (N. Ustryalov, *Pod Znakom Revolyutsii* (2nd
ed. 1927), pp. 212-218).

" national messianism ".[1] When Lenin introduced NEP, he set forth once again the two conditions of the success of the socialist revolution in backward Russia — " support at the right moment by a socialist revolution in one or several leading countries " and " a compromise between the proletariat . . . and the majority of the peasant population ".[2] Lenin did not, and could not, choose between the two conditions ; both were, in his thinking, essential. History had now forced a choice between them by indefinitely postponing the " socialist revolution in one or several leading countries ". Socialism in one country, the promulgation of which coincided with a marked intensification of the turn towards the peasant in Soviet policy, seemed to symbolize a frank acceptance of the choice. It rejected dependence on the socialist revolution in other countries. By the same token, it accepted dependence on a standing compromise with the peasant.

This appearance, like so much else in Soviet history of this period, proved illusory. Socialism in one country did, it was true, provide an answer to the dilemma of choice which Lenin refused to face. Socialism in one country did, it was true, start from rejection on dependence of other countries. But this did not involve acceptance of the alternative choice of dependence on the peasant. The ultimate significance of socialism in one country was that it denied (subject to the formal reservation about " final " victory) the necessity of either of the conditions posed by Lenin at the moment of the introduction of NEP, and thus, far from being the heir of NEP, boldly abandoned its basic presuppositions. In the years after 1925 socialism in one country, whatever the original intentions of its promoter and whatever the first impressions created by it, came to mean the opposite of NEP. Nor was this illogical ; for it was the recovery and the growing strength of the Soviet economy in the middle nineteen-twenties which pointed the way both to the superseding of NEP and to socialism in one country. What was now at stake was not the appeasement of the peasant, but the drive for industrialization. What was now to be realized " in one country " was not the peasant socialism of the old Russian tradition, but the industrial socialism of Marx.

[1] For Zinoviev see p. 163 below ; L. Trotsky, *Permanentnaya Revolyutsiya* (Berlin, 1930), p. 168.
[2] See *The Bolshevik Revolution, 1917–1923*, Vol. 2, p. 277.

The appeal to national sentiment was an appeal not to the Russia of the past, but to a new entity which would create a new world by its own resources. Self-sufficiency was proclaimed, not as an end, but as a necessary means. The appeal, though national (and potentially anti-Marxist) in one respect, was Marxist in another. Socialism in one country might look like the nationalization of the revolution ; but it was also its continuation. Through the process of industrialization the Soviet Union was to bring to fruition the socialist revolution, and to make itself a great and independent Power. Socialism in one country was a synthesis between socialist and national loyalties. It was the point at which Russian destiny and Marxism joined hands. By the same token it was a landmark in Russian history. Hitherto the economic development of Russia and the westernization of Russia had been integral parts of the same process. After 1925 they were separated. Industrialization would be pursued independently of the west and, if necessary, against the west. It was this self-reliance which distinguished industrialization under Stalin from industrialization under Witte.

By an odd paradox, the doctrine of socialism in one country, originally designed as a weapon against Trotsky, acquired its eventual importance in a quite different setting, and was used as a spear-head of quite different policies, including some that Trotsky himself had been most concerned to advocate. Socialism in one country seemed to be at the heart of all the economic, political and doctrinal disputes which flared up in the autumn of 1925. It fitted perfectly into the argument about the predominant character of the Soviet economy ; the theory that this was a form of state capitalism was the very negation of the belief in the possibility of building socialism in existing conditions. It fitted perfectly into the controversy about the nature of NEP ; if NEP was merely a retreat, then the Soviet Union was moving away from socialism, and the implication was clear that socialism in one country was a myth. It fitted perfectly into the dispute between the " industrial " school which desired, by a policy of rapid industrialization, to make the Soviet Union a self-sufficient economic entity and the " agrarian " school which advocated the expansion of agricultural exports in order to meet industrial requirements from abroad : the latter clearly rejected socialism in one country and looked forward to an indefinite prolongation of Soviet dependence on foreign countries. These issues lent topicality to a doctrine which had at first seemed purely abstract and scholastic. Socialism in one country suddenly emerged as the master-key which unlocked every door and served as the touchstone by which every issue could be judged and clarified.

But, above all, socialism in one country embodied the implicit — and later explicit — claim that Stalin alone offered, to the party and to the country, a positive and constructive policy, whereas his opponents had nothing to offer but negation and scepticism, and proposed to wait with folded arms for something to happen elsewhere. Theoretically the difference between the two views seemed almost to disappear under the weight of the argument. The supporters of socialism in one country did not at this stage dare to pretend that the building of socialism could be completely achieved in a backward and isolated country, but laid stress on the process of building. Its opponents did not deny that some progress could be made, but emphasized the inconclusive character of the work and the impossibility of bringing it to completion. Psychologically the difference was very great. Opponents of socialism in one country laid themselves open to the charge of implying that the revolution itself had been a mistaken or premature action, since it was now impossible to carry out the purposes for which it had been made ; and this charge stirred damning memories not only of Zinoviev's and Kamenev's "strike-breaking" opposition to Lenin in October 1917, and of the wavering of the party in face of the April theses six months earlier, but of the traditional view of Menshevism that backward Russia was not yet ripe for a socialist revolution. Alternatively, opponents of socialism in one country were exposed to the charge of rash adventurism to hasten at all costs the revolution in other countries — the reverse side of the medal of pessimism and lack of faith. This was declared to be the essence of Trotsky's " permanent revolution ", which Lenin had also condemned. It was easy, on the basis of the new doctrine, to depict Stalin as the true expositor of Bolshevism and of Leninism and his opponents as the heirs of those who had resisted Lenin and denied the Bolshevik creed in the past. Unwittingly Stalin had forged for himself an instrument of enormous power. Once forged, he was quick to discover its strength, and wielded it with masterful skill and ruthlessness.

CHAPTER 13

THE RIFT IN THE TRIUMVIRATE

THE rout of Trotsky in January 1925 removed the last solid support that underpinned the precarious structure of the triumvirate. Its collapse was now inevitable; and about the same time another event occurred which helped to shape the form and manner of the breakdown. Uglanov, whom Zinoviev and Kamenev had appointed secretary of the Moscow provincial party committee in the previous autumn to clean up the Moscow organization,[1] transferred his allegiance to Stalin. According to Uglanov's story, Zinoviev and Kamenev " carried on conversations with me from which I understood that they were trying in a roundabout way to fasten on me their disagreements with Stalin ". Uglanov, on his own showing, " declined this invitation ", and acted " with the firm intention to work in such a way as to bring the Moscow organization wholly and completely into line with the central committee ".[2] The first result of the change was the eclipse of Kamenev, who found himself ousted from any but an honorific function in his own party organization. After the defeat of Trotsky, Kamenev manifestly relapsed into a secondary rôle — a decline due, partly perhaps to his less ambitious and less pugnacious temperament, but mainly to his lack of the solid backing of any party machine. This left only Stalin and Zinoviev in the field as protagonists; and with Stalin in firm control both of the Moscow party organization and of the central party machine located in Moscow, and with Zinoviev's hold over Leningrad still unshaken, the clash between them was bound to take on the form of a struggle between the two capitals. The

---

[1] See p. 22 above.

[2] *XIV S"ezd Vsesoyuznoi Kommunisticheskoi Partii (B)* (1926), p. 193; that Uglanov moved over from Zinoviev and Kamenev to Stalin is confirmed in B. Bazhanov, *Stalin* (German transl. from French, 1931), pp. 37-38. The change may have been gradual; it cannot be precisely dated.

prestige of Zinoviev and of the powerful party organization in Leningrad might seem fairly matched against the prestige of Stalin and the Moscow organization, even though Moscow enjoyed the advantage of housing the central organs of the party.

The first occasion on which Leningrad could be said to have pitted itself against Moscow was the proposal to expel Trotsky from the Politburo, voiced by the Leningrad party committee and voted down by a large majority of the central committee.[1] This was followed by a demonstration of dissent and protest from the Leningrad committee of the Komsomol, which had taken a vocal part in the campaign for Trotsky's expulsion. The Leningrad committee — not, it was believed, without Zinoviev's encouragement — attempted to assert its independence of the central Komsomol organization in Moscow, and was called to order after a bitter struggle.[2] In another episode of these months the apparent triviality of the issue made the animus displayed in the Leningrad organization all the more striking. The conference of *rabkors* and *sel'kors* held in Moscow in December 1924 revealed a sharp division of opinion whether the *rabkors* and *sel'kors* should be organized round the newspapers to which they supplied information, and kept independent of the party, or whether they should be organized in territorial groups and made responsible to the local party organizations. The former view, which was said to encourage the recruitment of non-party workers and peasants, was endorsed by Bukharin, and was adopted by the conference. The latter view was that of the Leningrad delegation ; the Leningrad *rabkors* were apparently in fact organized on this basis.[3] The principal spokesman of the Leningrad view was a Leningrad party official named Sarkis, who had been active in organizing " patronage " of rural party organizations by the towns, and was singled out for praise by Zinoviev as " one of our best

---

[1] See p. 31 above.

[2] See pp. 95-98 below ; Bukharin later referred to this as the " second stage " in the attempt to create an independent opposition base in Leningrad (*Izvestiya*, January 10, 1926).

[3] For the conference see Vol. 1, p. 198, note 2. An article in *Leningradskaya Pravda*, December 12, 1924, sharply attacked the majority view as implying that " *rabkor* organizations have in general nothing at all to do with the party " ; Bukharin replied in an article reprinted in N. Bukharin, *O Rabkore i Sel'kore* (1925), pp. 68-73. For the history of this question see an article in *Leningradskaya Pravda*, February 4, 1925.

workers ".[1]   At the Leningrad provincial party conference in
January 1925 Sarkis launched a vigorous attack on Bukharin,
whom he accused of " syndicalist, non-Bolshevik " views ; [2] and
the controversy was carried on for some time in the columns of
Pravda and *Leningradskaya Pravda*.[3]   Another Leningrad party
official, Vardin, published a pamphlet attacking Bukharin and the
decisions of the conference, which was sharply reviewed by one of
Bukharin's disciples, Slepkov.[4]   In June 1925 a pronouncement of
the Orgburo, which was clearly intended to close the argument,
laid it down that *rabkors* and *sel'kors*, while serving as " conductors
of proletarian communist influence to the broad masses of toilers ",
should not be formally linked with party or trade union organizations.[5]   The discussion then petered out.   But references to it at
the fourteenth party congress in December 1925 showed how
deep were the mutual animosities engendered by it.   At that time
40 per cent of *rabkors* and 26 per cent of *sel'kors* were said to be
party members.[6]

The struggle within the triumvirate thus gradually acquired,
though this was no part of the design of either of the protagonists,
a geographical basis.   The peculiar jealousies which had existed
between the " two capitals " of Tsarist Russia reappeared in
an equally potent form under the Soviet order.   In the eyes of
the first generation of Bolsheviks, Petrograd was the shrine of the
revolution.   Here the revolution had been planned ; it was the
proletariat of Petrograd which had led the assault ; here the first
workers' and peasants' government had been proclaimed.   The
unfortunate sequel — the shift of the capital owing to the military

[1] G. Zinoviev, *Litsom k Derevne* (1925), pp. 66-67 ; for " patronage ", see
pp. 342-344 below.   Whatever Sarkis's other qualities, he was evidently something of a *frondeur* ; a violent attack by him on party education in *Leningradskaya
Pravda*, March 18, 1925, provoked several angry replies and an eventual editorial
disclaimer (*ibid.* March 31, 1925).

[2] Quoted in Stalin, *Sochineniya*, vii, 380, from the stenographic record of
the conference ; Sarkis's speech was briefly reported in *Leningradskaya Pravda*,
January 28, 1925.

[3] See, for example, *ibid.* February 13, March 3, 1925 ; *Pravda*, February 28,
1925, where the Leningrad *rabkors* were severely criticized.

[4] *Bol'shevik*, No. 13-14, July 31, 1925, pp. 65-75 ; for Vardin see p. 80,
note 3 below.

[5] *Izvestiya Tsentral'nogo Komiteta Rossiiskoi Kommunisticheskoi Partii
(Bol'shevikov)*, No. 22-23 (97-98), June 22, 1925, pp. 1-2.

[6] *XIV S"ezd Vsesoyuznoi Kommunisticheskoi Partii (B)* (1926), p. 61.

vulnerability of Petrograd, the collapse of industry, and of the heavy metal industries in particular, the depopulation of Petrograd — had not altogether eclipsed these memories. The renaming of the city after the dead leader, coinciding with unmistakable signs of a revival of industry, seemed an augury of a brighter future. But jealousy of Moscow had become endemic in Leningrad, and led to incessant exaggerated reminders of the city's revolutionary pre-eminence. *Leningradskaya Pravda* hailed the Leningrad city Soviet, on the occasion of a session in April 1925, as " the first Soviet of the proletarian dictatorship " ; [1] and Sarkis boasted on the same occasion that the party cell in factories was a Leningrad invention.[2] It sometimes seemed as if credit was claimed by Leningrad for every achievement of the party :

> Everywhere we see only advances. Who has done this ? First of all, the workers' organization of the city of Leningrad. Who of you can say where another such organization can be found, where so much initiative is shown as by us ? [3]

A piece of Leningrad arrogance which particularly enraged Moscow was the habit of treating the newspaper *Leningradskaya Pravda* (the name had been changed from *Petrogradskaya Pravda* on January 30, 1924) as the lineal descendant of the *Pravda* founded by the party in Petersburg in 1912. The title *Pravda* was printed in large capitals with the geographical epithet small and scarcely noticeable ; the year of issue reckoned from 1912 appeared under the title in every issue ; and, if occasion arose to mention the *Pravda* published in Moscow, the paper of the party central committee and the true heir of the *Pravda* of 1912, it was always referred to as the *Moskovskaya Pravda*. *Leningradskaya Pravda* managed to celebrate its thirteenth anniversary in its issue of May 5, 1925, without mentioning the existence of the Moscow *Pravda* at all.[4]

The Leningrad claim to pre-eminence in the revolutionary

---

[1] *Leningradskaya Pravda*, April 11, 1925.   [2] *Ibid.* April 16, 1925.
[3] *Ibid.* November 18, 1925 ; this passage was quoted by Rudzutak at the fourteenth party congress (*XIV S"ezd Vsesoyuznoi Kommunisticheskoi Partii (B)* (1925), p. 342).
[4] A speech of Safarov on the occasion, reported in *Leningradskaya Pravda*, May 13, 1925, also ignored the Moscow *Pravda* ; the annoyance of Moscow was expressed at the fourteenth party congress (*XIV S"ezd Vsesoyuznoi Kommunisticheskoi Partii (B)* (1926), p. 388).

landscape had an ideological character. Leningrad was the city of the proletariat. It had never quite lost its status acquired under the Tsars as the original seat of Russian industry and especially of Russian heavy industry. It was uniquely accessible to the west, still the key-point of industry and world trade. Even the poverty of the soil made it easier here than in Moscow to recruit an industrial proletariat divorced from the land. Leningrad was the stronghold of the class-conscious, organized proletariat, of the workers in heavy industry who had provided from the earliest days the hard proletarian core of Bolshevism. Leningrad, said Safarov, was " the chief commanding height of the proletarian dictatorship in our country ", and " the most important proletarian summit in the USSR ".[1] Leningrad, said Zinoviev, possessed " traits which distinguish it from other centres " : it was predominantly proletarian ; private trade was less developed there ; it was " a proletarian centre administering itself from the bottom to the top ".[2] The claim was constantly made that the composition of the party in Leningrad was more " proletarian " than in Moscow. This was difficult to establish from current statistics of membership. Of 50,000 party members and 40,000 candidates in the Leningrad province in September 1925, 72 per cent were returned as workers, 11 per cent as peasants and 17 per cent as officials ; of a somewhat larger total in the Moscow province, 71 per cent were workers, 5 per cent peasants and 24 per cent officials.[3] But more detailed analysis made possible by the party census of January 1927 revealed significant differences. In the first place, Leningrad province had a higher proportion of party members to population (362 to every 10,000 inhabitants) than Moscow (285 to every 10,000 inhabitants), and by far the highest proportion in the Soviet Union, where the general average was only 78 party members to 10,000 inhabitants. Secondly, of Leningrad workers who were party members 36·4 per cent were metal workers — " the most advanced and most conscious workers " ; of Moscow workers who were party members only

[1] *Leningradskaya Pravda*, November 21, 1925.
[2] *Ibid.* December 6, 1925.
[3] *Izvestiya Tsentral'nogo Komiteta Rossiiskoi Kommunisticheskoi Partii (Bol'shevikov)*, No. 40 (115), October 19, 1925, p. 6 ; No. 43-44 (118-119), November 16, 1925, pp. 11-12 ; the criterion of classification was, of course, social origin, not current occupation (see Vol. 1, pp. 91-92).

15·3 per cent came from the metal industries and 55 per cent
from the textile industries, more than half of these being women
— " a more backward element than the men and more difficult to
draw into political life ".[1]   There was force in Zinoviev's claim
that Leningrad was relatively free from the phenomenon of " new
workers " — peasants " who have not passed through the school
of factory and workshop, who have not in the past had any
hardening in the factory, and who have therefore acquired completely separate psychological traits ".[2]   It was undeniable that
the Leningrad workers, and especially the metal workers, had
behind them a longer and firmer tradition of trade union and party
membership than workers elsewhere in the Soviet Union, and
were politically more class-conscious and active.   It was also true
that the revival of heavy industry and the process of industrialization served in a special way to revive the prosperity, prestige and
authority of Leningrad.   Leningrad was still, at a time when other
large industrial centres had not yet been developed, the focal
point of heavy industry and of the industrial proletariat.   Current
boastings had some foundation in reality.   A social fact was
elevated and inflated into an article of faith.

Once, therefore, the struggle for power within the triumvirate
took on the geographical form of a rivalry between Leningrad and
Moscow, this factor also determined the ideological mould in
which it was cast ; and a curious reversal of attitudes occurred.
The triumvirate had come into power on what could without
much exaggeration be called a peasant platform.   The solid
achievements of its economic policy were the closing of the
scissors, the currency reform and the full realization of NEP.
Zinoviev, as the leading member of the triumvirate, had made
the " link " between the peasantry and the countryside the theme
of countless speeches, and as recently as the autumn of 1924 had
launched the slogan " Face to the countryside ".   " ' Face to the
countryside ' seriously, for a long time, for ever ", Zinoviev had
written in January 1925,[3] quoting and characteristically distorting
Lenin's slogan on NEP.   He had from time to time made routine
pronouncements about the revival of the metal industry.   But

[1] *Sotsial'nyi i Natsional'nyi Sostav VKP(B)* (1928), p. 19.
[2] *Leningradskaya Pravda*, December 9, 1925.
[3] *Ibid*. January 13, 1925.

c*

now, in allusion to Lenin's famous remark about changing over
from the " beggarly peasant *muzhik* horse " to the " horse of
large-scale machine industry ", he observed complacently :

> Some time will pass before the leader of revolution, the
> proletariat, will be able to say : " Now I have outgrown the
> peasant nag, now I have a race-horse ; let us now mount and
> travel more quickly ".[1]

It was Zinoviev and Kamenev who attributed peasant discontent
to jealousy of the superior privileges of the worker. According to
Zinoviev, the peasants protested " because on the silver half-ruble
piece the hammer is engraved above the sickle and not *vice
versa* " ;[2] according to Kamenev, they considered " that the
workers work little and live better than the peasants, and that
therefore we ought to introduce the ten-hour working day ".[3] It
was Zinoviev and Kamenev who led the attack on Trotsky for
neglecting the interests of the peasant, and who turned the helm
of party policy sharply towards concessions to the well-to-do
peasant at the fourteenth party conference in April 1925. Stalin,
though he never dissented from this policy, seemed the most eager
of the three triumvirs to recall from time to time that the peasant
was necessarily subordinate to the proletariat in the eyes of the
Marxist. In the spring of 1924, Stalin had resisted the plausible
suggestion to include " peasants from the plough " as well as
" workers from the bench " in the " Lenin enrolment·", and three
months later had rejected the view that the peasant question was
" the fundamental in Leninism ".[4] In a speech of January 1925
he had shown himself a less than whole-hearted supporter of
Zinoviev's " Face to the countryside " slogan.[5] At the time of
the fourteenth party conference in April 1925 the triumvirate
stood solidly united for the last time to secure party approval for
a policy of concessions to the peasant — the reduction in the
agricultural tax and the sanction given to the leasing of land and
the hiring of labour. After the conference, Kamenev and Zinoviev

---

[1] *Leningradskaya Pravda*, February 5, 1925 ; Lenin's remark was made in
one of his last articles *Better Less but Better* (*Sochineniya*, xxvii, 417). Zinoviev's speech was delivered at the Leningrad provincial party conference on
January 26, 1925.   [2] See the speech quoted in the preceding note.
[3] L. Kamenev, *Stat'i i Rechi*, xii (1926), 94.
[4] See *The Interregnum, 1923–1924*, pp. 340, 359.
[5] See Vol. 1, p. 243.

both defended the line adopted with unreserved approval ; and it was Stalin who — if only behind closed doors — deprecated Bukharin's extreme interpretation of the policy.[1]

These attitudes were, however, as the sequel showed, pragmatic and accidental ; they rested on no firm or lasting foundation of conviction — and least of all in the case of Zinoviev. Zinoviev had adopted the policy, and proclaimed the slogan, of appeasement of the peasant as spokesman of a party leadership united against Trotsky. But a rift in the leadership was now clearly impending — personal jealousies and incompatibilities had become too strong for unity to hold much longer ; and when, in the early summer of 1925, Zinoviev began to discover to his dismay the strength of Stalin's hold over the central organization in Moscow,[2] and his own consequent dependence on the rival organization in Leningrad, the opinions of the Leningrad organization on current issues of policy began for the first time to acquire major importance. On any question of agrarian policy, the attitude of the party in Leningrad was never in serious doubt. The Leningraders, said Yaroslavsky, believed that only they had " genuine class feeling ", and that all other organizations in the party were " infected with a petty-bourgeois deviation ".[3]   It was Moscow which was the home of the peasant orientation, Moscow where even the proletariat had scarcely emancipated itself from its peasant background and affiliations. In 1918 the Petrograd Bolsheviks had come out strongly for the committees of poor peasants ; Zinoviev may have remembered the congress at which, bound by party loyalty, he had induced his reluctant followers to approve the muzzling of these committees in the interests of conciliation in the countryside.[4] The workers' opposition, the only attempt at organized opposition to NEP, had its strength and its centre in Petrograd. The promotion of heavy industry in 1924 to the front rank of

---

[1] For the speeches of Kamenev and Zinoviev, and for Stalin's reservations, see Vol. 1, pp. 270-274, 283-284.

[2] This was the moment when the signs of Stalin's supremacy first became plainly visible. An acute observer from Moscow wrote in *Sotsialisticheskii Vestnik* (Berlin), No. 11-12 (105-106), June 20, 1925, p. 21 : " Judging from certain indications, Stalin will be the hero of the day. His portrait is on the cover of illustrated journals ; his bust is in the windows of book-shops ; his speeches are printed in separate editions the day after their delivery."

[3] *XIV S"ezd Vsesoyuznoi Kommunisticheskoi Partii (B)* (1926), p. 197.

[4] See *The Bolshevik Revolution, 1917-1923*, Vol. 2, pp. 158-159.

party concern was also a move for the revival of Leningrad, and the subsequent turn towards the peasant, culminating in the pro-*kulak* policy of the spring of 1925, can have had few supporters in the Leningrad organization. So long as Zinoviev was at the head of a united triumvirate committed to support of this policy, the Leningraders could do little to make their voice heard. But, once Zinoviev became dependent on Leningrad as his sole remaining base, the opinion of Leningrad became a paramount consideration, and he swung over almost automatically to the Leningrad line. As Trotsky afterwards put it, " the leaders of the opposition in their struggle for self-preservation were compelled to adapt themselves to the class-consciousness of the Leningrad proletariat ".[1]

The change was abrupt. In the second half of May 1925 Zinoviev defended without reservation before a party audience in Moscow the turn towards the peasant executed on the mandate of the fourteenth party conference, though it is noteworthy that on this occasion he sought and obtained from the Politburo against some opposition, presumably from Bukharin, authority to characterize the new policy as a " retreat ".[2] A few days later he reminded a provincial trade union congress in Leningrad that " the question of the countryside is the central economic and political question of our days ", and spoke of the " obligations " which " the present state of affairs places on the working class of our country ".[3] Early in June 1925 came the embarrassing episode of Krupskaya's article attacking Bukharin, which a majority of the Politburo refused to publish, Zinoviev and Kamenev voting in the minority.[4] This was the first direct split between Zinoviev and Bukharin, and the first occasion on which Zinoviev and Kamenev ranged themselves with Krupskaya against a majority of their colleagues in the Politburo. Before the end of the same month, Zinoviev made and published a speech which

---

[1] Unpublished memorandum of December 22, 1925 (see p. 168 below). Zinoviev himself recognized the same truth in an inverted form : " This attempt to smash the Leningrad organization . . . is bound up in the closest way with the whole social set-up in the country " (*XIV S"ezd Vsesoyuznoi Kommunisticheskoi Partii (B)* (1926), pp. 451-452).

[2] See Vol. 1, p. 281 ; for the significance of the term " retreat " in this context see pp. 68-69 below.

[3] *Leningradskaya Pravda*, May 31, 1925.

[4] See Vol. 1, p. 285.

proclaimed in unmistakable terms that the policy of concessions to the peasant had gone to dangerous lengths,[1] and for the rest of the year continued to propound this view with growing emphasis and consistency. Within a few weeks Zinoviev was transformed from the principal promoter into the principal opponent of the peasant policy, and a few months later went down to defeat denouncing concessions to the *kulaks* which he had ardently supported less than a year before. The violence of the change could only confirm his reputation for shiftiness and instability, while Stalin, who had carefully steered clear of extreme commitments, could readjust himself without apparent effort to meet the challenge, moving almost imperceptibly between positions a little to the Left and a little to the Right of centre as day-to-day tactics required.

Throughout these proceedings Trotsky, whose action in the previous autumn had put the spark to the train, remained inactive and almost silent. He was still convalescent in Sukhum, the capital of the miniature Abkhazian autonomous SSR on the shores of the Black Sea, when VTsIK held its session of March 1925 in Tiflis.[2] When the session was over, Myasnikov, deputy president of the Sovnarkom of the Transcaucasian SFSR, and two other important officials of the republic, set out on March 22, 1925, for Sukhum to attend — or perhaps to organize — a congress of Soviets of the Abkhazian republic. The aeroplane in which they were travelling crashed, and all were killed.[3] Trotsky afterwards came to believe that they had been sent by Stalin to Sukhum to establish contact with him. But, apart from other difficulties about this story, these were hardly the men whom Stalin would

---

[1] See Vol. 1, pp. 286-287. A speech of June 1925 in which Zinoviev drew attention to current unrest in Morocco and in China and concluded that " a genuine *world* revolution, and not merely a European revolution, is being kindled before our eyes " (*Izvestiya*, June 16, 1925), and an article on the same theme entitled *The Epoch of Wars and Revolutions* (*ibid.* June 28, 1925) may be thought to mark a growing revulsion against " socialism in one country " ; but the peasant orientation seems to have been the major factor in Zinoviev's change of front.   [2] For this session see p. 240 below.

[3] The accident was reported, with obituary notices of the victims, in *Pravda*, March 24, 1925; for Myasnikov see *The Bolshevik Revolution, 1917–1923*, Vol. 1, p. 308, note 4.

have chosen for a delicate mission. Later, Trotsky was visited
by Rakovsky and I. N. Smirnov: according to Trotsky, though
they made no overtures to him, they too had been sent to visit
him by Stalin in order to frighten Zinoviev.[1] Beyond doubt
Trotsky knew that Stalin had been less implacably hostile to him
in the debates of the central committee than Kamenev and
Zinoviev; and Stalin counted on this knowledge to prevent any
danger that Trotsky would throw his weight on the side of
Kamenev and Zinoviev in the impending break-up of the triumvirate. Stalin left little to chance, and would certainly have missed
no opportunity of keeping himself informed of Trotsky's state of
mind and intentions. But that he attempted or desired to make
any direct approach to Trotsky at this time is improbable. In
May 1925 Trotsky, having returned to Moscow, was appointed to
three separate posts — president of the chief concessions committee, president of Glavelektro, the administration of the electrical
industry, and president of the scientific-technical council, the last-
named being a body concerned with the application of science
and scientific research to industry.[2] During the summer he made
a number of non-political speeches on secondary occasions, maintaining the pose of a technical worker in uncontroversial fields.[3]
His most important article of the period was *Towards Capitalism
or Socialism?* inspired by Gosplan's first control figures.[4]

An embarrassing incident occurred at this time in connexion
with a small volume by Max Eastman, *Since Lenin Died*, published
in New York at the beginning of 1925 and in a French translation

[1] Trotsky's account is in *Byulleten' Oppozitsii* (Paris), No. 73, January 1939,
pp. 11-12; by this time imagination had begun to play a substantial part in
Trotsky's reconstructions of the past.

[2] L. Trotsky, *Moya Zhizn'* (Berlin, 1930), ii, 261. The second of these
appointments gave him an early interest in the Dnieprostroi project (see Vol. 1,
p. 335); for the third see N. Ipatieff, *The Life of a Chemist* (Stanford, 1946),
pp. 412, 423-424, according to which Trotsky refused to "accept any responsibility" for its work and soon ceased to attend meetings. Trotsky was relieved
of the presidency of Glavelektro in January 1926 "at his own request" (*Ekonomicheskaya Zhizn'*, January 28, 1926); the routine phrase was probably for
once accurate.

[3] Among these were a commemorative speech on his former collaborator
Sklyansky (*Izvestiya*, September 23, 1925; Sklyansky's death in America had
been announced, *ibid.* August 29, 1925, with an obituary notice by Trotsky —
for Sklyansky see p. 397 below), and a speech in honour of Mendeleev at a
chemical congress (N. Ipatieff, *The Life of a Chemist* (Stanford, 1946), p. 417).

[4] See Vol. 1, p. 505.

a few months later. Eastman began by recalling Trotsky's intimate association with Lenin since 1917 ; mentioned a letter received by Trotsky from Krupskaya a few days after Lenin's death in which she assured him that Lenin's attitude towards him had not changed from the time of their first meeting till the day of his death ; [1] related the attempt of certain members of the Politburo to suppress Lenin's last article ; [2] described and quoted Lenin's " testament " ; and then plunged into a detailed account, from a frankly Trotskyite point of view, of the struggle of the triumvirate against Trotsky, beginning in December 1923 and ending with Trotsky's resignation of his office in January 1925. The compromising feature of the book was that Eastman had been in Moscow from the autumn of 1923 to June 1924, and was known as an American supporter of Trotsky ; and, while he stated that he had seen Trotsky only twice for brief periods while the dispute was raging, and had received no documents from him, much of the information in the book was of a kind which could have come only from circles close to Trotsky and, it was felt, with his tacit approval or connivance. On returning to Moscow at the end of April 1925 Trotsky found awaiting him a telegram from Jackson, the editor of the British Left-wing paper *Sunday Worker*, asking for a statement for publication regarding the authenticity of Eastman's story. Trotsky at once issued a statement that he had not seen the book, and that he rejected " in advance and categorically " any attacks on the party which it might contain.[3] Thereupon Inkpin, the secretary of the Communist Party of Great Britain, sent him a copy of the book, and other copies soon reached Moscow. Trotsky was now under pressure, no longer from British communists whom he could easily put off, but from his colleagues in the central committee, to give the lie to Eastman's indictment.

Trotsky was once again faced with the familiar dilemma of having either to give battle on a secondary issue and on ground

[1] The text of the letter is in L. Trotsky, *Moya Zhizn'* (Berlin, 1930), ii, 251-252. The accuracy of Eastman's reference to it makes it probable that he had seen the letter : this was apparently the first mention of it in print.

[2] See *The Interregnum, 1923–1924*, p. 265.

[3] Jackson's telegram and Trotsky's statement were published in *Pravda*, May 9, 1925 : the statement appeared in the *Sunday Worker*, May 10, 1925, where it was accompanied by a hostile review of Eastman's book by Jackson headed *Poor Trotsky*.

unfavourable to himself, or to submit and disown his supporters. Once again he chose the second alternative. On July 1, 1925, he signed a statement which was, as he wrote three years later, "*forced on me by* a majority of the Politburo ".[1] After correcting a few minor errors in Eastman's account, he came to the main point :

> In certain passages of the book Eastman speaks of the fact that the central committee " concealed " from the party a number of extremely important documents written by Lenin in the last period of his life (this concerns letters on the national question, the so-called " testament ", etc.); this can only be called a slander on the central committee of our party. From the words of Eastman it might be deduced that Vladimir Ilich intended these letters, which had the character of advice on internal organization, for the press. In fact this is absolutely untrue. Vladimir Ilich after he fell ill several times addressed himself to leading institutions of the party or to his colleagues with proposals, letters etc. All these letters and proposals were, it goes without saying, always delivered to their destinations, were brought to the knowledge of the delegates to the twelfth and thirteenth congresses of the party, and always, of course, had their proper influence on the decisions of the party ; and, if not all these letters were printed, this was because they were not intended by their author for the press. Vladimir Ilich left no " testament " ; the very character of his relations with the party, and of the party itself, precluded the possibility of such a " testament ". In the guise of a " testament " mention is frequently made in the *émigré* and foreign bourgeois and Menshevik press (in a form distorted to the point of being unrecognizable) of one of Vladimir Ilich's letters containing advice of an organizational character. The thirteenth congress of the party paid the greatest attention to this letter as to the others, and drew conclusions from it in accordance with the conditions and circumstances of the time. All talk of a concealed or

---

[1] The authorities for this incident are Trotsky's statement of July 1, 1925, published in the *Sunday Worker*, July 19, 1925, and in *Bol'shevik*, No. 16, September 1, 1925, pp. 67-70, and his letter from Alma-Ata of September 11, 1928, published in *Byulleten' Oppozitsii* (Paris), No. 19, March 1931, pp. 38-39. Trotsky's attempt, in his letter of 1928, to share the responsibility for his decision to sign with " the leading group of the opposition " was a pathetic evasion ; nor was the excuse that the statement " did not cast any kind of aspersion, personal or political, on comrade Eastman " strictly correct. This was one of the actions in his career on which Trotsky must have looked back with least satisfaction.

destroyed " testament " represents a malicious invention, and is entirely at variance with the real will of Vladimir Ilich and with the interests of the party created by him.

Trotsky then attempted to refute the scandalous story of the attempt to suppress Lenin's last article.[1] He quoted a declaration signed by all members of the Politburo and Orgburo on January 27, 1923, to the effect that " in the internal work of the central committee there are no circumstances which might give rise to fear of a ' split ' ". Unfortunately Trotsky had confused Lenin's two articles on Rabkrin. The declaration referred to the first, which was written in January 1923 and which ended with some reflexions on the danger of a " split " between worker and peasant ; this was promptly published in *Pravda* of January 25. It was the second article which some members of the Politburo had wished to suppress ; and this was not written before February 6, 1923. Trotsky's memory on points of fact was generally exact. It is difficult to say whether it betrayed him on this occasion, or whether he contemptuously put his signature to a document drafted for him by others without caring about the truth or falsehood of what it contained. Finally he denied the reports that the central committee had " confiscated or held up in one way or another pamphlets or articles of mine in 1923 or 1924 or at any other time ". Trotsky's statement was published in the *Sunday Worker* of July 19, 1925, and then, with some delay, in the issue of the party journal *Bol'shevik* for September 1, 1925.[2]

Krupskaya was also inveigled into making her contribution to the discrediting of Eastman and, at the same time, of Trotsky. A discursive letter which bore clear marks of her own composition appeared in the *Sunday Worker* of August 2, 1925. It began by denouncing Eastman's book as " a collection of all sorts of common slanders ". Krupskaya then explained the letter which she had written to Trotsky after Lenin's death : it had been written because her husband " thought comrade Trotsky a talented worker devoted to the cause of the revolution ", not because he

---

[1] For the story see *The Interregnum, 1923–1924*, p. 265 ; Trotsky himself narrated it in his letter of October 24, 1923 (see *ibid.* p. 299).

[2] Since the Russian texts of this statement and of Krupskaya's letter (see below) must be the originals, I have made my own translation of them in preference to using the clumsy, though not substantially inaccurate, English versions of the *Sunday Worker*.

always agreed with Trotsky or regarded Trotsky as his successor.
She went on to speak of Lenin's " letters to the party congress " :

> Max Eastman relates all sorts of fables about these letters
> (calling them a " testament "). M. Eastman completely mis-
> understands the spirit of our party . . . [Lenin's] speeches at
> congresses were always marked by special seriousness and
> thoughtfulness. His letters on internal party relations (the
> " testament ") were also written for the party congress. . . .
> The letter contained among other things character-sketches of
> some of the most respected party comrades. The letters imply
> no kind of lack of confidence in those comrades to whom Lenin
> was bound by long years of common work. . . . The letters
> were intended to help the comrades who remained to direct the
> work along the right line, and for this reason the shortcomings
> of these comrades, including Trotsky, were noted, side by side
> with their merits, since these had to be taken into account in
> order to organize the work of the leading group of the party.
> All the members of the congress were acquainted with the
> letters, as V. I. desired.

Krupskaya ended rather abruptly by recalling her own past differences with Trotsky : she had been against him, and for the central
committee, in the controversy started by *Lessons of October*, and
had written an article in *Pravda* about it at the time. A Russian
text of Krupskaya's letter appeared in the issue of *Bol'shevik* of
September 1, 1925, immediately after Trotsky's statement.

The successful pressure placed on Trotsky to disown Eastman,
and on Krupskaya to disown both Eastman and Trotsky, was the
last, and not least remarkable, achievement of the united triumvirate. The double *coup* could have been carried out only by the
joint efforts of Stalin, Zinoviev and Kamenev, and proves that in
July and August 1925, whatever divisions of policy had begun to
appear, Zinoviev and Kamenev were still more afraid of Trotsky
than of Stalin. Nearly four months had still to elapse before the
final and open disruption of the triumvirate. But within a few
days of the delayed publication in *Bol'shevik* of Trotsky's statement
and Krupskaya's letter a new grouping had taken shape directed
primarily and undisguisedly against Stalin. On September 5,
1925, Zinoviev, Kamenev, Sokolnikov and Krupskaya met to sign
a document afterwards known as " the platform of the four ".
The platform of the four was not published and no clear

account of its contents has ever appeared in print.[1] Given the character and opinions of the signatories, it is unlikely to have been an original or constructive document. Fear and detestation of Stalin was the one link which united the four. Zinoviev, alarmed by the signs of Stalin's growing strength and truculence, had become conscious of his dependence on his own Leningrad supporters, and under pressure from them had turned sharply away from the pro-peasant, pro-*kulak* policy of the winter and spring of 1924–1925. Kamenev, lacking any independent base of his own, and keenly mistrustful of Stalin, who had taken the control of the Moscow organization out of his hands, followed in Zinoviev's wake. Krupskaya, mindful of her husband's early association with Kamenev and Zinoviev, always seems to have had kindly feelings towards them. She had taken strong exception to recent manifestations of the pro-peasant policy, and found it easy to come to terms with Zinoviev at the moment when he was turning his back on it. But, above all, Krupskaya was moved by a strong antipathy to Stalin arising out of the incidents that had occurred during Lenin's illness.[2] Any combination directed against Stalin was likely to have her support. The most enigmatic figure of the four was Sokolnikov. Ever since the introduction of NEP he had stood on the extreme Right of the party, upholding the principles of sound finance, the maximum freedom of the market, and respect for the interests of the peasant. He seemed the embodiment of that " dictatorship of finance " which was anathema to Trotsky and to the champions of industrialization and planning. To these he was firmly opposed ; and he had played a consistent, if minor, part in the campaign against Trotsky. His present *rapprochement* with Zinoviev and Kamenev paradoxically came at a moment when they were abandoning the policies which he supported. But here too antipathy to Stalin was the dominant factor. The ambition of Kuibyshev to intervene in financial policy had evidently been encouraged by Stalin, and had already resulted in a curbing of Sokolnikov's hitherto

---

[1] It was circulated to the delegates at the fourteenth party congress " with the permission of the presidium " (*XIV S"ezd Vsesoyuznoi Kommunisticheskoi Partii (B)* (1926), p. 527) ; it was somewhat melodramatically described by Andreev as " an ultimatum to the majority of the central committee in the guise of a platform " (*Leningradskaya Organizatsiya i Chetyrnadtsatyi S"ezd* (1926), p. 72).   [2] See *The Interregnum, 1923–1924*, p. 266.

undisputed authority.[1] This cannot have been agreeable to
Sokolnikov's pride, even though he can scarcely have foreseen
that it would be a prelude to Stalin's eventual overthrow of everything for which he had stood. Sokolnikov was a sophisticated
intellectual of western background, whose outlook almost inevitably ranged him with Kamenev against Stalin. In June 1925 he
had unexpectedly come out in favour of wage increases for the
workers — an apparent attempt to win popularity in a new
quarter ; and this may have paved the way to the present move.
But, as the sequel was to show, the differences between Sokolnikov
on the one hand and Kamenev and Zinoviev on the other on
questions of economic policy were profound ; and this cleavage
was one of the basic weaknesses of the opposition of 1925. The
platform of the four, which cannot have had any very solid economic foundation, probably consisted in the main of pleas for free
discussion and " party democracy " — the staple, but unsubstantial, diet of all oppositions.

Like all disputes in the party, however, the rift in the triumvirate in the summer of 1925 quickly found expression, not only
in differences of policy, but in differences of doctrine. It revived
the unsettled controversy, which had been latent, though never
far beneath the surface, since 1921, about the character of NEP.
Was NEP a forced retreat from positions which had been in-
correctly taken up only in the sense that it had proved impossible
to hold them, and which would one day have to be reoccupied ?
Or was it a retreat from positions which were in themselves incorrect, and at the same time a regrouping of forces for an
advance on a different and more promising path ? Was NEP a
temporary withdrawal from socialism into capitalism ? Or was it
a fresh advance towards socialism ?[2] Couched in these terms,
the argument appeared scholastic, and had only a certain historical
interest. But, like all questions of doctrine, it masked an argument about policy. If the first hypothesis were accepted, then
the aim must be to terminate as soon as possible the concessions

---

[1] See Vol. 1, pp. 461-462.
[2] For these questions see *The Bolshevik Revolution, 1917–1923*, Vol. 2,
pp. 274-279.

made to the peasantry under NEP (the ending of the retreat). If the second hypothesis were right, then the extension and development of NEP through fresh concessions to the peasantry was the logical conclusion.[1] A perfectly concrete debate about policy was conducted in the language of doctrine.

So long as the triumvirate remained united behind the slogan " Face to the countryside ", the view of NEP as a step on the road to socialism was the orthodox doctrine. It was challenged only by Trotsky, who now openly regarded NEP as a distasteful but transient episode, and described it as " a diversion in the revolutionary trajectory ", denouncing those for whom " the diversion in fact determines the whole direction of the trajectory ".[2] It was logical that, when in the summer of 1925 Bukharin emerged as the leading apologist of the peasant policy, he should have announced that the aim of that policy was to develop NEP " far more widely in the countryside than hitherto ",[3] and that his disciple Slepkov should have defended the policy as a " broadening of NEP ".[4] It was logical that, when Zinoviev in the same period went into opposition and denounced the policy of concessions to the peasant, he should also have begun to insist that NEP was primarily a retreat — " a retreat movement of Leninism on the broadest front " : this was the burden of a long chapter in Zinoviev's *Leninism* published in September 1925.[5] A fierce battle was fought on this doctrinal issue both before and during the fourteenth party congress, the principal weapons on both sides being an array of quotations from Lenin, who had notoriously taken divergent, if not contradictory, views of NEP.

Behind the question whether NEP was to be regarded primarily as a retreat or as a prelude to a fresh advance lay, however, another question about the character of NEP which assumed even greater

[1] It is interesting to note that, when the policy which ultimately took shape as NEP first began to be canvassed in 1920, Osinsky, later associated with the workers' opposition, at once attacked it as a " pro-*kulak* policy " (see *The Bolshevik Revolution, 1917–1923*, Vol. 2, p. 171, note 5).

[2] L. Trotsky, *Literatura i Revolyutsiya* (1923), pp. 73, 80.

[3] *Leningradskaya Pravda*, June 18, 1925 ; the speech was delivered at the all-union Komsomol conference in Moscow.

[4] Zinoviev at the fourteenth party congress (*XIV S"ezd Vsesoyuznoi Kommunisticheskoi Partii (B)* (1926), p. 117) quoted and attacked this phrase from an article by Slepkov, which has not been traced.

[5] G. Zinoviev, *Leninizm* (1925), pp. 223, 226, 255.

prominence in the party controversy. The two questions were closely linked. Those who insisted on the character of NEP as a retreat also described it as a form of state capitalism. Those who regarded NEP as a step on the road to socialism denied or minimized the capitalist taint and considered that NEP was a form, even though an imperfect form, of socialism. The issue had a complicated history. In the autumn of 1917 Lenin, in *The Impending Catastrophe and How to Combat It* and again in *State and Revolution*, had used the term " state monopoly capitalism " for the latest stage in the evolution of capitalism, the last stage before capitalism was transformed by the revolutionary process into socialism. To call this state capitalism " state socialism " was heresy ; but it was " *a step on the road to socialism* ".[1] It was under the heading of " state capitalism " that Lenin advocated collaboration with, and concessions to, capitalists in order to set industry on its feet again ; and when, in the spring of 1918, the Left opposition assailed this policy as unbecoming for a workers' government, and Bukharin developed the argument that " state capitalism " was inconceivable under the dictatorship of the proletariat, Lenin replied in his pamphlet *On " Left " Infantilism and the Petty Bourgeois Spirit* that state capitalism was a real advance over earlier forms, and that " if we in Russia in a short space of time could get state capitalism, that would be a victory ".[2] With the development of war communism the issue lost its practical importance. But Bukharin, in his major theoretical work *The Economics of the Transition Period*, continued to maintain the incompatibility of the conception of state capitalism with the existence of a workers' state.

The introduction of NEP momentarily revived the controversy in a new setting. Lenin in his pamphlet of May 1921 *On the Food Tax* quoted in defence of NEP his argument of 1918 on the progressive quality of state capitalism ; NEP, which embodied various forms of capitalism, was none the less a step on the road to socialism.[3] Lenin enumerated four specific forms of state capitalism under NEP — concessions, the cooperatives, the sale

[1] Lenin, *Sochineniya*, xxi, 186-187, 416.

[2] For this dispute see *The Bolshevik Revolution, 1917–1923*, Vol. 2, pp. 89-93 ; Bukharin's attack on " state capitalism " was published in *Kommunist*, No. 3, May 16, 1918, pp. 8-11.

[3] See *The Bolshevik Revolution, 1917–1923*, Vol. 2, p. 276.

by private traders of products of state industry, and the leasing of industrial enterprises, forests, land, etc.[1]   Bukharin, though he fully accepted NEP, did not abandon the argument.   When Lenin wrote that NEP was a blend of capitalism and socialism, Bukharin sent him a private note arguing that the description was wrong and that " you misuse the word ' capitalism ' ".[2]   In an article in *Pravda* Bukharin, while admitting that the term was commonly used, publicly re-stated his objections to it ; [3] and Lenin at the eleventh party congress, in Bukharin's absence, once more defended it.[4]   Other purists besides Bukharin continued to maintain that, since the essence of capitalism was production for the sake of extracting surplus profit, any kind of capitalism was incompatible with socialism.[5]   Trotsky in his speech at the fourth congress of Comintern in November 1922 declined to use the phrase " state capitalism ", and thought it seriously misleading ; [6] and after Lenin's death he claimed that Lenin had always used the phrase " in inverted commas " or called it " state capitalism of a special kind " (as he had done in his last article on the cooperatives).[7]   Preobrazhensky in 1922 described the Soviet economy as pursuing socialist ends by capitalist means, and refused to call this " state capitalism " ; in the following year he thought that the term could be properly used only of mixed companies and concessions.[8]   On the other hand, a report of Narkomzem of 1924 applied the term without question to the current Soviet economy.[9] With the general acceptance of NEP, the controversy ceased to have any practical significance and again faded quietly out.

It was no accident that the argument about state capitalism

---

[1] Lenin, *Sochineniya*, xxvi, 334-337.
[2] *Leniniskii Sbornik*, iv (1925), 383-384.
[3] *Pravda*, February 8, 1922.   [4] Lenin, *Sochineniya*, xxvii, 236-237.
[5] See, for example, the substantial article in *Narodnoe Khozyaistvo*, No. 6-7 (June–July), 1921, pp. 20-42.
[6] *Protokoll des Vierten Kongresses der Kommunistischen Internationale* (Hamburg, 1923), p. 276.
[7] L. Trotsky, *Sochineniya*, xxi, 158-159 ; in the article referred to Lenin mentioned the doubts which some " young comrades " had felt about his views on state capitalism, and used some studiously vague phrases which could be taken to imply that state capitalism was now practically confined to concessions (Lenin, *Sochineniya*, xxvii, 395).
[8] *Vestnik Sotsialisticheskoi Akademii*, ii (1922), 182 ; vi (1923), 304.
[9] *Osnovy Perspektivnogo Plana Razvitiya Sel'skogo i Lesnogo Khozyaistva* (1924), p. 5.

should have flared up afresh when, in the spring of 1925, the developments of agrarian policy once more raised the question of the character and duration of NEP. It was no accident that Bukharin, the most ardent supporter of the peasant orientation, should have returned to his refutation of the description of the NEP economy as state capitalism ; for it was only by vindicating the socialist character of NEP that its present extension by further concessions to the peasantry could be justified. When Bukharin undertook this theoretical task in an article in *Krasnaya Nov'* of May 1925, he showed the same frankness, and the same lack of discretion, as had been manifested in his appeal to the well-to-do peasants to enrich themselves. He openly admitted that he had disagreed in this question with Lenin who, at the time of the introduction of NEP, had talked as if there was no socialism, or only " a tiny island of socialism ", in the Soviet economy, and " all the rest is state capitalism ". But he claimed that Lenin had subsequently " elucidated " his position in his last article on the co-operatives.[1] *Krasnaya Nov'* was a literary journal, and Bukharin's essay provoked no immediate reaction. But to proclaim one's dissent from Lenin, and to hint that Lenin had eventually come round to one's view, was a foolhardy enterprise, as the experience of Trotsky had demonstrated. Stalin of all people had no desire to be associated with an argument tending to prove that Lenin had after all been wrong. Bukharin had played into the hands of the opposition ; and, when Zinoviev published his treatise on *Leninism* in September 1925, he triumphantly proved, without mentioning Bukharin's name, that the party leadership was committed to an anti-Leninist view of NEP and of state capitalism. NEP he defined, in the words of Lenin, as " state capitalism in a proletarian state " :

> When we are asked " from what " we retreated when we introduced the new economic policy, we reply in the words of Lenin : " We gave up the direct transition to purely socialist forms, to purely socialist distribution ". When we are asked " to what " we retreated, we reply in the words of Lenin : " To state capitalism in a proletarian state ".

The " excellent, stable, Soviet chervonets " was the perfect example of this state capitalism : nobody would pretend that a

[1] *Krasnaya Nov'*, No. 4, May 1925, pp. 265-266.

stable currency was an index of socialism. The state trusts and the cooperatives contained undeniable elements of capitalism ; the workers would quickly perceive the hollowness of the leaders' pretensions " if we offer them sugary phrases about this being socialism ".

> No illusions ! No self-deceit ! [exclaimed Zinoviev in conclusion]. Let us call state capitalism state capitalism.[1]

The defenders of the official line countered with a passage from a late article in which Lenin had referred to Soviet state enterprises as being " of a consistently socialist type ".[2] But, so long as the argument revolved round quotations from Lenin, the opposition seemed to have the best of it.

This advantage was, however, outweighed by serious handicaps. The adhesion of Sokolnikov was not an asset of unalloyed value. Sokolnikov's opinions did not fit easily into the platform which Zinoviev was trying to construct for the new opposition to Stalin. When Zinoviev now identified NEP with state capitalism, this was intended not as a compliment, but as a reproach. His criticism of Bukharin and Stalin was that they treated NEP as the high-road to socialism, and complacently pretended that the state capitalist economy of NEP was already socialist in character : the argument about the possibility of socialism in one country fitted into this framework. When Sokolnikov, on the other hand, spoke of NEP as state capitalism, he complacently accepted it as something that had come to stay for a long time ; and as a practical man he was not very much concerned about the eventual road to socialism. His criticism of the party leadership turned on its failure to make a system of state capitalism work efficiently ; and this failure he attributed to its refusal to recognize consistently the primacy of finance and its tendency to make too many concessions to industry and to the planners. If therefore Sokolnikov could combine with Zinoviev and Kamenev in opposing Stalin, his positive aims differed widely from theirs, and gave an incongruous twist to the opposition programme. In the first place, Sokolnikov believed that an expansion of agricultural production must precede the expansion of industry ; and this belief, which he shared with

---

[1] G. Zinoviev, *Leninizm* (1925), pp. 234, 236, 251-258.
[2] Lenin, *Sochineniya*, xxvii, 395.

Bukharin, was difficult to reconcile with his belief in the necessity of a " class policy " directed against the *kulak* in the countryside, which he now shared with Zinoviev and Kamenev.[1] Secondly, Sokolnikov induced Kamenev to adopt his own sceptical and unfriendly attitude to the first control figures of Gosplan, and, by setting the opposition against planning, deprived it of what should logically have been the main constructive plank in its platform. Thirdly, Sokolnikov advocated a policy of imports of consumer goods to stimulate the production of grain for the market, and wished to give such imports precedence over imports of capital goods for the development of industry ; and, though this policy was never really endorsed by Zinoviev or by Kamenev, it exposed the opposition to the charge of wanting to surrender to foreign capitalists and to make the Soviet Union an agricultural colony of the west.

But the platform of the opposition suffered not only from these internal inconsistencies, but from the graver handicap of its negative character. The arguments of Zinoviev and Kamenev about NEP and state capitalism exposed them to a damning retort in the form of a counter-charge of pessimism and lack of faith.[2] To claim that NEP was merely a retreat, to describe the existing Soviet economy as state capitalism, was to deny that any advance towards socialism had been made, was being made, or could be

[1] For Sokolnikov's anti-*kulak* line see Vol. 1, p. 308. Sokolnikov accurately defined his position in the autumn of 1925 in the following terms : " I defended the point of view of the necessity, side by side with a guarantee of the rapid recovery of agriculture as the basis of a powerful industry, of a calculated class policy in the countryside " (*Entsiklopedicheskii Slovar' Russkogo Bibliograficheskogo Instituta Granat*, xli, iii (n.d. [1928], Prilozhenie, col. 87) ; but he did not explain how these two apparently incompatible aims could be reconciled.

[2] By one of the many paradoxes of this story, the charge had first been brought by the triumvirate against the opposition of 1923 at the time of the scissors crisis. " What have they in common ? " asked Kamenev at the thirteenth party conference in January 1924, bracketing Preobrazhensky and Krasin, and answered : " What they have in common is panic, a lack of belief that the elements of a socialist economy are really growing in our poor, beggared, plundered Russia " ; and Mikoyan took up the same theme : " This panic tone in the speeches of our opposition, especially in comrade Pyatakov's, has its roots in the temporary set-backs of the German revolution . . . in the absence of faith among these comrades in our strength " (*Trinadtsataya Konferentsiya Rossiiskoi Kommunisticheskoi Partii Bol'shevikov*) (1924), pp. 55, 77) ; Bukharin wrote a little later of " *concealed* sceptics " who " thought it a mark of bad form to speak of our forward advance " (*Bol'shevik*, No. 2, 1924, p. 8).

made, without aid from the outside world. This was pessimism, this was blind refusal to believe in the constructive capacities of the people of the Soviet Union. This was the demon of despair which the new faith in socialism in one country was destined to exorcize. Socialism in one country seemed at the outset still economically ambivalent : it could equally well be harnessed to a campaign to develop peasant production as to a campaign of intensive industrialization. Whatever its precise economic content, however, it was a declaration of faith that NEP did not mean a mere retreat into a dead end, that capitalism had been vanquished, and that, by its own efforts and under the leadership of the party, the Soviet Union had advanced, was advancing and would advance with ever-growing confidence to the goal of socialism. In the debates which preceded the fourteenth party congress, and again at the congress itself, the emotional effect of this appeal was more and more powerfully felt, and tipped the scale which the weight of quotations from Lenin had loaded in favour of the opposition.

But, before describing the prelude to the congress and the events of the congress itself, it is necessary to discuss two minor episodes which played some part in the struggle : the debate about literary policy, and the controversy in the Komsomol.

CHAPTER 14

THE DEBATE ABOUT LITERATURE

THE Soviet literary scene in 1923, when literary controversies first began to take on a political colour, was one of fruitful diversity. *Krasnaya Nov'* enjoyed pre-eminence as the leading literary journal and was the organ of the " fellow-travellers ", who alone attracted an extensive reading public. The advanced " October " group, which had broken away from the Smithy,[1] published a rival journal *Oktyabr'*, and the Smithy had its own *Rabochii Zhurnal*, which, while professing proletarian principles, was tolerant of fellow-travellers. Independent literary groups still flourished. The most powerful of these, thanks mainly to the influence of Mayakovsky, were the Futurists, whose journal *Lef* was published by Gosizdat.[2] The name was significant. The Futurists continued to identify literary innovation with " Leftism ", and sought to establish their dubious proletarian credentials by attacking the fellow-travellers. In June 1923 the " October " group founded a new critical journal under the title *Na Postu*, which was designed to provide an ideological counterblast to the heresies of the fellow-travellers. The titular leader of the *Napostovtsy* (as they came to be called) was Rodov, one of the original founders of the Smithy ; and among its prominent members were the poet Bezymensky, the political versifier Demyan Bedny, the novelist Libedinsky and a young man of 19 named Averbakh, who had good party connexions (he was a nephew of Sverdlov and a relative of Yaroslavsky) and was editor of the Komsomol journal, *Molodaya Gvardiya*.[3] The editorial

[1] For these groups see Vol. 1, p. 64.
[2] An account of this journal, by one of the participants, is in *Izvestiya Akademii Nauk SSR : Otdelenie Literatury i Yazika*, xiii (1954), 339-358 : seven numbers in all appeared between March 1923 and March 1925.
[3] *Literaturnaya Entsiklopediya*, i (1930), 28-29. Averbakh was evidently the promising young man of the party ; Trotsky wrote a preface to a volume published by him in 1923 under the title *Voprosy Yunosheskogo Dvizheniya i Lenin* (Trotsky, *Sochineniya*, xxi, 354-355, 507, note 124).

manifesto which appeared in the first issue of *Na Postu* unequivo-
cally demanded a break with the past :

> We shall stand firmly *on guard over a strong and clear com-
> munist ideology in proletarian literature*. In view of the revival
> ever since the beginning of NEP of the activity of bourgeois
> literary groups, all *ideological* doubts are absolutely *inadmissible*,
> and we shall make a point of bringing them to light.
> We shall fight those Manilovs who distort and slander our
> revolution by the attention they pay to the rotten fabric of the
> fellow-travellers' literary creation in their attempt to *build* an
> aesthetic *bridge between the past and the present*.[1]

The new group was not the first to treat literature as a battle-
ground of social and political opinions, or to denounce its opponents as reactionaries and enemies of society : this was an
old-standing tradition of Russian literary criticism. But *Na Postu*
introduced a new and shriller note of intolerance into its expressions of animosity against the " petty bourgeois " fellow-travellers,
and plainly hinted that measures of repression used against class
enemies were properly applicable to them. Among the " list of
contributors ", in the second issue of the journal, appeared the
names of Kamenev, Radek and Yarovslavsky. This was perhaps
less significant than it seemed, since party leaders often lent their
names to new journals without any serious intention of writing
for them. But it showed that the new venture had support in
party circles. Literary policy was subject to the same compromise
which was inherent in all the policies of NEP. The party had
decided to encourage the fellow-travellers. But it had not decided
to discourage the so-called proletarian writers who were their
bitter rivals and adversaries.

The clash of opposing opinions was therefore sharp and well-
defined when Trotsky took the field in the summer of 1923. On
the Left, a number of literary groups and movements claimed to
speak in the name of the revolution and to be the protagonists of
new forms of literature and art, which rejected the heritage of
the bourgeois past. On the opposite wing, the so-called fellow-
travellers accepted the Russian literary and artistic tradition as a

---

[1] Quoted in translation in G. Reavey and M. Slonim, *Soviet Literature :
An Anthology* (1933), p. 405 ; Manilov is the complacent land-owner in Gogol's
Dead Souls.

valid foundation on which a new Soviet literature could be created ; and the reading public followed the fellow-travellers or read the old Russian classics. In a speech of July 1923 Trotsky repeated Lenin's argument of the previous autumn against Pletnev, and maintained that Pushkin and Tolstoy were just as necessary to the victory of socialism as bourgeois technicians.[1] In September 1923 he published, under the title *Literature and Revolution*, a series of essays written at intervals during the past two years. The preface returned to the case against proletarian literature :

> It is fundamentally incorrect to set in opposition to bourgeois culture and bourgeois art a proletarian culture and proletarian art. These will never exist, since the proletarian régime is temporary and transitional.[2]

Trotsky in an essay on *Futurism* gave a very qualified approval to the efforts of the Futurists ; [3] and in an essay on *Party Policy in Art*, which incidentally described the approach of the Formalists as " superficial " and " reactionary ", he argued that just as the Soviet state under NEP tolerated the parallel existence of different forms of economic production, by no means all of them socialist, so it must tolerate different forms of literary and artistic production.[4] In effect, Trotsky, like Lenin, was on the side of the fellow-travellers.

The time had not yet arrived when the support of Trotsky was calculated to damn any cause. His influence with the young intelligentsia was particularly strong ; and there is no reason to doubt that his defence of the fellow-travellers carried weight, especially in those " advanced " circles where they were most likely to be attacked. The only direct public retort to Trotsky's article on party policy in art seems to have come from Demyan Bedny, one of the first to discover that a modest career might be made out of sly denigration of Trotsky. In a poem published in *Pravda* under the title *Insult* he described " Lev Davidovich's article " as " an undeserved insult " to the young proletarian writers, denounced the " stinking " Pilnyak and " the horde of

---

[1] Trotsky, *Sochineniya*, xxi, 157-159 ; for Pletnev see Vol. 1, p. 63.
[2] L. Trotsky, *Literatura i Revolyutsiya* (1923), p. 9.
[3] *Ibid.* pp. 159-168.   [4] *Ibid.* pp. 91-116.

clueless fellow-travellers ", and looked forward to a " proletarian nemesis ".[1] In October 1923 the "society of old Bolsheviks " in Moscow issued a declaration on "our literary policy " which appeared in a Moscow party newspaper, but failed to find a place in *Pravda*. The declaration drew attention to the danger of " a resurrection of bourgeois and petty bourgeois ideology at the side of NEP ". *Belles-lettres* could not fail to be " a powerful instrument for educating the masses in one direction or another " ; and " all this dictates to party and Soviet organs the indispensable necessity of laying down and strictly following a firm and consistent literary policy ". Meanwhile the fellow-travellers were being freely published in literary journals and received the praise of Trotsky, Bukharin and other party leaders, while young proletarian writers " find no outlet ". The declaration ended with a call for a " decisive review " of literary policy.[2] It seems to have made little immediate impression. At the height of the first campaign against Trotsky in the winter of 1923–1924, the party leaders had no time for literary debates. But the issue continued to simmer in literary circles, and in February 1924 the " October " group came out with a policy manifesto. On questions of literary form and language, it declared, the party could remain neutral. But, in so far as literature was a means of " acting on the will and consciousness of the reader ", the party must have " a firm policy ". So-called " non-party " and " non-political " literature was as dangerous as counter-revolutionary literature, which could be dealt with by the censorship. The manifesto attacked the leading fellow-travellers by name, and raised the banner of proletarian literature which " organizes the psychology and consciousness of the working class and of the broad working masses on the side of the final aims of the proletariat as the transformer of the world and the creator of communist society ". It concluded by calling on the party to disown the fellow-travellers and support proletarian literature.[3] The

[1] *Pravda*, October 16, 1923.

[2] Quoted from *Rabochaya Moskva* in a Proletkult publication, N. Chukhazh, " *Literatura* " (1924), pp. 74-76 ; Bukharin was, at this time, not generally associated with the fellow-travellers, but wrote a preface to the novel *Khulio Khurenito* by I. Erenburg, who was an old associate of his youth (see Vol. 1, p. 162).

[3] *Pravda*, February 19, 1924. The eight signatories were Averbakh, Bezymensky, Vardin, Volin, Ingulov, Lelevich, Libedinsky and Rodov.

principal fellow-travellers replied in a joint letter to the press section of the party central committee that " the paths of contemporary Russian literature and, therefore, our paths are united with the paths of Soviet post-October Russia ", and that "literature should be the reflector of this new life that surrounds us ".[1]

The party leaders could no longer evade the challenge ; and a conference was summoned by the press section of the central committee for May 9, 1924, in advance of the thirteenth party congress. Voronsky, the editor of *Krasnaya Nov'* and principal patron of the fellow-travellers, opened the proceedings [2] by defining the party attitude as one of support f r any group which " works and takes its stand on the point of view of the October revolution ", and condemned the contrary view as " anti-specialist, the same which has been outlived in other departments of our life ". Vardin [3] spoke first for the dissidents and contrived to give his speech a political flavour. He ostentatiously quoted a passage from a report by Molotov on the rise of the *kulak* and connected this with the development of anti-proletarian tendencies in literature. He professed to detect a mood of " retreat, weariness and scepticism " in a recent article of Bukharin, attacked the fellow-travellers in general and Pilnyak in particular, and coupled Trotsky and Voronsky in an evident attempt to discredit the latter. Finally he put forward the claims of the All-Russian Association of Proletarian Writers (VAPP) to become the instrument of the party for carrying out its literary policy.

A confused and heated debate followed these opening statements. Bukharin described his position as " very radical ", and thought that the party should have its specific line " in all fields of ideological and scientific life, even in mathematics ". But it would be wrong to " crush peasant literature " or to eliminate

[1] *K Voprosu o Politike RKP(B) v Khudozhestvennoi Literature* (1924), pp. 106-107.

[2] A report of the speeches was published in *K Voprosu o Politike RKP(B) v Khudozhestvennoi Literature* (1924) and reprinted in *Voprosy Kul'tury pri Diktature Proletariata* (1925), pp. 56-139.

[3] Vardin was of Georgian birth, his real name being Mgeladze (*Literaturnaya Entsiklopediya*, ii (1930), 105, contained an entry " Vardin *see* Mgeladze " ; but, by the time the appropriate volume was reached in 1934, members of oppositions were taboo, and the entry did not appear). He was a member of the Left opposition in 1918, and from 1922 to 1924 was director of the press sub-section of the party central committee (*Devyatyi S"ezd RKP(B)* (1934), p. 581).

" the writer from the Soviet intelligentsia " in the supposed
interests of the proletarian writer :

> If we take our stand for a literature which must be regulated
> by the state power and enjoy all sorts of privileges, we do not
> doubt that by this means we shall destroy proletarian literature.

Averbakh attacked Voronsky and the fellow-travellers, but cleverly
separated himself from Vardin and manœuvred himself into a
middle position by professing to agree with Bukharin.   Trotsky,
in what was apparently the longest and best reasoned speech of
the conference, repeated the defence of the fellow-travellers and
the exposure of the illusory character of proletarian art which
were already familiar from his articles.   But Trotsky's position
in the party, since his condemnation by the thirteenth party
conference in January 1924, was seriously compromised ; and
nobody was anxious to agree with Trotsky.   Lunacharsky asked
why, if there was a transitional proletarian state, there should not
be a transitional proletarian literature.   Bezymensky accused
Trotsky and Voronsky of " preferring strangers to our own ".
An interesting contribution came from Meshcheryakov, the
director of Gosizdat, who explained that " not one of our contemporary proletarian writers is in demand ", and that their books
were unsaleable.   As regards journals, Gosizdat had no criteria
for discriminating between them :

> We give an equal number of sheets to all groups.   We
> watch to see that there is nothing counter-revolutionary in this
> literature, but we cannot enter into their mutual arguments.

Vardin in a concluding speech summed up the programme of the
malcontents :

> Our slogan is not the dictatorship of VAPP, but the *dictator-
> ship of the party* in the field of literature : VAPP may become
> the instrument of this dictatorship.

The resolution adopted by a majority, at the end of the conference,
showed some marks of a compromise, but was in substance a re-
affirmation of the party line.   While praising worker and peasant
writers, the conference considered it " indispensable to continue
the party line in respect of the so-called ' fellow-travellers ' ",
and declared, in opposition to Vardin's claim on behalf of VAPP,

that " no single movement, school or group can or should act in
the name of the party ". At the same time it promised " more
systematic leadership " from the party in the field of *belles-
lettres*.[1]

The conference of May 1924 had given little clear guidance to
the thirteenth party congress which met a few days later. Bukharin
at the congress described the situation with his usual disarming
frankness :

> Are our central institutions qualified to pursue this ques-
> tion ? No. Our party institutions are also not qualified. We
> have no party line laid down.[2]

The results of the conference were, however, reflected in a resolution of the congress " On the Press ". The greater part of the
resolution was devoted to the work of the press and of publishing-
houses in bringing political and cultural enlightenment to workers
and peasants. But, in its final section, it observed, with no great
apparent relevance to what had gone before, that " the fundamental condition of a growth of worker-peasant writers is a process
of more serious artistic and political self-improvement, and
liberation from the narrow spirit of the clique ", and recommended
a continuance of " systematic support of the most gifted of the
so-called fellow-travellers ", who should be helped by " sustained
party criticism " to correct " mistakes resulting from insufficient
understanding by these writers of the character of the Soviet
order " and to overcome their " bourgeois prejudices ". The
conclusion was summed up in a two-edged paragraph :

> Considering that no one literary trend, school or group can,
> or should be allowed to, speak in the name of the party, the
> congress emphasizes the importance of regulating the question
> of literary criticism and of throwing the fullest possible light on
> patterns of *belles-lettres* in the pages of the Soviet-party press.[3]

It was the first time that non-political literature had been the
subject of a resolution at a party congress. It was the last time
that the party formally reserved its neutrality between different

---

[1] It was published in *Krasnaya Nov'*, No. 3 (20), April–May 1924, pp. 306-
307, with a note by Voronsky that it had been passed " by an overwhelming
majority ".
[2] *Trinadtsatyi S"ezd Rossiiskoi Kommunisticheskoi Partii (Bol'shevikov)*
(1924), p. 540.   [3] *VKP(B) v Rezolyutsiyakh* (1941), i, 602.

literary " trends, schools and groups " ; and this neutrality could in the long run scarcely prove compatible with the necessity of scrutinizing literary productions in a party light.

The proceedings of May 1924 were followed by a lull on the literary front. But, when in the autumn the struggle between Trotsky and the triumvirate broke out again with fresh ferocity, no issue in the party could remain independent of it. The supporters of VAPP eagerly seized the opportunity to smear Voronsky and the fellow-travellers as associates of Trotsky, and as the literary wing of the political opposition. This was the main theme of a first All-Union Conference of Proletarian Writers in January 1925, at which the ambitious Vardin appeared as a protagonist, and once more pressed the claims of VAPP to become the organ of a party dictatorship in literature. Demyan Bedny also spoke at the conference, bringing his prestige as a popular versifier to the support of the proletarian cause.[1] On a report by Vardin the conference adopted a set of theses declaring that " the supremacy of the proletariat is incompatible with the supremacy of a non-proletarian ideology and, consequently, of a non-proletarian literature ", and that what was required was " a seizure of power by the proletariat in the field of art ".[2]

This offensive was distasteful to the party leadership, which was in no hurry to carry the crusade against Trotsky into the dubious by-ways of literary policy. Bukharin, who was at this moment leading the campaign against Trotsky on the economic front and could not be accused of any taint of Trotskyism, stepped into the breach. At the conference in May 1924 he had already qualified his earlier support of proletarian literature and moved into a central position. He had now become the most active champion of the peasant in the councils of the party ; and this logically aligned him — in so far as these literary rivalries had a political background — with the fellow-travellers in literature.

[1]. His speech, though not the other speeches delivered at the conference, was inconspicuously reported in *Pravda*, January 15, 1925, with a note of dissent from some of his views.

[2] The resolution was published " for information " in *Pravda*, February 1, 1925 ; it is also in V. Polonsky, *Ocherki Literaturnogo Dvizheniya Revolyutsionnoi Epokhi* (2nd ed. 1929), pp. 173-174.

At the end of February 1925 the party central committee organized a discussion on literary questions at which Bukharin was the principal speaker.[1] He opened with the remark that the Marxist " walks on a razor-edge " in such debates, and proceeded to extricate himself from the dilemma with skill and with some frankness. After the routine attack on Trotsky for under-estimating the duration of the transitional stage of the proletarian dictatorship, Bukharin declared his belief in a specifically pro-letarian culture. He admitted that he had differed in this respect from Lenin, and claimed to have been responsible for softening the attack made by Yaklovev on Pletnev on Lenin's instructions.[2] Having thus established his credentials as a sympathiser with proletarian writers, he went on to the main business of his speech : an attack on Vardin and his theses. He argued, in terms which reflected his current political attitude, that " our policy does not follow the line of inflaming the class struggle, but conversely, from a certain standpoint, of moderating it ". He accused VAPP of wanting to establish a monopoly, and explained that " our relation to the fellow-travellers is determined by our general relation to social-political forms sympathetic to us ". Vardin and his supporters — this was the final cut — " occupy the same position in literary policy as Preobrazhensky occupies in economic policy ". Bukharin's concluding appeal for toleration all round showed how little the party leaders wanted to be compelled to take sides in this thorny question :

> Let there be 1000 organizations, let there be 2000 organiza-tions. Let there be side by side with MAPP and VAPP [3] as many groups and organizations as you please.

The other principal speaker was Frunze, who, as Lenin himself had done, compared Lenin's opposition to a specifically pro-letarian art and literature with his opposition to a specifically proletarian military doctrine. He argued that " the necessity of

---

[1] The speech was published in *Krasnaya Nov'*, No. 4, May 1925, pp. 263-272, and reprinted in *Voprosy Kul'tury pri Diktature Proletariata* (1925), pp. 140-152.   [2] For this incident see Vol. 1, p. 63.

[3] The conference of January 1925 had resulted in the creation of a new Russian Association of Proletarian Writers (RAPP) which took the place of the more or less moribund VAPP ; MAPP was its Moscow branch. After 1928 the initials VAPP reappear as the title of a new All-Union Association of Proletarian Writers (*Literaturnaya Entsiklopediya*, ix (1935), 519-521).

allowing within certain limits capitalist accumulation in the countryside " pointed to the toleration of similar non-party elements in literature. The injunction " Face to the countryside " carried with it an obligation for the *Na Postu* group to " turn their face to the fellow-travellers ".[1]

The discussion of February 1925 had no binding character, and no resolution seems to have been passed. It was not till four months later that the central committee made a formal pronouncement — the first since the thirteenth party congress a year earlier — which showed once more how reluctant the party was to commit itself on issues of literary policy. The resolution of the central committee of June 18, 1925, proclaimed that " in a class society there is, and can be, no neutral art ", but that, " though the class struggle does not cease, it changes its form under the dictatorship of the proletariat " ; that, while " the leadership in the field of literature belongs to the working class as a whole ", there was as yet " no hegemony of proletarian writers " ; that, " while struggling against the new bourgeois ideology which is developing among a section of the ' fellow-travellers ' of *smenovekh* stamp, the party should be tolerant of intermediate ideological forms " ; that " a tactful and careful attitude " should be adopted to the fellow-travellers, who were " qualified specialists in literary technique " ; and that " Marxist criticism " decisively rejected " all pretentious semi-literate self-satisfied communist boasting ".[2] This indecisive pronouncement served only to reopen the controversy. The party journal *Bol'shevik* published an article by Yakovlev convicting Vardin of a return to all the errors of Bogdanov and Proletkult.[3] But it also published, two months later, a sharp retort from the editors of *Na Postu*, which accused Yakovlev of " a revision of Leninism " ; and this in turn was answered by Bukharin's disciple Slepkov, who divided his shafts impartially between Trotsky on one side and the supporters of RAPP on the other.[4] The literary debate had now, mainly

[1] M. Frunze, *Sobranie Sochinenii*, iii (1927), 150-155.

[2] *Pravda*, July 1, 1925 ; it is also in *Spravochnik Partiinogo Rabotnika*, v, 1925 (1926), pp. 349-352.

[3] *Bol'shevik*, No. 11-12, June 30, 1925, pp. 9-19 ; for Proletkult see Vol. 1, pp. 48-50.

[4] *Bol'shevik*, No. 15, August 15, 1925, pp. 66-77; No. 16, September 1, 1925, pp. 58-65.

through the fault of the participants, become inextricably involved
in the party struggle. The official line of qualified support for the
fellow-travellers, purged of its association with Trotskyism, found
a champion in Bukharin and fitted in conveniently with the pro-
peasant policy.[1] The enthusiasts for proletarian literature —
notably Vardin, Lelevich and Rodov — logically joined Zinoviev's
Leningrad opposition, and attacked Bukharin's peasant orientation.
But these new alignments also produced a split in RAPP.[2] The
supple Averbakh, who as long ago as May 1924 had shown an
inclination for diplomatic compromise, read the political signs of
the times and broke with his proletarian associates on the cardinal
issue of toleration for the fellow-travellers ; and, since he managed,
perhaps with official backing, to keep the journal *Na Postu* —
henceforth re-named *Na Literaturnom Postu* — in his hands, his
former colleagues could be made to appear, like Zinoviev in the
party struggle, as the factious dissidents who had broken party
unity.

The issue of the party struggle was up to a certain point
decisive for the literary controversy. Vardin and his followers
had committed themselves to the political opposition ; he and
Lelevich, in particular, wrote fervent political articles in *Leningradskaya Pravda* attacking the Moscow party organization and
the central committee.[3] By this miscalculation they sealed their
own defeat. Averbakh emerged as the rising star in the literary
constellation, having contrived to dissociate himself from both the
fellow-travellers of the Right and the proletarian extremists of
the Left — the same tactics which Stalin so brilliantly applied in

---

[1] Slepkov, in the article quoted above, discussed the attitude to be adopted
to the fellow-travellers in language which clearly suggested the analogy with the
well-to-do peasant : " Not a policy of ' squeeze and crush ', but consistent
systematic criticism, comradely work to attract to our positions, our views, our
aims, our ideals, those elements of the non-proletarian part of our society which
are being drawn towards us ".

[2] *Literaturnaya Entsiklopediya*, ix (1935), 521, attributes the split directly
to the resolution of June 18, 1925 ; but it came somewhat later, and seems to
have reflected the developments of the party struggle. Averbakh later said that
his differences with the Left began six months before the party congress
(*Bol'shevik*, No. 7-8, April 30, 1926, p. 112) ; but he was by this time anxious
to push them back as far as possible. After the split Lelevich claimed, no
doubt correctly, that he, Vardin and Rodov commanded a majority in the
Leningrad section of RAPP (*ibid*. No. 9-10, May 30, 1926, p. 91).

[3] For these see p. 130 below.

the party struggle. But he achieved his victory by accepting the compromise of an All-Russian Union of Writers to which proletarian writers and fellow-travellers would be equally admitted ; and the literary controversy was allowed to continue unchecked in the party press. A collection of essays published by Averbakh early in 1926 under the title *For Proletarian Literature* was violently attacked in *Bol'shevik* by a critic of the Right, who declared that Averbakh's views were indistinguishable from those of Vardin and were the literary reflexion of the new opposition, and insidiously praised by Lelevich, who complained that Averbakh had executed " a turn of 120, if not 180, degrees " since writing these essays.[1] One significant fact was clearly revealed by this interchange. The party leadership was as reluctant as ever to take sides in these literary disputes, and desired nothing better than to tolerate all the conflicting groups and schools, subject only to the condition of loyalty to the revolution and to the régime. It was the young and ambitious writers of the proletarian group who, by representing the literary issue as essentially political and ideological, and by branding their literary opponents as associates of the political opposition, sought to persuade or compel the party to extend its exclusive patronage to them and to entrust to them the functions of a literary dictatorship. This aim was pursued in turn by Vardin and by Averbakh : Averbakh was merely the more skilful or more fortunate of the two. For the moment Averbakh's success was limited. The party, while it recognized him as leader of the proletarian writers so long as he accepted the policy of toleration for the fellow-travellers, was not prepared to protect him from the criticism of his rivals or to establish any form of literary dictatorship. But something had been achieved. The party had been obliged, in spite of itself, to renounce an attitude of neutrality in literary affairs and to take decisions about them. This was already a step in the direction desired by the literary Left and a victory for the view that art and literature were inseparable from politics. It would bear fruit in the ensuing period.

[1] *Bol'shevik*, No. 3, February 15, 1926, pp. 88-95 ; No. 4, February 28, 1926, pp. 37-48 ; No. 9-10, May 30, 1926, pp. 86-93. Averbakh wrote an article in defence of his position, *ibid*. No. 7-8, April 30, 1926, pp. 101-114 ; his trump-card was the argument that " the ultra-Left theses developed by Vardin were begotten by the political theories of the opposition ".

CHAPTER 15

THE KOMSOMOL

THE Russian Communist League of Youth (Komsomol) was founded at a congress held in Moscow at the end of October 1918. The congress seems to have been representative of a large and rather miscellaneous collection of youth organizations and groups throughout the country. Though Krupskaya is said to have given " great help " in organizing it, it was in no sense a party creation. The party central committee held aloof, and was not represented at the congress.[1] The new league described itself as " an independent organization ", but proclaimed its " solidarity with the Russian Communist Party (Bolsheviks)", its aim being " to spread the ideas of communism and to draw the worker and peasant youth into active participation in the building of Soviet Russia ".[2] Its aspirations received the blessing of the eighth party congress in March 1919 which expressed the view that " communist work among the youth can be successfully conducted only through independent organizations marching under the banner of communism, in which youth can display the maximum of independence ", and promised " ideological and material aid " to the Komsomol.[3] Notwithstanding these assurances, however, statements at the congress pointed to friction occurring between party and Komsomol organs ; [4] and this must have been intensified by extravagant claims of the Komsomol to rank not merely as the equal partner of the party, but as the " vanguard " of the party.[5] This state of affairs was plainly unacceptable to the party leadership. In August 1919 an " instruction " was issued jointly by the

[1] *Devyatyi S"ezd RKP(B)* (1934), p. 487.
[2] *VLKSM v Rezolyutsiyakh* (1929), p. 10.
[3] *VKP(B) v Rezolyutsiyakh* (1941), i, 311.
[4] A Komsomol delegate complained that many party members treated members of the Komsomol as " children who are busy with their toys and get in the way of the grown-ups " (*Vos'moi S"ezd RKP(B)* (1933), pp. 300-301).
[5] *Pervyi Vserossiiskii S"ezd RKSM* (3rd ed. 1926), p. 40.

party central committee and the central committee of the Komsomol which brought order into relations between the two organizations. This declared the Komsomol to be " an autonomous organization with its own statutes ", which, however, " works under the control of the party ", its central committee being subordinate to the party central committee and its local organs to local party committees.[1] Since the Komsomol was financially dependent on the party,[2] it was clearly destined to enjoy such autonomy as the party judged expedient.

At the second Komsomol congress in October 1919, two-thirds of the delegates with right of vote were already party members.[3] The congress was held under the shadow of Denikin's march on Moscow, and Yudenich's threat to Petrograd, and, after a report by Trotsky on the military situation, a resolution ordering the mobilization of all Komsomol members over the age of 16 in threatened areas was unanimously adopted.[4] This did not, however, prevent a member of the Komsomol central committee, Dunaevsky by name, from putting forward a proposal to establish direct relations between the Komsomol and the trade unions and to set up in the trade unions special youth sections [5] — a proposal which was emphatically rejected by the party leadership. Once the military crisis was over, friction between party and Komsomol organs recurred in many places ; [6] and the third Komsomol congress of October 1920 was a battle-ground for several disputes. In preparation for the congress the group led

[1] *Pravda*, August 24, 1919 ; *Spravochnik Partiinogo Rabotnika*, [i] (1921), 141-142.
[2] The first Komsomol congress passed a resolution in which it " demanded " subsidies from Narkompros for the organization of the League (*VLKSM v Rezolyutsiyakh* (1929), p. 11) ; a delegate to the congress afterwards related a visit of some of the delegates to Lenin, at the end of which Lenin wrote a note to Sverdlov, then secretary of the party, asking for an allocation of 10,000 rubles to the Komsomol central committee (A. Kirov and V. Dalin, *Yunosheskoe Dvizhenie v Rossii* (1925), pp. 244-245). Later, party control became tighter, regional agencies of the Komsomol being financed through the regional party committees (*Izvestiya Tsentral'nogo Komiteta RKSM*, No. 1, March 26, 1920, p. 1).
[3] *Vtoroi Vserossiiskii S"ezd RKSM* (3rd ed. 1926), p. 7.
[4] *VLKSM v Rezolyutsiyakh* (1929), pp. 15-16.
[5] *Vtoroi Vserossiiskii S"ezd RKSM* (3rd ed. 1926), p. 109.
[6] It was referred to by a Komsomol delegate at the ninth party congress of March 1920 (*Devyatyi S"ezd RKP(B)* (1934), pp. 368-369), which, however, passed no resolution on the Komsomol.

by Dunaevsky, which now demanded separate youth sections in the trade unions and in the Soviets, joined hands with a Ukrainian group, which apparently had affiliations with the workers' opposition in the party, wished to make the Komsomol an exclusively or predominantly proletarian organization (hence its name or nickname of *klassoviki*), and demanded freedom of discussion for workers (though not for other classes).[1] The party central committee treated seriously the threat to party authority. At the end of September 1920, it expelled Dunaevsky from the party for six months " in the hope of his reformation ", and declared once more that the Komsomol was " an organization subsidiary to the Russian Communist Party, a school of communism in which our proletarian and semi-proletarian youth builds its character in a communist spirit ".[2] On the eve of the congress Bukharin addressed the communist fraction, which comprised a " significant majority "[3] of the delegates : an article in *Pravda*, which may be presumed to contain as much of the substance of the speech as was suitable for publication, attacked Dunaevsky as " an unbalanced leader " and proclaimed the duties of party loyalty.[4]

The congress itself was evidently a ticklish affair. Lenin, appearing for the only time at a Komsomol congress, delivered a somewhat academic address on the need of youth to learn and on the nature of communist morality.[5] After this, the communist fraction kept the congress well in hand against occasionally vocal opposition. A list of seventeen names for election to the central committee was put forward in the name of the fraction, requests for discussion were rejected, and a demand for the inclusion of Dunaevsky and two of his supporters was ruled out of order by the president. The list was then voted *en bloc* with a few absten-

---

[1] A. Shokhin, *Kratkaya Istoriya VLKSM* (2nd ed. 1928), pp. 89, 92-94.
[2] *VKP(B) o Komsomole* (1938), pp. 80-82.
[3] *Tretii Vserossiiskii S"ezd Rossiiskogo Kommunisticheskogo Soyuza Molodezhi* (1926), p. 89.   [4] *Pravda*, October 3, 1920.
[5] Lenin, *Sochineniya*, xxv, 384-397. The speech was not very well received ; Lenin's replies to the " many notes " sent up to the platform were apparently not recorded (*ibid.* xxv, 636, note 192). According to an official history, the Komsomol audience, " just back from the glories of the civil war and standing at a low level of political experience, was not prepared to understand the full significance of Lenin's address " (A. Shokhin, *Kratkaya Istoriya VLKSM* (2nd ed. 1928), pp. 87-88).

tions.[1] An attempt to make the Komsomol more effectively proletarian by banning students and intellectuals was defeated.[2] The congress adopted a programme, which duly emphasized the subordination of the Komsomol to party organs, and a statute, which fixed the lower and upper age-limits for membership at 14 and 23. " Passive " (i.e. non-voting) membership might be retained beyond the age of 23 ; and passive members, if elected to membership of Komsomol organs, regained the right to vote.[3] The third Komsomol congress marked a turning-point in the process which overtook all party and Soviet organizations. Effective control passed from the congress to the central committee, and eventually from the central committee to an inner bureau or secretariat, where vital decisions came to be taken. The purge of 1921, which was applied to the Komsomol as vigorously as to the party itself, had the same effect of eliminating potential trouble-makers. But those who sought to manage and direct the Komsomol faced two characteristic obstacles : the recalcitrance of youth to discipline, and the continuous and rapid turn-over of membership. During the party struggles of the middle nineteen-twenties, it was a constant anxiety of the party leadership to prevent the Komsomol from becoming a focus of opposition.

The new phase, marked by the involvement of the Komsomol in disputes originating in the party, began in the crisis over the platform of the 46 and the publication of Trotsky's series of letters and articles, afterwards collected under the title *The New Course*, in December 1923. The fourth and fifth congresses of the Komsomol had passed off without incident in 1921 and 1922 ; the year 1923 was the first in which no congress was held, its place being taken by a conference. Trotsky had addressed three Komsomol congresses — the second in 1919, the fourth in 1921 and the fifth in 1922 ; and his prestige as a leader in the revolution and in the civil war, combined with his vivid and flamboyant

---

[1] *Tretii Vserossiiskii S"ezd Rossiiskogo Kommunisticheskogo Soyuza Molodezhi* (1926), p. 235 ; Dunaevsky was later amnestied, and reappeared at Komsomol conferences and congresses, but was not again elected to the central committee.

[2] *Ibid.* pp. 257-261.

[3] *VLKSM v Rezolyutsiyakh* (1929), pp. 42-51 ; Ryazanov at the tenth party congress in March 1921 wished to reduce the upper age-limit to 18, but failed to win support (*Desyatyi S"ezd Rossiiskoi Kommunisticheskoi Partii* (1921), p. 65).

personality, readily made him a hero in the eyes of the young.[1] The theme of Trotsky's campaign, an attack on party bureaucracy in the name of revolutionary ardour and enthusiasm, had an obvious appeal to the young, which he did not hesitate to exploit.[2] Whatever may have been true of the young industrial worker, the student, both inside and outside the Komsomol, was overwhelmingly on Trotsky's side. The opposition leaders believed, as Zinoviev noted six months later, " that support for the opposition from the Komsomol was assured, and that the RLKSM was virtually in their pocket ".[3] The anxiety of the leadership over this situation was shown by two measures taken at the turn of the year. On December 29, 1923, the Komsomol central committee issued a new regulation restricting the admission of students to the Komsomol. Students, even if they were the children of workers (and therefore entitled to " worker " status under the usual party rules [4]), were required to go through a probationary period, which might extend to eighteen months, as " candidates " before admission to the Komsomol as full members ; and for transfer from candidate to member status the recommendation of three party or Komsomol members, each of at least two years' standing, was necessary.[5] On January 1, 1924, *Pravda* published a statement by nine members of the central committees of the Komsomol and the Communist Youth International condemning Trotsky.[6] But this only served to draw attention to the deep-seated divisions in the Komsomol, being answered by a declaration of eight leading Komsomol members, including two members of the central committee, which was sent to Trotsky and published by him.[7] The revolt in the Komsomol at this time was evidently too widespread to be dealt with by ordinary measures of dis-

---

[1] A party pamphlet, *Trotskizm i Molodezh* (1924), pp. 4-5, refers deprecatingly to " the very widespread legend of Trotsky as ' leader of the youth ' ".
[2] For a typical passage from *The New Course* see *The Interregnum, 1923–1924*, 325-326.
[3] *Shestoi S"ezd Rossiiskogo Leninskogo Kommunisticheskogo Soyuza Molodezhi* (1924), p. 53.   [4] See Vol. I, pp. 91-92.
[5] *Spravochnik Partiinogo Rabotnika*, iv (1924), 255-257.
[6] See *The Interregnum, 1923–1924*, p. 326.
[7] L. Trotsky, *Novyi Kurs* (1924), pp. 100-104 : the signatories were V. Dalin and Fedorov, members of the central committee, Bezymensky, Penkov and Dugachev, described as founding members of the Komsomol, Delyusin and Treivas, former secretaries of the Moscow committee, and Shokhin, an official of the central committee (and future historian of the Komsomol).

cipline. A year later, the eight signatories of the protest, together
with Averbakh, the editor of the Komsomol journal, made a statement in which they referred penitently to their Trotskyite attitude
at this time.[1] It does not appear that any of them had been
penalized for it.

The condemnation of Trotsky by the party central committee in January 1924, and Trotsky's retreat from the arena,
made it fairly easy to re-establish order in the Komsomol in the
first months of 1924. The opposition leaders in the Komsomol
had veiled their sympathy for Trotsky in a " theory of neutrality ".
If the Komsomol was not permitted to follow a political line of
its own, then it was better to keep out of politics altogether and
take no side in current controversies. In January 1924, the
Komsomol central committee, with only two dissentients (presumably Dalin and Fedorov), denounced neutrality and proclaimed its
support of the party line.[2] The Leningrad Komsomol organization also came out strongly against the heresy of neutrality, which
was once again condemned by the thirteenth party congress in
May 1924.[3] The trouble appears to have been most persistent in
the Ukrainian and White Russian Komsomols. Efforts to bring
the White Russian Komsomol into line on the Trotsky controversy
included two summons of White Russian Komsomol leaders to
Moscow and two visits by headquarters representatives to Minsk.[4]
But, when Stalin addressed a conference of party and Komsomol
workers on youth questions in April 1924, he contrived to play
down the difficulties and to convey the impression that things
were working smoothly again. It was true that the Komsomol
central committee had kept silence in the party controversy when
it should have spoken out. But this was a case not of " neutrality ",
but of over-cautiousness.[5] Zinoviev at the thirteenth party congress in the following month observed no such restraint, and
trounced Trotsky's attempt to incite the younger generation to

[1] *Pravda*, December 21, 1924.
[2] A. Shokhin, *Kratkaya Istoriya VLKSM* (2nd ed. 1928), pp. 130-131.
[3] *VKP(B) v Rezolyutsiyakh* (1941), i, 613 ; an account of the heresy was
given at the sixth Komsomol congress of July 1924, where it was called an
" ostrich policy " (*Shestoi S"ezd Rossiiskogo Leninskogo Kommunisticheskogo
Soyuza Molodezhi* (1924), pp. 144, 349).
[4] *Ibid.* p. 177, where a White Russian delegate complained of the incessant
harrying of the local organization.　　　　　[5] Stalin, *Sochineniya*, vi, 65-68.

war against the older — an attitude which was " radically and decisively incorrect ".[1] The sixth Komsomol congress of July 1924 proved more docile than its predecessors. It listened to a further warning from Zinoviev against Trotsky's appeal to youth, and promised support to " the old Bolshevik core of the party " against the opposition.[2] More significant still, the congress saw the emergence of a new leader in the person of Chaplin, the secretary of the Komsomol central committee, who was evidently prepared to organize and lead the Komsomol on lines of strict fidelity to the party. " Never ", said Chaplin in his speech to the congress, " has the Komsomol been so conscious of leadership from the party as at present." [3] Chaplin's services were promptly recognized by his appointment as a candidate member of the Orgburo.[4]

The progressive increase in the membership of the Komsomol during these years, and especially in 1924, had the same paradoxical effect as the corresponding increase in party membership of making the organization more amenable to control. Starting with a membership of 22,000 at its first congress in October 1918, the Komsomol two years later boasted a total of 480,000 members. Two years later still, in October 1922, the purge policy of the NEP period had reduced the total to 260,000 members and 13,000 candidates. From this low point membership began once more to climb steadily. In January 1924 a claim was made of 406,000 members and 94,000 candidates, and six months later of 630,000 members and 110,000 candidates, a recruitment of 170,000 being attributed to an extension to the Komsomol of the Lenin enrolment. In January 1925 the membership had topped a million, and two years later approached two millions.[5] In a mass organization expanding at this rate, quantity had inevitably to some extent replaced quality. Membership became for many a matter of routine and, as in the party, an avenue to promotion and to material advantages. In the broad rank and file of the Komsomol,

[1] Trinadtsatyi S"ezd Rossiiskoi Kommunisticheskoi Partii (Bol'shevikov) (1924), pp. 157-159.
[2] Shestoi S"ezd Rossiiskogo Leninskogo Kommunisticheskogo Soyuza Molodezhi (1924), pp. 49-50, 349.
[3] Ibid. p. 143.   [4] Pravda, June 3, 1924.
[5] A. Shokhin, Kratkaya Istoriya VLKSM (2nd ed. 1928), p. 115 ; Shestoi S"ezd Rossiiskogo Leninskogo Kommunisticheskogo Soyuza Molodezhi (1924), p. 38. For the Lenin enrolment see The Interregnum, 1923-1924, pp. 352-356.

independence, whether the independence of individual opinion
or the independence of the Komsomol from the party, seemed not
merely a lost, but a forgotten, cause.

When, therefore, in November 1924 *Lessons of October* broke
like a bombshell over the party, the Komsomol was already tamed
and ready to follow the party lead. But, once the party leadership
was split, docility in the Komsomol had the paradoxical effect of
reproducing within it the lines of the party struggle and once
more threatening to tear the organization asunder. In the
Komsomol, more than in the party, the tradition of the priority
and supremacy of Petrograd in the great days of the revolution
had survived as a living force : the power and prestige of the
Leningrad organization were relatively greater in the Komsomol
than in the party, of the central authority in Moscow relatively
less. Thus, in the party struggle of 1925, the Komsomol tended
to follow the Leningrad line just as in 1923 it had tended to follow
the Trotskyite line, though for different reasons. In both cases
strong intervention from Moscow was required to bring it to
order.

The initial stage raised no difficulty. On November 6, 1924,
at the very outset of the campaign against *Lessons of October*, the
Komsomol central committee sent out a detailed instruction on
the propaganda line to be adopted against Trotskyism.[1] The
Komsomol played its full part in agitation and in organizing
meetings to denounce Trotsky : this time no word of sympathy
with Trotsky was heard in its ranks. A statement signed on
behalf of the central committee and of the Moscow and Leningrad
committees of the Komsomol, and published in the press on
November 12, 1924, denounced Trotsky and defended Zinoviev
and Kamenev, whose past errors had been " recognized and corrected ".[2] But the result of this enthusiasm was to create in the
Komsomol widespread support for Zinoviev's proposal to expel
Trotsky from the party. As early as November 21, 1924, a
meeting of the Leningrad Komsomol organization, following the
lead of the provincial party committee, voiced a demand " to tear

---

[1] *Trotskizm i Molodezh* (1924), pp. 41-47.
[2] *Leningradskaya Pravda*, November 12, 1924.

out Trotskyism by the roots ".[1]   When the party central committee decided, against the minority votes of Zinoviev and
Kamenev, to take no disciplinary action against Trotsky,[2] Zinoviev
encouraged an agitation in the ranks of the Komsomol against
this " compromising " decision, and won over a majority of the
Komsomol central committee.[3]   The committee, meeting on
January 27, 1925, prudently refrained from pronouncing on the
issue of substance.   But the split in the committee was revealed
when the Leningrad delegates proposed to add to the bureau two
additional representatives from Leningrad and the Urals, where
the Komsomol organizations were known to be hostile to the
party decision.   The proposal was carried by a majority of 25 to
15, an amendment to refer it in the first instance to the party
central committee being rejected by the same majority.[4]   This
act of insubordination provoked a direct intervention by the
Politburo of the party which on February 12, 1925, warned the
Komsomol central committee that " narrow group politics " of
this kind would lead to " all possible organizational conclusions ".[5]

The Leningrad committee of the Komsomol remained, however, in a defiant mood.   A conference of the Leningrad Komsomol
was due to take place in February 1925 : and the committee
decided to invite to it delegates from 15 provincial Komsomol

---

[1] *Trotskizm i Molodezh* (1924), p. 48.

[2] See p. 31 above.

[3] Chaplin at the fourteenth party congress at first said that " some members
of the Politburo " incited the Komsomol, and, when challenged to mention
names, named Zinoviev ; Zinoviev virtually admitted the charge (*XIV S"ezd
Vsesoyuznoi Kommunisticheskoi Partii* (*B*) (1926), pp. 376, 460).   Gorlov at the
seventh Komsomol congress in March 1926 said that the opposition in the
Komsomol was set in motion by the opposition in the party : it was " the first
exploratory detachment of our party opposition " (*VII S"ezd Vsesoyuznogo
Leninskogo Kommunisticheskogo Soyuza Molodezhi* (1926), p. 140).

[4] *XIV S"ezd Vsesoyuznoi Kommunisticheskoi Partii* (*B*) (1926), p. 845.

[5] N. Chaplin, *Partiinaya Oppozitsiya i Komsomol* (1926), p. 14.   A strong
move was made at this time, probably under the direction of Bukharin, to
impart a Stalinist flavour to the monthly Komsomol journal *Molodaya Gvardiya*,
which had existed since 1922.   From No. 2-3, February–March 1925, the
editorship was taken over by Vareikis, the head of the press section of the party
central committee and a follower of Bukharin.   No. 4, April 1925, came out
with a photograph of Stalin as a frontispiece (No. 1, January 1925, had carried
a similar photograph of Lenin in commemoration of the first anniversary of his
death) ; an article in No. 6, June 1925, pp. 64-77 (by Lominadze, a strong
Stalinist and also on the editorial board), on the results of the fourteenth party
conference, was mainly devoted to the theme of socialism in one country.

organizations throughout the Soviet Union, as well as " observers " from the Uzbek and Kazakh organizations.[1] This was a barely disguised attempt to mobilize Komsomol opinion against the party decision and to establish a rival centre in Leningrad. Such a step would hardly have been taken except with the backing of Zinoviev and in the belief that his backing would be strong enough to protect those responsible against reprisals. The conference was duly held, and the hall rang with denunciations of Trotsky.[2] The invited visitors apparently failed to appear. This did not, however, diminish the wrath of the party leaders, whose veto on " group politics " had been flouted ; and an endorsement of the Leningrad action by a majority of the bureau of the Komsomol central committee [3] showed that the whole Komsomol organization was out of hand. Zinoviev evidently attempted to defend his protégés. He spoke afterwards with feeling of the " incredible campaign " directed against him and Kamenev on the charge that they had " dragged the Komsomol into this affair " ; and Bukharin referred to the discussion as " one of the biggest conflicts which have occurred in our central committee ".[4] Zinoviev had, however, a poor case. The breach of discipline was undeniable ; he could only plead the youth and inexperience of those ostensibly responsible. On March 5, 1925, the party central committee decided to send a commission to Leningrad to investigate the Komsomol organization.[5] When, however, the commission, consisting of Yaroslavsky, Kaganovich, Uglanov, Ilin and Chaplin, reached Leningrad, the local party leaders professed complete ignorance of what had occurred, and Komsomol leaders denied any ulterior motive in the invitations sent to outside delegates. Back in Moscow, the commission summoned the bureau of the Komsomol central committee, which appears to have stuck to its guns. The divisions were now too deep to be cured without a surgical operation. The secretary of the Leningrad provincial

[1] *XIV S"ezd Vsesoyuznoi Kommunisticheskoi Partii (B)* (1926), pp. 377, 845 ; the list of those invited is in N. Chaplin, *Partiinaya Oppozitsiya i Komsomol* (1926), p. 15.
[2] *Leningradskaya Pravda*, February 24, 1925.
[3] N. Chaplin, *Partiinaya Oppozitsiya i Komsomol* (1926), pp. 15-16.
[4] *XIV S"ezd Vsesoyuznoi Kommunisticheskoi Partii (B)* (1926), p. 460 ; *Leningradskaya Organizatsiya i Chetyrnadtsatyi S"ezd* (1926), p. 88.
[5] The text of the resolution is in N. Chaplin, *Partiinaya Oppozitsiya i Komsomol* (1926), pp. 16-17.

Komsomol committee Tolmazov was removed and replaced by Rumyantsev : half the members of the committee are said to have been replaced. Safarov, who represented the Leningrad provincial party committee on the Komsomol committee, was also removed. Zalutsky, the secretary of the Leningrad party organization, was censured for his failure to intervene. The Komsomol central committee was severely purged ; five members were immediately transferred elsewhere, and the number of dismissals eventually rose to 15.[1] The purged central committee met on March 16-17, 1925, and was addressed by Bukharin and Andreev on behalf of the Politburo. But, though the revolt was over, restiveness was still in the air. A long resolution sharply condemning the past actions of the bureau was passed by the narrow majority of 21 to 18, the minority voting for an alternative resolution which simply accepted the decisions of the Politburo announced by Bukharin and Andreev and ignored the past altogether.[2] After this clash, however, counsels of prudence seem to have prevailed on both sides ; peace was restored, and some degree of reconciliation achieved. The old bureau, having been formally condemned for its errors, was none the less re-elected ; and " even the Leningraders " swore that they " would work in a friendly and united spirit and carry out the decisions of the party ".[3]

The next crisis in the chequered affairs of the Komsomol related to the composition of the organization. Though, like the party, it was in principle a proletarian organization, considerable emphasis had been laid from the start on work in the countryside. A speaker at its first congress in October 1918 had advocated the recruitment of " groups of village youth " whose function would be to " rally the village poor in support of the new order ".[4]

---

[1] Accounts of this purge are in N. Chaplin, *Partiinaya Oppozitsiya i Komsomol* (1926), p. 18, and in an unpublished report in the Smolensk archives (WKP 522, p. 6). Chaplin names the five who were removed from the Komsomol central committee ; Zinoviev in his speech at the fourteenth party congress mentioned a total of 15 who had "been sent all over the place" (*XIV S"ezd Vsesoyuznoi Kommunisticheskoi Partii (B)* (1926), p. 459), but did not specify to what precise period he was referring : there was also a technical argument whether they had been " removed " or had voluntarily resigned or accepted other appointments (*VII S"ezd Vsesoyuznogo Leninskogo Kommunisticheskogo Soyuza Molodezhi* (1926), p. 166).

[2] N. Chaplin, *Partiinaya Oppozitsiya i Komsomol* (1926), pp. 19-21.

[3] *XIV S"ezd Vsesoyuznoi Kommunisticheskoi Partii (B)* (1926), p. 378.

[4] *Pervyi Vserossiiskii S"ezd RKSM* (3rd ed. 1926), pp. 97-99.

The Ukrainian group which sought to make the Komsomol exclusively proletarian came out against the membership of peasants as well as of intellectuals.[1] But this was never the majority view, though it continued to be heard at all the earlier congresses. According to the new programme adopted by the fourth Komsomol congress in October 1921, the Komsomol " relies in the countryside on the poorest peasant and *batrak* youth, while also admitting to its ranks the best elements of the middle peasant youth which are making the transition to communism ".[2] When, however, after the scissors crisis, party policy turned towards further conciliation of the peasant, trouble recurred in the Komsomol. The report of the party central committee to the thirteenth party congress of May 1924 drew attention to the " incorrect " attitude of some Komsomol organizations in " holding up the influx of peasants " into the Komsomol.[3] The resolution of the congress " On Work in the Countryside " echoed this criticism. It referred to the " exceptional importance " of the Komsomol in the countryside, and thought that the Komsomol should seek to recruit " *batraks* and poor peasants (first of all), and the best part of the middle peasants ".[4] Under this impetus, the membership of the Komsomol in rural areas advanced even more rapidly than in the towns, and it began to lose its character as a predominantly urban organization. The Komsomol central committee in October 1924 devoted a long resolution to the tasks of the Komsomol in the countryside ; and a few weeks later the Orgburo of the party once more condemned attempts to restrict the admission of peasants.[5] On January 1, 1924, when the membership of the Komsomol had recovered from the post-NEP purges and exceeded 500,000, the proportion of rural members had reached 39·9 per cent. The total rose to 1,140,000 with 46·9 per cent of rural members on January 1, 1925, and to 1,770,000 with 58·8 per cent of rural members a year later : this proved to

[1] See p. 90 above.
[2] *IV S"ezd RKSM* (1925), pp. 266-267, 321-322 ; *VLKSM v Rezolyutsiyakh* (1929), p. 88.
[3] *Izvestiya Tsentral'nogo Komiteta Rossiiskoi Kommunisticheskoi Partii (Bol'shevikov)*, No. 5 (63), May 1924, p. 30.
[4] *VKP(B) v Rezolyutsiyakh* (1941), i, 593.
[5] *Izvestiya Tsentral'nogo Komiteta Rossiiskoi Kommunisticheskoi Partii (Bol'shevikov)*, No. 4 (9), October 27, 1924, pp. 8-10 ; No. 11 (16), December 15, 1924, pp. 3-4.

be the highest percentage of rural members ever attained.[1]   A
peculiarity of the rural membership of the Komsomol was that
over-age membership was more freely tolerated in the country
than in the town, for the reason that young workers were more
freely admitted to the party than young peasants, who tended
to remain in the Komsomol.   According to one observer, the
Komsomol in rural areas at this period consisted, " not of children
of 16, but for the most part of fathers and mothers of families ".[2]
This state of affairs helped to make the rural Komsomols more
influential and more vocal.

The change of balance between town and country soon led to
frictions and embarrassments.   The rural Komsomol organizations began to ask why, when they represented so large and so
rapidly growing a part of the whole, they should be regarded as
subject to leadership from the towns.   A Komsomol conference
in the Kiev province claimed that since 55 per cent of the membership in the province was peasant, the same proportion should be
observed in electing the central committee.[3]   In the autumn of
1924 a group of rural Komsomols went so far as to propose a reorganization of the party itself as a " Russian Worker-Peasant
Party (Bolsheviks) " with equal rights for workers and peasants.[4]
These signs of independence in the countryside provoked a
reaction at headquarters in the form of an attempt to reduce
admissions to the Komsomol in rural areas.   But this was strongly
condemned in the resolution of the thirteenth party congress of
May 1924,[5] and again in a resolution of the Orgburo of the party
of December 1, 1924, which reminded the Komsomol of " the
fundamental question of Lenin's teaching — *the union of workers
and peasants and the leading role of the proletariat in our country* ",
and called on rural members of the Komsomol to recognize its
task as " *the first assistant of the party* in the countryside ".[6]

The Komsomol was now so closely attached to the party that
it could no longer hope to avoid involvement in any major party
dispute.   In the winter of 1924–1925 it had been Zinoviev who

[1] *VLKSM za Desyat' Let v Tsifrakh*, ed. Balashov and Nelepin (1928),
p. 32.   [2] Yu. Larin, *Rost Krest'yanskoi Obshchestvennosti* (1925), p. 68.
[3] *Pravda*, December 31, 1924.
[4] L. Kamenev, *Stat'i i Rechi*, xi (1929), 205.
[5] See p. 99 above.
[6] *Spravochnik Partiinogo Rabotnika*, v, 1925 (1926), 395-397.

sought to mobilize the Komsomol in support of his demand to exclude Trotsky. In the spring of 1925 it was the sponsors of a peasant orientation in the party who sought to reinforce this view by imposing it on the Komsomol. In April 1925, at the critical moment of the fourteenth party conference, an article on the Komsomol by Gorlov, a member of the Komsomol central committee, appeared in the party journal *Bol'shevik*. The journal had received " a series of complaints from members of the Komsomol " to the effect that " *the RKP is setting its course on the* kulak, *and the conquests of the proletariat and the poor peasantry* are being surrendered to the *kulak* ". Gorlov replied, in accordance with the current party line, that the duty of the Komsomol was not to " fan class conflicts in the countryside, but on the contrary to alleviate them, to make them die away ". He attacked a claim said to have been made by a Komsomol journal in Leningrad that the Komsomol was " the most Bolshevistically-inclined organization ", and rejected a demand for the " Bolshevization " of the Komsomol, if this meant that the Komsomol was to imitate all the functions of the party. What was needed was stronger party leadership. The article ended with a sentence which led to sharp controversy :

> It is indispensable to explain to the whole mass of Komsomols, especially to its urban sector, that the Komsomol is in its essence not predominantly a proletarian organization, like our party, but an organization which is in its broad mass peasant and should so remain.[1]

Like Bukharin, who had just uttered the fatal words " Enrich yourselves ", Gorlov had gone too far ; his position was made worse by the appearance in the Komsomol newspaper of an article endorsing Bukharin's slogan.[2] Chaplin was allowed to write an article in *Pravda* which, without referring to Gorlov's indiscretion, declared that " the Komsomol, though in composition a worker-peasant organization, is in its class essence a proletarian organization in which the leading role belongs to the worker youth ".[3] In June 1925 Gorlov himself retraced his steps in an article in a Komsomol journal in which he described the Komsomol as being

---

[1] *Bol'shevik*, No. 8, April 30, 1925, pp. 35-45.
[2] For this article and the reaction of the secretariat to it see Vol. 1, p. 284.
[3] *Pravda*, May 8, 1925.

" by its essence, its significance, its role a proletarian organization ".[1] But this did not prevent the airing of the dispute at the
fourth all-union Komsomol conference, which met in the same
month, covert attacks on the alleged " peasant leanings " of the
Komsomol central committee being made by Rumyantsev, the
secretary of the Leningrad provincial committee.[2] The conference in its resolution, while refusing to fix a quota for different
social groups within the Komsomol, adopted Chaplin's formula :

> The RLKSM, being in membership a worker-peasant
> organization, is by the essence of its class tasks a proletarian,
> communist organization, in which the leading role belongs to
> the worker youth.[3]

On the other hand, the resolution of the conference on organization removed the restriction by which " middle peasant " youth
seeking admission to the Komsomol was required, like students,
to pass through a " candidate " stage ; [4] and this concession to the
middle peasant, which fully accorded with party policy at the time,
probably had more practical consequences than the formal recognition of the Komsomol's proletarian essence.[5]

The alleged danger of a peasant deviation in the Komsomol
continued to play a minor part in the great party controversy ;
and the Leningraders, in drawing attention to this deviation in the
Komsomol, as in the party, contrived to depict themselves as
custodians of true proletarian principles. In August 1925 the
central Komsomol journal *Molodaya Gvardiya* carried an article
insisting on the importance of the work of the Komsomol in the
countryside.[6] Zalutsky responded in *Leningradskaya Pravda* with
an article on the dangerous predominance of petty bourgeois

---

[1] Quoted in *VII S"ezd Vsesoyuznogo Leninskogo Kommunisticheskogo
Soyuza Molodezhi* (1926), pp. 137-138.

[2] N. Chaplin, *Partiinaya Oppozitsiya i Komsomol* (1926), pp. 25-26. The
records of the proceedings of this conference have not been available, but it
was briefly reported in *Pravda*, June 18, 19, 1925.

[3] *VLKSM v Rezolyutsiyakh* (1929), p. 196.

[4] *Spravochnik Partiinogo Rabotnika*, v, 1925 (1926), pp. 446-447.

[5] The number of middle peasants in the Komsomol increased in 1925 at
the expense of the poor peasants, though no exact figures were given (*VII S"ezd
Vsesoyuznogo Leninskogo Kommunisticheskogo Soyuza Molodezhi* (1926), p. 395) ;
complaints began to be heard that, owing to the low degree of education of the
poor peasants, " the middle peasants take the leadership into their hands "
(*ibid.* p. 423).

[6] *Molodaya Gvardiya*, No. 8, August 1925, pp. 101-112.

elements — " even priests' sons " — in the Komsomol, and on
the need to give " proletarian-revolutionary Leninist clarity and
definition " to the principle of proletarian leadership.[1] Tarkhanov,
a Leningrad member of the Komsomol central committee, published an article in a Leningrad party journal in which he expressed the fear that the Komsomol would become " the tail-end
of peasant democracy ". In a eulogy of the proletarian qualities
of the Komsomol he reverted to the old claim that it was " more
revolutionary than the party " and " the vanguard of the vanguard ".[2] This was too much for the party central committee in
Moscow, which officially condemned Tarkhanov's article and
requested that a correction of the " mistake " should be inserted
in a later issue of the journal.[3]

At this point the publication of Zinoviev's *Leninism* drew a
red herring across the path. The chapter on the Komsomol,
which apparently belonged to the part of the book written before
Zinoviev had been weaned from the peasant orientation, was
found to contain a passage favouring the development in the
countryside of " all possible *auxiliary* organizations, perhaps a
system of ' delegates ' etc."[4] Rumyantsev, anxious to propitiate
his party chief, at once obediently endorsed the proposal in
a report to a regional Komsomol conference which was published in the local Komsomol press.[5] These moves called for
corresponding counter-moves. Stalin, in an arranged interview
published in *Komsomol'skaya Pravda*, at once rebutted the suggestion : a special peasant union organized within the Komsomol
would inevitably " set itself against the existing union between
the youth and its leader, the RKP(B) ", and create " the danger
of a split of the Komsomol into two unions — a union of worker
youth and a union of peasant youth ".[6] Some peasant youth

[1] *Leningradskaya Pravda*, August 30, 1925.
[2] These quotations are taken from Chaplin's report at the seventh Komsomol congress in March 1926 (*VII S"ezd Vsesoyuznogo Leninskogo Kommunisticheskogo Soyuza Molodezhi* (1926), pp. 50, 52-53) ; the article has not
been available.
[3] *Izvestiya Tsentral'nogo Komiteta Rossiiskoi Kommunisticheskoi Partii
(Bol'shevikov)*, No. 39 (114), October 12, 1925, p. 3.
[4] G. Zinoviev, *Leninizm* (1925), p. 358.
[5] N. Chaplin, *Partiinaya Oppozitsiya i Komsomol* (1926), p. 34 ; Rumyantsev's report appeared in *Smena*, October 16, 1925.
[6] Stalin, *Sochineniya*, vii, 245.

meetings were said to have been held, and to have become "a mouthpiece of anti-proletarian moods ".[1] Zinoviev himself hastened to retreat from an untenable position, and in an article published at the same time as Stalin's interview declared that poor and middle peasants should be admitted to the Komsomol " only within the limits of the possibility of dealing practically with them, i.e. guaranteeing the leadership of the proletarian element ".[2] Meanwhile Rumyantsev was dealt with in a resolution of the bureau endorsed by the Komsomol central committee on November 10, 1925. This censured Rumyantsev for giving utterance to personal views on controversial questions without consulting the central committee, rejected the proposals made by him, and finally took note of a " declaration by the Leningrad comrades of their abandonment of their proposal for delegate conferences ".[3] Throughout this time Gorlov remained, like Bukharin at a higher level, a favourite whipping-boy for those who denounced the peasant deviation. Two members of the bureau of the Komsomol central committee attempted to introduce this question into the Komsomol report to the fourteenth party congress, connecting Gorlov's unfortunate article with the current " underestimate of the *kulak* danger ". But these proposals were rejected by a majority of the bureau, though twelve members of the Komsomol central committee protested against the failure of the report to deal firmly with the peasant deviation.[4] Attacks on Gorlov's article continued to be heard from the opposition both at the fourteenth party congress in December 1925 and at the seventh Komsomol congress in the following March.

A further incident illustrating the extent to which the Lenin-

[1] *XIV S"ezd Vsesoyuznoi Kommunisticheskoi Partii (B)* (1926), pp. 378-379 ; *Spravochnik Partiinogo Rabotnika*, v, 1925 (1926), 457-458, 461-471.

[2] *Leningradskaya Pravda*, October 29, 1925 ; the same article advocated the admission to the Komsomol of " a full 100 per cent of the worker youth ", 100 per cent of *batraks* and " the best part of the middle peasant youth ". According to a later statement of Zinoviev (*ibid.* December 9, 1925), the article " received the approval " of the party central committee. The issue of *Leningradskaya Pravda* in which it was published on the front page also carried Stalin's interview on a later page ; *Pravda*, October 29, 1925, carried Stalin's interview on the front page, and did not print Zinoviev's article at all.

[3] *Spravochnik Partiinogo Rabotnika*, v, 1925 (1926), pp. 457-458.

[4] This episode was described by Tarasov, one of the two ringleaders, at the seventh Komsomol congress (*VII S"ezd Vsesoyuznogo Leninskogo Kommunisticheskogo Soyuza Molodezhi* (1926), pp. 72-74).

grad Komsomol organization was involved in the party struggle occurred after the session of the party central committee in October 1925. Rumyantsev compiled a dossier (referred to as the " blue dossier ") of recent utterances on the peasant question by Bukharin and his followers, beginning with Bukharin's " Enrich yourselves " speech and designed to demonstrate the existence of a peasant deviation. Some of the documents were annotated with critical remarks (including one to the effect that " Bukharin rejects Lenin ") by Barbashev, a Leningrad Komsomol journalist. The collection bore the title *Materials on the Question of the Class Line of the Party in the Countryside* ; it was said to have been duplicated in 40 copies, and distributed to local Komsomol committees in the Leningrad province. The copy which eventually reached the party central committee carried the label " Highly Secret " ; but it was alleged that this was added by the clerk in the office of the Leningrad Komsomol who betrayed it to Moscow. When the party central control commission investigated the affair, the Leningrad party organization professed to know nothing about it. Members of the control commission believed, or affected to believe, that the " blue dossier " was the product of a secret " seminar " conducted by Zinoviev for young party and Komsomol members. The incident ended in an increase of exasperation on both sides. The central control commission recalled Rumyantsev from his position on the Leningrad Komsomol committee, and censured Naumov, the member of the Leningrad party committee in charge of Komsomol affairs.[1]

As the fourteenth party congress approached, it was clear that the split in the party between Moscow and Leningrad was reproduced in the Komsomol, and that both sides were prepared to use their Komsomol followers as auxiliaries in the struggle. But the superior fighting strength of the central organization in Moscow was revealed at the critical moment. A meeting of the Komsomol central committee was convened on December 17, 1925, the eve of the party congress ; and the majority submitted to the meeting, apparently without notice, a resolution approving the line of the party central committee and condemning the attitude of the

[1] *XIV S"ezd Vsesoyuznoi Kommunisticheskoi Partii (B)* (1926), pp. 280-281, 846-848 ; *VII S"ezd Vsesoyuznogo Leninskogo Kommunisticheskogo Soyuza Molodezhi* (1926), p. 123.

Leningrad opposition, Zalutsky, Sarkis and Safarov being attacked by name. The Leningrad delegates, caught unawares, resorted to delaying tactics, demanding a formal report and documents in support of the resolution. This was refused, and the resolution was put to the vote and carried by a majority, twelve delegates voting against it.[1] Since divisions in the Komsomol now automatically and accurately reflected the divisions in the party, the vote was an omen for the results of the party congress. It is difficult to discover any other purpose served by it.

While, however, recriminations about Komsomol activities figured extensively in the debates of the fourteenth party congress, no issue specifically affecting the Komsomol arose, and the formal pronouncements of the congress on it followed routine lines. Molotov defined it in now familiar terms as " a worker-peasant organization in composition ", but " a proletarian communist organization in essence ". He recorded a total of 1,600,000 members. The percentage of workers in its membership had fallen in the past year from 39 to 36, but the percentage of *batraks* had risen from 5 to 8, so that the proportion of " proletarians " was still 44 per cent.[2] The theses presented by Bukharin claimed that the Komsomol now covered 50 per cent of young workers. Note was taken of " a weakening of discipline and an increased turn-over of membership ", or, more specifically, of " the phenomenon of an *exit* of considerable dimensions from the ranks ". Failure of discipline had been aggravated " by the presence of unemployment in the towns and immense agrarian over-population ". The familiar dilemmas were pointed out. It was necessary to win the confidence of backward elements in country and town without renouncing the task of leadership, to give the Komsomol a character of its own without asserting its independence of the party in matters of doctrine. At the same time " neutralism " was once more condemned.[3] Neither the theses nor the discussion on them contained anything new or significant. The fourteenth party congress was a landmark in the history of the Komsomol not because it took any important decisions, but because it witnessed

---

[1] *XIV S"ezd Vsesoyuznoi Kommunisticheskoi Partii (B)* (1926), pp. 375, 830 ; the resolution was published in *Pravda*, December 18, 1925.
[2] *XIV S"ezd Vsesoyuznoi Kommunisticheskoi Partii (B)* (1926), p. 62.
[3] *VKP(B) v Rezolyutsiyakh* (1941), ii, 71-80.

the culmination of the long and gradual process by which the Komsomol had been welded into the structure of the party. The conception of a communist youth organization independent of the communist party had never really made sense. Its independence was placed in doubt at an early stage when it began to draw its finance from the party : this meant that it ceased to control its own appointments. It soon lost the right to hold opinions different from those of the party leadership, or even to remain neutral on issues which divided the party. Its fate was sealed when it became a happy hunting-ground for oppositions seeking to challenge the party leadership. It was natural and inevitable that successive oppositions should have exploited the turbulence and restiveness of youth. But it would be rash to claim that they were any more interested than the leadership in an independent Komsomol ; both wanted to use it as a minor adjunct and reinforcement in their respective campaigns. The fourteenth party congress marked the end of an illusion which, perhaps, had already ceased to be an illusion and become a pretence. Henceforth the Komsomol was a junior branch of the party, echoing its doctrines and practices, and following its fortunes, in every detail.

CHAPTER 16

MANŒUVRING FOR POSITION

THE drawing up of " the platform of the four " by Zinoviev, Kamenev, Krupskaya and Sokolnikov on September 5, 1925,[1] was the first formal act of a concerted opposition. There is no evidence to show how soon Stalin became aware of its existence and content. But he must have guessed that something was on foot. Zinoviev's article *The Philosophy of an Epoch*, first submitted within a few days of the drawing up of the platform, could well be treated as the first manifesto of a new group. Stalin clearly regarded it as such, and humiliated Zinoviev by having it submitted for revision to the central committee.[2] This incident was quickly followed by the publication of Zinoviev's *Leninism*, which was a declaration of war on a broad front.[3] The sequel showed, however, that, though relations between Zinoviev and Stalin were now irretrievably embittered, the leaders on both sides still hesitated to attack one another openly and publicly. While much of the latter half of Zinoviev's *Leninism* was devoted to a covert attack on Bukharin, and to a lesser degree on Stalin, neither of them was named ; and Bukharin and Stalin in return neither criticized Zinoviev openly nor allowed their subordinates to launch an attack on him. This convention of formal restraint held good on both sides when the party central committee held its

[1] See pp. 66-68 above.
[2] For this incident see Vol. 1, pp. 300-302. The first part of the article in *Leningradskaya Pravda*, September 19, 1925, contained two misprints, corrected in a note on the following day. The first, by an extraordinary coincidence, was the same mistake in a quotation from Lenin (" nepman Russia " for " NEP Russia ") for which Stalin had already criticized Kamenev (see p. 4 above) ; the second, in a quotation from Dan, substituted " the gospel of Leningrad " for " the gospel of Lenin ". Neither misprint occurred in the version published simultaneously in *Pravda*, though the spreading of the type in both passages is consistent with the conjecture that corrections were made at the last moment ; if this supposition is correct, the errors were in Zinoviev's manuscript.   [3] See Vol. 1, pp. 303-305.

session in October 1925 and unanimously passed a number of resolutions on economic policy.[1] But it required four meetings of hard bargaining to achieve this result,[2] and among the proposals made, but abandoned, on this occasion was one to appoint Stalin and Kuibyshev to STO — an open declaration of non-confidence in Kamenev.[3] It was Stalin and the secretariat in Moscow, rather than Zinoviev and the opposition in Leningrad, who now held the initiative, and could slacken or force the pace in order to bring the issue to a head at a tactically favourable moment. At the October session Stalin moved just far enough towards the Left to make a compromise possible with the opposition, and stave off a public rupture for another indeterminate period. The breakdown of the triumvirate was now certain ; in a sense, it had already taken place. But the moment when it would be brought into the open depended on a number of imponderables, and, most of all, on Stalin's patient determination to wait for the moment when the opposition could be goaded into placing itself patently in the wrong. Stalin's control of the central party organization was now complete. It was noticeable that, in the usual anniversary issue of *Pravda* for November 7, 1925, the first signed article was by Stalin and appeared on page 2 (the first page being entirely devoted to a photograph and to pronouncements of the dead leader) together with articles of Rykov and Kalinin ; Zinoviev followed on page 3.[4]

At the end of October 1925 an event occurred which was in all probability a pure accident, but which in the heated atmosphere of party recriminations subsequently lent itself to rumour and suspicion : the death of Frunze, who had succeeded Trotsky as People's Commissar for War in the previous January.[5] Frunze, though known for many years as a stubborn opponent of Trotsky on military questions, rarely spoke or wrote on other matters and does not appear to have committed himself one way or the other in the breach now opening between Zinoviev and Stalin.[6] In the

[1] See Vol. 1, pp. 305-308.
[2] *XIV S"ezd Vsesoyuznoi Kommunisticheskoi Partii (B)* (1926), p. 401.
[3] *Ibid.* p. 340.
[4] In the corresponding issue of 1924 Zinoviev's article had appeared alone on the front page with articles by Trotsky and Rykov on page 2 : Stalin did not appear at all. [5] See p. 33 above.
[6] In a speech of January 1925, on the anniversary of Lenin's death, Frunze went out of his way to refer to Zinoviev's and Kamenev's opposition to Lenin

autumn of 1925 he suffered from an internal malady,[1] and received conflicting or uncertain medical advice on the desirability of an operation. The question was referred to the Politburo, the final arbiter of the destinies of important servants of the party, which decided, after reading the medical reports, that the operation should take place : none of the accounts represents the decision as contested or not unanimous. Frunze underwent the operation on October 28, 1925, died three days later, and was buried with full honours to the accompaniment of many laudatory articles in the press. In the current situation any appointment to an important post was politically significant, and was an index to the balance of power in the party. Voroshilov, a friend and supporter of Stalin, was appointed to succeed Frunze, with Lashevich, an adherent of Zinoviev, as his deputy.[2] The decision accurately reflected both Stalin's superior strength and his unwillingness, at this time, to break absolutely with Zinoviev.

Frunze's death might have passed without further comment if the literary journal *Novyi Mir* had not published, six months later, a story by the novelist fellow-traveller Pilnyak with the fanciful title *A Tale of the Unextinguished Moon*. The hero of the tale is an army commander ordered by his political superiors to undergo an operation : he submits to it reluctantly and with premonitions of disaster, and in fact dies, the implication clearly being that his death was desired and actively promoted by some higher authority. To make matters worse, Pilnyak prefaced the tale with a note, dated January 28, 1926, stating that he scarcely knew Frunze and was ignorant of the circumstances of his death, and warning the reader not to seek " genuine facts and living persons " in the story. This publication evidently infuriated the authorities. The issue of *Novyi Mir* was withdrawn, and another issue substituted for it, in which the Pilnyak item was replaced by

in October 1917, though without naming them (M. Frunze, *Sobranie Sochinenii*, iii (1927), 22) ; in the following month, he quoted with approval a speech by Stalin on the four allies of the proletariat (*ibid*. iii, 75). These are straws in the wind, but do not suggest that Frunze inclined at this time towards Zinoviev rather than towards Stalin.

[1] According to K. Voroshilov, *Stat'i i Rechi* (1937), pp. 7-8, injuries sustained by Frunze in a motor accident some months earlier had led to internal haemorrhage ; but no contemporary evidence is available to confirm this.

[2] These appointments were announced in the press of November 7, 1925 ; Voroshilov's appointment was also in *Sobranie Zakonov, 1925*, ii, No. 86, art. 226.

another story. This withdrawal did not prevent the publication
in the following number of *Novyi Mir* of a letter from Voronsky,
to whom Pilnyak had dedicated his tale, indignantly repudiating
the dedication, and of a note of apology from the editors describing
the publication of the tale as " a flagrant and gross error ".
Six months later Pilnyak, who had been abroad when the scandal
broke, himself wrote a letter, which was also printed in *Novyi Mir*,
denying any intention to write a " malicious slander " on the party,
but declaring that he now regretted his " grievous errors " and
recognized that " much written by me in this tale consists of
slanderous inventions ".[1] These successive disclaimers merely
helped to crystallize the legend of Frunze as a man hounded by
Stalin to his death, and gave it a lasting place in party recriminations. Evidence is lacking to convict Stalin, in this affair, of anything more sinister than his usual astuteness in taking advantage
of every accident to strengthen his own position.

The agreement embodied in the October resolution of the
party central committee was not a treaty of peace between the two
factions. It was a temporary truce, concluded because neither side
was prepared to force the issue at this stage ; but both sides undoubtedly intended the truce to continue long enough to cover
the proceedings of the forthcoming fourteenth party congress.[2]
No truce, however, can oblige the parties to remain altogether
inactive and to refrain from attempts to improve their respective
positions. No such obligation was accepted in the interval
between the October committee and the December congress
either by the group which controlled the central machine or by
the group centring round Zinoviev and Kamenev. Zinoviev did
not repeat the mistake which Trotsky had made a year earlier of
restricting his attack on the official policy to spoken and written
argument. He recognized that argument must be reinforced by
organization, and he pitted the Leningrad party machine against
the central party machine in Moscow. The prestige of the
Leningrad proletariat, and its specific weight in the party, made

[1] A detailed account of the two issues of *Novyi Mir*, No. 5, May 1926,
and of the subsequent disclaimers (*ibid.* No. 6, June 1926, pp. 184-185 ; No. 1,
January 1927, p. 256) is given in *Soviet Studies*, x, No. 2 (October 1958),
pp. 162-164.
[2] This was confirmed by both parties at the congress (*XIV S"ezd Vsesoyuznoi Kommunisticheskoi Partii* (*B*) (1926), pp. 294, 361).

the enterprise seem not at all hopeless. But the Leningraders failed to realize the overwhelming strength now concentrated in the central party organization, or the tactical weakness of a position in which they were compelled constantly to appear as challengers of party unity. It was a situation calling for skilful and firm leadership if disaster was to be avoided. This Zinoviev was ill equipped to supply. He failed to restrain his followers from rash enterprises which he could neither wholeheartedly support nor effectively disown ; and the same irresoluteness paralysed him when the moment demanded a decisive stroke.

The first incident, which coincided with the October session, related to Zalutsky, the secretary of the Leningrad provincial party committee. Zalutsky's post made him a key figure in the Leningrad organization ; and he was particularly persistent and outspoken in his criticisms of the official Moscow line. His downfall was the work of one Leonov. Whether Leonov was an agent deliberately used by Moscow to entrap Zalutsky, or a loyal party member who was shocked by what he heard and thought right to report it, is still not clear. What is certain is that about the time of the October session Leonov wrote a letter to party headquarters in Moscow describing an alleged conversation with Zalutsky. Zalutsky had said that the party leaders were " creating a bourgeois state — what Lenin called a ' kingdom of peasant narrow-mindedness', but what they call 'the building of *socialism*'", and that " they do not reckon with Leningrad, they treat it as a province ". He accused them of " degeneration " and of seeking to bring about a " thermidor " — words which were apparently often on Zalutsky's lips — and compared Stalin's personal position with that of Bebel, who had attempted to stand midway between the orthodox and the " opportunists " in the German Social-Democratic Party.[1] The central control commission set up a

[1] The text of Leonov's letter, as read to the fourteenth party congress, is in *XIV S"ezd Vsesoyuznoi Kommunisticheskoi Partii (B)* (1926), pp. 358-360 ; cf. Bukharin's account, *ibid.* p. 140. According to a later version (*Bol'shevik*, No. 19-20, October 31, 1926, p. 4), Zalutsky also accused the central committee of " protecting comrade Trotsky " — an echo of the dispute of January 1925. Zalutsky's right-about-turn was as complete as that of Zinoviev ; at the Leningrad provincial party conference of May 1924 he had described the view that NEP meant " degeneration " as a " Menshevik thesis " (*Leningradskaya Pravda*, May 8, 1924). But nobody seems to have bothered to point this out.

committee to investigate the affair, and Zalutsky was summoned to appear before it. Zalutsky seems to have made the task of the committee easier by declaring that he subscribed to Leonov's report " with both hands ", and that it saved him from the necessity of making a speech since it said all that he wanted to say. But he qualified this admission, then or later, by excluding from it the remarks about " degeneration " and " thermidor " : such charges he had never made against the central committee, though he had expressed lack of confidence in Bukharin, Molotov and Bubnov.[1] Apprised of these facts, the central control commission requested the Leningrad provincial committee to change its secretary. By a majority vote, with nine dissentients, the provincial committee decided to accede to the request ; at a later meeting, at which members of regional organizations were present, the same motion was carried by the still narrower majority of 19 to 16.[2] Zalutsky was then removed from office by a unanimous decision of the bureau of the provincial committee. It was, however, alleged that the Leningrad organization took no trouble to explain to its members the reason for Zalutsky's removal, and allowed the impression to gain ground that this was due to unwarranted interference from headquarters in Moscow. Komarov, to whom Zalutsky's post was offered, declined it, according to his own account, on the ground that " the results of the voting convinced me that the dispute with the central committee would not come to an end ".[3]

Whatever the formal rights and wrongs of the Zalutsky affair, it clearly aroused new resentment among the Leningrad leaders. At an anniversary meeting on November 7, 1925, which occurred immediately after Zalutsky's dismissal, Zalutsky, Safarov and Zinoviev appeared on the same platform. Zalutsky and Safarov

[1] The story has to be pieced together from accounts given at the fourteenth party congress by Petrovsky, Voroshilov (both members of the investigating committee), Rykov and Zalutsky himself (*XIV S"ezd Vsesoyuznoi Kommunisticheskoi Parti (B)* (1926), pp. 169, 230, 393, 414) ; according to Rykov, Zalutsky at one moment pretended that his remarks had been made deliberately in order to mislead Molotov, whose emissary he believed Leonov to be.

[2] It was evidently at one of these meetings that Rumyantsev, secretary of the Leningrad Komsomol committee, exclaimed that " the central committee is hammering us because we carry on the correct Leninist line " ; the remark was kept off the record (*ibid.* p. 218), but probably represented the view of most of those present.   [3] *Ibid.* pp. 218-219, 361.

spoke of the *kulak* deviation ; and Zalutsky added that the Leningrad organization needed to have " a strong fist " [1] in order to deal with it. Zinoviev remarked that 15,000 bureaucrats had betrayed the German Social-Democratic Party and pointedly asked whether there were more or fewer bureaucrats in the Russian party. Another speaker expressed the conviction that " Leningrad will win ".[2] By this time relations between the Leningrad provincial committee and the central committee in Moscow were a burning issue. The central committee, anxious to avert further incidents and to strengthen its hold in Leningrad, proposed to send a permanent delegate to sit with the Leningrad provincial committee. The proposal was accepted, and Shvernik was despatched to Leningrad, though friction occurred between Stalin and Zinoviev about the precise work on which he was to be employed.[3] A nine-hour session of the bureau of the Leningrad committee on November 12, 1925, was remembered by all the participants as particularly stormy and difficult. It ended with a resolution promising support to the central committee. On the next day Zinoviev wrote to Komarov expressing regret for past misunderstandings, and undertaking to do everything possible " to work with the majority ".[4] But this olive branch merely meant that the Leningrad malcontents still recoiled from any irrevocable step. Covert agitation against the policy of the central committee continued at district party meetings in Leningrad. A worker delegate thought it strange " to read that we have a whole series of shortcomings ", and that " our organization is put on the same footing as some county organization ".[5] The attempt to maintain the proprieties was beginning to break down :

---

[1] *Kulak* means " fist " : hence the untranslatable pun.

[2] No formal record of the speeches was made, and this perhaps exaggerated account depends on the recollection of a hostile witness six weeks later (*XIV S"ezd Vsesoyuznoi Kommunisticheskoi Partii (B)* (1926), pp. 922-923). An article by Yaroslavsky in *Bol'shevik*, No. 19-20, October 31, 1926, p. 4, recalled the agitation in factories by Leningrad party spokesmen at this time against the central committee and in support of " the platform of the four ".

[3] The fullest account of this episode comes from Komarov (*XIV S"ezd Vsesoyuznoi Kommunisticheskoi Partii (B)* (1926), pp. 218-219).

[4] *Ibid.* pp. 219-220, 361.

[5] *Leningradskaya Pravda*, November 17, 1925 ; Tomsky caricatured this attitude of the Leningrad party organization : " We are not some Kaluga or Tula to make reports in the ordinary way " (*XIV S"ezd Vsesoyuznoi Kommunisticheskoi Partii (B)* (1926), p. 283).

Everyone said : " We are for the central committee, for its line ", and so forth ; but the policy of the central committee in the peasant question, in the question of the press, and in different questions of our party life, was explained in such a way that the leadership of the central committee was, to put it mildly, not approved of.[1]

In the battle of words which developed between *Leningradskaya Pravda* and the *Pravda* of Moscow, the publicists of Leningrad far outdid their rivals in pungency and aggressiveness. Two articles by Safarov of November 15 and 22, 1925, the first bearing the title, ironically borrowed from a Moscow party publicist, *But Socialism is Soviet Power plus the " Link "*, and the second *Leninism with Reservations*,[2] set a new standard of controversial bitterness which was to reach a crescendo in the ensuing weeks.

An example of this envenomed journalistic controversy was provided by a campaign waged almost single-handed by Sarkis, who had already crossed swords with Bukharin over the question of the *rabkors*.[3] The proletarianization of the party was a cause which no good Marxist could reject, and which lay near to the heart of the Leningraders, being associated with the time-honoured claim that the Leningrad organization contained a larger proportion of workers than any other, and that the industrial workers of Leningrad were more party-conscious and more highly organized than any other large industrial group in the Soviet Union.[4] The admission of workers to the party had been a constant topic of discussion since the days of the Lenin enrolment, though not much practical effect had been given to it. Two cognate issues were involved and were sometimes confused. In the first place, it seemed desirable that as large a proportion as possible of authentic industrial workers should be drawn into the party ; secondly, that as high a proportion as possible of the party membership should consist of industrial workers. Both these desiderata had been officially expressed at the thirteenth party congress in May 1924 on the occasion of the Lenin enrolment.

The time is approaching [declared the main congress resolution] when the whole basic mass of the proletariat of our union

---

[1] *Ibid.* pp. 361-362.
[2] Both were reprinted in *Novaya Oppozitsiya* (1926), pp. 119-125, 130-134.
[3] See p. 54 above.   [4] See pp. 56-57 above.

will enter the party. The congress instructs the central committee to conduct its work in the sense of ensuring that the
immense majority of members of the party in the very near
future should consist of workers directly engaged in production.[1]

As regards the proportion of workers in the party, Molotov in his
report at the same congress set it as an aim " to raise the proportion of workers in the party to 90 per cent ". The special congress
resolution on party organization more modestly but more precisely spoke of the hope that " in the course of the next year more
than half the membership of the party may consist of workers
from the bench ".[2] The fourteenth party conference in April
1925 recalled, though without particular emphasis, " the decision
that our party should contain not less than 50 per cent of workers
directly engaged in production ".[3]

The twin desiderata of the admission of a majority of workers
to the party and of the proletarianization of the party were thus
firmly embedded in party doctrine. Nobody contested them, but
in ordinary times not much attention was paid to them. In the
autumn of 1925, at the height of the party controversy, the ingenious Sarkis discovered in them a fresh talking-point for use by
the Leningraders against the central party organization in Moscow,
which could be convicted of lukewarmness towards proletarian
claims. In the middle of November 1925 Sarkis submitted to
Pravda in Moscow an article on the admission of workers to the
party, in which he quoted Molotov's proposal at the thirteenth
party congress " to raise the proportion of workers in the party
to 90 per cent ", adding as his own view that 50 or 60 per cent of
all industrial workers ought to be in the party, and that 90 per
cent of the party ought to consist of " workers from the bench "
by the time of the fifteenth congress (now presumably rather more

---

[1] *VKP(B) v Rezolyutsiyakh* (1941), i, 567.

[2] *Trinadtsatyi S"ezd Rossiiskoi Kommunisticheskoi Partii (Bol'shevikov)*
(1924), p. 533 ; *VKP(B) v Rezolyutsiyakh* (1941), i, 570. Molotov afterwards explained that in quoting a figure of 90 per cent he had not been thinking
of " workers from the bench " (*XIV S"ezd Vsesoyuznoi Kommunisticheskoi
Partii (B)* (1926), p. 78 ; for the distinction between " workers " and " workers
from the bench " see Vol. 1, p. 92). It should also be said that he was speaking
of the Ukraine, where the proportion of workers in the party was unusually high
(see *The Interregnum, 1923–1924*, p. 355, note 1) ; but his words were given a
general application.

[3] *VKP(B) v Rezolyutsiyakh* (1941), ii, 12.

than a year ahead).[1] Bukharin, as editor of *Pravda*, found the quotation from Molotov embarrassing and Sarkis's glosses on it unacceptable, and returned the article to Sarkis, through Zinoviev, with criticisms and suggested corrections, apparently on the assumption that, if these were made, the article would be published in *Pravda*.[2] Sarkis amended the article by including " rural workers " (meaning *batraks*) and by omitting the phrase " workers from the bench " and the reference to the fifteenth congress ; and the article appeared in this modified form — not, however, in *Pravda*, but in *Leningradskaya Pravda*, on December 3, 1925. It urged that in the years immediately ahead the aim should be to draw 50 to 60 per cent of all industrial workers into the party, and to raise the proportion of " industrial and rural workers " in the party to 90 per cent of the total membership.

By this time, the dispute had spread and tempers were heated. Before Sarkis's article appeared, Uglanov wrote an article in *Pravda* deprecating any mass entry of workers into the party ; and another article in *Pravda* explained that 13 per cent of the industrial workers of Moscow belonged to the party, and that the immediate task was " not so much an increase of quantity as of quality ".[3] Uglanov's sally provoked a leading article in *Leningradskaya Pravda* by its editor Gladnev, entitled *The Proletarianization of the Party — the Pledge of Inner-Party Democracy*, which reproached Uglanov with " panic fear of the masses ", and hinted at a connexion between unwillingness to admit workers to the party and repressive measures against the opposition.[4] *Pravda* retaliated with an article also headed *The Proletarianization of Our Party*, which recalled a Menshevik proposal of 1908 for a workers' party, and denounced Sarkis for wanting " a broad workers' party in the spirit of the Menshevik Axelrod or a reformist party of the MacDonald type ".[5] Finally, Sarkis had the last

---

[1] The original article is not extant, but its tenor can be judged from the account of it given by Sarkis himself at the fourteenth party congress (*XIV S"ezd Vsesoyuznoi Kommunisticheskoi Partii (B)* (1926), p. 346) and from an article published by him at the same time in the Leningrad party journal *Pod Znamenem Kommunizma* and quoted in *Novaya Oppozitsiya* (1926), p. 196).

[2] *XIV S"ezd Vsesoyuznoi Kommunisticheskoi Partii (B)* (1926), p. 132.

[3] *Pravda*, November 29, December 3, 1925.

[4] *Leningradskaya Pravda*, December 2, 1925.

[5] *Pravda*, December 5, 1925 ; a reply from Sarkis was printed with an editorial rejoinder, *ibid.* December 9, 1925.

word with an article *One Step Forward, Not Two Steps Back*, which, by giving a twist to the title of Lenin's famous pamphlet of 1904, rebutted the charge of Menshevism and turned it back on the heads of the Muscovites.[1] The controversy provided minor ammunition for the Leningrad and Moscow provincial party conferences that preceded the fourteenth party congress. Zinoviev in his speech at the former endorsed Sarkis's demand, and the resolution of the Moscow conference spoke of " ostentatious attempts immediately to introduce 50 per cent or more of all workers into the party " and reverted to the comparison with Axelrod. The issue even figured in the debates of the congress itself.[2] But it had no real substance except as an outlet for embittered feelings in Leningrad and Moscow.

These public recriminations were indicative of the acute animosity now prevailing between the two largest and most important party organizations. But there was little sign that the divisions had spread to the rest of the party. Local party conferences, held, as usual, all over the Soviet Union in preparation for the party congress, obediently took note of the two deviations recorded in the October resolution of the central committee, but showed no tendency to take sides. Control commissions were sometimes reproached at these conferences with " weakness and excessive leniency ", not, however, towards opposition or fractionalism, but towards the moral delinquencies of party members, " especially towards drunkenness ".[3] It was also significant that the leaders, though they cannot be acquitted of some degree of complicity in the indiscretions of their henchmen on both sides, did not openly participate in the campaign ; Zinoviev is said to have " poured cold water " on the " Leftists " among his followers who were spoiling for a fight.[4] The appearance of unity at the summit of the party was preserved, and it still seemed possible that the compromise patched up at the October session of the central committee might equally hold good at the December congress. Preparations went forward for the congress on this

[1] *Leningradskaya Pravda*, December 15, 1925.
[2] *Ibid.* December 8, 1925 ; *XIV S"ezd Vsesoyuznoi Kommunisticheskoi Partii (B)* (1926), p. 171.
[3] *Izvestiya Tsentral'nogo Komiteta Vsesoyuznoi Kommunisticheskoi Partii (B)*, No. 9 (130), March 8, 1926, pp. 3-4.
[4] *XIV S"ezd Vsesoyuznoi Kommunisticheskoi Partii (B)* (1926), p. 220.

assumption. In November Lashevich assured Mikoyan that the
Leningraders did not intend to fight at the congress, and that " a
single front " would be maintained.[1] Party leaders of both
factions spoke in different parts of the country without emphasizing differences or hinting at the danger of a split. Kamenev
and Mikoyan spoke from the same platform in Rostov, Sokolnikov
in Kazan.[2] Draft resolutions prepared for submission to the
congress by Kamenev on the economic situation, by Bukharin on
the Komsomol and by Tomsky on the trade unions, and the draft
of a revised party statute, were duly approved by the Politburo,
and published in the usual manner, two or three weeks in advance
of the congress. Bukharin's theses on the Komsomol contained
two incidental passages which were to be frequently quoted in the
subsequent debates. He denounced those " remnants of defeated
revolutionary parties, SRs and especially Mensheviks ", who
" depict our state enterprises of socialist type as simply capitalism
or as this or that form of state capitalism ", thus implicitly reaffirming his own gloss on Lenin's view of " state capitalism " ; [3]
and in a later passage he balanced a criticism of " *communist
boasting and excessive optimism* " with an attack on " *pessimism and
liquidationist lack of faith in the socialist paths of our development* ".[4]

The spark which ignited this inflammable material was
generated at the conferences of the Leningrad and Moscow provincial party organizations which preceded the party congress.
It was generated by a process of friction between them ; and
nothing is gained by attempting to blame or exonerate one rather
than the other. When the Leningrad conference opened on the
last day of November, feelings already ran high, and tempers

---

[1] *Ibid.* p. 186.   [2] *Ibid.* pp. 247, 302.   [3] See pp. 70-72 above.
[4] *VKP(B) v Rezolyutsiyakh* (1941), ii, 72, 75. According to a statement by
Rykov and Molotov which appeared in *Pravda*, December 15, 1925, and in
Leningradskaya Pravda two days later, Bukharin's theses were " approved by
the Politburo not unanimously, but by a majority vote ". Possibly Zinoviev
and Kamenev objected to one or other of these two passages, though it would
be equally plausible to suppose that they slipped unnoticed into a very long
document ; special attention was drawn to them in a leading article in *Pravda*,
December 5, 1925 — the day on which the Moscow provincial party conference
met. Bukharin's theses were originally printed in *Leningradskaya Pravda*,
November 29, 1925, in small type — perhaps merely because nobody thought
them very important.

were short. Zinoviev appears to have been genuinely anxious to
restrain his more aggressive followers.[1] On the second day of the
conference he presented a report on the work of the central committee which contained a conventionally balanced account of the
two deviations, and ended with a typical flight of rhetoric :

> I think, comrades, that I have received moral full powers
> from one and all of the members of this conference, from one
> and all of the members of our Leningrad provincial party
> organization, from every communist working man or woman,
> from every Komsomol, from every member of our great family,
> to say, wherever and whenever it may be necessary, that our
> Leningrad organization stands as one man for the central com-
> mittee, for a single Leninist line, for Leninism.[2]

But other orators were less discreet. Sarkis asserted that there
was no difference between Bukharin and Bogushevsky — " both
names begin with B " — and that Bukharin was the first important
party member, since Trotsky, to undertake a revision of Leninism.[3]
Safarov dwelt on " the incorrectness of the views of comrades
Vareikıs, Bogushevsky and others on the question of class differentiation in the countryside ", attacked Uglanov and stressed the
importance of proletarian leadership. Boastful appeals were made
to the proletarian pre-eminence of Leningrad.[4] Safarov, in a
passage which was particularly resented in Moscow, described
the Leningrad workers as " the salt of the proletarian earth, who
have carried on their shoulders the burden of three great revolutions ", and declared that it was the Leningrad proletariat which
had " produced such a leader as Vladimir Ilich Lenin ".[5] Yaro-

---

[1] Tomsky admitted that Zinoviev and Kamenev " tried to put a brake on
the radicalism of the Leningrad organization " — when it was already too late
(*XIV S"ezd Vsesoyuznoi Kommunisticheskoi Partii (B)* (1926), p. 292).

[2] The speech was published in successive issues of *Leningradskaya Pravda*
from December 4 to 8, and in an abbreviated form in *Pravda* and *Izvestiya*,
December 8, 9, 1925, and reprinted in part in *Novaya Oppozitsiya* (1926),
pp. 23-25.

[3] *XIV S"ezd Vsesoyuznoi Kommunisticheskoi Partii (B)* (1926), pp. 227,
587 ; owing to its provocative character, the speech was not published, and was
omitted from the official record of the conference (*ibid.* p. 451).

[4] See pp. 55-57 above.

[5] This passage was quoted with indignation by Lomov, one of the few
defenders of the central committee, at the conference itself (*Leningradskaya
Pravda*, December 10, 1925), by Rudzutak at the fourteenth party congress
(*XIV S"ezd Vsesoyuznoi Kommunisticheskoi Partii (B)* (1926), p. 342), and later
in I. Skvortsov-Stepanov, *Izbrannye Proizvedeniya*, ii (1931), 345.

slavsky, who was present at the conference as delegate of the central committee, paid a rather grudging tribute to Zinoviev's impartiality in dealing with both the deviations cited in the October resolution of the central committee, but accused other speakers of concentrating exclusively on the so-called *kulak* deviation.

I should not have spoken here on this question [he went on], had not there been a false emphasis on the side of one deviation and a forgetfulness of other dangers.

He would not defend those whose views he did not share — Bogushevsky and Vareikis for example ; but some of the comparisons made and loudly applauded at the conference were unseemly.[1] Nobody took up the challenge. On December 3, 1925, Zinoviev wound up the debate in another wordy, but conciliatory, speech ;[2] and a resolution was unanimously adopted which recorded full and complete approval of " the political and organizational line of the central committee ", repeated the ritual phrases about the two deviations, and ended with a declaration of confidence in the " Leninist unity " of the party.[3] It was submitted to the party central committee in Moscow, which formally endorsed it.[4] Having cleared this hurdle, the conference passed on to uneventful discussions of the work of the provincial party committee and provincial control commission.

While the Leningrad conference was thus occupied, the corresponding conference of the Moscow provincial party organization met in Moscow on December 5, 1925. Stalin, implicitly promoted to a place high above all local organizations, did not attend. After Uglanov had formally opened the proceedings,[5]

[1] These speeches were reported in *Leningradskaya Pravda*, December 2, 3, 4, 1925, and more briefly in *Pravda*, December 6, 1925.

[2] This was published in *Leningradskaya Pravda*, December 9, 1925, and belatedly in *Pravda* and *Izvestiya*, December 17, 1925.

[3] The resolution, which appeared in *Leningradskaya Pravda*, December 4, 1925, does not seem to have been published in the Moscow press, but was printed in *Novaya Oppozitsiya* (1926), pp. 25-27.

[4] *XIV Vsesoyuznoi Kommunisticheskoi Partii* (*B*) (1926), pp. 349-350.

[5] Uglanov's speech contained only one allusion which sounded like a reflexion on the Leningrad proceedings, but this was printed in heavy type in *Pravda* : " *Perhaps we may be reproached with making little noise about Leninism, but we try to act in accordance with* Lenin ; do not shout, but act — that is our fundamental principle " (*Pravda*, December 6, 1925). Uglanov later claimed that " not one word, not one phrase " had been uttered at the conference against the Leningrad organization or its leaders (*XIV S"ezd Vsesoyuznoi Kommunisticheskoi Partii* (*B*) (1926), p. 193).

E*

Rykov presented the report on the work of the central committee. While he refrained from any direct attack on the Leningrad positions, he was less careful than Zinoviev had been to hold the balance even between the two incriminating deviations. He repeated the familiar arguments about state capitalism, quoting an article of Safarov as an instance of prevailing heresies, and thought that, while the *kulak* danger was of course real, the current " panic " about it could not be justified.[1] A number of minor speakers made harmless contributions to the debate. Then Bukharin took a hand. He opened with a sly passage deprecating attacks on " the Leningrad organization of our party ". Though there had been " mistakes on the part of some leaders of the Leningrad proletariat ", that proletariat was " really the best part of our working class " ; and Bukharin expressed confidence that " the Leningrad comrades will march with the central committee of our party, with the party, and not against the central committee and against the party ". The rest of his speech mixed arguments on the issues of principle with envenomed shafts against Zinoviev, discharged without mentioning his name. The problem of the peasantry and of private capital would not be solved by general all-embracing " prattle " (boltologiya) about the *kulak* ; and the point was driven home with another reference to " prattling phrases ". Bukharin developed at some length his theory of the two stages in Lenin's attitude to the cooperatives,[2] and returned once more to pour scorn on the absent Zinoviev :

> Hysterical young ladies in our party cry : Perhaps some sin has been committed ; ought we not perhaps to turn back ?

What the party wanted from the central committee was " not hysteria, but a policy ".[3] Bukharin ended with some curious reflexions on leadership :

> We can at present have only a *collective* authority. We have no man who could say : I am without sin, and can inter-

---

[1] The speech was reported in *Pravda* and *Izvestiya*, December 8, 1925, and printed in an abbreviated form in *Novaya Oppozitsiya* (1926), pp. 28-35.

[2] For this see Vol. 1, p. 259.

[3] Lenin in the peroration of *Current Tasks of the Soviet Power* in April 1918 had written : " We do not need hysterical outbursts " (Lenin, *Sochineniya*, xxii, 468) ; every Bolshevik understood these allusions. Stalin at the fourteenth congress also accused Zinoviev of " hysteria, not a policy " (Stalin, *Sochineniya*, vii, 378).

pret Lenin's teaching absolutely to a full 100 per cent. Everyone tries, but he who puts up a claim to 100 per cent attributes
too large a rôle to his own person.

The party congress was the expression of this collective authority,
and would call to order anyone who stood out against it.[1]

Bukharin's speech, which breathed an intense personal dislike
of Zinoviev, was provocative, and was meant to be provocative.
Kamenev replied on the same day in milder terms, but turned
the edge of his criticism against Bukharin, referring to the article
of May 1925 in which Bukharin had recorded his dissent from
Lenin's view of " state capitalism ".[2] The only difference existing
in the central committee on the subject was " between the
Leninist conception of state capitalism and the Bukharinist conception of it ". Coming nearer to the business in hand, Kamenev
read the resolution adopted three days earlier by the Leningrad
provincial conference : this he described as unexceptionable and
designed to promote the party unity which the Moscow organization also had at heart. Molotov answered Kamenev. With somewhat ponderous jocosity, he pointed out that, whereas Kamenev's
economic theses for the fourteenth party congress had failed to
deal with the problem of state capitalism at all, the party line had
been accurately stated in the theses on the Komsomol which
were the work of Bukharin.[3] He referred to Kamenev's " very
awkward manner " of taking all criticisms personally, and proceeded, cautiously and by implication, to compare the Leningrad
opposition with the opposition of 1923, which had also accused
the central committee of failing to see dangers and had proposed
to " save " the party from this blindness. He ended by quoting
once more from Bukharin's Komsomol theses the passage about
" pessimism and liquidationist lack of faith in the socialist paths
of our development ". Krupskaya, explaining that illness had

---

[1] The debate of December 6 down to and including Bukharin's speech was
reported in *Pravda*, December 10, 1925 ; Bukharin's speech also appeared in
Izvestiya on the same day. At a later stage in the proceedings, exactly when
and under what pressure is not clear, Bukharin made a formal declaration
once more disowning his erroneous slogan " Enrich yourselves " : he pointed
out that he had already done this twice — in his article in *Pravda* on Ustryalov
and in a speech to the central committee of the Komsomol. The declaration
appeared in *Leningradskaya Pravda*, December 11, and in *Pravda*, December
13, 1925.   [2] For this article see p. 72 above.   [3] See p. 119 above.

prevented her from following the whole discussion, deplored " the tone in which the debates are being conducted ". She had not been present at the Leningrad conference, but had heard that Zinoviev " sharply stopped one of the orators with the remark that the debates could not be carried on in such a tone ". Her one point of substance was to disagree with Bukharin's interpretation of Lenin's views on the cooperatives. The coming into action of these big guns intensified the atmosphere of mutual animosity by making it plain that the differences were not confined to relatively unimportant members of the party, but extended to the topmost ranks of the leadership. Rykov wound up the debate with a theoretical disquisition on the issues of principle, but contrived in his pedestrian way to lower the temperature. The resolution finally adopted was long enough to contain something which gave satisfaction to everyone ; and, while a careful reading showed the scales heavily tipped against the Leningraders on particular points, it made no direct attack on them. It was adopted unanimously, Kamenev voting for it with the rest.[1]

The Leningrad provincial conference was still in session when the resolution of the Moscow conference and some of the remarks made in the debate (which doubtless lost nothing in the telling) were reported to it. A wave of indignation swept over the conference, and a closed session was held at which Zinoviev gave vent to his feelings :

> I must say that until this morning I did not understand this whole set-up, this whole front ; but today, having read the resolution passed by the Moscow provincial party conference on the report of the central committee, I finally see this front. . . . I affirm that there is here a definite political verdict, and not only on my real or imaginary errors ; here are words directly referring to the Leningrad organization, to the Leningrad workers. . . . You should clearly recognize that the affair

[1] The resolution, which was adopted on December 7, was printed in *Pravda* and *Izvestiya*, December 8, 1925 ; the remainder of the debate was printed in the issues of December 13, Rykov's concluding speech in *Pravda*, December 13, and *Izvestiya*, December 15, 1925. The resolution is also in *Novaya Oppozitsiya* (1926), pp. 36-40. A short leading article in *Pravda*, December 8, 1925, *On the Kulak Danger*, summed up the position : " A careful arrangement of the planned leadership of our economy is one of our central tasks, among other things, from the standpoint of our struggle with the *kulak* " ; on the other hand, the struggle with the *kulak* could not be conducted by " hysterical exclamations ".

is now being conducted under the slogan " Beat the Lenin-graders ! " [1]

It was apparently at the same session that Yaroslavsky made a particularly offensive speech which was shouted down by an indignant audience, and which Evdokimov described as the turning-point of the conference. Yaroslavsky accused the Leningrad leaders of failing to nominate Komarov and Lobov (another prominent Leningrad party man) to the presidium of the conference because they supported the line of the central committee, and declared that the conference did not represent the real opinion of the workers in the factories.[2] After this the battle was joined, and normal restraints abandoned. Zinoviev asked Komarov to make a statement at the conference that he shared all the views of the conference and would defend them when required, and threatened, if he refused, to exclude him from the provincial party committee and from the Leningrad delegation to the forthcoming party congress — a threat which was duly carried out.[3] Yaroslavsky added further fuel to the flames by demanding to see the uncorrected stenographic record of the closed session, openly expressing the suspicion that it was intended to expunge the more incriminating passages.[4]

The Leningrad conference ended on December 10, 1925, on a note of defiance. By a unanimous vote with three abstentions (presumably Yaroslavsky, Komarov and Lobov), it decided to address a letter of protest to the Moscow provincial conference. " A whole series of speeches directed against our organization ", as well as the resolution of the conference, threatened the unity of the party by setting its two major organizations in opposition to

---

[1] Quoted in *XIV S"ezd Vsesoyuznoi Kommunisticheskoi Partii* (*B*) (1926), p. 172 (cf. *ibid.* p. 292) ; Zinoviev afterwards said that the Leningrad conference fell into two parts — before and after the Moscow resolution (*ibid.* p. 451). Sokolnikov also treated this resolution as the factor which forced the break (*ibid.* p. 322).

[2] For references to this speech, which was evidently a major incident, see *ibid.* pp. 200, 217, 351.

[3] *Ibid.* pp. 220-221 ; according to Safarov, Komarov and Lobov, both members of the bureau of the provincial party committee, indicated for the first time on the eve of the conference that they were not in agreement with Zinoviev " on certain organizational measures " (*ibid.* p. 382).

[4] *Ibid.* p. 587 ; at the fourteenth party congress, Yaroslavsky asserted that provocative passages from Zinoviev's speech had been omitted, but later withdrew the charge (*ibid.* pp. 587, 604).

one another, and called for a reply. The charges made in Moscow were refuted under the five heads of " liquidationist lack of faith ", state capitalism, the attitude to the peasantry, " Axelrodism " and pessimism. No names (other than the inevitable Bogushevsky and Slepkov) were mentioned. But the defence constituted a vigorous challenge to the standpoint of the Moscow organization.[1] Though the text of the letter was not immediately published, the gist was widely known. On the day after the conference ended, a leading article in *Leningradskaya Pravda* protested against the attacks from Moscow, expressed the hope that " the fourteenth congress of our party will take its decisions with sufficient unanimity ", but explained that none the less the Leningraders were " not Tolstoyans, but Bolshevik-Leninists ".[2]

While the Leningrad leaders were thus burning their boats, the Moscow conference continued its debates. The most important event of the last days of the conference was a report on the work of the central control commission by Kuibyshev. Hitherto the two deviations had been balanced, and treated as equal, in official party pronouncements. Now Kuibyshev openly maintained that the deviation which consisted of " panic fear of the *kulak* " and " exaggeration of differentiation in the countryside " was more dangerous than the opposite deviation of " glossing over the growing differentiation and denying the existence of the *kulak* ".[3] The sin of Bogushevsky was thus pronounced more venial than the sin of Safarov, the charge that lay against Bukharin less heinous than that to which Zinoviev had exposed himself. The letter of protest from Leningrad arrived in time to be read at the last session of the Moscow conference on December 13, 1925. The drafting of a reply was left to the Moscow provincial party committee. The text was quickly completed, and lacked nothing in vigour and outspokenness. It answered the Leningrad indictment under the same five headings, adding a sixth on the cooperatives. It did not, like the Leningrad letter, ostensibly

[1] *Pravda*, December 20, 1925, reprinted in *Novaya Oppozitsiya* (1926), pp. 40-44.
[2] *Leningradskaya Pravda*, December 11, 1925 ; the article was signed by the editor, Gladnev.
[3] Kuibyshev's report was published in *Pravda*, December 11, 1925 ; the crucial passage was, quoted in an article *Where is the Chief Danger ?* in *Leningradskaya Pravda*, December 18, 1925 (see p. 130 below).

restrict its attacks to minor figures.   It took to task both Kamenev
and Zinoviev, who had upheld in the Politburo the pessimistic
view that " we shall be unable to cope with our internal difficulties
owing to our technical and economic backwardness unless we are
saved by international revolution ".   It continued with a passage
which was to be the keynote of innumerable speeches and articles
in the next twelve months :

> We, together with the majority of the central committee,
> think that we can build, and go on building, socialism not-
> withstanding our technical backwardness and in spite of it.   We
> think that this building will proceed, of course, far more slowly
> than in conditions of a world-wide victory, but none the less
> we are going forward and shall go forward.   We also believe
> that the point of view of comrades Kamenev and Zinoviev
> expresses lack of faith in the internal strength of our working
> class and of the peasant masses which follow it.   We believe
> that this is a departure from the Leninist position.

The attack was pressed home on points of detail.   Zinoviev, in
his book on *Leninism*, had shared the error of Evdokimov, Sarkis
and Safarov on the issue of state capitalism, and had sometimes
failed (the comparison with Trotsky remained implicit) to " notice
the peasant ".   The conclusion was an appeal to the verdict of
the congress :

> At the present time, when comrade Lenin is no longer with
> us, the pretension of individual persons, however much noise
> they may make, to a monopoly of 100 per cent Leninism is in
> truth ridiculous.   In the place of persons stands the collectivity.
> The supreme interpreter of the Leninist line can only be the
> central committee and the party congress.[1]

The contingency which the October agreement in the central
committee had been designed to avert, and which for so long
seemed unthinkable — an open breach between the leaders on the
floor of the party congress — was now imminent.   Only five days
separated the ending of the Moscow conference from the opening
of the fourteenth party congress which was fixed for December 18,
1925.   The interval was occupied in preparations and manœuvres,
in which the Leningraders found themselves out-gunned and out-
classed.   The majority leaders were confident of victory and were

[1] *Pravda*, December 20, 1925, reprinted in *Novaya Oppozitsiya* (1926),
pp. 44-50.

prepared to fight, provided only that the responsibility for the breach of party unity should not fall on them. The Leningraders vacillated on the question whether to fight or not and on what issues to fight. On December 15 the party central committee met to give formal approval to the draft resolutions already endorsed by the Politburo.[1] The vote was unanimous. On the same evening eight of the majority leaders — Kalinin, Stalin, Bukharin, Rykov, Rudzutak, Tomsky, Molotov, Dzerzhinsky — after what Kuibyshev called " lengthy consultations, exhortations, conversations and night vigils ", made written proposals for a truce to the Leningrad delegation. The terms which they offered were, in brief, (1) to adopt the Moscow resolution of December 7, 1925, as the basis of the main congress resolution, " softening particular formulations " ; (2) not to publish the letter from the Leningrad conference to the Moscow conference or the Moscow reply ; (3) to agree that members of the Politburo should not speak against one another at the congress ; (4) to disown the articles of Sarkis on the composition of the party and of Safarov on state capitalism ; (5) to reinstate Komarov, Lobov and Moskvin (who had been evicted from posts in the Leningrad organization owing to their support of the majority of the central committee) ; (6) to introduce a Leningrad representative into the secretariat ; (7) to add a Leningrad representative to the editorial board of *Pravda* ; and (8) to replace the present editor of *Leningradskaya Pravda* by a " stronger " editor chosen by agreement with the central committee.[2]

The terms were stiff, and the Leningrad delegation, apparently after some hesitation, rejected them. According to Rykov, the decisive point was the insistence of the majority on a " single centre " : the Leningraders regarded it as a *sine qua non* that " Leningrad should remain an independent, competing centre

---

[1] *XIV S"ezd Vsesoyuznoi Kommunisticheskoi Partii (B)* (1926), p. 197.

[2] Stalin, *Sochineniya*, vii, 389 ; in this version the names of Bukharin, Rykov, Rudzutak and Tomsky have been removed from the list of signatories, which is given in full in *XIV S"ezd Vsesoyuznoi Kommunisticheskoi Partii (B)* (1926), p. 507. The tone of the offer was reflected in a leading article in the party journal *Bol'shevik*, No. 23-24, December 30, 1925, pp. 3-6, which was obviously written on the eve of the congress. It dwelt on current " moods of panic and pessimism " in the party, but attributed them to " individual sceptically disposed comrades (such, unfortunately, exist, Safarov, Sarkis etc.) " ; it did not suggest that these " moods " were shared by the Leningrad leaders.

with its own press organ etc."[1]   Zinoviev described the offer as
" a demand for our capitulation without any guarantees for the
future " ; Zinoviev and Kamenev are said to have asked for a
guarantee of freedom for the expression of their opinions in
speeches and articles — meaning, presumably, an independent
press organ — which was refused.[2]   The few hours that now
remained before the congress began were spent by the leaders
in reinforcing their positions and testing their strength.   On
December 17, the eve of the congress, a meeting of the central
control commission passed a resolution endorsing the line of the
party central committee as " wholly and fully correct ", and
instructing its president to make on its behalf at the congress " any
necessary declarations for the maintenance of Leninist unity ".
In a body of some 150 members only one member of the presidium
(no doubt, Krupskaya) and four other members recorded their
dissent, and four abstained.[3]   On the same day a hastily convened
meeting of the central committee of the Komsomol passed its
resolution, with 12 dissentients, supporting the party central committee and condemning the attitude of the Leningraders.[4]   The
Leningrad delegation drew the logical conclusion from the stand
it had taken by deciding to put up Zinoviev with a " co-report "
(sodoklad) to Stalin's report on the work of the central committee.
This procedure had never before been invoked on the main
report at a party congress.   But congress rules authorized it on
the written request of 40 delegates.   It was the formal declaration
of hostilities by the opposition on the party leadership.

   The last days before the congress witnessed an intensification
of the press campaign, in which the fiercest and most telling blows
were still being dealt from the side of Leningrad.   In *Leningradskaya Pravda* of December 13, 1925, Zalutsky admitted that
certain of his " formulations " about state capitalism had been
incorrect.   But he made no reference to his more serious misdemeanours ; and, as the admission occurred in the course of an
attack on the minor Moscow leader Lominadze entitled *On Official*

---

[1] *XIV S"ezd Vsesoyuznoi Kommunisticheskoi Partii (B)* (1926), p. 413.
[2] *Ibid.* p. 297, 423.
[3] *Ibid.* p. 532 ; for the text of the resolution see *ibid.* p. 590.   It was presumably on this occasion that a last vain attempt was made to persuade Krupskaya to withdraw her signature from "the platform of the four" (*ibid.* p. 528).
[4] See pp. 105-106 above.

" *Orthodoxy* " *and the Falsification of Other People's Views*, the retractation was lost in the cloud of fresh insults. Two days later Sarkis, in his article rebutting the charge of Menshevism,[1] contrasted the proletarian line of " our whole Leningrad organization " with what he called the " Moscow-Urals-Tula line " of the central committee.[2] In the same issue Safarov once more attempted to refute the imputation of pessimism, and attacked the " liquidationist optimism " of Moscow ; this article was triumphantly reprinted in *Pravda* on December 17, 1925, with a retort by the Moscow publicist Astrov. On the same day an article in *Leningradskaya Pravda* by the VAPP writer Lelevich (it was dated from Moscow by way of showing that the Leningrad opposition had its supporters even in the capital) contained personal attacks on Bukharin and on Uglanov, who was described as " one of the clearest exponents of the degeneration of the party ". Finally, on December 18, 1925, the morning of the day on which the congress met, *Leningradskaya Pravda* featured an article by Lelevich's colleague Vardin under the heading *Where is the Chief Danger ?* which surpassed anything hitherto printed in the virulence of its attack on Bukharin and his followers. It struck first at Bukharin's record without mentioning his name :

> The old " Left communism ", which was akin to the Left SRs, has in fact survived in the ranks of our party ; it has at its head the old leaders, and against them the old Leninist-Bolshevik struggle is imperative.

Vardin then proceeded to attack Bukharin, Kuibyshev, Uglanov and Kaganovich, as well as lesser Moscow figures, by name, and ended with a call " to eradicate the current phenomenon of a Right deviation armed with Left SR phrases ".[3] How far this campaign was deliberately encouraged by the leaders on either side, it is difficult to say. But it helped to account for the mood of embittered exasperation in which the congress finally met. Zalutsky, Safarov and Sarkis, though not Lelevich and Vardin, were members of the Leningrad delegation.

[1] See p. 118 above.
[2] This phrase was particularly resented at the congress (*XIV S"ezd Vsesoyuznoi Kommunisticheskoi Partii* (*Bol'shevikov*) (1926), p. 240) ; Sarkis had unconsciously echoed an old taunt of Trotsky against the Bolsheviks (see Vol. 1, p. 17).
[3] The article was reprinted in *Novaya Oppozitsiya* (1926), pp. 62-67.

CHAPTER 17

THE FOURTEENTH CONGRESS

THE fourteenth party congress formally opened on the evening of December 18, 1925. After Rykov's brief speech of welcome from the chair, two minor wrangles gave a foretaste of what was to come. The first concerned the election of the presidium, the honorific group of forty or fifty prominent party men who occupied the platform throughout the proceedings. The council of senior party leaders, who acted as the steering committee of the congress, had met in advance to draw up a list for submission to the congress. The usual practice was to elect to the presidium one delegate from each of the major local party organizations, with two each from Moscow and Leningrad. On this occasion the Leningrad delegation put forward its two candidates. The council accepted the first of them, Evdokimov, but for the second, by a majority vote, substituted Komarov who, when excluded from the Leningrad delegation for his support of the central committee line, had been conveniently provided with another mandate. An attempt of the Leningrad delegation to re-open the question on the floor of the congress was voted down by a show of hands, and the list was formally adopted with sixteen abstentions.[1] The second incident turned on the place of meeting of the congress. The thirteenth party congress, perhaps influenced by the recent renaming of the city in honour of Lenin, or perhaps by a desire to pay a compliment to Zinoviev, had decided to hold the next congress in Leningrad. It was not even at the time a sensible decision; for a party congress was now a highly organized affair requiring a vast apparatus of secretaries and documents which could not easily be transplanted from Moscow. But

---

[1] *XIV S"ezd Vsesoyuznoi Kommunisticheskoi Partii* (*B*) (1926), pp. 4-6; the decision to exclude Komarov from the delegation was taken by the Leningrad party provincial committee (*ibid.* p. 343).

the circumstances in which the fourteenth congress was to meet
made its removal to Leningrad not only practically inconvenient,
but politically inopportune. The central committee, apparently
unanimously, agreed to convene the congress in Moscow and to
propose that it should annul the rash decision of its predecessor.
Even the Leningrad delegation, conscious of the weak position in
which it found itself, did not openly challenge the decision, only
asking that the congress should visit Leningrad and hold one or
two formal sessions there. This was rejected, and the decision to
sit in Moscow was taken with only three abstentions.[1]

Stalin then made his report on the political work of the central
committee. He opened, as usual, in terms of studied moderation,
attacking nobody and contenting himself for the most part with
a lengthy and deliberately prosaic factual review of the period
since the thirteenth congress nineteen months earlier. Since the
opposition was now committed to a co-report, he could leave it to
bear the onus of breaking party unity. Only two remarks towards
the end of his speech were potentially provocative. He took up
the distinction which Kuibyshev had made at the Moscow conference between the two deviations on the peasant question. He
refused to admit that one was " worse ", or even more dangerous,
than the other. But, while the party was ready and eager to
restrain the *kulak*, it was less well equipped to deal with those
who underestimated the importance of the alliance with the
middle peasant ; and for this reason the party should " concentrate its fire on the struggle with the second deviation ".[2] The
other significant remark referred to the prospective victory of
socialist over capitalist elements in the Soviet Union — the cause
of socialism in one country :

> He who does not believe in this cause is a liquidator and
> does not believe in socialist construction. . . . He who is
> tired, who is afraid of difficulties, who loses his head — let him
> give way to those who have kept their courage and resolution.[3]

The exhortation was general and even platitudinous. But nobody
could pretend not to know who was meant.

Molotov followed his chief with the report of the central com-

---

[1] *XIV S"ezd Vsesoyuznoi Kommunisticheskoi Partii* (*B*) (1926), pp. 7-8.
[2] Stalin, *Sochineniya*, vii, 337.   [3] *Ibid.* vii, 349-350.

mittee on organizational questions. He, too, was in a matter-of-fact and benign mood. He spoke in general terms of the need for "immense work in the struggle with deviations from Leninism ", noted with satisfaction that the output of " Leninist literature " had increased thirteenfold since the last congress, and poked mild fun at Sarkis, who had unearthed no less than nine deviations from Leninism.[1] On the second day, Zinoviev delivered his co-report. Considering the nature of the occasion, his tone was surprisingly restrained, and he was heard politely and without serious interruption, though the only applause seems to have come from the Leningrad delegation. He offered theoretical disquisitions, first on NEP and on state capitalism, then on the party attitude to the peasant : the latter involved the usual denunciation of the slogan " Enrich yourselves ", and an attack on Bukharin by name. He refuted the thesis of the greater danger of the " Leftist " deviation, attributing it to Kuibyshev, who had first propounded it at the Moscow conference. His only reference to Stalin's endorsement of it was a phrase which echoed that used by Stalin : " It is necessary to open fire in the other direction ". He similarly rebutted the charge of " tiredness " without mentioning its author. The name of Stalin did not occur throughout his speech.[2] It was less discursive and less rhetorical than most of Zinoviev's utterances, but seems to have made a mediocre impression. More plaintive than challenging, it did not sound like a call to action from a potential leader.

Bukharin began his reply by expressing satisfaction that Zinoviev had spoken " not in the shrill tone which we hear daily from the pages of *Leningradskaya Pravda*, but in the quiet tone in which it is becoming to speak at a party congress ". But it was Bukharin who introduced the first note of personal acrimony into the debate. Zinoviev's co-report showed that he had set himself against the majority of the central committee, and constituted " a phenomenon of immense political importance " — a theme taken up by almost every subsequent speaker for the majority line. Bukharin taunted the opposition with having no concrete alternative proposals to make : this not unreasonable charge was also a favourite theme of later speakers. Having insisted that " *the*

[1] *XIV S"ezd Vsesoyuznoi Kommunisticheskoi Partii (B)* (1926), pp. 83-84.
[2] *Ibid.* pp. 97-129.

relation between the working class and the peasantry " was the key
to the whole discussion, Bukharin traversed once again the familiar
issues of socialism in one country, NEP, state capitalism and the
cooperatives. A repetition of his threefold withdrawal of the
slogan " Enrich yourselves " enabled him to turn on the opposition
in an effective peroration :

> You are taking advantage of the fact that we do not apply
> to our opponents the policy which you apply, since we have
> never demanded of Zinoviev that he should publicly renounce
> his error.[1]

Everyone who heard these words must have been reminded not
only of Bukharin's own recent recantation, but of Zinoviev's
eloquent appeal to Trotsky at the previous party congress to confess the error of his opinions.[2]

At the next session Krupskaya answered Bukharin in a moving
speech. His slogan had done immense harm before it was withdrawn ; and the danger was increased by the number of his disciples, since " the Red professorate grouped round comrade
Bukharin [3] is a succession which is being prepared, a school of
the theorists who will determine our line ". Krupskaya repeated
her dissent, already expressed at the Moscow conference, from
Bukharin's version of Lenin's divergent views on cooperatives.
She incautiously courted the charge of " lack of faith " by suggest-
ing that " the successes of our industry have a little bit turned our
heads " ; the over-optimistic estimate of harvest prospects in the
autumn indicated the loss of some of the " sobriety " recommended in the past by Lenin. But the most important part of her
speech had a more general character. She deplored the suppression of free discussion in advance of the congress :

> Individual opinions were not expressed in the pages of our
> central organ, and, thanks to this omission, the party was not
> prepared for the discussion which descended on it like a bolt
> from the blue two weeks before the congress.

The attack on Zinoviev for having expressed his personal opinion
was not justified. The decisions of a party congress were binding ;

---

[1] *XIV S"ezd Vsesoyuznoi Kommunisticheskoi Parti (B)* (1926), pp. 130-153.
[2] See *The Interregnum, 1923-1924*, p. 362.
[3] For the Institute of Red Professors see pp. 188-189 below.

but the congress was not omnipotent, as the English House of Commons claimed to be.

> For us Marxists [Krupskaya went on] truth is what corresponds to reality. Vladimir Ilich used to say : the teaching of Marx is invincible because it is true. And it must be the business of our congress to seek and find the right line. That is its task. One must not lull oneself into the belief that the majority is always right.

In a passage which gave much offence Krupskaya recalled the party congress of 1906 in Stockholm, the majority at which had been formed by the Mensheviks, and the main decisions of which had been later reversed. The conclusion that, at the fourteenth congress, a Bolshevik nucleus round Zinoviev, Kamenev and Krupskaya was confronted with a Menshevik majority in temporary control of the party was not explicitly drawn, or perhaps intended. But the analogy lay not far beneath the surface, and was seen by all. Krupskaya ended with one of her favourite quotations from Lenin :

> There have been occasions in history when the teaching of great revolutionaries has been distorted after their death. Men have made them into harmless *ikons*, and, while honouring their name, have blunted the revolutionary edge of their teaching.[1]

It was a formidable and somewhat unexpected line of attack ; and Petrovsky was put up to give the official reply :

> In our Bolshevik view truth consists in the fact that the whole body, the representatives of the whole party, come together here and say : This is truth. Truth consists, in accordance with another principle often enunciated by Vladimir Ilich, in submission to the majority when the issue is decided. Nadezhda Konstantinovna here, at a communist congress, made a remark about a bourgeois parliament, the sense of which was the following : Even though decisions may be taken by a huge majority, yet, if someone disagrees, then perhaps this will not be the truth. This is not in the Bolshevik tradition.[2]

[1] *XIV S"ezd Vsesoyuznoi Kommunisticheskoi Partii (B)* (1926), pp. 158-166 ; Krupskaya had already quoted the simile at the Komsomol congress eighteen months earlier (see p. 3 above).

[2] *Ibid.* p. 167. Krupskaya's digression on the nature of truth had many echoes during the congress and after. "Comrade Krupskaya", observed Tomsky, "said that the concept of what is true and what untrue is a subjective

A delegate of Uzbekistan (few delegates from the remoter regions were heard in the debate) supported the official line, and added a personal note. When the land reform in Central Asia was under discussion, some members of the Politburo — he would name no names — " did not interest themselves at all in this question ". The most active support and sympathy came from Stalin and Kalinin.[1]

By this time the congress was in its third day, and the atmosphere had visibly deteriorated. Lashevich was the first opposition speaker to be forced on to the defensive by constant jeers and interruptions. To a noisily unsympathetic audience he protested against the " cutting off " of Zinoviev and Kamenev from the leadership of the party ; and his plea that " the minority should not have its mouth shut " was greeted with ironical calls of " freedom of groupings ".[2] After Mikoyan had retorted that nobody thought of " cutting off " Kamenev or Zinoviev, but only of requiring them to " submit to the iron will of the majority of the central committee ", Uglanov launched a personal attack on Kamenev, his predecessor in the Moscow organization. A noisy session closed with a speech from Yaroslavsky, who did everything to rub salt into the wounds of the opposition, and

concept. We have one measure. For the working class, led by its party, there can be only one measure — *the will of the majority of the Leninist party* " (*ibid.* p. 288). Kalinin got into deeper water : " Who will be the judge, the arbiter ? Who will decide where truth lies ? It seems to me that the judge can only be time." And, when interrupters exclaimed "The congress !", he retired to more practical ground : " The idea that truth is truth is permissible in a philosophical club, but in the party the decisions of a congress are binding even on those who doubt the correctness of the decision " (*ibid.* p. 321). The more sophisticated Bukharin did not speak on the issue at the congress, but dealt with it in his report on the congress to the Moscow party organization a few days later. He admitted the existence of "objective reality", and continued : " Of course, it goes without saying that the party as a whole may make a mistake, and the whole congress and individual leaders of the party may make a mistake. Even Lenin made mistakes, as Marx too more than once made mistakes. But why all this talk about it ? Did we not know this already ? Of course, we did. What then is the meaning of this talk ? What does it mean when, not in a philosophical club but in a political congress, the argument is used that truth consists not in what the majority votes, but in conformity with reality ? It is not difficult to imagine what is being got at. If we are to reject the decision of the majority and say that truth consists in conformity with reality — which is in itself true — the question at once arises : Who decides what *is* or *is not in conformity* with reality ? " (*Pravda*, January 10, 1926).

[1] *XIV S"ezd Vsesoyuznoi Kommunisticheskoi Partii* (*B*) (1926), p. 175.
[2] *Ibid.* pp. 185-186.

raised a new issue by quoting, to the accompaniment of indignant shouts from the Leningraders, alleged resolutions from Leningrad party groups dissociating themselves from the attitude of the Leningrad delegation.[1]

The morning session of December 21, 1925, was devoted almost exclusively to a long speech by Kamenev, which was by common consent the ablest and most effective contribution from the opposition side.[2] He shamed early interrupters into momentary silence with the challenge : " If you have instructions to interrupt me, say so openly " — a charge, probably well founded, that the demonstrations against opposition speakers were organized. He covered the same issues of principle as other leading speakers, but carried his analysis further. He quoted Stalin's claim that the pro-*kulak* deviation was less dangerous than its opposite, and proceeded to refute it :

> The whole social environment, the whole relation of classes in our country, the whole international situation, support and nourish the roots of that tendency which is disposed to paint NEP in rosy colours, not to overthrow it.

He then proceeded to a telling attack on Stalin's personal attitude :

> I have reproached comrade Stalin at a number of conferences, and I repeat it at the congress : " You do not really agree with this line, but you *protect* it, and this is where you are at fault as a leader of the party. You are a strong man, but you do not allow the party strongly to reject this line, which a majority of the party thinks incorrect." I said to comrade Stalin : " If the slogan ' Enrich yourselves ' has travelled round the party for half a year, who is to blame ? Comrade Stalin is to blame." I asked him : " Are you in agreement

[1] *Ibid.* pp. 197-206. Yaroslavsky showed that he spoke with Stalin's authority by reading extracts from the unpublished letter from the party secretariat to the editors of *Komsomolskaya Pravda* on the *kulak* deviation (see Vol. 1, p. 284); an extract was also read by Stalin later in the debate (*Sochineniya*, vii, 383-384).

[2] *XIV S"ezd Vsesoyuznoi Kommunisticheskoi Partii (B)*, pp. 244-275. Kirov paid tribute to Kamenev as having " made the greatest impression of all the speeches here from the opposition " (*ibid.* p. 365); and Molotov described his speech as the "most systematic " exposition of the opposition case (*ibid.* p. 473). According to *Sotsialisticheskii Vestnik* (Berlin), No. 1 (119), January 16, 1926, p. 16, it lasted five hours (if this is correct, it must have been substantially abbreviated in the official report) and was "the most successful speech at the congress in the judgment of the participants ".

with this slogan ? " No, not in agreement. " Then why do you prevent the party from clearly and decisively rejecting this slogan ? " Now I see, comrades, that comrade Stalin has become a total prisoner of this incorrect line, the author and genuine representative of which is comrade Bukharin.

In a moment of exasperation he accused the majority of the central committee of a policy of " deceit " — a charge which he later withdrew with an apology, though it remained in the official record.[1] But the part of Kamenev's speech which created a sensation was the concluding passage, in which Stalin's leadership was directly challenged :

> *We are against creating the theory of a " leader " ; we are against making a leader.* We are against having the secretariat combine in practice both politics and organization and place itself above the political organ. . . . We cannot regard it as normal, and we think it harmful to the party, to prolong a situation in which the secretariat combines politics and organization, and in fact decides policy in advance.

At this point there were some interruptions. Kamenev went on undaunted :

> I must say what I have to say to the end. Because I have more than once said it to comrade Stalin personally, because I have more than once said it to a group of party delegates, I repeat it to the congress : *I have reached the conviction that comrade Stalin cannot perform the function of uniting the Bolshevik general staff.*

Such words, brusquely tearing asunder the fiction of collective leadership in which Stalin's personal power was still coyly veiled, had not yet been publicly uttered in the Soviet Union. They provoked a storm of protest from the majority, demonstrations of approval from the Leningrad delegates, and counter-demonstrations of applause for Stalin. When the noise subsided, apparently after several minutes, Kamenev concluded his speech :

> I began this part of my speech with the following words : We are against the theory of individual control, we are against the creation of a leader. With these words I end my speech.

Kamenev's bombshell changed the face of the congress. He had blurted out what some, perhaps many, had thought, but nobody hitherto had dared to say. But he had also exposed the

[1] *XIV S"ezd Vsesoyuznoi Kommunisticheskoi Partii* (B) (1926), p. 875.

opposition to a fresh charge, made by nearly every subsequent official speaker in the debate : Kamenev had unmasked the real motive of the opposition platform — personal jealousy and animosity against Stalin — and revealed the hollowness of the alleged arguments of principle on which it was supported. Even now it is doubtful whether the apprehensions voiced by Kamenev of Stalin's personal power were widely shared by the rank and file of the party. The immediate retort of Tomsky, the next orator on the list, was a rough-and-ready denial :

> It is ridiculous to speak as some comrades have spoken here, attempting to represent someone as having concentrated power in his hands, while the rest of the majority of the central committee back him up.
>
> How could that happen ? No, comrade Kamenev, if you put the question that a system of individual leaders must not exist, we say : We have all the time struggled against it ; a system of individual leaders cannot exist, and will not, no, will not.

And Tomsky ended with what was rapidly becoming a staple argument of the official line, begging Kamenev and Zinoviev to " apply to yourselves the lesson which you taught comrade Trotsky " and " bow your heads before the will of the party ".[1]

Sokolnikov next intervened with a long and well-reasoned speech which threw into relief both his points of contact with the other opposition leaders and his divergences from them. He, too, issued a warning against " overestimating the ripeness of the socialist elements in our economy ", but drew a conclusion which was not shared by the Leningrad opposition, and smacked rather of the " Right " deviation, that peasant production should be developed in order to encourage agricultural exports. The anomaly of his position was illustrated by the fact that, while the rest of the opposition regarded Bukharin as standing far to the Right, Sokolnikov accused him of reviving the " Left-wing infantilism " of which he had once been accused by Lenin.[2] On the question of Stalin's personal position, however, he strongly supported Kamenev :

> In so far as the general secretary is on the one hand a member of the Politburo, and on the other the director of the

[1] Ibid. pp. 289-292.   [2] Ibid. p. 327.

secretariat, a situation is created, quite independently of comrade Stalin's personality, in which any difference of opinion arising in the Politburo on any political question is reflected in organizational operations, since in reality one of the members of the Politburo, who is general secretary, i.e. director of all organizational work, is in such a position that any difference of opinion on any question in the Politburo can be immediately reflected in one way or another in organizational measures.[1]

The debate had now reached its fifth day, and everything that could be said seemed to have been said. The opposition leaders created a diversion by circulating to the delegates for their information, though not for publication, a *Collection of Materials on Disputed Questions*. Among other documents, it contained — to Stalin's annoyance — the text of his interview in *Bednota*, which appeared to canvass a return to private tenure of land, and the authenticity of which he had denied ; Krupskaya's article which the central committee had refused to publish ; and Bukharin's also unpublished reply.[2] Rudzutak accused Kamenev of having sounded him during the congress itself about joint action to overthrow Stalin. An obscure delegate from Tula read the text of Leonov's letter to the central committee about his conversation with Zalutsky.[3] Voroshilov entered the lists with the first positive, but still cautious, eulogy of Stalin. Kamenev was president of the Politburo, yet he complained of the undue authority exercised by Stalin :

> Comrades, all this happens for a very simple reason. Comrade Stalin is evidently destined by nature or by fate to formulate propositions rather more successfully than any other member of the Politburo. Comrade Stalin is, I affirm, the leading member of the Politburo, without, however, ever claiming priority ; he takes the most active part in the settlement of questions ; his proposals are carried more often than anyone's. And these proposals are carried unanimously.[4]

---

[1] *XIV S"ezd Vsesoyuznoi Kommunisticheskoi Partii (B)* (1926), p. 335.

[2] The collection was several times referred to in the course of the debate (*ibid.* pp. 368-369,, 372, 388 ; Stalin, *Sochineniya*, vii, 362). For the *Bednota* interview see Vol. 1, pp. 183, 247-248 ; for the Krupskaya article and Bukharin's reply see Vol. 1, p. 285.

[3] *XIV S"ezd Vsesoyuznoi Kommunisticheskoi Partii (B)* (1926), pp. 344, 358-360 ; for Leonov's letter see p. 112 above.   [4] *Ibid.* p. 397.

Rykov wound up the debate from the floor by taunting the opposition with its lack of unity. " Nadezhda Konstantinovna supports comrades Kamenev and Zinoviev from the point of view of sympathy with the ' poor and oppressed ', comrade Sokolnikov supports them ' from the Right ' ", i.e. by advocating further concessions to capitalist elements. "Nadezhda Konstantinovna says that the slogan ' Enrich yourselves ' led to a plan to liquidate the monopoly of foreign trade, the author of which was comrade Sokolnikov." Everything came back to the personal issue : " The party has never fallen on its knees, and never will fall on its knees, before anyone, before Stalin, before Kamenev or before anyone else ". Rykov ended effectively by quoting Zinoviev's tirades against Trotsky's " fractionalism " at and after the thirteenth congress. The moral did not need to be drawn.[1]

The way was now clear for the concluding speeches of the three *rapporteurs*, Zinoviev, Molotov and Stalin, delivered in that order. The first half of Zinoviev's immensely long speech [2] was devoted to the well-known theoretical disputes : the only new point made by Zinoviev here was to draw attention to the passage in the first edition of Stalin's *Foundations of Leninism* which had appeared to reject the possibility of " socialism in one country ".[3] Then Zinoviev turned to questions of party organization. " For a whole year ", he exclaimed, " the Leningrad organization has lived in an atmosphere of rumours, in a state of semi-siege." From this point onwards he was subjected to continuous and noisy interruption. Every complaint of the unfairness of the treatment meted out to the Leningrad organization and of the charges brought against its leader was met by shouts of " What about Trotsky ? " At last he attempted to refute the damning parallel. In 1923, he explained, conditions were not ripe for full democracy in the party. But " the year 1926 is not 1921 and not

---

[1] *Ibid.* pp. 406-420.

[2] *Ibid.* pp. 422-469. According to *Sotsialisticheskii Vestnik* (Berlin), No. 1 (119), January 16, 1926, p. 16, it lasted four and a half hours, being exceeded only by Kamenev's five-hour speech : it occupies, however, far more space than Kamenev's in the official record.

[3] For this passage see *The Interregnum, 1923–1924*, pp. 358-359. Stalin had implicitly modified his view in his article of December 1924 (see pp. 39-42 above) ; and the passage in *Foundations of Leninism* was revised in editions appearing in 1925. But it was not till after the fourteenth party congress that Stalin formally admitted and explained his change of attitude (see p. 164 below).

1923 ; today we have different workers, greater activity in the masses, other slogans. . . . In 1926 we must proceed otherwise than in 1923." But even this ingenuous juggling with dates (only a year in fact separated the two episodes) did not make a feeble argument sound effective. Then Zinoviev made a declaration which for a moment reduced his audience to an astonished silence, and, when challenged, repeated it in identical terms :

> While permitting no fractions, and in the question of fractions maintaining our previous positions, we should at the same time instruct the central committee to draw into party work all the forces of all former groups in our party, and offer them the possibility to work under the leadership of the central committee.

The repetition was greeted with a cry of " What's your little game ? " which Zinoviev ignored. He ended by proposing to reorganize the organs of the central committee " from the angle of a Politburo with full powers and a secretariat of functionaries subordinate to it ". The secretariat, he remarked, " has now incomparably greater powers than it had under Vladimir Ilich " — his only specific allusion to Stalin's personal position.

Molotov and Stalin had an easy task in their replies, and could afford to maintain the posture of reasonableness and moderation which had served them so well. Molotov dwelt on the vagueness and lack of unity of the opposition ; poked fun at " Grigory the Bountiful " for offering to extend his grace to all groups and tendencies in the party ; and observed in conclusion that the " Politburo with full powers " for which Kamenev and Zinoviev asked meant a Politburo where " comrades Zinoviev and Kamenev will be in a majority ".[1] Stalin spoke at less than half the length of Zinoviev. He replied crisply to four specific points. It was significant that three of them had been made by Sokolnikov, the member of the opposition from whose policies — apart from any personal considerations — Stalin most sincerely and whole-heartedly dissented. He discussed once more the so-called issues of principle, briefly but with far more asperity than in his earlier speech. Krupskaya had talked " sheer nonsense " by identifying NEP with capitalism ; Zinoviev had been guilty of " incessant wobbling " over the peasant question. Stalin borrowed a phrase

[1] *XIV S"ezd Vsesoyuznoi Kommunisticheskoi Partii (B)* (1926), pp. 470-486.

which Bukharin had used of Zinoviev at the Moscow conference :
" this is hysteria, not policy ". A few minutes later, he indulged
in one of his rare purple patches by taking up and embroidering a
remark which Kalinin had aimed at the opposition earlier in the
congress : " You want the blood of Bukharin ".

> What in fact [Stalin now asked] do they want of Bukharin ?
> They demand the blood of comrade Bukharin. That is what
> comrade Zinoviev demands when in his concluding speech he
> sharpens the issue of Bukharin. You demand the blood of
> Bukharin ? We shall not give you that blood, be sure of
> that.[1]

He devoted some time to the history of the dispute before finally
reaching his peroration. He was against any " cutting off " of
leaders. But the party would insist on unity " *with* comrades
Kamenev and Zinoviev if they want it, *without them* if they do not
want it ".

The six-day oratorical tourney was over, and it remained to
record a decision. Uglanov presented a draft resolution. It
dotted the i's and crossed the t's of the official line, and thus
implicitly condemned the standpoint of the Leningraders, but
without openly attacking them and without repeating the charges
of defeatism, liquidationism and Axelrodism. In short, it represented the compromise offered by the majority to the opposition
on the eve of the congress — a resolution based on the resolution
of the Moscow conference, but " softening particular formulations ".[2] Its moderation was embarrassing to the opposition,
which found it more difficult than ever to take a clear-cut stand.
In the end Kamenev, in the name of the opposition, declared its
acceptance in principle of the resolution, but immediately nullified
this by proposing a series of amendments which included a specific

---

[1] For this passage see Vol. 1, p. 171. In a previous passage of the speech
Stalin had used the phrase : " We stand, and shall stand, for Bukharin " ; in
the later version (Stalin, *Sochineniya*, vii, 365) the words " and shall stand "
are omitted.

[2] That the resolution represented, from the Leningrad standpoint, an
improvement on the Moscow resolution was shown by the claim of *Leningradskaya Pravda* on the following day (see p. 144 below) and by the subsequent
remark of a Leningrad delegate that the " famous " Moscow resolution had
been " half, though unfortunately only half, buried, but still buried " by the
congress resolution (*XIV S"ezd Vsesoyuznoi Kommunisticheskoi Partii (B)*
(1926), p. 582).

withdrawal of the charges against the opposition and an endorsement of some at least of its theses. Stalin, on behalf of " the
delegations which proposed the draft resolution read by comrade
Uglanov ", made it clear in a few words that the majority had
offered its maximum concession and that the resolution must be
taken or left as it stood. After a proposal to refer the draft and
the amendments to a commission had been rejected, the resolution
was carried on a roll-call by 559 votes to 65 — the full voting
strength of the opposition.[1] It was late on the evening of December
23, 1925. The congress decided to rest from its labours on the
following day.

The decisive vote of December 23, 1925, shifted the centre of
interest from Moscow to Leningrad, where the attitude of local
party groups was now of cardinal importance. Throughout the
debate, *Leningradskaya Pravda* had continued to denounce the
majority line in bitter terms, Safarov again attacking Bukharin in a
leading article of December 20 ; several of its articles were quoted
with indignation by majority speakers at the congress.[2] On
December 22, while the debate was still in progress, the provincial
party committee in Leningrad issued an instruction to all party
organizations in the province to refrain from discussion of the
issues at stake before the end of the congress. On the same day
the committee of the Vyborg district of Leningrad, while formally
bowing to the veto, decided by a majority vote to protest against
it to the party congress and to send a message of greeting to the
congress ; and it was censured for this breach of discipline by the
provincial committee.[3] *Leningradskaya Pravda* duly printed in its
issue of December 24, 1925, the resolution adopted on the previous
evening by the congress, noting that it had " not been carried
unanimously ", but failing to report the figures of the voting. It
implied that the Leningraders had voted against it only because
their proposals to amend it had been rejected without discussion,
and claimed that it " differs *very substantially* from the resolution
of the Moscow provincial conference ". It declared that the
resolution must be carried out, but warned its readers against " a

[1] *XIV S"ezd Vsesoyuznoi Kommunisticheskoi Partii (B)* (1926), pp. 521-524.
[2] *Ibid.* pp. 158, 192.   [3] *Ibid.* pp. 591-592.

capriciously extended interpretation ", and ended with an appeal for " Leninist unity ". The situation was delicate when, after the adoption of the resolution, Zinoviev and most of the other leading members of the Leningrad delegation returned to Leningrad, leaving only a skeleton force to hold the fort in Moscow. From the other camp, Uglanov, Mikoyan and Orjonikidze also made the journey to Leningrad. The battle for the allegiance of the Leningrad party and of the Leningrad proletariat was soon in full swing.[1] *Leningradskaya Pravda* continued to protest its devotion to party unity, but found this theme difficult to reconcile with the vote of the Leningrad delegation against the congress resolution.

Meanwhile the congress had resumed its sessions in Moscow on December 25 before a depleted audience and in the absence of many of the principals. The debate on the report of the central control commission, introduced by Kuibyshev, was noteworthy for some frank speaking on the vexed question of " informing ", which had been raised in an acute form by Leonov's letter about Zalutsky.[2] Krupskaya, who began by saying that she had " watched the destinies of our party with extreme emotion ", called in question the contribution of the control commission to " the defence of the unity of the party ", and attacked the unlimited power of the Orgburo and the secretariat to transfer or remove party members. The central control commission was required to have " independence and objectivity of thought " (" independence of what ? " asked someone) : this was the reason for the rule that a member of the central committee could not also be a member of the commission. Krupskaya rashly objected to the action of Kuibyshev, as president of the commission, in helping to draft the declaration of the Moscow conference against the Leningrad opposition, and was reminded that she had signed " the platform of the four ". She spoke amid frequent interruptions, and ended with a belated and pathetically ineffectual plea for unity.[3]

---

[1] *Ibid.* pp. 618, 920 ; Orjonikidze was reported as addressing the Leningrad garrison (*ibid.* p. 922). For a particularly hostile speech for the opposition by the trade union delegate Glebov-Avilov see p. 213 below.

[2] For this discussion see pp. 220-221 below.

[3] *XIV S"ezd Vsesoyuznoi Kommunisticheskoi Partii (B)* (1926), pp. 571-575 ; for the passage about the powers of the Orgburo and the secretariat see p. 213 below.

Yaroslavsky once again quoted Zinoviev's summons to Trotsky at the thirteenth congress to confess his error, and struck an ominous note for the future : " I am convinced that at the fifteenth congress we shall have no such shameful spectacle as we have had here ".[1] Kuibyshev in his concluding speech produced the most outspoken eulogy of Stalin yet heard by the congress :

> In the name of the whole central control commission I declare that comrade Stalin, as general secretary of our party, is precisely the person who has been able, together with the majority of the central committee and with its support, to gather round him all the best forces in the party and to put them to work. It is absolutely incontestable that the present leadership of the central committee between the thirteenth and fourteenth congresses has been the best of any of the hitherto existing central committees in the way of an improvement in leadership and in contact with local organizations. . . . On the basis of real experience, of a real knowledge of our leadership, I declare in the name of the central control commission that this leadership and this general secretary are what is needed for the party in order to go on from victory to victory.

Yet Stalin could still be portrayed as the man of moderation and restraint. Kuibyshev himself had wished to go to Leningrad with other members of the commission at the time of the provincial party conference in order to intervene in the proceedings. It was Stalin who had deterred them from this course " because there was still hope that things would not go so far ".[2] The report of the commission was approved by the congress with forty abstentions : the reduced Leningrad delegation had not the spirit to vote against it.[3]

The congress dragged painfully and rather pointlessly through its second week — an inevitable anticlimax after the tumultuous excitements of the first. On December 28 Zinoviev returned to Moscow to make the report on the work of Comintern. This was uncontroversial and received some polite applause, though Manuilsky and Lominadze could not refrain from drawing attention to the unfortunate effect on Comintern of the attitude adopted by its president in the party dispute. On this occasion 101 stalwart

---

[1] *XIV S"ezd Vsesoyuznoi Kommunisticheskoi Partii (B)* (1926), p. 593.
[2] *Ibid.* pp. 628-629.   [3] *Ibid.* p. 630.

supporters of the majority demonstrated their dislike of the *rapporteur* by registering abstention from the vote.[1] On the same day the congress took three decisions of some consequence. The first was the adoption, on a motion of Kalinin, of an " Appeal to the Leningrad Organization of the RKP(B) ", which denounced the Leningrad leaders for threatening to break the unity of the party and begged the Leningrad organization " to correct the errors committed by the Leningrad delegation ". It was an appeal to party members in Leningrad against their leaders, and was carried by an overwhelming majority against 36 Leningrad votes.[2] The second was a more practical decision to take over control of the Leningrad party press. It drew its immediate inspiration from two articles in *Leningradskaya Pravda* of December 27, 1925. The first, unsigned and entitled *The Truth About Our Position*, reiterated the points of principle asserted by the Leningrad delegation at the congress and attempted to represent them as compatible with the congress resolution ; the second, signed by Safarov, declared that the " new school " sought to " argue with people by trying to cover their eyes and shut their mouth ", called Zinoviev and Kamenev " Lenin's closest disciples ", and announced that the Leningrad organization would remain " unalterably faithful " to the banner of Leninism.[3] This could plainly not be tolerated. The party central committee was instructed " to take immediate measures to alter and improve the editorial board of *Leningradskaya Pravda* ". The third decision, prompted partly by desire to snub Kamenev, and partly by unwillingness to prolong the congress any further, was to abandon altogether Kamenev's report on economic policy and the proposed debate on it.[4]

The next day was occupied by Tomsky's report on the trade unions,[5] and by Bukharin's on the Komsomol. The discussions on both questions were occasionally acrimonious, but on the whole lifeless. Nobody had anything new to say. Bukharin, in his reply to the debate on the Komsomol, turned aside to make fun of Zinoviev's dramatic appeal to bring back members of " former groups " into the party, and to point the moral of the continuity

---

[1] *Ibid.* p. 721.   [2] *Ibid.* pp. 710-711.
[3] Safarov's article was reprinted in *Novaya Oppozitsiya* (1926), pp. 7-12.
[4] *XIV S"ezd Vsesoyuznoi Kommunisticheskoi Partii (B)* (1926), p. 716 ; the voting strength of the Leningrad delegation against both the last decisions was 38.   [5] See Vol. 1, pp. 399-402.

of the present opposition with former oppositions. Zinoviev was
paraphrased as saying : " I'm drowning, drowning ! Save me,
rescue me, comrade Shlyapnikov, comrade Sapronov, comrade
Drobnis ! " [1] Finally, and still more briefly, the congress debated
a report by Andreev on the revision of the party statute. The
most difficult question here was the proposal to change the name
of the party from Russian Communist Party (Bolsheviks), which
it had borne since 1919, to All-Union Communist Party (Bolsheviks). The demand for the change, which came from all the
non-Russian sections of the party headed by the Ukrainians, was
logically irresistible. But it encountered keen objections at the
session of the party central committee which preceded the congress from conservatives who wanted to keep the traditional title.
After a short debate, the objections were overruled, and the new
title adopted.[2] Changes in the rules for admission to the party
were also approved.[3] The final text of the statute was not yet
ready, and a resolution was passed authorizing the party central
committee to complete it : it was finally approved by the committee in the following June.[4]

No delay occurred in putting into effect the decision to call
Leningradskaya Pravda to order. On the evening of the day on
which the decision was taken — December 28, 1925 — the central
committee met to consider a proposal endorsed by a majority
of the Politburo to appoint Skvortsov-Stepanov, the editor of
Izvestiya,[5] to replace Gladnev as editor of *Leningradskaya Pravda*.
Zinoviev invited the committee to ask the congress to reconsider
its decision, which would mean the complete disruption of the

[1] *XIV S"ezd Vsesoyuznoi Kommunisticheskoi Partii (B)* (1926), p. 957 ;
Bukharin was so pleased with this sally that he repeated it in a speech in Leningrad a month later (see p. 157 below). Shlyapnikov was a leader of the workers'
opposition ; Sapronov and Drobnis were democratic centralists.
[2] *Ibid.* pp. 876-894 ; for some details of the discussion see pp. 251-252
below.   [3] See pp. 183-184 below.
[4] *VKP(B) v Rezolyutsiyakh* (1941), ii, 60 ; the final text was, however,
included among the resolutions of the congress (*ibid.* ii, 80-90).
[5] Skvortsov-Stepanov (the first was his real name, the second a pen-name)
was the author of the current Russian translation of Marx's *Capital*. He had
succeeded Steklov as editor of *Izvestiya* in June 1925 ; after editing *Leningradskaya Pravda* for a short period, he returned to his post in Moscow, which he
continued to occupy till his death in 1928 (*Entsiklopedicheskii Slovar' Russkogo
Bibliograficheskogo Instituta Granat*, xli, iii (n.d. 1928), Prilozhenie, cols. 44, 127 ;
I. Skvortsov-Stepanov, *Izbrannye Proizvedeniya*, i (1930), pp. xxx-xxxii).

Leningrad provincial party committee. Dzerzhinsky, the spokes-man of the majority, argued that " a revolt . . . against the decisions of the party congress " could not be condoned in the name of " party democracy ".[1] Trotsky, Pyatakov and Rakovsky — the leaders of the Trotskyite group which had remained silent at the congress itself — all spoke against the proposal on the ground that local editors should not be nominated by the central organs of the party, and suggested that discussions should take place with the Leningrad provincial committee on how to carry out the congress decision. The central committee overruled all these objections, and carried the appointment of Skvortsov-Stepanov by a majority vote.[2] The new editor at once went to Leningrad to take charge. According to his own account, delegates from all sorts of local party organizations visited him with threats of violence if the paper came out with a " Moscow deviation " ; members of the staff walked out and denounced those who remained as spies and *provocateurs* ; and members of the Kom-somol were particularly hostile. Notwithstanding these obstruc-tions the first " really Leninist " *Leningradskaya Pravda* appeared on December 30, 1925.[3]

The change in the complexion of *Leningradskaya Pravda* appeared to coincide with an equally abrupt reversal of opinion among the rank and file. The last issue to appear under the old editorship, on December 29, 1925, carried reports purporting to show that a vast majority of district party organizations in Lenin-grad endorsed the attitude of the delegation at the congress. The issue of December 30, the first under the new editorship, reported a meeting in the Vyborg district of Leningrad addressed by Krupskaya, Komarov, Mikoyan and Kirov, at which 850 votes were cast for a resolution condemning the attitude of the delegation and only 50 against ; and similar resolutions were said to have been carried by majorities in the Petrograd district and in some other districts.[4] The extent to which the opposition citadel had

---

[1] F. Dzerzhinsky, *Izbrannye Proizvedeniya*, ii (1957), 233-234.

[2] E. Yaroslavsky, *Kratkie Ocherki po Istorii VKP(B)* (1928), pp. 361-362.

[3] *XIV S"ezd Vsesoyuznoi Kommunisticheskoi Partii (B)* (1926), pp. 926, 935.

[4] Four resolutions of local Leningrad organizations at this time supporting the attitude of the delegation, and a far larger number condemning it, are in *Leningradskaya Oppozitsiya i Chetyrnadtsatyi S"ezd* (1926), pp. 32-36, 41-54, 57-58 ; some of the latter retracted previous resolutions of support.

been permeated by the superior resources and tactics of the
central committee was revealed on the last day of the party congress in Moscow. Almost the whole session — the date was
December 31, 1925 — was occupied by the appearance on the
platform of successive delegations of various party organizations
and groups brought from Leningrad for the purpose. One or two
of these protested their solidarity with the opposition. But the
overwhelming majority proclaimed their allegiance to the decisions
of the congress, and denounced in stereotyped invective the
factious and anti-Leninist attitude of the Leningrad leaders. The
proceedings degenerated into a series of noisy demonstrations
and counter-demonstrations. But they served their purpose
by enabling the victors to proclaim, as the congress closed,
that the opposition had been not only decisively defeated, but
disowned by the constituents in whose name it professed to
speak.

Stalin and the other leaders of the majority had repeatedly
declared that they did not seek the " cutting off " of the leaders
of the opposition. The elections to party offices showed that, for
the present and for whatever motive, they meant what they said.
The elections to the party central committee and to the central
control commission were traditionally the last act of the congress.
All the opposition leaders were re-elected to the central committee. But Zinoviev's supporters suffered heavily. Of members
of the central committee who spoke for the opposition at the
congress, Zalutsky and Kharitonov disappeared altogether from
the list, together with Kuklin, who had said at a party meeting in
Leningrad that the central committee " winked at the *kulak*
deviation " ; Nikolaeva and Lashevich were reduced from
member to candidate status. Of former candidate members,
Safarov and Glebov-Avilov were dropped.[1] Krupskaya was re-

---

[1] The lists of members and candidates elected by the thirteenth and
fourteenth congresses are in the respective records of the congresses and in
VKP(B) v Rezolyutsiyakh (5th ed. 1936), i, 635-636, ii, 80-81 (they are
omitted in later editions). The members are arranged in alphabetical order,
the candidates (apparently) in order of votes received : Nikolaeva and Lashevich
occupied two of the last three places. For Kuklin see *XIV S"ezd Vsesoyuznoi
Kommunisticheskoi Partii (B)* (1926), p. 221 ; for Glebov-Avilov, a Leningrad
trade union worker who had been the first People's Commissar for Posts and
Telegraphs in 1917, see *ibid.* pp. 784-789, 896, 952 ; for Nikolaeva see p. 221
below.

elected to the central control commission, but lost her place in
the presidium. On January 1, 1926, the new central committee
met to appoint its subordinate organs. The number of the
Politburo was raised from seven to nine. Of its existing members,
Bukharin, Zinoviev, Kamenev, Rykov, Stalin, Tomsky and
Trotsky, all were re-elected except Kamenev, who was reduced
to the rank of a candidate ;· three new members were added —
Voroshilov, Molotov and Kalinin (the two last had been candidate
members since the previous congress). Of existing candidate
members Dzerzhinsky and Rudzutak were retained, and were
joined by Kamenev, Petrovsky and Uglanov ; Sokolnikov lost his
status as candidate. Minor changes of no political significance
were made in the membership of the Orgburo and the secretariat.
The five members of the secretariat were now Stalin, Molotov,
Uglanov, S. Kosior and Evdokimov.[1] An offer had been made to the
opposition on the eve of the congress to add a Leningrad representative to the secretariat. Notwithstanding the rejection of the
offer by the opposition, effect was now given to it by the inclusion
of Evdokimov. It was evidently an attempt, which did not prove
successful, to win over a Leningrad leader of the second rank.
Bukharin was confirmed in his post as editor of *Pravda* with
Manuilsky as his deputy.

Later in the month extensive governmental changes were
announced. Zinoviev, holding no government post, was not
affected. But Kamenev and Sokolnikov were both down-graded.
Kamenev was succeeded as president of STO by Rykov — a
purely formal appointment, since Rykov was already president
of Sovnarkom. He also ceased to be a deputy president of
Sovnarkom ; in his place two new deputies were appointed,
Kuibyshev, who held the combined post of People's Commissar
for Workers' and Peasants' Inspection and president of the party
control commission, and Rudzutak, who was People's Commissar
for Communications. Kamenev succeeded Tsyurupa as People's
Commissar for Trade. Sokolnikov was replaced as People's Commissar for Finance by Bryukhanov, and received the minor post of
deputy president of Gosplan. Frumkin became Kamenev's deputy
at Narkomtorg in succession to Sheinman, who secured the dual
appointment of deputy People's Commissar for Finance and

[1] These appointments were announced in *Pravda*, January 8, 1926.

president of the State Bank.[1] All in all, it could not be said that the victors had displayed undue vindictiveness towards their leading opponents. But this restraint had its reverse side. Its price was absolute submission, and abstention from any form of criticism or self-justification. This was demanded by the rigid pattern of party discipline.

[1] These appointments were announced in the press on January 17, 1926 ; the major appointments were made by formal decree (*Sobranie Zakonov, 1926*, ii, No. 3, arts. 13, 14, 16 ; No. 5, art. 29). For the career of Bryukhanov, an old party member of no particular distinction, see *Deyateli Revolyutsionnogo Dvizheniya*, v (1931), 514-517.

CHAPTER 18

NEW ALIGNMENTS

STALIN'S sweeping victory at the fourteenth congress was incomplete only at one point : the defeated minority under Zinoviev was still in formal control of the Leningrad party organization.· The last stage in the consolidation of the victory was a cleaning-up operation in Leningrad. The local party organ, *Leningradskaya Pravda*, had successfully been taken over. It remained to transform the Leningrad party provincial committee into a loyal bulwark and outpost of the central committee in Moscow. No time was lost. The party central committee, meeting on January 1, 1926, declared against " personal attacks on representatives of the minority ", but also insisted " on the necessity of criticizing the conduct of the minority at the congress and explaining the mistakes of the Leningrad delegation ".[1] At the same time, in the name of " Bolshevik unity ", it forbade members of the Leningrad opposition to speak on party platforms against the resolutions of the congress.[2] On January 5, 1926, a powerful delegation from the central committee, headed by Molotov,[3] descended on Leningrad to report to the Leningrad workers on the results of the congress. Zinoviev wrote a bitter letter to the members of the visiting delegation expressing the hope that they would be " correct enough " to explain to the Leningrad workers the reason for his silence.[4] There is no evidence that any of them

[1] I. Skvortsov-Stepanov, *Izbrannye Proizvedeniya*, ii (1931), 329.

[2] A brief report of Dzerzhinsky's speech in support of this decision is in F. Dzerzhinsky, *Izbrannye Proizvedeniya*, ii (1957), 235-236.

[3] The precise membership of the delegation is uncertain. Tomsky names Voroshilov, Kalinin, Kirov and Molotov in addition to himself (*Leningradskaya Organizatsiya i Chetyrnadtsatyi S"ezd* (1926), p. 65) ; Andreev also appeared among the speech-makers (*ibid.* pp. 69-77). An interview with Petrovsky in *Pravda*, January 22, 1926, shows that he, too, was a member.

[4] *Leningradskaya Organizatsiya i Chetyrnadtsatyi S"ezd* (1926), pp. 65-66. An immense number of pamphlets relating to the party controversy were published in the weeks after the congress (for a bibliography of them see

thought it necessary to do so. Tomsky sarcastically recalled that, in the days when he " took a beating ", it had not occurred to him to " write declarations ".[1]

Though the field had thus been cleared for them, the visitors to Leningrad found their task sufficiently delicate. They were greeted on their arrival with the news that the bureau of the Leningrad provincial party committee had arranged a meeting of leading party members on that very day to hear the report of the distinguished guests. Molotov thought that such a gathering would be " a far from true reflexion of the organization ", and quoted a resolution of the north-western regional party bureau — a higher organ in the party hierarchy — that the delegates should " begin from the lower ranks of party groups ".[2] In conformity with this instruction the delegates decided to speak directly to party groups of workers in the factories. It was a hard-fought campaign. *Leningradskaya Pravda* admitted that the atmosphere in some factories was " unhealthy ", and that the opposition " defends itself desperately ", and " shifts its forces from district to district, from factory to factory ".[3] Molotov in an interim report in *Pravda* on the first week's work, recorded 48 meetings addressed by members of the delegation and attended by 28,000 workers. In general, unanimity or " huge majorities " had been secured. But in one district the opposition had been particularly active ; and elsewhere " in separate enterprises a few dozens of people were found to vote against resolutions on which we had agreed ".[4] Kirov addressed 15 meetings at factories in a month.[5] Opposition was occasionally encountered, and " non-party workers or backward workers, under some influence or other, sometimes let out remarks against our government and our party ".[6] At a meeting in the Putilov factory on January 20,

Leningradskaya Organizatsiya i Chetyrnadtsatyi S"ezd (1926), pp. 185-188): all of them supported the official line, except that the speeches of Zinoviev and Kamenev at the congress were reprinted as pamphlets.

[1] *Ibid.* p. 66 ; for the " beating " of Tomsky see *The Bolshevik Revolution, 1917–1923*, Vol. 2, pp. 324-325.

[2] *Leningradskaya Organizatsiya i Chetyrnadtsatyi S"ezd* (1926), p. 138.

[3] *Leningradskaya Pravda*, January 7, 12, 1926, quoted in I. Skvortsov-Stepanov, *Izbrannye Proizvedeniya*, ii (1931), 327, 335.

[4] *Pravda*, January 19, 1926.

[5] S. Kirov, *Izbrannye Stat'i i Rechi, 1912–1934* (1939), p. 69.

[6] *Ibid.* pp. 187, 193.

1926, to which special importance was evidently attached, Tomsky made the principal speech and was supported by Kalinin, Molotov, Voroshilov and Petrovsky : Glebov-Avilov, Minin and Kuklin spoke for the opposition. The resolution approving the policy of the central committee and condemning the Leningrad opposition was carried by an " immense majority ".[1] When on the following day Molotov drew up a balance-sheet of the whole campaign, he reported that 652 out of 717 workers' groups in Leningrad had been addressed by one or other of the delegates. The meetings were attended by 63,000 workers, or 82 per cent of the party membership in the city. Each in turn passed resolutions approving the decisions of the party congress and condemning the factious attitude of the opposition, more than 60,000 votes being cast for the majority and rather more than 2,000 against. In the district where the opposition had enjoyed most support it had mustered only 10 per cent of the votes. In party cells in the Red Army and Fleet 89 per cent of members had attended meetings and 99 per cent of those present voted for the central committee.[2] What other measures may have been necessary to prise the Leningrad workers from the grip of Zinoviev and his immediate followers are not recorded. The suddenness with which comparatively large groups of party members could be swung over in the space of a few days from quasi-unanimous support of the opposition to quasi-unanimous acceptance of the party line suggests neither a genuine ideological conversion nor specific measures of pressure (which would scarcely have been practicable on so large a scale), but a widespread readiness to follow the dominant opinion. To attempt to analyse this readiness into its constituent parts, to determine how much of it was due to sheer indifference, how much to the belief that conformity paid, and how much to the familiar psychological impulse to be on the winning side, would be an unrealistic task.

While, however, the rank and file was thus easily won over, and while the top leaders had been silenced, the most stubborn resistance appears to have come from the middle ranks of party officials and leaders. Molotov's report admitted that those who

---

[1] *Pravda*, January 22, 1926.
[2] *Ibid.* January 22, 1926, partly reprinted in *Novaya Oppozitsiya* (1926), pp. 271-274.

had voted against the resolutions comprised " a significant percentage of party activists ". Of the 61 members of the Leningrad delegation to the fourteenth congress, only 3 took prompt steps to dissociate themselves from the defeated opposition.[1] Five members of the Leningrad provincial party committee are said to have protested against the attitude of the Leningrad delegation at the congress ;[2] and *Pravda* of January 15, 1926, carried a declaration from another member of the committee :

> I separate myself from the opposition, not through cowardice (since an honest communist cannot be suspected of this), and call on other members of the provincial committee of the VKP(B) to follow my example.

Other defectors from the Leningrad opposition registered their change of heart in the columns of *Pravda* in January 1926.[3] But the number was small enough to suggest that they were the exception rather than the rule. Meanwhile a resolution of the north-western regional party bureau accused " certain sections of the party bureaucracy " in Leningrad of trying to stifle rank-and-file opinion and to prohibit meetings favourable to the party line.[4] The initial decision of the visitors from Moscow to avoid a meeting of leading party members and to appeal directly to the " lower ranks " seems to have been amply justified. After a fortnight of intensive propaganda in the factories, the delegates from Moscow were confident enough of their success to move out into the open. A majority had been secured in the Leningrad provincial party committee, which decided to summon the twenty-third Leningrad provincial party conference for February 10, 1926, with district and county conferences to be held in the preceding week. The decision was confirmed by the north-western regional bureau on January 25 and by the party central committee on January 27.[5]

All preparations were now made to overwhelm the defeated

---

[1] *Leningradskaya Oppozitsiya i Chetyrnadtsatyi S"ezd* (1926), p. 55.
[2] *Pravda*, December 29, 1925.
[3] The file of *Leningradskaya Pravda* for the period, which would probably contain more evidence on this point, has not been available.
[4] *Leningradskaya Organizatsiya i Chetyrnadtsatyi S"ezd* (1926), pp. 59-60 ; the resolution is not dated, but evidently falls within the period of the factory campaign.
[5] *Ibid.* pp. 83-84 ; the announcement appeared in *Pravda*, January 29, 1926.

opposition at the forthcoming provincial party conference. The preliminary district and county conferences were the occasion for further displays of oratory by the visitors from Moscow. Bukharin arrived to reinforce the delegation, and delivered the principal speech at the conference of the Vyborg district, the main stronghold of the metal workers. He began by claiming that the party central committee had appealed " *to the lower ranks of the Leningrad organization* " as " the most democratic way " of liquidating the conflict. The main theme of the speech was to connect the " new opposition " with earlier oppositions, the opposition of Trotsky, the " workers' truth " group, and the workers' opposition. Zinoviev was again depicted as turning in desperation to the former leader of the workers' opposition : " I'm drowning, Shlyapnikov, save me ! ". Mindful that he was addressing a proletarian audience, Bukharin once more retracted the erroneous slogan " Enrich yourselves ", the effect of which had been to " spoil a barrel of honey with a spoonful of tar ".[1] Kirov, who spoke in the Petrograd district, complained that in the first nine months of 1925 only nine " peasants from the plough " had been admitted to the party as candidates by the Leningrad organization, and only three of them had become full members : the charge of neglecting the peasantry was not yet dead.[2] Molotov, speaking in the Volodarsky district, struck a subtler note. He thought it mistaken to suppose that " these differences are explained by some personal disagreements of individual comrades or by their personal shortcomings ". He asked what social strata were represented by the opposition, and found the answer in " new elements " of the proletariat, " especially from the countryside ", who had no faith in socialism, as well as in those elements among the workers " for whom the obligations of the working class to the countryside are not sufficiently clear ".[3]

The main conference, which sat from February 10 to 12,

---

[1] *Leningradskaya Organizatsiya i Chetyrnadtsatyi S"ezd* (1926), pp. 84-115.
[2] *Ibid.* pp. 115-121.
[3] *Ibid.* pp. 122, 132-133. A speaker at the Komsomol congress in March 1926 was still more precise on this point: " The party opposition was objectively the expression of those moods, those experiences, which are being brought into our factories, into our working class, by new strata of workers arriving from the countryside" (*VII S"ezd Vsesoyuznogo Leninskogo Kommunisticheskogo Soyuza Molodezhi* (1926), p..140).

1926, provided no surprises. The chief speaker was once more Bukharin, who reverted to the theoretical issues of NEP and state capitalism, and reproached the opposition, though in comparatively polite terms, for its failure to recognize the characteristics of the period — the possibility of building socialism " even in one country " and the need for conciliation of the peasant. He ended with a plea for " not sham, but real inner-party democracy ", leading up to the most pungent passage in the speech :

> It seems to me — and some comrades who are among the former leaders of the Leningrad organization will forgive me — that the former regime here can be described as a mixture of demagogy with sergeant-major methods of party administration. . . .
> Let there be fewer parades, less verbal sparkle, let there be less show, let there be less external brilliance, let there be less external effects, but more work of substance, and work carried on in a more democratic way. Everyone will readily understand why a directing apparatus of the old style in Leningrad so quickly lost its authority : not only because a number of members of the central committee descended on Leningrad (of course, this had its importance), but because the central committee found support here in the democratic discontent of the lower party ranks with the bureaucratic apparatus of the Leningrad organizers.[1]

It was a clear announcement that no quarter would be given to Zinoviev, but that any of his followers who were prepared to desert and disown him would be welcome in the fold. A large majority evidently chose to follow that path. Kirov, Molotov and Voroshilov all spoke at the conference, Voroshilov declaring that an end must be put to the system of " feudal principalities

---

[1] N. Bukharin, *Doklad na XXIII Chrezvychainoi Leningradskoi Gubernskoi Konferentsii VKP(B)* (1926), pp. 42-43. Stalin, two months later, dwelt with considerable unction on the same theme : " If members of our central committee with the help of Leningrad party workers succeeded in two weeks in driving out and isolating the opposition which was conducting a struggle against the decisions of the fourteenth congress, this was because the campaign to explain the decisions of the congress coincided with the democratic impulse which existed, which was trying to break through, and which finally did break through, in the Leningrad organization " (Stalin, *Sochineniya*, viii, 144-145). Trotsky in his unpublished memorandum of December 22, 1925, spoke of the " commissar tone " of the Zinoviev régime in the Leningrad party (see p. 168 below), though he would not have regarded the charge as any less applicable to the régime in Moscow.

in the framework of our party ".[1]   Only one speaker openly
defended the opposition, though the mood of many delegates was
certainly critical : Bukharin in his concluding remarks admitted
that " an extraordinary number of notes " had been sent up to
the platform after his speech.[2]   The resolution of the conference
condemned the errors of the opposition, including its " scepticism
and lack of faith in the inner resources of the working class of our
country, and consequent lack of faith in the victorious and successful building of socialism " ;   denounced the " localism and
separatism " of the old Leningrad party apparatus ; and ended
with an expression of confidence in party unity and in the central
committee.   Subsidiary resolutions, designed to stress the new
loyalty of the Leningrad party to headquarters in Moscow,
carried messages of greeting from the conference to the party
central committee, to *Pravda*, the central organ of the party, to
the Moscow party organization, and to the enlarged plenum of
IKKI at the moment in session in Moscow.   A list of 154 persons
elected to the Leningrad provincial party committee was headed
by Stalin, Kalinin, Molotov and Kirov.   Yaroslavsky was named
a member of the Leningrad control commission.[3]   All resolutions
were carried unanimously.   After the conference Kirov was
appointed first secretary of the Leningrad provincial party committee, and secretary of the north-western regional bureau.[4]   The
Leningrad opposition had been liquidated.   More than once
again opposition would rear its head in the party.   But never
again would it have a local base, or set one section of the party
apparatus against another.   Nowhere outside Leningrad had any
serious opposition to the decisions of the congress been encountered.[5]   Henceforth the party machine would work as a

---

[1] N. Bukharin, *Doklad na XXIII Chrezvychainoi Leningradskoi Gubernskoi
Konferentsii VKP(B)* (1926), p. 53.   [2] *Ibid.* pp. 44, 45.
[3] The resolutions were published in *Pravda*, February 13, 14, 1926 ; the
main resolution is also in *Novaya Oppozitsiya* (1926), pp. 302-304.
[4] S. Kirov, *Izbrannye Stat'i i Rechi, 1912–1934* (1939), p. 69 ; for his
concluding speech at the conference see *ibid.* pp. 231-233.
[5] A general report on party meetings throughout the country to explain
the results of the congress was complacent : " Opposition speeches at meetings
are isolated occurrences ; the context of these speeches is either of a plainly
demagogic character or reveals a lack of understanding, an insufficient study
of the question " (*Izvestiya Tsentral'nogo Komiteta Vsesoyuznoi Kommunisticheskoi Partii (B)*, No. 8 (129), March 1, 1926, p. 2).   The Smolensk archives
(WKP 522) contain a detailed report from the secretariat in Moscow on the

single indivisible unit under the firm directing hand of Moscow.

Corresponding measures to those taken in the Leningrad party organization were also applied to the Komsomol. According to a later source, " the central committee of the Komsomol, led by the Bolshevik party central committee, despatched a large number of comrades to the Leningrad organization " : among the group was one Kosarev,[1] afterwards to become an important Komsomol boss. Komsomol leaders demonstrated their allegiance to the party line. Averbakh loudly denounced Vardin in the Komsomol journal which he edited as " one of the most consistent ' theorists ' of the opposition ".[2] But the Leningrad Komsomol proved less docile than the Leningrad party, and it was admitted that " a majority of Leningrad Komsomols followed the opposition ".[3] At a meeting of the Leningrad Komsomol committee on January 14, 1926, the majority was willing to accept a motion declaring that the decisions of the fourteenth party congress were binding ; but an amendment proposing to recognize them as correct was rejected by 16 votes to 8.[4] The Leningrad Komsomol journal *Smena*, which had supported the opposition during the party congress, took refuge after the congress in an attitude of neutrality. The revolt was quelled only when the Komsomol central committee appointed a new regional bureau for the north-western region, and when the leaders of the Leningrad provincial committee had been replaced by more pliant successors.[5] In Moscow Chaplin made a long report to the Komsomol provincial committee on January 7, 1926, which was a review of the whole dispute as it had affected the Komsomol.[6] Here no special difficulties were experienced, though Uglanov complained of a lack of clarity in Komsomol organizations " on a large number of questions resulting from the resolutions of the party congress ".[7]

congress for use in explaining its decisions to the Smolensk provincial party conference.

[1] *Komsomol'skaya Pravda*, December 22, 1934.

[2] *Molodaya Gvardiya*, No. 1, January 1926, p. 139.

[3] *Leningradskaya Pravda*, January 8, 1926, quoted in I. Skvortsov-Stepanov, *Izbrannye Proizvedeniya*, ii (1931), 329.

[4] *Leningradskaya Organizatsiya i Chetyrnadtsatyi S"ezd* (1926), p. 140 ; *VII S"ezd Vsesoyuznogo Leninskogo Kommunisticheskogo Soyuza Molodezhi* (1926), p. 54.   [5] *Pravda*, January 30, 1926.

[6] This was printed in N. Chaplin, *Partiinaya Oppozitsiya i Komsomol* (1926).

[7] *Pravda*, February 28, 1926.

The seventh Komsomol congress in March 1926 was remarkable as the last occasion on which, as at the fourteenth party congress, the opposition leaders were given the floor and allowed to speak at length, though amid frequent interruptions.[1] Chaplin made the main report, accusing the opposition of attempting to set the Komsomol against the party. Tarasov, one of the expelled members of the provincial committee, who appeared as chief opposition spokesman, once more protested against " the transformation of our league into a peasant league ". Katalynov, another opposition leader, described the prevailing psychology :

> For whom are you ?   A Stalinist or not a Stalinist ?   If the man is not a Stalinist, crush him, throttle him, throw him out, do everything short of kicking him.[2]

Bukharin, Rykov and Voroshilov all spoke in defence of the official line. Bukharin does not seem to have relished his task. For four months now he had borne the brunt of the oratorical campaign against Zinoviev. He complained that he was " utterly tired out ", and that his " nose, throat, ears and other organs " were no longer functioning properly.[3] The main resolution condemned " the disorganizing behaviour of a minority of the central committee of the RLKSM and of the former opposition leaders of the Leningrad organization of the league ". Tarasov, on behalf of six opposition leaders, announced that they accepted any resolution of the congress as " unconditionally binding ", but considered the charges brought against them in the resolution as " incorrect ". The congress refused to receive this " lying " and " hypocritical " declaration, and carried the resolution unanimously.[4] Following the example of the party congress, the congress substituted " All-Union " for " Russian " in the title of the Komsomol, which henceforth became the All-Union Leninist Communist League of Youth (VLKSM). In things both

---

[1] *Pravda*, April 2, 1926, complained bitterly that, though the opposition had not a single voting delegate at the congress, its representatives " none the less tried to oppose to the Bolshevik line of the whole congress their own anti-Leninist line already condemned by the party ".

[2] *VII S"ezd Vsesoyuznogo Leninskogo Kommunisticheskogo Soyuza Molodezhi* (1926), pp. 69, 108.

[3] *Ibid.* p. 243.   [4] *Ibid.* pp. 502, 506-507.

great and small the VLKSM was firmly integrated into the pattern of a monolithic party leadership.

While the former stronghold of the opposition was thus being brought under the control of the central authority of the party, Stalin consolidated his victory on the ideological plane through the development and popularization of the doctrine of socialism in one country. Considering the importance which it was later to assume, socialism in one country played surprisingly little part in the controversial exchanges before and during the fourteenth congress. In September 1925 Vareikis, the head of the press section of the party secretariat, published a pamphlet entitled *Is the Victory of Socialism in one Country Possible ?*, in which he answered his question in the affirmative and praised Stalin's article of December 1924 as the only serious contribution to Leninist theory since the death of Lenin. A review by a minor Komsomol leader, Barbashev, in *Leningradskaya Pravda*, headed " On Communist Lomonosovs ",[1] criticized Vareikis, who was a disciple of Bukharin, for believing that the USSR had already reached the first stage of socialism, and for preaching a peasant socialism in the guise of NEP.[2] A few weeks later Zinoviev attacked socialism in one country in *Leninism*.[3] But it was not one of his main targets. In the flow of angry articles in *Leningradskaya Pravda* during November and December, only one — by an obscure writer named Soloviev — was devoted to an offensive against the new bulwark of party orthodoxy : this, by accident, appeared on the morning of the first meeting of the congress.[4] At the congress itself Bukharin approached the question by way of a rejection of permanent revolution, which, he said, contained " the seeds of doubt about the possibility of building socialism in one country ". " Among us," he added, leaving the pronoun

---

[1] The reference was to a passage in *What is to be Done ?* (Lenin, *Sochineniya*, iv, 413) in which Lenin ironically referred to Martynov as " our Lomonosov ", implying that under the pretext of making profound discoveries he had merely confused elementary truths.

[2] *Leningradskaya Pravda*, September 13, 1925.

[3] See Vol. 1, pp. 304-305.

[4] *Leningradskaya Pravda*, December 18, 1925 ; *Pravda*, December 29, 1925, identified Soloviev as a student at the Institute of Red Professors.

undefined, socialism in one country had always been considered
" a fundamental question ". He then confused the issue of
building socialism with the issue of making a revolution in a
backward country by connecting it with the defection of Zinoviev
and Kamenev in 1917.[1] Kamenev, ignoring this provocation,
enquired " whether we shall succeed in building socialism in this
country in spite of the delay in world revolution ", and answered
in the following terms :

> Yes, this is theoretically possible, and has been demon-
> strated by Lenin, and can be carried out in practice to the
> extent that we can correctly perceive all the difficulties, and
> correctly aim our fire at the target which is really dangerous, to
> the extent that we do not allow ideological differences to grow
> into an organizational struggle.[2]

Zinoviev, who had avoided the question in his opening speech,
touched on it in his reply in order to point out the inconsistency
of Stalin's present position with his pronouncement of 1924.[3] He
then quoted a somewhat flamboyant passage from an article in a
provincial journal, and enquired whether this " does not give off
a whiff of national narrow-mindedness ". But his only conclusion
was that the question was " unclear for the broad masses of the
party ".[4] Stalin did not attempt to answer Zinoviev on this
point. Few of the other speakers mentioned it at all. The resolution of the congress spoke of " the struggle for the victory of
socialist construction in the USSR " and of the need " to guarantee
to the USSR economic independence " by developing " the production of the means of production ". But the phrase " socialism
in one country " did not appear in it.

Stalin had, however, by this time perceived something of the
value and popular appeal of the new slogan. At the end of
January 1926 he wrote a substantial essay *On Questions of Leninism*
which was his considered reply to the doctrinal debates of the
fourteenth party congress. Dedicated " To the Leningrad
Organization of the VKP(B) ", it was published in the party
journal *Bol'shevik* on February 15, 1926, and appeared immediately afterwards as the first item in a volume of Stalin's

---

[1] *XIV S"ezd Vsesoyuznoi Kommunisticheskoi Partii (B)* (1926), pp. 135-137.
[2] *Ibid.* p. 273.   [3] See p. 141 above.
[4] *XIV S"ezd Vsesoyuznoi Kommunisticheskoi Partii (B)* (1926), pp. 429-431.

collected essays with the general title *Questions of Leninism*, which also contained *Foundations of Leninism* originally published in April 1924 and Stalin's intervening articles and speeches on socialism in one country.[1] The greater part of the new essay *On Questions of Leninism*[2] was devoted to an embittered polemic against Zinoviev on the issues on which they had crossed swords at the congress or earlier — the attitude towards the peasantry, the character of NEP, the dictatorship of the party. But it was chiefly remarkable for its renewed emphasis on the distinction between the two alleged obstacles to the building of socialism in the Soviet Union.[3] The first — the technical backwardness of the economy — was once more firmly rejected : to insist on this as an insuperable obstacle was the cardinal sin of the opposition. The second — the threat from the capitalist world outside — was accepted as the, and by implication the sole, obstacle to the final victory of socialism. The distinction was now used — this also by way of reply to Zinoviev's taunt of inconsistency — to explain the " incomplete " and " incorrect " formulation of the question in *The Foundations of Leninism* which had been corrected in editions of that work subsequent to December 1924. The original version[4] had been written at a time when the relation of the victorious revolution to the capitalist world had been the dominant issue ; the emergence of the new issue of building a socialist economy in the Soviet Union had made a new and more correct formulation imperative. Stalin offered a new exposition of the doctrine, couched in his usual flat, lucid and antithetical style :

> What is the *possibility* of the victory of socialism in one country ?
> It is the possibility of resolving the contradictions between

---

[1] For the original publication of *Foundations of Leninism* see *The Interregnum, 1923-1924*, p. 358. The title *Voprosy Leninizma* was appropriate for the first edition of the collected volume published in March 1926 ; but the numerous subsequent editions down to 1941 were swollen by the inclusion of Stalin's major current political pronouncements, so that the sense of the original title was forgotten.   [2] Stalin, *Sochineniya*, viii, 13-90.

[3] For the first appearance of this distinction see pp. 44-45 above.

[4] For the text see *The Interregnum, 1923-1924*, pp. 358-359. As Trotsky did not fail to point out (*XV Konferentsiya Vsesoyuznoi Kommunisticheskoi Partii (B)* (1927), p. 529), the explanation was lame ; the original text had explicitly referred to " the organization of socialist production ".

the proletariat and the peasantry by the internal forces of our country, the possibility of the taking of power by the proletariat and of the utilization of this power for the building of a full socialist society in our country, with the sympathy and support of the proletariat of other countries, but without the previous victory of the proletarian revolution in other countries.

Without such a possibility, to build socialism is to build without any prospect, to build without the conviction that socialism can be built. It is impossible to go on building socialism unless one is convinced that it is possible to build it, unless one is convinced that the technical backwardness of our country is not an *insuperable* obstacle to the building of a full socialist society. To deny such a possibility is to lack faith in the cause of the building of socialism, to desert Leninism.

What is the *impossibility* of a complete final victory of socialism in one country without a victory of the revolution in other countries ?

It is the impossibility of a complete guarantee against intervention, and therefore against a restoration of bourgeois conditions, without a victory of the revolution in, at any rate, a number of countries. To deny this incontestable proposition is to desert internationalism, to desert Leninism.[1]

Little of substance was afterwards added to, or subtracted from, the doctrine thus proclaimed. With the publication of the first edition of *Questions of Leninism*, socialism in one country was established as the mainstay of Soviet orthodoxy.

Once the doctrine was established, Stalin tended, in accordance with his usual practice, to recede into the background and to leave it to his supporters to make the running. From the time of the fourteenth congress, it was Bukharin who appeared as the most persistent propagandist of socialism in one country. In his report of January 5, 1926, on the results of the congress to the Moscow party organization, he recounted the questions put to him by a group of workers at the Dynamo factory :

If we know in advance that we are not equal to the task, then why the devil did we have to make the October revolution ? If we have managed for eight years, why should we not manage in the ninth, tenth or fortieth year ?[2]

[1] Stalin, *Sochineniya*, viii, 65-66.
[2] *Izvestiya*, January 10, 1926.

In his speech a month later at the Leningrad provincial party conference, he dwelt on the effect of divergent national characteristics in the growth of socialism :

> Our socialism develops in a certain sense on a different foundation from that on which socialism will develop in America. With us it develops in other, in Russian, conditions, not in American or French conditions. This is completely natural because, just as capitalism had its different features in different countries, so socialism in these countries will at first have its special features, which only in the end, when the whole world economy is united on an advanced socialist foundation, will be effaced and levelled out.

He returned triumphantly to his earlier argument. What were the consequences if one did not believe that it was possible to build socialism in Soviet Russia ?

> Then there was no reason for us to go to the barricades in October, then the Mensheviks would have been right when they said that in so backward a country as Russia it was pointless to plan a socialist revolution, then Trotsky would have been right in affirming that without state aid from a victorious western European proletariat we shall necessarily come into collision with the peasant, who will necessarily overthrow us.[1]

Kirov, at a party meeting in Leningrad, described socialism in one country as " the fundamental point in the differences between the majority and the minority of the party and of our congress ",[2] and devoted a good half of his address to a Leningrad Komsomol conference to the theme of building socialism in the USSR — a theme which could easily be made attractive to the rising generation.[3] It was left to Rykov at the session of VTsIK in April 1926 to give the new doctrine its most frankly patriotic expression :

---

[1] N. Bukharin, *Doklad na XXIII Chrezvychainoi Leningradskoi Gubernskoi Konferentsii VKP(B)* (1926), pp. 17, 37. The same argument was used in Stalin's *On Questions of Leninism* : " *It was wrong to take power in October 1917* — that is the conclusion to which the internal logic of Zinoviev's argument leads " (Stalin, *Sochineniya*, viii, 70). Trotsky appeared in his article *Towards Capitalism or Socialism ?* to leave the issue undecided : " If it should turn out that capitalism is still capable of fulfilling a progressive historical rôle . . . that would mean that we, the communist party of the Soviet Union, were too early in saying masses for it, in other words, that we took power into our hands too early for the building of socialism " (*Pravda*, September 20, 1925).

[2] *Leningradskaya Oppozitsiya i Chetyrnadtsatyi S"ezd* (1926), p. 118.

[3] S. Kirov, *Izbrannye Stat'i i Rechi, 1912–1934* (1939), pp. 190–195.

We achieved these successes in the sphere of our whole national economy without any help from outside. Our state is apparently the only one which was capable of recovering from unheard of destruction without recourse to foreign loans. . . . The workers and peasants know how to build their economy, organizing it better than under the bourgeois-feudal and capitalist order.

And he found in these achievements " a gigantic moral victory in the sense of a proof of the superiority of our system over the bourgeois-capitalist system ".[1]

The split in the triumvirate at the fourteenth party congress left behind it one puzzling enigma : the position of Trotsky. Hostility to Trotsky was the main foundation on which the triumvirate had stood. It seemed unlikely that the relation of both camps to Trotsky, or of Trotsky to them, could long remain unaffected by the new alignment of forces. Could Trotsky continue indefinitely to profess an indifferent neutrality in the clash between Zinoviev and Stalin ? Could Stalin and Zinoviev, now united in nothing else, continue to nourish the same equal and undeviating animosity towards Trotsky ? To expect so much rigidity in a changing world was to fly in the face of all political experience. The only questions were who would move first, how soon, and in what direction ?

Trostky's position seemed the most rigid. Though a delegate at the congress, he had sat haughtily through the proceedings, while the two new factions tore one another to pieces, without rising to speak. He is said, on somewhat doubtful authority, to have intended to come out at the congress against Zinoviev and Kamenev, but to have been dissuaded by some of his political associates.[2] He once broke silence, when Zinoviev was laboriously explaining that he had proposed Trotsky's expulsion from the

---

[1] *SSR : Tsentral'nyi Ispolnitel'nyi Komitet 3 Sozyva : 2 Sessiya* (1926), pp. 5-6.

[2] This statement rests on a letter written in 1927 by Antonov-Ovseenko and quoted by Rykov (*Pravda*, November 27, 1927) ; the memorandum of December 22, 1925 (see below), shows that Trotsky felt greater hostility at this time to Zinoviev than to Stalin.

Politburo because that was the logical conclusion of his condemnation by the central committee, to exclaim : " Quite right ".[1] A contemptuous aside about Bukharin did not reach the official record.[2] These were his only public comments on the debate. His private comments were made in an illuminating unpublished memorandum of December 22, 1925, while the main debate of the congress was in full spate. The current issue between the peasantry and industry reminded him of the old struggle of the Marxists against the *narodniks*. Delay in the international revolution had encouraged the growth in the younger generation of the party of " elements of Soviet *narodnichestvo* ", of which Bukharin was the theoretical exponent. But Zinoviev had also helped " the tendencies towards national-rural narrow-mindedness to develop and attain an already fairly sharp expression ". It was a paradox that the Leningrad leaders, whose position depended on " the class-consciousness of the Leningrad proletariat ", should have been accomplices in this deviation. (Trotsky here interjected a contemptuous mention of " the promotion of the idea of a closed national economy, a closed building of socialism " — his only reference to socialism in one country.) " The Leningraders ", he concluded, " are now calling by its right name the very danger in the ideological preparation of which their leaders played a principal part." He attacked the party régime established in Leningrad, and considered that " a replacement of the Leningrad leadership and the adoption by the Leningrad organization of less of a commissar tone in relation to the whole party " would be " incontestably factors of positive significance ". But the essence of the proceedings was the setting of the countryside against the town : " we have here only the first premonitions of a process which can, as it develops, become fatal to the rôle of the proletariat ". And finally : " The democratization of the inner life of these [i.e. the Moscow and Leningrad] organizations is an indispensable condition of their active and successful resistance to peasant deviations ".[3]

As often in Trotsky's writings, the analysis was exceedingly

---

[1] *XIV S"ezd Vsesoyuznoi Kommunisticheskoi Partii (B)* (1926), p. 459.
[2] For this see Vol. 1, p. 173.
[3] Typewritten memorandum, with Trotsky's signature, in the Trotsky archives, T 2975.

acute, the positive prescriptions theoretical and unrealistic. It was significant that, in a document which revealed his inmost thoughts, Trotsky still treated Zinoviev rather than Stalin as the principal target. But it contained not the faintest hint of any shift in his own position to take account of new alignments. If Trotsky had " come to Lenin fighting " in 1917, and only because he was convinced that the April theses marked a substantial identity with the views long held by himself, he was not likely to prove more amenable now. Nor was this rigidity merely a question of personal pride or inflexibility. In the crisis of 1925 Zinoviev — and Kamenev after him — had swung from one extreme opinion to its opposite ; Sokolnikov's adhesion to the opposition was, as Trotsky noted in passing in his memorandum, " an example of purely personal unprincipledness " ; Bukharin was a weakling ; Stalin took up a position so firmly in the centre that he sometimes seemed to have no opinions of his own, and to adjust his attitude from time to time to meet the requirements of his position as supreme party boss. Of Trotsky alone could it be said that his attitude would be determined, and his actions directed, by a profound and unchanging conviction of the correct course to pursue and by an indifference to personal factors if they seemed irrelevant to this conviction. This quality was a source of political weakness as well as of strength. But it won respect, and gave him a unique position. How eagerly he longed to return to public life is shown by his readiness to accept invitations to speak on non-political occasions. While the fourteenth congress was in session, on December 26, 1925, he found time to address the Society of Political Prisoners on the anniversary of the 1905 revolution, concluding his speech with a hymn of praise to the coming world revolution, which would find him and his hearers in their places to greet it.[1] But he had no programme in terms of current party tactics. He would approach nobody. If anybody

---

[1] *Izvestiya*, January 8, 1926. Among his other recorded utterances of this period were speeches to a conference on the protection of mother and child (December 7, 1925), to a conference of doctors (December 8, 1925), to a conference of *rabkors* (January 13, 1926) and to the " society of friends of radio " (March 1, 1926). All these were reprinted in his collected works (*Sochineniya*, xxi, 44-55, 384-396, 397-405, 410-423) ; none of them touched on controversial issues. Trotsky also delivered a speech on February 25, 1926, celebrating the fifth anniversary of the creation of the Georgian SSR (*ibid.* xxi, 405-409).

approached him, it would have to be on his own conditions.
On the other hand, both the new rival groups were, from the
first moment of the split, keenly conscious of the problem of their
future relations with Trotsky, though both fluctuated in their
approach to it. At the fourteenth congress, the temptation to
tar the opposition with the brush of " Trotskyism " was overwhelmingly strong ; and this course was followed by nearly every
defender of the official line. Bukharin dragged up an old quotation from Zinoviev's writings to prove that, like Trotsky, he had
ignored the rôle of the peasantry in the 1905 revolution. When
Krupskaya was speaking, someone called out : " Lev Davidovich,
you have new allies ". Polonsky declared that Trotsky had put
his Right foot, Zinoviev his Left foot, into " the bourgeois sack " :
that was the only difference between them.[1] *Pravda* of December
22, 1925, in a leader designed to establish a line of succession from
the workers' opposition through Trotsky to Zinoviev, dubbed the
Leningraders " the new opposition ". Rykov repeated the phrase
on the same day at the congress ; [2] and it passed into current
usage. The leader on the congress in the party journal *Bol'shevik*
was built round the theme that the new opposition was infected
with the same pessimism as Trotsky and disbelieved in the possibility of building socialism in the Soviet Union without world
revolution.[3] The opposition, unable to escape the fatal brand of
Trotskyism, ended by accepting it. At the congress Lashevich,
provoked by charges of Trotskyism from interrupters, turned on
them with the retort that " Trotsky said not only untrue, but also
true, things " ; [4] and, when Zinoviev made his proposals to bring
back " former groups " into party work,[5] the will to bury the
hatchet with Trotsky was unmistakable. At such moments a
new alliance must have seemed already in sight.

Certain gestures, however, also came from the other side. It
was not surprising that at the congress official spokesmen had
directed their keenest shafts at the new opposition, and had left
Trotsky comparatively unscathed. Tomsky, in replying to
Kamenev's attack on Stalin, reminded the congress that it was

[1] *XIV S"ezd Vsesoyuznoi Kommunisticheskoi Partii (B)* (1926), pp. 138, 166,
171-172.   [2] *Ibid.* p. 410.
[3] *Bol'shevik*, No. 1, January 15, 1926, pp. 3-13.
[4] *XIV S"ezd Vsesoyuznoi Kommunisticheskoi Partii (B)* (1926), p. 183.
[5] See p. 142 above.

Zinoviev and Kamenev who had called a year earlier for the most
ruthless reprisals against Trotsky :

> Some thought that, if somebody had erred — well, that's
> enough, beat him and kick him. Others thought that our party
> is not so rich in resources that it can afford, in the case of
> everyone who errs — and many of us have erred on various
> questions — instead of letting him enter the channel of normal
> work, to put forward the proposition : Finish him off. Such
> a proceeding was thought incorrect.

And Tomsky went on to compare Kamenev unfavourably with
Trotsky, who always had concrete proposals to make.[1] Stalin in
his second speech at the congress was careful to mention that he
and his supporters had resisted Zinoviev's and Kamenev's demands
to expel Trotsky from the party or from the Politburo. After the
congress both Tomsky and Bukharin struck a human note such
as had not been heard in dealing with Trotsky for more than two
years.

> It is not necessary to kick a man [Tomsky was reported as
> saying], not necessary to cut him off, as they wanted to do with
> Trotsky. But think of doing even a quarter of what was done
> to Trotsky! Even an Indian elephant would not have endured
> what was done to Trotsky.[2]

And Bukharin a few weeks later was more positive :

> Trotsky never said that our industry was state capitalist.
> No, he recognized our industry as socialist. . . . In the dis-
> cussions with Trotsky I was always against putting the issue in
> the form of saying that Trotsky was a Menshevik. Of course,
> Trotsky is not a Menshevik. He fought for the October revolu-
> tion, he achieved a large number of things for which the party
> is much indebted to him.[3]

Words like these, spoken by Tomsky and Bukharin, suggested
passing flashes of genuine remorse, though on the lips of others

[1] *XIV S"ezd Vsesoyuznoi Kommunisticheskoi Partii (B)* (1926), pp. 276, 290.
[2] Quoted from a speech made at the Putilov factory (for the occasion see
pp. 154-155 above) on January 20, 1926, in *Byulleten' Oppozitsii* (Paris), No. 29-
30, September 1932, p. 31. The speech was mentioned in *Pravda*, January 22,
1926 ; no report giving the text has been traced, but the quotation is probably
authentic.
[3] *Leningradskaya Organizatsiya i Chetyrnadtsatyi S"ezd* (1926), pp. 96, 108 ;
that Bukharin felt scruples about past treatment of Trotsky is suggested by the
correspondence between them at this time (see Vol. 1, p. 173).

they might have sounded like cold calculation. But such feelings probably did not go far. If some sections of the party would have liked to mitigate the severity of its past verdicts on Trotsky, others were indignant at the faintest indication that " the party has changed its attitude to Trotskyism ".[1] The only prominent Bolshevik who at this time actually tried to engineer a truce between Trotsky and Stalin was the ingenious Radek, who had special reason to detest Zinoviev as the author of his downfall, and was eager to emerge from the secondary position to which he had been relegated for the past two years. But nobody seems to have taken his effort seriously.[2] Trotsky would not move ; and Stalin, while he would no doubt have been glad to prevent or delay a prospective *rapprochement* of Trotsky with Zinoviev and Kamenev, was unlikely to court an alliance in which he would have been matched by an equal, or perhaps more masterful, partner.

The cards were, however, already stacked. Stalin's position was now so overwhelmingly strong that his opponents were bound to unite against him, and to compose whatever personal or ideological differences still separated them. What is perhaps surprising is not that it happened, but that it took so long to happen. The

[1] Apprehensions on this point were noted in an article in *Izvestiya Tsentral'-nogo Komiteta Vsesoyuznoi Kommunisticheskoi Partii (B)*, No. 10-11 (131-132), March 22, 1926, p. 9. A curious example of current attitudes towards Trotsky is provided by an unpublished speech of Lunacharsky in the Bol'shoi Theatre on January 21, 1926, at the anniversary commemoration of Lenin's death (a few insignificant lines were devoted to the speech in *Pravda*, January 22, 1926). Lunacharsky, always naïve in politics, was led to discuss the possibility that " some man who has acquired popularity and enjoys influence in the country " might attempt to " overthrow our hegemony " by enlisting the support of capitalist or petty bourgeois elements. He went on : " Do not suppose, please, that I am alluding here to L. D. Trotsky ; I ought to say that comrade Trotsky never thought of this, and is perhaps further from it than any of us ". Nevertheless, when Trotsky went into opposition, " they " (not further defined) were willing to offer him " a crown on a velvet cushion " and " hail him as Lev I ". But, when Trotsky returned to a " normal position ", they " ceased to love him and said that he was ' a communist like all the rest ' ". Uglanov later told Lunacharsky that Trotsky was displeased by this speech, and Lunacharsky sent Trotsky a letter of explanation on March 3, 1926, in which he wrote : " I do not at all wish you to have the impression that I am numbered among your enemies ". The letter and extracts from the speech are in the Trotsky archives.

[2] Trotsky reported it many years later in *Byulleten' Oppozitsii* (Paris), No. 54-55, March 1937, p. 11, adding : " It was at this moment that the unfortunate Mrachkovsky . . . uttered the winged phrase : ' Neither with Stalin nor with Zinoviev ; Stalin will cheat, and Zinoviev will rat ' ".

prime mover was Kamenev. It was probably late in March, or early in April, 1926, that he had a conversation with Trotsky : it was their first private meeting since March 6, 1923. The only record of it is a short passage in Trotsky's autobiography. Kamenev said to him : " It is enough for you and Zinoviev to appear on the same platform, and the party will find its true central committee ". Trotsky describes himself as having " laughed at this bureaucratic optimism ". He spoke of the disintegration of the party during the past three years and of the present domination of the party apparatus by its " Right wing ", and foresaw " a long and serious struggle ".[1] It is not certain how soon this conversation was followed by others, or when Zinoviev was first drawn into the discussions. But too much bad blood had been generated. Trotsky, who for two years had borne the concentrated insults and misrepresentations of the triumvirate, stood aloof. Progress was slow. No common front had been established, and no agreement about common tactics reached, when the party central committee met on April 6, 1926.

The session of the committee which lasted from April 6 to 9, 1926, was remarkable for the active reappearance of Trotsky, after nearly two years' absence, in the proceedings of a major party organ. The rift in the triumvirate had once more made it possible for him to play a rôle ; once more he dominated any debate in which he took part. In form, the discussion revolved round the alternative proposed by Trotsky to Rykov's draft resolution. In substance it was Trotsky who kept the discussion firmly focused on the cardinal issue of the relation between agriculture and industry.[2] Stalin clashed with him on what was in effect the question of the rate of industrialization : was the ambitious project of Dnieprostroi still premature and far-fetched ? Kamenev emphatically agreed with Trotsky on the need for a stronger line against the *kulak*, thus giving to the party the first hint of the impending foundation of a new bloc. Dzerzhinsky openly accused Trotsky and Kamenev of seeking to create a " new platform " based on the exploitation of the peasant.[3] Trotsky, anxious

---

[1] L. Trotsky, *Moya Zhizn'* (Berlin, 1930), ii, 265-266 ; for the meeting of 1923 see *The Interregnum, 1923–1924*, p. 266, note 1.

[2] For the sources for this debate, and its conclusions affecting industry and agriculture, see Vol. 1, pp. 325-328, 354-356.

[3] See Vol. 1, p. 535.

perhaps to disclaim too close an association, reproached Kamenev
for failing to realize how closely the problem of the *kulak* was
bound up with the policy of industrialization. Trotsky at one
moment announced his intention to vote against the resolution.[1] But he did not carry out his threat, and the resolution was
carried unanimously. In fact, no clear issue was before the committee. Rykov, in his subsequent report on the session to a
Moscow party meeting, dramatized it as a clash between the two
extremes of maximum support for agriculture at the cost of
postponing industrialization and intensive industrialization through
a process of exploiting the peasant, associating the former with the
name of Shanin and the latter with that of Preobrazhensky.[2] But
the first of these time-honoured deviations was now a lost cause
among the party leaders, and no longer found any open support.
The real outstanding issue was the tempo of industrialization.
But on this, the question of the stiffening of the agricultural tax
having been already settled,[3] no further decision would be taken
till after the harvest. One minor decision revealed Stalin's un-
failing attention, at this critical moment of the struggle for power
in the party, to party appointments. The experiment of including
Evdokimov, a member of the Leningrad opposition, in the
secretariat [4] had evidently not been a success or had outlived its
purpose. Evdokimov was relieved of his post " at his own
request ", and replaced by Shvernik.[5]

For the moment, however, politically as well as economically,
nobody was eager to stir the embers of past controversies. Rykov's
report on the session sounded a studiedly non-controversial note
and justified the eclectic character of the resolution :

> The fourteenth congress made the principal opposition
> leaders members of the central committee and of the Politburo.
> It did so in order to preserve unity, in the interests of the
> utilization of all the forces of the party in the building of
> socialism. It did so also in order that the central committee,

[1] His statement is recorded in the Trotsky archives, T 2982.
[2] *Pravda*, April 23, 1926 ; Rykov repeated the same point six months later
without mentioning names at the fifteenth party conference (*XV Konferentsiya
Vsesoyuznoi Kommunisticheskoi Partii* (*B*) (1927), p. 122).
[3] See Vol. 1, pp. 320, 327.   [4] See p. 151 above.
[5] *VKP(B) v Rezolyutsiyakh* (1941), ii, 91 ; the decisions of this session of
the central committee were published in *Pravda*, April 13, 1926.

taking into account all differences, all opinions arising in the discussion of actual problems, might fix the correct policy in accordance with the decisions of the congress.

He admitted that differences had arisen in the central committee, but he refused to speak in detail of the debates, " because I did not want this or that piece of information, even the most objective, to serve as a starting-point for a new discussion in the party ".[1] Stalin chose to make his now customary speech on the session of the central committee to a party meeting in Leningrad — evidently a tribute to the importance and to the new-found party loyalty of the Leningrad organization. The speech was plainly adapted to a Leningrad audience. The only attack on the opposition — a retrospective one — occurred in the passage in which he attributed its defeat to the fidelity of the Leningrad party to the principle of inner party democracy.[2] The main emphasis of the speech was on the process of economic recovery and the prospects of industrialization. Any polemical note was carefully avoided. Declaring that the work of the central committee had proceeded from the " basic slogan " of the industrialization of the country proclaimed by the fourteenth congress, Stalin devoted his peroration to the past achievements of the party and concluded :

> Now there stands before us a new task — the industrialization of our country. The most serious difficulties have been left behind. Is it possible to doubt that we shall be equal to this new task, the industrialization of our country ? Of course not. On the contrary we now have all the necessary factors to overcome difficulties and carry into effect the tasks set before us by the fourteenth congress of our party.[3]

It was grateful doctrine in the ears of the Leningrad Bolsheviks. Socialism in one country, in the guise of " the industrialization of our country ", became the supreme Bolshevik achievement.

Zinoviev, Kamenev and Trotsky all remained silent on the proceedings of the April session of the central committee, leaving the party to guess how much lay behind the partial, but not unqualified, agreement between Trotsky and Kamenev which had emerged in the debate. The situation was still obscure and embarrassing even to those most closely concerned. It was

---

[1] *Ibid.* April 23, 1926. [2] For this passage see p. 158, note 1 above.
[3] Stalin, *Sochineniya*, viii, 116-148.

Trotsky whose next move once more seemed cryptic and un-decypherable. Having taken a first step in the direction of the reconciliation which Kamenev and Zinoviev now ardently desired, he decided to seek medical advice in Berlin, and absented himself from Moscow for nearly two months. No recurrence is recorded in the winter of 1925–1926 of the " mysterious infection " which had attacked him during the acute political crises of the two previous winters,[1] and he had appeared frequently in public.[2] But now, faced with a new call to political action, he became once more preoccupied with the need for treatment of his malady. The Politburo, fearing some incident abroad, attempted to dis-suade him from the journey, but placed no formal obstacles in his way. He left " about the middle of April ". Kamenev and Zinoviev were disconcerted by the move. According to Trotsky, they " parted from me with an appearance of real feeling ", since they " did not relish being left *tête-à-tête* with Stalin ". In Berlin a succession of physicians failed to diagnose Trotsky's malady till a throat specialist advised the removal of his tonsils. The opera-tion was successfully performed, though it proved in the long run not to have touched the enigmatic causes of the disease.[3] While Trotsky was convalescent in Berlin in May 1926, a series of crises broke on the world. But, while their repercussions were plainly felt in the sensitive climate of Moscow, the activities of the party opposition were perforce suspended, or conducted only at lower levels, till the principal actor could return to take his cue.

[1] See pp. 29-30 above.   [2] See p. 169, note 1 above.
[3] L. Trotsky, *Moya Zhizn* (Berlin, 1930), ii, 266-268.

CHAPTER 19

THE MONOLITHIC PARTY

(a) Numbers and Composition

THE most conspicuous as well as the most important change in the Russian Communist Party (Bolsheviks) in the middle nineteen-twenties was its sudden and rapid growth. To keep the party small was Lenin's long-standing ambition; and during the last two years of his active life he had striven effectively to reduce it from the swollen dimensions (a maximum of 650,000 members) which it had reached in the civil war. But this conception, inherited from the tradition of the underground party before the revolution, was inappropriate to a party called on to provide the backbone of government and administration for a large country just emerging from the throes of war and revolution; and the " Lenin enrolment " which immediately followed Lenin's death marked the end of it.[1] Henceforth the party expanded to keep pace with the new developments. From a total of 472,000 (350,000 members and 122,000 candidates) at the beginning of 1924, it increased to 772,040 (420,670 members and 351,370 candidates) at the beginning of 1925, and 1,078,182 (638,352 members and 439,830 candidates) at the beginning of 1926.[2] In two years the number of party members had almost doubled, and the total of members and candidates together more than doubled. But the methods and character of the recruitment underwent a radical change. The Lenin enrolment was no longer the enrolment of individual enthusiasts for the revolutionary cause, but of masses of " workers from the bench " drafted into the party as the result of a deliberate decision of the party central committee; and the same was true of the attempt to organize an enrolment of peasants in the following year. The composition of the party

---

[1] For the Lenin enrolment and its first consequences see *The Interregnum, 1923–1924*, pp. 352-356.   [2] A. Bubnov, *VKP(B)* (1931), p. 613.

was determined less than heretofore by spontaneous action " from below ", by pressure from would-be recruits to the ranks, and more by policy decisions " from above ", by a conscious effort to shape and mould the party on specific lines for specific purposes.

The most contentious issue of these years in regard to the composition of the party was not the size of the membership — the necessity for a rapid expansion was now silently conceded almost everywhere — but the desirability of an increased intake of peasants. A certain ambivalence about the admission of peasants to the party of the proletariat was a legacy of its history. The dependence of the proletarian revolution in Russia on an alliance with the peasant was foreshadowed in 1905, demonstrated in 1917, further illustrated in 1919 when, at the height of the civil war, the party held out the hand of friendship to the middle peasant, and sealed in 1921 in the famous " link " between proletariat and peasantry. But this did not answer the question of the eligibility of peasants for party membership. That *batraks*, or hired workers in agriculture, whose existence was once more legally recognized after 1922, were eligible, nobody denied. That *kulaks* were eligible, nobody pretended. But the mass of peasants who fell into neither of these categories presented an awkward conundrum. It was impossible to exclude them on principle, since the régime depended on their good will. But to admit them in numbers would be to change the character of the party and to deny its proletarian essence.

The " Lenin enrolment " of the first months of 1924 had been confined to the proletariat — " workers from the bench ". Stalin had at that time resisted a proposal to extend it to " poor peasants and agricultural labourers " ; [1] and the resolution of the thirteenth congress in May 1924, while remarking that the " Lenin enrolment " brought into the party " substantial groups of workers connected with the country ", significantly refrained from recommending any large-scale admission of peasants, and proposed " the transfer of communists to the countryside . . . systematically and by way of a combination of the voluntary principle with selection ".[2] To bring the party to the peasant still seemed a more practicable enterprise than to bring the peasant into the party.

[1] See *The Interregnum, 1923–1924*, p. 340.
[2] *VKP(B) v Rezolyutsiyakh* (1941), i, 594–596.

The promulgation of the " Face to the countryside " slogan in the summer of 1924 brought no immediate change in this respect. Party orthodoxy still resisted dilution of the " workers' party " with peasant elements. The resolution of the central committee of October 1924 merely recommended in general terms " the continuous transfer of communists to the country " and " the training and promotion of party workers from among the peasantry itself ", and proposed that " access to Komsomol organizations, as distinct from the party, should be opened on a broad basis not only to *batraks* and poor peasant strata in the countryside, but to the better and more conscious sector of the middle peasants ".[1] The recommendation to admit more peasants to the Komsomol read like a compromise between those who wished to admit more peasants to the party and those who did not wish to admit more peasants at all.

This was not, however, the end of the matter. After the central committee had adjourned more positive counsels prevailed ; and on November 6, 1924, a cautious instruction to admit more peasants to the party issued from the secretariat to rural party organizations. Peasants showing signs of political consciousness were to be directed into Soviet work ; and " the best and most outstanding elements, the nearest to the party and the most devoted to the Soviet power ", were to be admitted to the party. No quotas of numbers to be admitted in individual provinces or counties were to be fixed in advance. The work of recruitment would be carried on " not in the form of a campaign, but in the course of daily routine ".[2] Notwithstanding its guarded tone, the results of this instruction soon became apparent. In 1924, of 316,000 newly admitted candidates only 11·1 per cent were peasants (and nearly all of these were admitted in the second half

---

[1] *Ibid.* i, 631-633.

[2] The circular was printed in a truncated form (accidentally omitting the last three paragraphs and Molotov's signature) in *Izvestiya Tsentral'nogo Komiteta Rossiiskoi Kommunisticheskoi Partii (Bol'shevikov)*, No. 7 (12), November 17, 1924, p. 7, and reprinted in full, *ibid.* No. 8 (13), November 24, 1924, p. 7. In both cases it was printed in small type in the part of the gazette usually reserved for documents of secondary importance ; the instruction was phrased in such a way as to minimize its novelty and importance. It was admitted later that up to the middle of November 1924 the party attitude to the admission of peasants had been " very indecisive ", and that this was a " turning-point " (*ibid.* No. 15-16 (90-91), April 21, 1925, p. 8).

of the year) ; of 321,000 similarly admitted in 1925 29·5 per cent were peasants.[1] This admission was sometimes referred to in later party literature as " the second Lenin enrolment ", though the term does not appear to have been applied to it at the time.[2]

The attempt to strengthen the influence of the party in the countryside by increasing its peasant component had perhaps less substance than the statistics suggested. The official statistics of party membership for these years show that, while the Lenin enrolment of 1924 was successful in substantially increasing the proportion of workers in the party at the expense of the third category (employees and intellectuals), the increase in peasant membership as the result of the enrolment of the following year was scarcely sufficient to keep pace with the increase in total membership, so that the proportion of peasants in the party remained stable or even declined slightly. The following percentages of party membership are given for the beginnings of the years named : [3]

	Workers	Peasants	Others
1924	44·0	28·8	27·2
1925	56·7	26·5	16·8
1926	56·8	25·9	17·3

But such figures are less informative than they appear about the social composition of the party, partly because the classification

[1] A. Bubnov, *VKP(B)* (1931), p. 616 ; a more detailed analysis showed that of candidates admitted in the first half of 1925 62·4 per cent were workers, 22·5 per cent peasants and 15·1 per cent officials ; in the second half of 1925 the corresponding percentages were 43·8, 39·6 and 16·6 (*Bol'shevik*, No. 12, June 30, 1926, p. 64).

[2] The term was applied in a leading article in *Leningradskaya Pravda*, February 19, 1925, to an intensified enrolment of candidates in the first weeks of 1925 without special reference to peasants ; Molotov referred to " the revitalization of the Soviets " as " a continuation of the Lenin enrolment ", but only as the next task of party policy (*Chetyrnadtsataya Konferentsiya Rossiiskoi Kommunisticheskoi Partii (Bol'shevikov)* (1925), p. 10).

[3] A. Bubnov, *VKP(B)* (1931), p. 615. The failure of the high proportion of peasant " candidates " admitted in 1925 to reflect itself in later statistics suggests that an unusually high proportion of them failed to stay the course ; the percentage of peasants among candidates continued to be higher than among full members (*Sotsial'nyi i Natsional'nyi Sostav VKP(B)* (1928), p. 44).

reflected origin and not present status,[1] and partly because, owing
to the increasing importance of the party's rôle in administration,
a large number of those admitted as workers or peasants soon
found themselves engaged in whole-time or part-time administrative work, and more or less quickly lost their worker or peasant
affiliations. According to a report submitted to the fourteenth
party conference in April 1925, the majority of peasant members
of the party had " entirely or to some extent broken with the
peasant economy ", so that, in spite of an official peasant membership amounting to 25 per cent, only 8 per cent of the party
membership consisted of persons living exclusively by agriculture.[2]
Molotov complained at the fourteenth party congress of December
1925 that " those who enter the party under the rubric of peasants
are very often not peasant elements at all, but sometimes that very
official group which is seeking to ease its way into the party ".[3]
When, on the basis of the party census of January 1927, an
attempt was made to classify party members and candidates
according to present occupation, it was found that 30 per cent of
them were at that time employed as workers, 10·1 per cent as
peasants, 38·5 per cent as officials, 8·1 per cent in the Red Army
and the rest in other categories.[4] What occurred during these
years among party members and candidates was " an exodus from
the working class and — in lesser degree — from the peasantry
into the state apparatus, into economic, trade union, social and
other work ". Of 638,000 members and candidates registered as
workers, and of 217,000 registered as peasants, 184,000 and

---

[1] For the rules of classification see Vol. 1, pp. 91-92. The rules stipulating
different conditions of admission for different categories provided a new motive
for fictitious registrations. When, as a sequel to the All-Union Congress of
Teachers in January 1925 (see Vol. 1, p. 121), the Orgburo directed that from
2,000 to 3,000 village teachers should be admitted to the party (*Spravochnik
Partiinogo Rabotnika*, v, 1925 (1926), p. 243), an instruction from the party
central committee laid it down that teachers " who come from the peasants
and have not lost touch with the peasant environment " should be treated as
second category party candidates (peasants), not third category candidates
(employees) (*Izvestiya Tsentral'nogo Komiteta Rossiiskoi Kommunisticheskoi
Partii (Bol'shevikov)*, No. 8 (83), February 23, 1925, p. 5).

[2] *Ibid.* No. 15-16 (90-91), April 21, 1925, p. 6 ; Molotov stated at the
conference that two-thirds of the rural members of the party were employees
(*Chetyrnadtsataya Konferentsiya Rossiiskoi Kommunisticheskoi Partii (Bol'-
shevikov)* (1925), p. 21).

[3] *XIV S"ezd Vsesoyuznoi Kommunisticheskoi Partii (B)* (1926), p. 76.

[4] *Sotsial'nyi i Natsional'nyi Sostav VKP(B)* (1928), p. 42.

56,000 respectively were now employed as " officials or social workers ". While only 258,000 party members and candidates were registered as officials, 440,000 were actually employed as such.[1] These figures certainly did not exaggerate the extent to which party members officially registered as workers and peasants were in fact otherwise engaged.

Light was thrown on changing attitudes towards the composition of the party in these years by periodical amendments to the regulations governing admission to it. Under the party statute of December 1919 (the first to be adopted after the revolution), persons were admitted as candidates on the recommendation of two party members of not less than six months' standing ; workers and peasants were required to pass through a probationary period of two months, and others of six months, as candidates before admission to the party itself.[2] These relatively easy conditions, characteristic of the civil war period, were considerably tightened up after the introduction of NEP. On the eve of the eleventh party congress in March 1922 Zinoviev sponsored a proposal that the candidate stage should be prolonged for workers and peasants to six months, and for others to a year.[3] This provoked a sharp reaction from Lenin, who sent to the central committee a counter-proposal that the six months' stage should be limited to genuine workers who had worked for at least ten years in " large industrial enterprises ", and that the stage should be extended to one and a half years for other workers, two years for peasants and Red Army men, and three years for others.[4] The central committee was evidently reluctant to make this marked discrimination and, in a decision of March 25, 1922, taken in Lenin's absence, compromised on six months for workers, a year for Red Army men, and a year and a half for peasants and others.[5] Even this did not satisfy the pertinacious leader who insisted that the party was " insufficiently proletarian ", and demanded once more a lengthening of all stages except for workers.[6]

Thus goaded, the eleventh party congress, meeting a few days later, drew up elaborate rules for admission to the party. It

[1] *Sotsial'nyi i Natsional'nyi Sostav VKP(B)* (1928), pp. 45, 47.
[2] *VKP(B) v Rezolyutsiyakh* (1941), i, 318.
[3] *Pravda*, March 17, 1922.   [4] Lenin, *Sochineniya*, xxvii, 209-210.
[5] Quoted *ibid*. xxvii, 528-529.   [6] *Ibid*. xxvii, 211-212.

established three categories : workers and Red Army men, peasants and handicraft workers, and " others (employees etc.) ". Persons belonging to the first two categories were admitted as candidates on the recommendation of three party members of three years' standing ; persons in the third category required the recommendation of five party members of five years' standing. The probationary period was six months for the first category, one year for the second, and two years for the third ; a two-year stage was required for all candidates who had come over from other parties.[1] These rules were embodied in the new party statutes approved in August 1922.[2] But they were soon subject to further revision. The twelfth party congress in April 1923 recognized, for the first time, a specially favoured category of " workers from the bench " ; these might be admitted as candidates on the recommendation of only two party members of two years' standing ; [3] and this concession was followed by the Lenin enrolment of workers from the bench in the first months of 1924. Then, in April 1925, when the party had executed its turn towards the peasant, the same concession was extended to " *batraks*, peasant-cultivators and Red Army men " ; and the rider was added that, when peasants and *batraks* desiring to enter the party were unable to find party members to recommend them, the local party organs should help to provide the necessary credentials.[4] A party instruction was issued to temper the rigours of party discipline for " peasants from the plough ". Too high a standard of political instruction was not to be demanded of them ; and exception was not to be taken to the retention of personal property (presumably livestock and implements) or even to occasional participation in religious rites.[5] Finally, when a revised statute was approved by the fourteenth party congress, the special emphasis on the peasant had receded, and further refinements were introduced in respect of the number and character of the recommendations required for admission of candidates. The first category was split into two groups — " industrial workers regularly occupied in physical labour for wages " (two party members of one year's standing) and non-industrial workers, Red Army men and *batraks* (two

---

[1] *VKP(B) v Rezolyutsiyakh* (1941), i, 432.   [2] *Ibid.* i, 454.
[3] *Ibid.* i, 503.   [4] *Ibid.* ii, 12.
[5] *Spravochnik Partiinogo Rabotnika*, v, 1925 (1926), 512-514.

party members of two years' standing). The second category required recommendations from three party members of two years' standing, the third category from five of five years' standing. Further special conditions were imposed on candidates coming from other parties.[1] By a special dispensation of the central committee which found no place in the statute, " admission without going through the candidate stage is allowed only in exceptional cases which have political significance for the party ".[2] This was a hint that promotion to party status was still a reward which might be bestowed for exceptional services. From this welter of regulations, however, two points clearly emerged. In the first place, now that the net of recruitment was more widely spread, the intellectual level of the party had declined. Secondly, the heterogeneous composition of the party encouraged and necessitated the exercise of a strong authority from the centre : the unity of the party was assured no longer by the spontaneously generated sense of a common purpose, but by the firm leadership of the presiding group.

(b) Party Education

Of the problems resulting from the large and miscellaneous enrolment of new members in the middle nineteen-twenties, the declining intellectual calibre of the party was the most constant theme of preoccupation among the leaders. During the first two years of the régime little systematic control had been exercised over the qualifications of those seeking entrance into the party. But scarcely was the civil war over when, at the party conference of December 1919, Bukharin submitted a report on work among the new party members which was duly approved by the conference. Bukharin refused to admit that the new members differed in *quality* from the old, but stressed the importance of teaching " illiterate communists " their letters and of setting up " funda-

---

[1] For the revised statute see p. 148 above. For a detailed analysis of the changes in the rules of admission see *Bol'shevik*, No. 23-24, December 30, 1925, pp. 53-58 ; the main provisions had been drafted by the Orgburo in the spring of 1925 before the fourteenth party conference (*Izvestiya Tsentral'nogo Komiteta Rossiiskoi Kommunisticheskoi Partii* (*Bol'shevikov*), No. 9 (84), March 2, 1925, p. 8).

[2] *Ibid.* No. 16-17 (137-138), May 3, 1926, p. 5.

mental and elementary lectures " for them on communism and on the party.[1] For the next few years the issue was raised at every party congress. At the ninth congress in March 1920, Kamenev spoke of the difficulty of coping with the influx of new members, and another delegate said that the party was " basically unprepared " to carry out the necessary education of the peasants who had been admitted to it.[2] Preobrazhensky, at the tenth congress a year later, spoke of " the immense gap between comrades in our party who have not sufficient communist education and old communists who have possessed this Marxist baggage from remote times ", and between " the communistically mature element " and young party members who " have not the patience to read *Capital* and other fundamental works ", while Ryazanov lamented that " the percentage of comrades who have had a fundamental Marxist schooling grows smaller every day ".[3] At the eleventh party congress in March 1922, Zinoviev declared that, as the result of " the rapid, dizzy growth of our party from 5000 to 500,000 members ", the party contained " many illiterate members ", and proposed to halt further admissions in order to raise the standard.[4] The congress resolution, while it did not endorse this extreme solution, registered the shortcomings of the existing situation :

> In the next year or years the RKP must unconditionally devote its attention not so much to an increase in the number of its members as to an improvement in its qualitative composition. . . . The stormy years of civil war did not allow of sufficient attention and sufficient resources being devoted to raising the standard of Marxist education and the cultural level of rank-and-file members of the party. The next years must be consecrated to this task of first-class importance.[5]

A year later the twelfth congress repeated that " a strengthening of the work of party education among the mass of party members is in the present conjunction of circumstances a task of first-class importance ".[6] Active efforts were made. But successive waves of

[1] *VKP(B) v Rezolyutsiyakh* (1941), i, 323-324.
[2] *Devyatyi S"ezd RKP(B)* (1934), pp. 324, 355.
[3] *Desyatyi S"ezd Rossiiskoi Kommunisticheskoi Partii* (1921), pp. 61, 66.
[4] *Odinnadtsatyi S"ezd RKP(B)* (1936), pp. 424-425.
[5] *VKP(B) v Rezolyutsiyakh* (1941), i, 431.   [6] *Ibid.* i, 504.

G*

fresh admissions seemed to stultify them. When the thirteenth party congress met in May 1924, the Lenin enrolment was in full swing. From a sample taken in the central provinces of the RSFSR, Stalin put the average proportion of " political illiterates " in the party at 57 per cent ; in some provinces it reached 70 per cent.[1] Molotov, admitting that the influx of new members made " party educational work " specially important, drew attention to the embarrassing fact that 41 per cent of responsible workers in party central organs engaged in this work were themselves former members of other parties : [2] too many new members and too few reliable teachers created an insoluble problem. The congress was content to conclude that " work with the Lenin enrolment must in the near future take precedence in the educational work of the party ".[3] At the fourteenth congress a year and a half later, Stalin claimed in general terms that " the ideological level of our leading cadres, young and old, has risen substantially ".[4] But Molotov's pronouncement on the subject was more cautious ; and Ryazanov maintained that, while " a certain level of elementary party literacy has reached such masses as we had never hitherto dreamed of ", the qualitative level of party education as a whole had " declined fearfully ".[5] A party journalist at the same date observed, with special reference to the enrolment of peasants, that " raw material not yet sufficiently ' worked up ' from the party standpoint is being admitted to the party ".[6]

It was in these conditions that " political education " became a primary function of party policy. Institutions for education in the principles of communism and of party doctrine — institutions for educating the masses and institutions for educating the educators — proliferated at every level. The highest such institution was the Communist Academy. Founded in 1918 (before

---

[1] Stalin, *Sochineniya*, vi, 205-206 ; a few weeks later Stalin put the proportion on the eve of the Lenin enrolment at 60 per cent, and feared that it would now rise to 80 per cent (*ibid.* vi, 255-256). Komsomol figures of the same period classified 66·6 per cent of members as " politically illiterate ", 24·6 per cent as " politically partly literate ", and only 8·8 per cent as " politically literate " (A. Shokhin, *Kratkaya Istoriya VLKSM* (2nd ed. 1928), p. 112).
[2] *Trinadtsatyi S"ezd Rossiiskoi Kommunisticheskoi Partii (Bol'shevikov)* (1924), p. 535.   [3] *VKP(B) v Rezolyutsiyakh* (1941), i, 573.
[4] Stalin, *Sochineniya*, vii, 348.
[5] *XIV S"ezd Vsesoyuznoi Kommunisticheskoi Partii (B)* (1926), pp. 82, 691.
[6] *Bol'shevik*, No. 23-24, December 30, 1925, p. 45.

the party had changed its name) as the Socialist Academy and reorganized in 1919, it purported from the first to have duties of teaching as well as of research.[1] But it seems to have remained inactive till the tenth party congress in March 1921 proposed not only to utilize the " scientific resources " of the academy in order to organize courses by " responsible old party workers " for " groups of young communist auditors ", but also to establish at the academy " systematic courses in the theory, history and practice of Marxism ".[2] The courses were organized with an initial enrolment of 48 — all party members of three or four years' standing, not over 26 years of age and with experience of party work.[3] In the following year it was decided that 40 per cent of the enrolment (as against 25 per cent in the first year) should consist of workers.[4] Stalin is said to have undertaken to conduct the seminar on Leninism for these courses in 1924.[5] But there appears to be no evidence that he did so.

Next in the hierarchy of party institutions of higher education (komvuzy) came the Sverdlov University, which was founded in 1919 under the title " Workers' and Peasants' Communist University named for Y. Sverdlov " on the basis of short courses for propagandists organized by the party in the previous year.[6] The Sverdlov University became the most important institution for the training of the higher party workers. Bukharin spoke at the first graduation ceremony in 1923 :

> For the first time we are getting a group of officials educated in Marxism, devoted to the party, knowledgeable and capable

---

[1] For its early history see *Vestnik Sotsialisticheskoi Akademii*, i (1922), 13-39 ; the decree of 1919 (*Sobranie Uzakonenii*, 1919, No. 12, art. 123) defined its task as " the preparation of scientific workers in socialism and responsible workers in socialist construction ".

[2] *VKP(B) v Rezolyutsiyakh* (1941), i, 381.

[3] For the history of these courses see *Bol'shevik*, No. 21, November 15, 1931, pp. 78-83 ; Ryazanov was the first president. For the conditions of admission see *Spravochnik Partiinogo Rabotnika*, ii (1922), 96.

[4] *Izvestiya Tsentral'nogo Komiteta Rossiiskoi Kommunisticheskoi Partii (Bol'shevikov)*, No. 7 (43), 1922, p. 6.

[5] *Vestnik Kommunisticheskoi Akademii*, viii (1924), 379.

[6] For its early history see V. Nevsky, *Otchet Rabochego-Krest'yanskogo Kommunisticheskogo Universiteta imeni Sverdlova* (1920) ; its foundation was the result of a decision of the eighth party congress in March 1919 " to organize a higher party school attached to the central committee " (*VKP(B) v Rezolyutsiyakh* (1941), i, 305).

of action, who, spread all over the country, will carry on the task of building socialism.[1]

Stalin, who delivered his original lectures *The Foundations of Leninism* at the Sverdlov University in 1924, and paid a return visit in 1925 to answer questions from students there, called the Sverdlov University " one of the most powerful instruments in training the party's commanding personnel to lead the masses ".[2] The year 1921 saw the foundation by the party in Petrograd of the Zinoviev University, modelled on the Sverdlov University in Moscow ; [3] of the Communist University of Toilers of the East ; and of the Communist University of National Minorities of the West. Within the next three years communist universities had been established in Kharkov, Kazan, Tiflis, Tashkent and other centres making a total of 13 in all. The Sverdlov University and the Universities of the East and West had more than 1000 students each, the Zinoviev University more than 800 ; the others were smaller. The total number of students at these universities in the middle nineteen-twenties was about 6000.[4]

The principal embarrassment in the organization of these institutions was the provision of teaching staffs ; for, while by 1924 73 per cent of the students were members of the party, and 21 per cent of the Komsomol, leaving only 6 per cent of non-communists, 60 per cent of the teaching staff was non-party.[5] The Institute of Red Professors was founded in 1921 for the purpose of breaking the bourgeois monopoly of learning and training workers for teaching posts in higher educational institutions, Pokrovsky being the first president. The number of students was, however, small : the original decree contemplated a

[1] *Zapiski Kommunisticheskogo Universiteta im. Sverdlova* (1924), ii, 253.
[2] Stalin, *Sochineniya*, vii, 215-216.
[3] *Izvestiya Tsentral'nogo Komiteta Rossiiskoi Kommunisticheskoi Partii (Bol'shevikov)*, No. 33, October 1921, p. 17 ; after 1925 it became the Leningrad Communist University, and was later called the Stalin University.
[4] For these figures see *Kommunisticheskoe Prosveshchenie*, No. 3-4, 1924, pp. 58-61 ; *SSSR : God Raboty Pravitel'stva, 1924-25* (1926), pp. 649-650; *id. 1925-26* (1927), p. 524.
[5] *Kommunisticheskoe Prosveshchenie*, No. 3-4, 1924, p. 62 ; the Agitprop department of the party central committee, however, kept a list of all teachers at communist universities and controlled their appointment (*Izvestiya Tsentral'-nogo Komiteta Rossiiskoi Kommunisticheskoi Partii (Bol'shevikov)*, No. 11-12, November–December 1922, p. 19).

total of 200 in Moscow and 100 in Petrograd.[1] But the Petrograd part of the project was not carried out, and it was many years before this number was attained in Moscow. Most of the first students were young party intellectuals. Like other students, they sided with Trotsky in the party dispute of the winter of 1923–1924;[2] and the institute was subjected to a serious purge.[3] To prevent a recurrence of this error, an attempt was made to reduce the preponderance of intellectuals in the student body ; and from this time the proportion of workers admitted to the institute began to increase. But it now fell under the influence of Bukharin,[4] and suffered heavily at the time of his downfall. In the six years from 1924 to 1929 the graduates from the institute numbered only 236 in all ; and the effective output, owing to its involvement in these two deviations, was smaller still.[5] This seems to have been the least successful of all the party's efforts to secure a hold over the intellectual life of the country.

These institutions were all of a restricted character, and admission to them was carefully regulated both by intellectual and by party standards. The mass organs for higher political education and training were the so-called " Soviet-party schools ". The original conception was enunciated by a delegate at the sixth

---

[1] *Sobranie Uzakonenii, 1921*, No. 12, art. 79.

[2] For the attitude of the students see *The Interregnum, 1923–1924*, pp. 325-326.

[3] A confused and unconvincing account of this was given by Yaroslavsky to the central control commission in October 1924. He denied the allegation that 60 per cent of the students of the institute were oppositionists, but admitted that one-third were expelled : a high proportion of these were former " Zionists, Bundists, SRs or Mensheviks ". He added that the Moscow control commission had reinstated more than one-third of those expelled, and eventually 80 per cent of the remainder (*Pravda*, October 8, 1924). The students of the Marxism-Leninism courses at the Communist Academy, unlike those of the Institute of Red Professors, are said to have taken sides against Trotsky in 1923–1924, though some of them supported the Leningrad opposition in 1925 (*Bol'shevik*, No. 21, November 15, 1931, pp. 82-83).

[4] For Krupskaya's attack on it on this ground at the fourteenth party congress see p. 134 above.

[5] *Partiinoe Stroitel'stvo*, No. 2, 1930, p. 25. An unsatisfactory and perfunctory article in *Bol'shaya Sovetskaya Entsiklopediya*, xxxiv (1937), 600-601, on the Institutes of Red Professors, puts the annual figure of graduates between 1921 and 1929 at from 75 to 140, of whom 7 or 8 per cent were workers ; the total seems much too high. The title of the article refers to institutes in the plural, but no institutes appear to have existed outside Moscow before the nineteen-thirties.

party congress held in the summer of 1917 before the October revolution :

> It is necessary to make propagandists and agitators out of workers, who are the only active people, . . . for which purpose it is indispensable to organize party schools.[1]

At the height of the civil war, in March 1919, the eighth party congress instructed the central committee " to prepare a general programme and plan of studies in local party schools ".[2] Little had, however, been done when, a year later, the ninth party congress again resolved that " special attention should be paid to the further development of party schools (of the higher, lower and training types) for preparation for economic-administrative work ".[3] In August 1920, with the civil war almost over, it was decided to create " an all-Russian network of communist party-Soviet schools, first in the provincial, then in the county, capitals ".[4] Admission to these schools was dependent on the possession of minimum educational qualifications, but was not restricted to party members.[5] An elaborate system was worked out at a " first all-Russian conference of Soviet-party schools " in December 1921. Second-grade schools offering a nine-months course to prepare either for propaganda and instruction or for practical Soviet or party work were to be set up in the provincial capitals ; first-grade schools offering an elementary three-months course " to raise the political consciousness of the masses " were established in county capitals.[6] The system thus attempted to combine higher education for the training of officials or propagandists with general courses of political education. But the main emphasis of the Soviet-party schools continued to rest on the former. In 1922 a decision of the central committee fixed the number of second-grade courses at 53 with 9430 students and of first-grade courses at 150 with 10,825 students.[7] In 1923 the courses in the

---

[1] *Shestoi S"ezd RSDRP(B)* (1934), p. 183.
[2] *VKP(B) v Rezolyutsiyakh* (1941), i, 305.   [3] *Ibid.* i, 343.
[4] *Spravochnik Partiinogo Rabotnika*, [i] (1921), 58 ; for the detailed curriculum of these schools see *ibid.* [i], 59-63.
[5] *Ibid.* ii (1922), 33.   [6] *Ibid.* ii. 57-60.
[7] *Izvestiya Tsentral'nogo Komiteta Rossiiskoi Kommunisticheskoi Partii (Bol'shevikov)*, No. 4 (52), April 1923 , p. 51 ; one-half of those attending the second-grade schools, and one-third of those attending the first-grade schools, were party members (*ibid.* No. 3 (51), March 1923, p. 126). A claim at the eleventh

second-grade schools were extended to two years, and in the first-grade schools to one year.[1] At the twelfth party congress in that year Stalin described the communist universities and the Soviet-party schools as " the apparatus with the help of which the party develops communist education, and creates its commanding staff for education, which sows among the working population the seeds of socialism, the seeds of communism, and thus binds the party by ideological ties to the working class ".[2] The Soviet-party schools were the main medium through which workers were trained for party and Soviet work. In 1925 the conditions of admission to them were further tightened up by a provision that not more than 25 per cent of the students could be non-party, and that all these must be either " workers from the bench " or " peasants from the plough ".[3] On the other hand, doubts were sometimes expressed whether workers in fact made better propagandists than intellectuals. Some critics argued that " lack of theoretical learning in the end outweighs the positive, as it were ' natural ', qualities of the worker-propagandist ".[4]

While the main preoccupation of the party authorities appeared to be the political education of potential leaders, the aim of mass indoctrination was not ignored. Lenin had spoken in 1918 of the need " to re-educate the whole Russian people ".[5] And two years later he added :

party congress in March 1922 that 70 second-grade and 200 first-grade schools were in operation with a total of 30,000 students (*Odinnadtsatyi S"ezd RKP(B)* (1936), p. 380) seems to have been inflated ; according to *Kommunisticheskoe Prosveshchenie*, No. 2, 1922, pp. 35-36, 102, statistics included many students who failed to complete the courses. Totals of 21,553 for January 1, 1925, and 29,789 for January 1, 1926, were given in *SSSR : God Raboty Pravitel'stva, 1924-25* (1926), pp. 649-650 ; *id. 1925-26* (1927), p. 524. Bukharin's *Teoriya Istoricheskogo Materializma* (1922) was written as a text-book for Soviet-party schools (*Izvestiya Tsentral'nogo Komiteta Rossiiskoi Kommunisticheskoi Partii (Bol'shevikov)*, No. 3 (39), March 1922, p. 7).

[1] *Kommunisticheskoe Prosveshchenie*, No. 4-5, 1923, pp. 231-232.
[2] Stalin, *Sochineniya*, v, 203.
[3] *Spravochnik Partiinogo Rabotnika*, v, 1925 (1926), pp. 322-323.
[4] *Kommunisticheskoe Prosveshchenie*, No. 2, 1927, pp. 36-38.
[5] Lenin, *Sochineniya* (1st ed.), xv, 415 ; the version of Lenin's speech to an all-Russian congress on popular education from which this quotation is taken originally appeared in *Pravda*, August 30, 1918, and is described as " a summary newspaper report ". Later editions of Lenin's works (2nd ed., xxiii, 197-199 ; 4th ed., xxviii, 66-69) contained a widely different, though equally brief, report of the speech, said to be taken from protocols of the congress published in 1919.

We must re-educate the masses, and only propaganda and agitation can re-educate them.[1]

Here, however, a paradox quickly revealed itself. Before the revolution, the party had been constantly hailed as the vanguard of the proletariat ; it was the party which would lead and instruct the masses. Now, after the victory of the revolution, and with the progressive expansion of the party, the vanguard was formed not by the party as a whole, but by a group within the party, which was to lead and instruct the mass party membership and at the same time the masses which still remained outside the party. The distinction between leaders and led, between vanguard and masses, no longer corresponded to the distinction between party and non-party. As time went on, the mass of the party and the non-party masses might even seem to have more in common with one another than the mass of the party with the party *élite*. The attempt to build a socialist order in a society predominantly primitive and backward was taking another of its revenges on orthodox party doctrine.

The confusion had its repercussions on organization. In November 1920 a department of Narkompros was set up by a decree of VTsIK under the name of the Chief Committee for Political Education (Glavpolitprosvet) with subordinate sections (Politprosvety) in the provinces. Krupskaya was its president ; and its functions included the running of libraries and adult schools, the combating of illiteracy and in general the spread of political enlightenment in the population.[2] But what were the relations of Glavpolitprosvet, which was a state organ, to the Agitprop section of the party central committee, which was concerned with the dissemination of political knowledge in the name of the party ? This question provoked an animated debate at the tenth party congress in March 1921.[3] The resolution of the congress offered a picture of intertwined functions and organizations, which was an early example of the impracticability of drawing a sharp frontier between party and state, between party

[1] Lenin, *Sochineniya*, xxv, 455-456.
[2] The decree of VTsIK is quoted in *Kommunisticheskoe Prosveshchenie*, No. 1, 1920, p. 49.
[3] *Desyatyi S"ezd Rossiiskoi Kommunisticheskoi Partii* (1921), pp. 54-75 ; the remarks of Preobrazhensky and Ryazanov have already been quoted (see p. 185 above).

and non-party. It was admitted that " the centre of gravity of the work of Glavpolitprosvet " lay in " work among the non-party masses " ; and that the centre of gravity of the work of Agitprop lay in " work within the party in raising the conscious-ness of its members and promoting their communist education ". But the functions of the party organs included " leadership of the corresponding organs of the Politprosvety " ; and the organs of Glavpolitprosvet were to be equally available for work among party members. Indeed, the Soviet-party schools, which were primarily intended for the training of party leaders, the schools of *politgramota* which were designed to impart the elements of party doctrine to candidates and new members, and even the communist universities, were financed through the funds of Glavpolitprosvet ; and though this may have been a matter of budgetary convenience rather than of principle, it showed how slender was the line between state and party organs of political education.[1] A year later the eleventh party congress referred to the frictions which had evidently occurred in carrying out this ambiguous resolution, and advocated " a personal union in the leading posts of the agitprop sections and the politprosvety ".[2] How far this solution was realized, remains uncertain. But there is no reason to doubt that the customary principle of the acceptance by state organs of party directions applied in full to the organiza-tions of mass propaganda.

By the middle nineteen-twenties, the more advanced provinces of the USSR (little evidence is available for the more backward regions) were covered with a network of institutions for propa-ganda among the masses. It is significant that few, if any, of these were restricted to party or to non-party people ; to almost all both categories seem to have been admitted. When the *polit-gramota* schools were first established in 1921, their purpose was defined in terms which made no mention of party membership :

> The aim of the *politgramota* campaign is to draw broad masses of workers and peasants into socialist construction by

[1] *VKP(B) v Rezolyutsiyakh* (1941), i, 379-380 ; for the financing of the *politgramota* schools and the communist universities see also *Izvestiya Tsentral'-nogo Komiteta Rossiiskoi Kommunisticheskoi Partii (Bol'shevikov)*, No. 8 (45), September 1922, p. 21 ; No. 11-12 (47-48), November–December 1922, p. 19.

[2] *VKP(B) v Rezolyutsiyakh* (1941), i, 448.

spreading elementary political knowledge, which enables the masses to realize the meaning and significance of the communist revolution and to understand current political events.[1]

Later the *politgramota* schools served primarily to provide instruction for new entrants into the party. An order of the party central committee of January 1924 " On the Liquidation of Political Illiteracy among Members of the RKP " was directed primarily to the strengthening of these schools ; special short-course schools were set up in 1924 to cope with the Lenin enrolment.[2] The Soviet-party schools were for higher education and training. But in 1925 evening Soviet-party schools with short courses were set up ; [3] these appear to have been mass propaganda schools, and the limitation on the percentage of non-party students [4] presumably did not apply. Workers' clubs, according to a resolution of the twelfth party congress in 1923, were to be " converted into real centres for mass propaganda and for the development of the creative capacities of the working class ".[5] Study groups for Marxism-Leninism were popular in towns and factories : they were under party control, but it is not clear how far they were restricted to party members. Travelling *politgramota* schools for the villages made their first appearance in 1925 when the " Face to the countryside " campaign was at its height.[6]

The division in the party between an *élite* leadership which instructed and directed and a mass membership which received instruction and direction was by far the most important consequence of the rapid expansion in the numbers of the party.

[1] *Kommunisticheskoe Prosveshchenie*, No. 1, 1922, pp. 107-108.
[2] *Spravochnik Partiinogo Rabotnika*, iv (1924), 152-154.
[3] *Ibid.* v, 1925 (1926), pp. 325-326.   [4] See p. 191 above.
[5] *VKP(B) v Rezolyutsiyakh* (1941), i, 506.
[6] The following table gives the number of students in institutions of mass political education for two years :

	1924–1925	1925–1926
Short-term *politgramota* schools	339,680	200,000
Ordinary *politgramota* schools	125,940	185,340
Evening Soviet-party schools	1,000	9,000
Study groups for Marxism-Leninism	63,500	53,000
Privately organized study groups	—	95,000

In addition, 1645 travelling *politgramota* schools are recorded for 1925–1926 (*Kommunisticheskoe Prosveshchenie*, No. 2, 1927, pp. 31-32).

The same phenomenon was discernible in the workers' parties of western countries, and indeed in all political parties. But it appeared in an exaggerated form where the mass of workers lived at so primitive an economic level, and was politically so backward and untrained, as in Russia. When the need to instruct and indoctrinate members in the aims of the party became a main preoccupation of the leaders, the character of the party changed in the same way as the character of the Soviet trade unions was changing under the influence of the same need.[1] No doubt other factors, especially those arising from the close identification of the party with the state, also helped to determine the evolution of the Russian Communist Party. In the civil war, a party congress could still enunciate the time-honoured doctrine that party members " have no privileges over other workers, they have only higher obligations ".[2] In the reaction which set in with NEP, the burdens of party membership began to seem anomalous and intolerable ;[3] and, apart from the shrinkage due to the purge, a voluntary exodus occurred from the party.[4] From the time of the Lenin enrolment of 1924 this attitude was reversed. The view of the party as a source of higher privilege rather than of higher obligation was firmly implanted ;[5] and, since equality of privilege is a concept always more difficult to realize than equality of obligation, the sense of the party as a privileged institution insensibly led to an extension of privilege within the party. Not only did party members as such feel themselves entitled to a privileged position in the community at large, but the party élite began to distinguish itself in the same way from the rank and file of the party. From 1923 onwards warnings constantly appeared

[1] See Vol. 1, p. 411.
[2] VKP(B) v Rezolyutsiyakh (1941), i, 343.
[3] Many examples of this attitude appeared in a discussion recorded in L. Trotsky, Voprosy Byta (2nd ed. 1923), pp. 112-113, 115, 121, 125. The party member was subject to direction to a job by the party authorities, while the non-party man was free to choose for himself. The party member had no time to spare for his family : even his wife was expected to "work like a horse " and was under pressure not to let down the prestige of her husband as a party man. Nobody wanted to marry a party woman, who would neglect her husband and family for the party.
[4] This was said to have amounted in 1922 to 10 per cent of the membership in some places (Izvestiya Tsentral'nogo Komiteta Rossiiskoi Kommunisticheskoi Partii (Bol'shevikov), No. 11-12, 1922, p. 30).
[5] See The Interregnum, 1923-1924, pp. 355-356.

against the personal enrichment of party members.[1] Such abuses occur, however, in any institution, and were not peculiar to the Russian Communist Party. The basic determining factors in its evolution were, first of all, the rapid and overwhelming rise in its numbers and, secondly, the relatively low political and intellectual calibre of the new recruits, which made instruction and indoctrination from above an imperative necessity. The increasing size, and declining quality, of the rank-and-file membership were the foundations on which the power of the central party machine insensibly grew into a vast, monolithic dictatorship.

(c) The Party Machine

The growing size and changing composition of the party provided an impregnable argument for stricter party discipline. Mere increase in the numbers of party members automatically strengthened the authority of the central organs. Concentration of power at the centre everywhere distinguishes modern mass parties from the small élite parties of the past ; and, within the central authority, the elected organ meeting periodically tends to lose power to the permanent bureaucratic machine staffed by appointment. The party central committee elected by the eighth party congress of 1919, which created the Politburo and the Orgburo, consisted of 19 members and 8 candidates. When Stalin became general secretary in April 1922, the central committee consisted of 27 members and 19 candidates ; and the Politburo, the Orgburo and the secretariat [2] were now already well on the way to displace the party central committee as the effective organs of power. Thereafter its numbers swelled continuously, rising to 40 members and 17 candidates in 1923, 53 members and 34 candidates in 1924, and 63 members and 43 candidates at the fourteenth party congress in December 1925. Its representative character could also be said to have increased. In the early days, when the central committee was a small group directing the affairs of the party, it never contained more than one or two workers. At the fourteenth party congress Molotov was able to boast that the existing central committee already contained 53 per

---

[1] See, for example, *Spravochnik Partiinogo Rabotnika*, iv (1924), 115.
[2] See *The Bolshevik Revolution, 1917–1923*, Vol. 1, pp. 193-195.

cent of workers.[1] But this rise in numbers and in representative
quality was accompanied by an atrophy of power. Lenin in one
of his last articles noted that the party central committee was in
process of developing into a " supreme party conference " meeting
once in two months, and leaving the transaction of current business
to the Politburo, Orgburo and secretariat : he agreed that this
development should be accepted and standardized.[2] Stalin's
efficiency, Stalin's ambition and Stalin's ruthlessness were scarcely
required to complete the process. The only issue still outstanding
was the distribution of power between the three ostensibly subordinate organs, or rather — since the Orgburo quickly became
little more than a presidium of the secretariat[3] — between the
secretariat and the Politburo.

Stalin began cautiously with a memorandum of " proposals of
the secretariat for a division of functions " among the organs of
the central committee, which was discussed by the central committee at the end of January 1923. The memorandum proposed
an increase in the numbers of the central committee to 50 (Lenin's
" testament " of December 25, 1922, which contained a similar
proposal, may already have been known at this time), and an
increase in the numbers of both the Politburo and the Orgburo
from five to seven, with four " candidates ". It is difficult not to
see in this scheme a calculated weakening of the effectiveness of
all these organs *vis-à-vis* the secretariat, which alone retained its
existing form intact. Stalin had, however, discovered a new and
ingenious tactical device : to weaken the Politburo by professing
to exalt the authority of the central committee. The draft placed
on the Politburo the obligation to submit " substantially important
political proposals " to the central committee ; and it was
specifically noted that this " diminishes the rights of the Politburo
in favour of the plenum of the central committee ", though whether
it was calculated to have this result in practice is another matter.
Most significant of all was the definition of the powers of the

---

[1] *XIV S"ezd Vsesoyuznoi Kommunisticheskoi Partii (B)* (1926), p. 81.
[2] Lenin, *Sochineniya*, xxvii, 402-403.
[3] Lenin, who regarded " the distribution of party forces " as the chief
function of the Orgburo, expected this body to be subordinate to the Politburo,
since organizational questions could not be independent of politics : this view,
first expressed in 1920 and repeated in April 1922 (Lenin, *Sochineniya*, xxv,
94, 112-113 ; xxvii, 264), overlooked the secretariat altogether.

secretariat. The secretariat was entitled to make appointments to all party posts " not higher than the provincial level ", that is to say, to posts up to and including that of secretary of a provincial party committee ; such decisions were to take effect unless protested within 48 hours by a member of the Politburo. Appointments to party posts at higher levels were to be submitted to the Orgburo. Decisions of the Orgburo were subject to protest by a member of the Politburo. Such protests had the effect of suspending the execution of the decision, whereas protests by members of the central committee against decisions of the Politburo had no such suspensory effect.[1]

Available records do not reveal the precise fate of these proposals. At this stage Trotsky appears to have been the strongest defender of the prerogatives of the Politburo against the encroachments of the secretariat ;[2] and this fact doubtless helped to keep the other members of the triumvirate faithful to Stalin. At the twelfth party congress in April 1923 Stalin again appeared as the defender of the rights of the central committee against the encroachments of the Politburo, and earned the praise of Osinsky, who made a strong attack on Zinoviev.[3] The resolution of the congress included Stalin's recommendation that important proposals of the Politburo should in future be brought before the central committee. It also raised the membership of the party central committee to 40, with from 15 to 20 candidates having the right to be present at meetings, though not to vote, and increased the numbers of the Politburo and Orgburo in accordance with the proposals of the Stalin memorandum.[4] What happened to the proposals defining the authority of the secretariat to make party appointments is not clear. Once more the secretariat profited from the general belief in its unimportance. The functions of the secretariat were a routine matter not worthy of discussion by a party congress. But in the summer of 1923 Zinoviev became

[1] The document is in the Trotsky archives with annotations made by Trotsky during the discussion on January 29, 1923 ; one of the notes reads: " Nothing to be confirmed today ".

[2] See Trotsky's memorandum to the central committee of February 22, 1923, in the Trotsky archives.

[3] Stalin, *Sochineniya*, v, 227 ; *Dvenadtsatyi S"ezd Rossiiskoi Kommunisticheskoi Partii (Bol'shevikov)* (1923), p. 122. For Osinsky's attack on Zinoviev see *The Interregnum, 1923–1924*, p. 284.

[4] *VKP(B) v Rezolyutsiyakh* (1941), i, 501–502.

suspicious of the increasing power wielded by Stalin in his capacity as general secretary, and at the famous cave meeting at Kislovodsk put forward his scheme to " politicize " the secretariat by effectively subordinating it to the Politburo.[1] The initial outbreak of friction between Stalin and Zinoviev took the institutional form of a struggle between the secretariat, where Stalin was the undisputed master, and the Politburo, where Zinoviev had uneasily donned the mantle of Lenin. The attempt to curb Stalin's authority quickly proved, abortive. The crisis which began with the platform of the 46 in October 1923 and ended with the condemnation of Trotsky by the thirteenth party conference in January 1924 played into Stalin's hands ; and the dilution of the party ranks with the untried recruits of the Lenin enrolment strengthened the control of the central party machine over the new mass membership.[2] The last echoes of the struggle were heard at the fourteenth party congress in December 1925, when Zinoviev once again demanded " a Politburo with full powers, and a secretariat of functionaries subordinate to it ", and Molotov retorted that " a Politburo with full powers " meant, in the understanding of Zinoviev, a Politburo in which " comrades Zinoviev and Kamenev will be in a majority ".[3] The Politburo had eclipsed the central committee. The party machine operated from the secretariat now overshadowed the Politburo. The party succumbed to the masterful sway of the general secretary.

The rising power of the secretariat led to the emergence of a new and prominent feature in the party and Soviet landscape — the " apparatus " and the " apparatus-man ", the body of obscure and anonymous officials who were the cogs of the smoothly and, for the most part, silently working party machine. Few statements were made about the number of these party officials. It was stated that at the thirteenth party congress there had been one party worker for every 22 members and at the fourteenth congress one for every 40 ; assuming that the figures of party membership were the totals announced at the respective congresses (which included candidates), this meant 27,250 party workers in 1924, and

[1] See *The Interregnum, 1923–1924*, pp. 290-291.
[2] For the consequences of the Lenin enrolment see *ibid.* pp. 354-357.
[3] *XIV S"ezd Vsesoyuznoi Kommunisticheskoi Partii (B)* (1926), pp. 468, 484; for this exchange see p. 142 above.

25,600 at the end of 1925.[1] But the category of " party workers "
included all party members holding party appointments all over the
country ; only 767 were said to be employed in the office of the
central party committee at the time of the fourteenth congress.[2]

The growth of this apparatus marked, perhaps, the most important single difference between the régime of Lenin and the
régime of Stalin. It was the chief shortcoming of Lenin as a
statesman that he never really faced the problem of large-scale
administration in modern society. The improvisations of the
period of the seizure of power and of the civil war could pass as
temporary expedients : the most important of these improvisations, the creation out of former Tsarist officers of an officer corps
for the Red Army, was the work not of Lenin, but of Trotsky.
Lenin continued to believe that the solution lay, in the words
of the party programme of 1919, in " the simplification of the
functions of administration accompanied by a rise in the cultural
level of the workers " ;[3] and, if he came to realize that the rise of
the cultural level would be a slow process, he never recognized
the Utopian nature of the demand for a simplified administration.
When, after the victory in the civil war and the introduction of
NEP, practical problems of administration began to beset him,
Lenin had little contribution to offer to their solution except a
series of powerful warnings against the evils of bureaucracy in the
state and, in the last months of his life, in the party itself. But
once Stalin had taken over the secretariat, and the restraint of
Lenin and of the Lenin tradition had been removed, every inhibi-
tion disappeared. If Lenin had failed to see the inevitability of
bureaucracy, Stalin was equally blind to its dangers and to the
requirement of safeguards against them. The concluding chapter
of Stalin's *Foundations of Leninism*, originally published in May
1924, was entitled " Style in Work ", and called for a combination
of " Russian revolutionary enthusiasm " with " American practicality ".[4] But, though Stalin, with the help of copious supporting
quotations from Lenin, carefully maintained the balance between

---

[1] *XIV S"ezd Vsesoyuznoi Kommunisticheskoi Partii (B)* (1926), pp. 76, 81 ;
for the 1924 figure see Stalin, *Sochineniya*, vi, 201 (the calculation in the text is
based on the figure of 600,000 members on May 1, 1924).

[2] *Ibid.* p. 89.

[3] See *The Bolshevik Revolution, 1917–1923*, Vol. i, p. 248.

[4] Stalin, *Sochineniya*, vi, 186-188.

the qualities and defects of both elements, it became clear as time
went on that Stalin's " style in work " contained much that Lenin
might have denounced as bureaucracy.   It would, however, be
erroneous to treat this as a personal idiosyncrasy of Stalin.   Lenin's
constructive work was done at a time when revolutionary enthusiasm was still in the ascendant and was the primary need if
the régime was to survive.   Stalin was the product of a period
when stable and orderly administration, the mastery of a complicated machine of government, was the main requirement ; and,
given the weakness of the human material available, and the
survival of a primitive bureaucratic tradition, the imposition of
a rigid and oppressive conformity was the consequence.   If the
party no longer encouraged independence of thought, it provided
safe careers for those who would serve it faithfully and efficiently.
Stalin's " apparatus-men " were in this sense the very antithesis
of the intellectuals whose far-ranging thought had provided the
inspiration of the revolution.   A fundamental animosity and incompatibility of temper sharpened every clash between the party
leadership and successive oppositions.   Order and discipline, not
revolutionary enthusiasm, were now the prime virtues of a party
member and of a party official.   It was these virtues which the
secretariat of Stalin strove to inculcate.

The central machine exercised its power over the party in two
main ways : by the making of appointments which enabled it
silently and unostentatiously to reward its supporters and to
penalize the lukewarm and the hostile, and by the application of
direct measures of discipline to recalcitrants.   The second of
these methods was the more dramatic and attracted more notice :
it was on this practice that critics outside the Soviet Union concentrated their attacks.   But, in building up the enormous power
which came to be concentrated in the central party machine and in
the person of the general secretary, the virtually unlimited right
to make appointments to key positions probably played a larger
rôle.   These two decisive instruments of power both require some
examination.

(d) The Power of Appointment

The power of appointment in the hands of the central party
machine dated from the moment when the section of the central

committee (in practice, a section of the secretariat) in charge of the recording of qualifications and allocation of party personnel (Uchraspred by its short name), transferred its attention from the " mass mobilizations " of the period of the civil war and war communism to the individual appointments to special functions, especially in the economic sphere, characteristic of the NEP period.[1·] This course was confirmed when, shortly after Stalin's appearance in the secretariat in April 1922, a thirty-year-old party official named Kaganovich was placed at the head of Uchraspred.[2] The conspicuous feature of the first year of his tenure of office was a reduction by one-half in the number of party members receiving assignments through Uchraspred, partly owing to the decline in " mass mobilizations ", partly owing to a deliberate attempt to relieve the central machine of appointments to routine or subordinate work : of the 10,000 appointments made by Uchraspred between April 1922 and March 1923 nearly 5000 were to " responsible " posts.[3] The twelfth party congress of April 1923, after listening to Stalin's remarks on the importance of Uchraspred, passed the appropriate resolution :

> The congress instructs the central committee to take all measures to extend and strengthen the account and distribution organs of the party at the centre and in the localities, in order to embrace the whole mass of workers who are communists or sympathizers with communism in any and every sphere of administrative and economic work.[4]

The congress had given its approval to the building up of a powerful machine at the centre with local branches to exercise absolute control over appointments of party members and reliable supporters to " any and every " post in the party or govern-

---

[1] See The Bolshevik Revolution, 1917–1923, Vol. 1, p. 229. Krestinsky gave an account of the mass mobilizations of the past year to the tenth party congress in March 1921 (Desyatyi S"ezd Rossiiskoi Kommunisticheskoi Partii (1921), pp. 22-23); the new conception of individual appointments requiring special qualifications dated from a decision of December 1921 (Izvestiya Tsentral'nogo Komiteta Rossiiskoi Kommunisticheskoi Partii (Bol'shevikov), No. 1 (49), January 1923, pp. 11-14).

[2] For Kaganovich's career see Bol'shaya Sovetskaya Entsiklopediya, xxx (1937), 514-518.

[3] Izvestiya Tsentral'nogo Komiteta Rossiiskoi Kommunisticheskoi Partii (Bol'shevikov), No. 3 (51), March 1923, pp. 39-40.

[4] VKP(B) v Rezolyutsiyakh (1941), i, 504.

mental hierarchy. In the hands of outstanding organizers like Stalin and Kaganovich, the opportunity would not be missed. The congress marked its confidence in the new régime by electing Kaganovich a candidate member of the party central committee ; he became a full member in the following year.

The next few months were spent in creating a machine which would run smoothly. In July 1923 the party central committee, on the recommendation of Uchraspred, laid down a list of 3500 posts in state and economic organs appointments to which were to be made " through the central committee ", and of a further 1500 posts appointments to which, though made by the organs concerned, must be notified to Uchraspred. A similar classification, the details of which were not disclosed, was established for leading party posts ; and " a regulation was worked out by Uchraspred on the forms of agreement between the central committee and departmental and local party organs on nominations and removals of workers in local institutions ". Three months later " the distributory apparatus of the section was finally organized on the framework laid down in the July resolution of the secretariat ".[1] A decision of the Orgburo of October 12, 1923, established or confirmed a complete classification of posts, and defined the degree of authority required for the making or approving of different categories of appointment; it remained for more than two years the charter of the secretariat in the matter of state and party appointments.[2] A month later, on November 8, 1923, a resolution of the central committee approved these arrangements. It indicated that the most important appointments to be made in the near future were to posts in the economic organs, in the countryside and in the Red Army, and dwelt on the need for Uchraspred to study the individual qualifications of candidates for appointment ; an attempt was to be made to combine " selection carried out by the central committee and local party committees with promotion from below, from provincial and county

---

[1] *Izvestiya Tsentral'nogo Komiteta Rossiiskoi Kommunisticheskoi Partii (Bol'-shevikov)*, No. 9-10 (57-58), October–November 1923, p. 33; No. 4 (62), April 1924, pp. 40-42 ; at this time Uchraspred had a modest staff of 1 director, 3 deputies and 12 assistants (*ibid.* No. 7-8 (55-56), August–September, 1923, p. 24).

[2] The text of the decision does not appear to have been published : it was referred to in the resolution of the central committee of November 8, 1923 (see below).

party organizations ".[1] But the political crisis arising out of the platform of the 46 and the letters of Trotsky were inimical to any relaxation of central control. This was, indeed, delicately hinted at in the report of Uchraspred :

> The inner-party tasks that confronted the party after the November discussion introduced into this system of work of Uchraspred only supplementary and partial changes, especially by way of making more precise the agreement about transfers and recalls.[2]

The pattern was now established, and subsequent changes were of a formal character. In 1924 Uchraspred was amalgamated with the former organization section [3] under the name of Orgraspred ; this reorganization was confirmed by an order issued by the secretariat (it is perhaps significant that confirmation by the central committee seems no longer to have been required) on March 13, 1925.[4] The scope of the work of Uchraspred and Orgraspred is indicated by statistics of the appointments handled by them between 1922 and 1925 :

	Responsible Officials	Subordinate Officials	Total
From XI to XII Congress	4738	5613	10,351
From XII to XIII Congress	4569	1519	6,088
From XIII to XIV Congress	9419	2858	12,277

In each case, a small proportion of the totals was accounted for by a continuance of mass mobilizations, but the majority of the appointments were individual. The decline in the figures for

---

[1] *Izvestiya Tsentral'nogo Komiteta Rossiiskoi Kommunisticheskoi Partii (Bol'shevikov)*, No. 1 (59), January 1924, pp. 64-67 ; for " promotion " see Vol. 1, pp. 107-109.

[2] *Izvestiya Tsentral'nogo Komiteta Rossiiskoi Kommunisticheskoi Partii (Bol'shevikov)*, No. 4 (62), April 1924, p. 42.

[3] This section was originally called the " organization and instruction section " and handled " the relations of the central committee with local organizations " (*Ibid.* No. 3 (51), March 1923, p. 3); it was now split in two, one half being amalgamated with Uchraspred to form Orgraspred, the other forming a new " information section ".

[4] *K XIV S"ezdu RKP(B)* (1925), p. 1 ; *Izvestiya Tsentral'nogo Komiteta Rossiiskoi Kommunisticheskoi Partii (Bol'shevikov)*, No. 17-18 (92-93), May 11, 1925, pp. 7-8.

the middle period was due to the determination of the central machine to relieve itself of the growing burden of routine appointments.   Most of these were now left to the discretion of the organization concerned, though some may have come under local party controls.   The rise in the figures for the third period was due partly to the longer interval between the thirteenth and fourteenth party congresses (more than 18 months instead of a year), but also to the increasing number of important appointments in an expanding economic and political society.   Most of the appointments were to posts in economic organs, in the co-operatives, in the trade unions and in the Soviet administrative machine.   But the most significant figure of all showed that of the 9419 appointments to responsible posts made between May 1924 and December 1925, 1876 were to responsible posts in the party.   These were the officials who formed the key supports of the whole political structure.   It was ultimately through them that the " dictatorship of the proletariat " was exercised.[1]

Finally, in January 1926, the system was once more reviewed, and a new classification adopted for 5500 posts, nominations to which required the formal approval of the central committee.   In future, appointments to 1870 of these posts (category 1) would still be submitted for approval to the central committee, the Orgburo or the secretariat as a whole.   Appointments to 1640 posts (category 2) would require the sanction of one of the secretaries, and would be carried higher only in the event of dispute.   A new group of 1590 " elective posts ", presumably in party and Soviet organs, was created, appointments to which would be agreed with commissions set up *ad hoc* by the central committee : this special procedure· was a recognition of the delicacy of the problem of reconciling the overriding authority of the centre with the right of election by local organs.   At lower levels, outside these categories, local bodies. made their own appointments, subject, however, at each level to the authority of the regional, provincial or lower party committee, which was entitled to draw up categories of posts for which its consent to appointments was required.   A minor point of interest in the decision was insistence on a proper demarcation of functions between the party central committee and the Moscow provincial

[1] *K XIV S"ezdu RKP(B)* (1925), pp. 27-29.

party committee which had hitherto apparently been neglected.[1]

The commanding position of Orgraspred had not been attained without prolonged controversy in the party. In theory, all posts in the party were supposed to be filled by election; but this theory was difficult to reconcile with the acknowledged right of the party authorities to dispose of the services of party members in whatever way the interests of the party might require. In the early days, the power of the central machine was openly used to override or annul the results of election by the local party organization. As early as April 1920, even before the establishment of Uchraspred, the dissolution of a recalcitrant central committee of the Ukrainian party was achieved by a simple order of the central committee in Moscow transferring its members to work elsewhere.[2] A party conference in September 1920 recognized " the indispensability of nomination to elective offices in exceptional cases ", though it preferred " recommendation " to " nomination ", and added the significant rider that appointments should not be influenced " by considerations of any kind whatever, other than practical ones ", and that " repressions of any kind " on the ground of opinion were " inadmissible ".[3] In March 1921, at the tenth party congress, Krestinsky (then one of the three members of the secretariat and in charge of Uchraspred) spoke of an unspecified transfer of the previous August which had caused " surprise, dissatisfaction and suspicion whether there had not been repressive action, some punitive element ", though he did not actually admit that the suspicion was well founded.[4] During the following year, when Molotov had replaced Krestinsky as member of the secretariat in charge of Uchraspred, it became necessary to take " decisive and radical measures " against fractional activities in the Samara provincial party organization by removing " the whole upper group of party and Soviet workers ".[5] If such exhibitions of naked authority were

<hr>

[1] The text of the decision, with a commentary, is in *Izvestiya Tsentral'nogo Komiteta Vsesoyuznoi Kommunisticheskoi Partii (B)*, No. 1 (122), January 18, 1926, pp. 2-5.
[2] M. Ravich-Cherkassky, *Istoriya Kommunisticheskoi Partii (Bol'shevikov) Ukrainy* (1923), appendix 12.
[3] *VKP(B) v Rezolyutsiyakh* (1941), i, 351.
[4] *Desyatyi S"ezd Rossiiskoi Kommunisticheskoi Partii* (1921), p. 12.
[5] *Odinnadtsatyi S"ezd RKP(B)* (1936), pp. 57-58.

afterwards generally avoided, this was because the lesson had been learned, and because the appointments machinery of Uchraspred worked smoothly and silently to eliminate sources of friction and level out difficulties without allowing them to come to a head.

The issue of principle, however, remained ; and war continued to be waged on the question of nomination *versus* election of secretaries of party committees. The exercise of control by the central committee, or by Uchraspred acting in its name, over provincial appointments grew up gradually. It was described by Krestinsky in cautious terms at the tenth party congress in March 1921 :

> We put comrades at the disposal of a provincial committee, we recommend them for this or that work, and we come to an agreement with the representatives of the provincial organizations.[1]

This was the thin end of the wedge. Once the power to remove the existing occupant of a post, under the guise of promotion or of overriding party interest, was conceded, and the right to " recommend " a successor taken for granted, it was only a short step to direct nomination. This step was taken at the party conference of December 1921, which proposed that secretaries of provincial and county committees should be " confirmed by a higher party authority ". (This meant that provincial secretaries would be " confirmed " by the party central committee, and county secretaries by the provincial authorities.) The proposal was endorsed by the eleventh party congress in March 1922.[2] It became henceforth an accepted party rule. A report of Uchraspred to the twelfth party congress of 1923 recorded that 37 secretaries of provincial or regional committees (more than one-third of the total number) had been transferred or removed in the past year, and 42 party workers been recommended to provincial or regional committees for appointment as secretaries.[3] Provincial and regional secretaries were the key men on whose capacity to organize and to direct the power of the party in the area primarily depended. It was important for the central

[1] *Desyatyi S"ezd Rossiiskoi Kommunisticheskoi Partii* (1921), p. 44.
[2] *VKP(B) v Rezolyutsiyakh* (1941), i, 412, 436.
[3] *Izvestiya Tsentral'nogo Komiteta Rossiiskoi Kommunisticheskoi Partii (B),* No. 3 (51), March 1923, p. 51.

authorities to have in these posts men whose efficiency and loyalty were beyond suspicion.[1]

Once effective control of key provincial and regional party appointments was assured, the central apparatus sought to extend its hold to the next level — that of county party secretaries, whose appointment had since 1922 required the " confirmation " of the provincial authorities. Here, apparently, the main difficulty had been to find suitable candidates for the posts. At the twelfth party congress in April 1923 Stalin declared that the greatest need in party personnel was for " a reserve of 200 or 300 county secretaries ".[2] Preobrazhensky, having paid an ironical tribute to Stalin's " clever " speech, complained that 30 per cent of existing secretaries of provincial party committees had been, " as the expression goes, ' recommended ' by the central committee ", and belatedly feared that the practice of recommendation, instead of being an exception, would become a system.[3] No direct reply was made to Preobrazhensky's protest. Rykov admitted that all the members of the party bureaus for the newly established regions had hitherto been nominated by the central committee, and thought that it might be possible gradually to introduce a system of election, though " with the greatest caution ".[4] This pious hope found, however, no place in the formal decisions of the congress. The resolution on party organization stressed the importance of " measures for the improvement and selection of the leading cadre of party workers, from the secretary of the provincial or regional committee down to the secretary of the party cell ", and instructed the party central committee " to take all steps to

---

[1] A table showing in percentages the social origin of secretaries of provincial committees at the time of the eleventh (1922), twelfth (1923) and thirteenth (1924) party congresses was published in 1924 :

	Workers	Peasants	Employees
1922	24·7	3·6	71·7
1923	44·6	0·9	54·5
1924	48·6	0	51·4

(*Izvestiya Tsentral'nogo Komiteta Rossiiskoi Kommunisticheskoi Partii (Bol'-shevikov)*, No. 4 (62), April 1924, p. 5).
   [2] Stalin, *Sochineniya*, v, 217-218.
   [3] *Dvenadtsatyi S"ezd Rossiiskoi Kommunisticheskoi Partii (Bol'shevikov)*
1923), p. 133.   [4] *Ibid.* p. 438.

broaden and strengthen the Uchraspred organs of the party ";
and it proposed " to organize as a matter of urgency a school,
attached to the central committee, for secretaries of county party
committees, with a membership of 200-300 ".[1] In the autumn of
1923 the school for county party secretaries was opened in Moscow.
The declared purpose was " to form cadres of qualified county
party secretaries " ; and the implication clearly was that the right
qualifications, rather than election from below, would determine
these appointments.[2] Meanwhile provincial party secretaries continued to be nominated from the centre. When Trotsky launched
his first attack on the party leadership in October 1923, the charge
that nomination to party posts was ten times as common as in
the worst days of the civil war, and that " nomination of secretaries
of provincial committees is now the rule ", figured prominently in
the indictment.[3] The platform of the 46, issued a few days later,
bluntly attacked the " secretarial hierarchy " and described the
rift opening in the party between " professional party officials
appointed from above and the mass of the party which does not
participate in the common life ".[4] The famous resolution of
December 5, 1923, which registered the short-lived compromise
between the triumvirate and Trotsky at the end of this controversy, recorded the need to " verify the usefulness " of the system
of confirmation of appointments of provincial party secretaries, and
concluded that " the right to confirm secretaries cannot be allowed
to be converted into their virtual nomination ".[5] But this remained,
and was intended by the triumvirate to remain, a dead letter.

The increase in the authority and influence of Orgraspred was
an automatic process which was accelerated by each succeeding
party crisis. The autumn crisis of 1923 was a landmark in the

[1] *VKP(B) v Rezolyutsiyakh* (1941), i, 504-505.
[2] *Izvestiya Tsentral'nogo Komiteta Rossiiskoi Kommunisticheskoi Partii*
(*Bol'shevikov*), No. 6 (54), July 1923, p. 84 ; No. 7-8 (55-56), August–September
1923, p. 95. On June 17, 1924, Stalin made an important speech at the school,
explaining that he had chosen this audience precisely because at this juncture
the county had become the nodal point in relations between the party and the
peasantry (Stalin, *Sochineniya*, vi, 259-260) ; Trotsky made a brief speech at
the conclusion of one of the courses on June 30, 1924, apologizing for having
failed, through illness, to deliver a lecture at an earlier stage of the course
(Trotsky, *Sochineniya*, xxi, 365-368).
[3] For Trotsky's letter of October 8, 1923, see *The Interregnum, 1923–1924*,
pp. 295-297.
[4] See *The Interregnum, 1923–1924*, p. 298.   [5] *Ibid.* p. 306.

process. It was the first concerted attack on the party leadership since the central party machine had begun to function under Stalin's efficient management. The struggle which ensued, apart from its political and personal aspects, was a struggle between the party organization and a spontaneous and untutored party opinion which, as commonly occurs in such situations, tended to side with an opposition professing " Leftist " principles. The result, which also conformed to the modern pattern of experience in other countries, was a victory of the party organization over unorganized mass opinion, which failed altogether to withstand the combined resources of propaganda and patronage at the disposal of a large-scale organization. It was significant that the opposition grew progressively weaker as time went on, and as the discussion moved from the provinces to the centre, and that it retained more of its hold on the intellectuals than on the workers.[1] What clearly emerged from the struggle was the power of the central party organization, professedly an instrument of the central committee elected by the party congress which was composed of delegates of local party organs, to dominate its ostensible masters by controlling their votes. The control was exercised through mass propaganda, through the power of appointment and through the threat of reprisals : it would be unrealistic to attempt to assess the relative weight of the three pressures. Nor were the controls and pressures purely negative. If opposition was curbed by fear of penalties, conformity was encouraged by hope of rewards. As always happens, careerism was the counterpart of intimidation. Though nothing suspicious had actually transpired at the twelfth party congress of April 1923, Trotsky in his letter of October 8, 1923, six months after the event, expressed " alarm at the methods and procedures by dint of which the twelfth party congress was constituted " ; and the " platform of the 46 " bluntly asserted that " the secretarial hierarchy of the party to an ever greater extent recruits the membership of conferences and congresses, which are becoming to an ever greater extent the executive assemblies of this hierarchy ".[2] Protests against " bureaucracy ", the " party apparatus " and the system of nomination formed the staple of the opposition campaign ; and

---

[1] See the account in *The Interregnum, 1923–24*, ch. xiii *passim*.
[2] *Ibid*. pp. 295, 369.

allegations of " pressure from the party apparatus " on the election of delegates to the thirteenth party conference in January 1924 were freely bandied about at the conference itself.[1] The overwhelming majority secured by the leadership at the conference on issues on which the opposition had a few weeks earlier appeared to enjoy widespread support in the party was the best evidence that these allegations had some foundation.

From 1924 onwards the machinery of Orgraspred operated smoothly and efficiently. Like the appointments department of any large organization, Orgraspred went about its work with discretion and with a minimum of publicity. Personal ambitions and personal incompatibilities had to be taken into account ; awkward and restive individuals had to be quietly got rid of or placed in posts where they could do no harm ; the real reasons for appointments or dismissals could not always be openly stated. In these circumstances it is not surprising that the extent of the political pressures exerted through Orgraspred is largely a matter of conjecture and must be inferred from hints that emerged from time to time. The process was inevitable and, in many cases, defensible on any standard of judgment. No well-run organization favours hardened dissenters. As Orgraspred grew more powerful and more self-assured, it could even afford to appease objectors by a certain outward relaxation in the exercise of its power. Early in 1924 the central committee directed Uchraspred to adopt " a cautious approach " to " removals and transfers of workers in elective organs ", and " the course was set for a renunciation of direct nominations to responsible elective posts in party, trade union etc. organs ".[2] In the summer of 1925 it was announced that party workers elected to trade union posts would not be transferred before the expiration of the period for which they had been elected, and that presidents and secretaries of provincial or regional trade union councils would not be transferred without explicit approval of the party central committee.[3] In October of the same year the party central committee, in an appeal to all party organizations and members of the party, urged

    [1] *Ibid.* p. 333.
    [2] *Izvestiya Tsentral'nogo Komiteta Rossiiskoi Kommunisticheskoi Partii (Bol'shevikov)*, No. 4 (62), April 1924, pp. 42, 77.
    [3] *Ibid.* No. 31-32 (106-107), August 24, 1925, p. 6.

that " elections to local leading party organs and elections to the [party] congress should proceed without any imposition of particular candidates ".[1] As the system was standardized, a face-saving formula was devised to cover the nomination by Orgraspred of secretaries of provincial or regional party committees ; the appointment was " proposed " by the local organization and " confirmed " by the central authority.[2] Strong efforts were made to pacify opposition by keeping up appearances. At the Orgburo in March 1926, Molotov protested against cases in which lists of candidates for leading posts had been settled behind the scenes at party conferences, so that everything on the surface might have a correct appearance, and Stalin indignantly exclaimed : " Parade ! "[3] Two months later an order was issued denouncing provincial party committees which handed down to county party conferences lists of those who were to be elected to county party committees.[4] But, whatever attempts were made to preserve the decencies of formal election, nothing was likely to shake the right of the higher party authorities to the last word on key party appointments.

In practice the authority of Orgraspred continued to expand. Rykov had expressed the hope at the twelfth party congress [5] that, as " regionalization " spread over the Soviet Union, and the larger and more important " regions " took the place of " provinces ", the right of the party central committee, acting through Orgraspred, to nominate not only the secretary of the regional party committee, but its whole presidium or bureau, would be abrogated in favour of election. This hope was not realized. The practice of nomination by the centre became stereotyped. A provision for " confirmation " of such appointments was formally included in the revised party statute approved by the fourteenth party congress in December 1925 ; and, when an

---

[1] *VKP(B) v Rezolyutsiyakh* (1941), ii, 45.

[2] The following was a typical announcement of the spring of 1926 : " In connexion with the selection of comrade Antipov as member of the secretariat and bureau of the Leningrad provincial committee, the central committee agreed with the proposal of the bureau of the Ural regional committee to confirm comrade Sulimov as first secretary of the Ural regional committee " (*Izvestiya Tsentral'nogo Komiteta Vsesoyuznoi Kommunisticheskoi Partii (B)*, No. 10-11 (131-132), March 22, 1926, p. 6).   [3] *Ibid.* pp. 3-4.

[4] *Ibid.* No. 19-20 (140-141), May 24, 1926, p. 1.

[5] See p. 208 above.

opposition delegate protested against this retrogression from an elective system, he received the reply that, on the contrary, it represented an advance in party democracy, since, when the regions were first created, the whole of a regional committee had been nominated by the central authority. In any case, added the *rapporteur*, " the interests of the party must rate higher than the interests of formal democracy ".[1] By the time the fourteenth congress met, nobody could ignore the immense power which the right of appointment, dismissal and transfer conferred on the central party machine, or the way in which it was used to control and organize votes. Krupskaya, who wished to limit the powers of the Orgburo and the secretariat to transfer and remove party members, argued that " these transfers, these removals from work . . . frequently create in the party an inability to speak out sincerely and openly ", and that this was incompatible with " inner-party democracy ".[2] Glebov-Avilov, the Leningrad trade union leader, reported to a meeting of party trade unionists, while the congress was still in progress, that " the mass of delegates were in agreement with us " ; that many delegates " came to us, saying that they were in agreement with us, and explaining why they did not vote for us " ; and that " the atmosphere of the congress " was such that " not everyone will hold up his hand in opposition in order to be sent as a result to Murmansk or Turkestan ".[3] It had by this time become difficult to distinguish between what was abuse and what was legitimate and recognized procedure. The task of the central control commission, declared the resolution of the congress, " should consist, in a greater measure than has been realized in the past, in actively assisting the appropriate party and Soviet organs in the selection of workers for economic and state posts " ; [4] and everyone knew that one of the qualifications most prized by the control commission was orthodoxy

[1] *VKP(B) v Rezolyutsiyakh* (1941), ii, 83 ; *XIV S"ezd Vsesoyuznoi Kommunisticheskoi Partii (B)* (1926), pp. 883, 885-886, 892-893.

[2] *XIV S"ezd Vsesoyuznoi Kommunisticheskoi Partii (B)*, p. 572 ; for a quotation from Krupskaya's speech see *The Interregnum, 1923-1924*, p. 333, note 1.

[3] *Pravda*, December 29, 1925. Glebov-Avilov complained in a written declaration to the congress (*XIV S"ezd Vsesoyuznoi Kommunisticheskoi Partii* (1926), p. 952) that he had been misrepresented ; but the denial apparently covered only the concluding remark.

[4] *VKP(B) v Rezolyutsiyakh* (1941), ii, 54.

of opinion. Such pressures were sometimes felt even beyond the sphere of party appointments. At the seventh Komsomol congress in March 1926 the allegation was heard that, besides members of the opposition dismissed or transferred to distant posts, workers who were supporters of the opposition had been dismissed from factory jobs, so that they " go about unemployed for months and stand at the labour exchange ".[1]

(e) Unity and Discipline

The indirect control exercised through the power of appointment and dismissal was so strong and effective that it might have sufficed by itself to make the central party machine the dominant and directing force in the party. But it was reinforced, though in this period cautiously and sparingly, by direct disciplinary action against dissidents ; and the fear of reprisals was undoubtedly a substantial factor in imposing conformity on those who were outside the scope of party appointments. The central control commission with its subordinate network of local commissions was the organ of party discipline. The control commission was first instituted in September 1920 as a concession to growing opposition within the party. Its primary function was to investigate complaints against party officials, including even members of the central committee ; this was the point of the proviso that no member of the central committee could also be a member of the central control commission.[2] But the tenth party congress in March 1921, by its condemnation of " fractionalism ", made organized opposition a major party offence ; and it was in this atmosphere that the control commission took shape in the years from 1921 to 1923. The first recorded joint meeting of the party central committee with the central control commission — a procedure often to be repeated in dealing with later oppositions —

---

[1] VII S"ezd Vsesoyuznogo Leninskogo Kommunisticheskogo Soyuza Molodezhi (1926), p. 113 ; another delegate at the congress cynically commented on these allegations in the words of a familiar proverb : " When trees are felled, chips fly " (ibid. p. 130).

[2] See The Bolshevik Revolution, 1917–1923, Vol. 1, p. 196. Dzerzhinsky and Preobrazhensky, who were also members of the party central committee, left the commission 'some time before the tenth party congress in March 1921 (Desyatyi S"ezd Rossiiskoi Kommunisticheskoi Partii (1921), p. 28) ; and the congress elected an entirely new central commission of seven.

was convened by Lenin in August 1921 to consider disciplinary measures against Shlyapnikov.[1] At this time, however, disciplinary action was not necessarily taken through the control commissions. V. Kosior complained at the eleventh party congress in March 1922 that he, Sapronov and Mrachkovsky had been removed from the Urals " for considerations of an absolutely non-service character ", apparently by direct action of the central committee or the secretariat :

> If anyone had the audacity, or thought it necessary, to come out with a criticism or to point out this or that defect in the sphere of party or Soviet construction, he was at once counted with the opposition, this was at once notified to the competent authority, and he was removed.

And he recalled that the Politburo had taken similar action against members of the presidium of the trade union central council who had been on Trotsky's side in the trade union controversy of the previous year.[2] The same party congress to which these complaints were made gave the control commissions their first formal statute, and drew attention to their particular importance " in the conditions of the new economic policy, in connexion with which there is a growing threat of the degeneration of the least reliable and disciplined members of the party ".[3] It reduced the number of members of the central control commission from seven to five, and once more changed its personnel ; Solts, who had reported on the work of the central commission at the tenth congress, was the only member to be reappointed by the eleventh congress — an honour which foreshadowed his future importance in the commission.[4] When the twelfth party congress in April 1923 increased the number of the central control commission to 50, amalgamated Rabkrin with it,[5] and put Kuibyshev at the head of the enlarged institution, the central control commission was launched on its

---

[1] See The Bolshevik Revolution, 1917–1923, Vol. 1, p. 208.

[2] Odinnadtsatyi S"ezd RKP(B) (1936), pp. 133-134 ; the reference to the trade union leaders may be a confused recollection of the action taken in May 1921 against Tomsky, Rudzutak and Ryazanov (see The Bolshevik Revolution, 1917–1923, Vol. 2, pp. 324-325).

[3] VKP(B) v Rezolyutsiyakh (1941), i, 441-442.

[4] The names of those elected at the tenth and eleventh congresses are listed ibid. (5th ed. 1936), i, 404, 462 ; they are omitted in later editions.

[5] See The Bolshevik Revolution, 1917–1923, Vol. 1, pp. 227-228.

career as a major party organ — the party inquisition and the
scourge of offenders against the party code of behaviour or against
party orthodoxy.

It would be misleading to suggest that the disciplinary authority
of the central control commission and its subordinate organs over
party members was at this time applied primarily to the suppression of dissentient opinion. The more avowable purpose of
maintaining a high standard of conduct among party members
and punishing infractions of the party ethical code accounted for
the greater part of its work. For several years, in accordance with
a provision in the party statute, lists of persons expelled from the
party were regularly published in the party gazette together with
the grounds of the expulsion. These were extremely various.
Sometimes the description of the offence was limited to " conduct discreditable to the party " or " infractions of party discipline ". But as a rule particulars were given. Drunkenness was
the most frequent single cause, sometimes with aggravating circumstances such as " persistent drunkenness and brawling with
prostitutes ". Official offences were often alleged. One official
was expelled for collecting a tax without giving a receipt, another
for " misuse of official position and exploitation of subordinates ",
a third for " giving a recommendation to a total stranger for
private gain ". A party official was expelled for " exceeding the
powers of the Penza provincial committee ", though it was stated
that he might be employed in Soviet work. Ideological grounds
were often quoted. One member was expelled as " a person with
an obscure past ", another as " a dubious and ideologically cor-
rupt element ". A " former officer of the army " had evidently
turned nepman, and was expelled from the party for having
" concluded contracts with private firms for personal profit ".[1] It

---

[1] The grounds of 2382 expulsions of party members (1766 candidates were
also excluded) in the first quarter of 1925 were classified in percentages as
follows : offences against communist ethics, 22·9 ; official misdemeanours,
18·3 ; drunkenness, 16·3 ; criminal offences, 15·4 ; incompatibility, 8·9 ;
infractions of party discipline, 8·8 ; abandonment of party, 5·8 ; participation
in religious observances, 3·3. Of those expelled, 57 per cent were admitted in
1919 and 1920 (when admissions were widely granted) ; only 1·5 per cent had
been members before 1917 (*Izvestiya Tsentral'nogo Komiteta Rossiiskoi Kommunisticheskoi Partii* (*Bol'shevikov*), No. 34 (109), September 7, 1925, p. 5).
46,600 party members were called on to answer charges of offences against the
party between July 1924 and July 1925, and 31 per cent of these were expelled ;

is, of course, possible, as Preobrazhensky once alleged,[1] that charges of moral turpitude were sometimes fastened on those whom it was desired to discredit on political grounds. But the amount of publicity given to cases of disciplinary action by the central control commission against the party opposition, and the care taken to justify them on the ground of formal infringement of party rules, indicates that such interventions were still fairly rare. Meanwhile the organization began to extend its tentacles all over the Soviet Union. According to figures given by Kuibyshev to the central control commission at its session in October 1924, 116 control commissions were then functioning in different centres.[2] The membership of the 76 commissions for which detailed figures were available was 832, as against 536 six months earlier.[3]

The scope of the functions and authority of the central control commission also grew apace. Its first prominent appearance as the custodian of doctrinal orthodoxy was in October 1923, when a joint session of the party central committee and the central control commission condemned Trotsky's letter of October 8 as a " profound political error " and the platform of the 46 as a " fractional grouping ".[4] The central control commission passed an important resolution on irregular opposition activities on the eve of the thirteenth party conference in January 1924, and played its part in the purge of opposition supporters after the conference.[5] The year 1924, which opened with the death of Lenin, followed by the Lenin enrolment and the beginnings of the cult of Leninism, was one of progressive loss of independence within

a majority of the accused were classified as " employees ". Drunkenness was the most frequent offence, followed by breaches of party discipline (*XIV S"ezd Vsesoyuznoi Kommunisticheskoi Partii (B)* (1926), pp. 534-535).

[1] See *The Interregnum, 1923–1924*, pp. 356-357.

[2] At this time control commissions seem to have been attached mainly to provincial or regional party committees : the party statute approved by the fourteenth party congress of December 1925 made provision for control commissions at the department (okrug) level (*XIV S"ezd Vsesoyuznoi Kommunisticheskoi Partii (B)* (1926), p. 880 ; *VKP(B) v Rezolyutsiyakh* (1941), ii, 87).

[3] *Leningradskaya Pravda*, October 8, 1924 ; of the 832 members, 158 were employed on Rabkrin work, i.e. the control and inspection of Soviet institutions — an interesting indication that this side of the work of the control commissions was quite overshadowed by their party work.

[4] See *The Interregnum, 1923–1924*, pp. 300-301.

[5] See *ibid.* pp. 329-330, 356-357.

the party. It was marked both by the final organization of Orgraspred and by the elaboration of the system of control commissions. It was marked also by a wave of suicides of party members sufficiently large to cause anxiety to the party authorities : [1] the most notorious of these — Lutovinov, Evgeniya Bosh, and Trotsky's secretary, Glazman [2] — were known or suspected to be the direct result of the new régime in the party. Inquisitorial action by the central control commission soon became a familiar and recognized procedure. In the aftermath of the first campaign against Trotsky, in February 1924, the commission expelled two party members for distributing banned documents.[3] The most serious case of underground opposition unearthed by the commission in the period between the thirteenth and fourteenth party congresses was the so-called " Pililenko affair ".[4] At the end of 1924, at the height of the Trotsky controversy, a party member in Moscow named Khorechko, a signatory of the platform of the 46 and a former member of the democratic centralism group, wrote to a certain Pililenko, who held a party post in Kharkov, urging him to come to Moscow for a discussion of " many questions of principle ". Pililenko sent a letter in reply by a party member named Kotsyubinsky who, he wrote, shared his views and would be able to explain them in detail. The letter is said to have openly looked forward to a split in the party. Pililenko proposed to canvass the new recruits of the Lenin enrolment and also non-party workers, and " by way of mass demonstrations of the rank and file, though not beginning in Moscow, to mobilize the sympathies of broad strata of the party ".[5] The letter was brought

---

[1] See Vol. 1, p. 25.

[2] For Lutovinov see *The Interregnum, 1923–1924*, p. 129, note 1 ; Bosh was the wife of Pyatakov, the spokesman of the opposition at the party conference of January 1924 (her death was reported without comment in *Pravda*, January 6, 1925) ; for Glazman see p. 7 above.

[3] See *The Interregnum, 1923–1924*, p. 357.

[4] This was the only such affair mentioned by the central control commission in its report to the fourteenth congress (*K XIV S"ezdu RKP(B)* (1925), p. vii). Medvedev's "letter to Baku", written in January 1924, seems to have been discovered by the commission some time in 1925, but was not disclosed till the summer of 1926, presumably because investigations were still on foot ; it will be discussed in a subsequent volume.

[5] Knowledge of the text of the letter is derived from quotations read by Yaroslavsky, not a very reliable witness, at the Leningrad provincial party conference in December 1925 (*Leningradskaya Pravda*, December 6, 1925).

not to Khorechko, but to Drobnis, who showed it to V. M. Smirnov, both Drobnis and Smirnov being Democratic Centralists and signatories of the platform of the 46. At some time during 1925, by unknown means, the letter fell into the hands of the central control commission, which interrogated all those implicated. In November 1925 the presidium of the central control commission issued its decision. Pililenko was expelled from the party ; Drobnis and Khorechko were severely reprimanded and warned that any further infraction of party discipline would lead to their immediate expulsion ; and V. M. Smirnov and Kotsyubinsky were severely reprimanded.[1] Expulsion from the party was the supreme sanction, and was applied with reluctance to prominent party members.

While, however, overt reprisals against the opposition were still kept within the bounds of moderation, the new concentration of power of which the central control commission was a symptom and symbol bred new attitudes towards the expression of dissentient opinion in the party. Already in 1921 Lenin had treated opposition as a luxury too dangerous to be tolerated in time of crisis. Since the fact, or the pretext, of crisis could always be invoked, this attitude became permanent. As the institutions of the state were more and more closely integrated with those of the party, disloyalty to the party was indistinguishable from disloyalty to the state. The maintenance of a formal and institutional separation of party and state did not affect the substantial identity between them in purpose, in policy, in doctrine and in directing personnel. The absence of other recognized parties playing a subsidiary rôle, or advocating alternative policies, in public affairs contributed to the same result. Liberal democracy had established a distinction between the concepts of loyalty to a party and loyalty to the state, and found a place for both. This distinction disappeared in the one-party state with significant consequences. On the one hand, loyalty to the state came to require acceptance of specific doctrinal conformities hitherto associated with party. On the other hand, dissent from party doctrine or prescriptions

---

[1] *Pravda*, November 22, 1925. It is significant that at this time party censure did not automatically involve exclusion from Soviet work ; *Vlast' Sovetov*, Nos. 3 and 4, January 17, 24, 1926, carried an article by Drobnis on the problem of homeless children.

incurred the moral stigma, and later the physical sanctions, hitherto reserved for disloyalty to the state.   These implications of the identity of party and state, already apparent when Lenin died, developed to the full with the growing power of the party central organs.   The mere existence of an efficient machinery of repression invited the use of it.   Opposition became a crime because the means were now available to track it down and punish it.   Theses submitted by Kuibyshev to the central control commission in October 1924 included among the functions of the commission " the final eradication of the differences which occurred in the party before the thirteenth party congress ".[1]

The change of attitude associated with the rise of the control commission was visible in two main ways.   In the first place, it encouraged the practice of informing, which in the realm of public law had already received approbation in the new criminal code.[2] The crowning offence of the two members expelled from the party for distribution of banned documents in February 1924 was that they refused to name those from whom they had obtained the documents.[3]   In the Pililenko affair, the offence alleged against Drobnis and Smirnov was that, after reading Pililenko's letter, they had not reported it to the commission.   At the fourteenth congress in December 1925 the " system of informing " was attacked by opposition delegates and defended by official spokesmen.   Bakaev, a Leningrad delegate, protested that the practice of informing " is taking such forms and such a character that friend cannot tell friend his sincere thought ".   Several delegates pointed out that a party member who knew that other members were attempting to form " ideological groupings ", and failed to report it, was falling short in his obligations to the party.   Gusev put this doctrine in its extreme form :

> Lenin once taught us that every member of the party ought to be an agent of the Cheka, i.e. to watch and inform.   I do not propose to set up a Cheka in the party.   We have the central control commission, we have the central committee, but I think that every member of the party should inform.   If

[1] *Pravda*, October 5, 1924.

[2] Under art. 89 of the criminal code of the RSFSR of 1922 " failure to give information " of counter-revolutionary crimes " known to have been committed or to be impending " was punishable by imprisonment for a maximum of one year.   [3] See *The Interregnum, 1923–1924*, p. 357.

we suffer from anything, it is not from too much informing, but from too little.

" If two people speak sincerely together about questions of party life or about politics in general," said Nikolaeva, a woman delegate from Leningrad, " one of them invariably writes to the central control commission " ; and Solts, the spokesman of the commission, interjected : " It depends what they are speaking about ". And when Nikolaeva went on to protest that the Cheka (the popular synonym for the OGPU was used throughout the discussion) was " an instrument directed . . . against our class enemy . . . against the bourgeoisie ", she was greeted with cries of " Not always ! " [1] The long-prepared coalescence of the functions of the OGPU and of the central control commission was now an established fact.

The other new development had been inaugurated by Zinoviev at the thirteenth party congress, when he appealed to Trotsky to confess from the tribune of the congress that he " had made a mistake, and the party was right ". [2] But this innovation encountered resistance, and no such demand was made by the cautious Stalin on the opposition at the fourteenth congress. [3] Nevertheless, whatever tactics may have been followed in public and in regard to the leaders, it was clear by this time that a party member penalized, whether through the appointments procedure of Orgraspred or through direct disciplinary action by a control commission, for opposition associations or activities could not hope to find his way back to favour without renouncing his past opinions and joining in the condemnation and persecution of those who continued to hold them. The now accepted doctrine was enunciated without comment, but with evident reference to the continued holding by the defeated opposition leaders of party and governmental posts, at the seventh Komsomol congress in March 1926 :

> If this or that comrade has not recognized his error, and if he is appointed to this or that leading work, that does not mean

---

[1] *XIV S"ezd Vsesoyuznoi Kommunisticheskoi Partii* (*B*) (1926), pp. 566, 570, 595-596, 600-601, 612-613.

[2] See *The Interregnum, 1923–1924*, p. 362.

[3] This restraint enabled Bukharin to score a point against Zinoviev (see p. 134 above).

that we have given him an amnesty. There can be an amnesty
. . . only when the comrade recognizes his error.[1]

It was not long before a demand for a recantation of past errors
became one of the regular instruments in the enforcement of
conformity by the central party machine. A new regulation made
at this time stipulated that a former party member, whether he
had been expelled from the party or had left it of his own volition,
could be re-admitted only by decision of the central control
commission.[2]

(f) The Leader

The concentration of power in the central apparatus in the
name of party unity and the enforcement of party discipline is
commonly associated with the name of Stalin, who was the
ultimate beneficiary of the process. It would, however, be misleading to regard it as the work of one man. The process was not
perhaps consciously planned by anyone ; but it was also not
consistently resisted by anyone. Leaders of the opposition protested when measures of party discipline were applied to them.
But they had themselves previously acclaimed the principle of
such measures. The beginning of the process may be found in
Lenin's impassioned pleas for unity, and in the resolution banning
fractions and groupings, at the tenth party congress in March
1921. In the immediately following years, the event which did
most to further it was the campaign against Trotsky in the winter
of 1923–1924, when dissentients within the party were for the
first time penalized on an extensive scale. The first appearance
of the epithet " monolithic " as applied to the party was in the
resolution of the thirteenth party conference of January 1924
which condemned Trotsky, and contrasted the alleged opposition
view of the party " as a sum of all kinds of tendencies and fractions " with the Bolshevik view of it " as a monolithic whole ".[3]
In May at the thirteenth party congress Zinoviev proclaimed the
need for " a monolithism a thousand times greater than what we

---

[1] *VII S"ezd Vsesoyuznoi Leninskogo Kommunisticheskogo Soyuza Molodezhi*
(1926), p. 96.
[2] *Izvestiya Tsentral'nogo Komiteta Vsesoyuznoi Kommunisticheskoi Partii (B)*,
No. 16-17 (137-138), May 3, 1926, p. 5.
[3] *VKP(B) v Rezolyutsiyakh* (1941), i, 542.

have now ".[1] But Trotsky, though he did not use the word, was not behindhand in protestations of fidelity to the principle :

> In no circumstances does inner-party democracy presuppose fractional groupings. . . . I never recognized and do not recognize freedom of party groupings, because in present historical conditions a grouping is only another name for a fraction.[2]

Of those who six months later were to become leading publicists of the Leningrad opposition, Zalutsky at this time declared himself emphatically against groupings and fractions in the party and for " unity of will, unity of political line, unity of political platform " ; and Safarov announced that " the party from the very bottom to the very top is a steel ingot ".[3] Not only Zinoviev, but his principal followers, were exposed to the charge of both preaching and practising an intolerance of dissent which they resented only when they themselves became dissenters. Stalin was at this time publicly less committed to the demand for a monolithic party than most of his future opponents.

Nor can any difference of attitude be traced between the leaders on the practical conclusions of " monolithism ". Zinoviev and Kamenev outdid Stalin in January 1925 in their insistence on the application of disciplinary penalties to Trotsky ; and there is no reason to suppose that they were any more backward in the victimization of Trotsky's followers. Uglanov's clean-up of the Moscow organization was apparently undertaken at the instance of Zinoviev and Kamenev ;[4] and, under Zinoviev's uncontested rule, " hundreds and hundreds of workers " had, according to Trotsky's private memorandum of December 22, 1925, been " expelled from Leningrad and scattered all over the country ".[5] If the selection of delegates to party congresses was now habitually " managed " by the local party bosses at the dictation of the central machine, circumstantial evidence was not lacking of such management by the Leningrad leaders in the recruitment of the

---

[1] *Trinadtsatyi S"ezd Rossiiskoi Kommunisticheskoi Partii* (*Bol'shevikov*) (1924), p. 112.
[2] *Ibid.* pp. 159-160.
[3] *Leningradskaya Pravda*, May 8, 28, 1924.
[4] See p. 22 above ; it resulted in the dismissal or transfer of " tens and perhaps hundreds " of Moscow party workers (*XIV S"ezd Vsesoyuznoi Kommunisticheskoi Partii* (*B*) (1926), p. 384).
[5] For Trotsky's memorandum see p. 168 above.

Leningrad delegation to the fourteenth party congress.[1] A hostile
critic put the situation clearly and succinctly :

> Neither in Moscow nor in Leningrad were the masses in-
> formed of the substance of the disputes. It was the apparatus
> that voted.[2]

Whatever was at stake at the fourteenth congress, it would be
erroneous to see in it a struggle of champions of " inner-party
democracy " on behalf of freedom of opinion and freedom of
election against the defenders of a monolithic conformity in
opinion and organization. But a new and sinister stage in the
development was none the less marked by this congress. The
procedure which had made its appearance at the thirteenth party
conference in January 1924, at the culmination of the first campaign
against Trotsky, of jeering at opposition speakers and shouting
them down [3] emerged at the fourteenth congress in December
1925 as a regular system, deliberately organized on the side of the
majority and perhaps even on that of the minority. What were
now heard on the floor of the congress were not the arguments
of rational and spontaneous dissent, but the shouts of well-drilled
factions contending for mastery. That so much of the debate was
still conducted in the esoteric language of party doctrine or
economic theory seemed a tribute to the habits of the past rather
than a reality of the present : the familiar arguments themselves
began to take on a scholastic and unsubstantial form. More plainly
than ever before in the history of the party, the decisions of the
fourteenth congress were the product of naked power. The victory
of Stalin over his former partners in the triumvirate was a triumph,
not of reason, but of organization.

The concentration of power in the party at the centre, whether
in the secretariat or in the central control commission, did not at
the outset seem to portend a drift towards personal dictatorship,
towards the greater prestige and influence of an individual leader.
This phenomenon first emerged in local organizations, and its
cumulative effect was plural rather than singular. From the
moment when the capital and the party headquarters were moved

---

[1] For the exclusion of Komarov see p. 135 above ; similar tactics were
doubtless pursued by both sides.
[2] *Bol'shevik*, No. 14, July 31, 1926, p. 59.
[3] See *The Interregnum, 1923–1924*, p. 336.

to Moscow in March 1918, Zinoviev remained the outstanding
figure in Petrograd, and came automatically to dominate the
Petrograd party organization. Accident and his personal character combined to make him the first conspicuous party boss.
Partly by way of imitation, Kamenev occupied a similar position
in the Moscow party organization, though this was overshadowed
by the continuous presence in Moscow of the other leaders and of
the central organs of party and state. Other local party organizations had their recognized bosses : Orjonikidze in Tiflis and
Kirov in Baku were noteworthy examples. Weak party organizations in backward regions were commonly run by bosses sent
from Moscow : Yaroslavsky, and later Lashevich, functioned in
this capacity in Siberia, Goloshchekin in Kazakhstan. This system
of " fiefs " or " principalities ", as it afterwards came to be
called, was for a long time generally accepted, and few members
of the party noticed that behind the power of the local bosses
the over-riding power of a central boss was being built up round
the secretariat and the central control commission. Before
the beginning of 1925 Zinoviev and Kamenev, as controllers
of the Leningrad and Moscow organizations, were assumed by
most people to wield more power than the general secretary,
Stalin.

The rift in the triumvirate and the controversies that led up to
the fourteenth congress revealed for the first time the underlying realities of the situation. It became apparent that Kamenev,
having yielded up to Uglanov the effective control of the Moscow
organization, had forfeited his local base, and had become a
politically dependent hanger-on of the Leningrad group. On
the other hand, the challenge of the Leningrad opposition to the
central party leadership threw a lurid light on the potential danger
of the system of " principalities ", which came under attack at the
congress from Komarov, the main Leningrad supporter of the
central committee. It is significant that the system was criticized
on the ground not that it made the local boss a dictator over the
local party organization, but that it weakened the unitary structure
of the party, which seemed less secure than it had been in the
days of Lenin. " To give Moscow to one, Leningrad to another,
Donbass to a third, and so on ", said Komarov, might have been
all right under Lenin ; but nowadays it would turn the party

central committee into a League of Nations.[1] Uglanov won applause by claiming that he worked in Moscow " in such a way as not to allow the possibility of dividing our party into spheres of influence of separate leaders " ; and Voroshilov expressed satisfaction that Moscow under Uglanov had ceased to be any-one's " fief ".[2] The argument seemed irresistible. Nobody wanted a repetition of the clash between the party central com-mittee and a powerful local party organization. The Leningrad delegation proclaimed more loudly than anyone its devotion to the " Leninist unity " of the party ; had it won, it would have taken over control of the central committee and the central party apparatus. The struggle which culminated at the fourteenth congress was bound, whichever side proved victorious, to end in the disappearance of conflicting centres of authority dominated by local bosses.

But, though this development was clearly foreseen and wel-comed by the congress as a whole, the conclusion was not drawn that the elimination of the local boss as an independent figure would be achieved at the cost of elevating one man to the central seat of power and authority, of creating a unique party boss. The congress again and again acclaimed with evident sincerity the ideal of collective leadership. It counted heavily against Zinoviev that he had seen himself so easily as Lenin's successor. One delegate quoted, amid applause, what he described as the opinion of a typical party member from the provinces :

> Lenin left behind him a trunk full of relics of all kinds ; but individual representatives, individual members of the central committee, are beginning to try on his mantle. This mantle does not fit anyone, it does not fit our co-reporter from the central committee. This legacy should be the legacy of our whole party and of the whole central committee.

" Now that the central committee is collectively led ", remarked another delegate, " I think we should abandon the idea of suc-cession and successors " : this, too, was greeted with " stormy applause ".[3] Kamenev's personal attack on Stalin was answered by Tomsky's passionate assurance that " a system of individual

---

[1] *XIV S"ezd Vsesoyuznoi Kommunisticheskoi Partii (B)* (1926), p. 221.
[2] *Ibid.* pp. 193, 394 ; it was an opposition speaker who called Moscow " the empire of comrade Uglanov " (*ibid.* p. 384).   [3] *Ibid.* pp. 173, 179.

leaders cannot exist, and will not, no, will not ", as well as by Voroshilov's explanation that, if Stalin was " the leading member of the Politburo ", he never claimed priority there.[1] These protestations were, in part, sincere and were believed by many. It was not yet understood that Uglanov now ruled Moscow in succession to Kamenev as an agent of Stalin, and that this had enabled Stalin to confront the Leningrad opposition with the dual strength and authority of the Moscow organization and of the central party machine. When Zinoviev, after his defeat at the fourteenth congress, was finally ousted from his control of the Leningrad machine, and Kirov, a faithful Stalinist, transferred from Baku to Leningrad to replace him, no local party organization was any longer strong enough to resist the central authority in Moscow. By the same token, no other party leader could stand up against Stalin. The concentration of power in the central organization also meant the concentration of power in the hands of one man.

[1] For these passages see pp. 139-140 above.

PART IV

THE SOVIET ORDER

CHAPTER 20

THE UNION AND THE REPUBLICS

THE year 1924 saw the constitution of the USSR in full operation on lines which were to remain substantially unchanged till 1936. The USSR included in its federal embrace the four original constituent republics, the RSFSR, the Ukrainian SSR, the White Russian SSR and the Transcaucasian SFSR, to which were to be added in the following year the Uzbek and Turkmen SSRs. The constitutional structure of each of these republics with its pyramid of Soviets was patterned on that of the USSR itself; the constitution of the USSR had followed the model of the original constitution of the RSFSR.[1] Since the RSFSR accounted for two-thirds of the total population of the USSR [2] and occupied 95 per cent of its total area, it was not surprising that the USSR should sometimes have seemed not so much a federal union of equal republics as a device to enable the RSFSR to assert and legitimize its ascendancy over the other republics. In form the principle of equality was observed. In practice the USSR inevitably appeared as the heir of the old RSFSR rather than as the joint creation of all the republics. The main central organs of the union — the Congress of Soviets, the All-Union Central Executive Committee (TsIK) and Sovnarkom — were direct successors of the corresponding organs

---

[1] For an account of the constitution of the USSR see *The Bolshevik Revolution, 1917–1923*, Vol. 1, pp. 399-409.

[2] The figures of population as given in the census of December 1926 were as follows :

RSFSR	100,891,244
Ukrainian SSR	29,018,187
White Russian SSR	4,983,240
Transcaucasian SFSR	5,861,529
Uzbek SSR	5,272,801
Turkmen SSR	1,000,914
USSR	147,027,915

of the RSFSR, while the RSFSR and the other constituent republics adopted, at a subordinate level and within the framework of the USSR, similar constitutions, and set up similar organs. The pyramidal structure of the Soviet system was retained and perfected. The whole USSR was now organized as a single pyramid with the Congress of Soviets of the USSR as its apex.

(a) The Organs of the Union

The constitution of the USSR recognized its Congress of Soviets as " the supreme organ of power ". The definition was from the outset purely formal. The Congress of Soviets of the USSR inherited from its predecessor, the All-Russian Congress of Soviets, not only its constitutional status, but the virtual atrophy which had paralysed that body even before the formation of the Union.[1] The first Congress of Soviets of the USSR in December 1922 had signed the treaty of union ; the second in January 1924 had ratified its constitution. After the third congress, which took place in May 1925, congresses met only in alternate years.[2] They took the form of mass demonstrations, attended by more than 2000 delegates, in the Bol'shoi Theatre in Moscow, at which reports were read by one or more members of Sovnarkom, speeches delivered by selected delegates, acts of lower organs ratified, and prepared resolutions passed by acclamation. Proposals for legislation were rarely or never introduced at a congress, and no business, except of a formal character, was transacted. The atmosphere of solemnity and publicity surrounding the Congress of Soviets made it a convenient occasional forum for debates on foreign affairs, the motive being to instruct opinion at home and to impress opinion abroad rather than to influence the policy of the Soviet Government.[3] It was sometimes called

[1] See The Bolshevik Revolution, 1917–1923, Vol. 1, pp. 214-215.
[2] Art. 11 of the constitution which prescribed a meeting " once a year " was amended by the fourth congress in April 1927 to " once every two years ". Even this was not maintained : no congress met between 1931 and 1935.
[3] At the thirteenth party congress in May 1924, Zinoviev had insisted that " no provincial congress of Soviets, or even a rural district congress of Soviets, should pass without a detailed report on the work of Narkomindel ", the aim being to popularize foreign policy among the peasants (Trinadtsatyi S"ezd Rossiiskoi Kommunisticheskoi Partii (Bol'shevikov) (1924), p. 50). At the third

on to confirm the budget, though, since it did not meet every year, this was an incidental and intermittent function. When it adjourned after a session which rarely lasted longer than a week, its powers devolved on the TsIK elected to replace it till the next congress should meet.

Since the ostensible purpose of the constitution was to re-concile the necessities of strong central government with the demand for some measure of independence or autonomy for the constituent units, its main theoretical interest centred on the novel organ designed to fulfil this purpose — the bicameral TsIK, consisting of the Council of the Union elected by the Congress of Soviets and the Council of Nationalities elected by the central executive committees of the republics, autonomous republics and autonomous regions.[1] While the authority of the Congress of Soviets progressively declined, TsIK seemed at first sight to take a fresh lease of life from its bicameral structure, which enhanced its importance as the much publicized counter-part of western " parliaments ". But even TsIK soon became uncomfortably large. In 1925, after the admission of the Uzbek and Turkmen SSRs to the union, the Council of the Union was increased in numbers from 414 with 220 candidates to 450 with 199 candidates, the Council of Nationalities from 100 to 131 with 53 candidates. The 450 members of the Council of the Union, of whom more than 300 were representatives of the RSFSR, included *ex officio* the ten People's Commissars of the union and — incongruously — the Soviet diplomatic envoys in London and Berlin. The composition of the Council of Nationalities, heavily

Union Congress of Soviets in May 1925 a number of delegates made speeches demanding a stiffer and more vigorous foreign policy, and Chicherin returned a reassuring answer on the intentions of the government (*Tretii S"ezd Sovetov SSSR* (1925), pp. 66-100, 114-117, 130-131, 145-147). Though it would be rash to deny any spontaneous character to these speeches, it was clear that they were calculated to strengthen the hand of the Soviet Government in negotiations with foreign Powers ; one of the critics referred to the presence of foreign diplomatic representatives in the audience (*ibid.* p. 147). The precedent of critical speeches on foreign policy was followed at later congresses, at which Litvinov replaced Chicherin ; speeches on domestic policy, following the traditional report by the president of Sovnarkom, were almost exclusively laudatory, and rarely touched controversial issues.

[1] The statute of TsIK, drawn up in November 1923, is in *Postanovleniya Tret'ei Sessii Tsentral'nogo Ispolnitel'nogo Komiteta SSSR* (1923), pp. 3-11, and in *Sobranie Uzakonenii, 1923*, No. 106, art. 1030.

weighted in favour of the smaller, and especially of the non-Russian, units (Union republics and autonomous republics alike had five delegates each irrespective of population, and autonomous regions one), seemed to make it the licensed custodian of the federal character of the Union. But, owing to the large number of autonomous republics and regions comprised in the RSFSR, 68 of the 131 members of the Council of Nationalities came from that republic.[1]

The first TsIK of the USSR had, by a constitutional anomaly, met in December 1922, before the constitution of the union was ratified, or even drafted : [2] it had not then acquired its bicameral form. The second TsIK had held its first session in February 1924 immediately after the ratification of the constitution. But its business had been mainly formal.[3] The two chambers did not meet separately and questions of procedure were not discussed. These first arose when the second TsIK assembled for its second session in October 1924. The session lasted a full fortnight — from October 17 to 29, 1924 ; and it was the only occasion on which broad constitutional issues involving the respective rights of the union and of the constituent republics were seriously debated. As Enukidze said, Soviet legislators had no experience of working in two chambers ; and it was decided when the session opened that, as a general rule, the two chambers should sit together to hear the reports of government spokesmen and then debate them separately.[4] This procedure was followed for the reports on the harvest, on internal trade and on finance. But Chicherin's report on foreign affairs was debated in joint session ; and the debate on the organization of the judiciary and on the principles of criminal law was begun in joint session, and continued in separate sessions. No explanation was offered of these variations in procedure. The reports on the harvest, on trade and on foreign affairs were non-contentious. Sokolnikov's report on finance covered much important ground.[5] But the debate, apart from a few complaints of the financial impotence of the republics, which were pleas for a lost cause, raised no

---

[1] *Tretii S"ezd Sovetov SSSR* (1925), pp. 541-545.

[2] See *The Bolshevik Revolution, 1917-1923*, Vol. 1, p. 398.

[3] See *The Interregnum, 1923-1924*, p. 351.

[4] *SSSR : Tsentral'nyi Ispolnitel'nyi Komitet 2 Sozyva : 2 Sessiya* (1924), p. 5.   [5] See Vol. 1, pp. 458-459.

contentious issues. It was the reports on the constitution of the judiciary and on the principles of criminal law which, being by nature concerned with legal niceties, provided the occasion for keen and sometimes acrimonious argument.

The question of legislative competence was one of the most confused and obscure in relations between the central authorities and the union republics. Before the creation of the USSR, the RSFSR had been the only one of the Soviet republics to possess the technical equipment and trained personnel required for the drafting of legislation on any important scale. Hence the habit grew up in the other republics of adopting as their own the laws and decrees of the RSFSR, sometimes tacitly, sometimes by identical enactment, sometimes by enactment with amendments designed to take account of local conditions. Attention was drawn to this anomalous situation when the RSFSR enacted its series of codes in 1922. The earliest of these, the criminal code of May 1922, was adopted by the Ukrainian and Transcaucasian republics with minor amendments, and by the White Russian republic without amendment.[1] When the agrarian, labour, civil and judicial codes were passed by the TsIK of the RSFSR in October 1922, it seems to have been assumed that they would be automatically extended to the other republics.[2] The assumption in this crude form might have been wounding to national susceptibilities. But the Ukrainian delegate (by one of those anomalies so frequent in Soviet constitutional practice, delegates from the Ukrainian, White Russian and Transcaucasian republics took part in the proceedings) found the perfect way out. He announced that the Ukrainian TsIK had authorized the Ukrainian government to enter into a " legal union " with the RSFSR and the other republics, and suggested that the TsIK of the RSFSR should instruct its presidium to make to the other republics " a friendly proposal to introduce also in the other republics the codes adopted by the fourth session of the all-Russian TsIK ". This

---

[1] *SSSR : Tsentral'nyi Ispolnitel'nyi Komitet 3 Sozyva : 2 Sessiya* (1926), p. 615 ; the Ukrainian criminal code came into force on September 15, 1922 (*Zbirnik Uzakonen' ta Rosporyadzhen'*, *1922*, No. 36, art. 554).

[2] According to M. Reikhel, *Soyuz Sovetskikh Sotsialistichestikh Respublik* (Kharkov, 1925), i, 47, the preambles to the codes as originally drafted contained a provision for their extension to the other republics ; if this is correct, any reference to this tactless formula has been expunged from the records of the session.

suggestion was unanimously agreed to without discussion,[1] and
was doubtless carried out, sometimes perhaps tacitly, sometimes
by specific enactment.[2] The situation was described at the
session of TsIK in October 1924 with little exaggeration by an
official of the RSFSR :

> The only legislation for the whole union, for all the republics,
> was the legislation of the RSFSR. So it was in practice, and
> this legislation was adopted by all the union republics, so that
> *de facto* community was secured.[3]

It was with this background of unity in mind that the framers
of the constitution of the USSR had reserved to the union the
right to lay down the " bases " of a common judicial structure
and a common civil and criminal legislation.[4] It was with this
background in mind that the newly fledged TsIK set out in
October 1924 to debate the reports on judicial organization and on
the principles of criminal law.

The two reports were debated together. But the most serious
contretemps occurred on the first of them. Under the constitution
a Supreme Court " attached to the Central Executive Committee of the USSR " was to be established for the purpose of
" strengthening revolutionary legality and coordinating the efforts
of the union republics in the struggle against counter-revolution ".
The question of the organization of the courts was to be regulated
in a special decree ; and a draft decree " on the foundations of
the judiciary of the USSR and of the union republics ", which
had already been approved by Sovnarkom, was now submitted
to TsIK for confirmation. Unexpectedly, and disconcertingly,
however, a violent attack on it was launched by Krylenko, who
was deputy People's Commissar for Justice of the RSFSR.
Krylenko's indictment rested on two arguments. In the first

---

[1] *IV Sessiya Vserossiiskogo Tsentral'nogo Ispolnitel'nogo Komiteta IX
Sozyva : Byulleten'*, No. 8, November 1, 1922, p. 21.

[2] The civil code was adopted by the Ukrainian SSR on February 1, 1923,
by the Armenian SSR on April 10, 1923, and by the Georgian SSR (with
amendments in the chapter on inheritance) on September 1, 1923 (*Das Recht
Sowjetrusslands*, ed. A. Maklezow (1925), pp. 253-354); the agrarian code was
adopted with amendments, by the Ukrainian SSR on November 29, 1922, by
the Georgian SSR on May 15, 1924, and by the White Russian SSR on February
24, 1925 (V. Gsovski, *Soviet Civil Law*, i (Michigan, 1948), 660, quoting a
Soviet text-book *Zemel'noe Pravo* (1940)).

[3] *SSSR : Tsentral'nyi Ispolnitel'nyi Komitet 2 Sozyva : 2 Sessiya* (1924),
p. 454.   [4] See *The Bolshevik Revolution, 1917–1923*, Vol. 1, p. 404.

place the draft purported to set up " a single system of courts "
for the USSR, the courts of the constituent republics, including
their supreme courts, being explicitly subordinated to the Supreme
Court of the union ; and this " centralization " was a breach of
the constitution, which had left the People's Commissariats of
Justice, as republican commissariats, under the exclusive control
of the constituent republics.   Secondly, the draft accorded to the
Supreme Court of the USSR a right of " review and annulment
of decisions of the supreme courts [of the republics] on grounds of
incompatibility with the constitution ".   This, Krylenko declared,
was " constitutional control, not judicial policy ".   The Soviet
authorities had always " rejected the fiction of the independence of
the judicial power ".   The draft overthrew this basic principle, and
attempted to introduce " the old theory of the separation of powers
and the supremacy of the judicial organs over the administrative
officers who represent the sovereign power ".   Krylenko summed
up both arguments in the demand that the respective People's
Commissariats of Justice of the Republics, not the Supreme
Court of the USSR, should constitute the highest judicial power.[1]

In the debate which followed, the first speaker, Antonov-
Saratovsky, accused Krylenko of seeking to destroy the union by
clinging to the letter of the constitution.   Kursky, the People's
Commissar for Justice of the RSFSR, tactfully sat on the fence,
not contesting the legal validity of Krylenko's arguments, but
holding that uniform legislation and uniform provisions for
judicial organization were indispensable throughout the union.
Skrypnik, the delegate from the Ukraine, alone whole-heartedly
supported Krylenko : [2]

> With profound hatred, with contempt, we remember the
> old times of the Tsarist empire, the single indivisible state.
> We have no single indivisible state.

But even Skrypnik rejected the idea that the USSR could be " a
mere confederation ".   Kalinin defended the Sovnarkom draft,
but mainly on the ingenuous ground that the issue was too

---

[1] *SSSR : Tsentral'nyi Ispolnitel'nyi Komitet 2 Sozyva : 2 Sessiya* (1924),
pp. 404-414.

[2] Piquancy was added to this alliance by the fact that Krylenko and Skrypnik
had been protagonists on opposite sides when the office of procurator was
created in May 1922 (see Vol. 1, p. 82) ; it was Krylenko who had altered his
tune.

technical to be understood by plain men. Larin confused it still further by an attempt to return to the legal philosophy of the first days of the revolution. The Sovnarkom draft, he declared, represented " a penetration of petty bourgeois tendencies into our concepts ". What was wanted was not constitutional regulation or a code of law — all this was merely a " transitional weapon " — but complete freedom for courts to pronounce verdicts according to their conscience — a view which Krylenko described as " decentralist, anarchist and federalist (in the worst sense of the term) ".[1]

At this point the Council of the Union and the Council of Nationalities, on the demand of the latter, divided, and continued the debate in separate sessions. It now drifted away from the question of judicial organization to the draft " principles of criminal legislation ".[2] These incurred criticism in the Council of Nationalities from jealous representatives of the republics who detected an inroad on their prerogatives. Delegates from Kazakhstan and Uzbekistan plausibly opined that principles of criminal law drawn up in Moscow would prove inapplicable in Central Asia, where blood-feuds and polygamy were still endemic. Skrypnik, with less practical arguments to support him, pointed out that the original treaty of union signed in December 1922 had reserved civil and criminal legislation for the central authority, and that the revised formula in the final constitution had been intended as a concession to the republics, which was now being whittled away.[3] At the end of these inconclusive and bewildering discussions, both the Council of the Union and the Council of Nationalities were glad to refer the issues to drafting commissions, which had the unenviable task of working out verbal compromises. These were announced at a later stage of the session. In the matter of judicial organization the principle of " a single system of judicial institutions " was maintained ; and " unity of judicial policy " was to be assured both by the Supreme Court of the USSR and by the People's Commissariats of Justice and supreme courts of the constituent republics.[4] In practice, like

---

[1] *SSSR : Tsentral'nyi Ispolnitel'nyi Komitet 2 Sozyva : 2 Sessiya* (1924), pp. 439-440, 452.   [2] For the " principles " see pp. 433-434 below.

[3] *SSSR : Tsentral'nyi Ispolnitel'nyi Komitet 2 Sozyva : 2 Sessiya* (1924), pp. 465-466, 469-470.

[4] *Ibid.* pp. 589-590 ; *Postanovleniya TsIK Soyuza SSR : 2 Sessiya* (1924), pp. 93-99.

everything else in the constitution, this represented a victory for
a firmly centralized control ; but the victory was due to factors
that lay altogether outside the constitutional field. A similar
compromise was recorded in the field of criminal law. The draft
principles were approved with a few minor amendments. The
elaboration of criminal codes remained the prerogative of the
Union republics. But " the presidium of TsIK has the right to
indicate to the Union republics in indispensable cases the kinds
and forms of crime for which the USSR deems it indispensable to
apply the definite line of a single penal policy ".[1] Security —
the main field in which the USSR would assert its " indispensable " authority in criminal legislation and administration — provided a powerful impetus to centralization.[2]

Although the questions of judicial organization and criminal
law were the only ones on which an open clash occurred — and
even then in a confused and muted form — an undercurrent of
jealous rivalry between the power of the Union and the rights
of the republics ran through all the proceedings of the session of
October 1924. It was Skrypnik, the Ukrainian, who persistently
sounded the note of republican intransigence, asserting it even in
the field of military affairs :

> We are changing over our Red Army to the Ukrainian
> language, and in Georgia, from the very beginning of the
> organization of the Red Army, orders of the day and the word
> of command have been given in the Georgian language.

On the other hand, Chicherin, speaking for the commissariat
whose centralized authority was least contested and most easily
taken for granted, firmly explained, in a report on the legal character of Soviet citizenship, that " our federal Soviet state is not at
all a union of states, but a single state ".[3] It was left to Enukidze
to provide an official summing-up :

> If we speak of the unity of the state, then of course our
> union of republics is the most unitary state in this sense of the
> word, and our unity exceeds a thousandfold the unity which

[1] SSSR : Tsentral'nyi Ispolnitel'nyi Komitet 2 Sozyva : 2 Sessiya (1924),
pp. 616-624.

[2] For a further discussion of this issue see pp. 441-442 below.

[3] SSSR: Tsentral'nyi Ispolnitel'nyi Komitet 2 Sozyva : 2 Sessiya (1924),
pp. 468, 491.

existed under the Tsarist autocracy. . . . Our unity is sealed
not by constitutional laws, not by this or that paragraph, but
by the common interests of the workers and peasants of all the
union of republics.

Yet the nationalities of the Union now for the first time enjoyed
" the full development of their language and of their national
culture ", and the central authority had never extended any preference or privilege to " the great Power nation in our Union ", i.e.
to the Great Russians.[1] The claim was not unfounded. But these
issues had little relation to the somewhat unreal framework of the
constitution, and were governed by considerations other than
those of constitutional propriety.

The session of October 1924 was the last, as well as the first,
occasion on which TsIK provided a forum for serious controversies on the respective rights of the USSR and of the constituent republics, or on which its bicameral status seemed to have
more than a historical interest. Article 8 of the constitution
prescribed that sessions both of the Congress of Soviets and of
TsIK should take place at the capitals of the constituent republics in rotation. In accordance with this rule, the session of
TsIK in March 1925 was duly held in Tiflis. Thereafter, the
rule was quietly forgotten, and all subsequent meetings held in
Moscow. According to article 21 of the constitution TsIK was
to meet three times a year. In fact it was convened at irregular
intervals as the exigencies or conveniences of policy dictated, but
rarely more often than once a year.[2] At first an attempt was
made to establish a practice of holding a general debate at each
session on the affairs of one of the constituent republics : thus
Transcaucasian affairs were debated at the session of March
1925, Ukrainian affairs in 1926, and White Russian affairs in 1927.
Thereafter this practice seems to have lapsed. Even the division
of TsIK into two chambers, which was the essential novelty of
the constitution and the great concession to the rights of the
constituent republics, was in danger of becoming blurred. At the

---

[1] *SSSR : Tsentral'nyi Ispolnitel'nyi Komitet 2 Sozyva : 2 Sessiya* (1924),
pp. 507-509.
[2] Particulars of the frequency and duration of its meetings are collected in
J. Towster, *Political Power in the USSR, 1917-1947* (N.Y., 1948), pp. 229-230;
in the period from 1923 to 1936 it sat on an average for less than ten days a year.

beginning of the session of March 1925 it was proposed that, following the precedent of the previous session, the two chambers should sit together to hear the report of Rykov as president of Sovnarkom. For the rest of the session, the chambers sat together without further comment, though votes, delivered by show of hands, continued to be counted separately ; and, in spite of an energetic protest by Skrypnik against the illegality of the procedure, a joint commission of the two chambers was appointed to examine the question of the agricultural tax.[1] There can be little doubt that the practice of separate sessions would have been allowed to lapse altogether but for a further protest from the indefatigable Skrypnik at the outset of the next meeting of TsIK in April 1926 ; this elicited a ruling from the chair that separate sessions were required unless there was unanimous consent to dispense with them.[2] At subsequent meetings, separate and joint sessions alternated. But, since important controversial issues were rarely raised, the elaborate constitutional machinery served no apparent purpose, and the debates of the two chambers needlessly duplicated each other. The device of the bicameral TsIK, though upheld in theory, had proved abortive and meaningless in practice.

The rapid decline in the prestige and authority of the TsIK of the USSR, while it had symptoms and characteristics peculiar to it, was also a direct continuation of the decline which had overtaken the corresponding organ of the RSFSR before the formation of the union, when the large, unwieldy and intermittent representative assembly was gradually replaced for all practical purposes by its own presidium. This process, originally set in motion by successive amendments to the constitution of the RSFSR,[3] was irreversible ; and the original draft of the constitution of the USSR, dating from December 1922, contained an article recognizing the presidium as " the supreme organ of power " between the sessions of TsIK. From the outset, therefore, the presidium

---

[1] *SSSR : Tsentral'nyi Ispolnitel'nyi Komitet 2 Sozyva : 3 Sessiya* (1925), pp. 8, 101-102.
[2] *SSSR : Tsentral'nyi Ispolnitel'nyi Komitet 3 Sozyva : 2 Sessiya* (1926), pp. 568-570.
[3] See *The Bolshevik Revolution, 1917–1923*, Vol. 1, pp. 215-216 ; for the various powers exercised by the presidium see J. Towster, *Political Power in the USSR, 1917–1947* (N.Y., 1948), p. 244.

established itself as the effective organ of TsIK empowered to take action in its name; and even its formal responsibility to the body from which it emanated became shadowy and unreal. At the session of TsIK in October 1924, Enukidze referred rather apologetically, though without explanation, to the long delay in convening the session and promised to make a full report on the activities of the presidium to the next session of TsIK or to the forthcoming Union Congress of Soviets. To the present session the presidium had nothing to offer but a list of laws and decrees passed and put into operation, and now submitted for the formal endorsement of TsIK. This, in conformity with precedent, was accorded without discussion.[1] In view of the symbolical importance of the budget, it was a significant symptom when the third Union Congress of Soviets in May 1925 specifically conferred on the presidium of TsIK the right to introduce changes in the budget " during the period that remains till the close of the budget year ", reporting any such changes to the next session of TsIK.[2]

The substitution of the presidium of TsIK for the plenary body as the legislative organ was therefore virtually complete from the first. In the summer of 1923, when the establishment of a bicameral TsIK was decided on, Skrypnik had already drawn the logical conclusion, and proposed to invest the presidium of each chamber of TsIK with full powers to act separately on its behalf, so that the small presidium of the Council of Nationalities would become the effective custodian of the interests of the republics. The implications of this manœuvre were, however, quickly detected. The party conference on national questions which was dealing with the constitutional issue pronounced an unequivocal verdict :

> The presidium of TsIK should be one. It should be elected by both chambers of TsIK with, of course, a guarantee of representatives for the nationalities — at any rate, for the largest of them. The proposal of the Ukrainians to form two presidiums with legislative functions, corresponding to the two chambers of TsIK, is impracticable. The presidium is the

---

[1] SSSR : Tsentral'nyi Ispolnitel'nyi Komitet 2 Sozyva : 2 Sessiya (1924), pp. 506-507, 515-517 ; Sobranie Zakonov, 1924, No. 19, art. 183.
[2] Tretii S"ezd Sovetov SSSR : Postanovleniya (1925), p. 30.

supreme power of the union functioning between sessions [of TsIK]. The formation of two presidiums with legislative functions is a division in the supreme power which would inevitably create great complications in practice. The chambers should have their own presidiums which should not, however, possess legislative functions.[1]

In accordance with this directive, the final text of the constitution prescribed that the presidium of the TsIK should consist of the seven members of the presidium of the Council of the Union, the seven members of the presidium of the Council of Nationalities, and seven others to be elected jointly by the two councils.[2] Thus the eclipse of TsIK by its presidium carried with it a formal retreat from the bicameral principle, and marked the final bankruptcy of this attempt to provide a safeguard of the rights of the republics. After 1925 the struggle between unification and federalism, between centralization and devolution, was removed from the constitutional plane and took on other forms.

As formerly in the constitution of the RSFSR, however, so now in that of the USSR, the authority of TsIK was progressively sapped, not only by its own presidium, but also — and more significantly — by Sovnarkom, which effectively acquired or arrogated to itself legislative as well as executive powers coterminous with those of TsIK. In the period which followed the adoption of the constitution of the USSR, the authority of Sovnarkom, now reduced in numbers to ten by the exclusion of the republican commissariats, continued to grow at the expense of TsIK and its presidium. The constitutional uncertainties about the division of competence between TsIK and the Congress of Soviets or between TsIK and its presidium equally governed

[1] *VKP(B) v Rezolyutsiyakh* (1941), i, 528.
[2] The number was raised to 27 (nine of each category) by an amendment approved by the third Congress of Soviets in May 1925 (*Tretii S"ezd Sovetov SSSR : Postanovleniya* (1925), p. 9). At the subsequent meetings of TsIK to elect its presidium, Enukidze submitted the lists "proposed" by the two councils, implying that they required the confirmation of TsIK acting as a whole ; Skrypnik protested against this interpretation, but without effect, though the issue was now plainly academic (*SSSR : Tsentral'nyi Ispolnitel'nyi Komitet 3 Sozyva : 1 Sessiya* (1925), pp. 11-13). Each chamber also had its own presidium, but these bodies were concerned solely with the organization of business, and had no legislative or executive powers.

the relations of all those organs to Sovnarkom. The powers conferred on the Sovnarkom of the USSR " for the immediate direction of the different departments of the state administration" were cursorily defined in the constitution itself.. But on July 17, 1923, within a few days of its appointment by TsIK, the new Sovnarkom formally announced to the TsIKs and Sovnarkoms of the Union republics that it had entered on its functions, and requested them to submit to it for examination " questions within its competence under the terms of the constitution ".[1] In November 1923 its powers and functions were defined in an elaborate statute approved by TsIK.[2] But they were defined in terms which, while they appeared to insist on the due subordination of the administrative and executive functions of Sovnarkom to the legislative functions of TsIK and its presidium, in fact conferred on Sovnarkom a right of " examination and ratification of decrees and decisions of all-Union importance within the scope defined by the constitution of the USSR " as well as of "the examination and execution of all measures necessary for the general administration of the USSR ".

The statute of Sovnarkom remained the formal charter of its constitutional authority. Within this ample framework of discretion, no act of Sovnarkom could easily be described as *ultra vires* ; and no such conception was recognized in the Soviet constitution. Even in the domain of treaty-making Sovnarkom acquired independent constitutional powers. Under the constitution the conclusion and ratification of international treaties was entrusted to the " supreme organs " of the union, i.e. the Congress of Soviets and TsIK. At its first business session in November 1923 TsIK formally debated and ratified an agreement with Finland on timber-floating on the Neva.[3] But at a later stage such formal agreements were not submitted to TsIK, or even to its presidium, for ratification. The statute of Sovnarkom empowered that body not only " to examine treaties and agreements

[1] *Sistematicheskoe Sobranie Deistvuyushchikh Zakonov SSSR*, i (1926), 30-31.

[2] *Postanovleniya Tret'ei Sessii Tsentral'nogo Ispolnitel'nogo Komiteta SSSR* (1923), pp. 13-15 ; it was followed by a general statute for People's Commissariats of the USSR (*ibid.* pp. 16-21). These documents also appeared in *Sobranie Uzakonenii, 1923*, No. 106, art. 1031 ; No. 107, art. 1032.

[3] *Tret'ya Sessiya Tsentral'nogo Ispolnitel'nogo Komiteta SSSR* (1923), pp. 68-73 ; *id. : Postanovleniya* (1923), p. 157.

with the governments of foreign states ", but also " to confirm such treaties as do not require special ratification " ; and this distinction between ordinary treaties confirmed by Sovnarkom and treaties submitted to the solemn form of ratification by TsIK or by its presidium [1] proved perfectly satisfactory. In practice it was difficult, if not impossible, to discover any constitutional division of competence between Sovnarkom, the presidium of TsIK, TsIK and the Union Congress of Soviets. Sovnarkom enjoyed practical pre-eminence in all day-to-day decisions, whether they issued in executive, administrative or legislative action ; and this pre-eminence was marked both by the attachment to Sovnarkom of auxiliary technical organs, such as a commission on legislative proposals and a commission on financial administration, and of important economic organs such as STO, Gosplan and the Chief Concessions Committee,[2] and by the presence in Sovnarkom of party members of higher standing than in any other governmental organ. Soviet constitutional lawyers sometimes speculated about the relative authority of Sovnarkom and of the presidium of TsIK.[3] The question was unreal, since neither body possessed independent power ; but, as an agent of the party for the execution of policy and for the transaction of day-to-day business, Sovnarkom was the more important.[4] The budget alone remained apparently exempt from constitutional compromise, since Sovnarkom was obliged both by the constitution and by its statute to submit the annual budget for approval

[1] The distinction was formalized by a decree of May 1925 (*Sobranie Zakonov, 1925*, No. 35, art. 258).

[2] For the statutes of these bodies see *Sistematicheskoe Sobranie Deistvuyushchikh Zakonov SSSR*, i (1926), 36-45, 52-54.

[3] Current speculations are quoted in J. Towster, *Political Power in the USSR, 1917-1947* (N.Y., 1948), p. 245, note 10.

[4] Light was thrown at the fifth Tatar congress of Soviets in 1925 on relations between the TsIK and the Sovnarkom of the Tatar autonomous SSR. Here the presidium of TsIK had been reorganized as a " small " Sovnarkom. This reorganization was " dictated mainly by considerations of formality, though it should be mentioned as a positive characteristic of the small Council of People's Commissars that the deputy president of the central executive committee is included in its composition, by means of which change a perfect coordination in the work of the central executive committee and the Council of People's Commissars is attained " ; as a further result of this reform, it was now rarely necessary to submit decisions of the Sovnarkom to TsIK for ratification (*Pyatyi S"ezd Sovetov Tatar'skoi SSR* (Kazan, 1925), pp. 34, 56, quoted in W. R. Batsell, *Soviet Rule in Russia* (N.Y., 1929), pp. 334-335).

by TsIK. This formality, insistence on which no doubt owed something to the time-honoured precedent of western democracy, constituted the last vestige of the status of TsIK as a representative assembly exercising popular control over the public purse. It was regularly complied with so long as TsIK continued to meet annually; thereafter its prerogative in respect of the budget passed to its presidium.

The haze of empirical ambiguity which surrounded the mutual relations of the central organs of government of the USSR extended equally to relations between the central executive committee of the USSR and the central executive committee of a Union republic, as well as to relations between the Sovnarkom of the USSR and the Sovnarkom of a Union republic. For, while it was constantly asserted in official documents that " supreme power " in the territory of the republics was vested in the congress of Soviets of the republic in question,[1] the overriding " supreme power " of the Union Congress of Soviets and the organs dependent on it was explicitly reserved. Under articles 19 and 20 of the constitution, all " decrees, resolutions and orders " of TsIK were to be carried out immediately throughout the territory of the USSR, and TsIK had the right to " suspend or cancel " decrees or orders of congresses of Soviets or central executive committees of the Union republics. The rights of Sovnarkom under article 38 were defined in slightly less uncompromising terms:

> The Sovnarkom of the USSR, within the limits of the rights accorded to it by the central executive committee of the USSR and on the basis of the statutes of the Sovnarkom of the USSR, issues decrees and decisions which must be executed throughout the territory of the USSR.

But even the formal limitation related only to organs and enactments of the USSR, not of the republics ; it left the authorities of the USSR the sole arbiters of constitutional propriety. Where the basic conception of a judicially determinable and legally enforceable limitation or separation of powers was rejected, and a constitution was regarded as a code of convenient and, if necessary, flexible rules of procedure, the over-riding authority of the

---

[1] See, for example, art. 3 of the constitution of the RSFSR of May 1925 (*Sobranie Uzakonenii, 1925*, No. 30, art. 218).

higher organ automatically asserted itself. This process was probably helped rather than hindered by the formal provision for extensive representation of the republics " in a consultative capacity " at sessions of Sovnarkom. Not only did each of the republics appoint a " permanent representative to the Council of People's Commissars of the USSR ",[1] but the large number of officials entitled to attend sessions of the Sovnarkom of the USSR in a consultative capacity included the presidents of the TsIKs and Sovnarkoms of the Union republics, as well as People's Commissars of those republics for matters within their competence.[2] There is no evidence to suggest that this procedure was regularly applied or acquired any practical significance. But it helped to establish the fictitious hypothesis that decisions of the Sovnarkom of the USSR were taken in consultation with the republics and were therefore binding on them.

The most delicate situation arose over the powers not of TsIK, or of the Sovnarkom as a whole, but of individual People's Commissariats of the USSR. In the three-tier system of commissariats — all-Union, unified and republican [3] — the highest layer was formed by the all-Union commissariats having no counterparts in the republics. Their position was clear enough. Article 53 of the constitution provided that such commissariats " have plenipotentiary representatives directly subordinate to them attached to the Union republics " ; and, under article 12 of the regulating statute of the commissariats, these plenipotentiaries " participate in the sessions of the Sovnarkoms of the union republics either with a consultative or with a deciding vote, as determined by the TsIK of the Union republic or by its presidium ".[4] The position of the unified commissariats, which

---

[1] For the decrees of the RSFSR and the White Russian SSR creating these posts see *Sobranie Uzakonenii, 1924*, No. 70, art. 691 ; *Sobranie Uzakonenii SSR Belorussii, 1924*, No. 21, art. 185, which prescribed that the White Russian representative " takes part in sessions of the presidium of TsIK, Sovnarkom and STO of the USSR ". The title " representative " had a quasi-diplomatic flavour which was no doubt flattering to the republics.

[2] *Sistematicheskoe Sobranie Deistvuyushchikh Zakonov SSSR*, i (1926), 33-34.

[3] See *The Bolshevik Revolution, 1917–1923*, Vol. i, pp. 403-405.

[4] *Sistematicheskoe Sobranie Deistvuyushchikh Zakonov SSSR*, i (1926), 68-72 ; a decree of the RSFSR is on record granting to Voroshilov, as " plenipotentiary of the People's Commissariat of Military and Naval Affairs of the USSR to the Sovnarkom of the RSFSR ", the right to attend its sessions with full voting powers (*Sobranie Uzakonenii, 1925*, No. 55. art. 416). A decree

occupied the second tier of the structure, was, however, full of ambiguities. While the republican commissariat was clearly subordinate to the Union commissariat, the constitutional authority of the Union commissariat was not unlimited. Article 59 of the constitution allowed the central executive committees of Union republics to suspend the application to their territories of decrees of People's Commissars of the USSR (but not apparently of TsIK or of Sovnarkom as a whole) if these were " in flagrant contradiction " with existing legislation.[1] But the central executive committee exercising this right was to report that it had done so to the Sovnarkom of the USSR and to the commissariat of the USSR concerned ; and it was to be presumed, though it was not explicitly stated, that the eventual decision of the Sovnarkom of the USSR was final. On the other hand, the Union commissariats under their general statute could " suspend and annul " decisions of the corresponding republican commissariats which " contravened directions given by them on all-union legislation ", though this right did not extend to decrees issued by a republican commissariat on the specific authority of the republican Sovnarkom.[2]

These obscure and mutually frustrating provisions opened the way to an unresolved constitutional deadlock. In October 1924 Enukidze assured the TsIK of the RSFSR that, while decisions of unified commissariats of the RSFSR could in principle be overruled by the corresponding commissariats of the USSR, this did not apply to decisions taken on the express authority of the Sovnarkom or of the presidium of the TsIK of the RSFSR.[3] The new constitution of the RSFSR of May 1925 was prudently

of the White Russian SSR similarly provided for the attachment to the White Russian Sovnarkom of " a plenipotentiary of the People's Commissariat of Communications of the USSR " (*Sobranie Uzakonenii SSR Belorussii, 1924*, No. 27, art. 240). From art. 11 of the statute of the Sovnarkom of the Moldavian autonomous SSR, of which a translation is in W. R. Batsell, *Soviet Rule in Russia* (N.Y., 1929), pp. 628–632, it appears that representatives of these plenipotentiaries were also attached to the Sovnarkoms of the autonomous SSRs.

[1] This article was based on art. 17 of the original treaty of December 30, 1922, which was the foundation of the Union; the original article contained the qualifying words " in exceptional cases ", which were dropped from the text of the constitution.

[2] *Sistematicheskoe Sobranie Deistvuyushchikh Zakonov SSSR*, i (1926), 71.

[3] *Vserossiiskii Tsentral'nyi Ispolnitel'nyi Komitet XI Sozvya : Vtoraya Sessiya* (1924), p. 286.

silent on this point. Article 10 of the statute of the Sovnarkom of the RSFSR adopted in August 1925 laid it down that, while decisions of unified commissariats of the RSFSR could be " suspended, amended or annulled " by the corresponding commissariats of the USSR, decisions taken by commissariats of the RSFSR on the authority of the Sovnarkom of the RSFSR could be overruled only on an appeal by the corresponding commissariat of the USSR to the Sovnarkom of the USSR.[1] This concession did not, however, satisfy the central authorities ; and in September 1925 an additional decree of the RSFSR was issued making it clear that the onus of making the appeal against a suspension or annulment rested on the commissariat of the RSFSR and that the lodging of the appeal did not suspend the operation of the contested decision.[2] This was merely one further instance of the progressive concentration of effective power at the centre which marked the history of the Soviet constitution.[3]

The constitutional position of the republican commissariats, which occupied the third and lowest tier, seemed at first sight clear and impregnable, since they had no union counterpart and might be supposed to enjoy exclusive powers. But here, too, the central authority imposed itself through the right conferred on the Union to lay down " foundations " and " general principles " and " fundamental laws " in spheres nominally reserved for republican jurisdiction ; and this constitutional right was buttressed by the patent necessity of establishing some measure of coordination and uniformity and by the lack of trained and experienced personnel which hampered the activities of all the republics (with the exception of the Russian, and the partial exception of the Ukrainian, republics). The situation of the republican commissariats differed far less from that of the unified commissariats of the republics, and had changed far less since the days when legislation of the RSFSR was tacitly or explicitly adopted by the other republics, than constitutional doctrine pretended. Decrees or orders were

---

[1] *Sobranie Uzakonenii, 1925*, No. 70, art. 553.
[2] *Ibid*. No. 72, art. 569.
[3] See *The Bolshevik Revolution, 1917-1923*, Vol. 1, pp. 408-409 ; a Soviet commentator cautiously invoked the parallel of Woodrow Wilson's doctrine of " implied powers " as explaining the growing predominance of federal authority (M. Reikhel, *Soyuz Sovetskikh Sotsialisticheskikh Respublik* (Kharkov, 1925), i, 96-100).

I*

freely issued by the supreme organs of the USSR on all important
and controversial matters. Whether or not the drafters of these
decrees or orders remembered to observe the constitutional
proprieties, the effect was the same. The formal confusion was
immense.

> As the result of the large number of republics in our union
> [wrote a jurist of the Narkomvnudel of the RSFSR] . . . we
> have at least two tiers of legislation : Union legislation and
> republican legislation. Both are extremely abundant, very dis-
> persed and not systematized. On the other side there remains
> a vast heritage from the periods preceding the formation of the
> Union, part of it *de facto* dead, part of it amended by subsequent
> laws. In this chaos, not only a cossack with a pike, but the
> best qualified professional jurist, will lose his way.[1]

In practice the confusion was less great. Whenever the central
authorities stepped in, their prerogative was never openly contested, though marked differences might occur between republics
in the interpretation and application of these rulings. Centralizing
tendencies were always at work. At the session of TsIK in April
1926 a Ukrainian delegate complained that " ideas of founding
Union commissariats of justice and education are quite deeply
implanted ", and that " comrade Semashko is not at all opposed
to the creation of a Union commissariat of health " ; the recent
establishment of a Union council for physical culture was a step
in that direction.[2] Krylenko on the same occasion complained
that officials of Narkomvnutorg were so ignorant of the constitution that they had recently written a letter to a non-existent
Narkomyust of the Union, advocating an " all-Union code for
foodstuffs ".[3] But a large field remained in which the organs of
the USSR, whether through lack of interest or lack of qualification, did not intervene ; and here the republics continued to enjoy
a provisional measure of constitutional autonomy.

The complexities and ambiguities of these constitutional
arrangements would have made them quite unworkable without
the reality that lay behind them : the over-riding power of the
party. Under the Soviet view of law, constitutional enactments

[1] *Sovetskoe Stroitel'stvo : Sbornik*, iv-v (1926), 92.

[2] *SSSR : Tsentral'nyi Ispolnitel'nyi Komitet 3 Sozyva : 2 Sessiya* (1926),
p. 625.   [3] *Ibid.* p. 632.

were the expression of the will of the sovereign power, and could not be invoked in opposition to it ; the notion of constitutional safeguards, interpreted and protected by judicial authority, was inappropriate and meaningless. Under the Soviet system, all constitutional appearances were in some measure illusory, since ultimate decisions on major issues of policy were taken by party organs and handed down by them to the constitutional authorities for execution. Lenin's death, while it in no way changed the essence of the situation, tore away some of the disguises. The prestige which he had conferred on Soviet institutions by his regular appearance with a major policy speech at the All-Russian Congress of Soviets, and, above all, by his presidency of Sovnarkom, was now seen to be largely factitious. Of the new leaders, Zinoviev had never held office in Sovnarkom ; Stalin had laid down both his former offices ; even Kamenev's appointment as president of STO was less conspicuous and important than his party functions as chairman of the Politburo and as head of the Moscow organization. The other leaders who now played the principal rôles in the TsIK and Sovnarkom of USSR — Kalinin, Rykov, Tsyurupa, Dzerzhinsky, Sokolnikov, Chicherin — were men of secondary rank in the party hierarchy. The subordination of Soviet to party organs was more apparent, if not more real, than in the days when Lenin dominated both.

The singular and preponderant rôle of the party makes it appropriate to record, as the final act in the process of constitution-making which created the USSR, the change in the party's name effected by the fourteenth party congress in December 1925.[1] The name " Russian Communist Party (Bolsheviks) " had been adopted in March 1918 [2] when the original constitution of the RSFSR was in the making, and corresponded to the period when the RSFSR had been the effective directing nucleus of the multi-national group of Soviet republics. Now that a decent veil had been drawn over Russian constitutional predominance by re-organizing the group in the form of a Union of Soviet Socialist Republics, and reducing the RSFSR to the status of a unit of the group, it was logical that a similar readjustment should be made in the name and organization of the party. The change

[1] See p. 148 above.
[2] See *The Bolshevik Revolution, 1917–1923*, Vol. 1, p. 190.

encountered resistance which explained the delay in making it. In the party non-Russian elements were weaker than in the governmental machine, and the forces of tradition stronger ; it seemed " difficult to part with the old, tried name ".[1] What was achieved at the fourteenth party congress was in fact a compromise. The name of the party was changed, not without some opposition from a Bolshevik old guard headed by Polonsky, to " All-Union Communist Party (Bolsheviks) ". On the other hand, the logical proposal to form a separate Russian party on the same footing as the other national parties [2] within the union was decisively rejected. This, said the *rapporteur*, would be " the greatest evil for the party ", since, in view of " the specific weight of the Russian section ", it would mean having " two central directing organs ".[3] The reality behind the argument was clear. Both in the state and in the party the organs which had formerly carried the Russian label were re-named to take account of the susceptibilities of other national groups. But they remained in essence the same organs : continuity was maintained. In the state a new set of subordinate organs was created in the form of the RSFSR. In the party this precedent was not followed. Division of executive and administrative authority was tolerable and even salutary. Division of authority at the policy-making summit was not.

(b) The RSFSR

The formation of the USSR presented the RSFSR with a unique constitutional problem. The constitution of the RSFSR, which dated back to 1918, the first of all Soviet constitutions and the model on which the constitution of the USSR was itself based, was now clearly unsuited to one of the constituent republics of the USSR. In January 1924, when the constitution of the USSR had been officially ratified, the eleventh All-Russian Congress of

---

[1] *XIV S"ezd Vsesoyuznoi Kommunisticheskoi Partii (B)* (1926), p. 891.

[2] The national units of the party were by courtesy called parties — the Ukrainian party, the White Russian party, the Georgian party, etc.; but it was made clear from the outset that they were not independent parties and enjoyed the rights only of regional committees of the united party (see *The Bolshevik Revolution, 1917–1923*, Vol. 1, p. 370). A proposal to deprive them of the title of parties was rejected on the ground that " it would throw a certain shadow on our national policy " (*XIV S"ezd Vsesoyuznoi Kommunisticheskoi Partii (B)* (1926), p. 892).   [3] *Ibid.* p. 881.

Soviets took cognizance of its diminished status by instructing the All-Russian TsIK to make the necessary amendments in its constitution.[1] Three months later TsIK appointed a commission of twelve to go into the question.[2] The task was delicate ; adjustment was required in the relations of the RSFSR not only to the new USSR, but to the autonomous republics still included in it. When TsIK met in October 1924, immediately before the session of the TsIK of the USSR, no agreement had been reached. Enukidze explained that the constitution had undergone many amendments since 1918, and that to bring it up to date in present conditions would " demand very much time, the more so as these changes are bound up with changes in the constitutions of the autonomous republics ". He consolingly added that only people " whose view of the world has been nourished on bourgeois jurisprudence " thought it essential that " everything should be smoothly put together on paper and one letter not contradict another ". In the Soviet view, it was common experience for a constitution " to go out of date, to fall into partial contradiction with our practice or with this or that fundamental decision " : this merely meant that the constitution must from time to time be changed and " perfected ".[3] For the moment nothing was done but to approve the composition of the Sovnarkom of the RSFSR as established during the past nine months.

The interval before the twelfth All-Russian Congress of Soviets met in May 1925 was occupied in constitution-making behind the scenes. When the congress assembled, Kursky, the People's Commissar for Justice of the RSFSR, explained that the mere amendment of the constitution originally contemplated had proved impracticable. A new constitution embodying parts of the old would be required ; and a draft of this was submitted to the congress.[4] The preamble relating to general principles contained

[1] S"ezdy Sovetov RSFSR v Postanovleniyakh (1939), p. 285 ; Sobranie Uzakonenii, 1924, No. 27, art. 258.

[2] D. Kursky, Izbrannye Stat'i i Rechi (1948), pp. 107-111, contains a speech apparently delivered to this commission, in which Kursky already pointed to the conclusion that amendment would not be enough, and that a new constitution would be required : the date is not stated.

[3] Vserossiiskii Tsentral'nyi Ispolnitel'nyi Komitet XI Sozyva : Vtoraya Sessiya (1924), pp. 282-283, 288.

[4] XII Vserossiiskii S"ezd Sovetov (1925), pp. 136-178 ; the draft constitution was published in Izvestiya, May 3, 1925.

some interesting changes. The Declaration of Rights of the Toiling and Exploited People, which had been incorporated at the last moment on Lenin's initiative in the constitution of 1918,[1] was omitted, though reference was made to it in the first article. It had been something of an anomaly even in the earlier constitution, and much of its terminology must now have seemed quaint and obsolete.[2] Apart from this omission, certain changes of phrase were significant. The function of the constitution of 1918 had been " to guarantee the dictatorship of the proletariat for the purpose of crushing the bourgeoisie, of abolishing the exploitation of man by man and of establishing socialism, in which there will be neither division into classes, nor state power ". The constitution of 1925, in adopting this formula, substituted for the words " establishing socialism " the words " realizing communism ", thus recalling the Marxist distinction between the two stages, and preparing the way for the acceptance of a " socialism in one country " which would be compatible with the survival of state power. Other signs of the times could also be discerned. Where articles 14-17 of the old constitution had spoken of the " poor peasantry " or the " poorest peasants " as partners of the " workers " or the " working class ", the corresponding articles of the new constitution knew only the partnership of " the working class and the peasantry " or of " workers and peasants " ; in the spring of 1925, the policy of splitting the peasantry was in abeyance. The main innovations were an article (art. 27) confirming the power of the presidium of TsIK to act in its name in the intervals between its sessions (this had been entirely a growth of the period since 1918 [3]) ; an important new chapter " On the Autonomous Soviet Socialist Republics and Regions " ; and a much enlarged chapter " On Local Govern-

---

[1] See The Bolshevik Revolution, 1917–1923, Vol. i, p. 150.

[2] Apparently it was Gosplan which first raised objections to the retention of the declaration, and won the support of the Sovnarkom of the RSFSR (Ekonomicheskaya Zhizn', April 29, 1925). The declaration had inter alia commended " the Soviet law on workers' control " and the introduction of " universal labour service ", of which the former had quickly proved unworkable, and the latter had ended with war communism. The new constitution also omitted the quotation, " He that does not work, neither shall he eat ", and confined itself to the statement that the RSFSR " recognizes labour as an obligation of all citizens of the republic " (art. 9).

[3] See The Bolshevik Revolution, 1917–1923, Vol. i, pp. 215-216.

ment ". These indicated the two main constitutional preoccupations of the moment : the strengthening of the multi-national
structure of the USSR through a federalized hierarchy of republics
and autonomous republics and regions, and the attempt to build
up a more effective system of local government, especially in the
countryside — the so-called " revitalization of the Soviets ". The
debate on the new constitution was confined to the discussion of a
few minor details, and it was then adopted without more ado.[1]
The rest of the agenda of the congress was devoted to agriculture,
to health, and to the subordinate and much diminished budget
of the RSFSR. It was, as Kalinin, a little ruefully recalling past
glories, remarked, " extremely modest ".[2]

The procedure of the congress served to bring out, more
vividly than the routine debate on the constitution, some anomalies
of the new status of the RSFSR. Formally the RSFSR was
merely a constituent unit of the USSR, on a par with the Ukrainian
and White Russian SSRs and the Transcaucasian SFSR. In
reality the RSFSR was the foundation on which the USSR had
been constructed and still provided the solid framework of the
larger structure. Its capital was Moscow, the capital of the
USSR ; Rykov was president of the Sovnarkom of the RSFSR as
well as of the USSR ; the All-Russian Congress of Soviets and
the TsIK of the RSFSR conveniently held their sessions at or
about the same time as those of the corresponding organs of the
USSR. When the twelfth All-Russian Congress of Soviets met,
the proposal was at once made, and carried without discussion,
that the delegates should attend the ensuing session of the third
Congress of Soviets of the USSR to hear Rykov's report on the
work of the government of the USSR. No question arose of a
separate report by Rykov on the government of the RSFSR.
Having prematurely completed its business in a five-day session
on May 11, 1925, the All-Russian Congress of Soviets adjourned
till May 13, when the major congress was due to open. On that
day its members attended the Congress of Soviets of the USSR
to hear Rykov's report to that body ; and, thereafter, questions of
competence being conveniently ignored, the report was briefly

---

[1] *XII Vserossiiskii S"ezd Sovetov* (1925), pp. 252-253 ; for the final text of
the constitution see *id. : Postanovleniya* (1925), pp. 5-23.
[2] *XII Vserossiiskii S"ezd Sovetov* (1925), p. 267.

debated in the All-Russian Congress of Soviets and unanimously approved.[1] The realities of the situation emerged more clearly from some remarks of a delegate of the RSFSR to the Union congress than from the perfunctory proceedings of the Russian congress. What had happened was that the machinery of the unified commissariats (as well as of the commissariats now allocated exclusively to the USSR) had been taken over as it stood from the RSFSR by the new Union authorities, leaving to the RSFSR the task of creating new commissariats for its own subordinate functions. Thus, " our Union has occupied all the commissariats of the RSFSR, so that in reality the RSFSR has no personality of its own ", and " the functions of the Komvnutorg of the RSFSR have been transferred to the Komvnutorg of the Union ". On the other hand, the republican commissariats found it difficult to divest themselves of the wider functions which they had formerly exercised by tacit consent, and to limit themselves to the confines of the RSFSR : Lunacharsky was accused of behaving as if he were People's Commissar for Education for the whole of the USSR.[2] Many of the first laws and decrees of the USSR appeared in the official collection of the RSFSR ; it was not till September 1924 that the USSR began to issue its own collection of laws.[3] The difficulty of effecting a real divorce in practice between the machinery of the RSFSR and of the USSR evoked the heroic suggestion to move the capital of the RSFSR to Leningrad and that of the USSR to Nizhny-Novgorod — a suggestion reinforced by the argument that congestion in Moscow was becoming as bad as in London, and that it was " impossible to move ".[4] It was a long time before the RSFSR effectively developed its own institutions ; and the history of the USSR was subtly influenced by the fact that its major organs of government had at the outset been taken over from the RSFSR.

The new chapter of the 1925 constitution (arts. 44-48) devoted

[1] *XII Vserossiiskii S"ezd Sovetov* (1925), pp. 6, 261-267.

[2] *Tretii S"ezd Sovetov SSSR* (1925), pp. 133-134.

[3] The first issue of the *Sobranie Zakonov* of the USSR was dated September 13, 1924, and contained laws and decrees dating back to July 1, 1924.

[4] *Tretii S"ezd Sovetov SSSR* (1925), p. 133 ; Ryazanov proposed that Moscow and Leningrad should be made joint capitals of the RSFSR (*Tret'ya Sessiya Vserossiiskogo Tsentral'nogo Ispolnitel'nogo Komiteta XI Sozyva* (1925), p. 69).

to the status of the autonomous republics and regions within the
RSFSR, which had been created since the enactment of the constitution of 1918,[1] represented an assertion of the continuing
authority of the RSFSR over its subordinate units. A proposal
to detach from the RSFSR these lesser national units in its
federal structure, and to attach them directly to the USSR, had
been rejected in principle at an early stage,[2] though this procedure
was in fact adopted when the Uzbek and Turkmen SSRs were
created as constituent republics of the USSR early in 1925.[3]
Minor readjustments were made from time to time within the
existing framework. In July 1924 the autonomous Mountaineers'
republic was broken up into the North Osetian and Ingush
autonomous regions, this being a part of the arrangements for the
creation of a North Caucasian region.[4] Earlier in the same year
the Volga German autonomous region, and in the following year
the Chuvash autonomous region, became autonomous republics
of the RSFSR ; these were promotions presumably awarded for
material progress and loyalty.[5] On the other hand, the Kalmyk,
Chechensk, Kabardino-Balkarsh and North Osetian autonomous
regions received a reproof for their presumption in describing
their regional executive committees as " central executive committees " — a more honorific title reserved for republics ;[6] and
the Karachaevo–Cherkessian autonomous region was divided " on

---

[1] For a list of them see The Bolshevik Revolution, 1917–1923, Vol. 1,
p. 393, note 4.
[2] See ibid. Vol. 1, pp. 393-394 ; the case against the proposal was argued
in Stalin, Sochineniya, v, 151-152.
[3] For this change, and for the consequent constitutional readjustments in
Central Asia see pp. 267-270 below.   [4] See pp. 286-287 below.
[5] Sobranie Uzakonenii, 1924, No. 7, art. 33 ; No. 20, art. 199 ; Sobranie
Uzakonenii, 1925, No. 26, art. 184 ; No. 43, art. 319. The act of the regional
congress of Soviets of the Volga German autonomous region proclaiming the
region an autonomous republic, dated January 4, 1924, ended with a belated
appeal reflecting revolutionary hopes in Germany in the preceding autumn :
" The congress calls the attention of the struggling German proletariat to our
small autonomous unit, and once more emphasizes the difference between free
democratic Germany, oppressed by domestic as well as by foreign capital, and
the real freedom of nations united in the USSR " (E. Gross, Avtonomnaya
Sotsialisticheskaya Sovetskaya Respublika Nemtsev Povolzh'ya (Pokrovsk, 1926),
pp. 33-34).
[6] Sobranie Uzakonenii, 1926, No. 11, art. 82 ; in September 1925 the
Kabardino-Balkarsh autonomous region, on the fourth anniversary of its
creation, had petitioned in vain for promotion to the status of autonomous
republic (Vlast' Sovetov, No. 43, October 25, 1925, pp. 9-10).

grounds of nationality " into a Karachaev autonomous region
and a Cherkessian autonomous department, the latter being
included in the North Caucasian region.[1] The highly complex
constitutional arrangements required to give life to this vast
system of autonomous republics and regions seem to have remained, in part at any rate, a dead letter. The autonomous units
of the RSFSR ranged from the Volga German autonomous
republic, which contained perhaps the most advanced rural
population in the RSFSR, to the Oirot autonomous region, which
had no written language of its own and, at its first congress of
Soviets, renounced all legislative functions, so that it enjoyed
in practice less autonomy than some purely Russian regions.[2]
Article 44 of the constitution of the RSFSR provided that constitutions for the autonomous republics and statutes for the
autonomous regions should be adopted by their own congresses
of Soviets and submitted to the TsIK of the RSFSR and to the
All-Russian Congress of Soviets for confirmation ; and these
constitutions and statutes were presumably intended to lay down
the powers of the republics and regions, which had remained undefined in the constitution of the RSFSR. Several autonomous
republics drafted constitutions for themselves, including the
Volga German, Dagestan and Bashkir republics. But exception
was taken to the first two drafts on the ground that they both
referred to the republics as " states ",[3] and to the draft Bashkir
constitution for stating that the Bashkir autonomous SSR " enters
freely into the RSFSR and is united through it in the USSR ".[4]
In spite of the direct representation of the autonomous republics
and regions in the Council of Nationalities, any hint of a direct
relation between them and the USSR over the head of the RSFSR
excited the jealous resentment of the authorities of the RSFSR.
By the end of 1926 no constitution of an autonomous republic
had been approved in Moscow. Thereafter the question lapsed

---

[1] *Sobranie Uzakonenii, 1926*, No. 25, art. 198 ; for the constitution of the
North Caucasian region, see pp. 285-286 below.

[2] Quoted in V. Durdenevsky, *Ravnopravie Yazikov* (1927), p. 237.

[3] *Sovetskoe Stroitel'stvo : Sbornik*, iv-v (1926), 113-117 ; for the Volga
German constitution see also *Vlast' Sovetov*, No. 15, April 11, 1926. Later,
the autonomous republics were recognized as " socialist states of workers and
peasants " (A. Vyshinsky, *Sovetskoe Gosudarstvennoe Pravo* (1938), p. 284).

[4] *Sovetskoe Stroitel'stvo*, No. 3-4, October–November 1926, p. 33.

for several years. Interest now centred on the new division of the USSR into regions defined primarily by economic considerations, and on the building up of a system of local government. These issues were of concern to the economic planner and to the practical administrator, but not to the constitutional lawyer, whose intervention would only have confused them. In the practice of administration the opposing principles of concentration and devolution were often at war. The degree of recognition of the special status of national groups, large and small, varied considerably from time to time. But these disputes and these variations were governed by political decisions lying quite outside the constitutional sphere. The notion of constitutional rights and constitutional safeguards was as remote from the theory of Marxism as it had been from traditional Russian practice. Nothing was likely to implant it in the constitutional procedures of the Soviet Union.

(c) The Ukrainian and White Russian SSRs

The Ukrainian SSR possessed a constitution which had been adopted on March 10, 1919, at the height of the civil war, and which closely resembled the original constitution of the RSFSR.[1] Unlike the RSFSR, it did not adopt a new constitution to take account of its incorporation in the USSR, but was content to refurbish the old one. The eighth Ukrainian Congress of Soviets of January 1924, after having heard a report by Skrypnik delivered in Ukrainian, formally ratified the new constitution of the USSR and instructed the Ukrainian TsIK to draft the necessary amendments in the Ukrainian constitution.[2] This process occupied more than a year. The final decision to amend the constitution was taken by the ninth Ukrainian Congress of Soviets on May 10, 1925, a few days in advance of the adoption of the new constitution of the RSFSR. Certain amendments were approved forthwith ; and TsIK was instructed to prepare and complete an amended text for the next Ukrainian congress. The Ukrainian constitution, as now amended, revealed three significant divergencies from the new constitution of the RSFSR. In the first place, the Ukrainian constitution retained in several articles without

---

[1] See The Bolshevik Revolution, 1917–1923, Vol. 1, p. 301.
[2] Proletarskaya Pravda (Kiev), January 22, 1924.

amendment the mention of " the poor peasantry " as the ally of
the proletariat which was so carefully expunged from the constitution of the RSFSR; in the densely populated Ukraine the
problem of the *batrak* was perennial and unescapable. Secondly,
the Ukrainian constitution announced, in terms more emphatic
than anything that appeared in the Russian constitution, that
" the Ukrainian SSR enters into the composition of the USSR
as an independent treaty republic, its sovereignty being restricted
only within the limits indicated in the constitution of the USSR
and only in matters within the jurisdiction of the USSR "; the
thesis of the formal sovereignty of the republics was more vigorously asserted in the Ukraine than in any other of the constituent
republics. Thirdly, while the revised constitution of the RSFSR
treated the constitutional arrangements of the autonomous republics as a purely practical question, the Ukrainian constitution
used the establishment of the autonomous Moldavian SSR, the
only sub-unit included in the Ukrainian SSR, as an occasion for
an eloquent declaration of principle :

> Striving to create a free, voluntary and therefore all the
> more perfect and stable union of the toiling masses of all nations
> inhabiting the Ukrainian SSR, and fully recognizing the right of
> all nations to self-determination to the point of separation, the
> Ukrainian SSR, taking note of the firmly expressed desire of
> the Moldavian people to establish their own political existence
> within the framework of the Ukrainian SSR, unites with it on
> the basis of the formation within the Ukrainian SSR of the
> Moldavian Autonomous SSR.

The recognition of the national rights of the Moldavian people
within the Ukrainian republic served implicitly as a proclamation
of the similar rights of the Ukrainian people within the USSR.[1]
The promptness with which these constitutional arrangements
were carried through was a tribute to the relative efficiency and
independence of the Ukrainian SSR, and probably owed much
to Skrypnik's clear-headedness. Nor does any objection to them
appear to have been registered at the time in Moscow. Vyshinsky
much later recalled that " the revision of the constitutions of the

[1] The decision of May 10, 1925, is in *Rezolyutsii Vseukrains'kikh Z'izdiv
Rad* (1932), pp. 218-223, or in Russian in *S"ezdy Sovetov v Dokumentakh*, v
(1964), 149-155.

Union republics [in 1925–1927] proceeded in conditions of struggle with Trotskyist-Right elements and their nationalist allies ", who tried to secure " ' constitutional guarantees ' for the unimpeded development of capitalist elements under cover of NEP ".[1] But this struggle, at any rate in the Ukraine, appears to have followed rather than preceded the constitutional amendments of 1925.

The autonomous Moldavian SSR had been set up by a decision of the Ukrainian TsIK of October 12, 1924.[2] Its constitution, modelled on the constitutions of the autonomous republics set up within the RSFSR before the creation of the USSR, was voted by the first Moldavian Congress of Soviets at the Moldavian capital, Balta, on April 19, 1925. It was approved by the ninth Ukrainian Congress of Soviets in the following month with one significant amendment designed to make it clear that the Moldavian re~ 'blic was subordinated exclusively to the Ukrainian SSR and had no direct relations with organs of the USSR.[3] The Ukrainian SSR was as jealous as the RSFSR of any claim by its autonomous offspring to assert independence of the parent republic.

The White Russian SSR lacked altogether the vitality of its Ukrainian counterpart. White Russia was from the first a largely artificial creation ; [4] and, as a White Russian spokesman later observed, " it is only since 1923 that the Soviet structure has begun to establish itself in White Russia — far later than in the other republics ".[5] At this time the White Russian SSR occupied only the former province of Minsk with about 1,500,000 inhabitants. In March 1924 the TsIK of the RSFSR and the TsIK of the White Russian SSR agreed on a cession of territory designed to include in the White Russian republic all areas having a majority of White Russian population. This concession, which

---

[1] A. Vyshinsky, *Sovetskoe Gosudarstvennoe Pravo* (1938), p. 110.

[2] W. R. Batsell, *Soviet Rule in Russia* (N.Y., 1929), pp. 354-356.

[3] The resolution of the Ukrainian congress, the resolution of the Moldavian congress, and the text of the constitution are in *Rezolyutsii Vseukrains'kikh Z'izdiv Rad* (1932), pp. 223-231 ; the Moldavian congress was briefly reported in *Vlast' Sovetov*, No. 20, May 15, 1925, p. 14. The text of the Moldavian constitution was originally published in *Zbirnik Uzakonen' ta Rosporyadzhen', 1925*, No. 51, art. 313. Both the revised Ukrainian and the Moldavian constitutions are in *Konstitutsiya USSR ta AMSSR* (Kharkov, 1927).

[4] See *The Bolshevik Revolution, 1917–1923*, Vol. 1, pp. 307-311.

[5] *SSSR : Tsentral'nyi Ispolnitel'nyi Komitet 3 Sozyva : 3 Sessiya* (1927), p. 67.

transferred large parts of the Vitebsk and Gomel provinces and a small part of the Smolensk province to the White Russian SSR, and increased the population of the republic to over four millions, was extolled in a special declaration of the presidium of the TsIK of the USSR as a shining example of the neighbourly relations prevailing between the Soviet republics.[1] In the following year a further territorial readjustment was made in favour of the White Russian SSR, this time mainly at the expense of the Ukrainian SSR;[2] though less extensive than its predecessor, this new accretion of territory added a further 650,000 inhabitants to the population of the republic. Simultaneously with the territorial expansion of the White Russian republic in March 1924, the constitutional issue was taken in hand. The sixth extraordinary White Russian Congress of Soviets, which had been summoned to ratify the new territorial acquisitions, instructed the TsIK of the republic to amend its constitution in accordance with the newly ratified constitution of the USSR.[3] The process proved difficult, perhaps because of the insistence of White Russian nationalists on the unqualified assertion of sovereignty of the constituent republics of the USSR;[4] and it was not till three years later, on April 11, 1927, that the eighth White Russian Congress of Soviets formally ratified the new constitution.[5]

[1] *Sobranie Uzakonenii, 1924*, No. 24, art. 237 ; No. 39, art. 357 (for the declaration see *ibid.* No. 47, art. unnumbered) ; *SSSR : Tsentral'nyi Ispolnitel'nyi Komitet 3 Sozyva : 3 Sessiya* (1927), p. 93. A detailed account of the stages by which this decision was reached is given in *Istoricheskie Zapiski*, xlvi (1954), 291-292 ; it was discussed by the local and central party organs between May and December 1923, and confirmed by the fifth White Russian Congress of Soviets in January 1924.
[2] For an account of the negotiations between White Russia and the Ukraine leading up to this transfer see *Sovetskoe Stroitel'stvo : Sbornik*, ii-iii (1925), 184-185 ; the original proposal was for an exchange, but in the end the White Russian SSR gave practically nothing. The agreement was ratified by the TsIKs of the two republics (the White Russian ratification is in *Sobranie Uzakonenii SSR Belorussii, 1925*, No. 8, art. 72), and finally by the presidium of the TsIK of the USSR on October 16, 1925 (*Izvestiya*, January 31, 1926).
[3] *Istoriya Sovetskoi Konstitutsii v Dekretakh* (1936), pp. 268-269 ; for the embryonic constitution of the White Russian SSR of 1919 see *The Bolshevik Revolution, 1917-1923*, Vol. 1, pp. 309-310.
[4] This is hinted at in V. Ignatiev, *Sovetskii Stroi* (1923), p. 113.
[5] It was printed in four languages — White Russian, Russian, Polish and Yiddish — as an annex to the proceedings of the congress (*Vos'my Usebelaruski Z"ezd Sovetau* (Minsk, 1927)) ; it is also in *Sobranie Sovetskikh Konstitutsii i Konstitutsionnykh Aktov*, ed. A. Malitsky (Kharkov, 1928), pp. 63-76.

(d) The Transcaucasian SFSR

The constitutional problems of the Ukrainian and White Russian republics turned on their relations with the USSR. The constitutional problems of Transcaucasia arose from the unparalleled national diversity of the population of the region and the inextricable intermingling of its peoples, which made some kind of federal structure unavoidable, if Transcaucasia was to be treated as a constitutional unit. But the three major Transcaucasian peoples — Georgians, Armenians, Azerbaijani — reacted differently to the setting up of the Transcaucasian Socialist Federal Soviet Republic (ZSFSR). The Georgians were the most advanced of the three peoples, and might have profited from a Transcaucasian federation in which Georgia's superior material resources and political experience would have enabled her to play a dominant rôle. Such a federation had in fact been created in the troubled days of 1918 ; but Georgia had not been strong enough to assert her predominance, and, with German encouragement, quickly broke away and declared her independence.[1] Four and a half years later, the setting up of a Transcaucasian federation dominated by Moscow, in which Georgia would be in a position of equal partnership with Armenia and Azerbaijan and have to share her natural advantages with them, held few attractions for the Georgian intelligentsia. As the capital of the federation, Tiflis, already the home of a mixed Armenian, Georgian and Russian population (in that numerical order), acquired still more of an international, as opposed to a national Georgian, character. The federation, which brought increased security and prestige to the other two major peoples of Transcaucasia, seemed to diminish the independent status of Georgia. The Armenian intelligentsia, not less numerous and influential than the Georgian, was more loyal to the Soviet régime in virtue both of its jealousy of the Georgians and of its fear and hatred of the Turk. Azerbaijan possessed no native intelligentsia ; the intelligentsia of Baku was mainly Russian and in part Armenian. Thus only the Georgian intelligentsia remained as a whole hostile to the Soviet régime, and continued to nourish dreams of independence or autonomy. But

[1] For these events see *The Bolshevik Revolution, 1917–1923*, Vol. 1, pp. 340-343.

it was increasingly isolated, and constituted a threat to authority only in the event of grave peasant discontent which it could mobilize and lead. The Georgian rising of August 1924[1] had this mixed social and national character. But it was suppressed after a few days ; and the Georgian SSR thereafter took its place side by side with the Armenian and Azerbaijani republics, without further disturbance of the peace, in the Transcaucasian federation.

The constitution of the ZSFSR of December 12, 1922,[2] unlike the original constitutions of the RSFSR and the Ukrainian SSR, had been drafted with a view to the entry of the republic into the USSR, then in course of formation, and did not therefore call for fundamental change. But a series of amendments were adopted by the Transcaucasian TsIK in September 1924 and ratified by the third Transcaucasian Congress of Soviets on April 14, 1925. The effect of the most important of these was to establish the competence of the ZSFSR as against that of its three constituent republics in such matters as " principles for the development and use of land ", " the bases of judicial organization and legal procedure and of civil and criminal law ", " the direction of internal trade ", and " labour legislation ". The supreme organs of the ZSFSR could also set aside decrees of organs of the constituent republics which might conflict with the constitution. On the other hand, the constitution recognized the formal sovereignty of the constituent republics, as limited only by the constitutions of the ZSFSR and the USSR. The congress of Soviets at the same time authorized TsIK to draft a new chapter to be added to the constitution, making it clear that, just as the budget of the ZSFSR formed an integral part of the budget of the USSR, so the budgets of the three republics formed an integral part of the budget of the ZSFSR. This instruction was carried out at a session of the Transcaucasian TsIK held at Erivan on January 29, 1926, and confirmed by the presidium of TsIK on February 15, 1926.[3] The

---

[1] See Vol. 1, pp. 198-199 ; its national aspects will be discussed in a subsequent volume.

[2] See *The Bolshevik Revolution, 1917–1923*, Vol. 1, p. 396.

[3] The constitution in its final form, together with the resolutions of April 14, 1925, January 29, 1926, and February 15, 1926, approving and amending it are in *Osnovnoi Zakon (Konstitutsiya) Zakavkazskoi Sotsialisticheskoi Federativnoi Sovetskoi Respubliki* (Tiflis, 1926) ; the constitution is also in *S"ezdy Sovetov v Dokumentakh*, vi (1964), 39-49.

effect of these provisions, as of all other constitutional provisions of the period, was a strengthening of the central authority.

The constitutions of the three republics forming the Transcaucasian federation — Georgia, Armenia, Azerbaijan — dated from 1920 and 1921, long before the ZSFSR or the USSR had been in contemplation, and were clearly incompatible with the new arrangements. The Armenian republic seems to have been first in the field ; the fourth Armenian Congress of Soviets voted in March 1925 in favour of constitutional amendment.[1] But it was not till 1926 or 1927 that the Georgian, Armenian and Azerbaijan SSRs all possessed approved constitutions.[2] The constitutional anomaly of the region was the Abkhazian republic occupying a small coastal strip on the Black Sea with its capital at Sukhum. This was commonly referred to as an autonomous SSR within the Georgian republic. In fact, its relations with Georgia resulted from a treaty between the two republics signed on December 16, 1921,[3] and it was officially described as a " treaty republic ". It acquired a constitution approved by the Abkhazian TsIK on October 27, 1926, under the terms of which it " enters in virtue of a special treaty into the Georgian SSR, and through it into the Transcaucasian SFSR ".[4] In spite of the greater elaboration of its constitution, no practical difference seems to have distinguished it from an ordinary autonomous republic.

(e) The Central Asian Republics

The changes already described took place within the constitutional structure of the USSR as initially established in 1923. In 1924, after the formation of the USSR, a major territorial rearrangement was undertaken, which had the effect of removing the greater part of Soviet Central Asia from the orbit of the RSFSR, and creating two new member republics of the USSR. In 1921 the greater part of the Central Asian territories of the former Tsarist empire had been organized as the Turkestan

---

[1] *Vlast' Sovetov*, No. 14, April 5, 1925, p. 15.
[2] For these see *Sobranie Sovetskikh Konstitutsii i Konstitutsionnykh Aktov*, ed. A. Malitsky (Kharkov, 1928), pp. 89-106, 107-129, 147-163.
[3] *Ibid.* pp. 204-205.
[4] *Ibid.* pp. 129-146.

autonomous SSR within the RSFSR, with the former principalities of Khorezm and Bokhara remaining as formally independent Soviet republics.[1] This arrangement had, from the outset, a provisional character, both because it cut across ethnographical divisions and because the " Soviet republics " of Khorezm and Bokhara were admittedly a transitional form to full socialist status. The two major ethnic groups forming a majority of the population of the Turkestan republic were the Uzbeks and the Turkmens, both of Turkic stock and speech. As early as 1921 a distinction was drawn between the two groups by naming the western part of the republic " the Turkmen territory ".[2] Inhabiting a desert steppe, the Turkmens were a more primitive people than their Uzbek kinsmen who formed the core of the population further east. Divided into several tribes, many of them were still nomads ; settled agriculture was almost everywhere dependent on artificial irrigation, and land was still commonly held in family or tribal units. The south-western sector of the Turkestan autonomous SSR was occupied by the Tajiks, a people of Iranian stock and speech, and the Kirgiz, a Turki-speaking group less far removed by social conditions than the Turkmens from the Uzbek majority. The Soviet republics of Khorezm and Bokhara had no distinctive ethnographic basis, both containing Uzbek majorities and Turkmen minorities. Finally, to the north of the Turkestan autonomous SSR lay the Kazakh autonomous SSR, a desert steppe occupied by a nomadic people also of Turkic origin and speech, but presenting different problems from those of Turkestan and politically separated from it, though two provinces inhabited mainly by Kazakhs were provisionally included in the Turkestan republic.

The formation of the USSR in 1923 provided the impetus for a revision of these arrangements. Stalin, in his speech at TsIK on the original treaty of union in December 1922, had referred to the republics of Khorezm and Bokhara as likely one day to be included.[3] At the twelfth party congress of April 1923, while the constitution of the union was still under discussion, Stalin spoke again of Khorezm and Bokhara in a passage of his speech which

[1] See The Bolshevik Revolution, 1917–1923, Vol. 1, pp. 335-338.
[2] Voprosy Istorii, No. 2, 1950, p. 7.
[3] Stalin, Sochineniya, v, 151.

dealt with the dangers of " aggressive " local nationalism, and the conflicts between majorities and minorities provoked by it.¹ This was followed by the arrest of Sultan-Galiev, the charges against him including one of attempting to establish relations with Turkestani and Kazakh nationalists.² At the party conference which discussed this affair, Stalin took occasion to dwell on the backwardness of Turkestan, where the situation was " the most unfavourable, the most disturbing " of any in the national republics : Turkestan was " the weak point of the Soviet power ". He went on to speak of the poor state of the party in Khorezm and Bokhara, and of the inadequacy of the Bokharan government. Bokhara, it appeared, wanted to join the USSR. The question, Stalin insisted with rather heavy irony, was whether she deserved to be admitted.³ Nevertheless, it was clear that a movement to bring Khorezm and Bokhara into the union was overdue. During the next few months pressure was exercised on all concerned for a far-reaching reorganization of the whole area on national and ethnographic lines.⁴

The first formal steps were taken in September and October 1923, when the Bokharan and Khorezm congresses of Soviets passed resolutions providing for the transformation of their respective republics from " Soviet " into " Soviet socialist " republics and declaring their desire to be admitted to the USSR.⁵ But this was only to be the prelude to a far more ambitious scheme. In March 1924 the central committee of the Turkestan Communist Party recorded its decision in favour of a national redistribution of the whole area, and in the following month the

¹ *Ibid.* v, 249-250.   ² See *The Interregnum, 1923-1924*, pp. 286-287.
³ Stalin, *Sochineniya*, v, 328-333.
⁴ Circumstantial accounts of the difficulties experienced in finding representative spokesmen for the different groups and of the arrest and " internment " in a Moscow hotel of members of the Bokharan government are given in Baymirza Hayit, *Turkestan im XX. Jahrhundert* (Darmstadt, 1956), pp. 108-109, 140-141 ; they apparently rest on oral information and, though not lacking in plausibility, must be treated with caution.
⁵ *Voprosy Istorii*, No. 2, 1950, p. 8. The decision of the Bokharan congress of Soviets is said to have been accompanied by orders to remove " officials, merchants and priests " from posts in the government and deprive them of the franchise, and to confiscate the property of " capitalist classes or elements " (Baymirza Hayit, *Turkestan im XX. Jahrhundert* (Darmstadt, 1956), p. 141, where, however, no source is quoted) : this would have been a logical sequel of the transition to socialist status.

Central Asian bureau of the party central committee in Moscow set up a commission to work out details.[1] By the autumn of 1924 everything was ready for the official machinery to be set in motion. On September 17, 1924, a resolution was adopted by the TsIK of the autonomous SSR of Turkestan declaring that the time was ripe to reorganize the republic into " nationally homogeneous states ". The republic itself was to disappear ; the Uzbek population was to form a new Uzbek SSR within the USSR, the Turkmen population a new Turkmen SSR within the USSR ; the Kazakh provinces were to be incorporated, in accordance with a long-standing promise,[2] in the Kazakh (here still called Kirgiz) autonomous SSR, an autonomous republic of the RSFSR ; the Kirgiz (here called Kara-Kirgiz) population was to form a new autonomous region within the RSFSR ; and the Tajik population, the only non-Turki-speaking group in the area, was to form a new Tajik autonomous SSR within the Uzbek SSR. Each of the proposals in turn was justified by a reference to " the declared general will of masses of the workers and dekhans " of the peoples concerned.[3] A few days later the fifth Bokharan congress of Soviets decided to dissolve the Bokharan Soviet republic proclaimed four years earlier, and to approve the incorporation of its Uzbek and Turkmen populations in the proposed Uzbek and Turkmen republics respectively.[4] On October 2, 1924, a similar step was taken by the fifth congress of Soviets of Khorezm.[5] The formal, but totally unreal, independence of the two " Soviet republics " of Central Asia was thus brought to an end.

The scene now shifted to Moscow, where a delegate of the

---

[1] *Voprosy Istorii*, No. 2, 1950, pp. 10-11.

[2] See *The Bolshevik Revolution, 1917–1923*, Vol. 1, p. 339; for the nomenclature see *ibid*. Vol. 1, p. 316, note 2.

[3] The resolution was read at the session of the TsIK of the RSFSR of October 1924 (*Vserossiiskii Tsentral'nyi Ispolnitel'nyi Komitet XI Sozyva : Vtoraya Sessiya* (1924), pp. 320-322), and is also in *Sobranie Uzakonenii, 1924*, No. 87, art. 874.

[4] The decree, dated September 20, 1924, is in F. Ksenofontov, *Uzbekistan i Turkmenistan* (1925), pp. 31-33 ; an exchange of notes in the same sense between the RSFSR and the Bokharan republic was published in *Pravda*, October 5, 1924.

[5] *Voprosy Istorii*, No. 2, 1950, p. 11 ; according to a somewhat dubious source, the decision was taken under duress, the hall where the congress met having been surrounded by the Soviet envoy with Soviet troops (Baymirza Hayit, *Turkestan im XX. Jahrhundert* (Darmstadt, 1956), p. 157).

autonomous Turkestan SSR laid the proposals before the TsIK of the RSFSR at its session in October 1924, justifying them on the ground that they would make for " clearer and simpler mutual relations between the peoples of Central Asia " through the creation of units homogeneous both in national and in social and economic composition. The otherwise complete harmony of the proceedings was faintly marred by a Kazakh delegate who pressed for a further readjustment of the frontier in favour of Kazakhstan. The proposals of the Turkestan TsIK were then read and endorsed in their entirety.[1]   Later in the same month the Bokharan communist leader Faizulla Khodzhaev appeared at the VTsIK of the USSR to support the incorporation of Bokhara in the proposed Uzbek SSR ; and the whole project received without further debate the approval of the highest organ of the union.[2]   A few days later it was formally endorsed by the party central committee.[3]   At the beginning of 1925 another minor territorial readjustment was made. The sparsely populated mountain region of the Pamirs, hitherto split between the Kirgiz autonomous region and the Tajik autonomous SSR, was united to form a single autonomous region within the Tajik republic.[4]

The formal establishment of the new Uzbek and Turkmen SSRs was proclaimed in their respective capitals in February 1925.[5]   It was ratified three months later by the twelfth All-Russian Congress of Soviets, and by the third Union Congress of Soviets, which admitted them as fifth and sixth constituent republics of the USSR.[6]   The proceedings were uneventful. At the Union Congress of Soviets, declarations of greeting were read

[1] *Vserossiiskii Tsentral'nyi Ispolnitel'nyi Komitet XI Sozyva : Vtoraya Sessiya* (1924), pp. 309-324.

[2] *SSSR : Tsentral'nyi Ispolnitel'nyi Komitet 2 Sozyva : 2 Sessiya* (1924), pp. 542-548, 561 ; *Sobranie Zakonov, 1924*, No. 19, art. 187.

[3] L. Kamenev, *Stat'i i Rechi*, xi (1929), 189-190.

[4] *Sistematicheskoe Sobranie Deistvuyushchikh Zakonov SSSR*, i (1926), 207.

[5] The declarations of the first Uzbek and Turkmen Congresses of Soviets are in *Istoriya Sovetskoi Konstitutsii v Dekretakh* (1936), pp. 271-277. A brief account of the Uzbek congress which was held in Bokhara (presumably as a gesture of conciliation to the defunct republic) on February 14-18, 1925, is in *Vlast' Sovetov*, No. 11, March 15, 1925, pp. 16-17. A TsIK consisting of 160 members and 44 candidates was elected, 20 per cent being non-party ; Faizulla Khodzhaev was elected president of Sovnarkom.

[6] *S"ezdy Sovetov RSFSR v Postanovleniyakh* (1939), p. 331 ; *Sobranie Uzakonenii, 1925*, No. 31, art. 222 ; *Sobranie Zakonov, 1925*, No. 35, arts. 244, 245.

on behalf of the Uzbek and Turkmen SSRs and the Tajik autonomous SSR, and an Uzbek peasant presented a portrait of Lenin
in mosaic.[1] Point was added to the creation of the Tajik republic
when it was referred to by one of its delegates as the " Iranian
Soviet republic ".[2] Constitutions for the Uzbek and Turkmen
SSRs were finally adopted in 1927.[3] No further addition was
made to the number of constituent republics till 1929.

The reunion of the Kazakh provinces of Turkestan with the
Kazakh autonomous SSR was celebrated at the fifth Kazakh
congress of Soviets in the spring of 1925. The congress, which
was held at Kzyl-Orda, the Kazakh capital, was said to have been
the first representative Kazakh congress of Soviets, mustering
394 delegates, of whom 59 per cent were Kazakh and 30 per cent
Russian, and of whom 75 per cent were illiterate.[4] Immediately
after the congress, a decree of the RSFSR confirmed the new
territorial settlement, and established part of the ceded territory
as the Kara-Kalpak autonomous region of the Kazakh autonomous SSR.[5] Finally, at the request — it was stated — of the
fifth Kazakh congress of Soviets, the vexed question of nomenclature was tackled. By decrees of the RSFSR of May and June
1925 what had at first been officially styled the Kara-Kirgiz
autonomous region was re-named the Kirgiz autonomous region,
and what had hitherto been officially known as the Kirgiz autonomous SSR became the Kazakh autonomous SSR.[6] Both these
peoples thus regained the historical names of which they had
been deprived for a century or more by the usage of the Russian
Empire. About the same time the predominantly Russian-
speaking province of Orenburg, hitherto included in the Kazakh
autonomous SSR, was transferred to the RSFSR.[7]

The most serious problem presented by this complicated reorganization of a primitive region was the lack of any trained
personnel or of any substantial number of local intellectuals
qualified to hold administrative posts at any level. In Turkmen-

---

[1] *Tretii S"ezd Sovetov SSSR* (1925), pp. 14-16, 18-21.
[2] *Ibid.* p. 135.
[3] *Sobranie Sovetskikh Konstitutsii i Konstitutsionnykh Aktov*, ed. A. Malitsky
(Kharkov, 1928), pp. 164-186, 187-200.
[4] *Vlast' Sovetov*, No. 23-24, June 14, 1925, pp. 24-26.
[5] *Sobranie Uzakonenii, 1925*, No. 31, art. 222.
[6] *Ibid.* No. 36, art. 259 ; No. 43, art. 321.
[7] *Ibid.* No. 49, art. 377.

istan " the whole state apparatus had to be constructed anew, in new conditions, from completely new persons, and for new purposes ".[1] Except in Uzbekistan, which inherited the administrative machinery of the defunct Turkestan republic, these deficiencies were acute throughout the area. A minor embarrassment was revealed by the difficulty of finding suitable capitals for the new republics. The surprising decision was at first taken to make Samarkand, not Tashkent, the capital of the Uzbek SSR. This may have been a gesture of conciliation to Bokharan susceptibilities over the loss of Bokharan independence, though it was officially attributed to a desire to keep Tashkent, the only large city in Central Asia, as a centre for the whole territory and not for any one part of it. But the decision proved too inconvenient to be maintained. Samarkand was an ancient bazaartown without any modern pretensions ; and the capital returned to Tashkent. The capital originally designed for Turkmenistan was Charjui-Leninsk. But this turned out to be no more than an " uncompleted station " at the point where the Central Asian railway crossed the Amu-Darya river ; and, after a brief period, the capital was fixed at Poltoratsk (the former Ashkhabad) on the railway near the frontier of Iran, the seat of a glass-bottle factory, one of the few factories in the area. The first capital of Kazakhstan Kzyl-Orda, formerly Perovsk, was a remote township in an irrigated oasis in desert country south of the Aral Sea : this was later replaced by Alma-Ata, a mountain resort in the extreme south-eastern corner of the republic. Only the Kirgiz autonomous region and the Tajik autonomous republic permanently retained their original capitals. But the Kirgiz capital, Pishpek, re-named Frunze in 1926, was a small market town which had only just been connected by railway with the outside world ; and the Tajik capital, Dyushambe, later renamed Stalinabad, had no railway and " not a single presentable building of European appearance " when it acquired its new status, so that the People's Commissariats of the Tajik republic had to be accommodated in " sheds ".[2] These conditions make it unusually clear that it is

---

[1] *Vlast' Sovetov*, No. 13, March 28, 1926, p. 5.

[2] *Planovoe Khozyaistvo*, No. 11, 1925, p. 246 ; *Tretii S"ezd Sovetov SSSR* (1925), p. 136. These difficulties were not confined to Central Asia. For the vain search to find a capital for the Kalmyk autonomous region to replace Astrakhan, a Russian city separated from the region by the Volga estuary, see

dangerous and inappropriate to generalize about the character and working of Soviet institutions, even those bearing the same name and possessing the same formal functions, throughout the vast and diverse expanse of the USSR.

Sovetskoe Stroitel'stvo : Sbornik, iv-v (1926), 120-121 ; the Adygeisk autonomous region had its capital at Krasnodar, which lay outside its territory (*Planovoe Khozyaistvo*, No. 5, 1926, p. 224).

CHAPTER 21

REGIONALIZATION

DURING the first seven years of the régime the structure of Soviet power throughout the country continued to rest on the territorial divisions and subdivisions inherited from Tsarist Russia — the village (selo), the rural district (volost'), the county (uezd) and the province (guberniya). The lowest unit of rural government was the village Soviet [1] consisting of delegates elected by the village meeting (skhod). The village Soviets sent delegates to a rural district congress of Soviets, which generally met once a year, and whose principal function was to appoint a rural district executive committee; this constituted, apart from some primitive functions discharged by the village Soviet, the lowest executive organ. At the next stage country and town met for the first time. The rural district congresses of Soviets of each county, as well as the city and factory Soviets of the county capital, elected delegates to the county congress of Soviets which in turn appointed a county executive committee. The county congresses of Soviets of each province, together with the city and factory Soviets of the provincial capital, elected delegates to the provincial congress of Soviets. Finally, the provincial congresses of Soviets elected delegates to the All-Russian Congress of Soviets. A decree of December 1918 invited provinces to group themselves into regions (oblasti) with regional congresses of Soviets as an intermediate stage between the provincial congresses and the All-Russian Congress of Soviets.[2] This project proved abortive;[3] and in the turmoil of the civil war and its aftermath,

[1] For the elasticity of the term "village" see *The Bolshevik Revolution, 1917–1923*, Vol. 1, p. 126, note 1.

[2] *Sobranie Uzakonenii, 1917–1918*, No. 99, art. 1019.

[3] Four "regions" of the RSFSR (Moscow, Ural, Northern and Western) were actually formed, but were all liquidated by May 1918 (L. Kaganovich, *Mestnoe Sovetskoe Samoupravlenie* (1923), pp. 51-52, quoted in *Voprosy Ekonomicheskogo Raionirovaniya SSSR*, ed. G. Krzhizhanovsky (1957), p. 237).

little of this formal structure of local government can have remained intact. The effective trend down to 1922 was towards decentralization, and the multiplication of units of local authority. In the territory of the RSFSR (for which alone statistics were available), the 56 provinces, 476 counties and 10,606 rural districts existing in 1917 had risen five years later to 80 autonomous regions and provinces, 601 counties and 12,363 rural districts.[1]

Simultaneously with this spontaneous process, however, quite different policies were being canvassed by the central authorities. In the last years of the Tsarist régime, the inconvenience of having so large a number of provinces (97 for the whole Russian Empire) as the highest form of administrative unit had come to be recognized; and the practice had grown up of classifying the provinces into 19 regions (krai or oblasti), though this division had no administrative effect.[2] After the revolution the renewed impulse to administrative reorganization was to come from the economic planners, who were concerned not only to have a more manageable number of units, but to bring into existence a new system of divisions and subdivisions which would conform, not to ancient historical traditions, but to current economic realities. The seventh All-Russian Congress of Soviets in December 1919 instructed TsIK " to work out the practical question of a new administrative-economic division of the RSFSR " ;[3] and TsIK duly set up a so-called " administrative commission " to deal with the project.[4] The ninth party congress of March 1920, in the same resolution which had for the first time propounded the desideratum of " a single economic plan ",[5] cautiously drew attention to the importance of creating large-scale " regional economic organs " :

> For broad areas [6] remote from the centre and distinguished by special economic conditions, the congress regards it as

[1] A. Luzhin, Ot Volosti k Raionu (1929), p. 15.
[2] A detailed proposal to group the 97 provinces (including Finland) into 14 regions (krai) was made by Mendeleev, the scientist and geographer, Witte's adviser, in 1896 (D. I. Mendeleev, Sochineniya, xxi (1952), 197-212); when the results of the 1897 census were published, the 89 provinces (excluding Finland, where the census was not taken) were grouped in 19 regions.
[3] S"ezdy Sovetov v Dokumentakh, i (1959), 116.
[4] Raionirovanie SSSR, ed. K. Egorov (1925), p. 18.
[5] See The Bolshevik Revolution, 1917–1923, Vol. 2, p. 370.
[6] The word used is raion, which had not yet acquired its technical sense as a minor unit (a " district ") to replace the " rural district " (volost') : the whole process of administrative reorganization was commonly known as raionirovanie.

absolutely indispensable in the near future to create strong and competent regional economic organs on the principle of delegation from the corresponding state authorities.

These regional bureaus, composed of experienced workers adopting the standpoint of general state interests, should have wide powers in the sphere of the immediate direction of local economic life, so that by uniting both provincial sovnarkhozy and area administrations, they may carry out, on the basis of a plan confirmed by the centre, all necessary changes, transfers of raw materials and of labour power etc. etc. which are required by the circumstances. . . .

The delimitation of the regional boundaries necessary for the creation of regional agencies of the central authority must be conducted on the basis of economic considerations.[1]

Taking its cue from this resolution, the eighth All Russian Congress of Soviets in December 1920 pronounced in favour of " a new administrative-economic division of the Russian Socialist Federal Soviet Republic primarily on the basis of economic affinity ".[2] At this time, however, interest turned mainly on agricultural development, and the purpose of the project was to group together areas where conditions and problems were similar.[3]

> The region should be formed [ran a report of TsIK of this period] by separating a distinct, and so far as possible economically complete, territory which, thanks to a combination of natural qualities, of the cultural acquisitions of former times and of a population prepared for productive activity, can represent one of the links in the general chain of the national economy.[4]

Other lines of advance contributed more directly to the ultimate acceptance of regionalization. The eighth All-Russian Congress of Soviets also gave its approval to a project of electrification which, with the personal encouragement of Lenin, was worked

---

[1] *VKP(B) v Rezolyutsiyakh* (1941), i, 332.

[2] *S"ezdy Sovetov v Dokumentakh*, i (1959), 145.

[3] This conception persisted to a much later date and was the theme of B. N. Knipovich, *Sel'skokhozyaistvennoe Raionirovanie*, a work issued by the planning department of Narkomzem in 1925 ; a long study of " agricultural regionalization " from this point of view, apparently written early in 1926, appeared in *Entsiklopedicheskii Slovar' Russkogo Bibliograficheskogo Instituta Granat*, xli, ii (n.d. [1927]), cols. 42-133.

[4] Quoted in *Planovoe Khozyaistvo*, No. 11, 1936, pp. 145-146.

out during the following year by a commission on electrification (Goelro).[1] Electrification was necessarily organized on a regional basis ; and the Goelro plan provided for a division of Soviet territory into seven broad regions, each of which was to have its own plan of electrification.[2] Meanwhile the foundation of Gosplan made it certain that the project of an administrative reorganization of the whole country on economic lines would be kept well in view, and shifted the emphasis from agricultural to industrial development. In the summer of 1921 Gosplan set up a " regionalization section ", and issued a pamphlet written by the head of the section, Alexandrov, under the title *The Economic Regionalization of the RSFSR*, which was described in the journal of Gosplan as the first attempt at " a profoundly thought out, revolutionary, and at the same time fully scientific and purely Marxist approach " — a collection of epithets designed to convey that it looked to the future as well as to the present, and was concerned with economic expansion rather than with administrative convenience. The outline of the scheme was a division of the European provinces of the RSFSR together with the new industrial regions of western Siberia into 13 regions, each of which would have its own plan of economic development.[3] Later in the year Alexandrov prepared a more detailed scheme for the creation of 21 regions, 12 in European and 9 in Asiatic Russia, which received the endorsement of Krzhizhanovsky.[4] Contact was now established with the " administrative commission " of TsIK, which gave its approval in principle to these projects ; and they formed the basis of the discussions of an all-Russian conference of workers on " regionalization " which met in Moscow in February 1922 under the presidency of Rykov.[5] As a result of these discussions the commission submitted a set of theses to the presidium of TsIK, which were \ approved by that body on April 13, 1922, for submission to the forthcoming session of

[1] See *The Bolshevik Revolution, 1917–1923*, Vol. 2, pp. 375-378.
[2] The original plan was reprinted as *Plan GOELRO* (1955).
[3] *Sotsialisticheskoe Khozyaistvo*, No. 4, 1925, pp. 73-79 (the promised continuation of this article never seems to have appeared) ; *Planovoe Khozyaistvo*, No. 3, 1925, pp. 235-236.
[4] Both Alexandrov's projects were reprinted in an abbreviated form, together with Krzhizhanovsky's article, in *Voprosy Ekonomicheskogo Raionirovaniya*, ed. G. Krzhizhanovsky (1957), pp. 66-101.
[5] *Planovoe Khozyaistvo*, No. 3, 1925, pp. 235-238.

TsIK.[1] The regional reorganization foreshadowed in the theses was to provide for the reduction in the number of administrative units recommended by the ninth All-Russian Congress of Soviets.[2] It was to be based on the " economic principle ", which was understood to imply " a practical division of labour between different regions " as well as " the best utilization of all the potentialities " of each. The twenty-one regions proposed by Gosplan were provisionally adopted, and the scheme was to involve a threefold hierarchy of units : the region (oblast'), the department (okrug) which was to supersede the existing province and the existing county and be half-way between them in size, and the district (raion) which was to replace the existing rural district (volost'). Autonomous national republics or regions would be fitted into the regions without altering their boundaries or diminishing their political rights. The place to be taken in the scheme by republics linked by treaty with the RSFSR [3] could, of course, be determined only by fresh treaties. The theses, together with a long report by the commission,[4] were submitted to the session of TsIK in May 1922, and were discussed by a special conference of interested delegates. Here objections were evidently raised (though no detailed records were published) to the implied curtailment of the rights of national or local units. It was apparently the absence of representatives of the outlying regions, or perhaps the opposition of some of them, which induced TsIK to refrain from taking any decision on the project. Gosplan was at this stage simply invited to circulate it for further consideration.[5]

The national issue, thus, for the first time, cast its shadow across the path of the reformers. Alexandrov's original Gosplan projects of 1921 were criticized in the organ of the People's Commissariat of Nationalities on the ground that they diminished the substance of autonomy in the national republics and regions.[6] About the

---

[1] For the theses see *Raionirovanie SSSR*, ed. K. Egorov (1925), pp. 47-50, or *Voprosy Ekonomicheskogo Raionirovaniya*, ed. G. Krzhizhanovsky (1957), pp. 102-108 ; their approval by the presidium is recorded *ibid.* p. 305.

[2] For this recommendation see p. 295 below.

[3] For these republics see *The Bolshevik Revolution, 1917–1923*, Vol. 1, p. 380.

[4] *Voprosy Ekonomicheskogo Raionirovaniya*, ed. G. Krzhizhanovsky (1957), pp. 109-174 : this is said to be an abbreviated version of the report.

[5] *III Sessiya Vserossiiskogo Tsentral'nogo Ispolnitel'nogo Komiteta IX Sozyva*, No. 12 (May 28, 1922), pp. 16-20.

[6] *Zhizn' Natsional'nostei*, No. 21 (119), October 10, 1921.

time of the discussions in TsIK a representative of the Chuvash
autonomous region protested that, " if the autonomous regions
and republics are to enjoy only political rights, there is no point
in calling them autonomous national regions and republics ".[1] No
formula really resolved the dilemma. On the one hand, it was
clear that a re-division of Soviet territory on economic lines was
liable to cut across the division on national lines so ardently proclaimed in the first stage of the revolution ; and there were
certainly those who saw in territorial planning under the name of
regionalization a corrective to the evils of national separatism. It
was not only in Soviet Russia that a potential clash could be discerned between the claims of national self-determination and the
claims of economic progress.[2] On the other hand, the Bolshevik
doctrine of self-determination had sought to escape from this
dilemma by insisting on the principle of equal economic development and equal economic opportunity as an indispensable condition of equality between nations, and therefore of national
independence.[3] The assertion that one of the main objectives of
planning, and of the territorial and administrative rearrangements
designed to facilitate it, was to carry the advantages of industrial
development to the more backward regions of the country, to
integrate them with the more advanced regions, and thus promote
a policy of uniformity and equality which removed the last traces
of discrimination between ruling and subject nations, was not
devoid of substance. All the national republics and autonomous
republics or regions, with the single exception of the Ukraine,
were economically backward regions with a low proportion of
industrial development and urban population. Most of them
were thinly populated and suffered from undeveloped communications ; some were still entirely primitive. They therefore
offered a vast and largely virgin field for development. But a
working compromise had still to be reached between those who

---

[1] *Zhizn' Natsional'nostei*, No. 12 (147), June 15, 1922.

[2] The manifesto of the second congress of Comintern in July 1920, having
noted that " the workers' state is capable of painlessly harmonizing national
demands with economic demands, purifying the former of chauvinism, and
freeing the latter of imperialism ", went on : " Socialism strives to combine all
regions, all districts, all nationalities, in the unity of an economic plan " (*Kommunisticheskii Internatsional v Dokumentakh* (1933), p. 151).

[3] For a discussion of these questions see *The Bolshevik Revolution, 1917–
1923*, Vol. 1, pp. 365-367, 378-379.

wished to sacrifice everything to the rapid attainment of uniformity and equality and those who wished to leave open the widest scope for national differences and to stress the separate and particular status of national units within the broader framework.

The initial obstacles came, however, not only from national opposition, but also from the vested interests of existing units — what Krzhizhanovsky called " the ' parish pump ' of our former provinces ".[1] Gosplan hastened, on the basis of its provisional scheme of " regions ", to appoint regional planning commissions ; but these for a long time failed to secure recognition or cooperation from the provincial authorities.[2] Little or no practical progress had been made when the matter was taken up by the twelfth party congress in April 1923. Rykov made the report with a show of reluctance, and admitted that some party members had not wanted to have it raised at the congress. He dwelt on the importance of the rural district organization which was the point of contact with the peasant masses ; the rural districts should be enlarged in order to make them more efficient. The other crucial level in the governmental structure was the region, which was particularly associated with economic planning. Rykov's report provoked no discussion, and the resolution put forward by him was unanimously adopted.[3] It displayed an unusually acute consciousness of the difficulties involved. While it recognized " the former administrative-economic division of the republic " as obsolete, it admitted that the introduction of a new system " requires a cautious approach and a long lapse of time for its final realization ". It treated the Gosplan project approved by the commission of TsIK as a " preliminary working hypothesis which needs to be supplemented, verified and elaborated on the basis of experience ". Having noted the work already proceeding in the Ukraine, it instructed the central

[1] *Planovoe Khozyaistvo*, No. 3, 1926, p. 39; " its own belfry " is the Russian idiom. Jealousy was not confined to vested bureaucratic interests ; a case was quoted in which, several rural districts having been amalgamated to form a new district, the peasants insisted on outsiders being brought in to man the district executive committee, lest it should fall under the control of any one of the old rural districts (*Soveshchanie po Voprosam Sovetskogo Stroitel'stva 1925 g. : Yanvar'* (1925), p. 153).

[2] *Planovoe Khozyaistvo*, No. 3, 1926, p. 205.

[3] *Dvenadtsatyi S"ezd Rossiiskoi Kommunisticheskoi Partii (Bol'shevikov)* (1923), pp. 429-438, 574-575.

committee of the party to carry out the project of re-division " for a beginning " in two regions, one industrial, the other agricultural. Plans for other " regions, national republics and provinces " should continue to be studied, but were not to be put into effect till the lessons of two initial experiments had been digested. The " absolute necessity for the existence and further development of national republics " was reaffirmed, and attempts to subordinate them to a central power condemned. The need for contact with the masses was once more stressed : any scheme for the enlargement of the rural districts must be " carried out with the greatest caution and with full regard for the interests of the broad masses of the peasant population ".[1]

During the next three years the process of regionalization went forward on the lines laid down by the twelfth party congress of April 1923. The reference in the congress resolution to the Ukraine was significant. The Ukraine, though relatively small in area, contained nearly 20 per cent of the population of the USSR ; it produced 28 per cent of the grain of the USSR and 52 per cent of the marketable surplus of grain, 80 per cent of the sugar, 70 per cent of the pig iron and 65 per cent of the iron ore.[2] It had also enjoyed under the Tsars a more developed form of local government. At the same time, the Ukraine suffered more than any other part of the union from the chronic problem of agrarian over-population, and the devastation of the civil war had fallen on it more severely than on any other region. For these reasons it was a particularly important and potentially fruitful area for planning. But the Ukraine, more than any other constituent republic of the USSR, jealously asserted its independence ; more than any other, it was in a position to act for itself and to make good its own point of view. The Ukrainian SSR embraced with enthusiasm the principle of regionalization. Already in 1922, in advance of any other Soviet republic, it had reduced the number of its provinces from twelve to nine, and within these replaced its counties (uezdy) by a smaller number of departments (okruga), and its rural districts (volosti) by a smaller

---

[1] *VKP(B) v Rezolyutsiyakh* (1941), i, 497-498.
[2] These figures are quoted in *Planovoe Khozyaistvo*, No. 6, 1926, p. 179.

number of districts (raiony).[1] This new organization was provided for in a series of decrees in the spring of 1923 immediately before and after the twelfth party congress.[2]

Here, however, a controversy arose between the Ukrainian SSR as established by the constitution of the USSR of 1923 and the central authorities of Gosplan. The original scheme of Gosplan for 21 regions included a proposal to create, on the territory of the Ukrainian republic, two separate regions, a mining-manufacturing region centring on Kharkov and an agricultural region centring on Kiev. This division would, in the view of the Ukrainian authorities, have perpetuated the dichotomy in the body of the Ukrainian republic which was already a threat to its national character. It merely reproduced and emphasized the existing division between the predominantly agricultural (and overwhelmingly Ukrainian) sector of the country on the right bank of the Dnieper and the predominantly industrial (and partially Russianized) sector on the left bank ; and the scheme was made all the more obnoxious by the Gosplan proposal to include in the Kharkov region a sector of territory of the RSFSR including the port of Rostov. An alternative proposal by the Ukrainian Gosplan — the creation of a third region centring on Odessa — did not remove this objection.[3] The Ukrainian SSR, rather than submit to the Gosplan proposal, decided to dispense with any provincial or regional divisions. Under the final scheme of reorganization the Ukrainian SSR was divided into 41 departments (okruga), the departments corresponding not merely to the departments (the enlarged counties), but also to the regions, of the rest of the USSR. This so-called " three-tier system " (centre, department, district) was approved in the summer of 1925, and

---

[1] The relevant decisions were taken by the TsIK of the Ukrainian SSR at its session of October 1922 (*Raionirovanie SSSR*, ed. K. Egorov (1925), p. 112).

[2] The decrees on the provinces were dated March 7, 1923 (*Zbirnik Uzakonen' ta Rosporyadzhen', 1923*, No. 18-19, arts. 306-314 ; No. 20-21, art. 317), those on the departments and districts May 30, 1923 (*ibid.* No. 20-21, arts. 318-319) ; the history of the process is traced in a resolution of the ninth Ukrainian Congress of Soviets in May 1925 (*Puti Ukrepleniya Raboche-Krest'yanskogo Bloka* (1925), p. 90).

[3] For this controversy see *Planovoe Khozyaistvo*, No. 6, 1926, pp. 180-181 ; *SSSR : Tsentral'nyi Ispolnitel'nyi Komitet 3 Sozyva : 2 Sessiya* (1926), p. 406 ; *Voprosy Ekonomicheskogo Raionirovaniya*, ed. G. Krzhizhanovsky (1957), p. 320.

brought into effect on October 1, 1925.[1] The Moldavian autonomous SSR had a status corresponding to that of a department.
The White Russian SSR made haste to follow the Ukrainian
example. The impetus to regionalization appears to have come
from the large increase in territory by cession from the RSFSR
in March 1924,[2] which made reorganization imperative. As in
the Ukraine, it was decided to make the republic a single regional
unit and to create no divisions larger than the department.[3] The
former province of Vitebsk together with its capital having been
transferred to the White Russian SSR, the provincial administration at Vitebsk was suppressed and its functions transferred to
the capital of the republic, Minsk.[4] In the summer of 1924 the
republic was subjected to a process of " economic-administrative
division ", which provided for 10 departments (instead of 15
counties), 100 districts (instead of 238 rural districts) and 1202
(instead of 3405) villages having village Soviets.[5] It took twelve
months to complete these complex arrangements ; and the new
administrative organization of the White Russian SSR came into
force on August 1, 1925.[6] A novelty which does not appear to
have been reproduced elsewhere in the USSR was the establishment of " local " Soviets for small market towns which were the
capitals of districts.[7] The increase in the size of the district
unit automatically produced the need for these supplementary
Soviets.

The two regions, in which the two first experiments in

[1] The decree of the Ukrainian TsIK of July 1, 1925, was printed in Ukrainian
and Russian in *Radyan'ska Ukraina*, No. 3 (9), July 25, 1925, pp. 52-67 ; for
an exposition of the system, followed by a speech of Chubar to representatives
of the dissolved provincial and newly created departmental executive committees, see *ibid*. No. 4 (10), August 1925, pp. 7-15.

[2] See p. 261 above.

[3] Here, as in the Ukraine, Gosplan had in the first instance tried to impose
a division into regions (*SSSR : Tsentral'nyi Ispolnitel'nyi Komitet 3 Sozyva :
2 Sessiya* (1926), p. 452).

[4] *Istoricheskie Zapiski*, xlvi (1954), 297 ; no similar problem arose in Gomel
or Smolensk since, while parts of the provinces had been transferred, the capital
cities remained in the RSFSR.

[5] The relevant decrees are in *Sobranie Uzakonenii SSR Belorussii, 1924*,
No. 13, arts. 113-117 ; for summaries of the reform see *Vlast' Sovetov*, No. 6,
September 1924, p. 204 ; *Sovetskoe Stroitel'stvo : Sbornik*, i (1925), 260 ; *Istori-
cheskie Zapiski*, xlvi (1954), 296-299.

[6] *Sobranie Uzakonenii SSR Belorussii, 1925*, No. 2-3, art. 12 ; No. 31,
arts. 289-291.   [7] *Ibid*. No. 19, art. 177 ; No. 31, art. 292.

regionalization prescribed by the twelfth party congress, industrial
and agricultural, were to be made, were the Urals and the Northern
Caucasus. The regionalization of the Urals was a straightforward
piece of planning for the development of industry. The rich iron
deposits of the Urals had been extensively and successfully worked
for two centuries. But the disappearance of the serf labour on
which the iron-masters of the Urals had relied struck the industry
a crippling blow. Primitive equipment, obsolete methods of
production and lack of communications contributed to the
decline ; [1] and in the latter part of the nineteenth century the
more favoured position of the Ukrainian iron and coal fields had
made them the centre of Russia's nascent iron and steel industry.
The war of 1914, while it exposed the Ukraine to the ravages of
enemy occupation, spared the Urals ; and substantially the same
experience was repeated in the subsequent civil war, when fighting
in the Ukraine was more intense than in any other area, and
continued for a year after the region of the Urals had been re-
conquered and incorporated in Soviet territory. When, therefore, Soviet heavy industry reached its lowest ebb in 1920 and
1921, the prospects of an expansion of heavy industry in the
Urals seemed brighter than those of a revival of the derelict
industry of the Ukraine. By 1923 the recovery in the Ukraine
had partially redressed the balance ; but the Urals remained an
ideal ground for experiments in industrial planning, and were
naturally chosen as the scene for the initial experiment in
regionalization. In November 1923, six months after the resolution of the twelfth party congress, a statute for the Ural region
was adopted by the TsIK of the RSFSR and issued in the form of
a decree of the RSFSR.[2] National and constitutional problems
were avoided by not attempting to include in it the Bashkir
autonomous SSSR, a department of which remained embedded
as an enclave in the new region.

The establishment of the Ural region set the pattern for the
whole subsequent policy of regionalization, and revealed its
pragmatic character. The novelty of the new region was that it

[1] This was described by Lenin in 1899 in a passage of *The Development of
Capitalism in Russia* (*Sochineniya*, iii, 376-379), with which all Soviet planners
and administrators would have been familiar.
[2] *Sobranie Uzakonenii, 1923*, No. 104, art. 1028.

broke boldly through old geographical and administrative divisions
by including territory on both sides of the Urals range, thus
combining a sector of western Siberia (broadly corresponding with
the former provinces of Ekaterinburg, Tyumen and Chelyabinsk)
with the eastern fringes of European Russia (part of the former
province of Perm). On the other hand, the initial conception of
regions as economically homogeneous had gone by the board.
The new region, in area twice as large as France, and with a
population estimated at 6,200,000, was divided into 15 departments, of which five were predominantly industrial and nine
predominantly agricultural, while one (Tobolsk), the largest in
area but smallest in population, consisted mainly of uninhabited
tundra.[1] The departments were divided into districts (an average
of 14 to each department), and the districts into villages (an
average of 16 to each district).[2] In accordance with the usual
Soviet pattern, the highest constitutional authority of the region
was the regional congress of Soviets with its executive committee ;
beneath it stood the department congresses of Soviets and executive committees ; and beneath them the district congresses and
committees ; and the base of the pyramid was formed by village
Soviets sending delegates to the district congresses, and town and
factory Soviets sending delegates to district, department or
regional congresses according to their size and status. The Ural
statute contained one unique feature. The famous five-to-one
ratio between the coefficient of representation for rural and urban
Soviets, which had been the basis of the original amalgamation
of peasants' with workers' Soviets and was embodied in all subsequent constitutions,[3] was abandoned in favour of a ten-to-one
ratio. The purpose of this innovation was evidently to weight
the coefficient of representation still further on the side of the

---

[1] A great deal of literature appeared on the Ural region ; *Vestnik Finansov*,
No. 3, March 1925, pp. 131-146, contained a full description of its organization,
and *Planovoe Khozyaistvo*, No. 11, 1925, pp. 215-245, a review of plans for
industrial and agricultural development.

[2] *Ibid.* No. 3, 1926, p. 200. The Ural region was afterwards quoted as
an instance of " regionalization from above ", i.e. the departments were formed
first, and the subdivisions came later (*ibid.* No. 5, 1926, p. 190; No. 3, 1927,
p. 258) ; much of this was newly developed territory, and there were fewer
vested interests to contend with than elsewhere.

[3] For the origin and character of this differentiation see *The Bolshevik
Revolution, 1917–1923*, Vol. 1, pp. 126, 143-144.

proletariat in a region whose industrial development was a major objective. It was not imitated in any of the other new regions, and disappeared in the Ural region when the statutes of the regions were standardized in 1928.[1]

The second region indicated in the resolution of the twelfth party congress was the Northern Caucasus. Here the process of regionalization occupied the greater part of the year 1924, and was concerned with quite different problems from those of the Ukraine or the Urals.[2] The slopes of the Northern Caucasus were inhabited by a population of extreme diversity engaged in primitive agriculture, viticulture and forestry ; politically they were divided between the Dagestan and Mountaineers' autonomous SSRs, and the Kabardino-Balkarsh, Karachaevo-Cherkessian, Adygeisk and Chechensk autonomous regions, all within the RSFSR. The major decision, which now determined the shape and destinies of the new region, was the inclusion in it of the small but important industrial area of the Lower Don with a large Russian and Ukrainian population, which had been joined in the original Gosplan scheme to the Kharkov industrial region, and might more logically have been grouped with the projected Lower Volga region : Rostov at the mouth of the Don was to be the capital of the new region. This arrangement had the undoubted advantage of linking a rich industrial area with a potentially rich agricultural area and, by the same stroke, of linking a predominantly Russian and predominantly proletarian population with the backward and ethnically diverse population of the Caucasian slopes.[3] It was still accepted doctrine at this time that autonomous republics could not be incorporated in " regions ", and the Dagestan and Mountaineers' autonomous SSRs were therefore excluded. Autonomous regions could be included ; but the determination of future relations between the executive committees of the four autonomous regions and the main central

---

[1] *Sobranie Uzakonenii, 1928*, No. 70, art. 503.

[2] It was contrasted with the Ural region in the passages already quoted (see p. 284, note 2 above) as a case of regionalization from below.

[3] In the words of a contemporary report : " Districts which have passed through a period of tempestuous economic growth find themselves side by side with districts completely backward both economically and culturally ; the region has lived in an atmosphere of national animosities sustained by differences of status " (*Planovoe Khozyaistvo*, No. 3, 1926, p. 229).

executive committee of the region with its seat at Rostov was a matter of some delicacy. By an agreement reached in November 1923 at a conference between the newly created regional authorities and the authorities of the autonomous regions concerned, the division of competence between them was said to be based on the same principles as the division between the USSR and the constituent republics under the constitution of the USSR. This meant that, in all matters dealt with under that constitution by unified commissariats, though not in matters left to the competence of republican commissariats, the authorities of the autonomous region would be subordinated to the central regional authorities. Autonomous regions retained the right to send delegates to the Council of Nationalities of the USSR, and had direct access to the central organs of the RSFSR.[1] It was presumably in order to avoid the apparent anomaly of including an autonomous region (oblast') in another region that the North Caucasian region was officially designated not as an oblast', but as a krai. An official announcement of the intention to create the North Caucasian *krai* issued from the presidium of the TsIK of the RSFSR on June 2, 1924.[2]

Before the project could be completed, however, a further and more dramatic change was made. On July 7, 1924, a decree of the TsIK of the RSFSR dissolved, in accordance with the alleged wish of the nationalities inhabiting it, the autonomous SSR of the Mountaineers; the territory was divided on the basis of nationality into two autonomous regions of Northern Osetia (Yugo-Osetia, south of the Caucasus range, was already an autonomous region in the Georgian SSR) and Ingushetia. A peculiar feature of the arrangement was that Vladikavkaz, the only large city in the region, was to remain the seat of administration of both autonomous regions, and was itself to become an " independent administrative unit " directly responsible to the

[1] Much discussion took place about the status of the four autonomous regions included in the North Caucasian region, which was evidently felt to constitute a precedent : see *Vlast' Sovetov*, No. 3-4 (June–July), 1924, pp. 94-97 ; *Planovoe Khozyaistvo*, No. 4, 1925, pp. 275-280 ; *Sovetskoe Stroitel'stvo : Sbornik*, ii-iii (1925), 262. Like most questions of constitutional theory in the Soviet Union, it had no great influence on subsequent practice.

[2] *Raionirovanie SSSR*, ed. K. Egorov (1925), p. 120 ; *Sovetskoe Stroitel'-stvo : Sbornik*, ii-iii (1925), 253.

TsIK of the RSFSR ; and a similar independent status was reserved for the Sunzhensk department in which Vladikavkaz was situated.[1] The autonomous SSR of the Mountaineers had never been ethnically homogeneous ; the failure to find a national name for it was significant. Racial jealousies and the primitive character of its native population may have made it unsatisfactory as an autonomous republic. It is reasonable to assume that the decision to break up the republic was dictated partly by the difficulty of handling notoriously turbulent and unruly populations, and was to this extent an application of the familiar principle " divide and rule ",[2] and partly by the desire to bring the territory into the North Caucasian region — a solution hitherto debarred by its status as an autonomous republic.

The formal decision creating the North Caucasian region was taken by the TsIK of the RSFSR at its session in October 1924, the drafting of a detailed statute being left to the presidium of TsIK.[3] The statute was finally issued on January 26, 1925. It differed in some respects, partly owing to the greater complexity of the region, from the statute of the Ural region. At the head stood the regional congress of Soviets with its executive committee, and beneath it the congresses of Soviets of the autonomous regions and of the departments, all with their executive committees. But, while both autonomous regions and departments were to be divided into districts, no provision was made for district congresses of Soviets or executive committees : village and factory Soviets sent their delegates direct to the congresses of the autonomous regions and departments to which they belonged. The most interesting chapter of the statute related to the rights of the autonomous regions, which were said to " enter into the region (*krai*) in the capacity of independent administrative-economic

---

[1] *Sobranie Uzakonenii, 1924*, No. 66, art. 656.

[2] A writer who was a child in the area at the time records this event as follows : " By July 1924 the growing aspirations of the North Caucasians towards full independence resulted in a Moscow decree which terminated their partial independence. Leading national communists were arrested ; others were sent to far distant regions of the Soviet empire." He adds that " at the time the significance of all this naturally escaped my own generation " (G. A. Tokaev, *Betrayal of an Ideal* (1954), pp. 14-15). While there is no independent evidence of arrests or deportations, it would have been in accordance with Soviet practice, once the decision was taken, to remove potential troublemakers from the scene.

[3] *Sobranie Uzakonenii, 1924*, No. 87, art. 881.

units with reservation of the indefeasible rights granted to them by the decisions creating them ". In the constitutional structure the autonomous regions stood side by side with the departments without any apparent distinction of right or function, except that the autonomous regions, unlike the departments, were directly represented in the All-Russian Congress of Soviets and in the TsIK of the USSR. An elaborate attempt was made to carry out the understanding of November 1923 by allocating to them a certain measure of autonomy in matters which under the constitution of the USSR fell within the competence of the constituent republics, and a right of executive action, subject to the direction of the central organs, in matters dealt with under the constitution of the USSR by unified commissariats. But these distinctions can have had little reality. The cardinal provision of this chapter of the statute was that the regional executive committee and the executive committee of the autonomous region could, in the event of disagreement between them, each appeal against the decisions of the other to the TsIK of the RSFSR. But there was a significant difference in terminology. The regional executive committee could " protest ", the executive committee of an autonomous region could " complain " ; and this difference doubtless meant that the " protest " of the superior organ had the effect of suspending the contested decision till judgment was given from Moscow, whereas the " complaint " of the subordinate organ had not.[1] Moreover, behind these constitutional niceties, as behind all others in Soviet constitutional practice, lay the ultimate control of the party over major decisions of policy and key appointments. This sanction assured the smooth operation of many arrangements which might otherwise have seemed unworkable.

The first congress of Soviets of the North Caucasian region assembled within a few days of the issue of this decree, on January 31, 1925. Rykov, who attended it as representative of the TsIK of the RSFSR, unexpectedly described the region as "a state within a state ".[2] A month later, the formation of the region was at length completed by the incorporation in it of the four units of the dissolved Mountaineers' republic — the North Osetian and

---

[1] *Sobranie Uzakonenii, 1925*, No. 11, art. 76.
[2] *Sovetskoe Stroitel'stvo : Sbornik*, ii-iii (1925), 253.

Ingush autonomous regions, the department of Sunzhensk and the city of Vladikavkaz.[1] The Dagestan autonomous republic remained outside it as an independent unit of the RSFSR.[2] An interesting feature of the new region was the resettlement in the predominantly Russian Kuban area in the west of 15,000 Cossacks who had fought on the anti-Soviet side in the civil war and had fled abroad. These now returned to their homes and, having " bowed their heads before the Soviet power ", were granted an amnesty and restoration of political rights.[3] The third Union Congress of Soviets in May 1925 was made the occasion of public gestures of reconciliation. A Cossack delegation of five, including one woman, appeared carrying two banners, a sheaf of ears of corn and a bouquet of giant sunflowers ; and it was announced that Kalinin, Bukharin, Rykov, Stalin and Chicherin (the omission of Zinoviev and Kamenev is perhaps significant of rifts that were just opening) had been elected " honorary Cossacks ". A " non-party Cossack " declared that " the Cossacks have turned their face to the Soviet power " and demanded " the return of the Cossacks carried off by Wrangel and Denikin ".[4]

In spite of the prominence given by the racial diversity of the North Caucasian region to national questions, the central purpose of the new regional structure, here as in the Urals, was to promote economic planning and economic development. A regional economic council and its planning commission had been established long before the formal constitution of the region : these were indeed the organs which prepared the way for its creation. It was the regional planning commission which in the winter of 1924–1925 elaborated and submitted to Gosplan the first project for a canal to link the Volga to the Don and for a deep-sea port at Rostov, the whole scheme to be completed by 1930–1931 at a

[1] *Sobranie Uzakonenii, 1925*, No. 18, art. 118.
[2] This led to a complaint that the Ingushes were separated from pastures in Dagestan which they had used from time immemorial (*Planovoe Khozyaistvo*, No. 5, 1926, p. 222).
[3] *SSSR : Tsentral'nyi Ispolnitel'nyi Komitet 2 Sozyva : 3 Sessiya* (1925), pp. 83, 90 ; the party central committee noted that this implied a restoration of rights to existing Cossack communities, and proposed that, in Cossack districts, the mention of " Cossack deputies ", which appeared in the original title of the Soviets after the revolution, but had long fallen into disuse, should be reinstated (*VKP(B) v Rezolyutsiyakh* (1941), i, 649–650).
[4] *Tretii S"ezd Sovetov SSSR* (1925), pp. 23–24, 139–140.

cost of 130–140 million rubles.[1] In May 1925 a commission
appointed by Rabkrin visited the area to study local agricultural
conditions.[2] By the beginning of 1926 there were in existence
a " completed plan for the development of industry ", covering large-scale enterprises controlled by the Vesenkha of the
USSR, like Donugol' and Grozneft', enterprises controlled by
the Vesenkha of the RSFSR, and enterprises controlled by the
regional economic council, and a transport plan including the
construction of highways, which were almost entirely lacking in
the region.[3]

Next to the Ural and North Caucasian regions, no part of the
RSFSR more urgently demanded the application of regional
planning than the vast expanse of Siberia. In one of its original
projects in 1921, Gosplan had provisionally divided the whole
territory into six regions, three west of Lake Baikal — western
Siberia or the basin of the Ob with its capital at Omsk, a Kuznetsk-
Altai region with its capital at Novo-Nikolaevsk, and the basin of
the Enisei with its capital at Krasnoyarsk ; and three east of Lake
Baikal — Yakutia with its capital at Yakutsk, a Lena-Baikal region
with its capital at Irkutsk, and a Maritime region with its capital at
Vladivostok.[4] So long as Japanese troops remained in eastern
Siberia, such planning was an academic exercise ; and the inter-
lude of the Far Eastern Republic created a certain administrative
unity over eastern Siberia, though its demise was followed by the
creation in 1923 of Buryat-Mongol and Yakut autonomous SSRs.
A further blow was struck at the original Gosplan scheme when
a large part of the proposed western Siberian or Ob region was
incorporated in the Ural region. Meanwhile the vested interests
of the two bodies still responsible for the administration of western
and eastern Siberia, the Siberian Revolutionary Committee
(Sibrevkom) and the Far Eastern Revolutionary Committee
(Dalrevkom), hardened against any further partition of their
respective areas. Agreement was reached without much difficulty
to constitute the whole of Siberia west of Lake Baikal, with the

---

[1] An outline of the scheme is in *Planovoe Khozyaistvo*, No. 4, 1925, pp. 327-
328.
[2] The record of some of its conclusions (*ibid.* No. 10, 1925, pp. 31-42) has
already been quoted (see Vol. 1, p. 239).
[3] A vague account of these and other projects is in *Planovoe Khozyaistvo*,
No. 3, 1926, pp. 232-236.   [4] *Ibid.* No. 9, 1925, p. 239.

exception of the area included in the Ural region, as a Siberian region with its capital at Novo-Nikolaevsk,[1] this region incorporating the Oirot autonomous region already established in 1922.[2] A statute providing for the division of the region into 17 departments and setting up administrative machinery similar to that of the Ural region, was duly adopted by the TsIK of the RSFSR at its session of October 1925.[3] The first regional Siberian congress of Soviets opened at Novo-Nikolaesvk on December 3, 1925.[4] Early in 1926 Novo-Nikolaevsk changed its name to Novo-Sibirsk.[5]

The future of eastern Siberia was the subject of a prolonged controversy, Gosplan standing out for its independent Lena-Baikal industrial region, and Dalrevkom seeking to keep the whole of eastern Siberia, outside the two autonomous republics, under a single jurisdiction. A conference in Chita in 1924 was followed by a further conference in Moscow in April and May 1925, which produced no agreed conclusion. In October 1925 the difference was referred to the presidium of the TsIK of the RSFSR, which passed a resolution to constitute a Far Eastern region with its capital at Khabarovsk and to substitute the new administrative system of departments and districts for the old system of provinces, counties and rural districts. But this resolution still failed to settle the disputed question whether the whole of eastern Siberia was to be included in the new region; and Gosplan continued throughout the autumn of 1925 to fight a losing battle for its scheme, which seems to have been a relic of the initial, but long discarded, conception of economically homogeneous regions. Finally, in January 1926 the presidium of TsIK decided on the inclusion of the whole of Transbaikalia in the Far Eastern region.[6] The decision did not affect the project to create

[1] *Sobranie Uzakonenii, 1925,* No. 38, art. 268.
[2] *Sobranie Uzakonenii, 1922,* No. 39, art. 550.
[3] *Vserossiiskii Tsentral'nyi Ispolnitel'nyi Komitet XII Sozyva : Vtoraya Sessiya : Postanovleniya* (1925), pp. 25-61 ; *Sobranie Uzakonenii, 1925,* No. 85, art. 651.   [4] *Izvestiya,* December 5, 1925.
[5] *Sobranie Zakonov, 1926,* No. 9, art. 73.
[6] *Sobranie Uzakonenii, 1926,* No. 3. art. 8 ; for the preceding discussions and decisions see *Planovoe Khozyaistvo,* No. 9, 1925, p. 239 ; No. 5, 1926, pp. 196-197. The Gosplan case for a separate Lena-Baikal region was argued at length in an article *ibid.* No. 9, 1925, pp. 239-257, where it was maintained that the Lena-Baikal region was necessary as " a bridge to the Far East and an indispensable economic base in its rear " (p. 253), and in further articles *ibid.* No. 10, 1925, pp. 259-271.

eventually an important industrial base in the Lena area, though this took second place to the industrial development of the Kuznetsk-Altai area west of Lake Baikal. The Far Eastern region thus constituted was the largest in area of all the existing or projected regions except the Siberian region and the Yakut autonomous SSR, and had the smallest population of any except the Buryat-Mongol and Yakut autonomous SSRs. It covered four former provinces — Maritime, Amur, Transbaikal and Kamchatka. It was now to be divided into nine departments — Vladivostok, Khabarovsk, Nikolaevsk, Amur, Zeisk, Sretensk, Chita, Kamchatka and Sakhalin ; and a small gold-bearing area of the Yakut SSR was to be annexed to the gold-mining department of Zeisk.[1] The first regional congress of Soviets of the Far Eastern region was held at Khabarovsk in the spring of 1926.[2]

The fourteenth party congress in December 1925 was already able to speak of " the successful carrying out of regionalization ", through which the Soviet power had " placed a material-economic foundation beneath the regions, autonomous republics and union republics " ;[3] and it gave orders to reshape the local party organizations to take account of these changes.[4] A few months later, the whole process of regionalization, including the creation of departments and districts, with the appropriate organs at each level, was said to be complete in the Ural, North Caucasian, Siberian and Far Eastern regions of the RSFSR, as well as in the Ukrainian, White Russian and Turkmen SSRs.[5] In October 1926 the Uzbek SSR constituted itself as a region divided into 11 departments ; at the same time a joint economic council with planning functions was set up for all the Central Asian republics.[6] The initial regional organizations, including planning commissions, had been established in 1923 for the Central Industrial and Lower

---

[1] *Planovoe Khozyaistvo*, No. 5, 1926, pp. 203-220.
[2] *Vlast' Sovetov*, No. 17, April 25, 1926, pp. 18-20.
[3] *VKP(B) v Rezolyutsiyakh* (1941), ii, 47.
[4] *XIV S"ezd Vsesoyuznoi Kommunisticheskoi Partii (B)* (1926), pp. 878, 885-886.
[5] *Planovoe Khozyaistvo*, No. 5, 1926, p. 189. Under the final scheme the RSFSR was divided into 19 regions ; the Ukrainian and White Russian SSRs, the Transcaucasian SFSR and the Uzbek and Turkmen SSRs each formed one region.   [6] N. Arkhipov, *Sredne-Aziatskie Respubliki* (1927), pp. 135-137.

Volga regions, and in 1924 for the North-Eastern, Western, Central Black-Earth and Vyatka-Vetluga regions.[1] But these had not yet completed their work; the establishment of the Lower Volga region was still a bone of contention between different local authorities affected.[2] In the Transcaucasian SFSR hardly anything had been done. In general, progress was slowest in regions where the old administrative machinery had been most fully developed and put up most resistance to plans to supersede it. Cases occurred where the old provincial authorities refused to recognize the new-fangled regional planning commissions.[3] In the Middle Volga region, protests were made against the intervention of the provincial authorities at Samara, even before the region was constituted, in the economic affairs of the Tatar and Chuvash autonomous republics.[4] But the opposition was eventually overruled. By a constitutional innovation, which had hitherto been successfully resisted,[5] both of these republics were incorporated in the Middle Volga region. The fifteenth party congress in November 1927 resolved that regionalization should be carried to its conclusion within the period of the first Five-Year Plan;[6] and by 1928, when the first Five-Year Plan was introduced, the reform was on its way to completion. Throughout the USSR the old administrative structure of provinces, counties and rural districts was being replaced by the new structure of regions, departments and districts.[7]

The process of regionalization was from the outset closely

[1] *Planovoe Khozyaistvo*, No. 3, 1926, p. 204.

[2] See a series of articles in *Planovoe Khozyaistvo*, No. 4, 1927, pp. 247-286.

[3] *Ibid.* No. 3, 1926, p. 205.

[4] The protests were recorded at the fifth Tatar congress of Soviets in 1925 (*Pyatyi S"ezd Sovetov Tatar'skoi SSR* (Kazan, 1925), pp. 24-25, quoted in W. R. Batsell, *Soviet Rule in Russia* (N.Y., 1929), p. 648); the Chuvash autonomous region was promoted in 1925 to the status of an autonomous republic (see p. 257 above).

[5] In 1928 it was for the first time formally laid down that an autonomous SSR might be incorporated in a region of the RSFSR " on principles of voluntary consent " (*Sobranie Uzakonenii, 1928*, No. 79, art. 554); in 1926 such a step had been described, even by an official of Gosplan, as " untimely and inappropriate " (*Planovoe Khozyaistvo*, No. 5, 1926, p. 194).

[6] *VKP(B) v Rezolyutsiyakh* (1941), ii, 244.

[7] Precise figures showing the process of replacement are in *Pyatiletnii Plan Narodno-Khozyaistvennogo Stroitel'stva SSSR* (1929), iii, p. xii; for a convenient sketch-map showing the division of the USSR into regions at the date of the census of December 1926 see F. Lorimer, *The Population of the Soviet Union* (Geneva, 1945), between pp. 44 and 45.

connected with the adoption of the policy of planning. In the governmental machine Gosplan was the strongest and most persistent advocate of the reform, which was declared to rest on " the fundamental principle that politics is concentrated economics ".[1] The new regions had all been shaped with a view to economic considerations, though the criterion applied was not uniform. Sometimes the declared aim was to make an economically homogeneous region, sometimes to combine complementary opposites, the contrasting methods being labelled " integral regionalization " and " differential regionalization ".[2] Sometimes the purpose in view was to perpetuate and organize existing forms of production, sometimes to create and develop new forms — a difference which had a certain analogy with the clash between " genetic " and " teleological " conceptions of planning.[3] While one of the main purposes of regionalization was said to be " the decentralization of state economic policy and the establishment of a planned economy for broad economic regions ",[4] and while the regional planning commissions played an important part in the scheme, the total result was in the long run to confirm the power, prestige and effectiveness of the central authorities, and especially the Gosplan of the USSR, which now became the ultimate source of major economic policy. The new regional organs were, first and foremost, the organs of a planned economy. Without regionalization, the five-year plans could not have worked.

Regionalization was, however, not only an " economic ", but a " social-political " process,[5] and had its effects beyond the economic sphere. It was an administrative as well as an economic reform — a way of reducing the number of administrative units and simplifying the administrative machine. This process had already begun in 1922 by way of reaction against the multiplication of units in the early years of the régime,[6] and for motives

[1] *Planovoe Khozyaistvo*, No. 5, 1926, p. 193.
[2] *Ibid.* No. 6, 1927, p. 240.
[3] See Vol. 1, pp. 495-497.
[4] *Planovoe Khozyaistvo* No. 3, 1926, p. 209; provinces before they were " regionalized " had no planning organs, the deficiency being made good by the central organs of Gosplan (*Kontrol'nye Tsifry Narodnogo Khozyaistva SSSR na 1927–1928 god* (1928), p. 410).
[5] *Planovoe Khozyaistvo*, No. 5, 1926, p. 192.
[6] For this see p. 274 above.

unconnected with those of the economic planners. The initial reasons for the policy of " enlargement " of counties and rural districts (as the reduction in their numbers was generally called) were shortage of man-power and shortage of money. The demand for more efficient local administration revealed the acute lack of competent and trustworthy officials ; and the economy campaign inaugurated by NEP, and especially the re-establishment of provincial budgets in the autumn of 1921,[1] set up powerful pressures for a contraction in the number of administrative units. The ninth All-Russian Congress of Soviets in December 1921 voted " to reduce the number of provincial executive committees by combining neighbouring provinces " ;[2] and it was logical that the reduction in the number of provinces should be accompanied by corresponding reductions in the lower units. Between the summer of 1922 and the summer of 1924 " enlargement " at every level of local administration went on apace throughout the European provinces of the RSFSR and the Ukraine, and more spasmodically elsewhere. In the European provinces of the RSFSR (for which alone full statistics are available) the process of enlargement and reduction in number was applied sparingly, and in some provinces not at all, to the counties, but drastically to the rural districts, the number of which was reduced in proportions varying from one-third to two-thirds ; while in 1922 few rural districts had a population of more than 10,000, by 1924 hardly any had less than that number, and rural districts with 20,000 or 30,000 inhabitants were not uncommon.[3] In the European provinces of the RSFSR 5854 rural districts with an average population of 7480 were transformed in these two years into 2389 rural districts with an average population of 21,237.[4] Occasional statistics from the autonomous republics reproduce the same picture. A decree of the Tatar autonomous SSR of March 1924 reduced the number of rural districts in the republic from 223 to 125 ; in the Bashkir autonomous SSR it was reduced from 295 to 117.[5] According to comprehensive but perhaps less reliable statistics, the total number

[1] See *The Bolshevik Revolution, 1917–1923*, Vol. 2, pp. 347-348.
[2] *S"ezdy Sovetov RSFSR v Postanovleniyakh* (1939), p. 221.
[3] See the tables in A. Luzhin, *Ot Volosti k Raionu* (1929), pp. 47, 63.
[4] *Raionirovanie SSSR*, ed. K. Egorov (1925), p. 221.
[5] *Sobranie Uzakonenii Tatar'skoi Respubliki, 1924*, No. 17, art. 128 ; *X Let Sovetskoi Bashkirii* (Ufa, 1929), p. 415.

of rural districts in the RSFSR fell from 7325 in 1922 to 3368 in 1924.[1] In the whole territory of the USSR the number of rural districts, which had stood at 13,913 in 1917, had fallen by 1924 to 6840.[2]

This process of " enlargement " of existing units, while it was initiated independently of regionalization and for different motives, was gradually overtaken by the broader policy and incorporated in it. The corollary of this replacement of the province (guberniya) by the region (oblast' or krai) was the replacement of the county (uezd) by the department (okrug), and of the rural district (volost') by the district (raion) ; and all these changes meant the substitution of a larger for a smaller unit of administration. Calculations for the RSFSR in 1924 showed that the average population of a province was 1,380,000, of a county 180,000 and of a rural district 14,500 ; the corresponding figures for the whole of the USSR were somewhat lower, but the areas of the units were three or four times as great.[3] The population of the new " regions " varied from just over one million in the Turkmen SSR to 29 millions in the Ukrainian SSR, both of which constituted single regions ; the population of the newly created European regions of the RSFSR varied from about five to ten millions. The population of a department varied from 50,000 to more than a million ; about 500,000 (or nearly three times as great as the average of the county) was a normal figure. Districts with up to 50,000 inhabitants (or nearly two-and-a-half times as great as the average of the rural district) were common, and substantially larger figures were not unknown.[4] Concentration was generally most intense in the most thickly populated regions ; in sparsely populated areas distance put some limitations on the process. In the province of Tula, where regionalization at the lower levels preceded the incorporation of the province in the still unformed Central Industrial region, 56 new districts replaced 229 rural districts. In the Ukraine 49 departments replaced 102 counties and 706 districts 1898 rural districts.[5] In the Ural region one-

[1] *Vserossiiskii Tsentral'nyi Ispolnitel'nyi Komitet XI Sozyva : Vtoraya Sessiya* (1924), p. 50.

[2] G. Zinoviev, *Litsom k Derevne* (1925), p. 38.

[3] *Vlast' Sovetov*, No. 7, 1924, p. 205.

[4] For examples of the population of departments and districts at the time of their formation see *Raionirovanie SSSR*, ed. K. Egorov (1925), pp. 285-296.   [5] *Ibid.* p. 241.

half of the 205 districts corresponded approximately to the old rural districts or were occasionally made by dividing them ; the other half were combinations of anything from two to seven of the old rural districts.[1]

The enlargement of the rural districts had as its corollary the enlargement of the unit of administration next below it, the village, though this also was no part of the original intention of those responsible for regionalization, and was dictated by the same practical considerations as the enlargement of the rural district : as Kaganovich said, it " took place not on a basis of planned economy, but out of need and shortage of funds ".[2] While the village had always been a locality of varying size, the constitution of the RSFSR of 1918 laid down for the establishment of Soviets a fixed ratio of one deputy for every 100 inhabitants, village Soviets consisting of not less than three and not more than 50 deputies : this implied that villages should contain not less than 300 and not more than 5000 inhabitants. The abortive statute for village Soviets of January 1922,[3] apparently forgetful of this constitutional provision, fixed 400 inhabitants as the lowest number entitled to form a village Soviet, but had laid down the ratio of one deputy to 200 inhabitants with a maximum of 25 deputies, thus maintaining the maximum of 5000 inhabitants for a " village ". That this was not intended as a limit was shown, however, by another article which permitted a village Soviet representing more than 10,000 inhabitants to set up an executive committee — a provision applied to all Soviets in the 1918 constitution which appears never to have been carried out in the villages. The amended statute of October 1924 [4] returned to the figure of 300 inhabitants as the minimum qualification for a village Soviet, and to the ratio of one deputy for every 100 inhabitants, but declared that a village Soviet should be composed of not less than three, and not more than 100, deputies ; this meant that a village might have anything from 300 to 10,000 inhabitants.[5]

---

[1] *Vestnik Finansov*, No. 3, March 1925, p. 132.
[2] *Soveshchanie po Voprosam Sovetskogo Stroitel'stva 1925 g. : Aprel'* (1925), p. 13.   [3] See p. 305 below.   [4] See p. 322 below.
[5] The constitution of the RSFSR of 1925 retained the limit of 50 deputies (and 5000 inhabitants) for the village Soviet ; but little attention was paid to such constitutional rules.

These wide limits left ample discretion to the reformers ; and the number of " villages " (in the sense of units having village Soviets) in the RSFSR fell from 80,000, each containing on an average 200 households or 1000 inhabitants, in 1922, to between 50,000 and 55,000, each containing 300 households and 1500 inhabitants, in 1924. Before this process of enlargement, half the villages in the RSFSR had less than 1000 inhabitants ; after it, only 31 per cent had so few. The proportion of villages with more than 1500 inhabitants rose from 15 to more than 45 per cent.[1] In the Ural region the number of villages was reduced from 6000 to rather more than 3000 with an average population of 1825.[2] In the Bashkir autonomous SSR the number fell from 3698 to 1905 with the result that some peasants were living more than 20 or 30 versts from the seat of their village Soviet.[3]   In the Ukraine the reduction was from 15,696 to 9307, with an increase of 1607 in 1925.[4]   In the Crimea the average village had more than 4000 inhabitants, living up to 30 versts from the seat of the Soviet ;[5] and a case was quoted of a village of 6000 inhabitants, some of them living 60 versts from the centre, in the Sochi district on the Black Sea.[6]   A " village ", according to an official spokesman, had come to be an administrative unit with a population of anything from 300 to 13,000 persons.[7]

Large claims were made for the economies effected by these changes. In the Ural region the number of administrative units had been reduced from 7080 to 3430, in the North Caucasian region from 1470 to 1252.[8]   How far the reduction relieved the

[1] *Sovetskoe Stroitel'stvo : Sbornik*, i (1925), 44-46.
[2] *Vestnik Finansov*, No. 3, March 1925, p. 134.
[3] *Vlast' Sovetov*, No. 45, November 8, 1925, p. 15.
[4] *Raionirovanie SSSR*, ed. K. Egorov (1925), p. 258 : similar figures are quoted in *SSSR : Tsentral'nyi Ispolnitel'nyi Komitet 3 Sozyva : 2 Sessiya* (1926), p. 406.
[5] *Soveshchanie po Voprosam Sovetskogo Stroitel'stva 1925 g. : Yanvar'* (1925), p. 176.
[6] *Sovetskoe Stroitel'stvo : Sbornik*, iv-v (1926), 148.
[7] *Soveshchanie po Voprosam Sovetskogo Stroitel'stva 1925 g. : Aprel'* (1925), p. 72. For the average number of inhabitants of an " enlarged " village in different regions and republics see the tables in *Raionirovanie SSSR*, ed. K. Egorov (1925), p. 263 ; the figure varied from 1500 to over 4000.
[8] *Planovoe Khozyaistvo*, No. 3, 1926, p. 200 ; No. 5, 1926, p. 222. The term " administrative unit " seems, however, to have been elastic, and a different calculation is made *ibid.* No. 3, 1927, p. 260. Another account (*ibid.* No. 2, 1927, p. 233) even claimed that the number of administrative units in the

growing weight of bureaucracy is doubtful. In the Ukraine it was claimed that the number of officials had been reduced from 92,304 to 49,811.[1] In the North Caucasian region, the total number was said to have been reduced by 24 per cent, and in the Ural region by 39 per cent.[2] But the last claim was not borne out by other sources, which alleged that only a 5-per-cent reduction had been achieved in the Ural region, and that the number of officials was once more growing.[3] In view of the expansion of public services and activities of all kinds it is unlikely that any temporary reduction in the number of officials was maintained. But there is no reason to question the claim that regionalization constituted a substantial measure of rationalization.

Regionalization served, however, other political purposes besides a simplification of the administrative machine. The compromise between national and economic factors effected in the early days of regionalization was not static ; and the battle continued to rage. In 1925 Alexandrov, who had drawn the first fire of national critics in 1921,[4] was subjected to particularly violent accusations of *smenovekh* tendencies and Great-Russian chauvinism.[5] In March 1926 the president of the Ukrainian Gosplan complained that " the Gosplan of the USSR organizes its work on the basis of vertical divisions of the national economy — metal, coal, grain, transport — without taking sufficient account of its branches in the republics, and is little interested in assessing the role of the republics as self-contained units of the economy ".[6] The Ukraine might resist proposals to weaken its unity in the name of regionalization, and Transcaucasia or Uzbekistan fight a delaying action

North Caucasian region had increased so that " government had moved nearer to the population " as the result of regionalization : this seems to be confirmed by comparative figures in *Raionirovanie SSSR*, ed. K. Egorov (1925), p. 279.
[1] *SSSR : Tsentral'nyi Ispolnitel'nyi Komitet 3 Sozyva : 2 Sessiya* (1926), p. 406.
[2] *Planovoe Khozyaistvo*, No. 5, 1926, p. 222 ; No. 3, 1926, p. 200.
[3] *Vestnik Finansov*, No. 3, March 1925, p. 135 ; comparative figures in *Raionirovanie SSSR*, ed. K. Egorov (1925), p. 279, relate only to officials of district executive committees and village Soviets. [4] See p. 277 above.
[5] *Bol'shevik*, No. 5-6 (21-22), March 25, 1925, pp. 115-125. The attack appeared to reflect jealousy of Gosplan in Vesenkha circles ; most of the Gosplan experts were non-party and therefore vulnerable. This time Alexandrov replied in *Planovoe Khozyaistvo*, No. 11, 1925, pp. 297-301, and was again attacked in *Bol'shevik*, No. 5, March 15, 1926, pp. 70-75.
[6] *Ekonomicheskaya Zhizn'*, March 14, 1926.

against the introduction of the new system. But the weaker national units had no such resources : and the over-all uniform authority of Gosplan and its agents dimmed the reality of the original picture of federal diversity. Within the RSFSR the same process moved more rapidly still. In theory, the accepted principle was still to regard " not only the union republics, but each separate autonomous republic and region as a national unit with an economic organism of its own ".[1] Of the 11 autonomous SSRs within the RSFSR, the seven largest — the Bashkir, Crimean, Dagestan, Buryat-Mongol, Yakut, Kazakh and Kirgiz[2] SSRs — were independent units enjoying the status of regions ; the remaining four — the Karelian, Tatar, Chuvash and Volga German SSRs — were incorporated as units in the regions to which they geographically belonged, and were assimilated to the status of ordinary departments, having, in effect, the same measure of administrative independence — neither more nor less.[3] The Bashkir SSR, assimilated to the status of a region, divided itself into districts in such a way as to create compact and self-contained national units of Bashkirs, Russians and other minorities. But this arrangement worked badly owing to the difficulty of finding qualified native officials for the national units.[4] The autonomous regions had the administrative status of departments of the regions in which they were incorporated.[5] Everywhere " separate terri-

---

[1] *Planovoe Khozyaistvo*, No. 5, 1926, p. 194.

[2] The Kirgiz autonomous region became an autonomous SSR in April 1927 (*Sobranie Uzakonenii, 1927*, No. 40, art. 258).

[3] The Moldavian autonomous SSR, the Abkhazian and Ajarian autonomous SSRs, and the Tajik autonomous SSR had the same status within the Ukrainian, Georgian and Uzbek SSRs respectively.

[4] *XII Vserossiiskii Tsentral'nyi Ispolnitel'nyi Komitet : Vtoraya Sessiya* (1925), p. 209.

[5] The RSFSR contained 12 autonomous regions — the Adygeisk, Cherkessian, Kabardino-Balkarsh, North Osetian, Ingush and Chechen autonomous regions, included in the North Caucasian region ; the Komi autonomous region, included in the North-Eastern region; the Mari and Votyak autonomous regions, included in the Vyatka region ; the Kalmyk autonomous region, included in the Lower Volga region ; the Oirot autonomous region, included in the Siberian region ; and the Kara-Kalpak autonomous region, included in the Kazakh autonomous SSR. The Transcaucasian SFSR contained the Yugo-Osetian autonomous region, included in the Georgian SSR, and the Nakichevan autonomous SSR and the Nagorny-Karabakh autonomous region, both included in the Azerbaijan SSR. The Nakichevan autonomous SSR, populated by Turks, was included administratively in Azerbaijan, though it was separated from Azerbaijan by Armenian territory, lying on the Turkish frontier of Armenia.

torial units were left after the reform with even reduced rights " ; and the enemies of the scheme denounced its " exaggerated centralization ".[1] Throughout this period the theory was proclaimed that " the national principle (the principle of the self-determination of nationalities in the USSR) and the principle of economic regionalization merely complement each other ".[2] But national diversities, while they were not repudiated and continued to enjoy respectful recognition, came to seem less important, and were viewed with increasing impatience by practical administrators. The new order was based on other criteria. A proposal by the eccentric lawyer Reisner to transform the Council of Nationalities into a Council of Economic Regions [3] was not taken seriously. But it was a logical expression of the current trend.

Finally, regionalization had the effect of breaking down the old administrative system and substituting one professedly inspired by new and revolutionary ideas. In some respects, no doubt, the regions, departments and districts were merely the old provinces, counties and rural districts writ large : a good many of the old capitals and centres were retained, and many officials were inherited by the new régime from the old. But what remained intact was less striking than what was changed.

> All over Russia [wrote an enthusiastic commentator] the conventional boundaries of the old territorial units are being broken down, giving place to a better conjunction of human, natural and technical resources in the interests of the maximum economic development of each sector of territory and population.[4]

The old county capitals, which were " petty bourgeois towns, nests of the gentry, the landowners, the officials, the bourgeoisie ", were being superseded by new " productive proletarian centres ".[5] The disappearance of the old landmarks and the old names, the delimitation of new divisions and subdivisions, the arrival from Moscow of specialists and experts in planning, were a visible symbol of the consolidation of the revolution in the countryside.

---

[1] *Planovoe Khozyaistvo*, No. 2, 1927, p. 231.
[2] *Pyatiletnii Plan Narodno-Khozyaistvennogo Stroitel'stva SSSR* (1929), iii, 11.   [3] *Sovetskoe Stroitel'stvo : Sbornik*, i (1925), 192-207.
[4] *Sotsialisticheskoe Khozyaistvo*, No. 3, 1925, p. 234.
[5] *Raionirovanie SSSR*, ed. K. Egorov (1925), pp. 13-14.

The revolution had evolved its own administrative structure ; and emphasis was laid on concentration rather than on devolution.

The territory has in any case not been divided [ran another contemporary statement], but organized. Regionalism is not a measure of decentralization, but on the contrary one of the important methods of concentrating resources, attention, will, management and organization on Soviet construction.[1]

The newly built pyramid of regions, departments and districts had much the same significance as the creation of the Napoleonic departments in France in the aftermath of the French revolution. At one stroke, it swept away the administrative trappings of the past, cut across local loyalties, traditions and diversities, and laid the foundation of a uniform centralized system.

The full balance-sheet of regionalization had, however, its debit as well as its credit entries. It was essentially an administrative measure directed to rationalize the structure of the administration. It was designed by bureaucrats to provide a foundation or a framework for an efficient bureaucracy. Its importance in this respect should not be underestimated. The administrative machine inherited by the revolution from the Tsarist régime was a by-word for backwardness and inefficiency. Since no modern state can exist without a large-scale bureaucracy, an efficient bureaucracy is a condition of survival. But it is also true that, the more efficient and more highly centralized the administrative machine, the greater its divorce from the daily concerns of the population which it purports to serve, and the more intolerant it becomes of the diversity and irrationality of local needs and local claims. While in one sense Bolshevism was of necessity a great promoter of bureaucracy, hostility to the spirit of bureaucracy (" bureaucratism ") was deeply ingrained in the Bolshevik tradition. The campaign of Lenin's last years was waged not merely against inefficient bureaucracy, but against "'bureaucratism " as such.

How is it possible to end bureaucratism [he wrote] except by bringing in workers and peasants ? . . . If we want to struggle against bureaucratism, we must bring in the lower ranks.[2]

---

[1] *Ekonomicheskoe Obozrenie*, March 1926, p. 188.
[2] Lenin, *Sochineniya*, xxv, 495-496.

Regionalization, imposed from above in the interest of a more efficient and more centralized authority, not only took no account of the " lower ranks ", but, by curtailing the number and increasing the size of the smallest units of administration throughout the country, appeared to limit rather than to expand the contacts of the administration with the masses.   It is therefore not surprising that it should have provoked a healthy reaction in the form of a demand to strengthen the administrative structure at those lowest levels which the regionalization policy had ignored or sought to contract, and thus to provide increased opportunities for the participation of the " lower ranks ".   This was an important element in the campaign which began in the autumn of 1924 for the " revitalization of the Soviets ".

CHAPTER 22

REVITALIZING THE SOVIETS

(a) The Soviets in Decline

THE constitutional theory embodied in the Bolshevik slogan
" All power to the Soviets " had regarded each and every
local Soviet of workers or peasants as the repository and
representative of the will of the sovereign people, the source from
which congresses of Soviets and their executive organs derived a
delegated authority. Already in the first months of the régime
the anarchic implications of this theory clashed with the practical
needs of an efficient central government ; and the transformation
of Soviets into organs of local administration and agencies of the
central power had begun.[1] The civil war radically affected this
process in several different ways. It swept away altogether a large
part of the precarious Soviet structure built up after the revolution. Where Soviets survived in the cities, they were quickly
integrated into the governmental machine and lost their independent or representative character. Where they survived in rural
areas, they tended to assume a non-party or sometimes even SR
complexion, and, especially after the grain requisitions and the
Bolshevik experiment with the committees of poor peasants,
became open or covert rallying-grounds for potential opposition
to the régime. During the civil war it was opposition spokesmen
who most loudly championed the Soviets. At the seventh All-
Russian Congress of Soviets in December 1919 Martov complained of " a dying-out of the fundamental institutions on which
the Soviet constitution rests " ;[2] and a year later the SRs submitted to the eighth congress a resolution complaining that " the
Soviets have never been convened or, if they have, have met only
to approve work already done by their central executive com-

[1] For the first steps in this process see The Bolshevik Revolution, 1917–1923,
Vol. 1, pp. 133-135.　　　　　[2] 7¹ Vserossiiskii S"ezd Sovetov (1920), p. 61.

mittees and presidia ", and that " millions of peasants " had been deprived of their political rights.[1] About the same time Lenin admitted that a majority of delegates at a Moscow provincial conference of rural Soviets had " openly or indirectly abused the central power ".[2] The slogan " Soviets without communists " at the time of the Kronstadt insurrection was a legacy of this opposition. When the civil war ended, and the introduction of NEP heralded a return to stable conditions, two different tasks confronted those who attempted to restore the shattered structure of local administration. The first was to overcome anarchy and disorganization by setting up an efficient and more or less uniform system : and this implied a large measure of centralized discipline and control. The second was to build up a body of loyal support for the régime in the countryside : and this implied political methods of conciliation and compromise to match the economic methods of NEP. The problem of discharging these tasks under the leadership of a party whose rural membership was both quantitatively and qualitatively weak was a facet of the broader problem of establishing and maintaining in a predominantly peasant community a régime whose personnel and programme were predominantly urban.

The reconstitution of the hierarchy of Soviet institutions after the civil war was a gradual process and proceeded from the centre outwards and from the top downwards. In the central provinces, the administrative machinery of the provinces and counties had survived the civil war or was gradually restored. Decrees providing for the setting up of county congresses of Soviets and executive committees, of rural district congresses of Soviets and executive committees and of village Soviets, were issued as early as January 1922.[3] But it is doubtful whether these were effective at the lower levels. The restoration of Soviet institutions at the higher levels presented no insuperable difficulties. A statute defining the powers, and governing the proceedings, of provincial congresses of Soviets and their executive committees was adopted in October 1922.[4] County congresses of Soviets and

---

[1] *Vos'moi Vserossiiskii S"ezd Sovetov* (1921), pp. 55-56.
[2] See *The Bolshevik Revolution, 1917–1923*, Vol. 2, p. 170.
[3] *Sobranie Uzakonenii, 1922*, No. 10, arts. 91, 92, 93.
[4] *Ibid.* No. 72-73, art. 907 ; for an amending statute of the following year see *Sobranie Uzakonenii, 1923*, No. 103-104, art. 1026.

executive committees began to re-establish their authority. At these levels, and in the central provinces,[1] the complex system worked with reasonable regularity and formal efficiency, though congresses of Soviets appear to have met at less frequent intervals than was originally intended. But in the purely rural parts of the machine — the rural district congresses and executive committees and the village Soviets — irregularities and abuses were the rule rather than the exception. These organizations were the weakest link in the Soviet chain.

The rural district executive committee was the lowest Soviet executive organ in regular contact with the peasant population. It was nominally elected by the rural district congress of Soviets composed of delegates from the villages. But the electoral system at this time clearly did not work effectively, or sometimes did not work at all. Where it worked, the results might be disconcerting. Rykov at the twelfth party congress of April 1923 complained that the rural district executive committees had become simply the tools of " kulak power " in the countryside.[2] Zinoviev at the party central committee in October 1924 quoted a sarcastic comment on cooperation between " a drunken priest and a drunken rural district executive committee " as the perfect example of the " link " between worker and peasant. Worse still, " the poor peasant comes with a request and will get nowhere ; but when a man comes who knows how to make requests, everything will be done for him — yes, because he will give a bribe ".[3] Rykov declared that " bribery, driven from the railways and from the higher provincial and central apparatus, still exists in the lower [Soviet] apparatus ", where officials were paid only 20 chervonets rubles a month.[4] At the same time the familiar charge of bureaucratic arrogance on the part of the higher Soviet authorities may not have been wholly unfounded.

> The provincial and county organizations [wrote one critic] adopt an inexcusably domineering and pompous attitude to

[1] Subject to variations in local conditions, it is broadly true to say that in the eastern republics, autonomous republics and autonomous regions the system of local Soviets scarcely existed before the middle nineteen-twenties (see pp. 364-365 below).

[2] *Dvenadtsatyi S"ezd Rossiiskoi Kommunisticheskoi Partii (Bol'shevikov)* (1923), p. 432. [3] G. Zinoviev, *Litsom k Derevne* (1925), p. 68.

[4] A. I. Rykov, *Sochineniya*, iii (1929), 93.

rural district workers, and this is passed on by the rural district workers to workers in the village.[1]

The lower Soviet organs were harried by a continuous flow of instructions from above :

> In every decree there is a point where it is laid down that this or that People's Commissariat has to work out an instruction in order to give effect to it. Our countryside, our lower Soviet apparatus, lives on these circulars.[2]

The administrative apparatus was overloaded, inexperienced and out of touch with a scattered and politically untutored peasantry. It is not surprising that it creaked in every joint.

The primitiveness and inefficiency of the rural district organization was multiplied tenfold at the level of the village Soviet. In the countryside, as Enukidze said, " every social cause comes up against lack of culture ".[3] The village Soviet itself was still an alien institution. So long as it remained, in accordance with the original intention, a general assembly of citizens, it had followed the well-understood pattern of the ancient village meeting or *skhod*.[4] But once the village Soviet had everywhere become a

---

[1] *Na Agrarnom Fronte*, No. 5-6, 1925, pp. 209-210.
[2] *SSSR : Tsentral'nyi Ispolnitel'nyi Komitet 2 Sozyva : 3 Sessiya* (1925), p. 63.
[3] *Soveshchanie po Voprosam Sovetskogo Stroitel'stva 1925 g. : Yanvar'* (1925), p. 140.
[4] The *skhod*, which dated from Tsarist times, was the village meeting ; where the communal system of land tenure still prevailed, the *skhod* was also the assembly of the *mir* or *obshchina*. The president of the *skhod* was the *starosta* or village elder. It was not, strictly speaking, a public body. It had no constitutional status, no officially recognized duties except the periodical redistribution of the land and the collection and payment of tax ; but it sometimes performed primitive functions of local government. In a society where the boundary between public and private law was undefined, and "ownership" of land was an uncertain and fluctuating concept, no clear distinction was drawn between the village as an administrative unit and the *mir* as the community in which the land was vested ; and the *skhod* functioned indifferently as the assembly of both. The original constitution of the RSFSR referred (art. 57) to " the general assembly of electors " of the village, which elected deputies to the village Soviet, or, " where this is recognized as realizable ", itself constituted the Soviet. But no light was thrown on the identity or otherwise of the assembly of electors with the traditional *skhod*. The agrarian code of 1922 drew a distinction between administrative and economic units, recognizing the village Soviet as a state organ and the *mir* or *obshchina* as an association enjoying rights of utilization of land, the *skhod* being the organ of the *mir*. But here too the question of its identity with the general assembly of citizens was left obscure ;

body of delegates elected by the population, unfamiliar procedures were invoked. The *skhod* had normally, though not always, been confined to heads of *dvors* or households ; where this had been the practice, it was difficult to convince the peasant that all adults were entitled to participate in elections to the Soviets. The head of the *dvor* came to vote on the assumption that " he alone can represent his whole family ".[1] In a society totally unused to decisions taken by majority vote, the view of the franchise as a right of the individual made no sense.

> The peasantry takes little part in elections [said one observer] not from evil intent, but simply because it has poor education and poor understanding of the meaning of elections.

And another added :

> Historical conditions with us were such that the masses of peasants and workers never took part in electing organs of government : it goes without saying that we could not in seven years transform the views of the peasantry on government, on elections, on participation in state administration.[2]

Though the size of the village made it increasingly difficult for all voters to travel to the centre, individual and separate voting would have been inconceivable ; for an election to be valid it must be conducted by an assembly of electors all meeting together in the same place. One such electoral meeting was described as having lasted from 2 o'clock in the afternoon till 5 o'clock next morning ; on this occasion the party officials apparently refused to nominate candidates, and left the peasants to decide for themselves.[3] This collective procedure raised the difficulty that many village centres did not possess a building large enough to hold all the electors ; and the argument that the elections should be held at a time when no work could be done in the fields clashed with the argument that they should be held in summer when the meeting could take place in the open air.[4] Lack of electoral experience was also

and it can be assumed that, whatever legal or constitutional theories were propounded in Moscow, the assembly of peasants which gathered to elect the village Soviet regarded itself as the village *skhod*.

[1] *Soveshchanie po Voprosam Sovetskogo Stroitel'stva 1925 g. : Yanvar'* (1925), pp. 26, 173 ; *id. : Aprel'* (1925), p. 31.

[2] *Id.: Yanvar'* (1925), pp. 77, 173. [3] *Ibid.* p. 152.

[4] *Tretii S"ezd Sovetov SSSR* (1925), p. 297 ; *Na Agrarnom Fronte*, No. 5-6, 1925, p. 74 ; *Vlast' Sovetov*, No. 22, May 30, 1926, p. 21.

suggested by a system of " net " votes sometimes adopted. Where this method was in force, electors were entitled to cast votes " for " or " against " each candidate on the list : the " net " vote was obtained by subtracting votes " against " from votes " for ", and determined the place of the candidate in the final list.[1] What happened if no candidate obtained a net surplus is not disclosed. The method of election of delegates to the rural district congress of Soviets also varied : sometimes they were elected by the village Soviet (this seems to have been the original intention) and sometimes by the meeting which elected the village Soviet.[2] Nor did shortcomings end with the elections. Model village Soviets existed such as one in the Ukraine which met nineteen times during the year, discussed repair of roads and buildings, the supply of fuel to the village school, the liquidation of illiteracy and other topics : 44 out of 46 members of this Soviet were literate.[3] Another village Soviet in the Ukraine set up a commission on abortion presided over by a doctor, and " without the consent of the doctor no abortion can be arranged " — a totally irregular, but perhaps salutary, arrogation of powers.[4] But such active Soviets were rare. Probably more typical was the village Soviet 75 miles from Odessa which had never heard of the statute of village Soviets : complaints were common that village Soviets, and even rural district executive committees, did not possess the official codes of law and collections of decrees, and were entirely dependent on orders and circulars received from higher local authorities.[5]

One of the perennial obstacles to the creation of a working system of local government was the difficulty of delimiting the functions and competence of organs at different levels of the Soviet hierarchy. The theory that the sovereign authority resided in the Soviet as such was never formally abandoned ; and this meant that no conception of *ultra vires* could ever apply to the action of a Soviet. If the village Soviet could in fact levy contributions from the peasants, or impose labour service on them, no higher authority would interfere. A professor at the Institute

---

[1] *Bol'shevik*, No. 7-8, April 30, 1926, p. 64.
[2] *Na Agrarnom Fronte*, No. 5-6, 1925, p. 60.
[3] *Soveshchanie po Voprosam Sovetskogo Stroitel'stva 1925 g. : Yanvar'* (1925), pp. 52-53.   [4] *Ibid.* p. 85.   [5] *Ibid.* pp. 82, 121.

of Soviet Construction (an offshoot of the Communist Academy) held up to ridicule a series of regulations issued by the Yaroslav provincial executive committee and attacked regulations issued by other local authorities. But the point was that the regulations were absurd in content, not that they were *ultra vires*.[1] Some local authorities claimed the right to decide on what date decrees issued in Moscow were to come into effect in the territories under their jurisdiction. Peasants complained that, if a decree arrived which conferred some benefit on the population, its application was delayed by the rural district authorities, whereas, if a decree was received which "takes something from the population", it was put into force at once.[2] On the other hand, the authority of the lower Soviets was limited by lack of funds and of any power of enforcement beyond what they could derive from local tradition, and complaints were frequent that village Soviets had no rights at all.[3] Sovkhozy notoriously refused to recognize any authority lower than that of the province, and would have no dealings with the village Soviets or even with the rural district committees in whose areas they were situated.[4] But the *mir* and the kolkhoz, though they were required by the agrarian code to register with the village Soviet, were equally unamenable to its control.[5] Where so much theoretical confusion and uncertainty prevailed, the reality of the authority exercised by Soviet institutions at all levels depended largely on finance. It is significant that the first serious attempt to define the legislative powers of district and rural district executive committees by decree of the RSFSR [6] should have been made in April 1925 at the moment when independent district budgets were being introduced.[7] A decree of about the same time authorizing village Soviets to call on compulsory labour for dealing with forest fires or repairing

[1] *Sovetskoe Stroitel'stvo : Sbornik*, iv-v (1926), 78-81.
[2] *Ibid.* iv-v, 93-94.
[3] Such a complaint from Dagestan is picturesquely recorded in *Vlast' Sovetov*, No. 28-29, July 19, 1925, p. 25.
[4] *Soveshchanie po Voprosam Sovetskogo Stroitel'stva 1925 g. : Aprel'* (1925), pp. 20, 55.
[5] *Ibid.* p. 51 ; the speaker who made this complaint repeated the common failure to distinguish between public and private law by arguing that the cause of the recalcitrance of land-owning associations to public control was that they were recognized as juridical persons.
[6] *Sobranie Uzakonenii, 1925*, No. 24, art. 170.
[7] See Note A : " Local Finance " (pp. 455-465 below).

roads [1] was an odd anomaly which must have been provoked by some now forgotten emergency. The powers exercised in practice by the village Soviet were certainly not limited to these contingencies, and did not rest on decrees. At a level where a monetary economy was not yet effective, tradition and habit were still major factors determining the competence of the lower Soviet organs.

It was in part a cause, and in part a symptom, of these defects that the communist party had not yet acquired any firm foothold in the countryside. In 1925 only one out of every 25 or 30 villages contained a party cell,[2] and an observer still later recorded the impression that " in the countryside the party exists mostly on paper ".[3] Of a total of nearly 700,000 party members in the autumn of 1924, only 150,000 lived and worked outside the towns. Of these, 45,000 were in the central provinces of the RSFSR and 16,000 in the Ukraine. In remoter regions the crust of rural party members was very thinly spread ; at the bottom of the scale, the White Russian SSR had only 3700 and the Far Eastern region 3000. Of this total it was estimated that only 35 per cent were actively engaged in agricultural work, and only 15 per cent employed exclusively in it. From 20 to 30 per cent were party officials sent from the centre to run the local party organizations and without original connexions with the locality. With members so widely scattered, meetings of party cells were rare, and were suspended altogether in the summer when all hands were required for the harvest. The low morale of the party members themselves was no doubt partly attributable to their isolation. The proportion of resignations from the party and of expulsions for misconduct was significantly higher in the countryside than in the towns.[4] In these conditions party control of administration outside the large centres was tenuous and precarious. The proportion of communists in Soviet organs of the RSFSR (for which alone these

[1] *Sobranie Uzakonenii, 1925*, No. 57, art. 455.
[2] *Bol'shevik*, No. 23-24, December 30, 1925, p. 44.
[3] A. M. Bolshakov, *Sovetskaya Derevnya, 1917–1927* (1927), p. 425.
[4] *Na Agrarnom Fronte*, No. 2, 1925, pp. 103-112 — a balanced and informative account ; for the presence of " elements which discredit the party in the countryside " see *ibid.* No. 5-6, 1925, p. 207.

statistics were available) varied on a consistent pattern : it was higher in the higher organs than in the lower, in the towns than in the country, and in the executive committees than in the congresses of Soviets which appointed them. In the town and factory Soviets of provincial capitals of the RSFSR the proportion of communists early in 1924 was as high as 91 per cent ; in the town Soviets of county capitals it reached 61 per cent. At the county level, the congresses of Soviets contained 54·5 per cent of communist delegates, the executive committees 81 per cent. Below county level, communists were everywhere in a minority in the Soviet organs. In the rural district executive committees the proportion reached 40 per cent, but fell to 11·7 per cent in the rural district congresses consisting of delegates from the villages, and to 6 per cent in the village Soviets, though even this was said to represent an improvement on the figures of two years earlier. Moreover, of party members in Soviet organs about one-half appear to have been not authentic workers or peasants, but " employees " — a good many of them probably party officials sent from headquarters on an unpopular assignment.[1] The numerical weakness of the party in the countryside confronted the leaders with a constant dilemma. If the party refrained from intervening actively in the work of the lower Soviet organs, these fell under the control of the minority of well-to-do peasants, and the cry was raised that the Soviets were in the hands of the *kulaks*. If the party instructed its nominees to enforce party policy, the charge of party dictatorship was unavoidable. Both these evils came to a head, and impinged strongly on the con-

[1] For these figures see the tables in *Sovety, S"ezdy Sovetov i Ispolkomy* (NKVD, 1924), pp. 11-53 : they were quoted by Stalin at the thirteenth party congress (Stalin, *Sochineniya*, vi, 200-201). They presumably relate to the Soviet organs as they resulted from the elections of 1923 ; figures for 1923 in *Perevybory v Sovety RSFSR v 1925-1926 godu* (1926), ii, 19, 39, differ in some details, but present the same general picture. The ratio of " employees " to communists in Soviet organs varied fairly consistently round 50 per cent : on the reasonable assumption that virtually all the " employees " were party members, this means that about one-half of all party members in Soviet organs were " employees ". Molotov gave the proportion of party members in the rural district executive committees after the elections in the autumn of 1924 as 61 per cent (*XIV S"ezd Vsesoyuznoi Kommunisticheskoi Partii (B)* (1926), p. 66) : this figure related to the whole of the USSR, and indicates a higher proportion of party members in the executive committees of the other republics than in those of the RSFSR (where the corresponding proportion was 40 per cent).

sciousness of the party leaders, in the autumn of 1924.

The growing economic influence of the *kulaks*, which first plainly declared itself at the time of the harvest of 1924, was quickly and automatically translated into political influence. From the earliest days, when rural Soviets were generally controlled by SRs and dominated by the " *kulak*-bourgeois element ",[1] the well-to-do peasants had probably always had a numerical majority in them, the poor peasant being often afraid to attend meetings or lacking the leisure or transport to enable him to do so.   In the latter part of 1924, when more than 90 per cent of the membership of village Soviets was peasant, only about 10 per cent of the members were " horseless " peasants.[2] What was new was the organized exploitation of the opportunities created by this predominance.   In June 1924 Rykov complained of exemptions from agricultural tax secured by " *kulaks* sitting in the village and rural district Soviets ".[3]   A little later a story was told from the department of Poltava of an order to restore 200 desyatins of land " stolen " by *kulaks* which was cancelled by the secretary of the village Soviet under *kulak* pressure.[4]   But the important thing was that *kulak* influence was no longer confined to illicit transactions, but was coming out boldly into the open. Bukharin thus described the situation in August 1924 :

> Complicated processes are going on in the countryside ; the difference between poor and rich is increasing ; on the other hand an active Soviet-minded peasant youth is growing up ; teachers and agronomists are turning toward us.   At the same time the *kulak* often worms his way into organs of administration or keeps the local authority in a position of economic dependence.[5]

" *The activity of* kulak *elements is growing* ", said Kamenev with emphasis in September 1924, " *and not only economic, but political, activity.*"   The *kulak*, whose power had been increased by the poor harvest, was penetrating the lower levels of the Soviet

---

[1] See *The Bolshevik Revolution, 1917–1923*, Vol. 2, p. 48.

[2] *Vlast' Sovetov*, No. 1, January 4, 1925, p. 9.

[3] A. I. Rykov, *Stat'i i Rechi*, iii (1929), 120.

[4] *Soveshchanie po Voprosam Sovetskogo Stroitel'stva 1925 g. :   Yanvar'* (1925), p. 107.

[5] N. Bukharin, *O Rabkore i Sel'kore* (2nd ed. 1926), p. 66.

system.[1] A month later Kamenev spoke to the Moscow provincial party committee :

> Since . . . the *kulak* elements have the possibility of orientating themselves more quickly, acquiring the necessary knowledge and thus putting pressure on the organs of Soviet power, their influence grows ever stronger.[2]

Nor was it possible unreservedly to condemn this unwelcome phenomenon. Politically, as well as economically, the *kulak* might well appear as a progressive force. It was the well-to-do peasant from whom the demand for an improved administration in the countryside mainly proceeded. An observer in January 1925 offered a convincing diagnosis of the source of the new discontent :

> Has our apparatus really become worse in comparison with the past ? No, comrades, our apparatus is, all the same, improving. It was bureaucratic before, it is bureaucratic now, but even in its bureaucratic form it has begun to improve. But now its irregularities have become more conspicuous, our peasantry has grown up a little in comparison with the past, and, in particular, a well-to-do element has grown up in the village which reacts quickly to every trifle, every irregularity, and quickly knocks at the right door. That is why we have become conscious of this caprice, these shortcomings, which exist in the village.[3]

The dilemma was constant :

> There is in the countryside no " Soviet action group " which could organize the countryside round itself. It does not exist, but its place may be taken, if we are not wide awake, by an " anti-Soviet action group ".[4]

The other current evil, which appeared to be the only practical alternative to domination of the rural Soviets by *kulaks*, was the dictatorship of a handful of party officials and workers. Both opposite evils were encountered side by side. Party cells are said to have rarely existed in the rural district executive committees or, *a fortiori*, in the village Soviets, so that party influence could not make itself felt at all. An observer in January 1925 summed up the weakness of the party in a graphic phrase : " in the village,

---

[1] L. Kamenev, *Stat'i i Rechi*, xi (1929), 109. [2] *Ibid.* xi, 204.
[3] *Soveshchanie po Voprosam Sovetskogo Stroitel'stva 1925 g. : Yanvar'* (1925), p. 94. [4] *Sovetskoe Stroitel'stvo : Sbornik*, iv-v (1926), 135.

as a rule, the Soviet apparatus eats up the party apparatus ",
whereas in the cities, " the provincial party committee often
interferes in questions of Soviet organization in which, by rights,
it ought not to interfere ".[1] But cases also occurred in the countryside in which a party fraction entirely usurped the functions of
the presidium of a rural district executive committee.[2] Generally
speaking, the party directives were conveyed to the lower Soviet
organs in the countryside by a single party official who easily
incurred the imputation of dictatorial behaviour. A common
pattern was for a " qualified party worker " to be elected president
of the village Soviet. He then conducted the business of the
Soviet with a secretary, and rarely convened meetings of the
Soviet, calling on the mass of members only when some piece of
work had to be done to carry out the orders of the rural district
executive committee.[3] Complaints were frequent that elections
at all levels were turned into a farce by party nominations. When
party officials from headquarters, the " county bosses ", urged the
peasants to vote, the peasants answered : " Why should we come
to the elections ? It makes no sense ; you have brought the list
of the new executive committee with you in your pocket." [4] In
Kazakhstan the local party secretary was said to appear at elections with a ready-made list of candidates, which he put forward
at the meeting with the enquiry " Who is against ? " [5] In a
Siberian village, when the peasants refused to vote the list proposed by the electoral commission, the commission simply
adjourned the meeting to the following day. This was repeated
for seven days on end ; on the seventh day, the peasants stayed
away, and the list was voted.[6] In the Stavropol department,
village Soviets were in the habit of inviting the local party secretary,
or the whole party cell, to participate in their deliberations ; in
one case the president of a village Soviet offered to divide his
salary with the party secretary in return for the latter's help and
guidance.[7]

The general picture resulting from these arrangements was

---

[1] *Soveshchanie po Voprosam Sovetskogo Stroitel'stva 1925 g. : Yanvar'*
(1925), p. 164.   [2] *Na Agrarnom Fronte*, No. 5-6, 1925, p. 210.
[3] *Soveshchanie po Voprosam Sovetskogo Stroitel'stva 1925 g. : Yanvar'*
(1925), pp. 62, 64, 69.   [4] *Ibid.* p. 152.
[5] *Na Agrarnom Fronte*, No. 9, 1925, p. 118.
[6] *Ibid.* No. 5-6, 1925, p. 61.   [7] *Ibid.* No. 10, 1925, p. 10.

one of almost complete divorce, and consequent mutual distrust, between the few party officials and the mass of peasants of whatever category. " Party workers who are deficient in class consciousness or in experience ", said a party report of March 1923, " quickly lose authority with the peasantry." [1] The party worker from the city had no sympathy with the peasant : the more efficient he was, the less patience he had. " We have beards for show purposes in our executive committees ", one of these was reported as saying, " and need nothing more. What sense do you expect from peasants ? " [2] When questions were asked by peasants at meetings of village Soviets or rural district executive committees, the party official who did not know the answer got out of it by abusing the questioner as a counter-revolutionary or a Menshevik.[3] Numerous stories were told of high-handed treatment of peasants. One president of a rural district executive committee, a party nominee, was alleged to use a whip on the peasants or to " arrest peasants without any cause and then, after keeping them for some time in a cellar, let them go just as capriciously as he had arrested them ".[4] One party official summoned peasants who were late with tax payments to his office and made them stand in the corner.[5] The peasant retaliated by treating the party member as an alien and an interloper. The peasants to whom Stalin gave an interview in March 1925 explained that " almost everywhere the party cells hold aloof from the peasants " ; " they live their way, we live our way ", said a peasant from Tambov.[6] According to another observer, most peasants regarded communists as " clever fellows who could get a horse elected to the rural district executive committee if they wanted to ".[7]

Even more serious resentment was felt against members of

---

[1] *Izvestiya Tsentral'nogo Komiteta Rossiiskoi Kommunisticheskoi Partii (Bol'-shevikov)*, No. 3 (57), March 1923, p. 53.

[2] *Soveshchanie po Voprosam Sovetskogo Stroitel'stva 1925 g. : Aprel'* (1925), p. 7.   [3] *Id.: Yanvar'* (1925), p. 163.   [4] *Ibid.* (1925), p. 142.

[5] Many instances of the high-handed behaviour and unpopularity of party officials are quoted in *Sovetskoe Stroitel'stvo : Sbornik*, ii-iii (1925), 356-357 ; A. M. Bolshakov, *Sovetskaya Derevnya, 1917–1927* (1927), pp. 329-331.

[6] *Bednota*, April 5, 1925 ; for this interview see Vol. 1, p. 183 ; for a general discussion of the shortcomings of party work in rural areas see *Bol'shevik*, No. 3-4 (19-20), February 25, 1925, pp. 74-86.

[7] *Soveshchanie po Voprosam Sovetskogo Stroitel'stva 1925 g. : Yanvar'* (1925), p. 126.

the Komsomol, who first became active in rural areas in 1924, especially after the encouragement given to such activity by the thirteenth party congress in May of that year.[1] A circular from the Komsomol central committee in February 1924 warned members of rural branches of the Komsomol against an attitude of "aloofness" from the peasant.[2] But the imputation of aloofness was soon less common than that of active interference. A delegate from the neighbourhood of Moscow complained of Komsomol members who appeared at elections with ready-made lists :

> When we learn that out of 27 members elected to our Soviet, nine were women and nine Komsomol members, I doubt whether such a village Soviet would have authority with the peasant, who is accustomed to see in a village Soviet not Komsomol members and not women, but bearded elders.[3]

In December 1924 the Orgburo inveighed against anti-religious excesses of Komsomol members in the countryside ; and six months later a Komsomol conference issued a warning of " the inadmissibility of incautious and clumsy methods of anti-religious propaganda " among the peasants.[4] Other common and well substantiated charges against Komsomol members were of drunkenness and hooliganism.[5] The sins of the Komsomol aggravated the unpopularity of the party, since no clear line was drawn between them, and further complicated the task of establishing party authority in the countryside.

These resentments and embarrassments accumulated slowly in the first years of NEP. The symptom which caused most disquiet in party circles was that participation in elections to Soviets, after rising sharply in 1923, fell back in the following year. According to returns quoted by Kaganovich (covering, however, only 12 provinces), 22.3 per cent of electors voted in 1922, 35 per

---

[1] See p. 99 above.

[2] *Spravochnik Partiinogo Rabotnika*, iv (1924), 255.

[3] *Soveshchanie po Voprosam Sovetskogo Stroitel'stva 1925 g. : Yanvar'* (1925), p. 93 ; for the prejudice against women in the Soviets see p. 322, note 4 below.

[4] *Spravochnik Partii'nogo Rabotnika*, iv (1924), 396 ; v, 1925 (1926), 431.

[5] A. M. Bolshakov, *Sovetskaya Derevnya, 1917–1927* (1927), p. 334 ; Stalin in April 1925 referred to the shortcomings of Komsomol work in the countryside (*Sochineniya*, vii, 80-82).

cent in 1923 and only 31 per cent in 1924.[1] What appear to be
the fullest available figures show that in 1923 in 68 provinces 14
million out of a potential 37·6 million voters went to the polls
(or 37 per cent), and in 1924 in 49 provinces 8·4 million out of a
potential 29·2 million (or 28·9 per cent). In 1923, in one-half of
the provinces covered, the proportion of those voting ranged from
35 to 50 per cent; in only one-third did the proportion fall
below 35 per cent. In 1924 it fell below 35 per cent in three-
quarters of the provinces covered.[2] Since these figures were likely
to relate to provinces where voting had been most active, the
estimate in a party report that only from 15 to 20 per cent of
qualified electors voted in the 1924 elections as a whole [3] may
well be correct. What increased the disquiet was that, while the
proportion of those voting declined, the proportion of communists
elected rose substantially. The proportion of members of the
party and the Komsomol elected to village Soviets increased from
7·8 per cent in 1923 to 12 per cent in 1924, to rural district congresses from 17·8 per cent to 27 per cent and to rural district
executive committees from 48·5 per cent to 61·4 per cent.[4] But,
as Molotov later asserted, there was " much that was inflated,
unstable and insecure " in this progress, and " this seeming,
external, statistical increase in the leadership of the countryside
by the party did not bear witness to a real improvement in that
leadership ".[5] On the contrary, the increasing apathy of the
ordinary voter at a time when more communists were entering
the village Soviets seemed to point to a growing indifference or
hostility in the mass of the peasantry to the party and to the
régime.

(b) " Face to the Countryside "

Such were the conditions when, in the autumn of 1924, the
party for the first time turned its serious attention to the question
of the rural Soviets, to the backwardness of local administration
and to the scarcity of suitable officials, especially at the lowest

---

[1] *Soveshchanie po Voprosam Sovetskogo Stroitel'stva 1925 g. : Yanvar'*
(1925), p. 111.   [2] *Sovetskoe Stroitel'stvo: Sbornik*, i (1925), 39-40.

[3] *Izvestiya Tsentral'nogo Komiteta Rossiiskoi Kommunisticheskoi Partii (Bol'-
shevikov)*, No. 9 (84), March 2, 1925, p. 1.

[4] *Sovetskoe Stroitel'stvo : Sbornik*, i (1925), 51.

[5] *XIV S".ezd Vsesoyuznoi Kommunisticheskoi Partii (B)* (1926), p. 66.

levels. Administrative decentralization was part of the general reaction against the rigours of war communism. At first it was applied mainly to the organization of essential industries, and did not extend to the less urgent sphere of political administration, especially in the countryside, where few party or Soviet workers were available, and where peasant mistrust was a formidable barrier to innovation.[1] It was only from 1923 onwards, as the peasant became more and more the focus of economic policy, that notice began to be taken of the political importance of the Soviet machine in the countryside. Stalin in his speech at the twelfth party congress of April 1923 attacked the " simplified " form of administration in which everything was decided at the centre, and went on :

> In our Soviet land we put into effect a different system of administration, a system of administration that permits us to anticipate with accuracy all changes, everything that is going on among the peasants, among the nationalities, among the so-called " other races " and the Russians ; the system of supreme organs must include a series of barometers which will detect every change, will record and forestall . . . any possible tumults or discontents. That is the Soviet system of government.[2]

This was evidently an idealized picture of how the system ought to work, not a description of how it actually did work. But it was symptomatic of a new recognition of the problem. The resolution of the congress on party work in the countryside (the first special resolution on this subject passed by a party congress) drew emphatic attention to present shortcomings :

> The rural district and village apparatus of the Soviet power is filled to a large extent by those elements of the rural semi-intelligentsia who have from of old been connected mainly with the well-to-do strata in the countryside, and introduce into the Soviet apparatus the traditions of the period of serfdom with its roughness, its contempt for the peasant and his needs, its haughty indifference to his backwardness, his illiteracy, his inability to find his way about in the Soviet apparatus.

By way of prescription, however, the resolution had little to offer but general exhortation. The " rural district and village apparatus

---

[1] *Sovetskoe Stroitel'stvo: Sbornik*, i (1925), 5-8.
[2] Stalin, *Sochineniya*, v, 259-260.

of power " must be strengthened ; in place of " the old rural
district clerk who was one of the basic instruments for oppressing
the peasant masses ", a peasant who had been through the civil
war and the school of party teaching should be installed as secretary
of the rural district executive committee. But candidates with
these qualifications were scarce ; and the concrete recommendation to send reliable party officials from headquarters to occupy
key posts in the countryside was too unpopular among party
officials themselves to be widely adopted.[1] A year later, at the
thirteenth party congress, the same recommendation was repeated.
By this time the rising power of the kulaks was beginning to
attract attention ; the freeing of the " lower Soviet and party
apparatus in the countryside " from kulak influence, as well as an
improvement of its quality, was proclaimed as the goal.[2] But the
discussion which took place on that occasion about the peasant
committees of mutual aid revealed the reluctance of powerful
elements in the party to disturb the existing situation, which left
the control of local administration in the countryside largely in
the hands of well-to-do peasants friendly to the new policies
of the régime.[3] Reforming influences progressively lost their
strength the further from the centre they were required to operate.

In the autumn of 1924 the situation had become too grave to
be ignored. The harvest had been a partial failure ; the Georgian
rising and the Dymovka scandal were popular themes of discussion in party circles ; and Zinoviev had recently proclaimed
the slogan " Face to the countryside ". Zinoviev, now at the
zenith of his career and of his ambitions, again took the lead. To
meet the growing menace of inefficiency and dissatisfaction in
the countryside, a new slogan — " The Revitalization of the
Soviets " [4] — was launched in an article in Pravda of October

[1] VKP(B) v Rezolyutsiyakh (1941), i, 516-519. From 1923 onwards a
journal under the title Sovetskaya Volost' was issued by Narkomvnudel ; files
of it have not been available.
[2] VKP(B) v Rezolyutsiyakh (1941), i, 595.
[3] See The Interregnum, 1923-1924, pp. 148-149 ; for subsequent attempts
to make use of the committees see Note B : " Peasant Committees of Mutual
Aid " (pp. 466-467 below).
[4] The phrase came from Lenin, who in his letter to Myasnikov of May
1921 (see The Bolshevik Revolution, 1917-1923, Vol. 1, p. 208) had coined, or
endorsed, the watchword : " to revitalize the Soviets, to attract non-party
people, to use the non-party people to check the work of party members "

11, 1924, which was evidently intended to sound the key-note for
the forthcoming sessions of TsIK and of the party central committee. " Large successes ", Zinoviev claimed, had been achieved
in improving administration at the provincial, and in part at the
county, level. Reform must now be extended to the rural district
and the village. He admitted that the question had been raised
many times before, though without result. The slogan " Down
with the *kulaks* and their stooges " must not be taken to imply that
only party members should be admitted to Soviets and Soviet
organs. To identify the party with the Soviets was an old heresy ;
in order to revitalize the Soviet apparatus it was necessary " to
bind the local Soviets by unbreakable threads to the non-party
masses of workers and peasants ". The directives were : " Face
to the countryside ; more attention to non-party elements ; revitalization of the Soviets in the localities at all costs ".

It was in the first flush of this campaign that the TsIK of the
RSFSR debated in October 1924 draft statutes for county and
rural district congresses of Soviets and executive committees and
for village Soviets. Kiselev, the official spokesman, announced
that wider powers would be given to local organs. Now that
" the economic potentialities of the rural district " had begun to
be developed, it was time to think about the development of its
rights. Rural district congresses of Soviets and executive committees would henceforth be qualified to discuss " all state
questions ", including questions " of the militia and of criminal
investigation ", and rural districts would for the first time have
independent budgets. On the subject of village Soviets he was
more guarded, admitting that they had hitherto had " only
obligations and scarcely any rights ". But " with the enlargement
of the rural districts it has become necessary to confer on village
Soviets such rights as were, to some extent, enjoyed by rural
district executive committees ".[1] In the ensuing debate Larin
complained of the non-participation of women in the elections
to village Soviets : in 1923 only 3 million women had voted as

---

(Lenin, *Sochineniya*, xxvi, 474) : the context suggests that the phrase may have
been borrowed or adapted by Lenin from Myasnikov's letter or pamphlet, which
have not been available. It is significant that the revitalization of the Soviets
was from the outset connected with the recruitment of non-party elements.

[1] *Vserossiiskii Tsentral'nyi Ispolnitel'nyi Komitet XI Sozyva : Vtoraya
Sessiya* (1924), pp. 44-50.

against 16 million men, and the proportion of women elected
had been lower still. Another speaker praised the proposal " to
create Soviet responsibility in the countryside under the leadership of the communist party ".[1] Kalinin took exception to a
reference to the rural district executive committees as " organs
of local self-government ", and propounded, for what must have
been almost the last time, the classic doctrine of the sovereignty
of the Soviets :

> Our rural district and other Soviet institutions are in
> principle not identical with organs of self-government.   In
> drawing up the " statute " for our executive committees —
> county, rural district and village — the chief principle is that
> they are infused with the unitary principle of power.   Any one
> of our Soviets is a fragment of the sovereign power, which is
> fully embodied in the Union Congress of Soviets.
> Even the village Soviet, strictly speaking, has all the rights
> of the union congress, including international rights, within
> the limits of its territory.   It does not have envoys in other
> countries only because its territory is bounded by the Soviet
> Union.   In principle, it seems to me, this is a unitary power.
> Our statute ought, therefore, to be infused with the unity of
> power.[2]

But this was a lost cause, or an excursion into Utopia.   What
TsIK was debating was not the theory of political power, but the
practical problem of creating a system of local government.   At
the end of the discussion, on October 16, 1924, three decrees were
duly adopted, on county congresses of Soviets and executive committees, on rural district congresses of Soviets and executive
committees, and on village Soviets.[3]   The usual constitutional
ambiguity was apparent in the statute of the village Soviets.
The village Soviet " carries out all legal decisions of the general
meeting (skhod) of citizens ", by which it was elected.   But it was
at the same time " responsible to the appropriate rural district
committee ".   A separate decree was passed on the need to encourage women to participate in the work of the Soviets.[4]   Corre-

---

[1] Vserossiiskii Tsentral'nyi Ispolnitel'nyi Komitet XI Sozyva : Vtoraya
Sessiya (1924), pp. 56, 64.   [2] Ibid. p. 71.
[3] Ibid. p. 422 ; Sobranie Uzakonenii, 1924, No. 82, arts. 825, 826, 827.
[4] Ibid. No. 82, art. 828.   Spasmodic attempts were made throughout the
ensuing campaign to increase the representation of women in the Soviets,
but encountered strong resistance.   Peasants were accustomed to see " not

sponding decrees of the Ukrainian and White Russian SSRs established a similar system of local government for these republics.[1]

The party central committee, which met on October 25, 1924, was concerned to see that these decrees should not once more remain a dead letter. On the eve of the meeting Stalin and Kaganovich addressed a gathering of secretaries of rural party cells. Stalin reiterated Zinoviev's programme : to revitalize the Soviets, to establish links between party members and the non-party masses in the countryside (the Georgian insurrection was attributed to failure to do this), and to draw politically active peasants into the work of administration. Kaganovich described the function of the Soviets as " the coupling of the dictatorship

women, but bearded elders " in village assemblies ; to elect a woman meant " an empty place ", since " she is not summoned to meetings of the village Soviet, or, if she is summoned, her opinion is not asked " (*Soveshchanie po Voprosam Sovetskogo Stroitel'stva 1925 g. : Yanvar'* (1925), pp. 93, 95). Stories were told of a peasant who, on learning that his wife had been elected to the Soviet, locked her up to prevent her from attending, and of women members of the Soviet who were set to wash the floor of the Soviet office (*Sovetskoe Stroitel'stvo : Sbornik*, ii-iii (1925), 359). The campaign had some effect, the proportion of women in village Soviets rising from 2·2 per cent in 1923 to 9 per cent in 1924–1925 and 10·5 per cent in 1925–1926, in rural district congresses of Soviets from 2·6 to 7·6 and 8·8 per cent, and in rural district executive committees from o·6 to 7·1 and 9 per cent in the same years (G. Mikhailov, *Mestnoe Sovetskoe Upravlenie* (1927), p. 426). But this was attributed to a " definite pressure " on the electorate : " once a higher percentage of women was required, it was produced ; but it has not been produced as the result of a declared wish of the peasantry to introduce women into government " (*Soveshchanie po Voprosam Sovetskogo Stroitel'stva 1925 g. : Aprel'* (1925), p. 67). A woman complained that everyone in the Soviets, including the party workers, treated the women as " nincompoops " because they were illiterate (*ibid.* p. 104). In the re-elections of the spring of 1925 the number of women elected was said to have decreased in places where pressure had previously been exercised to secure a quota of women in the Soviets, but ncreased elsewhere (*Na Agrarnom Fronte*, No. 5-6, 1925, pp. 70, 72). In February 1926 a party conference was held on party work among worker and peasant women. A resolution on its conclusions was issued by the Orgburo (*Izvestiya Tsentral'nogo Komiteta Vsesoyuznoi Kommunisticheskoi Partii (B)*, No. 9 (130), March 8, 1926, Prilozhenie, pp. 1-4) ; and the full text of its recommendations was published (*ibid.* No. 12-13 (133-134), April 5, 1926, Prilozhenie, pp. i-vi). But the impression prevails that this was routine business to which no great importance was attached.

[1] *Sovetskoe Stroitel'stvo : Sbornik*, i (1925), 5-8, discusses a number of differences of detail between the republics : the White Russian decrees had been adopted in July 1924 in advance of those of the RSFSR (*Sobranie Uzakonenii SSR Belorussii, 1924*, No. 13, arts. 113-116).

of the proletariat with the immense, unparalleled independence and support of millions of toilers " and " the coupling of the centralism of state power with the broadest local self-government ".[1] Both Stalin and Zinoviev spoke on the topic in the central committee.[2] Molotov in his report sat delicately on the fence in criticizing the party attitude to the *kulak* :

> Instead of, in the person of the party and the Soviet power, isolating, and isolating ourselves from, the relatively small percentage of *kulaks* in the countryside, we sometimes include in the general rubric of *kulaks* a large percentage of the rural population which, in its majority, not only is not hostile, but need in no case become hostile, to the Soviet power.[3]

The resolution prescribed, in considerable detail, the functions of the party in the revitalization of the Soviets. The first point was to secure the election to rural Soviets and executive committees of a larger number of non-party peasants and peasant women, " especially those who enjoy authority in peasant circles ", and to secure the election of a proportion of non-party peasants to the republican and union congresses of Soviets. The principle of free election was to be observed, and the party was to " avoid illegal interference " in the work of the Soviets. On the other hand, " in order to strengthen political leadership of the work of the Soviets ", it was necessary " to strengthen the work of the communist fractions in the Soviets and local executive committees ". The line between avoiding illegal interference and strengthening political leadership through the party fractions would, obviously, prove difficult to draw. Finally the resolution demanded " a particularly cautious approach to questions of antireligious propaganda ", and placed a ban on " measures of administrative action (closing of churches etc.) which in the majority of cases achieve the opposite results ".[4]

[1] Stalin, *Sochineniya*, vi, 302-312 ; *Izvestiya*, October 26, 1924.

[2] Stalin *Sochineniya*, vi, 313-320; G. Zinoviev, *Litsom k Derevne* (1925), pp. 67-72. Zinoviev delivered two further speeches in the next few days, emphasizing the importance of the decisions taken (*ibid*. pp. 73-84).

[3] *Pravda*, November 1, 1924. *VKP(B) v Rezolyutsiyakh* (5th ed. 1936), i, 645, records a co-report by A. P. Smirnov ; the reference to it is omitted from later editions of this work, and it does not appear to have been published. Smirnov, who was People's Commissar for Agriculture of the RSFSR, belonged to the party Right, and probably, like Kalinin, inclined towards the *kulaks*.

[4] *VKP(B) v Rezolyutsiyakh* (1941), i, 630-633.

The policy of improving the machinery of administration was actively pursued. On October 20, 1924, the Orgburo had appointed a party commission to study ways and means of strengthening Soviet work.[1] The commission was presided over by Kaganovich, the rising star in the party firmament.[2] It reported in general terms, early in December 1924, on the tasks to be performed, and recommended the appointment of a governmental commission attached to the TsIK of the USSR to prepare the necessary measures.[3] Effect was given to this recommendation by a decision of the presidium of TsIK on December 19 to appoint a conference of some 50 delegates " on questions of Soviet construction ".[4] Before, however, the conference could meet, a fresh example of the weakness of party work in the countryside confronted the party leaders. The results of the annual elections to the Soviets, which had been spread over the months September to November 1924, showed a marked decline in the already low proportion of electors who thought it worth while to record their votes.[5] Strong measures to counteract the growing apathy of the peasant towards the régime seemed imperative. A decree of TsIK of December 29, 1924, drew attention to " irregularities and omissions in the work of the electoral commissions ", as a result of which " the electors did not participate fully enough in the elections " ; where such abuses had occurred, or where less than 35 percent of the electors had voted, it proposed to the TsIKs of the Union republics and autonomous republics and to the executive committees of regions and provinces to cancel the elections already held and to hold new elections.[6] This was to be the principal and most dramatic move in the campaign for the revitalization of the Soviets.

The conference " on questions of Soviet construction ", which was designed as a conference on the revitalization of the Soviets, held two sessions in January and April 1925. Its proceedings

[1] *Izvestiya Tsentral'nogo Komiteta Rossiiskoi Kommunisticheskoi Partii (Bol'shevikov)*, No. 3 (8), October 20, 1924, p. 8.   [2] See pp. 202-203 above.
[3] *Izvestiya Tsentral'nogo Komiteta Rossiiskoi Kommunisticheskoi Partii (Bol'shevikov)*, No. 11 (16), December 15, 1924, pp. 1-2.
[4] *Pravda*, December 21, 1924.   [5] See pp. 317-318 above.
[6] *Sobranie Zakonov, 1925*, No. 1, art. 3.

are a substantial source of information on the Soviet countryside ;
and its resolutions laid the foundation of Soviet policy in local
administration for several years.[1]   The principal report at the
January session, which was presided over by Kalinin and also
addressed by Rykov, Enukidze and Kiselev, was entrusted to
Kaganovich.   Four years after the introduction of NEP, declared
Kaganovich, the weariness of the civil war had been overcome,
prosperity was rising everywhere, and the masses were displaying
a " broad political activity ".   This activity must be canalized
into the Soviets, which should exchange the " methods of compulsion " current in the civil war period for methods consistent
with " the social self-activization of the masses ".   The chief task
before the conference was " *to improve the work of the Soviets in the
countryside* ".   This meant the carrying out of the decision of
TsIK to hold re-elections where the proportion of voters had
fallen below 35 per cent, and to establish an improved procedure
for the elections.   Kaganovich admitted that the peasant, in many
places, did not yet look on the Soviets as " his own elected organs " ;
and he and other speakers quoted instances where lists of candidates had been forced on reluctant electors by party secretaries,
by Komsomol groups or even by the local electoral commission :
only in the Ukraine (where the komnezamozhi [2] still existed) had
the poor peasants sometimes ventured to nominate candidates
of their own.   In conclusion Kaganovich put forward two further
points.   The first was the need for independent rural district
budgets — a condition of real local self-government.   The second
was the strengthening of " revolutionary legality " : the peasant
must feel himself protected " from caprice, from abuses, from
illegality, from infringement of the revolutionary laws ".[3]

It was an unspoken premiss of any campaign to revitalize the
rural Soviets and improve local administration that non-party
elements sympathetic to the régime should be induced to col-

---

[1] Its proceedings were published as *Soveshchanie po Voprosam Sovetskogo
Stroitel'stva, 1925 g.* (2 vols. sub-titled *Yanvar'* and *Aprel'*) (1925).
[2] For these see Vol. 1, p. 288.
[3] Kaganovich's speech is in *Soveshchanie po Voprosam Sovetskogo Stroitel'-
stva, 1925 g. : Yanvar'* (1925), pp. 97-117 ; for the other points cited see
ibid. pp. 88, 95-96.   The conference was fully reported in *Pravda*, January
7-11, 1925.   For the question of rural district budgets see Note A (pp. 455-465
below) ; for " revolutionary legality " see Note C (pp. 468-471 below).

laborate with it. The attempt to make up for the inadequate strength of the party cadres by an appeal to non-party people to participate in Soviet work went back to the thirteenth party congress of May 1924. On that occasion Stalin emphatically declared that " without giving particular attention to the task of drawing non-party people into Soviet work in the provinces and counties, serious constructive work is impossible ", and that without this " broadening of the base " of Soviet administration, " the Soviets may seriously lose weight and influence " ; [1] and the congress resolution rather more cautiously pronounced that, " together with party comrades, non-party workers should also be drawn into all this work ".[2]   Conferences of non-party peasants were held under party auspices to explain the " significance of the Soviets and of the re-election campaign ".[3]   Kalinin's opening speech at the conference on the revitalization of the Soviets in January 1925, was a covert apologia for the non-party worker, whose " fundamental aim is restricted to the thing on which he is actually working ", who has " no ultimate, remote perspectives ", and who " fixes his gaze on what is at the moment being immediately done under his eyes " : this, Kalinin implied without saying it, was a healthy corrective to the " bureaucratism " which was the vice of the party man.[4]   The movement was, however, liable to have awkward implications.   Later in the same session Kiselev referred to talk in the villages that " there should be Soviets without communists " and that, just as the workers were organized in trade unions, so the peasants ought to have their own organizations.[5]   The proposal to organize non-party peasants as a separate group clearly marked off from workers and party members stirred immediate apprehensions of *kulak* or SR predominance ; and perhaps for this reason the recruitment of non-party peasants into the Soviets was not specifically mentioned either in Kaganovich's report or in the resolutions of the conference.   The conference recommended the holding of re-elections

---

[1] Stalin, *Sochineniya*, vi, 213.
[2] *VKP(B) v Rezolyutsiyakh* (1941), i, 584.
[3] *Soveshchanie po Voprosam Sovetskogo Stroitel'stva 1925 g. : Aprel'* (1925), p. 9 ; the Smolensk archives (WKP 279) contain records of such meetings in the districts and rural districts of White Russia.
[4] *Soveshchanie po Voprosam Sovetskogo Stroitel'stva 1925 g.: Yanvar'* (1925), pp. 5-8.   [5] *Ibid*. p. 144.

for all Soviets where less than 35 per cent of electors had voted in the elections of the autumn of 1924, or where irregularities had occurred, and drew up draft instructions to electoral commissions which prohibited these commissions from putting forward lists of candidates, gave electors unlimited freedom to nominate candidates either in advance or when the electoral meeting assembled, and made provision for electoral meetings at local centres, and not merely at the headquarters of the village Soviet.[1] The recommendation for fresh elections was promptly carried into effect by a decree of TsIK of January 16, 1925.[2] On this occasion the right of TsIK to legislate on elections seems to have been assumed, and the constitutional rights of the constituent republics were silently ignored.[3]

The decision raised one important practical issue. Under article 65 of the original constitution of the RSFSR, and corresponding articles of those of the other constituent republics, persons employing hired labour or living on interest from capital were, among other categories, deprived of the franchise. The constitution of the USSR was silent on the subject, since electoral rights were a matter for the republics. On the other hand, the republics, apart from the formal declaration of principle in their constitutions, treated the question as of no practical importance, and, with the single exception of the Ukrainian SSR,[4] appear to have passed no legislation to define the manner in which the principle should be applied. It was not at this time the practice to draw up lists of voters ; when elections took place, the decision

---

[1] *Soveshchanie po Voprosam Sovetskogo Stroitel'stva 1925 g. : Yanvar'* (1925), pp. 221-229 ; the provision for voting to take place at local centres was important because, with the increased size of the village, only peasants living near the headquarters of the village Soviet could be expected to attend a meeting held there in full strength (*Na Agrarnom Fronte*, No. 5-6, 1925, p. 60).

[2] *Sobranie Zakonov, 1925*, No. 6, art. 54.

[3] The TsIK of the White Russian SSR issued on January 31, 1925, a decree in the same terms as the decree of VTsIK of January 16 (*Sobranie Uzakonenii SSR Belorussii, 1925*, No. 16, art. 112) ; this was followed by a proclamation of February 21, 1925, recording the decision to hold re-elections where less than 35 per cent had voted, and appealing to the population to vote (*ibid.* No. 9, art. 74). Similar decrees were presumably issued by the other republics.

[4] Decrees of April, July and October 1921 are in *Zbir Zakoniv i Rosporyadzhen', 1921*, No. 7, art. 202 ; No. 13, art. 355 ; No. 22, 620. These decrees rigidly excluded all peasants employing hired labour ; for their provisions on the franchise for town Soviets see p. 358, notes 5 and 6 below.

on those to be excluded was left to the caprice of the electoral commission.[1] Many stories were afterwards told of the way in which this discrimination had been exercised. A Red Army man had been deprived of the right to vote because his grandfather kept a village shop in 1902.[2] Russian peasants in Kazakhstan were disqualified for having belonged in the past to church councils.[3] Elsewhere peasants were said to have been disfranchised on such charges as stealing a goat, or " slaughtering the cow of a poor peasant ", or taking bribes, though none of these charges had been brought before a court ; another peasant was deprived of the vote because he worked in his spare time as coachman for a well-to-do merchant. One county was said to have disqualified all peasants who had ever been fined for distilling illicit spirit. A case was quoted from the province of Saratov where 30 per cent of the peasants of a district were excluded from the vote.[4] What is clear is that between 1921 and 1924 the issue excited no interest : a policy of " silent indifference to questions of electoral law "[5] prevailed everywhere.

The revival of this constitutional conundrum was a direct consequence of differences on agrarian policy. The disfranchisement of employers of hired labour, in its application to the peasantry, was the political counterpart of the provision in the law of February 19, 1918, on the socialization of the land, which confined the right to use land " to him who cultivates it with his own labour ".[6] The right to use land and the right to vote went together. When, therefore, the " fundamental law " of May 1922 and the agrarian code of October 1922 cautiously sanctioned, in certain circumstances, the leasing of land and the hiring of labour,[7]

---

[1] The conference on revitalization recommended that lists of disqualified persons should be publicly exhibited in advance of the election (*Soveshchanie po Voprosam Sovetskogo Stroitel'stva 1925 g. : Yanvar'* (1925), p. 224). This was the practice in the Ukraine (*Radyan'ska Ukraina*, No. 13 (19), April 1926, p. 34) ; but this formality does not seem to have been observed elsewhere.

[2] *Pravda*, May 27, 1925.   [3] *Na Agrarnom Fronte*, No. 9, 1925, p. 116.

[4] *Sovetskoe Stroitel'stvo : Sbornik*, iv-v (1926), 76-77, 105.

[5] *Ibid.* i (1925), 127. Although much play was made with the exclusions, their number was probably small ; according to Yu. Larin, *Rost Krest'yanskoi Obshchestvennosti* (1925), p. 12, only 1·4 per cent were disqualified in 1922 and 1923, and only 40 per cent of these were disqualified on grounds of social and economic status.

[6] For this law see *The Bolshevik Revolution, 1917–1923*, Vol. 2, pp. 45-47.

[7] See *ibid.* Vol. 2, pp. 289, 296.

some political concession seemed the natural corollary. It was not, however, till the summer of 1924 that desire in the party to conciliate the well-to-do peasant had become strong enough to enforce a change. On August 11, 1924, the presidium of the TsIK of the RSFSR issued an order that persons employing hired labour in accordance with the terms of the agricultural code, or holding monetary deposits, were not to be disfranchised on that account ; and similar decrees were issued a little later by the Ukrainian and White Russian SSRs.[1] Since the middle peasant had never been disfranchised for his hiring of extra labour for the harvest, the concession clearly applied to peasants rich enough, and working on a large enough scale, to employ permanent labour. This decision did not escape criticism at the session of the TsIK of the RSFSR in October 1924, when Larin vigorously demanded the exclusion of *kulaks* from the franchise in accordance with the terms of the constitution.[2] If, however, it was now desired to conciliate the only element among the peasantry in which competent administrators, even at the lowest level, might be found, it was necessary to abate the rigour of the law. On October 23, 1923, TsIK laid it down, regardless of the constitutional position, that persons employing hired labour within the terms of the agrarian code " are not deprived of electoral rights ".[3] The decree of TsIK of January 16, 1925, prescribing fresh elections, was accompanied by another decree of the same date which, in even more flagrant contravention of the rights of the republics, explained that persons formerly disfranchised on

[1] *Sobranie Uzakonenii, 1924*, No. 71, art. 695 ; *Zbirnik Uzakonen' ta Rosporyadzhen', 1924*, No. 34, art. 235 ; *Sobranie Uzakonenii SSR Belorussii, 1924*, No. 19, art. 177. The Ukrainian decree was more detailed than the others, and attempted to provide a positive definition of those entitled to vote (these included " foreigners belonging to the working class or to the toiling peasantry ") ; in one Ukrainian village where 250 peasants had been disqualified in 1924, all but 46 had regained the franchise in January 1925 (*Soveshchanie po Voprosam Sovetskogo Stroitel'stva 1925 g. : Yanvar'* (1925), p. 57).
[2] *Vserossiiskii Tsentral'nyi Ispolnitel'nyi Komitet XI Sozyva : Vtoraya Sessiya* (1924), p. 59. According to Yu. Larin, *Rost Krest'yanskoi Obshchestvennosti* (1925), p. 44, Kalinin at the session of the party central committee in October 1924 opposed a suggestion that the electoral commissions for village Soviets and rural district executive committee elections should be instructed to ensure that *kulaks* should be debarred from voting : the suggestion was, however, adopted.
[3] This order is quoted in *Bol'shevik*, No. 13, July 15, 1926, p. 24, but has not been traced elsewhere.

this account might regain their right to vote on production of evidence that they were now living on the proceeds of their own labour, and that persons employing hired labour within the provisions of the agricultural code and persons having deposits in savings banks were not subject to disfranchisement.[1] A further decree of the presidium of TsIK of April 8, 1925, repeated these regulations, and pointed out that definite evidence was required to justify disfranchisement : mere " declarations of individual citizens " were not enough. According to the same decree, some local authorities had disfranchised artisans who had set up " subsidiary " businesses, as well as servers, singers or organists in churches and members of church councils ; exclusion on such grounds was declared to be unjustified.[2] A minor difficulty arose over peasants who formerly served in the police and who, under the constitution of the RSFSR, were liable to disfranchisement on this ground ; the practice appears to have grown up of restoring electoral rights to such persons if the other inhabitants of the locality petitioned on their behalf.[3]

Party exhortations were redoubled to secure as large a vote as possible. An instruction of the party central committee signed by Kaganovich spoke of the necessity " to bring non-party people (especially women) into the Soviets far more extensively than in previous electoral campaigns ". Non-party people were to be allowed to put forward their own lists of candidates, and " the attempts of some Komsomol members which have been observed in the past to dictate their will rudely and tactlessly to the electors " were to be resisted. No attempt should be made to exclude

[1] *Sobranie Zakonov, 1925*, No. 6, art. 55. The preamble of the decree cited arts. 9 and 10 of the constitution of the USSR ; but these articles dealt solely with the method of election to the Union Congress of Soviets, and did not establish the competence of the Union to legislate for elections at a lower Soviet level. A Soviet commentator observed that the provisions of this decree " cannot be regarded as consonant with the letter or meaning of the Soviet constitution, the more so since the orders were issued even without a sessions of TsIK " (M. Reikhel, *Soyuz Sovetskikh Sotsialisticheskikh Respublik* (Kharkov, 1925), i, 66). A writer in a Ukrainian journal criticized the two degrees of TsIK of January 16, 1925, on the holding of re-elections and on the definition of the franchise as intruding on matters reserved for the republics ; instructions had also been sent out which contravened the decree of the Ukrainian SSR of September 1924 (*Radyan'ska Ukraina*, No. 1-2 (7-8), July 1925, pp. 27-29 ; for the Ukrainian decree see p. 330, note 1, above).

[2] *Sobranie Zakonov, 1925*, No. 42, art. 313.

[3] *XII S"ezd Sovetov RSFSR* (1925), p. 178.

" individual peasants who in one degree or another have criticized
actions of local organs of the Soviet power " : even Cossacks
were not to be excluded merely on the ground that they fought
against the Soviets in the civil war.[1] Orjonikidze, in a speech in
Baku in January 1925, declared that every non-party peasant
should take part in Soviet work, and that communists guilty of
malpractices should be " chased out of the party and of the
countryside ". He added with provocative emphasis :

> The non-party peasant must be made to feel that he is master
> of the land, and the party member must be shown that he is not a
> person who cannot in any circumstances be touched.[2]

The columns of *Pravda* during February 1925 were full of warnings against potential abuses by party members in the electoral
campaign — in particular, the unjust disfranchisement of peasants
and the imposition of party candidates. Kaganovich, at the April
session of the conference on revitalization, spoke with great
emphasis against " *illegal deprivation of electoral rights* " both at
the original elections and at the re-elections. The term *kulak*
had been interpreted very widely : definitions were required " so
that the constitution may not be interpreted in an extensive and
capricious manner ". Voters had been disqualified on the ground
of " opposition to the Soviet power ", merely because they had
come out with criticisms of the president of a rural district
executive committee or village Soviet.[3] The mood of the moment
was most frankly expressed in a statement " on the question of
depriving so-called ' *kulaks* ' of electoral rights " made by Kalinin
to the conference in April 1925 :

> Undoubtedly abuses often occur in this matter. It is quite
> understandable that the independent peasantry, even if it is in
> a minority, or in other words the independent minority of the
> peasantry, should sometimes find a way to dictate its will to the
> impoverished majority. That is correct. But all the same, in
> spite of that, I think that we ought to be very cautious about
> taking away electoral rights.[4]

---

[1] *Izvestiya Tsentral'nogo Komiteta Rossiiskoi Kommunisticheskoi Partii (Bol'-
shevikov)*, No. 6 (81), February 9, 1925, p. 2.
[2] G. Orjonikidze, *Stat'i i Rechi*, i (1956), 374.
[3] *Soveshchanie po Voprosam Sovetskogo Stroitel'stva 1925 g. : Aprel'* (1925),
pp. 11-12.   [4] *Ibid.* p. 163.

Practice varied from place to place. Orjonikidze recorded the extreme case of a man with three cows who sold his third cow in order not to be branded as a *kulak* and deprived of the franchise.[1] But apparently few peasants were excluded from voting in the spring of 1925 on the ground of being *kulaks*. A later critic, who included among the errors committed at this time " the extension of the right to vote to categories of persons who were deprived of that right under the constitution ", added the consoling re-flexion that this had had " substantially " little effect.[2] Under the electoral system prevailing, it was moral rather than numerical preponderance which counted.

Re-elections to village Soviets began in February 1925 and continued sporadically till May or June. Material difficulties, and official and party obstruction on the spot,[3] prevented the full realization of the programme. But when the conference on the revitalization of the Soviets met for its second session early in April, Kaganovich was able to report that complete re-elections had taken place or were in progress in ten provinces, and partial re-elections in several others.[4] Six weeks later the third Congress of Soviets of the USSR was told that one-third of all village Soviets had been re-elected.[5] Bukharin gave an encouraging account of the proceedings to a session of IKKI :

> The peasant has become far more active than before. His political horizon has broadened ; his independence has in-creased ; he feels the need to take part more energetically in political life, in the organs of state administration, in the village Soviets, the cooperatives, etc.[6]

The general verdict was that " the electoral meetings as a whole passed off in a much livelier and more business-like way than before ".[7] Some striking increases were quoted in the percentages

---

[1] G. Orjonikidze, *Stat'i i Rechi*, i (1956), 405.
[2] *Sovetskoe Stroitel'stvo*, No. 1, August 1926, p. 31.
[3] Examples of obstruction are quoted in *Na Agrarnom Fronte*, No. 5-6, 1925, pp. 61-63.
[4] *Soveshchanie po Voprosam Sovetskogo Stroitel'stva 1925 g. : Aprel'* (1925), pp. 4-5.
[5] *Tretii S"ezd Sovetov SSSR* (1925), p. 302.
[6] *Rasshirennyi Plenum Ispolkoma Kommunisticheskogo Internatsionala* (1925), p. 370.
[7] *Na Agrarnom Fronte*, No. 5-6, 1925, p. 68.

of those voting in the re-elections — from 25 to 57 in the Gomel province, from 13 to 38 in Ryazan, from 25 to 39 in Voronezh, from 20 to 55 in Irkutsk, from 23 to 61 in Kharkov.[1] But these were exceptional cases. Total figures of elections in the RSFSR for 1924–1925 showed a percentage of 41·1 voting in elections to village Soviets as against 37·2 in 1923. But these figures included the uncancelled elections of the autumn of 1924 as well as the re-elections of the spring of 1925.[2]

Even greater success seems to have attended the other declared purpose of the re-elections : to increase the participation of non-party people in the Soviets. Whereas the elections in the autumn of 1924 had revealed " a sharp rise in the percentage of communists and of poor peasant elements in the countryside, and at the same time a clearly marked absenteeism among the electors ", the re-elections in the spring of 1925 showed "a sharp fall in the percentage of communists and poor peasants in the Soviets and a high rate of activity among the electors ".[3] The percentage of communists in the Soviets declined as a result of the re-elections from 12 to 7 per cent (or, according to another computation, by one-half) ; since the total membership of the Soviets had risen with the increased number of voters, this was said to represent an absolute decline of from 30 to 35 per cent in the number of communist deputies. The decline was frankly attributed not only to the decision of the party central committee to encourage the election of non-party candidates, but also " in a remarkable degree " to the rejection of " worthless communists " by the peasant electors in the first comparatively free elections.[4] The term " communists " in this context included not only party members and candidates, but members of the Komsomol. The number of these declined to one-fifth or one-seventh of the previous total : their marked unpopularity was attributed in part to their reputation for unruly behaviour, in part to their active campaign against religion, but most of all to the reluctance of the peasants to elect untried youths to the Soviets.[5]

[1] *Na Agrarnom Fronte*, No. 5-6, 1925, p. 68 ; *Soveshchanie po Voprosam Sovetskogo Stroitel'stva 1925 g. : Aprel'* (1925), p. 28.
[2] *Perevybory v Sovety RSFSR v 1925–1926 godu* (1926), i, 10-11.
[3] *Sovetskoe Stroitel'stvo*, No. 1, August 1926, p. 15.
[4] *Na Agrarnom Fronte*, No. 5-6, 1925, pp. 71, 209.
[5] *Ibid.* pp. 69-70, 72.

(c) The Kulak and the Party

While, however, the re-elections had apparently been successful in realizing the purpose for which they were designed, they
brought to the surface crucial dilemmas of party policy. The
results of the re-elections were perhaps not foreseen by all. At
first, some well-to-do peasants are said to have feared that they
would produce an influx of poor peasants and *batraks* into organs
where the well-to-do had hitherto predominated ; [1] and Larin,
probably with his tongue in his cheek, called them " a clear act in
pursuance of our anti-*kulak* line ".[2] The sequel contradicted any
such expectations. Statistical evidence fails in the absence of any
precise definition of the different categories of peasant. But the
results, on the whole, justified those who saw, in the re-elections,
" a refusal of the party and of the Soviet power to support the
poor peasantry and a turn to the side of the strong peasant, into
whose hands the leadership of the village was being given ".[3]
The conspicuous feature of the elections was " the fearful eagerness of the *kulaks* to creep into power ".[4] " The well-to-do and
kulak strata in the countryside ", in the words of another commentator, " showed an immense interest in the new elections, and
prepared for them very intensively." [5] In the Ukraine, the
revitalization of the Soviets meant that " the *kulak* element is
studying the laws in order to utilize them for its group interests ".[6]
According to one estimate, the proportion of middle peasants
elected to the Soviets had risen from 30-40 per cent to 70-75 per
cent.[7] This, too, was significant ; for the *kulak* often sheltered
behind the middle peasant, " who stands nearer to the *kulak* than

[1] *Ibid.* No. 3, 1925, pp. 97-98. The Cossacks of the North Caucasian
region were said to have suspected a trick : " There is no point in reading
us reports about the revitalization of the Soviets ; give us practical orders
how to work " (*Tretii S"ezd Sovetov SSSR* (1925), p. 298) ; in Kazakhstan
the elections were at first mistrusted as an attempt to stir up strife between
families and tribes (*Soveshchanie po Voprosam Sovetskogo Stroitel'stva 1925 g. :
Yanvar'* (1925), p. 122).

[2] Yu. Larin, *Rost Krest'yanskoi Obshchestvennosti* (1925), p. 21.

[3] *Na Agrarnom Fronte*, No. 5-6, 1925, p. 65.

[4] *Soveshchanie po Voprosam Sovetskogo Stroitel'stva 1925 g. : Yanvar'*
(1925), p. 26.   [5] *Na Agrarnom Fronte*, No. 5-6, 1925, p. 66.

[6] *Byulleten' Vseukrain'skogo Tsentral'nogo Vykonavchego Komitetu*, No. 2,
February 16, 1925, p. 231 ; the speaker was Petrovsky.

[7] *Na Agrarnom Fronte*, No. 5-6, 1925, p. 209.

to the poor peasant ".[1] " In a large number of the districts of
our country ", observed Stalin a little later, " *the middle peasant
took his stand at the side of the* kulak *against* the poor peasant." [2]
The poor peasants, ignorant and incapable, were subordinate to
the *kulak* or middle peasant on whom they depended for their
daily bread. In the absence of strong party leadership and support
they remained politically passive, and seem everywhere to have
lost ground.[3] After the re-elections, the proportion of " horseless " peasants in the village Soviets is said to have sunk to 4 per
cent,[4] while *batraks* and non-agricultural hired workers together
accounted for only 2·9 per cent.[5]

These phenomena had been particularly conspicuous in outlying regions remote from central control, where the well-to-do
peasant had been able to exert his influence without restraint or
disguise. A delegate from the northern Caucasus to the fourteenth
party conference of April 1925 drew a picture which, though
perhaps somewhat over-coloured (the *kulaks* had always been
particularly powerful in this region), was true in outline for other
parts of the USSR. At first the new slogans had been regarded
with mistrust, as a " trick ". But, when the new elections were
held, the well-to-do peasants changed their attitude.

> As soon as they were persuaded that the local communists
> had really stopped issuing orders, that there were none of the
> hated obligatory lists, that there was a chance of electing indi-
> viduals, a chance even of throwing out the communist who
> had blacked their eyes and made a scandal over their work, the
> large peasants and Cossacks believed us, and flocked to the
> elections, and the authority of the Soviet power in these regions
> all at once increased remarkably.

Unfortunately these proceedings had led to the eclipse both of
the communists and of the poor peasants :

> In some places the powerful, well-to-do peasant and Cos-
> sack, and in places even the genuine *kulak*, who went to the

---

[1] *Soveshchanie po Voprosam Sovetskogo Stroitel'stva 1925 g. : Yanvar'*
(1925), p. 62.   [2] Stalin, *Sochineniya*, vii, 123.
[3] *Na Agrarnom Fronte*, No. 5-6, 1925, pp. 65-66, 70-71, 211.
[4] According to a pamphlet of Larin reviewed in *Vestnik Finansov*, No. 9,
September 1925, pp. 269-270 ; for the earlier estimate of 10 per cent see
p. 313 above.   [5] L. Kaganovich, *Partiya i Sovety* (1928), p. 86.

elections meticulously organized, got complete leadership into his hands.[1]

In the Kuban district, " the course ' Face to the countryside ' was understood as a turning towards the well-to-do peasants : freedom of elections meant a refusal by the party to lead the electoral campaign and the Soviets ". A reversion to " liberal " conceptions of freedom had resulted, as Marxists maintained that it must result, in the supremacy of the capitalists, and had encouraged the participation in the elections of " former atamans, white guard officers and other anti-Soviet elements ".[2] In the elections in Bashkiria " the class principle was not at all observed, and *kulaks* and priests often got into the Soviets", the reason being that "the Soviet apparatus in general was very weak, and the number of ideologically reliable leading workers in the local Soviets and executive committees was insufficient".[3] In Uzbekistan, Russian *kulaks* threatened to boycott the Soviets and employ no more hired workers if they were deprived of their electoral rights.[4] In Kazakhstan " Soviet construction in the village (*aul*) was accepted in form, but not in substance ; the social basis of power remained as before ; the Soviets were in the hands of beys who were tribal chiefs ". Not only the Soviets but the party organs were subject to infiltration ; old members of Alash-Orda " tried to plant their counter-revolutionary organizations under the flag of cells of the RKP(B) " and distributed party tickets to their adherents.[5] In one county of Kazakhstan " the *kulaks* and beys displayed great activity in driving the poor peasants to elect their candidates", one of these being a mullah.[6]

The anxiety provoked in party circles by these untoward symptoms was difficult to allay. The attempt to swamp the rural Soviets with non-party peasants and reduce, relatively and even

---

[1] *Chetyrnadtsataya Konferentsiya Rossiiskoi Kommunisticheskoi Partii (Bol'-shevikov)* (1925), pp. 24-25 ; the account in *Na Agrarnom Fronte*, No. 5-6, 1925, p. 65, also mentions that in the northern Caucasus, " as the result of the re-elections, a considerable part of the Soviets passed into the hands of middle peasants and well-to-do Cossacks ".

[2] *Bol'shevik*, No. 7-8, April 30, 1926, p. 56.

[3] *X Let Sovetskoi Bashkirii, 1919–1929* (Ufa, 1929), p. 413.

[4] *Vlast' Sovetov*, No. 20, May 15, 1925, p. 20.

[5] *Voprosy Istorii*, No. 10, 1946, pp. 5-7, quoting an unpublished report of 1925 ; for Alash-Orda see *The Bolshevik Revolution, 1917–1923*, Vol. 1, p. 323.

[6] *Vlast' Sovetov*, No. 20, May 15, 1925, p. 20.

absolutely, the number of party members in them, was deeply resented in many party circles, especially in the remoter outposts. One commentator diagnosed " bewilderment and despondency in the mood of rural communists ", who bitterly resisted the proposal to " throw overboard party members who took part in the civil war ".[1] Another described the attitude of party members in Siberia :

> Their state of mind was distracted, even panic-stricken. The turn of the party " Face to the countryside " shocked them. It seemed a dangerous retreat before the *kulak* element, a step far more important and hazardous than NEP.[2]

Bukharin a year later recalled how at this time many communists had been " distracted ", and " disoriented, not knowing how to act ".[3] Nothing had occurred to change the balance of social forces in the countryside. The revitalization of the Soviets, accompanied by a larger measure of self-abnegation on the side of the party, seemed merely to have put a new instrument of power in the hands of enemies of the régime. A speaker at the Moscow provincial party conference in January 1925 had ominously noted that " definite SRs and well-to-do peasants who sometimes seem to run the countryside appear in the guise of non-party peasants ".[4] At the April session of the conference on revitalization Kaganovich confirmed that " at the re-elections of some village Soviets SRs had slipped through under the guise of non-party peasants, and had come out with the slogan ' Soviets without communists ' — the old Milyukov slogan ".[5] At the fourteenth party conference later in the same month, he again insisted on the proved need for party leadership in the Soviets,

---

[1] *Na Agrarnom Fronte*, No. 5-6, 1925, pp. 199-200 ; this anonymous article clearly had an authoritative character. Another protest of the same kind is recorded *ibid*. No. 10, 1925, p. 11.

[2] *Sovetskoe Stroitel'stvo : Sbornik*, ii-iii (1925), 357.

[3] A. I. Rykov and N. Bukharin, *Partiya i Oppozitsionnyi Blok* (1926), p. 71.

[4] *Ekonomicheskaya Zhizn'*, January 27, 1925 ; the speech containing these remarks was omitted, probably by accident, from the report of the conference in *Pravda*, January 28, 1925.

[5] *Soveshchanie po Voprosam Sovetskogo Stroitel'stva 1925 g. : Aprel'* (1925), p. 10 : Molotov at the fourteenth party congress in December 1925 described such references to " Soviets without communists " as " dreams of white-guardists " and " expressions of panic " (*XIV S"ezd Vsesoyuznoi Kommunisticheskoi Partii (B)* (1926), p. 68).

while admitting that, if the party fraction settled all the business of the Soviet in advance, "no great liveliness will be shown in it". But no escape was offered from the dilemma except to make party leadership " more flexible, more elastic ". Finally, Molotov, in winding up the debate, explained that " the revitalization of the Soviets" could not imply "any weakening or softening in relation to political groups hostile to the Soviet dictatorship " ; the hand of friendship and participation was being held out not to " Mensheviks, SRs etc.", but to "the broad non-party masses".[1] The resolution of the conference spoke of " the restoration and reinforcement of the work of communist fractions " in Soviet and other organs, and of the desirability of electing non-party peasants and workers " generally devoted to the Soviet power " to these organs.[2] The application of these principles to the well-to-do peasants and kulaks was not further elucidated.

The third Union Congress of Soviets, which met a month after the party conference, showed less embarrassment over the results of the elections. Kalinin listed the defects of the rural Soviets : " an insufficiently broad participation of workers, especially of women, and especially in our autonomous republics and regions and in border territories of the Union"; "a diminution of the rôle of the Soviets as organs of genuine popular power, and their replacement by individual presidents of executive committees " ; and " a reduction of the Soviets to the rôle of institutions to register prepared decisions ". He alleged that party representatives still indulged in " mechanical manipulations " to secure the acceptance of prepared lists of candidates, and — true to his policy of favouring the well-to-do peasant — complained of " the exclusion from the electoral lists of unamenable voters under the guise of kulaks ".[3] The resolution of the congress on Kalinin's report, which endorsed the recommendations of the conference on revitalization, contained nothing but well-worn platitudes.[4] But the leadership had good reason to be satisfied. The " wager on the kulak " was now at its height. The revitalization of the Soviets served as its political counterpart. When an

[1] Chetyrnadtsataya Konferentsiya Rossiiskoi Kommunisticheskoi Partii (Bol'-shevikov) (1926), pp. 38-39, 58.
[2] VKP(B) v Rezolyutsiyakh (1941), ii, 8.
[3] Tretii S"ezd Sovetov SSSR (1925), pp. 261-262.
[4] Sobranie Zakonov, 1925, No. 35, art. 247.

official journal hailed the new policy as proof of a determination to elect to the Soviets men who " know how the crops grow ",[1] it expressed both a literal and a metaphorical truth. The well-to-do peasants were not only the best farmers, but the people who were most likely to run the rural Soviets efficiently : in default of trained administrators sent from the centre — who were not in any case available in any number — they were the only people who could do so. The revitalization of the Soviets, like the wager on the *kulak*, was a policy of building on the most efficient. In the summer of 1925 it was a policy which, except to a few party stalwarts and doctrinaires, seemed to make unimpeachable good sense. Meanwhile the congress of Soviets, not content with endorsing the revitalization policy, contributed to the advancement of non-party people by electing 146 of them to the newly constituted TsIK, forming 22 per cent of the total membership. In the previous TsIK only 11 per cent of members had been non-party.[2] The TsIK elected by the twelfth All-Russian Congress of Soviets, which met at the same time, went a step further by demonstratively electing a non-party peasant and a non-party worker to its presidium.[3]

If, however, the revitalization of the Soviet organs was pursued at this time mainly by seeking new support outside the party ranks, party pressure was strong enough to ensure that the second purpose proclaimed by the thirteenth party congress — " to strengthen the influence of the party in these organs " — was not forgotten. Indeed, though the two purposes might at the outset have seemed incompatible, it became clear in the long run that, in a state entirely dominated and directed by the party, the

[1] *Vlast' Sovetov*, No. 20, May 15, 1925, p. 19.
[2] *Tretii S"ezd Sovetov SSSR* (1925), p. 542. According to Enukidze (*ibid.* p. 543), " the union republics, as well as the local authorities — provinces and regions — were recommended to nominate at the elections to the central executive committee more workers direct from the bench and the plough, in other words to lower the percentage of persons occupying administrative or party positions " : to increase the percentage of manual workers meant automatically to reduce the percentage of party members.
[3] *Vserossiiskii Tsentral'nyi Ispolnitel'nyi Komitet XII Sozyva : Pervaya Sessiya* (1925), p. 6 ; the TsIK itself contained 60 (or 26 per cent) non-party members as against 49 (or 16 per cent) in its predecessor (*id.: Vtoraya Sessiya* (1925), p. 540).

machine of local administration would not run smoothly and efficiently unless it were subjected to a strong infiltration of party influence. More specifically, in a country where the relations of the central government with the peasantry, and with different sections of the peasantry, were the major issue of policy, it was impossible for the party controlling the central government to be indifferent to the question what sector of the peasantry controlled the organs of local administration ; and the more efficient these organs became (since it was a matter of policy to increase their efficiency), the less indifferent could the party afford to remain. Hence, at a time when the party was loudly proclaiming its desire to draw "non-party elements" into the work of the Soviets and to reduce such direct control as had previously been exercised by the party, opposite forces were driving it more and more insistently towards intervention. Increased influence of the party in the countryside could theoretically have been best promoted by an increased recruitment of peasants into the party. But, when this method had been tried, and was limited by ever-present inhibitions about the undue dilution of the party with non-proletarian numbers,[1] nothing remained but the alternative method of sending party members to the countryside as missionaries of party aims and executors of party policy. Yet this method, too, was limited by the shortage of available workers, by general unwillingness in party circles to undertake a despised and uncongenial assignment, and by the inherent difficulties of the task.[2]

The general recommendations of the thirteenth party congress of May 1924 and of the central committee in October 1924 to transfer party members to rural areas produced little or no response.   In December 1924 the party central committee " sanctioned a decision " of the central committee of the Komsomol to transfer 600 Komsomol workers to rural posts[3] — an indication of the unavailability of party workers for the purpose. But this was a manifest evasion of party responsibility. In the

[1] See pp. 178-180 above.
[2] These had already been noted in a party report of 1923 (*Izvestiya Tsentral'-nogo Komiteta Rossiiskoi Kommunisticheskoi Partii (Bol'shevikov)*, No. 3 (51), March 1923, p. 53) ; in addition to unwillingness to move to the country, " unreliable communists, when they reach the country, are unable to oppose communist discipline to the rural element, and quickly go to pieces ".
[3] *Ibid*. No. 12 (17), December 22, 1924, p. 8.

spring of 1925 Molotov, on behalf of the party secretariat, paid a
visit to party organizations in the provinces of Tambov, Kursk
and Tula ; and the most important recommendation made by
him on his return was for the despatch of more party workers to
the rural areas.[1] In April 1925, with the revitalization campaign
at its height, the fourteenth party conference decided that 3000
party propagandists, together with 1000 party workers to act as
instructors to the county party committees, and 2000 Komsomols
to strengthen local youth organizations, should be sent to the
countryside before September 1.[2] The decision was carried out.
The 6000 were distributed over the countryside. But an un-
official account of the enterprise in the following summer revealed
some of its embarrassments. Many complaints were registered of
an " unskilful and tactless approach of individual comrades to
work in the countryside ". On the other hand, local parties had
sometimes not given the new arrivals " practical support ", and
had treated them as " outsiders ". Discontent at being sent to
the country and desire to return to the cities had been general.
Of those sent 5 per cent had abandoned the work (these were
referred to as cases of " desertion ") : in some areas the proportion was higher. Though formal approval was expressed of what
had been achieved, the impression was plainly conveyed that the
campaign had not been a success.[3] Such were still the practical
difficulties, in the middle nineteen-twenties, of giving reality to
the link between proletariat and peasantry, and establishing party
authority in the rural areas of the Soviet Union.

A device extensively employed or recommended at this time
to raise the level of party work in the countryside was the institu-

[1] For Molotov's report and the resolution of the central party committee
on it see *Izvestiya Tsentral'nogo Komiteta Rossiiskoi Kommunisticheskoi Partii
(Bol'shevikov)*, No. 13-14 (88-89), April 6, 1925, pp. 3-4.

[2] *VKP(B) v Rezolyutsiyakh* (1941), ii, 11, 13 ; according to a detailed instruction issued by the party central committee in July 1925, the 3000 propagandists were to set up schools of political instruction (*politgramota*) in the rural
areas (*Izvestiya Tsentral'nogo Komiteta Rossiiskoi Kommunisticheskoi Partii
(Bol'shevikov)*, No. 29-30 (104-105), August 10, 1925, pp. 1-2).

[3] *Izvestiya Tsentral'nogo Komiteta Vsesoyuznoi Kommunisticheskoi Partii (B)*,
No. 21-22 (142-143), June 7, 1926, pp. 1-2 ; it was admitted at the Komsomol
congress in March 1926 that many cases had occurred of a " flight from the
country " of " comrades sent there to strengthen basic positions for the establishment of proletarian leadership " (*VII S"ezd Vsesoyuznogo Leninskogo Kommunisticheskogo Soyuza Molodezhi* (1926), p. 185).

tion of so-called " patronage " (sheftstvo).[1] This meant that a party organization of workers took under its protection a corresponding rural organization, extending to it advice, material assistance and, above all, the help of experienced party workers. Lenin had several times spoken of the need for such support of the country by the town and factory.[2] The creation of an office or institution to sponsor and promote " patronage " appears to have dated from the beginning of 1923. The thirteenth party congress of May 1924 recommended the creation of special societies of workers in order to strengthen " the general work of cultural patronage over the countryside ", and mentioned with approval the " workers' societies for the cultural link between town and country " already created by the Leningrad party organization.[3] But it was only in the winter of 1924–1925 that, with the introduction of the " Face to the countryside " slogan and the campaign to revitalize the rural Soviets, the scheme began to develop. In November 1924 the party central committee passed a resolution attempting to define the character of " cultural patronage work ". It was a deviation to concentrate exclusively on agitation and cultural propaganda or exclusively on material aid : what was required was a combination of both.[4] The second anniversary of the scheme was celebrated by articles in the press in the new year of 1925.[5] In the following month the Leningrad party organization proclaimed a " week of the link between town and country ", and held a conference of " workers' societies for the cultural link ". " Patronage " received the endorsement of the party in a resolution of the fourteenth party conference in April 1925, though a warning was issued against

[1] The first application of " patronage " was apparently the adoption by cities of units of the Red Army. Trotsky explained that this was a substitute for the adoption of Tsarist regiments by members of the imperial family, who became their nominal " chiefs " or " patrons ": " the workers' and peasants' army will henceforth also have its ' patrons ' " (L. Trotsky, *Kak Vooruzhalas' Revolyutsiya*, iii, i (1924), 74, 322-323).

[2] The earliest occasion was in 1918 (Lenin, *Sochineniya*, xxiii, 216) ; the most specific reference to the scheme was in notes for an undelivered speech of December 1922 (*ibid.* xxvii, 384).

[3] *VKP(B) v Rezolyutsiyakh* (1941), i, 594.

[4] *Pravda*, November 23, 1924 ; *Izvestiya Tsentral'nogo Komiteta Rossiiskoi Kommunisticheskoi Partii (Bol'shevikov)*, No. 9 (14), December 1, 1924, p. 2. An account of the Leningrad societies had appeared *ibid.* No. 7 (12), November 17, 1924, p. 6.   [5] *Izvestiya*, January 3, 1925 ; *Pravda*, January 4, 1925.

such mistakes as " ill-considered political and anti-religious propaganda " and " combining the patronage campaign with holiday diversions ".[1] By the end of the year it had expanded so far that Molotov was able to claim a million members of " patronage organizations ", of whom 60 or 70 per cent were workers ;[2] and an all-union conference on patronage was held in Moscow in April 1926.[3] " Patronage " was an accurate expression of the cardinal party doctrine of the leadership of the proletariat, through which alone the backward peasantry could be shepherded into the revolutionary fold. It also provided a suitable means for inducing the urban party worker to undertake party duties in the countryside ; and, since such inducements were always hard to find, this was perhaps its main practical significance. It continued to figure extensively in party propaganda and party exhortations for several years.

The campaign for re-elections to the Soviets reached its climax, simultaneously with the broader agrarian policy of support for the *kulak*, in May 1925. Then a mood of criticism and disillusionment set in, which seems to have reflected the changing alignments in the party. Abuses had undoubtedly occurred. In some places, the zeal of the local authorities is said to have outrun even that of the official decree : they demanded a 70 per cent poll, and cancelled elections where this condition was not fulfilled. In other places, militiamen were used to order voters to the poll, and those who failed to appear were threatened with fines.[4] In June 1925, when Stalin was already manœuvring to damp down the ardour of the pro-*kulak* enthusiasts,[5] he also turned his critical attention to the revitalization policy, publicly admitting

---

[1] *VKP(B) v Rezolyutsiyakh* (1941), ii, 11. The " diversions " were liable to take the form of drinking bouts ; a complaint was made about this at the fourteenth party congress in December 1925 (*XIV S"ezd Vsesoyuznoi Kommunisticheskoi Partii (B)* (1926), p. 815).   [2] *Ibid.* p. 60.

[3] *Bol'shaya Sovetskaya Entsiklopediya*, lxii (1933), cols. 366-371, art. Sheftsvo ; the conference was briefly reported in *Pravda*, April 20, 1926, when the institution was said to " enjoy great popularity in the working masses ". A favourable report on the Leningrad " societies for the cultural link " appeared in *Izvestiya Tsentral'nogo Komiteta Vsesoyuznoi Kommunisticheskoi Partii (B)*, No. 24-25 (145-146), June 28, 1926, pp. 4-5.

[4] These particulars come from a later account in *XV Let Sovetskogo Stroitel'stva*, ed. E. Pashukanis (1932), pp. 439-440.   [5] See Vol. 1, pp. 283-284.

that hitherto " in a large number of districts the elections of
Soviets in the countryside have not been real elections, but an
empty bureaucratic procedure for forcibly bringing in ' deputies '
by way of a large number of tricks and of pressure by a small group
of rulers who are afraid of losing power ", though he claimed that
" an end is now being put to such electoral practices in the
countryside ".[1] An official party report two months later was
even more sweepingly critical :

> Little good can be said of the way in which party directives
> about the revitalization of the Soviets have been realized in
> practice ; achievements here are extremely insignificant.
> Measures taken to this end in many localities have not gone
> beyond the limits of paperwork.[2]

At this moment the party line on the orientation towards the
peasant was still wavering and uncertain. The policy of the revitalization of the Soviets would henceforth be firmly geared to
that line.

The most significant barometer of shifting opinions was the
discussion about the extension of the franchise, which had more
symbolical than practical importance and continued throughout
the summer and autumn of 1925. During the first months of
1925 a new constitution for the RSFSR had been in leisurely
preparation.[3] The logical course was evidently to incorporate in
it the new rules laid down in the January decree of TsIK,
admitting to the franchise those who employed hired labour
under the now authorized conditions, and those in receipt of
interest on savings.[4] This course was adopted ; and, when the
draft of the revised constitution was submitted to the TsIK of
the RSFSR at the beginning of May 1925,[5] it was found to repeat
the provisions of the January decree on this point. But objections were felt to this open abandonment of what had once been
regarded as fundamental principles of the constitution. It could,
after all, be argued that the " temporary rules " permitting hired
labour on farms were not intended to last, and that it would be

---

[1] Stalin, *Sochineniya*, vii, 184.
[2] *Izvestiya Tsentral'nogo Komiteta Rossiiskoi Kommunisticheskoi Partii (Bol'-
shevikov)*, No. 31-32 (106-107), August 24, 1925, p. 1.
[3] See p. 253 above.
[4] See pp. 330-331 above.   [5] See pp. 253-254 above.

improper to base constitutional provisions on them. In the text
finally adopted, article 69 of the new constitution was a precise
reproduction of article 65 of the old, with a few verbal changes
which did not affect these provisions : " persons resorting to
hired labour in order to extract surplus value " and " persons
living on unearned income, such as interest on capital . . ." were
once more declared incapable of electing or being elected to
Soviet organs. This demonstrative assertion of revolutionary
principle may be explained either as a last throw by the doctrinaires
of the early period of the revolution, or as an early symptom of the
reaction against the pro-*kulak* policy of the spring of 1925 ; it
probably combined both elements. It had no practical effect.
Since no elections were immediately pending, the conflict between
the new constitution of the RSFSR and the decrees of VTsIK
remained academic. Undeterred by the text of the constitution,
the People's Commissariat of Justice of the RSFSR issued a
month later, on June 18, 1925, an instruction that hand-workers
and artisans employing not more than two apprentices were not
to be regarded as exploiting hired labour, or deprived of the
right to vote.[1]

Since the re-elections ordered after the autumn elections of
1924 were not everywhere completed till June 1925, some latitude
was allowed about the date of the next elections ;[2] and these were
spread over the last two months of 1925 and the first months of
1926.[3] The balance of emphasis was now somewhat altered. At
the end of September 1925, with a crucial session of the party
central committee due to take place in the first week of October,
a lengthy instruction to local party organizations was issued over
the signature of Molotov. It began by claiming a "substantial
improvement in the link between worker and peasant " as a result
of the revitalization of the Soviets, and demanded a continuance
of the campaign. The new note was the emphasis given to the
need to organize the poor peasants and to bring the middle
peasants into alliance with them.[4] On October 2, 1925, on the eve

---

[1] *Sbornik Dekretov, Postanovlenii, Rasporyazhenii i Prikazov po Narodnomu
Khozyaistvu*, No. 23 (44), August 1925, p. 161.
[2] *Sobranie Zakonov, 1925*, No. 68, art. 506.
[3] *Perevybory v Sovety RSFSR v 1925–1926 godu* (1926), i, 5-6.
[4] This instruction appeared, in the place usually devoted to a leading
article, in *Pravda*, September 29, 1925.

of the session, *Pravda* published Molotov's report to the central committee "on work among the poor peasants", which contained a specific injunction to local party organizations to organize special meetings of poor peasants in advance of the elections; and this was endorsed by the central committee. This seemed an important concession to anti-*kulak* opinion in the party, and staved off any danger of a break with Zinoviev and Kamenev on this point.[1] But the balance was to some extent readjusted, after the committee had adjourned, by a decree of the RSFSR of October 14, 1925, which, ignoring the constitutional anomaly, repeated the provisions of the January decree of TsIK, admitting to the franchise employers of hired auxiliary labour under the provisions of the agrarian code.[2] At the same time TsIK issued a decree proposing to the TsIKs of the union republics (a rare gesture to constitutional propriety) to set up in each republic a central electoral commission " for the general direction of the electoral campaign and to review complaints against the actions of regional and provincial electoral commissions ".[3] In spite of this injunction, it is clear that uniformity was not achieved in the granting or withholding of the franchise, and that practice varied from place to place, the main determining factor being the varying extent of the influence of the *kulaks* and of the inclination of the local authorities to placate them. But the exemptions appear on the whole to have been generously applied. The number of those disqualified in rural areas of the RSFSR fell from 541,000 in the elections of 1924–1925 to 416,000 in the elections of 1925–1926 : these figures were said to represent 1·3 per cent and 1 per cent

---

[1] For the proceedings of this session of the party central committee see Vol. 1, pp. 305-308, and pp. 108-109 above.

[2] *Sobranie Uzakonenii, 1925*, No. 79, art. 603 ; in the following year, when the reaction against the *kulaks* had set in, this decree was attacked in the party journal as inconsistent with the constitution of the RSFSR (*Bol'shevik*, No. 9-10, May 30, 1926, pp. 40-42). The corresponding decree of the Ukrainian SSR of November 27, 1925, listed as entitled to the franchise members of the free professions, teachers, hand-workers and artisans not employing more than two apprentices, household workers, small traders holding first category licences (for these categories see *The Bolshevik Revolution, 1917–1923*, Vol. 2, p. 337, note 2), and peasants employing auxiliary labour within the limits of the law (*Zbirnik Uzakonen' ta Rosporyadzhen', 1925*, No. 97, art. 531).

[3] *Sobranie Zakonov, 1925*, No. 68, art. 506 ; the decree of the RSFSR carrying this proposal into effect only came four months later, in February 1926 (*Sobranie Uzakonenii, 1926*, No. 8, art. 59).

respectively of the population of voting age in these areas.[1]

The instruction to organize special meetings of poor peasants had little effect and does not seem to have been taken very seriously. When Kamenev was asked at a party meeting in Moscow immediately after the session of the central committee how these meetings were to be arranged, he replied that " the central committee did not lay down a precise organizational form, and did not do it advisedly " ; and, when another questioner enquired whether these groups would not amount to a revival of the kombedy and a return to class war in the countryside, he explained that the party could now achieve its ends " not by the procedure of civil war, but by the procedure of civil peace, having the whole state apparatus in our hands ".[2] Some local party organizations, firmly wedded to the peasant orientation, postponed or obstructed the carrying out of the instruction, pretending that its terms were not clear, that no representative groups of poor peasants could be found or that no *kulak* activity had been in evidence.[3] In some places, the local organization adopted " a position of peculiar neutrality in regard to the electoral campaign, eliminating itself from the leadership of the toiling masses in the elections to the Soviets ".[4] Where meetings of poor peasants were convened, they were broken up by *kulaks* ; elsewhere *kulaks* " strive by all ways and means to deck themselves out as ' champions of the interests of the poor peasantry ' ".[5] The purpose of using the

---

[1] *Perevybory v Sovety RSFSR v 1925–1926 godu* (1926), i, 6-7 ; of those disqualified 37·6 per cent in 1924–1925 and 46·7 per cent in 1925–1926 were disqualified as employing hired labour or engaged in trade (G. Mikhailov, *Mestnoe Sovetskoe Upravlenie* (1927), p. 425). The proportion of those disqualified in the towns was far higher than in the country (see p. 362 below). *Radyan'ska Ukraina*, No. 13 (19), April 1926, p. 37, gives the proportion of those disqualified in the Ukraine as 1·5 per cent ; in the Kuban 1·4 per cent were disqualified, 45 per cent of these being merchants, 11 per cent priests, 9 per cent former members of the police and 8 per cent entrepreneurs (*Bol'shevik*, No. 7-8, April 30, 1926, p. 64).

[2] L. Kamenev, *Stat'i i Rechi*, xii (1926), 409-411.

[3] Examples of this attitude from several widely separated centres were quoted in an article in *Leningradskaya Pravda*, December 25, 1925.

[4] *Sovetskoe Stroitel'stvo*, No. 1, August 1926, p. 32.

[5] *Izvestiya Tsentral'nogo Komiteta Vsesoyuznoi Kommunisticheskoi Partii* (*B*), No. 2 (123), January 25, 1926 ; this report also mentioned opposition by some party workers to the organization of poor peasants. A writer in *Pravda*, June 26, 1926, bluntly said that party decisions in favour of the poor peasant had been sabotaged.

meetings to select poor peasant candidates for the elections seems rarely to have been fulfilled. As before, the situation was particularly bad in the outlying regions. In Kazakhstan, though 62 per cent of electors are said to have voted, the elections proceeded on family lines, and " the beys . . . in most cases came out victorious ".[1] In the Caucasus the *kulaks* joined hands with " former beys " and members of the gentry, and both physical violence and bribes in the form of loans of produce or stock were used to drive the poor peasants to support them.[2] Siberia, where population was relatively sparse and many large holdings survived, seems to have been the paradise of the politically minded *kulak* ; an outside observer reported in 1926 that " the Soviets in Siberia are even today thought to be too dependent on village psychology, and therefore on the strong peasants, to be fully accepted by the party ", and that agents of the party and the government " incur the particular hatred of the threatened peasants, and are frequently enough exposed not only to beatings, but to the danger of being murdered ".[3]

Vigorous propaganda was once more conducted to secure a large vote. Early in November 1925, when the new elections were about to begin, a firm warning was issued over the signature of Kalinin that any widespread failure to vote would entail another cancellation of the elections.[4] When Molotov drew up an interim balance-sheet of the campaign at the fourteenth party congress six weeks later, he cautiously claimed that " this revitalization of the Soviets has begun, or here and there, truth to tell, is only just beginning ". The proportion of electors voting had risen in the recent elections to 45 per cent — a 50 per cent advance on the previous year, and a healthy sign of interest among the " non-party masses ".[5] When the final figures of the elections of the winter of 1925–1926 were complete, they showed that in the RSFSR 47·3 of eligible electors had voted as against 41·1 per cent in 1924–1925. Whereas in the earlier year the percentage had fallen below 35 in 27·5 per cent of all provinces, regions and

[1] *Voprosy Istorii*, No. 10, 1946, pp. 8-9.
[2] *Leningradskaya Pravda*, December 13, 15, 1925, quoting the Tiflis newspaper *Zarya Vostoka*.
[3] G. Cleinow, *Neu-Siberien* (1928), pp. 402-403.
[4] *Izvestiya*, November 8, 1925.
[5] *XIV S"ezd Vsesoyuznoi Kommunisticheskoi Partii (B)* (1926), p. 65.

autonomous republics of the RSFSR, in 1925–1926 not one had
failed to attain this minimum level.[1] The other republics registered
still higher proportions : the Ukraine, 54 per cent (against 46·6
per cent in 1924–1925) ; White Russia, 46·5 per cent ; Armenia,
47·9 per cent ; Georgia, 51·3 per cent ; Azerbaijan, 60·2 per
cent ; Uzbekistan, 45·7 per cent ; Turkmenistan, 52 per cent.[2]
Whether the proportion of communists elected had continued to
decline is uncertain. Molotov in his interim report of December
1925 claimed that it had, but arrived at this conclusion by lumping
together the results of recent elections with those of the re-
elections in the spring of 1925.[3] According to later figures, the
proportion of communists elected, after its sharp fall in 1924–
1925, rose again slightly in the elections of 1925–1926.[4] This
would have accorded with the new turn in party policy which,
from this time onward, began to react sharply against the appeasement of the well-to-do peasant practised in 1925.

It may, however, be erroneous to infer that this new turn of
policy was sufficiently defined to exercise any serious influence on
the Soviet elections of 1925–1926. Molotov in his report spoke
again openly of increasing class differentiation in the countryside,
of the strengthening of " the *kulak* offensive ", and of the difficulty
of organizing the poor peasant.[5] Most contemporary evidence suggests that, whatever the other achievements of the revitalization of
the Soviets, it had brought an accretion of the influence and self-
assurance of the well-to-do peasant. An optimistic report from
the Kuban district stated that there the *kulak* had been less active
in the elections of January and February 1926, the poor peasant
better organized, and the middle peasant less inclined to work
hand-in-glove with the *kulak*.[6] But this, if true, appears to have
been exceptional. Bukharin, in January 1926, declared that the
kulak had " crept " into the Soviets, though only because " the
middle peasant and perhaps also the poor peasant voted for

[1] *Perevybory v Sovety RSFSR v 1925–1926 godu* (1926), i, 10-11.

[2] *Sovetskoe Stroitel'stvo*, No. 1, August 1926, p. 12 ; the relatively high
percentage for some of the more backward republics may be regarded with
scepticism, especially as it is doubtful whether full lists of electors can really
have existed there.

[3] *XIV S"ezd Vsesoyuznoi Kommunisticheskoi Partii (B)* (1926), pp. 65-66.

[4] *Sovetskoe Stroitel'stvo*, No. 1, August 1926, p. 16.

[5] *XIV S"ezd Vsesoyuznoi Kommunisticheskoi Partii (B)* (1926), p. 67.

[6] *Bol'shevik*, No. 7-8, April 30, 1926, pp. 57-60.

him " ; [1] and a little later he added that the *kulak* was following
one of two lines, either " winning himself a place in the Soviets ",
or, if he was foiled there, " going into the cooperatives " in order
" to seize such organizational ' commanding heights ' as exist in
the countryside ".[2] A later commentator recorded that, in the
elections of 1925–1926, " hostile class elements " penetrated the
Soviets, and that *kulaks* even sat in the election committees.[3]
The ambiguous situation was reflected in a contemporary party
report which, after asserting that " the confusion of mind of rural
communists is being overcome ", went on to admit " that by
these very measures dissension is being sown in the countryside,
and that the *kulak* may by way of counterweight create his own
following, which will at the elections take power into its hands ".[4]
The elections of 1925–1926 showed that much had been done to
revitalize the Soviets by making elections partially free and by
bringing electors to the vote, but that this had been achieved at
the cost of placing an instrument of potential power in the hands
of the well-to-do peasant, who might now be in a position to
translate into political terms the economic consequences of " the
wager on the *kulak* ".

A minor consequence of the campaign to revitalize the Soviets
was to stimulate a reaction against the policy of " enlargement "
of rural districts and villages.[5] While this process was at its
height, the twelfth party congress in April 1923 in its resolution
on regionalization issued a guarded warning that the enlargement
of rural districts should be carried out " with the greatest caution
and with full regard for the interests of the broad masses of the
peasant population ".[6] Not much notice was taken of this *caveat*.
The greater remoteness of the rural district centre from the more
distant parts of an enlarged area could not fail to affect the

[1] N. Bukharin, *Doklad na XXIII Chrezvychainoi Leningradskoi Gubernskoi Konferentsii VKP(B)* (1926), p. 29.
[2] *VII S"ezd Vsesoyuznogo Leninskogo Kommunisticheskogo Soyuza Molodezhi* (1926), p. 254.
[3] *XV Let Sovetskogo Stroitel'stva*, ed. E. Pashukanis (1932), pp. 436, 459.
[4] *Izvestiya Tsentral'nogo Komiteta Vsesoyuznoi Kommunisticheskoi Partii (B)*, No. 2 (123), January 25, 1926, p. 2.   [5] See pp. 295–298 above.
[6] *VKP(B) v Rezolyutsiyakh* (1941), i, 498 ; for this resolution see p. 280 above.

participation of the population in district affairs. A complaint that
the duration of district congresses of Soviets had been cut down
to four or five hours, which gave no time for serious discussion,
provoked the retort that peasant delegates to a lengthy congress
in a distant place would have to be lodged and fed — for which
no official funds were available.[1] One consequence of the enlargement of districts was that the proportion of peasants in district
executive committees declined, since fewer of them could afford
the time, or provide the transport, to travel to the district centre.
In the province of Tula where concentration had been extreme,
56 districts replacing 229 old rural districts, the proportion of
peasants in the executive committees fell from 80·9 per cent to
54·8 per cent ; the proportion of party members had at the same
time increased from 38·6 to 89·3 per cent.[2] The district executive
committees had doubtless become more efficient ; but they had
at the same time become less representative of the peasant outlook, and more obviously dominated by party or official nominees,
being sometimes sarcastically referred to as " rural district
Sovnarkoms ".[3] This was the very opposite of the result desired
from the revitalization of the Soviets.

The same issue presented itself in a more serious form when
the policy of enlargement was extended to the villages. A critic
discovered in the whole process a tendency " not to bring the
village Soviets and the Soviets in general nearer to the population,
but on the contrary to draw the lower Soviet organs nearer to
the higher ones, so that they could be more easily ordered
about " ;[4] and the desire of the higher authorities to have a more
manageable number of larger local units to deal with was certainly
a conscious or unconscious factor. This was an aspect of the
clash between centralized efficiency and decentralized representation which was inherent in the issue of the revitalization of the
Soviets. When the rural district was swallowed up in the larger
district, the unit next below it — the village Soviet — inevitably
acquired greater importance. The village came in some sense to

[1] *Soveshchanie po Voprosam Sovetskogo Stroitel'stva 1925 g. : Aprel'* (1925),
pp. 12-13, 37.

[2] *Vlast' Sovetov*, No. 8, November 1924, p. 27 ; this feature is discussed in
Yu. Larin, *Rost Krest'yanskoi Obshchestvennosti* (1925), pp. 152-153.

[3] *Sovetskoe Stroitel'stvo*, No. 1, August 1926, p. 9.

[4] *Sovetskoe Stroitel'stvo : Sbornik*, iv-v (1926), 94.

replace the old rural district in the administrative hierarchy : one case was cited in which a rural district had simply been re-classified as a village.[1] But, whatever the motives of the enlarge-ment of the village Soviets and the consequent reduction in their number, the consequences for the rural population were not in doubt. " With our enormous distances, lack of roads and dispersal of inhabited points, with a population of which almost one-half have no horse ", the enlargement and increased remoteness of the lowest unit of administration was " inexpedient from the stand-point of the communications of the population with the village Soviet ".[2] The conference of 1925 on the revitalization of the Soviets at its April session passed a resolution declaring that the enlargement of village Soviets was contrary to the provision of the statute of October 1924 allowing populations of 300 and upwards to constitute village Soviets, and drawing attention to its " negative results ". Even the enlargement of rural districts, while it was admitted to have brought about " a certain improve-ment in the rural district Soviet apparatus ", had the drawback of " greater distance of the villages from the rural district centre ", and should be carried out " with all necessary caution and without haste ".[3]

By this time the dangers and drawbacks of the enlargement of the village Soviet had become sufficiently apparent to put an end to the process. But to reverse what had already been done was far more difficult. The recommendation of the conference on this point lacked formal authority, and was carried out by the provincial authorities, who seem to have had the decisive voice, " reluctantly and sparingly ".[4] It was not till a year later, in April 1926, that the official journal of the Narkomvnudel of the RSFSR came out with a strong declaration that a process of " de-enlarge-ment " of village Soviets was necessary ; and later in the month a decree to this effect issued from the presidium of the TsIK of the RSFSR, though with reservations about the financial practicability of the proposal.[5] But the real remedy was found in another and quite different direction.

---

[1] *Ibid.* iv-v, 131.   [2] *Ibid.* iv-v, 149.
[3] *Soveshchanie po Voprosam Sovetskogo Stroitel'stva 1925 g. : Aprel'* (1925), pp. 180-182.   [4] *Sovetskoe Stroitel'stvo : Sbornik,* iv-v (1926), 151.
[5] *Vlast' Sovetov,* No. 14, April 4, 1926, pp. 7-8 ; No. 21, May 23, 1926, pp. 1-2.

The enlargement of the village Soviet had the unexpected result of increasing the importance of the traditional *skhod*, which continued to operate in the smaller area of the old village.[1] When the first steps were taken to restore the village Soviets after the disruption of the civil war, not much notice was taken of the *skhod* by party or state officials, who considered these primitive gatherings " not worthy of attention ".[2] In practice, while the Soviet institutions proved difficult to establish, it was precisely the traditional character of the *skhod* which accounted for its vitality.

> In the countryside [said one observer] the *skhod* still exists today as it has existed, very likely, since the days of the tribal moot, and, very likely, there are to this day still church bells by which, as formerly in ancient Russia, people are summoned to the *skhod*.[3]

The inclination of the peasant to treat the *skhod* as the main vehicle of local self-government could only be strengthened by the policy of diminishing the number of village Soviets. " In the localities ", wrote a subsequent commentator, " the idea became rooted that the highest authority in the village was not the village Soviet, but the village *skhod*." [4] The *skhod* undertook necessary local work such as the repair of roads, and sometimes imposed fines on those who refused to participate. This was probably illegal (unless, indeed, the *skhod* was acting in the name of the *mir* in respect of land vested in it) ; but nobody objected.[5] The *skhod* usefully filled a gap left by the failure of the Soviet system to work at the lowest level.

The result of these developments, as the conference diagnosed it at the beginning of 1925, was transparently clear. Party members had " tried to stand aside from the *skhod* " ; the *skhod* had fallen into the orbit, not of the Soviets, but of " our enemy the *kulak* ".[6] The remedy was not to ignore the *skhod*, but to bring it into the Soviet system. It was necessary, said Kaganovich

[1] For the *skhod* see p. 307 , note 4 above.
[2] *Vlast' Sovetov*, No. 6, February 7, 1926, p. 13.
[3] *Soveshchanie po Voprosam Sovetskogo Stroitel'stva 1925 g.* : *Yanvar'* (1925), p. 153.   [4] *Sovetskoe Stroitel'stvo*, No. 5, December 1926, p. 44.
[5] *Vlast' Sovetov*, No. 52, December 27, 1925, p. 20.
[6] *Soveshchanie po Voprosam Sovetskogo Stroitel'stva 1925 g.* : *Yanvar'* (1925), pp. 85, 153.

at the April session of the conference, " that the village Soviet should make it its task to direct the *skhod*, that every peasant should be trained in the *skhod* to participate in local organs of government, and to participate in the administration of the state as a whole ". Thus exhorted, the conference included in its main resolution on the work of the Soviets a chapter " on the improvement of the work of the *skhody* ". The resolution maintained the formal sovereignty of the *skhod* by reiterating the doctrine, already embodied in the statute of village Soviets, that " the village Soviet as the organ elected by the population of the village is bound to render an account of its work at the general assemblies (*skhody*) ". But the unmistakable effect of the operative clauses was to establish the authority of the village Soviet over the *skhod*. The village Soviet was to be responsible for summoning the *skhod* not less than once a month, for preparing its agenda and for directing the proceedings. The Soviet was to be " the one directing organ of government in the countryside ".[1] But, while the conference had spoken clearly enough, much else that seemed more urgent had to be done. It was not till nearly two years later that a decree was issued giving effect to this recommendation.[2] The formal incorporation of the *skhod* into the Soviet system was the logical culmination of a long process. When the village Soviet became an organized and established institution with an office and a paid staff, taking its orders from some higher authority, removed both by distance and by its bureaucratic character from the daily life of the peasant, the need was felt for a smaller, more informal, more local body, through which the peasant could express himself and which he could regard as his own. This need was filled by the *skhod*. What had happened was that institutions at each level had acquired increased size and importance and moved up in the hierarchical scale. As the rural district became, in Kaganovich's words, " almost a little

---

[1] *Id.* : *Aprel'* (1925), pp. 12, 172-173.

[2] *Sobranie Zakonov, 1927*, No. 51, art. 333. The decree placed on the village Soviet, as the recommendation had failed to do, the responsibility for carrying out decisions of the *skhod*, which was thus deprived of executive functions ; the village Soviet could appeal to the district executive committee against decisions of the *skhod*. The *skhod* was now for the first time clearly recognized as a public body — a " general assembly of citizens " — and distinguished from the " general assembly of members of the land-holding association ".

county ",[1] as the village Soviet approached, both in size and in
the nature of its functions, the initial design of the rural district
executive committee, so the *skhod* rose up from below to assume
the initial form of a village Soviet. It was paradoxical that the
institution in the countryside which most closely conformed to
the original Bolshevik conception of a Soviet should have been
one which did not bear the name.

(d) The City Soviets

The city Soviets [2] were less conspicuous than the rural Soviets
in the revitalization campaign, partly because less attention was
paid to them in a period when party policy was concentrated on
the countryside, and partly because they were overshadowed both
by the more important party organizations and by the provincial
or county Soviet organs which had their headquarters in the city ;
they were thus politically less significant than the rural Soviets,
which were often the sole point of contact between the authorities
and the local population.   In January 1922 TsIK had promulgated, simultaneously with the statutes for county and rural
district Soviet organs, and for village Soviets, a statute for city
Soviets of the RSFSR.[3]   The statute retained enough of the
traditional language of the revolution to describe the city Soviet
as " the highest organ of power within the city limits ". But it
defined the functions of the Soviet in terms too broad to have any
precise meaning, and it contained no provision for independent
executive organs to make it an effective instrument of government.   The executive committees, which the city Soviets, like
other Soviets, had originally been expected to form, were still-
born or withered away in the civil war.   In cities which were
capitals of provinces or counties, i.e. in all cities of any size,
no attempt was made to revive them.   The city Soviet was
" directly responsible to the corresponding provincial and county

---

[1] *Soveshchanie po Voprosam Sovetskogo Stroitel'stva 1925 g. : Aprel'* (1925),
p. 12.
[2] The translation is conventional ; " cities " included all kinds of conurba-
tion from great cities like Moscow and Leningrad to small and remote county
towns.
[3] *Sobranie Uzakonenii, 1922*, No. 10, art. 90 ; for the other statutes see
p. 305 above.

congresses of Soviets and to executive committees of higher rank ". In practice the executive committee of the provincial or county congress of Soviets acted as the executive organ of the city Soviet ; the departments which managed municipal enterprises, finance, education, health and administrative services were common to the province or county and to the city,[1] and were responsible to the provincial or county executive committee, which appears in all cases to have had the final word. One important new provision was included in the decree. The city Soviet could form " sections ", or committees, of its members to supervise particular departments of local government. The creation of " sections " was optional, not obligatory. They had no executive powers ; and their subordinate status was marked by the fact that the head of the department presided over the corresponding section of the Soviet. But they represented a first serious attempt to bring the members of the Soviet into contact with current administration.

Evidence on what happened to the city Soviets between 1922 and 1924 is sparse. The pioneer Soviets in the organization of " sections " are said to have been " Moscow and Leningrad and Nizhny-Novgorod and, up to a certain point, Ekaterinoslav and a number of other cities ".[2] The Kazan city Soviet was a particularly flourishing institution, with its members actively participating in the sections. But here no provincial executive committee existed, the city Soviet had an independent presidium, and its president had direct access to the Sovnarkom of the Tatar autonomous republic.[3] Kamenev claimed that five or six thousand party and non-party workers were taking part in the sections of the Moscow Soviet in December 1924.[4] If, however, a few of the leading city Soviets were gradually developing into effective organs of local government, complaints were frequently heard of shortcomings and irregularities in the Soviet machinery of cities

[1] This was true even of Moscow, where 95 per cent of the business of the departments of the Moscow provincial executive committee is said to have been devoted to city affairs (*Soveshchanie po Voprosam Sovetskogo Stroitel'stva 1925 g. : Yanvar'* (1925), p. 92, cf. *ibid.* pp. 149, 153). In Moscow and Leningrad the city was so large that the province became an adjunct of the city ; elsewhere the opposite generally happened.

[2] *Id. : Aprel'* (1925), p. 132.   [3] *Ibid.* p. 145.

[4] L. Kamenev, *Stat'i i Rechi*, xi (1929), 271-272 ; a figure of 5000 was cited in *Soveshchanie po Voprosam Sovetskogo Stroitel'stva 1925 g. : Yanvar'* (1925), p. 91.

of secondary importance.[1] Even in the most active Soviets, more time was spent in listening to reports or in sessions of a ceremonial character than in the discussion of current issues ; and the sections, where they existed, seldom or never dared to criticize the work of the departments.[2]

The statute of January 1922, while citing the franchise disqualification article of the constitution, laid down no special rules for elections to city Soviets. But an instruction of the electoral commission of the Moscow Soviet for the elections of 1922 shows how much of the initial professional basis of the Soviet still survived :

> Elections take place on the basis of factories, workshops and railway-shops, of enterprises in the city, of trade unions, and of Red Army and militia units, and also at special assemblies convened by district electoral commissions.[3]

Some city Soviets introduced a discriminatory franchise in imitation of the discrimination between workers and peasants in the original constitution of the RSFSR : [4] examples are quoted of elections to city Soviets conducted on the basis of one deputy for every 50 organized workers and for every 200 of the unorganized population, or of one deputy for every 100 workers or Red Army men and for every 300 officials or other qualified voters.[5] Voters in elections to city Soviets were at this time confined mainly to organized workers. Other strata of urban population, even if not legally disqualified, were politically aloof.[6] In 1923 32 per cent of those qualified to vote voted in elections to city Soviets in the

---

[1] A number of complaints are quoted from the Soviet press in *Das Recht Sowjetrusslands*, ed. A. Maklezow (1925), p. 110 ; for a reference to the " ' dying away ' of the city Soviets " see *Soveshchanie po Voprosam Sovetskogo Stroitel'stva 1925 g. : Yanvar'* (1925), p. 149.   [2] *Id. : Aprel'* (1925), pp. 127-128.

[3] *Sovetskoe Stroitel'stvo : Sbornik*, i (1925), 136.

[4] See *The Bolshevik Revolution, 1917-1923*, Vol. 1, pp. 143-144.

[5] *Sovetskoe Stroitel'stvo : Sbornik*, i (1925), 138-139 ; the only republic where a discriminatory franchise in local elections was prescribed by decree was the Ukraine (*Zbir Zakoniv i Rosporyadzhen', 1921*, No. 7, art. 202 ; No. 13, art. 355 ; No. 22, art. 620).

[6] A Ukrainian decree of July 1921 on city Soviets excluded from the franchise persons " not being, for whatever reason, members of trade unions " (*Zbir Zakoniv i Rosporyadzhen', 1921*, No. 13, art. 355). As late as 1924 in elections to the Moscow and other large city Soviets, workers and officials voted, and artisans and nepmen stayed away (Yu. Larin, *Rost Krest'yanskoi Obshchestvennosti* (1925), p. 13).

USSR and 38 per cent in the RSFSR.[1] In 1924–1925 the proportion for the RSFSR rose to 40·5 per cent, though this was un-
evenly spread ; the proportion was regularly higher in the larger
than in the smaller cities, and in no less than 125 of the latter
(41 per cent of the total number of " cities ") the percentage fell
below 35.[2] If these figures were somewhat lower than the corresponding figures for the rural Soviets,[3] the explanation was not
far to seek. In Nizhny-Novgorod, where the high proportion of
43 per cent of all eligible electors voted in the elections for the
city Soviet in 1924, the percentage sank to 32 in the non-factory
districts of the city ; and of those voting 62 per cent were members
of trade unions.[4] In the same year, of all Red Army men qualified
to vote in elections to city Soviets, 72 per cent actually voted, and
of trade unionists, 39 per cent ; of other qualified electors only
16 per cent used their votes, and in many cities the proportion of
" other " voters was negligible.[5] In elections to the city Soviets
of the Tatar autonomous republic, outside Kazan, nobody except
trade unionists voted.[6] Of deputies elected to city Soviets in the
RSFSR in 1922 and 1923, more than 69 per cent were party
members, candidates or members of the Komsomol [7] — a striking
contrast to the insignificant percentage of communists in village
Soviets.

The decision of the presidium of TsIK of December 19,
1924, setting up the conference " on questions of Soviet construction " [8] included among its tasks the improvement of the
activity of the city Soviets ; and these received intermittent
attention at both January and April sessions of the conference.
The January resolution on the holding of re-elections where less
than 35 per cent of the electorate had voted applied to city as well
as to rural Soviets. But re-elections were apparently not held in
the cities. More significant was the recommendation of the conference that, in addition to elections to the city Soviets organized

[1] Sovetskoe Stroitel'stvo : Sbornik, i (1925), 113 ; L. Kaganovich, Partiya
i Sovety (1928), p. 86.
[2] Perevybory v Sovety RSFSR v 1925–1926 godu (1926), i, 47-48.
[3] See pp. 333-334 above.
[4] Soveshchanie po Voprosam Sovetskogo Stroitel'stva 1925 g. : Yanvar'
(1925), p. 33.   [5] Id. : Aprel' (1925), p. 129.   [6] Ibid. p. 145.
[7] Perevybory v Sovety RSFSR v 1925–1926 godu (1926), i, 66.
[8] See p. 325 above.

on the factory and trade union basis, elections should be organized
on the basis of territorial units "for citizens not employed in
enterprises and not organized in trade unions, such as artisans,
housewives, cab-drivers etc." [1] An instruction of the party central
committee of January 27, 1925,[2] called for a special effort in the
cities to draw the "so-called unorganized population" of the
cities into the Soviets ; this was the counterpart of the appeal to
non-party peasants in the countryside. In April 1925 the conference heard a formal report on city Soviets, mainly devoted to the
defects in their working, and recommended a new draft statute
to replace the statute of January 1922. The draft statute made
the sections a normal part of the organization of the city Soviet,
and specifically gave the Soviet authority to decide on differences
of opinion between the presidium and the sections, thus at one
and the same time enhancing the power of the Soviet itself and
raising the status of the sections. But a complete separation of the
authority of the city Soviet from that of the Soviet of the province
or county in which the city was situated was felt to entail the
danger of "dual power". The executive committee of the province or county continued to have responsibility for city administration, and was to render an account of its work twice a year to
the city Soviet.[3] This recommendation, like the other recommendations of the conference, received the endorsement of the
third Union Congress of Soviets in May 1925.[4] But, with attention
riveted on the struggle within the party and on issues of agrarian
policy, the reform of the city Soviets had no compelling urgency ;
as Kamenev complacently pointed out to the Moscow Soviet, it
was the rural Soviets which most needed to be "revitalized".[5]
It was not till October 1925 that a new statute, based on the
recommendations of the conference, was approved and promulgated by the TsIK of the RSFSR, a year after the corresponding
statute of the rural Soviets. Under the new statute all urban

[1] *Soveshchanie po Voprosam Sovetskogo Stroitel'stva 1925 g. : Yanvar'*
(1925), p. 227.
[2] *Izvestiya Tsentral'nogo Komiteta Rossiiskoi Kommunisticheskoi Partii (Bol'-
shevikov)*, No. 6 (81), February 9, 1925, p. 2.
[3] For the report see *Soveshchanie po Voprosam Sovetskogo Stroitel'stva 1925
g. : Aprel'* (1925), pp. 125-135 (cf. also p. 17) ; for the resolution and draft
statute see *ibid.* pp. 186-196.   [4] See p. 339 above.
[5] L. Kamenev, *Stat'i i Rechi,* xii (1926), 273.

settlements having upwards of 10,000 inhabitants or 2000 electors were entitled to form city Soviets ; cities of more than 50,000 inhabitants were divided into districts (*raions*) with district Soviets. All workers' settlements had factory Soviets irrespective of numbers. City and factory Soviets, like rural Soviets, were elected annually, and were expected to meet twice a month.[1] A city Soviet formed a presidium of not more than 11 (this figure might be exceeded by the Moscow and Leningrad city Soviets), which exercised control over the " city economy " and certain special city services ; apart from these, ultimate control still rested with the provincial executive committee, and the city Soviets still had no independent budget.

In the cities, as in the countryside, the success of the campaign for the revitalization of the Soviets was measured by the increased number of those voting in the elections, and by the increased participation of non-party voters and delegates. The proportion of electors voting in elections for city Soviets in the RSFSR rose from 40·5 per cent in 1924–1925 to 52 per cent in 1925–1926 ; and a table was issued showing, in percentages, the social status of those elected to the city Soviets :[2]

	1922	*1923*	*1924–1925*	*1925–1926*
Workers	44·0	36·6	46·0	38·8
Employees	40·9	49·9	35·7	39·2
Red Army	7·7	7·4	5·1	4·8
Others	7·4	6·1	13·2	17·2

These returns presented two interesting features. The first was the rapid rise in the percentage of " employees " in the first years of NEP, checked in 1924 partly by the campaign for the revitalization of the Soviets, and partly by the Lenin enrolment of workers in the party. The second feature was the rapid increase in " other " delegates, which was a direct result of the revitalization campaign, reflecting the appeal to the non-party and non-proletarian elements of the population to participate in the

[1] *Sobranie Uzakonenii, 1925*, No. 91, art. 662.
[2] L. Kaganovich, *Partiya i Sovety* (1928), pp. 86, 87 ; according to *Perevybory v Sovety RSFSR v 1925–1926 godu* (1926), i, 47-48, the proportion voting in elections to city Soviets of the RSFSR in 1925–1926 was 48·7 per cent, and 14 cities (as against 125 in 1924–1925) still failed to reach 35 per cent.

elections. On the other hand, the proportion of those disfranchised on grounds of social and economic status was, not
unnaturally, higher in the cities than in the countryside, reaching
a percentage of 8·2 in 1923 and 5·3 in 1924 ; the larger the city
the higher the proportion of those disqualified. Some 75 per cent
of ˊthose excluded were said to be merchants or employers of
hired labour.[1] The proportion of communists among those
elected to city Soviets fell from the high point of 69 per cent in
1923 to 57 per cent in 1924–1925 and 45·5 per cent in 1925–1926.[2]

(e) The Balance-Sheet

In the summer of 1926, when the elections for 1925–1926
were at length complete, an attempt was made to draw up a
balance-sheet of the whole campaign. A discouraging report was
given to the Orgburo of the results of the mobilization of 6000
party and Komsomol workers for work in the countryside, which
fully confirmed the earlier unfavourable account. The start of the
work had been delayed by caution or obstruction, and had been
made only after the fourteenth party congress in December.
The report condemned the error of treating the poor peasants
as constituting a special branch of party work and of attempting
to organize them as a separate entity ; conferences of poor
peasants had been summoned in secret as if they were conspirators,
middle peasants had been excluded. What was required was to
organize the poor peasants into the Soviets, the cooperatives, the
krestkomy, etc. But the positive directives were obscure, and
were not made any plainer by a speech of Molotov and a resolution
of the Orgburo.[3] Party policy had moved in the direction of the
poor peasant and away from the kulak, but was still indecisive
and ambivalent.

The same qualities were apparent in a resolution adopted, on
a report by Molotov, by the joint session of the party central
committee and central control commission in July 1926.[4] This

[1] Sovetskoe Stroitel'stvo : Sbornik, i (1925), 110.
[2] Perevybory v Sovety RSFSR v 1925–1926 godu (1926), i, 66.
[3] Izvestiya Tsentral'nogo Komiteta Vsesoyuznoi Kommunisticheskoi Partii (B),
No. 23 (144), June 14, 1926, p. 1 ; No. 26 (147), June 30, 1926, p. 3 ; No. 29-30
(150-151), July 26, 1926, pp. 1-2. For the earlier account see p. 342 above.
[4] VKP(B) v Rezolyutsiyakh (1941), ii, 103-111 ; the report was printed in
Pravda, August 20, 1926.

noted a gratifying rise in the proportion of electors voting in the countryside, which in the RSFSR had now reached 47 per cent. " New strata of workers and especially new strata of peasantry, hand-workers, employees, village intelligentsia (teachers), etc." had been drawn into " the work of Soviet construction ". The *kulaks* had been compelled to abandon " the open defence of their class interests and their anti-Soviet policy ", and were concealing their machinations under the guise of " the interests of the poor peasantry " and " revolutionary legality ". The resolution also noted increased participation in elections to city Soviets in the RSFSR by " proletarian strata not organized in the trade unions (wives of workers, unemployed, workers not belonging to trade unions etc.), and toilers of the petty bourgeois strata (small craftsmen, artisans etc.) ", and estimated the percentage of participation among these groups at 37 for 1925–1926 as against 24 for 1924–1925. On the other hand, the goal of the " revitalization of the Soviets " was defined, in harsher terms than had hitherto been used, as being " finally to explode the remains of the influence of bourgeois elements (nepmen, *kulaks* and bourgeois intelligentsia) on the toiling masses ". The resolution sharply condemned both " deviations which occurred in the drawing up of electoral instructions ", and the " unduly broad application " of these instructions, in the matter of the franchise : these errors had led to an unwarranted " curtailment of the number of persons deprived of electoral rights, at a time when a certain increase of bourgeois elements is occurring both in the town and in the country ".[1] The " renunciation of methods of dictation and nomination in regard to the Soviets ", though necessary and praiseworthy, had sometimes led to the opposite extreme of " renunciation of the leadership of the party, and adoption of a 'tail-endist'[2] interpretation of its tasks in the electoral campaign ". But the two-sided obligation imposed on the party — to exercise

[1] Two successive issues of the party journal *Bol'shevik*, No. 13, July 15, 1926, pp. 23-44, No. 14, July 30, 1926, pp. 13-30, carried a long article attacking the " wholesale extension of electoral rights to new strata of the population which have hitherto not enjoyed them " ; according to the opposition platform of October 1927, " the penetration of the Soviets by the lower *kulak* and ' semi-*kulak* ' elements and the city bourgeoisie, which began in 1925 ", was " partially stopped by the attacks of the opposition " (L. Trotsky, *The Real Situation in Russia* (n.d. [1928]), p. 97).

[2] For this heresy see *The Bolshevik Revolution, 1917–1923*, Vol. I, p. 18.

effective leadership in Soviet affairs and Soviet elections without incurring the charges of " dictation " and " nomination ", and to broaden the social basis of the Soviet power without sacrificing the claim of the party to exclusive leadership and to an unchallenged right of final decision — was easier to define than to discharge. The resolution wound up with appeals to increase the participation of non-party workers and peasants and to continue and intensify " the truly Leninist policy of the revitalization of the Soviets ".

A novel feature of the resolution was the introduction of a paragraph devoted to the need for new electoral procedures in " nomadic and semi-nomadic districts " and for work in the autonomous republics and regions where " the task of creating and strengthening the Soviets as real organs of the Soviet power" still, " in many cases ", lay ahead. In most of these outlying regions, where primitive native peoples were interspersed with more or less numerous Russian settlers, the creation of a Soviet machinery had scarcely begun, and authority, both formal and real, remained with the organs of the central administration of the region. In the Kalmyk autonomous SSR there were, in 1925, except in one district, no village Soviets ; the lowest organ was the rural district executive committee.[1] According to a report of the same year from the Bashkir autonomous SSR, " village Soviets do not exist ", though there were unorganized village meetings ; elsewhere in Bashkiria Soviets were said to have fallen under the control of " worthless individuals who won popularity by the dishonest manipulation of tax assessments, insurance claims etc." [2] In Uzbekistan and in the Buryat-Mongol republic " many village Soviets never meet after the day of the elections ". In Kazakhstan the president of the district executive committee or the chief of the militia ruled single-handed.[3] In the parts of the republic of Bokhara taken over by Turkmenistan no Soviets had hitherto existed, and they were first created in 1925.[4] In Kirgizia, there was a movement for " tribal Soviets " or " Soviets without communists ", which had no class basis and became the tool of beys

---

[1] T. Borisov, *Kalmykiya* (1926), p. 62.
[2] *Vserossiiskii Tsentral'nyi Ispolnitel'nyi Komitet XII Sozyva : Vtoraya Sessiya* (1925), pp. 89-90.
[3] *Bol'shevik*, No. 21-22, November 30, 1925, p. 54.
[4] *Vlast' Sovetov*, No. 10, March 7, 1926, pp. 9-10.

and manaps.[1] In the autonomous region of the Pamirs no Soviet machinery was set up till 1927.[2] At the fifteenth party congress in that year Molotov confessed that " there is no single country-side ", and that " in connexion with a number of areas, especially of the Soviet east, we have to speak not of the revitalization of Soviets, but of the creation of Soviets ".[3]

The specific campaign for the revitalization of the Soviets ended in the summer of 1926 and was not subsequently renewed. But the policies then inaugurated were continued, and extended to regions where they had not hitherto been applied. The campaign indubitably coincided with a growth of political self-consciousness in the countryside : how far this was due to the increased material well-being of the NEP years, how far to the sharpness of the issues presented by the new " differentiation " between strata of the peasantry, and how far to the campaign itself, is a matter of speculation. Nor can it be doubted that the Soviets themselves became more efficient, and that Soviets were created where they had not hitherto existed. Elections were regularly held, and voters voted on lists which had been some-how settled in advance by a process of compromise between nomination and negotiation. Soviets, executive committees and congresses of Soviets met at intervals : current business was transacted by paid secretaries and by presidiums. The machine worked. It worked not only more efficiently but more smoothly. Explanation and persuasion played a larger rôle, dictation and compulsion a smaller one, than in the earlier years. To this extent the revitalization of the Soviets implied some progress towards government by consent of the governed.

Yet it is also clear that in the clash between the two original aspects of the Soviet — its function as a representative body of the sovereign people and its function as an organ of local government carrying out the behests of a central authority — the dice were more and more heavily loaded as time went on in favour of the second. This was due in large part to the increasing authority and efficiency of the central government, especially with the development of planning and the extension of regionalization.

---

[1] *Bol'shevik*, No. 13, July 15, 1926, pp. 73-75.

[2] *Revolyutsiya v Srednei Azii*, ii (Tashkent, 1929), 193.

[3] *XV S"ezd Vsesoyuznoi Kommunisticheskoi Partii (B)* (1928), p. 1047.

The Soviet Union was not the only country where the growing intervention of the government in economic and social policy characteristic of the modern world strengthened the rôle of the central power ; and in territories so vast, and with populations so disparate, as those of the Soviet Union some degree of imposed uniformity and centralization was probably a condition of survival. But the progressive encroachment of the centre was also due in part to the weakness of the representative principle in the Russian political tradition. The original and easily comprehensible concept of a Soviet as a group of workers or peasants meeting together to order their affairs in common had of necessity been replaced by the concept of a Soviet of delegates chosen by the vote of a majority to speak in the name of the community ; and this no longer had the same appeal or evoked the same faith. The aroma of unreality which clings to Soviet representative institutions was the product of apathy from below as well as of dictation from above.

When, therefore, the Bolshevik leaders spoke of revitalizing the Soviets, they had in mind two different and perhaps incompatible processes. The first was to create throughout the country an efficient machine of local government to which decisions of a central authority could be handed down for punctual execution ; over a large part of the Soviet Union the middle and later nineteen-twenties saw substantial progress towards this end. The second purpose was to woo the loyalty of the masses, in town and country, by enlisting the direct or indirect support of as large a proportion as possible of the population in the conduct of government, and by making them feel that the Soviets in some sense represented their views and their interests. This purpose was very imperfectly fulfilled. A régime which, while pursuing long-term aims that had a universal and popular appeal, was compelled by the dilemma of its seizure of power in a backward country to pursue these aims by way of short-term policies that placed an enormous burden on the masses of workers and peasants, could not be popular. There was no room in Soviet conditions for a slow growth of popular representative institutions and traditions such as had formerly occurred in western Europe ; nor was the time any longer propitious for such a development. The process of " revitalizing the Soviets " was quite different. It was an

attempt by the leaders to bridge from above the gap which traditionally divided government and people ; and, though some forms
of representative institutions borrowed from the west were used
in the process, the operation was essentially one of propaganda
and organization, an effort to create a link by a conscious act of
policy.

> We gradually draw the non-party peasants, i.e. in essence
> the petty bourgeoisie, into the lower levels [said Bukharin],
> while we maintain from above a secure proletarian leadership.
> We re-make the peasants in our manner, draw them into the
> system of our work, teach them to work on new lines, drawing
> them into the process of socialist construction.[1]

It was part of a process of political education, of the endeavour to
create the " new type " of Soviet man.[2]

But at this point yet another contradiction was found to lurk
in the policy of revitalizing the Soviets — a reflexion of the
innate contradiction of the agrarian policy of these years. The
revitalization of the Soviets had begun, or at any rate developed,
as the political counterpart of the economic " wager on the
kulak ", and had had the same implications. It was denounced
by the opposition as a " swamping " of the party by the petty
bourgeoisie, and as " our abdication, a slipping of our state power
from the proletarian track " ;[3] and an authorized party commentator went far to confirm this view when he wrote that " the
widening of the circle of electors in the countryside, by drawing
in the exploiting elements, is accompanied by a simultaneous
narrowing of the participation in political life of the semi-
proletarian and proletarian elements and by a lessening of the influence of the party in the Soviets ".[4] This could not, however,

[1] A. I. Rykov and N. Bukharin, *Partiya i Oppozitsionnyi Blok* (1926), p. 68 ;
the quotation is from a speech of Bukharin of July 28, 1926, to a Leningrad
party meeting.   [2] See Vol. 1, pp. 131-132.
[3] The phrases were attributed to the opposition by Bukharin (A. I. Rykov
and N. Bukharin, *Partiya i Oppozitsionnyi Blok* (1926), pp. 70-71). It is difficult
to find a contemporary opposition statement ; but an unpublished memorandum
of 1927 of the Democratic Centralism group denounced the revitalization of the
Soviets as " the slogan of the extension of petty-bourgeois democracy " and
demanded " a restoration of genuine worker Bolshevik Soviets " (p. 37 of the
memorandum preserved in the Trotsky archives).
[4] *Pravda*, July 8, 1926. The same writer, in an article on the city Soviets
in *Pravda* on the following day, similarly noted that " the widening of the
circle of electors, by drawing in the urban petty bourgeoisie, is accompanied by

remain the ultimate goal. The reaction against "the wager on the *kulak*", which began in the autumn of 1925, equally affected the revitalization policy, and placed the emphasis on the other aspect of its original design — the drawing of the masses of the middle and poor peasantry into the Soviet orbit. In this respect it was an important concomitant of the campaign against illiteracy and the spread of education in the countryside. Its success was limited by chronic shortages of man-power and of material goods. Everywhere in the history of the revolution too much was being attempted with too few resources. Yet, in the period of relaxed tension and growing material prosperity which followed the consolidation of NEP, something was achieved. A form of local administration was established, and spread by slow degrees over the country, which was not only more efficient technically than anything known in the past, but was also accepted in some degree as a point of contact between the masses and the remote and all-powerful central government. This was the ultimate purpose, and the imperfect — but still real — achievement of the " revitalization of the Soviets ".

A constant and characteristic feature of Soviet elections, which was intensified rather than diminished by the policy of revitalization, was the extremely rapid turn-over of delegates at all levels of the Soviet hierarchy. The use of the Soviets to carry out the principle of direct participation by the maximum number of citizens in the work of government was a deeply cherished ideal. The party programme of 1919 had demanded :

(1) The obligatory introduction of every member of the Soviet into some definite work in the administration of the state ;
(2) regular rotation of these tasks so that they may gradually include all branches of administration ;
(3) the gradual drawing of the entire toiling population, down to the last man, into state administration.[1]

Re-election of the same individual merely diminished the number of those who were able to enjoy the experience. In practice, the

---

a certain simultaneous decline in the specific weight of the proletarian sector of the electorate in their broad masses, and by far smaller activity on their part than on the part of new electors from the petty bourgeoisie ". But in the cities — at any rate, in the large cities — the "proletarian sector" was far stronger, and the petty bourgeois element far weaker, than in the countryside. The parallel hardly applied. 　　　[1] *VKP(B) v Rezolyutsiyakh* (1941), i, 286.

incidence of re-election increased with the responsibility of the post. Of those elected presidents of rural district executive committees, only 25·8 per cent in 1924–1925 and 30·1 per cent in 1925–1926 were serving their first term ; in the same years 51·2 per cent and 47 per cent respectively were serving a second term, and the rest had a longer record of service.[1] But, except in such outstanding posts, re-election was the exception rather than the rule. Of all those elected between 1918 and 1927 in the RSFSR to village or city Soviets, to congresses of Soviets or to executive committees, two-thirds sat for a one-year term and were never re-elected.[2] Of those elected to the Moscow city Soviet in 1925, 74 per cent were serving for the first time.[3] The situation in party committees was similar. Of members elected to county, department or city district committees in 1925, only 26·4 per cent had served previously.[4] It is, moreover, significant that party members of Soviet committees were more often re-elected for a second term than non-party members. Of all members of provincial and county executive committees in the RSFSR elected in 1924–1925 and 1925–1926, about 50 per cent were elected for the first time ; the percentage of non-party members elected for the first time was well over 80 in both years.[5] Such continuity as there was in the personnel of Soviet representative organs was assured by the party members.

The initial belief in a rapid turnover of delegates as a desirable means of giving as many as possible of the citizens the experience and privilege of participating in organs of government was both persistent and sincere, though party leaders also became sensitive

---

[1] G. Mikhailov, *Mestnoe Sovetskoe Upravlenie* (1927), p. 429.

[2] L. Kaganovich, *Partiya i Sovety* (1928), pp. 60–61.

[3] *Sovetskoe Stroitel'stvo : Sbornik*, ii–iii (1925), 267.

[4] *Partiinye, Professional'nye i Kooperativnye Organy i Gosapparat* (1926), p. 16. It is more remarkable that excessive mobility should have occurred in the early years even among high party officials. Molotov at the fourteenth party congress in December 1925 complained that of 767 officials of the party central committee 704 had changed their job since the previous congress, and that it was " necessary really to stabilize the technical apparatus of the central committee " (*XIV S"ezd Vsesoyuznoi Kommunisticheskoi Partii (B)* (1926), p. 89) ; this was followed by a party circular denouncing " the mass-scale unplanned shifting round of party members, which is to a significant degree a survival of the times of war communism " (*Izvestiya Tsentral'nogo Komiteta Vsesoyuznoi Kommunisticheskoi Partii (B)*, No. 1 (122), January 18, 1926, p. 3).

[5] *Perevybory v Sovety RSFSR v 1925–1926 godu* (1926), ii, 43.

at a later date to the value of rotation in reducing opportunities
for organized opposition.[1] But, whatever the motive, repeated and
sweeping changes inevitably prevented the accumulation of any
administrative experience in the rank-and-file membership of
Soviet organs, which fell the more inevitably under the control of
party fractions or of presidents and secretaries who were generally
party members — a result due not so much to cunning calculation
as to misunderstanding at all levels of the conditions of the
effective functioning of democratic administration. The same
result probably accrued from the policy of increasing the proportion of peasants and workers among delegates to Soviets and Soviet
congresses. Like the policy of the " Lenin enrolment " in the
party, this seemed a laudable and unexceptionable project. But
it produced in the long run, not a more active and independent,
but a more docile and submissive, body of delegates. While the
efficiency of Soviet administration at all levels certainly increased
in this period, it is not clear that the campaign for the revitalization of the Soviets had any success in making democratic representation more effective, or in increasing the participation of
elected delegates in the proceedings of the Soviets. Nor could
this easily be achieved so long as current views of the function
of representation continued to prevail. When a writer in the
journal of Narkomvnudel suggested triennial instead of annual
elections to Soviets, on the ground that delegates elected for a
single year had no time to gain experience or to prove themselves,
the retort was quickly returned that the proposal ran counter to
the policy of revitalizing the Soviets and drawing into them the
maximum proportion of the population.[2]

It was no less characteristic of the early phase of the Soviet
theory and practice of government that no clear line was drawn
between the functions of elected representatives and of paid
officials. At the outset it seems to have been taken for granted
that the exiguous paper work of village Soviets, and even of rural
district executive committees, could be easily handled by a

[1] Zinoviev in 1924 specifically recommended " fairly frequent changes "
in the leading posts of the Komsomol as a safeguard against deviations (*Shestoi
S"ezd Rossiiskogo Leninskogo Kommunisticheskogo Soyuza Molodezhi* (1924),
pp. 64-65).
[2] *Vlast' Sovetov*, No. 10, March 7, 1926, p. 14 ; No. 19, May 9, 1926,
pp. 21-22.

president and secretary who were elected members of the bodies concerned. Before long it became the practice to assign meagre salaries to presidents and secretaries for the discharge of these functions ; the statute of village Soviets of January 1922 had provided that presidents of village Soviets should be paid out of the funds of the provincial executive committee — the lowest organ at that time possessing a budget.[1] But since these officials were rarely re-elected, at any rate at the village Soviet level, the problem of continuity remained. It was first seriously faced by an official spokesman at the April session of the conference of 1925 on the revitalization of the Soviets :

> The question of secretaries is a big question. It seems to me that the question of secretaries must be settled in such a way as to make secretaries permanent. The confusion which is created in the rural district executive committees, when delegates of the rural Soviets change in rotation and secretaries almost as fast, must be brought to an end at a moment when we are giving more rights to village Soviets ; we must return to the situation which existed formerly. Formerly a clerk sat for years on end, and knew all the business by heart ; but with us, frequent changes bring about such a mess that sometimes you can get no sense at all out of the village Soviet or the executive committee. . . . Let the secretary be non-elective, let him serve for a wage, be a hired worker, but let him be a specialist in the business, so that there will be a president who will change frequently and a secretary who will sit permanently, completely master the job and play an important rôle in the rural district.[2]

This simple lesson was too much at variance with current party conceptions of self-administration to be readily digested, and no formal ruling appears to have been given on it. The increase in the size and in the powers of village Soviets, and the creation of independent rural district budgets, gradually made the paid

---

[1] For this statute see p. 305 above. Salaries are mentioned ranging from 6 to 15 rubles a month (*Soveshchanie po Voprosam Sovetskogo Stroitel'stva 1925 g. : Yanvar'* (1925), pp. 79, 128, 136-137). This was less than a living wage ; rural school teachers at this time received 22½ rubles a month (*id. Aprel'* (1925), p. 99). Kamenev said in October 1924 : " In order to improve the lower Soviet apparatus it is necessary to pay such salaries that bribes are not taken " (L. Kamenev, *Stat'i i Rechi*, xi (1929), 207).

[2] *Soveshchanie po Voprosam Sovetskogo Stroitel'stva 1925 g. : Aprel'* (1925), pp. 76-77.

permanent official an indispensable and familiar figure in local administration. But this progressively widened the gap between the permanent official who knew everything and the constantly changing delegate who knew nothing. As late as 1928 it was officially admitted that there were still " village Soviets whose plenums do not meet regularly, and where the work of the village Soviet is equivalent to the work of its president and secretary ".[1] It is indisputable that the machinery of local government improved enormously throughout the Soviet Union in the middle and later nineteen-twenties ; and this improvement was in part the product of the campaign for the revitalization of the Soviets. But its representative character remained its weakest point.

[1] L. Kaganovich, *Partiya i Sovety* (1928), p. 78.

CHAPTER 23

THE RED ARMY

MORE than one paradox underlay the creation and organization of the Red Army which emerged victorious from the civil war. Socialists of every complexion had always been particularly hostile to the conception of a standing army, the strongest bulwark of the power which they sought to overthrow. In theory, the world-wide victory of socialism would one day render all military force obsolete : the army would die away with the state which it served. But even the Russian Social-Democrats did not think in terms of this distant Utopia. The immediate aim of a socialist revolution would be to destroy the standing army and set up in its place what was commonly called a " people's militia ". In 1905 Lenin had written of the " reactionary character of a standing army " and the " full practicability of a people's militia ".[1] He firmly reiterated this idea after the February revolution :

> The people must learn down to the last man to bear arms, and down to the last man to enter the militia which replaces the police and the standing army.

Thus would be formed " a militia of the whole people ", men and women, with election and right of recall of all commanders and officials.[2] The militia thus conceived was essentially a territorial organization, composed of men (and women) mustered for local defence or for the maintenance of order, but not detached from their homes and normal occupations. The units of the Red Guard which took part in the October revolution in Petrograd and some other cities were — for obvious reasons of practical necessity — organized on this basis.

The Red Army which was called into being immediately after

---

[1] Lenin, *Sochineniya*, viii, 397.   [2] *Ibid.* xx, 204-205.

the Brest-Litovsk treaty [1] owed little or nothing in conception to the people's militia of socialist doctrine. It was the instrument of the dictatorship of the proletariat ; its specific function was to overthrow and destroy the bourgeoisie, not to embody the principles of the future classless socialist order. Hence it was a class organization. The workers who had seized power must take up arms to defend the revolution, and deny arms to the enemies of the régime. Military training and service were to be confined to workers and peasants ; other elements were to be enrolled in unarmed labour battalions behind the front. The distinction between the Red Army and the people's militia of the future was clearly enunciated in the party programme adopted by the eighth party congress in March 1919 at the height of the civil war :

> The Red Army, as the arm of the proletarian dictatorship must of necessity have an openly class character, i.e. be recruited exclusively from the proletariat and semi-proletarian strata of the peasantry which stand close to it. Only in connexion with the abolition of classes will such a class army be transformed into a socialist militia of the whole people. [2]

The Red Army had two features particularly disconcerting to orthodox party opinion. In the first place, it rejected the principle of territorial formations proper to the militia system, which was incompatible with the exigencies of war. The civil war period was marked, in Trotsky's words, by a struggle " for the creation of a *centralized, disciplined army*, supplied and administered from a single centre ". [3] Secondly, the officer corps of the Red Army had been formed to a large extent out of officers taken over, under the equivocal title of " specialists ", from the former Tsarist army — a practice announced and defended by Trotsky at the session of TsIK in July 1918. [4] The anomaly of this arrangement was mitigated, but not removed, by the attachment to each commanding officer of one, or more often two, " political commissars " representing the views and interests of the party ; though ostensibly military appointments, the commissars were always party men. While they had no pretension to technical

---

[1] For the beginnings of the Red Army see *The Bolshevik Revolution, 1917–1923*, Vol. 3, pp. 59-67.　　[2] *VKP(B) v Rezolyutsiyakh* (1941), i, 287.
[3] L. Trotsky, *Kak Vooruzhalas' Revolyutsiya*, i (1923), 17.
[4] See *The Bolshevik Revolution, 1917–1923*, Vol. 3, p. 67.

military competence, they enjoyed supreme authority. Even operational orders were counter-signed by them as a guarantee that the order was " dictated by operational and by no other (counter-revolutionary) considerations ".[1] Nevertheless, it was the " specialists " who constituted the officer corps and effectively commanded the Red Army. A system so anomalous and so repugnant to traditional party beliefs could not fail, even in the crisis of the civil war, to incur criticism. At one extreme Smilga, a party stalwart who had been from the outset a member of the Revolutionary Military Council, came early to believe that full responsibility should be vested in the military commanders, and proposed to abolish the political commissars.[2] But a more common and influential criticism came from a group largely composed of former " Left communists " of 1918 and more or less identical with the newly formed group of " democratic centralists ".[3] These objectors reacted strongly against the conventional system of military organization and discipline which Trotsky had imposed on the Red Army, and upheld the doctrine of " partisan warfare ", locally organized and led, which had been successfully practised on some occasions in the civil war.

This group emerged at the eighth party congress of March 1919 in the guise of a " military opposition ". Trotsky, called to the front by military emergencies, was not present ; and the theses which he had prepared [4] were presented to the congress by Sokolnikov, who made the report on military affairs. Sokolnikov argued that all the issues raised by the opposition turned on the

---

[1] The institution of political commissars appears to have originated in the " dual power " of the February revolution : TsIK from an early date attached political commissars to the Petrograd garrison and to other military units in Petrograd, and the practice was inherited by the Revolutionary Military Council set up after the October revolution. The first order regularizing the status of political commissars was dated April 6, 1918 (for the text see L. Trotsky, *Kak Vooruzhalas' Revolyutsiya*, i (1923), 406-407). Trotsky relied heavily on the commissars to overcome party resistance to the use of Tsarist officers : " every specialist ", he said at TsIK in July 1918, " must have a commissar on his right and a commissar on his left, each with a revolver " (*Pyatyi Vserossiiskii S"ezd Sovetov* (1918), p. 80).

[2] A pamphlet by Smilga entitled *Stroitel'stvo Armii* containing this proposal was quoted by Sokolnikov in his report at the eighth party congress in March 1919 (*Vos'moi S"ezd RKP(B)* (1933), pp. 152, 499, note 51).

[3] See *The Bolshevik Revolution, 1917-1923*, Vol. i, pp. 195-196.

[4] The theses have not been published in their original form, but only minor amendments were made in them by the congress (see p. 377, note 1 below).

central question of a partisan *versus* a regular army : this applied
to the campaign against the specialists, to the demand for election
of officers and commissars, and to the demand to give greater
authority to party cells in the army. Sokolnikov admitted that
what was in course of creation was " a regular, standing army ".
This was " the army of the transition period " ; and the criticisms
of the opposition were misguided attempts to introduce into this
army " traits which existed in the partisan army and which will
revive only in a communist militia ". The time was not yet ripe
for the transition to the militia (though this was proclaimed as the
ultimate goal in the party programme adopted by the congress).
Those who wished to put the effective control of the Red Army
in the hands of its communist members were " party syndi-
calists ". On the other hand, Smilga's proposals, which amounted
to the abolition of the political commissars, were premature.[1]
V. M. Smirnov, who made a co-report on behalf of the opposition,
denied that the opposition rejected the use of specialists or
demanded an immediate transition to a militia. But it disliked
the growing emphasis on centralization as against the methods
of partisan warfare waged by autonomous local formations, and it
wished to increase the authority of the political commissars.[2]

After these two main speeches in plenary session the debate
was transferred to a " military section " of the congress consisting
of 66 members,[3] which met in secret and whose proceedings were
not published. Both Lenin and Stalin addressed the section in
support of Trotsky's theses. Stalin, according to extracts from
his speech published some years later, argued for " a strictly disciplined regular army " on the ground that loosely organized
militia levies would be untrustworthy : " the non-worker elements
who constitute the majority of our army will not fight voluntarily
for socialism ".[4] But the opposition was evidently also vocal.
At the end of the debate a drafting committee of five members
was appointed — Zinoviev, Pozern and Stalin for the majority,
Safarov and Yaroslavsky for the opposition.[5] But, with the civil
war in a critical phase, the objections were not pressed, and

[1] *Vos'moi S"ezd RKP(B)* (1933), pp. 146-155.
[2] *Ibid.* pp. 155-160.   [3] *Ibid.* p. 464.
[4] Stalin, *Ob Oppozitsii* (1928), pp. 668-669 ; some phrases are toned down
or omitted in the version in Stalin, *Sochineniya*, iv, 249-250.
[5] *Vos'moi S"ezd RKP(B)* (1933), pp. 273, 465.

Trotsky's original theses were embodied with minor drafting amendments [1] in a resolution which was then unanimously adopted by the congress. The resolution discredited the slogan of a " people's militia " by associating it with the Second International and comparing it with the demand for a constituent assembly. But this did not imply a break with " the programme of a militia as such ". To oppose " the idea of partisan detachments " to " an army organized and centralized in accordance with a plan " was " the creed of ' Left ' Social-Revolutionaries and their like " and " a caricature of the political thought or absence of thought of the petty bourgeois intelligentsia " : " to preach partisan warfare as a military programme is the same thing as to recommend a return from large-scale industry to artisan handicrafts ". To recruit a real " worker-peasant militia " would be a work of years or at any rate of months. The present army was transitional : " a class army in social composition, it is not a militia, but a ' standing ', ' regular ' army in its method of recruitment and training ". The " class militia army " of the future would have to be an army " equipped and organized according to the last word of military science ". Even after several years, however, when the army was thoroughly organized, " there would be no reasons of principle to refuse to draw into the work those elements of the old officer corps who have sincerely rallied to the point of view of the Soviet power ". The resolution ended with renewed demands for the creation of " separate labour battalions " for " *kulak* and parasitical elements " (which was " at present not realized, contrary to official decisions "), for the recruitment and training of " proletarians and semi-proletarians " as officers, and for strengthening the authority of the political commissars, who were described as " not only the direct and immediate representation of the Soviet power, but first and foremost the bearers of the spirit of our party ". The existing " all-Russian bureau of military commissars " was to be replaced by a " political section " of the Revolutionary Military Council — later renamed the " political administration of the Red Army " or PUR.[2]

[1] *Ibid.* p. 337 ; Trotsky accepted responsibility for the final form of the resolution by reprinting it in L. Trotsky, *Kak Vooruzhalas' Revolyutsiya*, i (1923), 186-195.

[2] *VKP(B) v Rezolyutsiyakh* (1941), i, 296-302 ; for the order of the Revolutionary Military Council of April 18, 1919, creating the political section, and

N*

This resolution, which was published with the other resolutions of the congress, appeared to represent an unqualified victory
for Trotsky and a vindication of his views. But this was not the
whole story. Trotsky's military opponents had been able to profit
by the personal antipathies and jealousies which Trotsky excited
among the other leaders. As the result of a compromise behind
the scenes, the published resolution of the congress was accompanied by an unpublished resolution instructing the party central
committee to take steps to improve the working of the Revolutionary Military Council, to increase the representation of the party
in the general staff, and to arrange for periodical conferences of
party workers at the front.[1] The unpublished resolution was
presented to the party central committee with a report by Zinoviev,
which made clear its character as a snub to Trotsky. The report
expressed sympathy for the attitude of the " Left " military
opposition, demanded a changed attitude to communists in the
Red Army, and by implication denounced the severity of the
discipline applied by Trotsky to them. The central committee
apparently confined itself to an instruction to send the unpublished
resolution, together with Zinoviev's report, to Trotsky. Zinoviev
carried out the instruction with an accompanying letter to Trotsky,
in which he explained the resolution as a necessary concession to
the opposition, and advised Trotsky to treat it as a " warning ".[2]
Trotsky evidently had reason at this time to regard Zinoviev, rather
than Stalin, as his chief rival and enemy among the leading Bolsheviks. The congress was shortly followed by another blow to
Trotsky's authority. The commander-in-chief, Vatsetis, who had
been appointed by Trotsky in September 1918, vetoed the pro-

the subsequent order of May 26, 1919, transforming it into the political administration of the Red Army see A. Geronimus, *Partiya i Krasnaya Armiya* (1928),
p. 80. One sequel to the resolution was the foundation in Petrograd of the
Tolmachev institute for training qualified political instructors for the Red
Army ; an account of the institute was given on the occasion of its fifth anniversary in *Leningradskaya Pravda*, May 25, 1924.
    [1] This resolution was apparently published for the first time in *VKP(B) v
Rezolyutsiyakh* (1941), i, 303; it was not included in earlier editions of this
work.
    [2] This episode is known in detail from a long and angry reply from Trotsky
preserved in the Trotsky archives : Trotsky accepted the terms of the resolution, though he claimed that some of them rested on a misunderstanding of the
situation, but described Zinoviev's report as " completely incorrect " and
defended the need for discipline in the army.

posal of an influential general and former Tsarist officer, Sergei
Kamenev, for an offensive against Kolchak. At the beginning of
July 1919 the party central committee, against Trotsky's advice,
dismissed Vatsetis and appointed Kamenev commander-in-chief
in his place. Trotsky tendered his resignation, which was refused
by the central committee.[1]

So long as the civil war lasted, the settlement of March 1919
held good, and the conception of an efficient, centralized military
force approximating as closely as possible to a regular army was
not seriously contested. The appointment of so stout a champion
of the military specialists as Smilga as the first head of PUR was
significant of a determination to put the claims of military
efficiency above those of the party doctrinaires. At a conference
of political workers in the Red Army early in December 1919
Smilga defended, in everything but name, the conception of a
regular army, and demanded " the reorganization of the Red
Army on the principle of one-man command ". This was a
return to the proposal for the suppression or subordination of the
political commissars. The potential clash between the system of
political commissars and the principle of " one-man command "
had been apparent from the outset. Trotsky, as early as the
autumn of 1918, had been looking for a way out :

> The more the commissar begins to penetrate into combatant
> work, and the commander to assimilate political work, the
> nearer we are to one-man command.[2]

But this was an evasion rather than a solution of the problem ;
and Trotsky, at the conference of December 1919, rather half-
heartedly supported the system of political commissars as a
scaffolding which was at present necessary to the rising edifice
of the Red Army, but would one day be removed.[3]

---

[1] For this episode see L. Trotsky, *Moya Zhizn'* (Berlin, 1930), ii, 185-186 ;
correspondence relating to it is in the Trotsky archives.

[2] L. Trotsky, *Kak Vooruzhalas' Revolyutsiya*, i (1923), 184.

[3] *Ibid.* ii, i (1924), 76-82 ; Smilga's view had originally been put forward
in the journal *Voennaya Mysl'* (*ibid.* ii, i, 453, note 31). About the same time
a former Tsarist officer, Svechin, wrote an article in the journal *Voennoe Delo*
demanding that the Red Army should be freed from " all upsets in the form
of militias, universal military training (Vsevobuch), military councils and little
councils, and of the curtailment of the real authority of every officer and, above
all, of the commanding officer " (*ibid.* ii, i, 454, note 37).

This military mood was, however, too much the product of a military emergency, and too much at variance with current party doctrine, to survive the victorious ending of the civil war. When Trotsky addressed the seventh All-Russian Congress of Soviets at the end of December 1919, the defeat of both Denikin and Kolchak was already assured ; and the atmosphere was markedly different from that of the military conference a few weeks earlier. Trotsky now quoted Jaurès's socialist classic, *L'Armée Nouvelle*, and declared that the idea of a militia " confronts us as the only possible prospect for our permanent armed force in time of peace ".[1] The enthusiasm generated by the victorious ending of the civil war was at its height when the ninth party congress met in March 1920, and issued a message of greeting to " the Red Army and Red Fleet of the RSFSR ".[2] At a moment when the attention of the party was being switched from military questions to what Lenin called the " bloodless front of economic reconstruction ", Trotsky made a balanced and cautious report on military organization.[3] He once more quoted Jaurès, though he admitted that both Jaurès and Bebel, in their approach to military questions, indulged in " democratic, i.e. in essence petty bourgeois, illusions ". He was, however, clearly influenced at this time by Jaurès's vision of the organization of the socialist armed forces of the future in the form of local militias organized round units of production — farms or factories — where the men would continue to work while enrolled in military units for military training ; Trotsky saw the employment of units of the Red Army on productive work — the so-called " militarization of labour " [4] — as a practical realization of this idea. This seemed to Trotsky, at this time, the main point of the militia system :

> A militia has the fundamental advantage over a standing army, that it does not separate defence and labour, does not divide the working class from the army.

But his conclusion was less dogmatic. He argued that the militia and the standing army should not be opposed to one another as " two abstract, absolute principles ", and went on :

[1] 7ᶥ *Vserossiiskii S"ezd Sovetov* (1920), p. 93.
[2] *VKP(B) v Rezolyutsiyakh* (1941), i, 347-348.
[3] *Devyatyi S"ezd RKP(B)* (1934), pp. 405-418.
[4] See *The Bolshevik Revolution, 1917–1923*, Vol. 2, p. 212.

For a certain period divisions recruited on the old model and militia divisions capable of standing on their own feet will exist side by side.

The congress, relieved to be no longer faced with the chronic military emergency of the last two years, did not consider it necessary to debate Trotsky's report, and somewhat light-heartedly passed a resolution " On the Transition to the Militia System ". This emphasized that " the essence of the Soviet *militia system* must consist in bringing the army by all means as close as possible to the productive process ", and in adapting units to the territorial distribution of industry, so that workers might provide " the core of the militia units ". But it sounded a suitable note of caution. The transition must be effected with " an indispensable gradualness, in accordance with the military and international diplomatic situation of the Soviet republic ", and with a view to the overriding condition of maintaining efficiency in defence.[1]

The ninth party congress of March 1920 was held at a moment of rising self-confidence, when victory in the civil war seemed already won. It was followed by a series of dramatic events. Piłsudski launched an invasion of the Ukraine in May 1920; this was answered by the advance on Warsaw in August 1920, followed by the no less rapid retreat ending in the October armistice. Wrangel, the last of the White generals, reopened the front in the south, and was not finally driven out till the latter part of November 1920. Civil war had now reached its end. A long respite was in sight, and the demobilization of the Red Army began. But these events powerfully influenced military thinking and led to the formation of new groupings in the party, which gathered strength throughout the winter, and took the field at the tenth party congress in March 1921.

Two of these groups represented opposite extremes. The first put forward the logical demand that, now the emergency was over, the regular army should be demobilized and a complete transition made to a militia system. This group was headed by Podvoisky, one of the military leaders of the October *coup* in

[1] *VKP(B) v Rezolyutsiyakh* (1941), i, 345.

1917, but seems to have been the weakest of the three groups
and to have had little following in military circles.[1] The second
group was headed by Smilga, who pursued his campaign for the
maintenance of a regular army with renewed vigour and with
fresh arguments. The defeat before Warsaw in August 1920
was widely attributed to the weakness of half-trained peasant
units ; and during the following autumn and winter the spread
of peasant discontent threw further doubt on the reliability of
local levies as a basis for the national army. Smilga seized the
occasion to present to a private meeting of military delegates to
the eighth All-Russian Congress of Soviets in December 1920 a
set of theses which, on the experience of the civil war, condemned
the militia system root and branch :

> The militia system, the essential mark of which is its
> territorial basis, encounters an insuperable obstacle to its intro-
> duction in Russia in the form of our political régime. Con-
> sidering the small number of the proletariat in Russia, we
> *cannot* guarantee proletarian leadership in such units. . . . To
> return to this form of organization would be a crude and totally
> unjustifiable mistake.[2]

Having secured the approval of his theses by the meeting, Smilga
submitted them on January 18, 1921, to the Moscow party committee, which also accepted them in principle, the intention being
to bring them up at the forthcoming party congress.[3] Trotsky,
who was at this moment mainly preoccupied by the trade union
controversy,[4] still held a middle position between the two extremes.
In a speech of February 1921, he again quoted Jaurès and proclaimed his fidelity to the principle of a militia, but admitted that
" it is impossible to make the transition to it all at once, just as
it is impossible all at once to make the transition to socialism ".[5]

The third group, which was destined to eclipse the other two
in importance, was formed on the basis of what was called " the
single military doctrine ". The doctrine reduced itself to the

[1] *VKP(B) i Voennoe Delo* (2nd ed. 1928), p. 282 ; the theses presented by
Podvoisky to the tenth party congress are in *Desyatyi S"ezd RKP(B)* (1933),
pp. 674-676.
[2] The theses were published in I. Smilga, *Ocherednye Voprosy Stroitel'stva
Krasnoi Armii* (1921), pp. 15-18.
[3] An account of these proceedings is given in *VKP(B) i Voennoe Delo*
(2nd ed. 1928), p. 283.
[4] See *The Bolshevik Revolution, 1917-1923*, Vol. 2, pp. 221-226.
[5] L. Trotsky, *Kak Vooruzhalas' Revolyutsiya*, iii, i (1924), 10-14.

assertion, which had been more than once made in the controversies of the preceding years, that there was a specifically Marxist,
proletarian, revolutionary theory of military affairs, in the light
of which all military problems could and should be resolved,
though its supporters remained discreetly uncommitted on questions of application, including the controversial militia issue.
The simplicity and vagueness of the doctrine were a source of
strength rather than weakness in a movement which combined
several disparate elements, and whose main appeal was to per-
sonalities. The leader of the group was Frunze, a former Tsarist
non-commissioned officer of Moldavian origin born at Pishpek
(later re-named Frunze) in Kirgizia, who had risen rapidly in the
Red Army. He had been in command in Turkestan in 1919 ; [1]
and, as the commander on the southern front against Wrangel in
the autumn of 1920, he now enjoyed the prestige of the crowning
victory of the civil war. The theorist of the group was Gusev,
an ambitious party worker in military affairs. The party proletarian flavour of the movement secured for it the adhesion of
many members of the military opposition of 1919. It was marked
— perhaps, indeed, inspired — by a thinly veiled antagonism to
Trotsky, who was a known opponent of the introduction of class
theory into questions of military policy.[2] In this way, it attracted
those exponents of partisan warfare who had been snubbed and
superseded as a result of Trotsky's insistence on regular, centralized
organization and command ; the newly trained officers with a
party or proletarian background who were jealous of the former
Tsarist professional officers ; and, in general, other party leaders
who, now that the civil war was over, were jealous of Trotsky's
military renown and ascendancy. Voroshilov, a partisan leader
who had clashed with Trotsky and enjoyed the patronage of
Stalin in 1919, and Budenny, a dashing cavalry commander in the
civil war and in the Polish campaign of 1920,[3] were both members

---

[1] See *The Bolshevik Revolution, 1917–1923*, Vol. 1, p. 336.

[2] In 1919 Trotsky had inveighed against a writer who objected to the employment of former Tsarist officers on the ground that they " do not understand or
recognize the class policy of the proletariat " (L. Trotsky, *Kak Vooruzhalas'
Revolyutsiya*, ii, i (1924), 59, 452, note 26).

[3] Both Voroshilov and Budenny had been praised by Trotsky by name at
the ninth party congress in March 1920, though perhaps with the veiled implication that their exploits had little relevance to current conditions (*Devyatyi S"ezd
RKP(B)* (1934), p. 405).

of the group. Tukhachevsky, who had been in command of the advance on Warsaw and was recognized as the ablest of the rising generation of younger officers, occupied an anomalous position. Nobody insisted more emphatically on a specifically proletarian military doctrine permeating strategy, tactics and organization. Tukhachevsky believed that the character of the Red Army should be determined by its mission to carry the proletarian revolution to other countries ; and he advocated " preparation for foreign class war " through the creation of a military general staff for Comintern.[1] But, while these extreme views disposed him to whole-hearted acceptance of the " single military doctrine ", they also led him to share Smilga's out-and-out rejection of the militia system, not only on the ground alleged by Smilga that territorial units would be dominated by *kulaks* and constitute " counter-revolutionary armies against ourselves ", but also on the plea, not advanced by Smilga, that a militia would be incompatible with " Soviet Russia's present military mission to disseminate the socialist revolution throughout the world ".[2] Tukhachevsky thus remained a slightly eccentric member of the Frunze group. The first attempt to formulate the " single military doctrine " and to provide a programme for the group was a set of theses drafted by Gusev and Frunze in the Ukraine in the winter of 1920–1921. The aim set forth in the theses was to transform the Red Army into " a single organism, welded together from top to bottom not only by a common political ideology, but also by unity of view on the character of the military problems facing the republic and on the method of solving those problems, as well as on the system of combat and training ".[3] They apparently received the endorsement of the Ukrainian party central committee in January 1921.[4]

The tenth party congress met, in March 1921, in the mood of acute alarm inspired by the Kronstadt rising — the reverse of the

[1] M. Tukhachevsky, *Voina Klassov* (1921), pp. 57-59 ; for his letter to Zinoviev at the time of the second congress of Comintern in July 1920 see *ibid*. pp. 138-140.

[2] *Ibid*. p. 71 ; the article *Red Army and Militia* propounding these views was published among the party " materials " for the tenth party congress.

[3] The twenty-one theses are in *Desyatyi S"ezd RKP(B)* (1933), pp. 676-682, and in S. Gusev, *Grazhdanskaya Voina i Krasnaya Armiya* (1925), pp. 91-96 ; the last six, said to have been the work of Frunze, are also in M. Frunze, *Sobranie Sochinenii*, i (1929), 205-206.

[4] A. Geronimus, *Partiya i Krasnaya Armiya* (1928), p. 124.

atmosphere of security and triumph which had prevailed at the ninth congress a year earlier. The three sittings which the congress devoted to military questions were held in secret, and the records of these have not been published. The two extreme views for and against the militia system, and for and against the political commissars, were played off against one another and apparently gave little trouble. The theses on the single military doctrine were more embarrassing, and the opposition seems to have concentrated on them, attacking Trotsky for his lack of interest in Marxist military theory and his empirical attitude to military questions.[1] The clash might have been serious, had not Lenin, in a private conversation, dissuaded Frunze from pressing his plan. Lenin compared the notion of a proletarian military doctrine with that of a proletarian literature and art. He repeated to Frunze what he had previously said to Bukharin :

> Please learn, train up your youthful forces. But if you now come out with your theory of proletarian art, you will fall into the error of " communist boasting ".[2]

Under this persuasion the opposition refrained from placing the theses on the formal agenda, and they remained among the unpublished material of the congress.[3]

It thus came about that the resolution of the congress "on the military question ", which was not published in full till some years later,[4] passed over in silence the question of doctrine, and confined itself to practical issues of military organization. In the face of Smilga's proposals to abolish the political commissars and other

---

[1] L. Trotsky, *Kak Vooruzhalas' Revolyutsiya*, iii, ii (1925), 258.

[2] M. Frunze, *Sobranie Sochinenii*, iii (1927), 150 ; Bubnov, in his preface to the collected edition of Frunze's works, confirmed that Lenin was opposed to the "single military doctrine" (*ibid.* i (1929), p. xxvi). Frunze did not specify the occasion of Lenin's intervention ; but the statement in *Desyatyi S"ezd RKP(B)* (1933), p. 682, that the Frunze-Gusev theses were withdrawn " by agreement with Lenin " makes the identification reasonably certain.

[3] A brief account of these proceedings is in Trotsky, *Sochineniya*, xxi, 453-454, note 2 ; the writer of the note claims that Trotsky " persuaded them [i.e. Frunze and Gusev] to withdraw these theses from discussion by the congress ".

[4] An abbreviated version appeared in *VKP(B) i Voennoe Delo* (2nd ed. 1928), pp. 90-92, being quoted from a party journal of April 1921 (*ibid.* p. 282). It was omitted from the original proceedings of the congress, and was apparently published in full for the first time in the later edition of the proceedings, *Desyatyi S"ezd RKP(B)* (1933), pp. 617-621 ; it is also in *VKP(B) v Rezolyutsiyakh* (1941), i, 392-394.

political organs of the Red Army, and to entrust political work in the army to organs of the party,[1] the congress decided " to preserve the political apparatus of the Red Army in the form which it has assumed in the three years of war " and to strengthen its links with local party organs while maintaining its " full independence ". But it also advocated the transfer of " commissars who have acquired the appropriate experience " to command posts. On the issue of the militia the resolution was emphatic and categorical. While no revision of the party programme was called for, " the methods and tempo of the transition to a militia depend entirely on the international and domestic environment, on the duration of the breathing-space, on mutual relations between town and country etc." In the immediate future, the Red Army in its present form must remain "the foundation of our armed forces". A partial exception was admitted " only in respect of regions with the densest proletarian population (Petrograd, Moscow, the Urals) " ; and, where such militia units were formed, " special communist detachments " were to be assigned to them to provide the necessary stiffening. Only when the success of NEP had restored confidence in the loyalty of the peasant would a wider extension be given to the militia system.

The withdrawal of the " single military doctrine " at the tenth party congress was not a defeat, but a tactical retreat. Its champions were soon once more in the field. An article of Frunze of July 1921, which appeared both in the military journal *Armiya i Revolyutsiya* and in the literary journal *Krasnaya Nov'*, attempted a fresh definition of the doctrine :

> The " single military doctrine " is a doctrine which, adopted in the army of a given state, determines the character of the structure of the armed forces of the country, the methods of military training of its forces and their leadership, on the basis of the views prevailing in the state on the character of the military tasks that lie before it and on the methods of resolving them — methods which derive from the class essence of the state and are defined by the level of development of the productive forces of the country.

These vague generalities now found concrete expression in the doctrine of the offensive : since " the working class will be com-

---

[1] I. Petukhov, *Partiinaya Organizatsiya i Partiinaya Rabota v RKKA* (1928), pp. 57-58.

pelled by the very course of the historical revolutionary process to pass over to the offensive against capital ", it followed that the offensive must be the basis of the tactics and training of the Red Army.[1] This theory harked back to the old civil war controversies about partisan warfare and the specialists. In the summer of 1919 one Tarasov-Rodionov had published an elaborate article in the military journal attacking the specialists for clinging to the old-fashioned tradition of a war of " positions ", insisting on " the character of manœuvre of class warfare ", and demanding that attention should be given to the tactics of cavalry, motor-cyclists and light artillery.[2] The theory of the offensive, now revived by Frunze, became the main burden of the " single military doctrine ", and the effective point of contact between Frunze and Tukhachevsky. The theory had a certain romantic appeal to the rising generation of young officers who made Tukhachevsky their idol, and enjoyed a wide popularity. Lenin, who was now mainly preoccupied by the problems of NEP and of bureaucracy, and whose activity was soon to be restricted by failing health, made no further incursion into military affairs ; and Trotsky's position was correspondingly weakened. Meanwhile two new appointments, in the autumn of 1921, indicated the growing influence of the opposition group. Gusev succeeded Smilga as head of PUR ; and Tukhachevsky became director of the military academy.[3]

In the autumn, Trotsky took the field publicly against the new doctrine. He developed his objections at length in a speech at the Military Scientific Society :

> It is necessary to exercise the greatest vigilance in order to escape falling into some mystical or metaphysical trap, even though such a pitfall were camouflaged by revolutionary

[1] M. Frunze, *Sobranie Sochinenii*, i (1929), 207-227.

[2] The article was quoted and refuted in an article by Trotsky entitled *The Partisans and the Regular Army* (L. Trotsky, *Kak Vooruzhalas' Revolyutsiya*, ii, i (1924), 59-60, 452, note 26). Trotsky was no advocate of the war of " positions " : he contrasted the static character of the world war with " our war ", which had been " full of mobility and manœuvre " (*ibid.* iii, i (1924), 156), and after a period of initial scepticism became an enthusiastic supporter of Budenny's cavalry (*ibid.* ii, i (1924), 287-288). But he objected to the proclamation of a doctrine of mobility or the offensive, and to its association with proletarian ideology.

[3] *Entsiklopedicheskii Slovar' Russkogo Bibliograficheskogo Instituta Granat*, xli, i (n.d. [1927]), Prilozhenie, col. 109 ; iii (n.d. [1928]), Prilozhenie, col. 163.

terminology. . . . We want a concept which is concrete, precise, and filled with historical content.

Borrowing an argument which had done service in the literary controversy, he declared that " to invent something better than the *tachanka* [1] one must take lessons from the bourgeoisie ", and, denouncing " boastfulness and revolutionary superficiality ", added that, " when strategy is developed from the point of view of young revolutionaries, chaos results ". He attacked Tukhachevsky for his opposition to the militia system and for his theory of the offensive.[2] Frunze was not present, having been sent on a diplomatic mission to Turkey.[3] But Trotsky's sallies did not pass without reply. According to his own account, " some comrades from among our young commanders who had been on the civil war fronts, excellent men, reliable, brave, decorated with the Order of the Red Flag ", continued to maintain that offensive tactics were " particularly appropriate to a revolutionary army ".[4] Trotsky carried on the campaign a few weeks later in a further speech in which he compared the doctrine of the military offensive with the doctrine of the revolutionary offensive preached by German and Italian Leftists and condemned at the third congress of Comintern in the previous summer, and specifically attacked Tukhachevsky's advocacy of an international general staff, as being both unrealizable, till a world-wide proletarian revolution had occurred, and incompatible with current policies of temporary accommodation with capitalist countries.[5] A long article of December 1921, entitled *Military Doctrine and Pseudo-Military Doctrinairism*, which originally appeared in the journal of Comintern and later as a separate pamphlet, was devoted to a detailed refutation of the views of Frunze, Gusev and Tukhachevsky.[6] No immediate necessity arose for a party pronouncement on the main issue. But in the same month a resolution of the party conference declared it a task of the party " to transform the

---

[1] A primitive peasant cart used in the civil war for transporting artillery.

[2] L. Trotsky, *Kak Vooruzhalas' Revolyutsiya*, iii, ii (1925), 201-209.

[3] See *The Bolshevik Revolution, 1917-1923*, Vol. 3, p. 475.

[4] L. Trotsky, *Kak Vooruzhalas' Revolyutsiya*, iii, i (1924), 63.

[5] *Ibid.* iii, i (1924), 88-89 ; for the condemnation of the " revolutionary offensive " by Comintern see *The Bolshevik Revolution, 1917-1923*, Vol. 3, pp. 386-387.

[6] *Kommunisticheskii Internatsional*, No. 19, December 17, 1921, cols. 4995-5028 ; L. Trotsky, *Kak Vooruzhalas' Revolyutsiya*, iii, ii (1925), 210-241.

barracks into a parallel section of the party schools " and to ensure that the Red Army man should emerge from his two years' service " with knowledge not less than that of the graduates of a provincial party school ".[1] The supporters of the single military doctrine could derive some satisfaction from this recognition of the importance of Marxist indoctrination in military training. A resumption of the struggle at the eleventh party congress in March 1922 was now unavoidable. A preliminary trial of strength occurred at a military conference in Kharkov at the beginning of the month. In the Ukraine Frunze was on his home ground, and enjoyed widespread support. He reiterated his view of the Red Army as a proletarian class army " strongly welded " by ideological unity, and dwelt once more on the superiority of the offensive over the defensive, of a war of manœuvre over a war of position ; Vatsetis, Trotsky's first commander-in-chief in the civil war, was attacked for having at one critical moment advocated a strategy of retreat on the eastern front.[2] At the party congress the tradition established in previous years of holding military discussions in secret was maintained. In the public session a formal report on the Red Army was made by Trotsky. At the end of a mainly non-controversial speech, he referred in slighting terms to the single military doctrine, and deplored some of the things that had been said at the Ukrainian conference. He suggested that supporters of the doctrine erred through idealization of the past and of the experience of the civil war, and would be better employed in such practical tasks as getting rid of illiteracy and lice in the army. He concluded by inviting interested delegates to attend the meeting of military experts to be held on the following day.[3]

---

[1] *VKP(B) v Rezolyutsiyakh* (1941), i, 414.

[2] M. Frunze, *Sobranie Sochinenii*, i (1929), 389-409 ; Frunze was evidently criticized in the discussion, and in his closing remarks toned down his claims, protesting that the single military doctrine was not " an ossified dogmatic system " (*ibid.* i, 415). The attack on Vatsetis reflected his dispute with Sergei Kamenev (see pp. 378-379 above).

[3] *Odinnadtsatyi S"ezd RKP(B)* (1936), pp. 299-311 ; Trotsky's speech was reprinted in L. Trotsky, *Kak Vooruzhalas' Revolyutsiya*, iii, i (1924), 119-130. When Lenin was speaking at the congress of the danger of " communist boasting ", Trotsky turned to Frunze (according to Frunze's story) and said : " Vladimir Ilich's whole speech hits at you " (M. Frunze, *Sobranie Sochinenii*, i (1929), 463) ; the note in Trotsky, *Sochineniya*, xxi, 454, attributes the initiative in raising the question to " Voroshilov and Frunze ".

When the meeting opened, Trotsky embarked on an elaborate refutation of the single military doctrine, which he attributed to Frunze and Gusev, analysing in detail the theses put forward at the Kharkov conference.

> War [he argued] is not a science ; war is a practical art, a skill. : . . War is a " profession " for those who correctly learn military business. . . . How can the maxims of the military profession be determined with the help of the Marxist method ? That would be the same thing as to create a theory of architecture or a veterinary text-book with the help of Marxism.

Men were more important than doctrine. Military doctrine could not be built on idealization of the exploits of the civil war. To proclaim a theory of the offensive was like believing that the player who first gave check at chess would win the game.[1] Frunze replied. Having begun by professing that no differences of principle existed, but only differences of application, he vigorously upheld the theory of the offensive, comparing Trotsky's objections to it with the attitude of the " liquidators " in the party after 1905 and of the Mensheviks and SRs in 1917.[2] He eloquently rebutted Trotsky's accusation of idealizing the past ; here Trotsky, with his customary neglect of the psychological factor, had evidently wounded the pride of many young officers by appearing to depreciate the glories of the civil war.[3] Among the speakers

---

[1] L. Trotsky, *Kak Vooruzhalas' Revolyutsiya*, iii, ii (1925), 242-258. Trotsky's reference to war as an art was a quotation of a well-known passage in an article of Marx : " Insurrection is an art, just as war is, like other forms of art, and is subject to definite rules " (Marx i Engels, *Sochineniya*, vi, 99). Later Trotsky distinguished " science as an objective knowledge of what is from art which teaches how to act " (L. Trotsky, *Kak Vooruzhalas' Revolyutsiya*, iii, ii 1925), 201).

[2] Frunze's speech is in M. Frunze, *Sobranie Sochinenii*, i (1929), 459-471. He reverted to the charge of Menshevism and liquidationism in his concluding remarks (*ibid.* i, 472-473) ; this seems to be the first recorded attempt to introduce these ancient controversies into the campaign against Trotsky. A note in the 1936 edition of the proceedings of the congress accused Trotsky *inter alia* of " worship of bourgeois military science " (*Odinnadtsatyi S"ezd RKP(B)* (1936), p. 770, note 133).

[3] Three years later Frunze contrasted the part of the officer corps " inherited from the old Tsarist army ", which was inclined to " underestimate the experience of the civil war ", with the part that had " grown up in the body of the Red Army itself, socially and politically united with the working class and the

in the debate were Voroshilov and Budenny, who praised the theory of the offensive, Tukhachevsky, who agreed with Trotsky " with reservations ", and Muralov who protested that well polished boots and buttons were " not everything ". Trotsky answered them briefly and mildly.[1] Theoretical agreement was not in sight, but no immediate practical issue was involved. The conclusions of the meeting of military delegates were presented to the congress not by Trotsky, but by Frunze. Only a brief and apparently uncontroversial resolution about the problems of demobilization and the rôle of the party in the army was submitted : this was declared carried on a show of hands by a " clear majority ".[2] But Frunze admitted that two questions discussed by the meeting did not appear in the resolution. One was the question of military discipline and the need to maintain " revolutionary-military courts " : this, Frunze explained, would have to be dealt with by Soviet organs. While this explanation was formally correct, the meeting had in fact adopted a resolution on the subject which it would have been indiscreet to publish. It noted that " recent statistical data show a menacing increase in desertion and other specific military crimes ", and recorded that the military command " cannot fail to be perturbed about the real fighting capacity of the Red Army ".[3] The second question, which turned on relations between PUR and Glavpolitprosvet,[4] incidentally raised the thorny issue of the single military doctrine. The theses adopted by the meeting, which were approved by Trotsky, dwelt on the need to kindle the Red Army man's " interest in military affairs " and to make him " a good fighter ", and argued that political instruction should start " not from the theory of class warfare, but from the concrete political situation of the present day ". Here the failure to bring the issue to the congress was probably due to obstructive tactics on the part of the supporters of the single military doctrine, who could not

peasantry ", which was inclined to " overestimate the experience of the civil war ", and claimed that " objective truth " had proved to be on the side of the latter (M. Frunze, *Sobranie Sochinenii*, iii (1927), 249).

[1] L. Trotsky, *Kak Vooruzhalas' Revolyutsiya*, iii, ii (1925), 258-270.

[2] The resolution is in *VKP(B) v Rezolyutsiyakh* (1941), i, 449-450 ; for Frunze's short speech see *Odinnadtsatyi S"ezd RKP(B)* (1936), pp. 522-524.

[3] It was eventually published *ibid.* p. 693.

[4] For this question see p. 407, note 2 below.

count on a victory over Trotsky, and did not wish to expose themselves to defeat.[1]

Trotsky returned once more to the " single military doctrine " in an address to the Military Scientific Society on May 8, 1922, on *Military Knowledge and Marxism*.[2] But, by this time, it was clear that the theme had more importance for the personal vendetta against Trotsky than for questions of military organization. The controversy on military doctrine died away after the eleventh party congress, not because any decision had been taken by the congress on the issues involved, but because, with the progressive demobilization of the Red Army, these issues had ceased to seem relevant. The spirit of NEP, with its sharp reaction from the experiences and ways of thought of the civil war, was unpropitious to any form of military enthusiasm, and brought the Red Army to its lowest ebb, numerically and psychologically. The year 1922 was still one of demobilization ; and it was not till the following year that the problem of rebuilding the Red Army on a permanent peace-time footing was seriously taken in hand. Even now no great initiative was shown. Trotsky's main interest had been diverted after the civil war, on his own showing, from military to economic questions.[3] The twelfth party congress in April 1923 was the first since the revolution which held no discussion of military questions.

During this lull in party controversy, the shape and organization of the Red Army for the next ten years were settled almost automatically and without further debate. The resolutions of the eighth and ninth party congresses in favour of the transition to a territorial militia system were on record. But it may be doubted whether, when the critical moment arrived, these were as decisive as the practical arguments which dictated the raising of the first

[1] The theses have not been published, but quotations from them may be found in *Bol'shevik*, No. 1 (17), January 15, 1925, pp. 58-60, and in A. Geronimus, *Partiya i Krasnaya Armiya* (1928), pp. 160-161.

[2] L. Trotsky, *Kak Vooruzhalas' Revolyutsiya*, iii, ii (1925), 271-289.

[3] L. Trotsky, *Moya Zhizn'* (Berlin, 1930), ii, 242. According to a note in *Desyatyi S"ezd RKP(B)* (1933), pp. 865-866, he tendered his resignation as People's Commissar for War on January 12, 1921, to the party central committee, which refused it ; this appears to have been prompted not by dissent on military issues, but by preoccupation with other matters.

territorial levies in the autumn of 1923. The size of the army had been reduced from 4,400,000 in March 1921 to 560,000 at the end of 1923.[1] In the mood of 1923, and with a strictly limited budget, an increase in the numbers of the regular army was unthinkable. Yet, if a regular army of this size were the sole military force, less than one-third of the available annual contingent would be called up, and the number of trained reserves available in some future emergency would fall perilously low. On the one hand, the strained resources of the Soviet budget were not equal to the maintenance of a large regular army such as had been maintained in the latter days of the Tsarist régime when a million and a half men were constantly under the colours.[2] On the other hand, a small regular army could be regarded as efficient in terms of modern warfare only if it were mechanized and fully equipped with modern weapons. While military opinion remained sceptical of the military value of half-trained territorial formations, the essential argument in support of the militia system was the backwardness of Soviet industry. It was not possible in the middle nineteen-twenties to look forward to a time when Soviet industry would be able to provide equipment for a modern regular army which would enable it to match, either in quantity or in quality, the armies of western Europe.[3] Industrial backwardness compelled the Soviet régime to rely, in army organization as elsewhere, on an abundance of man-power in default of a sufficiency of mechanical equipment. This made it impracticable to dispense with raw and ill-equipped militia levies. In the autumn of 1923, when the time came to call up further classes for

---

[1] A. Geronimus, *Partiya i Krasnaya Armiya* (1928), p. 148 ; L. Trotsky, *Kak Vooruzhalas' Revolyutsiya*, iii, i (1924), 144, put the total number at the end of 1920 at 5,300,000.

[2] The numerical comparison was made by Frunze in a speech of February 24, 1925 (M. Frunze, *Sobranie Sochinenii*, iii (1927), 101) ; the budget as a limiting factor in the size of the army was stressed by Frunze in his speech of November 16, 1924 (*ibid.* ii (1926), 130-131). In 1925–1926 military expenditure accounted for 15·8 per cent of the state budget as against 30·5 per cent in 1913 (V. Dyachenko, *Sovetskie Finansy v Pervoi Faze Razvitiya Sovetskogo Gosudarstva*, i (1947), 460).

[3] M. Frunze, *Sobranie Sochinenii*, iii (1927), pp. 92, 168, 267 ; " until recently ", Frunze said in November 1924, Polish artillery had been more than twice as powerful as Soviet artillery : he claimed that the Red Army was now a match for its neighbours in this arm (*ibid.* ii (1926), 132). A month later he repeated : " We lag behind the bourgeois states, our resources are limited " (*ibid.* ii, 197).

military service, it was decided to call up the whole annual contingent. But only about one-fourth of these would be required to man the cadres of the regular army. The remainder would be enrolled in rotation, for short periods of training, in territorial units, for which regular army units would serve as a stiffening. In two respects the prescription for a militia laid down by the ninth party congress proved obsolete. No attempt was made either to base the territorial militia on industrial centres or to associate it with compulsory labour service. Its composition in rural areas was exclusively peasant and its function purely military.

A beginning was quickly made, though only 17 per cent of the army had been put on a territorial basis by the end of 1923,[1] and 100,000 of those available were not called up, apparently as a measure of financial economy.[2] The first call-up coincided with the abortive revolutionary *coup* in Germany, and was accompanied by rumours of mobilization for war.[3] When a Bessarabian division was enrolled in the Ukraine, desertions amounted to 50 per cent. In general, the enrolment is said to have passed off better than was expected : the total proportion of defaulters was only 2 per cent.[4] Once the peasants realized that they were not being mobilized to fight, or even torn away from their homes, but merely called up for periods of training, they accepted the new system with equanimity. The old argument against the militia system based on the alleged disloyalty and unreliability of the peasant faded away. The new territorial Red Army became a symbol of the reconciliation of the peasant with the régime — a typical product of the NEP period.[5]

Scarcely was the new system under way when the summits of the Red Army were ruffled by the first party campaign against

[1] *X Let Krasnoi Armii : Al'bom Diagramm* (1928), p. 19.
[2] M. Frunze, *Sobranie Sochinenii*, ii (1926), 131.
[3] *VKP(B) i Voennoe Delo* (2nd ed. 1928), p. 337.
[4] L. Trotsky, *Kak Vooruzhalas' Revolyutsiya*, iii, ii (1925), pp. 162-164 ; Frunze later put the total percentage of deserters from the Red Army at 7·5 for 1923, 5 for 1924 and 0·1 for 1925 (M. Frunze, *Izbrannye Proizvedeniya* (1934), p. 436).
[5] It was admitted that difficulties occurred over the call-up in the autumn of 1924 owing to the prevalence of discontent among the peasants at this time (M. Frunze, *Sobranie Sochinenii*, iii (1927), 313) ; but these disappeared after the more favourable attitude to the peasantry adopted at the fourteenth party conference in April 1925 and the third Union Congress of Soviets in May 1925 (*K XIV S"ezdu VKP(B)* (1925), p. 156).

Trotsky, which raged through the winter of 1923–1924. Trotsky undoubtedly enjoyed the sympathy of the higher " professional " groups in the Red Army, the " specialists " whom he had recruited and defended in the dark days of the civil war. What was more important, he had the support of many party cells in the army,[1] and in particular of the party intellectuals who formed the backbone of PUR. The dismissal of Antonov-Ovseenko, the head of PUR, who had signed the platform of the 46 and was one of Trotsky's chief adherents,[2] was the prelude to Trotsky's own condemnation at the thirteenth party conference in January 1924. The resolution condemning Trotsky significantly contained a clause prescribing punishment of " particular severity " for attempts to introduce " fractional activities " into the Red Army.[3] Though it did not deprive Trotsky of his office, it marked the end of his effective authority in military affairs. At the end of the conference, the party central committee set up a commission under the presidency of Frunze (in which Trotsky, convalescent in Sukhum, did not participate) on the reorganization of the Red Army.[4] This was a prelude to far-reaching changes, and clearly marked out Frunze as Trotsky's future successor.

The most urgent step taken was the appointment of Bubnov to succeed Antonov-Ovseenko as director of PUR. The choice was at first sight surprising. Bubnov had lived down his association with the " Left communists " of 1918. He became director

---

[1] According to *VKP(B) i Voennoe Delo* (2nd ed. 1928), p. 350, resolutions supporting the opposition were passed by one-third of the party cells in the Moscow garrison, and by party cells in units in the Ukraine and in the western and Volga military districts. Some of the discontent is said to have taken the form of demands for the election of political commissars and even of military commanders (A. Geronimus, *Partiya i Krasnaya Armiya* (1928), pp. 157-158) — a revival of the old " party syndicalism " of the military opposition of 1919 (see p. 376 above) ; this had little in common with Trotsky's views.

[2] See *The Interregnum, 1923–1924*, pp. 324-325 ; Antonov-Ovseenko had succeeded Gusev as director of PUR in the autumn of 1922 (*Entsiklopedicheskii Slovar' Russkogo Bibliograficheskogo Instituta Granat*, xli, i (n.d. [1927]), Prilozhenie, col. 10).   [3] See *The Interregnum, 1923–1924*, p. 339.

[4] This was recorded in Gusev's article in *Pravda*, December 17, 1924 (see pp. 20-21 above). No earlier announcement has been traced ; but this is not surprising, since decisions relating to military matters were normally kept secret. K. Voroshilov, *Stat'i i Rechi* (1937), p. 563, describes the commission as " headed by comrade Gusev ". According to *VKP(B) i Voennoe Delo* (1928), pp. 335-336, a joint commission of the party central control commission and Rabkrin was set up in 1923 to investigate the condition of the Red Army ; its report led to the appointment of the commission of January 1924.

of the propaganda section of the party secretariat in 1922, and was elected a candidate member of the party central committee at the twelfth congress in April 1923.[1] But in the autumn of that year he had lapsed from grace by signing (though with reservations) the platform of the 46. He was, however, one of the few who had hastened to recant when the crisis broke in December ; and his prompt conversion to orthodoxy was now rewarded. Bubnov signalized his appointment by cancelling Antonov-Ovseenko's peccant circular of December 24, 1923,[2] and issuing a fresh circular of February 3, 1924, on " inner-party democracy " in the Red Army. It was now clearly laid down that party discussion was limited by the requirements of military discipline, and that the party apparatus in the Red Army, except at the level of regimental party cells, was appointed from above, not elected from below.[3] Bubnov proved an efficient head of PUR. He was elected to the party central committee by the thirteenth congress in May 1924, and for many years his loyalty to the party leadership was unimpeachable.

The Frunze commission reported to sessions of the party central committee in February and April 1924, uncompromisingly concluding that " the Red Army in its present form is unfit to fight ".[4] Though the verdict did not lack foundation,[5] its edge was deliberately sharpened as a weapon against Trotsky, and it was followed by a general purge in the army administration, in which the Frunze-Gusev group evidently played the leading part.

[1] Entsiklopedicheskii Slovar' Russkogo Bibliograficheskogo Instituta Granat, xli, i (n.d. [1927]), Prilozhenie, col. 49.
[2] See The Interregnum, 1923–1924, p. 324.
[3] I. Petukhov, Partiinaya Organizatsiya i Partiinaya Rabota v RKKA (1928), p. 73. The circular was not published ; according to VKP(B) i Voennoe Delo (2nd ed. 1928), p. 350, it " laid down the correct lines of party organization in the army within the established framework of party leadership and construction in the army ". A year later the elective principle had been so far eliminated that " the bureau of the cell is frequently nominated from above, and pressure is exercised at elections " ; and this was said to be adversely affecting party work in the Red Army (Izvestiya Tsentral'nogo Komiteta Rossiiskoi Kommunisticheskoi Partii (Bol'shevikov), No. 15-16 (90-91), April 21, 1925, p. 21).
[4] K. Voroshilov, Stat'i i Rechi (1937), p. 563.
[5] It was reiterated in December 1924 by Frunze : " Our estimate in the spring and summer was such that we knew by and large that throughout the summer and autumn of this year we must not allow ourselves to be provoked into any kind of armed action whatever " (M. Frunze, Sobranie Sochinenii, ii (1926), 194).

Unshlikht, deputy president of the Cheka and of the GPU from 1921 to 1923, was transferred, after a difference of opinion with his chief Dzerzhinsky in the autumn of 1923,[1] to the People's Commissariat of War, and became an active member of the group. Early in 1924 a deputation from the party central committee, consisting of Tomsky, Frunze, Pyatakov and Gusev, visited Trotsky, who throughout this period was sick or convalescent in Sukhum, to secure his endorsement of changes in the organization and personnel of the People's Commissariat of War. Trotsky describes the visit as " the purest comedy ", since " the replacement of personnel had been going on for a long time behind my back ". It culminated in March 1924 in the appointment of Frunze as deputy People's Commissar for War in succession to Sklyansky, who had held the post since 1918 and was now transferred to economic work.[2] In the reconstruction of the high command, the post of commander-in-chief was abolished, and Sergei Kamenev became inspector-general of the Red Army.[3] Lebedev, a professional soldier who had been chief of staff for several years and had kept aloof from current controversies, seems to have been silently retired ; " the duties of chief of staff " were taken over by Frunze.[4] Tukhachevsky became deputy chief of staff with the special mission of army reorganization.[5] Trotsky, while remaining titular People's Commissar for War and president of the Revolutionary Military Council, acquiesced in changes patently designed to eliminate his supporters and destroy his authority in military affairs. Frunze, whose status was enhanced by his election after the thirteenth party congress in May 1924 as a candidate member of the Politburo, played the leading rôle

[1] See *The Interregnum, 1923–1924*, p. 223, note 1.

[2] L. Trotsky, *Moya Zhizn'* (Berlin, 1930), ii, 253-254 ; in Trotsky's view Frunze was " a serious person ", but " far inferior to Sklyansky as a military administrator ". Frunze's appointment was announced in *Izvestiya*, March 14, 1924.

[3] *Entsiklopedicheskii Slovar' Russkogo Bibliograficheskogo Instituta Granat*, xli, i (n.d. [1927]), Prilozhenie, col. 178.

[4] See the biographical notice in M. Frunze, *Izbrannye Proizvedeniya* (1950), p. 10 ; no public announcement has been traced. According to a statement in *Forschungen zur Osteuropäischen Geschichte*, ii (1955), 324, based on the unpublished archives of Brockdorff-Rantzau, Lebedev had been relieved of his duties in May 1923.

[5] *Entsiklopedicheskii Slovar' Russkogo Bibliograficheskogo Instituta Granat*, xli, iii (n.d. [1928]), Prilozhenie, col. 163.

in the large body of military reforms undertaken during 1924, while Trotsky stood helplessly and indifferently aside. Trotsky's numerous speeches during the year 1924 included no significant pronouncement on military affairs. In the fresh campaign against Trotsky provoked by *Lessons of October* in the autumn of 1924, Gusev repeated the old attacks on Trotsky's military policies ; reverting to the half-forgotten controversy about the single military doctrine, he accused Trotsky of divorcing military science from Marxism, and resuscitated Frunze's old charges of Menshevism and liquidationism.[1] But these were mere rivulets in the spate of denunciation. When in January 1925 Trotsky was at length deposed from his military office, and succeeded by Frunze, with Unshlikht as his deputy,[2] these appointments merely regularized a situation which had existed *de facto* throughout the past year. In May 1925 Kamenev became chief of staff,[3] Tukhachevsky remaining as deputy chief of staff.

The reforms introduced by Frunze and associated with his name covered a wide range, and laid the foundations on which the Red Army developed for the next decade. The two most important and contentious were concerned with the composition and reorganization of the army, and with the relation of the political commissars, and of political work generally, to the military command. The main lines of the future organization of the Red Army — a combination of regular and territorial formations — had in fact been determined by the call-up of the autumn of 1923. It was decided to stabilize the armed forces on the basis of existing numbers. Of an available annual contingent of 800,000 or 900,000 men, 280,000 would be taken each year for two years' service in the regular army, which would thus be maintained at the figure of 560,000. This would be an army living in barracks and trained in the use of modern weapons : it included navy, air force and technical units. A further 250,000 men would be enrolled annually in territorial units, in which they would receive a short period of annual training for five years

[1] For Gusev's articles see p. 21, note 1 above ; for Frunze's charges see p. 390 above.   [2] See p. 33 above.

[3] *Entsiklopedicheskii Slovar' Russkogo Bibliograficheskogo Instituta Granat,* xli, i (n.d. [1927]), Prilozhenie, col. 178.

(not more than two months in any one year). The remainder of the annual contingent would be liable to be called up for military training where practicable, but would not be taken away from their homes or normal occupations.[1] These arrangements formed the basis of the call-up in the autumn of 1924, and were embodied in a formal resolution of the Revolutionary Military Council at the end of November 1924 which was published in the press.[2] The announcement appeared at the height of the embittered argument over Trotsky's *Lessons of October*, and excited little controversy. Military opinion as reflected by the officer corps would have preferred a larger regular army on grounds of greater efficiency if this had been practicable.[3] Frunze himself had specifically rejected the doctrinaire view of a militia as " perfect in itself and best adapted to our conditions ", defending the militia system as necessary " from the financial and general economic point of view ", but making reservations about its efficiency.[4] At the moment of the 1924 call-up he issued a warning that the militia, if not treated by party, Soviet and trade union organs " with sufficient seriousness ", might become " a source of weakness for us ".[5] The mixed system adopted in 1924 was in no sense ideal. It was an expression both of the country's industrial backwardness and of the compromise with the peasant which marked the whole NEP period. The Red Army of the nineteen-twenties was still an army which relied primarily on man-power.[6]

---

[1] This elementary military training was at first not organized by the army at all, but by rifle clubs, physical culture groups, schools and other educational institutions (*K XIV S"ezdu RKP(B)* (1925), p. 174).

[2] *Pravda*, December 3, 1924. The council sat from November 26 to December 1, 1924 ; its proceedings were apparently published, but have not been available.

[3] " Of course, if we had the choice between a regular army of $1\frac{1}{2}$ or 2 million men and the present militia system, from the military point of view all the data would be in favour of the former solution " (M. Frunze, *Sobranie Sochinenii*, iii (1927), 289). Trotsky wrote at this time : " It does not at all follow that the proletariat after its rise to power, supported by an extremely low level of productive capacity, can on the next day create a tactic which will in principle correspond to the higher productive capacities of the future socialist society " (*Pravda*, March 28, 1924).

[4] M. Frunze, *Sobranie Sochinenii*, ii (1926), 52.   [5] *Ibid.* ii, 109.

[6] Frunze noted, by way of contrast, that " in the largest bourgeois countries the living man is beginning to give place to the machine ", but offered the far-fetched explanation that this was due to their inability to rely on armed forces consisting of workers and peasants (*ibid.* iii (1927), 376).

It remained to give the compromise of November 1924 legislative sanction. This was achieved during 1925 in a leisurely manner which suggests divided opinions behind the scenes. The principle of combining regular with territorial formations was once more laid down and approved at the third congress of Soviets of the USSR in May 1925.[1] In the following month a draft decree was prepared by the Revolutionary Military Council for submission to Sovnarkom and VTsIK.[2] It was finally issued on September 18, 1925, to come into effect on October 1. All citizens from the age of 21 to 40 were liable to military service (with pre-military training from 19 to 21 [3]). Service might take one of three forms : enrolment in the regular army for two years ; enrolment in a territorial unit, involving service for a period of 8 to 12 months spread over five years (not more than 3 months in any one year) ; or military training for not more than 6 months in all without enrolment. Citizens who had no political rights were to be enrolled for non-combatant service.[4] Some anxiety was clearly felt in party circles about the reception of the new regulations. On the eve of the issue of the decree, the party journal published an article strongly defending the territorial system on the ground that it had won the confidence of the peasantry.[5] Shortly afterwards a leading article in the military newspaper sought to overcome the hostility or contempt evidently felt by the professional soldier for the territorial levies. Carrying the

---

[1] *Tretii S"ezd Sovetov SSSR : Postanovleniya* (1925), pp. 38-44 ; the resolution is also in *Sobranie Zakonov, 1925*, No. 35, art. 249.

[2] *Leningradskaya Pravda*, June 30, 1925.

[3] Pre-military training, mainly concerned with physical culture, was in the hands of a special department called Vsevobuch (universal military training) ; it must have been confined, at any rate at first, to the large centres.

[4] *Sobranie Zakonov, 1925*, No. 62, arts. 462, 463. The principle that " non-toilers " should not bear arms was still strongly insisted on in theory, though not always in practice (M. Frunze, *Sobranie Sochinenii*, iii (1927), 188) ; Trotsky, in speaking of the first territorial levies in the autumn of 1923, had demanded the greatest vigilance in excluding " traders and *kulaks* " (L. Trotsky, *Kak Vooruzhalas' Revolyutsiya*, iii, ii (1925), 163). Labour battalions had disappeared after the civil war, and these " non-toiler " elements, sometimes referred to as *nepy*, served as batmen or in menial occupations (*Krasnaya Zvezda*, January 3, 1925).

[5] *Bol'shevik*, No. 16, September 1, 1925, pp. 40-50 ; Frunze had claimed in May 1925 that " the commanding and political personnel is beginning to enjoy more respect and gratitude from the peasantry " (M. Frunze, *Sobranie Sochinenii*, iii (1927), 235).

title *Face to the Territorial System*, it explained that the system
had already been approved by the ninth party congress in 1920,
that " a good half " of the army was already on this basis, and
that " the position of the USSR is such that its defence depends
chiefly on the territorial units ", which should be regarded as
" the foundation of our armed forces ". It was wrong to treat
them as if they were on the same footing as the regular army ;
but to approach them with scepticism was equally wrong. Another
article in the same issue argued that junior officers for the territorial units should be drawn from the region itself — another
attempt to apply the regional principle.[1] The decree of September
18, 1925, settled the form of the Red Army for almost a decade. By
1926 65 per cent of the Red Army was raised on a militia basis.[2]

The drastic reduction in the size of the Red Army brought
with it a corresponding reduction in the officer corps. It was
natural that an attempt should have been made to dispense first
with the services of former Tsarist officers : of an original total
of more than 30,000 some 12,500 were said to have been retired
in 1921.[3] But the first systematic reorganization of the officer
corps was undertaken by Frunze in the spring of 1924, and was
connected in part with the general process of reform in the Red
Army and in part with the campaign against Trotsky. Trotsky
had been known as the protector of Tsarist officers and as the
opponent of the class principle in the army, and had been attacked
both by the old military opposition of 1920 and by the later
Frunze-Gusev group on both counts. When in April 1924
Frunze announced a comb-out in the officer corps he was careful
to deny that any " general persecution of specialists " was intended. He laid stress on the need to promote younger and
newly trained men from below whose capacities had hitherto
been denied an outlet, and clinched the argument with an implicit
criticism of Trotsky's policy :

> Had we taken this course earlier and more firmly, there
> would probably be no necessity now for the general shake-up
> which is at present being carried out.[4]

[1] *Krasnaya Zvezda*, October 17, 1925.
[2] *X Let Krasnoi Armii : Al'bom Diagramm* (1928), p. 19.
[3] *Grazhdanskaya Voina, 1918–1921*, ed. A. Bubnov, S. Kamenev and
R. Eideman, ii (1928), 97-98.
[4] M. Frunze, *Sobranie Sochinenii*, ii (1926), 35-36.

A few months later he once more announced that " preference
will be given to those who have risen from below, who have a
broad fighting experience, and have retained their vigour un-
impaired ".[1] In the higher age-groups all junior officers and a
considerable proportion of field officers are said to have been
retired.[2] The older officers liable to dismissal were in the nature
of things predominantly former Tsarist officers. A far larger
number of officer and higher administrative personnel was retired
in 1924 than in 1923 (9400 as against 2750), and the proportion
among them returned as " former whites " was also much higher
(1500 as against 50).[3] On the other hand, those retained were
finally relieved of the stigma of a separate classification as " former
white officers " in Red Army records.[4] " We want ", exclaimed
Frunze in January 1925, " to have a single officer corps fully
equal in rights, not dividing it for service purposes into party
and non-party men."[5] The " shake-up " of 1924 in the officer
corps would seem to have been more directly aimed at supporters
of Trotsky than at former Tsarist officers. After the process was
complete, 16·8 per cent of Red Army officers had received their
whole training, and 7·5 per cent part of their training, in the
Tsarist army.[6] Voroshilov, in a eulogy of the " old specialists "
in February 1926, declared that there was now " scarcely any
difference " between them and other Red Army commanders.[7]
Prejudices nevertheless died hard. More than a year later
Voroshilov himself complained of a lack of a " closely welded
collective of the commanding and political personnel " which
sometimes drove the older officers to " despair ".[8]

An important element in the Frunze reforms was the search
for an increase in efficiency through an improvement in the status
of the officers, and in the discipline and training of both officers
and rank and file. The first step towards the creation of an
efficient officer corps was an improvement in its material condi-

[1] M. Frunze, *Sobranie Sochinenii*, ii (1926), 171.
[2] *Ibid.* ii, 194.
[3] *Grazhdanskaya Voina, 1918–1921*, ed. A. Bubnov, S. Kamenev and
R. Eideman, ii (1928), 101, 103.
[4] *Ibid.* ii, 107.
[5] M. Frunze, *Sobranie Sochinenii*, iii (1927), 33-34.
[6] *X Let Krasnoi Armii : Al'bom Diagramm* (1928), p. 37.
[7] K. Voroshilov, *Stat'i i Rechi* (1937), p. 50.
[8] K. Voroshilov, *Oborona SSSR* (1927), pp. 75-76.

tions. In the days of the civil war and with the prejudice against specialists at its height, Trotsky issued an appeal for " greater equality " between all ranks in the Red Army ; [1] and a party directive of February 1921 instructed political commissars to live with their men in barracks and share in the life of the party cells and to maintain the principle of equality between officers and men.[2] But, with the coming of NEP, a different trend soon declared itself. The tenth party congress in March 1921 decided, in view of the fact that the army had now become a " permanent profession ", to " take measures for a real improvement in the material position of the officer corps, especially of its lower ranks ".[3] For some time, with demobilization actively in progress, little was done. In February 1923 a regular scale of pay for officers was for the first time fixed in goods rubles, and in August of the same year, when the foundations of the territorial system were being laid, substantial increases were granted.[4] The reforms of 1924 brought junior and field officers two successive increases in pay, said to have amounted on an average to nearly 30 per cent.[5] In February 1925 Frunze claimed that the material conditions of the officer corps had so improved that they were no longer obliged " to think continually about their crust of bread ", and could " devote all their energy to the business of training Red Army men ".[6] But three months later, at the third Union Congress of Soviets, he instituted a comparison between the pay of Soviet officers and of the officers of other European armies, purporting to show that the pay of officers in other armies was substantially higher than in the Red Army, and in the British army from five to ten times as great. Moreover, 70 per cent of Red Army officers were inadequately housed, and married officers were living with their families in a single room.[7] Voroshilov, who

[1] L. Trotsky, *Kak Vooruzhalas' Revolyutsiya*, ii, i (1924), 83-87.

[2] *Izvestiya Tsentral'nogo Komiteta Rossiiskoi Kommunisticheskoi Partii (Bol'-shevikov)*, No. 30, April 4, 1921, pp. 6-7.

[3] *VKP(B) v Rezolyutsiyakh* (1941), i, 393 ; Trotsky strongly supported the proposal in a speech of October 1921 (L. Trotsky, *Kak Vooruzhalas' Revolyutsiya*, iii, i (1924), 54).

[4] Figures from a contemporary publication are quoted in *VKP(B) i Voennoe Delo* (2nd ed. 1928), pp. 313-314.

[5] M. Frunze, *Sobranie Sochinenii*, ii (1926), 144-145.

[6] *Ibid.* iii (1927), 100.

[7] *Ibid.* iii, 226.

succeeded Frunze in November 1925, admitted that officers of the Red Army were not as highly paid as officers of other armies, and that they did not aspire to " the rates of pay of generals ", but promised that their economic status would improve with rising prosperity in the country.[1] An important decree of March 1926 made extensive provision for social insurance and pensions for Red Army officers, and claimed to provide for them full " state security ".[2] The measures reflected not only improved material conditions, but a recognition of the rising status of the officer corps of the Red Army in the Soviet hierarchy.[3]

As material conditions slowly improved, progress was made with the more delicate question of military discipline. Here, too, revolutionary egalitarianism in its extreme form did not survive the civil war. But it left marked traces on the practice of the ensuing period. Towards the end of the civil war the party instructed " members of revolutionary military councils, commissars and other persons holding official posts " in the Red Army to " apply revolutionary discipline "; but they were, all the same, to " struggle decisively against the routine of the old military system ".[4] During the demobilization period after the civil war, when material conditions were at their worst, discipline throughout the army also sank to a low ebb. To restore it was one of the tasks of the reform of 1924. Bukharin, at the fifth congress of Comintern in June 1924, was led into an unexpected digression on Red Army discipline :

> Our army is in a high degree similar to the quite ordinary bourgeois army. Once upon a time we thought that the structure of our army would look quite different : no forced discipline, only conscious discipline. But experience showed that the forms of conscious discipline in this literal sense are inapplicable, though naturally this consciousness plays a larger rôle with us than in other armies. Therefore we have various measures of compulsion in the army, and that is absolutely necessary : we even shoot deserters. . . . The formal structure

---

[1] K. Voroshilov, *Stat'i i Rechi* (1937), p. 27 ; for further details see *VKP(B) i Voennoe Delo* (2nd ed. 1928), p. 313.

[2] *Sobranie Zakonov, 1926*, No. 20, art. 131.

[3] According to E. Wollenberg, *The Red Army* (2nd ed. 1940), pp. 188-189, Voroshilov in 1926 not only increased officers' pay, but introduced separate officers' messes, which had not hitherto existed in the Red Army.

[4] *VKP(B) v Rezolyutsiyakh* (1941), i, 352.

is like that of a bourgeois army. But that is not the decisive
thing. The decisive thing is its different class character.[1]

In a speech to army officers of November 1924 Frunze attacked the
slackness of some officers and commissars in matters of discipline :

> In many cases instead of a firm and categorical request to
> carry out an official duty we have an unprincipled " currying
> favour " with the rank and file of Red Army men, a desire to
> display a special " democratic spirit ".
> This " democratic spirit " is the crudest perversion of any
> and every rule of discipline in our Red Army. A command is
> a command. To persuade and exhort men to carry out orders
> is in itself a crude breach of discipline.[2]

In a speech a month later he used a recent incident to refute the
common notion that communism and military discipline did not
go together. A territorial unit on the march was " straggling
badly, notwithstanding all the efforts of the commanding officer ",
who " made a remark in sharp and cutting terms ". The communist cell met and passed a vote of censure on him, thus proving
that they understood nothing of military discipline. In capitalist
countries, discipline was " based on the class inferiority of the
rank-and-file soldier ". In the Red Army it was based " on the
necessity for a correct division of labour, correct leadership and
correct responsibility ".[3] But to treat " military precision, the
discipline of the line, external order " as " something harmful,
unrevolutionary and unnecessary " was " absolute nonsense ".[4]
At the Komsomol conference of June 1925 Frunze reproved the
organization for its poor standard of discipline. Members of the
Komsomol formed in 1924 30 per cent of the crews of the Baltic
fleet, but committed 61 per cent of the disciplinary offences. In
the Ukrainian and North Caucasian military districts more than
30 per cent of mobilized members of the Komsomol had been
punished for disciplinary offences in the first three months of
1925, though Frunze consolingly added that most of the offences
had not been grave.[5] At the end of the year PUR reported to the
fourteenth party congress an improvement in the discipline of

---

[1] *Protokoll : Fünfter Kongress der Kommunistischen Internationale* (n.d.),
ii, 527.   [2] M. Frunze, *Sobranie Sochinenii*, ii (1926), 146.
[3] *Ibid.* ii, 186-188.   [4] *Ibid.* iii (1927), 32.   [5] *Ibid.* iii, 296-298.

the Red Army, both in general and among mobilized members of the party and of the Komsomol.[1]

The most delicate and controversial question with which Frunze had to cope was the relation of party control in the Red Army, and especially of the political commissars, to the military command. In capitalist countries relations between politicians and soldiers had often been uneasy. The Red Army, since the early days of the specialists, had always reflected in an acute form the tension between the professional expert and the spokesman of party policy. In theory, nobody contested the principle of unity of command ; Lenin was on record as having hailed with satisfaction in 1920 the " approach to one-man command " in the army.[2] In practice, compromise was inevitable so long as the distinction between party and non-party was significant, and so long, in particular, as a substantial proportion of the professional experts were identified with the traditions of the old régime.[3] Nor was this an issue which divided different groups in the party. Trotsky was known as a defender of the interests of the specialists and professionals, and the advocates of the single military doctrine prided themselves on their party and proletarian outlook. Yet Trotsky at the eleventh party congress in 1922 had emphatically declared that there could be no question of abolishing the political commissars, even where the military commander was a party member ;[4] and Frunze, when he rose to a position of authority, became the unhesitating champion of the rights and interests of the officer corps.

The keenness of the rivalry between the political commissars and the military supporters of unity of command tended, however,

---

[1] *K XIV S"ezdu RKP(B)* (1925), p. 165.

[2] Lenin, *Sochineniya*, xxv, 18.

[3] The compromise was expressed in the formally ambiguous position of PUR, which was an organ both of the Revolutionary Military Council and of the party central committee : from 1924 onwards its director was always a member of both these bodies. The new party statute authorized by the fourteenth party congress in December 1925 described PUR as " the military section of the [party] central committee ", responsible for " the direction of party work in the Red Army and the Red Fleet " (*VKP(B) v Rezolyutsiyakh* (1941), ii, 88).

[4] *Odinnadtsatyi S"ezd RKP(B)* (1936), p. 306.

to obscure the subtle change which had occurred in the issue at stake. The title of political commissar remained. But the function exercised by the original commissars of supervising the loyalty of the military commanders to whom they were attached became to all intents and purposes obsolete at the end of the civil war. Such a function was largely meaningless in time of peace ; and after the introduction of NEP the loyalty of the former Tsarist officers remaining in the Red Army was not in serious doubt. The main function of the political commissars in the NEP period was to supervise not the loyalty of the commanders, but the morale of the rank and file. This was a task of party propaganda and political education, and became highly important in an army dependent mainly on raw peasant levies. The likelihood of jealousy and friction between the political commissar and the non-party military commander still existed. But it was clearly less acute than in the days when the presence of the commissar was an expression of doubt of the commander's loyalty. On the other hand, friction now sometimes arose between the political commissar and other party authorities, since the commissar attempted to use his military position to assert an independence not enjoyed by other party functionaries. This created in some party circles a certain mistrust of political commissars who allowed their allegiance to the army to predominate over their allegiance to the party.

The first occasion on which these new aspects of party work in the army, and of the functions and status of the political commissars, figured in a party resolution appears to have been at the party conference of September 1920 when the civil war was reaching its end. The conference drew the attention of members of revolutionary military councils, commissars and other officials to the task of fostering " revolutionary discipline " in the army by establishing close contact with the rank and file, though it also declared any separation between such work and " general party life and work " to be inadmissible ; [1] and the tenth party congress in March 1921 cautiously insisted both on the " complete independence " of the political apparatus of the Red Army, and on the need to "*strengthen* its link with local party organizations".[2] The

[1] *VKP(B) v Rezolyutsiyakh* (1941), i, 352, 354.
[2] *Ibid.* i, 393. Another resolution of the congress introduced a fresh element of confusion by making Glavpolitprosvet responsible for political

next two or three years were marked by growing attention to the importance of party and political propaganda in the Red Army. One result of the demobilization at the end of the civil war had been to reduce to a minimum the number of party members in the Red Army : in 1922–1923 scarcely any were to be found outside the commanding and political staff.[1] The army was largely composed of peasants. The peasant had become a central factor in party and Soviet policy ; and the call-up provided the best — indeed, almost the only — opportunity to inculcate in the peasantry the virtues of party doctrine and loyalty to the régime. Stalin, at the twelfth party congress in 1923, spoke of the Red Army as " a meeting-place of workers and peasants " — " the only meeting-place where workers and peasants of different provinces, sundered from one another, come together, and, coming together, work out their political views " ; [2] and the thirteenth congress a year later commended the transition to the territorial militia system on the ground that it would become a medium linking party and state with the peasantry.[3] The growing importance of this work increased the insistence of the party authorities on the strict subordination to them of PUR and the political commissars ; and

education in the army and subordinating the commissars to it for this purpose (*VKP)B*) *v Rezolyutsiyakh* (1941), i, 379-380 ; for Glavpolitprosvet see pp. 192-193 above) ; this state of affairs lasted till the summer of 1922 when political education in the army was once more transferred from Glavpolitprosvet to PUR (*VKP(B) i Voennoe Delo* (2nd ed. 1928), p. 297).

[1] A. Geronimus, *Partiya i Krasnaya Armiya* (1928), p. 154. This situation improved only slowly. The thirteenth party congress in May 1924 proposed to " increase the number of communists among Red Army men and sailors " (*VKP(B) v Rezolyutsiyakh* (1941), i, 568) ; a party circular of April 1925 deplored the low proportion of party members among Red Army men (*Izvestiya Tsentral'nogo Komiteta Rossiiskoi Kommunisticheskoi Partii (Bol'shevikov)*, No. 13-14 (88-89), April 6, 1925, p. 5). About the same time Frunze claimed that 12 per cent of the armed forces were members of the Komsomol (M. Frunze, *Sobranie Sochinenii*, iii (1927), 299) ; according to Molotov at the fourteenth party congress, the proportion of " communists " (i.e. members of the party or of the Komsomol) in the Red Army rose from 11 per cent in 1924 to 15 per cent in 1925 (*XIV S"ezd Vsesoyuznoi Kommunisticheskoi Partii (B)* (1926), p. 70). Even so, it was far lower than the proportion among officers (see p. 415 below). [2] Stalin, *Sochineniya*, v, 204.

[3] *VKP(B) v Rezolyutsiyakh* (1941), i, 594. Trotsky paradoxically used the same argument to justify the maintenance of " regular " divisions ; the " Red barrack " must be retained as an educational influence on the young peasant (L. Trotsky, *Kak Vooruzhalas' Revolyutsiya*, iii, ii (1925), pp. vii-xii ; this preface originally appeared as an article under the title *Step by Step* in *Pravda*, November 1, 1924).

this in turn tended to weaken the prestige of the commissar *vis-à-vis* the military commander.

The party controversy of the winter of 1923-1924 adversely affected the position of the political commissars. That Trotsky should at this time have found such strong support in PUR and among the political commissars in the Red Army, drawn for the most part from the ranks of party intellectuals, tended to discredit these institutions in the eyes of the party leadership. Bubnov had heralded his appointment to PUR by an instruction which, in reversing his predecessor's encouragement of free political discussion, had seemed to imply that the work of the political commissars was in future to be subordinated to the requirements of military discipline.[1] For some months the current set in this direction. The commission on the reorganization of the Red Army appointed in January 1924 reported three months later that one-man command was " the practical question towards the solution of which the whole system of our work of military construction is advancing ", though it admitted that it was impossible at present " to force the introduction of one-man command ".[2] In June 1924 the Orgburo made a pronouncement in favour of unity of command as " the practical principle for the organization of the Red Army ", but left it to the organs of the Red Army to work out details of application.[3] When in the following month Bubnov said that the essence of the military reforms in progress was " the liquidation of the survivals of war communism ",[4] he used a favourite catch-phrase to which many different meanings were attached. But one of its meanings in this context was a curbing of the authority of that characteristic institution of the civil war period — the political commissars of the Red Army. About the same time Frunze described the institution of political commissars as " temporary ", and spoke of the " firm course " set by the party for " a transition to the so-called unity of command ". He admitted that the completion of the reform had been delayed, but " the Revolutionary Military

---

[1] See p. 396 above.

[2] A. Geronimus, *Partiya i Krasnaya Armiya* (1928), pp. 170-171 ; for the commission see p. 395 above.

[3] Quoted in *VKP(B) i Voennoe Delo* (2nd ed. 1928), p. 343.

[4] *Shestoi S"ezd Rossiiskogo Leninskogo Kommunisticheskogo Soyuza Molodezhi* (1924), p. 308.

Council recognizes its obligation, so soon as favourable conditions for the unity of command are realized, to carry it unflinchingly into effect ".[1]

The solution was, however, by no means so simple. The fundamental need for a compromise between the authority of the military experts and the authority of the party remained ; and the vested interests of the political commissars were strong. A conference of political workers in the army in November 1924 insisted that " one-man command in the army cannot be treated‹ as the liquidation of the institution of commissars ", since these were a necessary element of "party leadership and political education in the army ".[2] The November resolution of the Revolutionary Military Council on army reform bore witness to the prevailing embarrassment.[3] It restated all the elements of the dilemma ; and its main contribution seems to have been the invention of a new and ambiguous formula. Two forms of one-man command were now distinguished. One was the concentration of military, economic and administrative powers in the hands of the commander, while political functions remained with the commissar (this appeared to abrogate the control of the commissar·in non-political matters, but fell short of what had hitherto been understood as one-man command). The other was the concentration of all functions in the hands of the commander ; this was conceivable only if the commander was a party man enjoying the full confidence of the party authorities. Frunze admitted that this second form could not be a " widely spread phenomenon ", since the personal conditions for it were very strict, and that the first would be the " prevailing form of one-man command ".[4] Some party stalwarts interpreted the resolution as a " decisive rejection " of those " tendencies to subordinate the political organs to the military staffs " which had manifested themselves earlier in 1924.[5] But Frunze's interpretation in a speech delivered

[1] M. Frunze, *Sobranie Sochinenii*, ii (1926), 83.
[2] *VKP(B) i Voennoe Delo* (2nd ed. 1928), pp. 343-344.
[3] *Ibid.* pp. 344-345.
[4] The text of the resolution has not been available (for this session of the Revolutionary Military Council see p. 399, note 2 above), but a fairly full account of it was given in two speeches of Frunze (M. Frunze, *Sobranie Sochinenii*, ii (1926), 152-153, 176-183).
[5] This interpretation is represented in N. Kharitonov, *Politicheskii Apparat Krasnoi Armii* (1929), pp. 30-32.

a few weeks later was more tactful and cautious. Most military commanders, he said, even if they were communists, would have to be content with supreme authority in the spheres of combat, administration and supply, leaving the political sphere to the commissar. But he added with emphasis that " the non-party section of the command personnel should regard the decisions of the plenum on this question as an expression of the complete confidence of the Soviet Government and of the Communist Party in it " ; and he spoke of " the process of transition to one-man command " as likely to be realized in the forthcoming year.[1]

In January 1925 Frunze succeeded Trotsky as People's Commissar for War and president of the Revolutionary Military Council,[2] and from this time began to lean more openly to the side of the military commanders. Blame for conflicts within the Red Army was laid at the door of political workers who failed to support the military command in maintaining discipline ; some of them were accused of attempting to curry favour with the rank and file by posing as protectors of its interests against the military commanders.[3] But the obstacles to a clear-cut solution were formidable. An ordinance of the Revolutionary Military Council of March 2, 1925, prescribed that important orders were to be signed jointly by the military commander and by the commissar, and routine orders by each independently within his own sphere ; but the attempt to clarify the demarcation of functions between them was vague and unsuccessful. A significant point was that, though the commissar could appeal to higher authority against the order of a commander, the appeal did not have the effect of suspending the validity of the order pending a decision.[4] This ordinance was followed up by a circular issued in the name of the party central committee and bearing the title " On One-Man Command in the Red Army ". The circular declared that " the tasks of the corps of commissars . . . must be radically changed ". Operational and administrative functions were entirely in the hands of the commander, and the commissar was " freed from day-to-day control over them ", though he " retains

---

[1] M. Frunze, *Sobranie Sochinenii*, ii (1926), 182-185.
[2] See p. 33 above.
[3] M. Frunze, *Sobranie Sochinenii*, ii (1926), 188.
[4] *Ibid.* ii, 310-311, note 86.

the direction of political and party work in the unit and is responsible for its social-political condition ". Where the military commander was a party man and capable of exercising these functions, the military and political functions might be combined in the same person. The instruction did not apply to national military units or to the Red Fleet, where the introduction of one-man command must proceed more slowly.[1] A conference of secretaries of party cells in the army, which was addressed by Frunze, emphasized the change which the party apparatus in the army had undergone. If the function of the political commissar had once been to keep watch on the military commander, his function and that of the party cells throughout the army was now to " help the whole military apparatus in the task of establishing iron discipline in the ranks of the army and fleet ".[2] Meanwhile Frunze, commenting a few weeks later on the March circular, optimistically declared that the principle of unity of command had been " settled in an entirely precise and definite way " : the only thing that delayed its full and immediate application was the need to re-train and re-allocate the political commissars, who were too influential to be simply dispossessed.[3] In June 1925 Frunze told a party conference of the Leningrad Military Region that a fully responsible officer corps was indispensable to the Red Army, that " our former system of dual power, demanded by political considerations, hindered the development of this officer corps ", and insisted that even the non-party military commander would henceforth have full authority except in party matters.[4] Gusev more realistically noted the growing influence of the party in military affairs and recognized the strength of the opposition to " one-man command ", though he consolingly added that the objections were not to the principle, but to " the forcing of the question ". Undeterred by these doubts, the conference passed a resolution advocating " the militarization of the political staff ".[5]

[1] *Izvestiya Tsentral'nogo Komiteta Rossiiskoi Kommunisticheskoi Partii (Bol'-shevikov)*, No. 11-12 (86-87), March 23, 1925, p. 16. The circular appeared in small print in an inconspicuous place on the back page ; this treatment, unusual for so important a pronouncement, suggests that some party circles were either out of sympathy with the decision or apprehensive of the reaction to it.

[2] *Ibid.* No. 13-14 (88-89), April 6, 1925, pp. 4-6.

[3] M. Frunze, *Izbrannye Proizvedeniya* (1934), pp. 407-409.

[4] M. Frunze, *Sobranie Sochinenii*, iii (1927), 316-317.

[5] *Leningradskaya Pravda*, June 21, 24, 1925.

Following on this campaign, the Revolutionary Military Council issued at the end of July 1925 a " temporary statute for military commissars of the Red Army and the Red Fleet ", based on the ordinance and the party circular of the preceding March.[1] But none of these efforts was successful in eradicating a stubborn opposition. Frunze, in February 1925, had admitted that some party members were seeking to delay the establishment of one-man command till all military commanders were party men, though "this will never be, and we do not desire it ".[2] Six months later, he again noted "a negative attitude among a certain part of our commissar personnel to the whole of this reform ", as a result of which very little had yet been achieved ; [3] according to a party report, resistance among commissars and other party workers in the army was so strong that some had been asked to be demobilized from army work.[4] At the end of 1925 unity was reported to have been achieved in 73·3 per cent of corps commands, in 44 per cent of divisional commands, and 33·4 per cent of regimental commands, by one of the two now recognized forms of one-man command.[5] At the height of the campaign for unity of command, these percentages represented something far short of complete success.

When, therefore, the split in the triumvirate became apparent in the autumn of 1925, the first of the two major issues of military policy — the size and form of the new army — had been settled by the decree of September 18, 1925.[6] The second — the relation between military commanders and political commissars — seemed well on the way to a settlement which favoured the military element, but still encountered strong resistance in the party. It is a tribute to the strength of the party tradition to avoid public dispute on military questions that this controversial issue never played any visible part in the party struggle. But a situation in which party capital might have been made out of any unpopular move was inimical to decisive action. Any step forward was bound to offend an influential body of opinion in the party ; and

---

[1] K. Voroshilov, *Oborona SSSR* (1927), p. 80 ; the text has not been traced.

[2] M. Frunze, *Sobranie Sochinenii*, iii (1927), 125.   [3] *Ibid.* iii, 359.

[4] *K XIV S"ezdu RKP(B)* (1925), pp. 165, 167-168.

[5] *Ibid.* p. 165.   [6] See p. 400 above.

the enforcement of·unity of command in the Red Army appears to have made little progress during the summer and autumn of 1925.[1] Frunze's death at the end of October 1925 no doubt encouraged a further postponement. At the Leningrad provincial party conference early in December 1925, a delegate named Shelavin feared that " an intention is evidently gaining ground to subordinate the political organs to the [military] command ", and thought that more attention should be given to " deviations occurring in such an important field as the Red Army ".[2] At the ensuing fourteenth party congress Shelavin was mildly derided by Molotov for having discovered a " Trotskyist deviation " in party work in the Red Army, and more solemnly reproved by Orjonikidze.[3] But the question was not otherwise discussed, and neither Stalin nor Zinoviev nor any other of the leaders openly took sides on it. When Voroshilov was appointed to succeed Frunze, with Lashevich as his deputy, Tukhachevsky replaced Sergei Kamenev as chief of staff of the Red Army.[4] But Tukhachevsky, though his sympathies were probably on the side of the military commanders, was also an astute politician ; and Voroshilov, a man of far less character and independence than Frunze, showed no great eagerness to insist on the awkward issue of unity of command. The uneasy compromise between the authority of the military command and the political and party element represented by PUR and by the political commissars remained a source of friction throughout the nineteen-twenties.

Meanwhile, the scales were decisively weighted in favour of ultimate victory for the military element in this controversy by a single basic factor. The system of independent political commissars had been created at a time when the régime was compelled

[1] *Krasnaya Zvezda*, October 27, 1925, on the eve of Frunze's death, carried correspondence expressing divergent views on the " militarization of the political staff ", as if this was still an open question.

[2] Quoted in A. Geronimus, *Partiya i Krasnaya Armiya* (1928), p. 184 ; Shelavin's speech was, perhaps significantly, not mentioned in *Leningradskaya Pravda*, which reported the conference fairly fully.

[3] *XIV S"ezd Vsesoyuznoi Kommunisticheskoi Partii (B)* (1926), pp. 84, 226.

[4] *Entsiklopedicheskii Slovar' Russkogo Bibliograficheskogo Instituta Granat*, xli, iii (n.d. [1928]), Prilozhenie, col. 163 ; Kamenev reverted to his post as inspector-general, which he had combined since May 1925 with that of chief of staff (*ibid.* xli, i (n.d. [1927]), Prilozhenie, col. 178).

to rely on an officer corps ideologically alien, and even hostile, to it. When the régime had time to train an officer corps reared in its own traditions, and when a large proportion of high army officers, as of leaders in other professions, were party members, this justification for the anomalies and inconveniences of divided responsibility would disappear. Discrepancies occur in the figures of " communists " (i.e. members of the party or of the Komsomol) in the officer corps of the period. Molotov at the fourteenth party congress claimed that the percentage had risen from 19 in 1924 to 29 in 1925.[1] But considerably higher percentages are quoted elsewhere — 22·5 for 1922, 32 for 1924, 43 for 1925 and 47 for 1926.[2] Two factors were at work in accelerating this process. In the first place, a high proportion of the young officers passing out of the military schools now had party or Komsomol membership.[3] Secondly, senior officers, even if they had originally served under the Tsar, were now often admitted to the party in recognition of their services ; in 1926 all corps commanders, 75 per cent of heads of military schools and 55 per cent of commanders of divisions were party men, the proportion among field and junior officers being about 38 per cent.[4] The middle nineteen-twenties were a period of transition from the predominantly " specialist " officer corps of the civil war to an officer corps predominantly composed of party members ; and for the present the vested interests of the political commissars, who were party members to a man and could in the last resort count on high party backing, were a serious obstacle to reform. Once the transition to a predominantly party officer corps was complete, the demand for unity of command would prove irresistible. But the Red Army would retain enough *esprit de corps* to attract recurrent suspicion in party quarters, and the issue of

---

[1] *XIV S"ezd Vsesoyuznoi Kommunisticheskoi Partii (B)* (1926), p. 70.

[2] K. Voroshilov, *Oborona SSSR* (1927), pp. 184-185 ; A. Geronimus, *Partiya i Krasnaya Armiya* (1928), p. 166. For the much lower percentages in the rank and file see p. 408, note 1 above.

[3] Of 2000 graduating in August 1925, 65 per cent were members of the party and 15 per cent of the Komsomol (*Leningradskaya Pravda*, August 8, 1925).

[4] A. Geronimus, *Partiya i Krasnaya Armiya* (1928), p. 179 ; as late as 1925 former Tsarist officers predominated in the high command and had a virtual monopoly of staff appointments (S. Gusev, *Grazhdanskaya Voina i Krasnaya Armiya* (1925), p. 190).

political commissars would revive in a different form in the remote future.

The civil war had meant the virtual end of the Soviet navy. It had cut off the central power from every ice-free outlet ; of former Russian naval bases only Petrograd remained in Soviet hands. The larger ships of the Black Sea fleet were carried off by Wrangel, and found asylum in French North Africa at Bizerta. With all resources concentrated on the Red Army, such ships as remained were entirely denuded of men and supplies. Trotsky later recalled an occasion in 1920 on which the party central committee debated whether to lay up the ships or to sink them, since it was difficult to believe that they would ever again serve a useful purpose.[1] The Kronstadt mutiny of March 1921 cast discredit on what was left of the fleet ; as Trotsky said, " the Kronstadt fortress, the sailors' base, has become at the same time the symbol of revolt against the Soviet power ".[2] It was, nevertheless, the tenth party congress, sitting at the moment of the suppression of the Kronstadt revolt, which announced " measures to revive and strengthen the Red fighting fleet ". Recruits were to be enrolled " predominantly from factory workers " ; the Revolutionary Military Council and PUR were to be instructed to give their attention to the fleet ; and political commissars, preferably " communist sailors ", were to be appointed to it.[3]

It was an uphill task, which proceeded slowly. In December 1921 a conference of military delegates to the ninth All-Russian Congress of Soviets, in which Trotsky played a leading part, " decided to remind the whole country of the glorious rôle of Kronstadt in the birth and development of the revolution ", and declared that Kronstadt had once more become, after the " tragic episode " of March 1921, " an outpost of the proletarian revolution ".[4] It was once more Trotsky who, at a Red Fleet conference in April 1922, declared that so complex and specialized an organization " will in the nature of things develop slowly " and spoke of

---

[1] L. Trotsky, *Kak Vooruzhalas' Revolyutsiya*, iii, i (1924), 81.
[2] *Ibid.* iii, i, 34.
[3] *VKP(B) v Rezolyutsiyakh* (1941), i, 394.
[4] *Pravda*, January 4, 1922.

the need to " lay the first foundation-stone ".[1] Since the Red Fleet, unlike the Red Army, could not rely on a primitive peasantry to supply its rank and file, man-power was a perennial problem. In an attempt to solve it, the Komsomol was induced at its fifth congress in October 1922 to become the " patron " of the Red Fleet : 2000 members of the Komsomol were said to have joined it already, and more were urged to do so.[2] In his speech at the congress Trotsky expressed the hope that the Komsomol recruits would counteract both what was left of the old " narrowness " of the " privileged, arrogant and prejudiced corporate spirit ", characteristic of navies throughout the world, and the new " military-revolutionary arrogance ", which had made its appearance since 1917.[3] In the same month, Trotsky visited the destroyer squadron in the Black Sea. On his return he sent a message in which he noted " significant progress . . . in the revival of the Red Fleet ", and promised that the Revolutionary Military Council would " apply all its efforts to improve the position of the sailors and, in particular, of the officers and the quartermaster staff ".[4] In December 1922 the party central committee instructed PUR and the central committee of the Komsomol jointly to organize a navy week to be held in all provincial capitals and sea-coast towns from January 15 to 22, 1923, to popularize the Red Fleet.[5]

These methods of recruitment sufficed to keep the Red Fleet in being, and to give it a somewhat different character from the Red Army. Bubnov in 1924 boasted that of the new recruits for the navy 75 per cent were workers (63·5 per cent metal-workers — " workers from the bench ") : 74 per cent of recruits

[1] L. Trotsky, *Kak Vooruzhalas' Revolyutsiya*, iii, i (1924), 130-132. According to a French secret report quoted in *Les Relations Germano-Soviétiques*, ed. J.-B. Duroselle (1954), pp. 156, 158, arrangements for the rehabilitation of the Soviet navy with the aid of former German naval officers were discussed during a visit of Hintze (see *The Bolshevik Revolution, 1917–1923*, Vol. 3, pp. 314-315, 437, note 4) to Moscow in May 1922, and approved by Sovnarkom on September 1, 1922 : no evidence has been found that they ever became effective.

[2] *VLKSM v Rezolyutsiyakh* (1929), 101-102 ; for " patronage " see p. 343, note 1 above.

[3] L. Trotsky, *Kak Vooruzhalas' Revolyutsiya*, iii, i (1924), 136-141.

[4] *Ibid.* iii, i, 185.

[5] *Izvestiya Tsentral'nogo Komiteta Rossiiskoi Kommunisticheskoi Partii (Bol'-shevikov)*, No. 1 (49), January 1923, p. 71 ; *VKP(B) o Komsomole* (1938), pp. 251-252.

were members of the Komsomol, 25 per cent party members or candidates. In the whole Red Fleet at this time 42 per cent of the personnel were workers. Partly owing to the purge after Kronstadt and partly to these conditions of recruitment, no Trotskyite opposition appeared in the Red Fleet in 1923–1924. On the other hand, the same problems of discipline manifested themselves in the fleet, especially among Komsomol members, as had appeared in the army : they were said to be on the way to a solution.[1] The fifth congress of Comintern in June 1924 sent a delegation to visit the Baltic fleet, and revolutionary greetings were exchanged.[2] Frunze's first pronouncement on the Red Fleet seems to have been made in his speech of November 1924, when the recent de jure recognition of the Soviet Government by France had kindled hopes of a return of the ships interned in Bizerta. Frunze claimed that " a gigantic step forward " had been taken during the preceding year, and saw no reason to " put a cross over our naval construction ", though, in view of straitened resources, it would probably have to be confined to " small ships of a defensive character ".[3] In the Black Sea a Soviet fleet of 26,000 tons was confronted by Turkish, Rumanian and Bulgarian fleets amounting in all to 63,000 tons. In the Baltic, on the other hand, the Soviet fleet mustered 83,000 tons as against the 18,000 of other Baltic countries.[4] An exercise of the Baltic fleet in the summer of 1925 was said to have caused anxiety in neighbouring countries ; and Frunze, who had visited the fleet during the exercise, declared that a strong Baltic fleet was necessary to the defence of Leningrad.[5]

[1] Shestoi S"ezd Rossiiskogo Leninskogo Kommunisticheskogo Soyuza Molodezhi (1924), pp. 320-325 ; this account given to a Komsomol congress is likely to have erred on the side of optimism.

[2] Protokoll : Fünfter Kongress der Kommunistischen Internationale (n.d.), i, 452-453.

[3] M. Frunze, Sobranie Sochinenii, ii (1926), 146-147 ; for this speech see p. 405 above.

[4] M. Frunze, Sobranie Sochinenii, iii (1927), 185-186. According to a statement furnished by the Soviet Government to the commission set up under the Straits convention concluded at Lausanne in 1923 (see The Bolshevik Revolution, 1917–1923, Vol. 3, p. 489), the Soviet Black Sea fleet at the beginning of 1925 consisted of one cruiser, three submarines and a number of smaller craft fully manned, and of one battleship, one cruiser and a number of smaller craft " with reduced crews " (League of Nations : Official Journal, No. 9, November 1925, pp. 1687-1688) ; the Swedish navy seems to have been omitted from the Baltic calculations, presumably as constituting a neutral factor.

[5] M. Frunze, Sobranie Sochinenii, iii (1927), 237, 454-455.

The resolution of the third Union Congress of Soviets on the Red Army noted " significant achievements in the creation of the worker-peasant fleet ".[1] But the exclusion of the navy from the attempt to impose unity of command [2] showed plainly that, whatever the social or political complexion of the rank and file, the naval commanders did not yet enjoy the unqualified confidence of the party. Meanwhile, enthusiasm in the Komsomol seems to have fallen off : its seventh congress in March 1926 registered with regret a decline in " patronage work with the Red Fleet ".[3] The navy was now being maintained, and recruitment for it had been stabilized. But it can have had little or no value as a fighting force ; and it attracted only spasmodic attention in influential party and Soviet circles. No new ships appear to have been built or acquired in this period.

Aviation played no rôle in the civil war. The Soviet air arm seems to have owed its inspiration in part to German guidance and collaboration resulting from the secret agreements of 1922,[4] and in part to the international crisis of the first months of 1923 following the French occupation of the Ruhr. In March 1923 Trotsky declared that " with very great efforts and with the loss of much time " the question of Soviet aviation had " at last been placed on the agenda ", and announced the foundation of a Society of Friends of the Red Air Fleet (ODVF) ; in the following month he addressed the society on the importance of its work.[5] The Curzon ultimatum of May 8, 1923, came at an opportune moment to stimulate the new development. An " aviation week " was held at the end of May ; [6] and the first Soviet air squadron received the honorific name of " Ultimatum ".[7] Two years later ODVF was amalgamated with Dobrokhim, the society for chemical defence, to form a joint society known as Aviakhim.[8]

---

[1] For this resolution see p. 400, note 1 above.   [2] See p. 412 above.
[3] VII S"ezd Vsesoyuznogo Leninskogo Kommunisticheskogo Soyuza Molodezhi (1926), p. 241.
[4] For these see The Bolshevik Revolution, 1917–1923, Vol. 3, pp. 370-372, 436 ; they will be further discussed in Part V in the following volume.
[5] L. Trotsky, Kak Vooruzhalas' Revolyutsiya, iii, ii (1925), 181-184, 185-190.
[6] Ibid. iii, ii, 192-195 ; the article, entitled The Weapon of the Future, originally appeared in Pravda, May 30, 1923.
[7] M. Frunze, Izbrannye Proizvedeniya (1950), p. 572, note 69.
[8] In 1927 Aviakhim was amalgamated with the Society for the Promotion of Defence (OSO), which was the successor of the old Military Scientific

In the following year a number of Soviet aeroplane factories were united in an aviation trust, which was said by 1925 to be capable of supplying the needs of the Soviet air fleet ; and Frunze looked forward to " the liquidation of aeronautical illiteracy " in the Soviet Union.[1]

Society, to form Osoaviakhim, by which name it was thereafter known (*Bol'-shaya Sovetskaya Entsiklopediya*, xliii (1939), 468).

[1] M. Frunze, *Sobranie Sochinenii*, ii (1926), 198 ; iii (1927), 162.

CHAPTER 24

ORDER AND SECURITY

SECURITY, in the sense of the defence of the régime against its internal enemies, had been a major preoccupation since the first days of the revolution. As early as 1905 Lenin, echoing Marx, had written that " the great questions in the life of nations are settled only by force ", that it was the reactionaries who used force first, and that revolutionary dictatorship meant " defence against counter-revolution and everything that contradicts the sovereignty of the people ".[1] In 1908 he used the familiar argument from the Paris commune, which had been defeated because it failed to use sufficiently ruthless measures of repression against its enemies.[2] The traditional revolutionary use of terror to combat counter-revolution was familiar to every Bolshevik, and was freely canvassed long before it was brought into play. On the other hand, the conception of crime as the product of a disordered society and of punishment as an act not of retribution, but of reclamation and education, was deeply implanted in the thinking of the Bolsheviks, as of other Left parties. This conception found its fullest expression in the party programme adopted in March 1919, which looked forward to " a fundamental alteration in the character of punishment, introducing conditional sentences on an extensive scale, applying public censure as a means of punishment, replacing imprisonment by compulsory labour with retention of freedom, and prisons by institutions for training, and establishing the principle of comradely courts ".[3] The paradox of the tension between ultimate humanitarian ideals and the immediate necessities of a revolutionary situation was here particularly acute. The tension could be

[1] Lenin, *Sochineniya*, ix, 111-112.
[2] *Ibid.* xii, 163 ; Stalin in 1927 quoted " the mistakes of the Paris commune " in order to repel foreign criticisms of the OGPU (Stalin, *Sochineniya*, x, 234). [3] *VKP(B) v Rezolyutsiyakh* (1941), i, 288.

resolved only on the heroic assumption that the harshest penalties
applied to class enemies were temporary measures necessitated
by the revolutionary struggle for power, and had nothing in
common with the permanent methods and policies of the régime.
For the present, this assumption allowed the two systems to grow
up side by side without apparent incompatibility between them.
It was even claimed in the programme that the Soviet power had
set up " a single people's court in place of a system of different
courts ".

The dichotomy reflected itself from the very first moment in
an attempt to draw a distinction between ordinary crimes, which
could be dealt with by humanitarian methods of education and
correction, and " counter-revolutionary " crimes, which were
subject to repression by revolutionary terror. The distinction,
though seldom expressed in this form, was between crimes against
the individual and crimes against the state ; and it was commonly
implied, though not often categorically stated, that, whereas
workers and peasants might be guilty of crimes of the former
kind, " counter-revolutionary " crimes were normally, and even
necessarily, the work of class enemies. These assumptions supported and justified the distinction between the two systems.
It was significant of this dual attitude that the first decree of
November 1917 on the constitution of Soviet courts contained a
final article providing for the establishment of special " revolutionary tribunals " to deal with counter-revolution and profiteer-
ing ; [1] and this was followed on December 7/20, 1917, by the
constitution of the Cheka, whose undefined powers to deal by
extra-judicial methods with all forms of counter-revolutionary
activity grew with each successive emergency. By the summer of
1918 three different organs were engaged in imposing penalties
for various kinds of crime : the ordinary courts, the revolutionary
tribunals and the organs of the Cheka.[2] The first were concerned
with crimes which did not affect or threaten the security of the
state. The second and third were both concerned with crimes

[1] *Sobranie Uzakonenii, 1917–1918*, No. 4, art. 50.
[2] For an analysis of the origins and status of the Cheka see *Soviet Studies*, x,
No. 1 (July 1958), pp. 1-11 ; a resolution of VTsIK of February 17, 1919,
regulating relations between the Cheka and the revolutionary tribunals is in
Sobranie Uzakonenii, 1919, No. 12, art. 130. For the name Cheka see *The
Bolshevik Revolution, 1917–1923*, Vol. 1, p. 159, note 1.

which threatened state security. But, while the revolutionary tribunals purported to be judicial organs, the Cheka was frankly an administrative organ, whose actions were not subject to any legal rules of procedure or limited in scope by any legal definition or restriction. The distinction between different categories of crime and the distinction between different types of jurisdiction were thus embedded from the outset in Soviet practice.

These ambiguities were reproduced in the early history of Soviet penal policy. Marx in the *Critique of the Gotha Programme* had attacked the practice of treating criminals as "cattle" and referred to "productive labour" as "the only method of correction" capable of reforming the criminal.[1] Reformation and repression struggled side by side as twin elements in Bolshevik penal theory and practice : the term "corrective labour" seemed to cover them both. "Obligatory social labour" made its appearance in a decree of December 19, 1917/January 1, 1918,[2] as one of the penalties which might be imposed by a revolutionary tribunal ; and under a decree of the following month prisoners could be formed into "labour brigades to carry out necessary state work".[3] Everything pertaining to prisons had already been placed under the control of a "collegium" of the People's Commissariat of Justice (Narkomyust).[4] The first attempt to systematize penal regulations was a decree of Narkomyust (characteristically called a "temporary instruction") of July 23, 1918, "On Deprivation of Liberty as a Measure of Punishment and on the Method of Undergoing it".[5] This laid down the basic principle that a sentence of deprivation of liberty always involved forced labour, though sentences of "forced social labour" without deprivation of liberty could be imposed up to a maximum of three months. Sentences of deprivation of liberty were served either in "ordinary places of confinement (prisons)"[6] or in "reformatories and agricultural colonies" : the latter were "especially for young offenders". Both kinds of institution were

---

[1] Marx i Engels, *Sochineniya*, xv, 287.
[2] *Sobranie Uzakonenii, 1917–1918*, No. 12, art. 170.
[3] *Ibid.* No. 19, art. 284.   [4] *Ibid.* No. 15, art. 223.
[5] *Sobranie Uzakonenii, 1917–1918*, No. 53, art. 598.
[6] The term prison (*tyur'ma*) included convict camps and settlements for long-term sentences, but not concentration camps for political offenders which were at this period in a different category (see p. 425 below).

under the authority of the penal department of Narkomyust. The choice between them was made not by the court pronouncing the sentence but by a special " distributing commission ", whose members were appointed by, or in agreement with, the penal department.[1] This decree also for the first time made provision for " special prisons (isolators) " for prisoners guilty of disciplinary offences or of resistance to forced labour ; a prisoner transferred to an " isolator " was regarded as incorrigible.[2] In addition to these institutions, houses of detention (these in practice were generally town prisons) were established for persons awaiting trial or condemned persons awaiting transportation to distant places of confinement. These were under the authority of Narkomvnudel, presumably as the department which controlled the police.

The dichotomy between the jurisdiction of the courts and the administrative action of the Cheka soon, however, extended to penal institutions. The Cheka quickly established places of confinement under its own control for persons arrested by it ; and, side by side with the regular system of places of confinement authorized by the order of July 23, 1918, a different and independent penal system came into existence for those whose activities or potential activities constituted a threat to security. Like the other proceedings of the Cheka, this system was at first subject to no legal authority or precise legal definition. The first mention of concentration camps in the Soviet period seems to have been in August 1918 when, on the occasion of an armed rising in Penza, Lenin telegraphed to the local authorities to use " merciless mass terror against *kulaks*, priests and white guards ", and confine suspects in concentration camps outside the city.[3] Shortly afterwards, the " Red terror " decree of September 5, 1918, laid down

---

[1] Another function of the " distributing commission " was to pronounce on petitions from prisoners for conditional release before the end of the term for which they were sentenced. In 1924–1925 70 per cent of sentences to deprivation of liberty did not run their full term ; later the proportion fell to half or less (B. Utevsky, *Sovetskaya Ispravitel'no-Trudovaya Politika* (1934), p. 14).

[2] Class enemies were regarded as *ex hypothesi* incorrigible ; " we do not propose ", wrote Krylenko, " to correct the class enemy by inoculating him in prison with communist ideas or with sympathies for communist society " (*Entsiklopediya Gosudarstva i Prava*, ii (1925–1926), 933).

[3] Lenin, *Sochineniya*, xxix, 489.

the principle that " the Soviet republic should be made secure against class enemies by isolating them in concentration camps ".[1] The function of the original concentration camps was not punitive, but preventive. Confinement in a concentration camp was an administrative, not a judicial, act ; and the camps appear from the outset to have been under the control of the Cheka. The resolution of VTsIK of February 17, 1919, which attempted to define relations between the Cheka and the revolutionary tribunals,[2] limited the right of the Cheka to carry out executions to cases of armed insurrection, counter-revolution and banditry, but recognized its unlimited right to confine in concentration camps. But this transition from the firing squad to the concentration camp as the predominant instrument of repression in the hands of the Cheka [3] was accompanied by a change in the character of the camps. Hitherto, since the function of the camps had been regarded as primarily preventive, the principle of " forced social labour " had not been applied, or not systematically applied, in them. In introducing the resolution of February 17, 1919, to VTsIK Dzerzhinsky made it clear that the time had come to end this anomaly. Having spoken of the need to retain " administrative sentences and, in particular, concentration camps ", he went on :

> At this present moment, we are far from utilizing to the full the labour of prisoners on public work ; and I am proposing to retain these concentration camps, and to utilize the labour of prisoners, for gentlemen who live without occupation, for those unable to work without a certain compulsion ; or, if we take Soviet institutions, such a measure of punishment should be inflicted for an irresponsible attitude to work, for disorderliness, for unpunctuality, etc.[4]

---

[1] *Sobranie Uzakonenii, 1917–1918*, No. 67, art. 710.

[2] For this resolution see p. 422, note 2 above.

[3] That such a transition occurred is confirmed by one of the rare sets of figures available from a Cheka source. In 1918, in 20 provinces of the RSFSR, 6300 persons were shot by order of Chekas (454 by order of the Ve-Che-Ka), 21,988 sent to prison and 1791 to concentration camps ; in the first seven months of 1919 the corresponding figures were 2089 (327 for the Ve-Che-Ka), 12,346 and 7305 (M. Latsis, *Dva Goda Bor'by na Vnutrennem Fronte* (1920), pp. 75-76). There is no reason to doubt that from this time the number of inmates of concentration camps grew rapidly.

[4] *Istoricheskii Arkhiv*, No. 1, 1958, p. 10.

The new insistence on forced labour rather than the death penalty as the proper means of dealing with counter-revolutionary activities thus brought with it an ever-widening conception of the crimes dealt with by the Cheka. The main threat to state security, as Dzerzhinsky explained in his speech, now came not from " mass insurrection ", but from individual " sabotage, corruption etc." [1] From this moment the punitive character of the concentration camp was for the first time fully established, and its gates were open to receive not only dangerous political enemies who had to be kept out of the way, but offenders whose crimes, though not political in character, were particularly detrimental to the régime. To this extent, the Cheka encroached on the ordinary administration of justice.

An attempt was now made in a decree of April 1919, supplemented and in part amended by a further decree of the following month,[2] to regulate the status of forced labour camps. Offenders could be sent to these camps by people's courts or revolutionary tribunals as well as by Chekas or " other Soviet organs ". But, apart from this tenuous link, these camps were divorced from the ordinary system of criminal law, and were not, like ordinary penal establishments, under the control of Narkomyust. Responsibility for organizing them rested on the provincial Chekas. One camp, capable of accommodating 300 inmates, was to be set up in each province ; in special cases camps might also be established in county capitals. The administration of the camp was in the hands of a " forced labour section " of Narkomvnudel. The commandant of the camp was responsible to the provincial executive committee, but " temporarily " also to the Cheka, as well as being required to report to the forced labour section. These complicated arrangements probably reflected inter-departmental rivalries. But nothing in these decrees affected the right of the Cheka to maintain concentration camps under its own control or to commit persons to them by administrative action. By accident or design the

---

[1] After the civil war ended this change of emphasis was naturally intensified : a Cheka order of January 1921 described " the economic front " as " far more dangerous than the counter-revolutionary front " (*Istoricheskii Arkhiv*, No. 1, 1958, p. 14).

[2] *Sobranie Uzakonenii*, *1919*, No. 12, art. 124 ; No. 20, art. 235 ; for the labour regulations in these camps see *The Bolshevik Revolution, 1917–1923*, Vol. 2, pp. 210-211.

resolution of VTsIK of February 17, 1919, confirming this right [1] was published in the same issue of the official gazette which contained the first decree on forced labour camps. Thus the tripartite system of criminal jurisdiction — people's courts, revolutionary tribunals and the Cheka — was paralleled by a tripartite system of penal establishments — ordinary places of confinement and corrective labour institutions under the control of Narkomyust,[2] forced labour camps under the control of a special section of Narkomvnudel, and concentration camps under the control of the Cheka.

With the ending of the civil war and the consolidation of the régime under NEP, the dichotomy between ordinary criminal jurisdiction and the repression of counter-revolutionary crimes by exceptional procedures, and the bewildering multiplication of these procedures, lost any apparent justification. In December 1921 VTsIK resolved to " narrow " the powers of the Cheka by " reserving for the judicial organs the struggle against violations of the laws of the Soviet republics " and by " strengthening the principles of revolutionary legality " ; and in February 1922 the Cheka was abolished and replaced by the GPU as a regular department of Narkomvnudel.[3] The logical consequence of the abolition of the Cheka was the adoption of the criminal code of May 1922,[4] which brought all crimes, whether against individual persons and property or against public security, within the scope of the same statute law and the same courts. As a corollary of this reform, the revolutionary tribunals also went out of existence at the beginning of 1923, subject to the right of VTsIK to reconvene them for a specific purpose.[5] Both administrative action and the special procedure of the revolutionary tribunals for dealing with counter-revolutionary crimes appeared to have been eliminated from the Soviet system. A further logical corollary

---

[1] See p. 422, note 2 above.

[2] These were regulated by a detailed decree of November 15, 1920 (*Sobranie Uzakonenii, 1921*, No. 23-24, art. 141).

[3] For the resolution of VTsIK and the decree creating the GPU see *The Bolshevik Revolution, 1917–1923*, Vol. i, pp. 180-181.

[4] See Vol. i, pp. 76-78.

[5] *Entsiklopediya Gosudarstva i Prava*, iii (1925–1927), 686 ; no relevant decree has been traced.

of the reform would have been a unification of the penal system. In particular, it seems to have been assumed that, with the abolition of the Cheka, the concentration camps organized and controlled by it would also disappear.[1] These expectations proved, however, illusory. In appearance the reform set out to obliterate the distinction between different categories of crime, between different forms of criminal jurisdiction and between different types of penal establishments. In practice it served to strengthen and perpetuate all these distinctions.

In the first place, the criminal code of May 1922, in purporting to bring all crimes within the same framework of law, had in fact consecrated in legal form the distinction between ordinary crimes and " state crimes " (the phrase seems to have appeared here for the first time in an official enactment) by attempting to define such crimes and the penalties attaching to them with legal precision. The death penalty, hitherto an exceptional measure of reprisal, an act of war rather than of law, was now introduced, under the deprecatory periphrasis of " the highest measure of punishment " and with a passing reference to its temporary character,[2] into the regular practice of Soviet criminal law. The most important crimes to incur this penalty were a group of counter-

---

[1] A later textbook actually states in a footnote that both concentration camps and forced labour camps were liquidated " about 1922 " (*Ot Tyurem k Vospitatel'nym Uchrezhdeniyam*, ed. A. Vyshinsky (1934), p. 33) ; but no formal record of a decision to abolish them has been traced.

[2] What may be called the traditional party view was reiterated during the discussion of the code in TsIK by Ryazanov, who did not object to the use of terror in cases of emergency as a political weapon, but thought that " from the criminal code, in so far as it is designed not for a year, but for a more permanent and lengthy time, any deprivation of life, any annihilation, should be absolutely excluded " (*III Sessiya Vserossiiskogo Tsentral'nogo Ispolnitel'nogo Komiteta IX Sozyva : Byulleten'*, No. 9 (May 25, 1922), p. 4). But this view was now obsolescent : an amendment of February 1923 removed from the code even the casual and inoperative reference to the temporary character of " the highest measure of punishment " (*Sobranie Uzakonenii, 1923*, No. 15, art. 192). On the other hand, Dzerzhinsky, in a private note to Unshlikht of August 1923 (*Istoricheskii Arkhiv*, No. 1, 1958, pp. 20-21), continued to argue that the death penalty, " whether by sentence of a court or by our decisions ", should be regarded as " an exceptional measure " applied only to " state traitors (spies), bandits and those starting an insurrection ", and not as " a permanent institution of the proletarian state " : he wished to substitute " forced labour (convict labour) camps involving the colonization of uninhabited regions and iron discipline " (for Dzerzhinsky's advocacy of concentration camps as a measure of colonization see p. 446 below).

revolutionary crimes defined under the famous article 57 as " any
action directed towards the overthrow, destruction or weakening
of the power of the workers' and peasants' Soviets . . . or any
action directed to assist that part of the international bourgeoisie
which does not recognize the equal status of the communist
system that has taken the place of capitalism, and strives to
overthrow it by way of intervention or blockade, espionage,
financing of the press, etc." [1] The succeeding articles elaborated
this theme in further detail, including under the head of counter-
revolutionary crimes " the organization for counter-revolutionary
purposes of armed risings or of the invasion of Soviet territory
by armed detachments or bands ", and " relations with foreign
governments or with their individual representatives designed to
persuade them to undertake armed intervention in the affairs of
the republic, to declare war on it or to organize a military expedi-
tion against it " (arts. 58, 59).   An article which introduced the
principle of retroactive justice [2] permitted the application of " the
highest measure of punishment " by way of reprisal for " active
measures or active struggle conducted under the Tsarist régime
against the working class and the revolutionary movement "
(art. 67).   An amendment of 1923 included in the definition of
" counter-revolutionary crimes " any action which, in the knowledge of the person committing it, involved " an attack on the
fundamental political and economic achievements of the proletarian revolution ".[3]

Secondly, just as the attempt to create a comprehensive
system of criminal law had merely served to reinforce the distinction between ordinary and state crimes, so the project of
obliterating the distinction between ordinary and exceptional procedures for the repression of crime and bringing all offences
within the competence of the courts, ended with the paradoxical
result of emphasizing the distinction and lending greater power
and authority to the exceptional procedure.   The Cheka had been
a provisional expedient adapted to a period of disorder and civil

---

[1] The phraseology of this article was suggested by Lenin (*Sochineniya*,
xxvii, 296).
[2] It is possible to regard this not as a case of retrospective justice, but as an
early instance of reprisals against the potential criminal rather than against the
criminal act (see p. 434 below).
[3] *Sobranie Uzakonenii, 1923*, No. 48, art. 479.

war and not claiming judicial functions or a regular status : it was not for nothing that the epithet " extraordinary " appeared in its title. The GPU was from the first a regular and permanent organ, enjoying as such an authority and prestige never conferred on the Cheka. This accretion of power was indeed the principal difference which distinguished the new institution from its predecessor. Continuity was assured when the GPU took over the premises of the Cheka on Lubyanka Square, and no doubt inherited the major part of its staff. Dzerzhinsky, the head of the Cheka, was already also People's Commissar for Internal Affairs, and automatically became head of the newly established organ.[1] Unshlikht, who had been deputy chief of the Cheka since April 1921, occupied the same post in the GPU ;[2] and Yagoda, a leading official in the old institution, played an equally influential rôle in the new.[3] Though the GPU came into existence as an adjunct of the judicial system, its status as a department of Narkomvnudel showed that it had not shed the administrative character attaching to the Cheka.

Thirdly, the same fate overtook the penal aspects of the reform. The tripartite system under which places of confinement for different categories of offenders were divided between the authority of Narkomyust, Narkomvnudel and the Cheka, like the tripartite jurisdiction of people's courts, revolutionary tribunals and Cheka, was challenged by the reform which abolished the Cheka and brought the new criminal code into force in the spring of 1922. Under article 51 of the code " inspection and management of the execution of sentences to deprivation of liberty and

[1] The GPU was placed by the decree creating it " under the personal presidency of the People's Commissar for Internal Affairs or of his deputy appointed by the Council of People's Commissars " (*Sobranie Uzakonenii, 1922*, No. 16, art. 160).

[2] *Entsiklopedicheskii Slovar' Russkogo Bibliograficheskogo Instituta Granat*, xli, iii (n.d. [1928]), Prilozhenie, col. 178.

[3] According to the biography in *Bol'shaya Sovetskaya Entsiklopediya*, lxv (1931), 335, Yagoda was born in 1891, joined the party in Nizhny-Novgorod in 1907, was a member of the collegium of Vneshtorg in 1919 and of the presidium of the Cheka in 1920. The allegation in A. Orlov, *The Secret History of Stalin's Crimes* (1954), p. 260, that this account antedated his party membership by ten years lacks support. Independent evidence shows that he held an important military-administrative post (" commandant of Moscow ") early in 1918 (N. Ipatieff, *Life of a Chemist* (Stanford, 1946), p. 264) ; and in December 1920 he signed a Cheka document as " director of administration " (M. Latsis, *Chrezvychainye Komissii po Bor'be s Kontrrevolyutsiei* (1921), p. 62).

forced labour is entrusted to the central corrective labour section of the People's Commissariat of Justice and its local organs ". This victory was short-lived, and recoiled on the head of Narkomyust. The argument for unification of authority was irresistible. But the rights of Narkomvnudel and of its newly created department the GPU, the successor of the Cheka, were not so easily overridden. By a decision of Sovnarkom of July 5, 1922, the corrective labour section of Narkomyust was amalgamated with the forced labour section of Narkomvnudel to form a chief administration of places of confinement, which was set up not under Narkomyust, but under Narkomvnudel. The new administration came into existence on October 12, 1922.[1] The control of places of confinement had been taken entirely out of the hands of Narkomyust, which never regained it.

Meanwhile the GPU, assured of its status as a permanent department of Narkomvnudel, grew and prospered. The decree which established it in February 1922 required that persons arrested by it must within two months be either released or handed over to the courts for trial, unless special permission for continued detention were obtained from the presidium of TsIK.[2] The obtaining of this permission was never more than an empty formality. The GPU continued to enjoy in a legal form the powers of unlimited detention by administrative order which had been exercised outside the ordinary legal system by the Cheka. The attempt to subject its operations to the control of the courts proved too great a strain. The GPU rapidly emancipated itself from any kind of judicial revision, and arrogated to itself whatever powers it deemed necessary to the discharge of its functions. But it also soon acquired new legal powers. The first step seems to have been taken in August 1922, when, " in order to isolate persons who have participated in counter-revolutionary activities", the penalty was instituted of deportation of such persons abroad or to named destinations in the RSFSR ; the penalty was to be imposed, not by a court, but by a " special commission " presided over by the People's Commissar for Internal Affairs, and composed of representatives of the People's Commissariats of Internal Affairs and Justice. The duration of such " administrative

---

[1] *Spravochnaya i Adresnaya Kniga " Vsya Rossiya "* (1923), iii, 50-51.
[2] See *The Bolshevik Revolution, 1917–1923*, Vol. 1, p. 181.

deportation " was not to exceed three years. Persons deported to places in the RSFSR were to be under the supervision of local organs of the GPU.[1]   A corresponding decree of the Ukrainian SSR of September 6, 1922, added the rider that " deportation from the Ukrainian SSR to the territory of the RSFSR is carried out by agreement between the Ukrainian TsIK and the All-Russian TsIK ".[2]   As a Russian speaker later pointed out, the Ukrainian and White Russian SSRs had no " remote spots " of their own and were therefore compelled to "resort to the help of the RSFSR ".[3]   Both the RSFSR and the Ukrainian SSR passed decrees adding to existing categories of disfranchised persons " those banished by administrative order "[4] — a step which suggests that this class was becoming numerous.   An instruction of the Narkomvnudel of the RSFSR of January 1923 made liable to administrative deportation, on the recommendation of the GPU, persons whose residence in their present localities " appears dangerous from the point of view of revolutionary order ".   In addition to deportation from the RSFSR, it distinguished between two degrees of deportation within the RSFSR — simple deportation " with prohibition on living in named localities of the RSFSR ", and deportation to " a named region of the RSFSR " ;   the former generally meaning in practice a prohibition on living in the principal cities, the latter confinement to a remote region of Asiatic Russia.[5]   It is noteworthy that the enactment of Soviet codes of law in the latter part of 1922 should have been accompanied by this barely disguised revival of the procedures of Tsarist administrative justice.   But, apart from such powers which were nominally preventive, the GPU quickly acquired punitive powers.   On October 16, 1922, a few days after the control of ordinary places of confinement had been transferred from Narkomyust to Narkomvnudel, a further decree conferred on the GPU the right to inflict summary punishments, including

---

[1] *Sobranie Uzakonenii, 1922*, No. 51, art. 646.

[2] *Zbirnik Uzakonen' ta Rosporyadzhen', 1922*, No. 39, art. 586 ; this followed a decree of August 23, 1922, bringing into force for the Ukrainian SSR a criminal code closely modelled on that of the RSFSR (see p. 235, note 1 above).

[3] *Vserossiiskii Tsentral'nyi Ispolnitel'nyi Komitet XII Sozyva : Vtoraya Sessiya* (1925), p. 351.

[4] *Sobranie Uzakonenii, 1922*, No. 51, art. 646 ; *Zbirnik Uzakonen' ta Rosporyadzhen', 1922*, No. 39, art. 586.

[5] *Sobranie Uzakonenii, 1923*, No. 8, art. 108.

execution by shooting, in cases of banditry and armed robbery, and authorized the " special commission " set up by the earlier decree (on which GPU influence seems to have been predominant) to sentence those guilty of anti-Soviet activities to a maximum of three years' confinement in a concentration camp.[1] What in the days of the Cheka had been emergency measures justified on grounds of an exceptional situation now received formal and permanent sanction. Beside and beyond the ordinary procedures of criminal jurisdiction and punishment, a new and powerful organization possessing an entirely independent authority, and destined in a still distant future to play an important rôle of its own in the Soviet state machine, had been written into the Soviet legal system.

The establishment of the USSR in 1923 reinforced the growing importance of state security in Soviet criminal law, and strengthened the authority and prestige of the security organs. Under the terms of the constitution, the authorities of the USSR were empowered to " establish the bases . . . of the civil and criminal legislation of the union ". In October 1924 TsIK duly debated and approved a set of " principles " which would govern the criminal law of the Soviet republics.[2] The general view of crime as an infraction of the social order was taken over unchanged from the " leading principles " of 1919 and the criminal code of the RSFSR of 1922.[3] Though the phrase " state crimes " which had figured in the code of 1922 no longer appeared, new emphasis was given to the basic distinction between two categories of crime : crimes " directed against the foundations of the Soviet order . . . and therefore recognized as most dangerous " and " other " crimes. The former incurred, as in the 1922 code, minimum penalties not to be diminished by a court, the latter maximum penalties not to be exceeded by it. The principles thus remained the consistent and logical embodiment of a system in which offences against society were more heinous than offences against an individual, But a change had occurred in the climate

---

[1] *Sobranie Uzakonenii, 1922*, No. 65, art. 844.
[2] *Sobranie Zakonov, 1924*, No. 24, art. 205 ; for the debate see pp. 238-239 above. [3] For these see Vol. 1, pp. 71, 76-78.

of opinion. Virtually the only survival in the principles of
the humanitarian outlook of the earlier pronouncements was
in a note to article 13, which still treated shooting as a "temporary" measure of social defence. But, whereas the earlier
documents had retained the term "punishment", implying a
just balance between the crime committed by the criminal and
the sentence imposed on him, the principles of 1924 spoke only
of "measures of social defence".[1] Intensified emphasis on
state security as the over-riding aim of criminal law encouraged
the view that the repressive action of the law was directed to the
defence of the social order and not to the punishment of the
offender. The conception of individual guilt justifying an
equivalent penalty was replaced by the conception of potential
danger calling for measures of prevention. In the trial of two
Catholic priests for treason in the spring of 1923, Krylenko had
put forward the view that the actions of the individual accused
must be judged from the point of view of the "social danger"
presented by them; in judging the criminal, it was necessary to
take into account "not only what he has done, but what he may
do in the future".[2] Under article 22 of the principles of October
1924, deportation from one locality to another, or prohibition to
live in certain localities, might be imposed on "persons recognized
in the locality in question as socially dangerous in virtue of their
criminal activity, or connexion with a criminal milieu"; and this
sentence might be imposed on persons not convicted of any
specific crime or even on persons acquitted on a specific charge.

Here, however, a highly contentious issue arose. The theo-

[1] This was an amendment introduced in TsIK; the original draft of the
principles approved by Sovnarkom used the word "punishment" (*SSSR :
Tsentral'nyi Ispolnitel'nyi Komitet 2 Sozyva : 2 Sessiya* (1924), pp. 618-619).
[2] N. Krylenko, *Sudebnye Rechi, 1922-1930* (1931), p. 4. Krylenko repeated
this view in a speech of October 1925 in the TsIK of the RSFSR : " A cardinal
difference of principle exists between the structure of our criminal law and the
structure of criminal law in bourgeois countries. The idea of protecting our
new social order or protecting our socialist construction dictates to us measures
directed not only against persons who have committed this or that action and so
demonstrated their criminality at this particular moment, but also against the
very possibility of such crimes in the future. This idea is in sharp contradiction
with the individualistic idea of bourgeois law which, resting on the precept ' an
eye for an eye, a tooth for a tooth ', says that punishment is possible only when
a contravention of the law has already occurred " (*Vserossiiskii Tsentral'nyi
Ispolnitel'nyi Komitet XII Sozyva : Vtoraya Sessiya* (1925), p. 338).

retical conception of Soviet law as an instrument of class warfare, and of Soviet courts as " class courts against the bourgeoisie ",[1] had little practical effect on early Soviet legislation, which made no attempt to distinguish between offenders on grounds of class. When at the end of 1918 a prominent Cheka official argued that it was unnecessary to convict a suspect of positive anti-Soviet activity, and that " your first duty is to enquire what class he belongs to, what were his origin, education and occupation ", Lenin protested against this " absurdity ".[2] Such views quickly succumbed to the harsh necessity of maintaining law and order against infractions by members of any class. Belief that the treatment meted out to offenders should vary with their class origin proved more persistent. The only trace of class discrimination which survived in the "⁄leading principles " of 1919 was a recommendation to the judge to take the class status of the offender into account in fixing the penalty (art. 12). A Cheka order of January 1921 signed by Dzerzhinsky proclaimed the motto : " Prison for the bourgeoisie, comradely influence for workers and peasants " ; and, while the order cautiously admitted that " the crude marks of distinction between one's own and not one's own on a class basis " were obsolete, and that individual behaviour had to be taken into account, it firmly proposed " to isolate the bourgeoisie from worker and peasant prisoners " in all places of confinement and " to erect special concentration camps for the bourgeoisie ".[3] The class principle found no place in the 1922 criminal code of the RSFSR. But, paradoxically, it remained strong enough to influence certain provisions of the civil code of the same year. Article 4 prescribed that, where an issue was not covered by any specific rule, " the court decides it in accordance with the general principles of Soviet legislation and the general policy of the workers' and peasants' government " — an injunction interpreted by some as an invitation to the judge to apply the principle of class discrimination. Article 406 provided that where a wealthy defendant could not be proved liable under the terms of the code for an injury done to a poor plaintiff, damages should none the less be awarded in accordance with the relative material

---

[1] See Vol. 1, p. 73.
[2] Lenin, *Sochineniya*, xxiii, 458 ; Lenin's comment was, however, not published at the time.   [3] *Istoricheskii Arkhiv*, No. 1, 1958, pp. 13-16.

positions of the parties : and article 411 prescribed that the court, in assessing damages for breach of contract or other torts, should "always take into account the financial position of the two parties ". The growing demand for regularity and uniformity of legal decisions which marked the campaign for "revolutionary legality " soon made such discrimination seem anomalous.

The class principle was, however, too firmly embedded in party doctrine to be allowed to fade without a struggle out of Soviet legal theory and practice ; and it became involved as a minor item in the party controversies of 1924 and 1925. In February 1924 a commission appointed by the central control commission of the party, voicing the time-honoured party view, reported in favour of milder penalties for criminals of proletarian origin, and the substitution of education and reformation in labour colonies, where such offenders were concerned, for more drastic forms of punishment. Dzerzhinsky, reversing his position of three years earlier, protested vigorously against the proposal. Such a policy could result " at *the present time* " only in " an increase in crime and an increase in the number of criminals ". Dzerzhinsky rejected the application of any " distinguishing mark of class " to the criminal ; only the crime could be defined in terms of class, i.e. in terms of the threat which it involved to the government of workers and peasants. " The struggle against criminals ", Dzerzhinsky continued severely, " should be conducted by sharp, shattering blows " : the current practice of the courts was " mere liberal chatter ".[1]

Krylenko, a firm believer in the Marxist theory of law, and an old adversary of Dzerzhinsky in matters of penal policy, now fought a strong rearguard action to uphold the purity of proletarian doctrine. As procurator of the RSFSR Krylenko wielded an important influence in the legal sphere, though not beyond it. The theses which he presented to the fifth All-Russian Congress of Judicial Workers in March 1924 were significantly entitled " On Penal Policy and the Strengthening of the Class Principle in it ". They recommended " a complete separation between the two groups of criminals in respect of places of punishment ", the " special purpose isolators " being reserved for class enemies, and labour colonies, described as " agricultural or factory-workshop

---

[1] *Istoricheskii Arkhiv*, No. 1, 1958, pp. 23-24.

colonies ", for offenders who belonged to the class of toilers.[1] Another supporter of the same view complained bitterly that " the practice of the chief administration of places of confinement completely liquidates the class line indicated in the party programme ".[2] Krylenko defended his theses as representing the class principle upheld by the party in criminal law. But he proceeded to weaken his argument by admitting that the decision in a particular case could not be made to depend exclusively on the class origin of the offender, quoted the dictum that " a class policy is a policy directed to the attainment of class ends ", and conceded that offenders who, " though of the proletarian class, are unconditionally dangerous from the social point of view ", should be subjected to the same treatment as class enemies.[3] In a congress where the influence of Narkomyust predominated, Krylenko's theses, thus attenuated, seem to have won general support ; and even a spokesman of Narkomvnudel agreed that the special isolators ought to be reserved for " class enemies ".[4] One critic protested, however, that the criminal law knew no concept of " toilers ", that existing social classifications were unreliable, being sometimes by origin and sometimes by occupation, and that it was therefore impossible to define the class principle which Krylenko had made the key to his proposals.[5]

The resolutions of the congress lacked formal authority, but indicated the trend of legal opinion. An order of the Supreme Court of the RSFSR in July 1924 reminded the Soviet criminal court that it was, like other courts, a " class court ", and that it should in its judgments " draw a strict line between persons, on the one hand, who are alien in spirit to the proletarian state in consequence of their class affiliation, and persons, on the other hand, belonging to the toiling masses who have committed a crime ".[6] When TsIK, in the autumn of 1924, introduced into

---

[1] *V Vserossiiskii S"ezd Deyatelei Sovetskoi Yustitsii* (1924), pp. 21-24 ; for the theses as eventually adopted see *ibid.* pp. 294-297. For the distinction between isolators and labour colonies see p. 445 below.

[2] *Ibid.* p. 238.

[3] *Ibid.* pp. 227-232 ; this last concession was not in the original draft, but was embodied in the final text of the theses (*ibid.* p. 295).

[4] *Ibid.* pp. 234-235.

[5] *Ibid.* p. 239 ; another critic contested the view that art. 4 of the civil code justified class discrimination (*ibid.* pp. 249-250).

[6] *Ezhenedel'nik Sovetskoi Yustitsii*, No. 31, 1924, pp. 740-742.

its " principles " of criminal law the application of measures of social defence to persons recognized as " socially dangerous " even if they had not been convicted of a specific crime,[1] it opened the way to the assumption that a socially dangerous person was a class enemy, and that the class criterion would be the chief means of identifying him ; articles 31 and 32 of the principles further encouraged this assumption by declaring a " more severe measure of social defence " applicable to persons belonging in the past or in the present (an attempt to circumvent ambiguities of classification) to the class of exploiters of labour, and a " milder measure of social defence " to workers or working peasants. At the moment when TsIK adopted these principles, the TsIK of the RSFSR was drafting a new corrective labour code, and the *rapporteur* seized the occasion to drive home the same moral :

> The sharpness of our criminal repression is directed mainly against persons not belonging to the working class ; the introduction of the class element corresponds to the general policy of the Soviet power.[2]

But the text of the code did not fully bear out this profession : under article 47 those liable to be sent to special purpose isolators were " persons not belonging to the class of toilers who have committed a crime in virtue of class habits, opinions or interests, but also persons who, although belonging to the toilers, are recognized as especially dangerous to the republic or are transferred by way of disciplinary reprisal ".[3] Even where the principle was most loudly proclaimed, it was applied with reservations which went a long way to nullify it.

By this time the class principle in justice was beginning to clash with major directives of party policy. In the winter of 1924–1925, when " Face to the countryside " was being equated with the conciliation of the well-to-do peasant, and revolutionary legality was hailed as an important part of the policy of revitalizing the Soviets, the slogans and procedures of class warfare were out of fashion. The endorsement of revolutionary legality by the

---

[1] See p. 434 above.
[2] *Vserossiiskii Tsentral'nyi Ispolnitel'nyi Komitet XI Sozyva : Vtoraya Sessiya* (1924), p. 297.
[3] For the code see p. 445 below.

fourteenth party conference in April 1925 contained no hint of
discrimination between offenders on grounds of social origin or
status.[1] The Supreme Court of the RSFSR silently reversed its
attitude of July 1924, and by an instruction of June 29, 1925,
which referred to the " directives " of the third Union Congress
of Soviets on revolutionary legality, conveyed a specific warning
against class discrimination :

> Courts must remember that the application of a class
> approach to penal policy consists not in bringing to justice the
> " nepman " or the " kulak ", or in exonerating the toiler or the
> poor and middle peasant, but in a distinct and clear under-
> standing of the social danger of the actions of the citizen on
> trial, judged from the standpoint of the proletariat as a whole.
> First and foremost, a firm line must be drawn between actions
> punishable as crimes and actions which are indifferent from the
> point of view of criminal law, independently of who it is that
> commits them. It is completely inadmissible that, other con-
> ditions being identical, one citizen should be held responsible
> in criminal law, and the other not.[2]

Solts, the *rapporteur* on the question at the fourteenth party conference, knew well, as president of the central control commission
of the party, that opposition required equally firm handling
whether it came from workers or from former class enemies ;
and he became the protagonist in the reaction against class discrimination. When the drafting of a new criminal code was debated in the TsIK of the RSFSR in October 1925, even Krylenko
had shifted his ground, objecting to the " crude formula "
of article 32 of the " principles ", which prescribed milder
penalties for crimes committed by " a worker or a toiling peasant ",
and arguing that the penalty should depend not on " class affiliation ", but on " the dangerousness of the crime committed ".
Solts put in a *caveat* against the suggestion that the adoption of
measures against the " socially dangerous " person implied
acceptance of a class view of justice :

> We must not say that workers and peasants may commit
> offences because a worker-peasant government is in power. We

---

[1] For this resolution and that of the third Union Congress of Soviets see
pp. 469-470 below.
[2] *Ezhenedel'nik Sovetskoi Yustitsii*, No. 31, 1925, p. 1070.

should not soften their punishment in the light of their class origin. That is harmful.[1]

How rapidly opinion on this subject had evolved during the past year was shown when the TsIK of the RSFSR requested VTsIK to amend the articles of the principles to which these objections had been taken.[2]

A month after this noteworthy session Solts took the bull by the horns in an address to a conference of judicial officers which was published as an article in both *Pravda* and *Izvestiya* on November 24, 1925. Starting from the proposition that existing law could not be judged by the standards of the future communist society, he argued that " the question of practicality should determine the form of the law ". He rejected the notion that workers should be punished more mildly than other offenders : " for us there is no privileged class ", and " the government ought to think of the population irrespective of the class to which it belongs ". He referred contemptuously to " a part of the population living on the feelings of the civil war ", and added that " every government is interested, when civil war is over, that it should be quickly forgotten ". This brutally blunt revision of cherished party doctrine provoked some resistance. Krylenko protested with asperity and with some cogency that Solts's argument offered no justification for the epithet " revolutionary " as applied to legality.[3] But, doctrine apart, there was no doubt that Solts accurately represented a growing trend of opinion in party circles. The conception of Soviet law as the expression of the policy of a Soviet state, and of a community of Soviet citizens subject to that law, was in process of replacing the original view of a society differentiated on the basis of class. Three months later Bukharin, at a Komsomol congress, took occasion to poke fun at the im-

---

[1] *Vserossiiskii Tsentral'nyi Ispolnitel'nyi Komitet XII Sozyva : Vtoraya Sessiya* (1925), pp. 352-353, 383 ; Solts even desired the abandonment of the article in the principles which stipulated that no " measures of social defence " should be applied which " have as their aim the infliction of physical sufferings or the humiliation of human dignity ", on the ground that this stipulation was inconsistent with the retention of the death penalty (*ibid.* p. 385).

[2] *Id. : Postanovleniya* (1925), pp. 65-66.

[3] *Pravda*, December 8, 1925 ; Solts replied, not very effectively, *ibid.* December 16, 1925. Solts also replied to another attack in *Leningradskaya Pravda*, December 6, 1925, and was answered again *ibid.* December 8, 1925.

pression that, in the eyes of the law, " communist party membership, especially when combined with proletarian origin, and
especially if a man has two parents both workers from the bench,
or four grandparents and all four from the bench, serves as a
kind of absolute immunity ".[1] Solts at the session of TsIK in
April 1926 protested against the habit of raking up the past and
demanding " merciless reprisals for old counter-revolutionary
crimes ".[2] As time went on, the test applied in charges of socially
dangerous behaviour was not membership of a reprobate class or
group, but indulgence in words or actions appropriate to membership of such a class, so that the argument from class became
circular.   But the conception of potential guilt first clearly
established in the principles of October 1924 remained important
in the procedure, if not of the ordinary courts, at any rate of the
security organs.

Apart from issuing general instructions to the union republics
on the character and content of their criminal legislation, the
" principles " of October 1924 reserved to the USSR itself the
right to legislate on " military crimes ". Simultaneously with
the promulgation of the principles, VTsIK also issued on its
own account a decree " on military crimes ". Soviet legislation recognized no distinction between military law and ordinary
criminal law : the criminal code of the RSFSR of 1922 contained
a chapter on military offences. The new decree, while dealing
mainly with infractions of military discipline and regulations,
also prescribed the death penalty for " military espionage, i.e.
the collection, communication or transmission to foreign governments, counter-revolutionary organizations or hostile armies of
information about the armed strength or defence capacity of
the USSR ".[3] In the spring of 1925 the presidium of TsIK
approved plans " for the defence of revolutionary order " to be
put into effect in the event of an " exceptional situation " or a
state of war : the elaboration of appropriate measures was entrusted to a commission of three, consisting of the People's
Commissar for War, the Procurator of the Supreme Court of the

---

[1] *VII S":ezd Vsesoyuznogo Leninskogo Kommunisticheskogo Soyuza Molodezhi*
(1926), p. 256.
[2] *SSSR : Tsentral'nyi Ispolnitel'nyi Komitet 3 Sozyva : 2 Sessiya* (1926),
p. 612.   [3] *Sobranie Zakonov, 1924*, No. 24, art. 207.

USSR and the president of the OGPU.[1] A few months later a decree of the USSR defined espionage as " the transmission, or illicit acquisition or collection for purposes of transmission, to foreign states, counter-revolutionary organizations or private persons, of information which in virtue of its content affects specially protected state security ", and prescribed for it penalties of from three years' imprisonment to death by shooting. The collection or transmission of economic information whose publication was prohibited was punishable with imprisonment up to three years.[2] These successive measures mark the taking of security out of the sphere of ordinary criminal law and criminal jurisdiction. A working distinction had once more been established between ordinary criminal law and procedure promulgated by the republics and administered by the courts of the republics, and extraordinary law and procedure applied in security questions under decrees of the USSR and administered by the OGPU. The distinction was recognized and accepted by the TsIK of the RSFSR in October 1925 when, in preparing its own criminal code, it excluded the security provisions which had figured in the original draft, and referred them back to the authorities of the USSR for enactment.[3]

If the constitution of the USSR had intensified the distinction between measures of state security and the administration of ordinary criminal law, it also, and still more conspicuously, enhanced the status of the organ primarily responsible for such measures. In the earlier period the Cheka had existed on sufferance, and on the assumption that it would come to an end with the state of emergency which had justified its creation. The GPU had come into existence in 1922 as a permanent department of the Narkomvnudel of the RSFSR. But even the GPU was not an independent organ, and had no constitutional status of its own. On the creation of the USSR, the GPU of the RSFSR was

[1] *Sobranie Zakonov, 1925*, No. 25, arts. 166, 167.

[2] *Ibid.* No. 52, art. 390 ; a further elaboration of the definition of military and economic espionage occurred in a decree of April 1926 (*Sobranie Zakonov, 1926*, No. 32, art. 313).

[3] *Vserossiiskii Tsentral'nyi Ispolnitel'nyi Komitet XII Sozyva : Vtoraya Sessiya : Postanovleniya* (1925), pp. 65-66.

transformed into the Unified State Political Administration or OGPU of the USSR, and enshrined by name in the constitution, which required it " to coordinate the revolutionary efforts of the union republics in the struggle against political and economic counter-revolution, espionage and banditry ". Detached from its former subordination to the Narkomvnudel of the RSFSR, it became an independent department of the USSR with the status of a " unified commissariat ", having subordinate commissariats in the republics.[1] Its president was a member of Sovnarkom, though only in a consultative capacity. Its officials enjoyed in all territories of the Soviet Union the status and rights of members of the armed forces on active service. It had its own " special armies " under the direct command of the president of the OGPU or of his deputy. Its function was to " direct the work of the local organs of the state political administrations through its pleni-potentiaries attached to the Councils of People's Commissars of the union republics, acting in virtue of a special decree ". Henceforth the OGPU presided over security measures throughout the Soviet Union, being nominally responsible only to TsIK and Sovnarkom, and having only a tenuous association with normal criminal procedures in the courts. The status of the OGPU as an organ of the union, and its duty to deal with the most heinous and dangerous category of crimes, combined to confer on it an authority and prestige transcending those of the ordinary republican organs of justice.

It was a part of this process that the competence of the OGPU was gradually extended to cover an ever-widening circle of major crimes. From the outset the term " counter-revolutionary " had been applied in Soviet parlance to all serious forms of sabotage, espionage, banditry or speculation : the extra-legal character of the Cheka had made precise definition superfluous. In February 1919 Dzerzhinsky had declared his intention to use the concentration camps under the control of the Cheka as a place of punishment " for an irresponsible attitude to work, for disorderliness, for unpunctuality, etc." on the part of Soviet

---

[1] See *The Bolshevik Revolution, 1917–1923*, Vol. 1, p. 404 ; the statute of the OGPU, originally promulgated by the presidium of VTsIK in November 1923 (*Sistematicheskoe Sobranie Deistvuyushchikh Zakonov SSSR*, i (1926), 194-195), was confirmed by VTsIK in October 1924 (*Sobranie Zakonov, 1924*, No. 19, art. 183).

officials.[1] Where so wide an interpretation could be given to such conceptions as " sabotage " or " counter-revolution ", it was easy for a situation to develop in which not merely acts directed against state security in the strict sense, but any act seriously detrimental to the public interest, whether specifically covered by the criminal code or not, could be removed, at the discretion of the OGPU, from the ordinary courts, and dealt with behind closed doors by a procedure whose nature and rules were never made public.[2] Thus, while in the earlier period an impulse had been felt to obliterate the distinction by assimilating the procedure of the Chekha to that of the ordinary courts, the same drive to obliterate the distinction now led to the opposite result of making the authority and influence of the OGPU supreme in matters of criminal justice. The establishment of the USSR had two consequences. It intensified the predominance of the conception of security throughout the whole field of criminal law ; and it removed jurisdiction over major criminal offences, i.e. those affecting the security of state, from the republics and placed firmly in the hands of a highly centralized organ of the USSR. At the fourteenth party conference of April 1925, which passed a resolution in support of " revolutionary legality ",[3] the *rapporteur* on the subject, fortifying himself with quotations from Lenin, observed that measures might be required to deal with criminals " which may perhaps seem inappropriate from the point of view of the bourgeois law-maker ", and " which are not limited by the formal framework laid down in the law ".[4] At a discussion later in the same year at the newly founded Institute of Soviet Construction in the Communist Academy, it was forcefully argued that any attempt to oppose " revolutionary legality " to " revolutionary expediency " was non-Marxist, since no revolutionary

---

[1] See p. 425 above ; under the criminal code of the RSFSR of 1922 grave misdemeanours of officials shared with counter-revolutionary activities the distinction of incurring the " highest measure of punishment " (see Vol. 1, p. 77).
[2] A striking instance of an extension by the OGPU of the conception of " state security " occurred in May 1926 when three officials of Narkomfin were condemned and shot for " speculating in gold, currency and state securities " (see Vol. 1, p. 488) ; the sentence and execution were conspicuously announced in the principal newspapers of May 6, 1926.
[3] See p. 469 below.
[4] *Chetyrnadtsataya Konferentsiya Rossiiskoi Kommunisticheskoi Partii (Bol'-shevikov)* (1925), p. 248.

faced with such a choice could reject what was expedient to the revolution.[1]

The growing powers of the OGPU, like those of the Cheka in the early period, were intimately connected with its control of penal policy and penal institutions. Throughout this period, ordinary " places of confinement " remained under the authority of prison administrations which were departments of the Narkomvnudels of the union republics. In October 1924 the TsIK of the RSFSR adopted a corrective labour code which made provision for every kind of place of confinement, ranging from labour colonies, industrial and agricultural, whose main purpose was declared to be reformatory, to " special purpose isolators " designed for " those who do not belong to the class of toilers ".[2] But this restriction was not maintained in other articles of the code ; and it could be noted that, while the number of class enemies was certainly decreasing, the need was felt for a larger number of isolators. The fifth All-Russian Congress of Judicial Workers in March 1924 recommended that the number in the RSFSR should be increased to " at least 15 ".[3] According to official statistics, the total number of prisoners in all places of confinement in the Soviet Union was 144,000 on January 1, 1925 ; 149,000 on January 1, 1926 ; and 185,000 on January 1, 1927 ; the number of places of confinement rose from 571 in 1925 to 591 in 1926.[4] Whether these figures included all ordinary categories of prisoners and places of confinement or were in other respects complete, cannot be guessed.[5]

---

[1] *Sovetskoe Stroitel'stvo : Sbornik*, iv-v (1026), 98-102.

[2] *Sobranie Uzakonenii, 1924*, No. 86, art. 870 ; for the reservations in the application of this principle see p. 438 above.

[3] *V Vserossiiskii S"ezd Deyatelei Sovetskoi Yustitsii* (1924), p. 295.

[4] *Itogi Desyatiletiya Sovetskoi Vlasti v Tsifrakh, 1917–1927* (n.d.), p. 116 (for numbers of prisoners) ; *Statisticheskii Spravochnik SSSR za 1928 g.* (1929), pp. 898-899 (for numbers of places of confinement, with slightly higher totals of prisoners). Earlier figures seem incomplete and unreliable.

[5] By a curious anomaly the OGPU was responsible for the foundation in 1924 of a model " working commune " near Moscow for young offenders. Training was the keynote of the institution, and it was run as an " open prison " without apparent measures of compulsion, discipline being maintained by the collective action of the inmates themselves. Much publicity was obtained for it (*Ot Tyurem k Vospitatel'nym Uchrezhdeniyam*, ed. A. Vyshinsky (1934), p. 50). It is paradoxically significant of the status of the OGPU that the most humane, as well as the most brutal, of Soviet penal establishments should have been under its control.

Nothing, however, in these arrangements affected the concentration camps or other places of confinement which had been inherited by the OGPU from the Cheka and remained, now as before, outside the system of ordinary penal establishments.' It was significant that, while the corrective labour code of the RSFSR adopted in October 1924 made no mention of the OGPU or of places of confinement controlled by it, the first draft of the code had contained a clause excepting from the operation of the code " prisoners under the control of the judicial, investigating and other organs of the OGPU ". It was decided in the course of the debate in TsIK, apparently without discussion, to omit this clause.[1] The omission was evidently due to official discretion and not to any prospect of establishing control by republican organs over the proceedings of the OGPU. On the other hand, the view that confinement in a concentration camp was a preventive, not a punitive, measure died hard. Political prisoners continued to enjoy some of the respect and the leniency which had been accorded to them by the Tsarist régime.[2] They were not at this time generally required to engage in physical labour ; and confinement in a concentration camp was regarded as a lighter penalty than an ordinary sentence of deprivation of liberty.[3] This anomaly, which accorded preferential treatment to prisoners branded as enemies of the régime, had already been denounced by Dzerzhinsky in the days of the Cheka [4] — though apparently with less effect than might have been expected. It was Dzerzhinsky who now again appeared as the scourge of the political prisoner, and proposed to adapt the concentration camps to a " policy of colonization " by establishing them in remote and hitherto undeveloped territories, " where it will be possible to compel the inmates, whether they like it or not, to occupy themselves in productive work ".[5] Even where political offenders were not confined in concentration camps, but merely banished

[1] *Vserossiiskii Tsentral'nyi Ispolnitel'nyi Komitet XI Sozyva : Vtoraya Sessiya* (1924), pp. 444-446.

[2] For instances of this see pp. 449-452 below.

[3] As late as 1925 a protest appeared in the Menshevik journal in Berlin against the sentence of a Menshevik to ten years' imprisonment on the ground that previous sentences had been only for three years and only to a concentration camp (*Sotsialisticheskii Vestnik* (Berlin), No. 3 (97), February 18, 1925, p. 13).

[4] See p. 425 above.

[5] *V Vserossiiskii S"ezd Deyatelei Sovetskoi Yustitsii* (1924), p. 233.

to remote destinations, the economic motive was not overlooked. It appeared significantly in a resolution of the fifth All-Russian Congress of Judicial Workers :

> To recognize as correct the proposal to introduce banishment by order of a court for the most socially dangerous elements, as a substitute for their long-term imprisonment, to especially remote regions, where these exiles will be exposed to the necessity of engaging in productive labour in order to live.[1]

From this period dated the progressive transformation of concentration camps into penal establishments of a particularly severe kind — a process connected both with the increasing intolerance of political dissent inside and outside the party and with the growing pressure to raise productivity and to harness all available labour to the needs of an expanding economy. The long-standing conception of the civil war period of using enemies of the régime for " difficult and unpleasant work "[2] had been extended and systematized. No attempt can be made to estimate the number of those sent to concentration camps or deported by administrative order at this time. But by 1924 it was large enough to provoke the argument that the process sometimes had the effect of dislocating production rather than of contributing to it. Krasin noted privately in that year that "very many people sit in concentration camps who could be used for economic work if communists were more sensible and practical in economic and production matters ", and instanced the case of Eiduk, a former official of his department, who was in a camp building a railway in Semirechiya, a province of Kazakhstan.[3]

The tightening up of the machinery of repression was accompanied by a broader change in the attitude of the Bolsheviks towards political opposition. The trial of the SR leaders in the summer of 1922 was an important landmark.[4] Hitherto a certain

---

[1] *Ibid.* p. 295 : this clause was not in the original draft of the resolution.
[2] See *The Bolshevik Revolution, 1917–1923*, Vol. 2, p. 211.
[3] Pencilled note passed to Trotsky at a meeting of the party central committee and preserved in the Trotsky archives, T 809 ; the date was June 2, 1924.
[4] For the trial of the SRs and the attendant circumstances see *The Bolshevik Revolution, 1917–1923*, Vol. 1, pp. 182-183.

temporary and conditional tolerance of other Left wing parties, or of sections of those parties, had been practised from time to time ; and no obstacle had been placed in the way of the departure of members of these parties who wished to leave Soviet territory. Several new factors now made themselves felt. The increasingly rigorous demands for uniformity in party opinion after 1921 automatically favoured the demand for greater uniformity among those engaged in public affairs ; political discipline seemed all the more necessary in order to counter the economic relaxation of NEP. The alarm caused by the Kronstadt rising did not at once die down, and produced a stiffer attitude towards opposition in any form.[1] The opposition parties were becoming more and more openly a focus of anti-Soviet propaganda abroad ; [2] and this sealed the view of them, in official circles, as implacable enemies who deserved no quarter. When the so-called bourgeois parties were outlawed in the early stages of the civil war, and no longer had any overt adherents in Soviet territory, the only surviving opposition had consisted of anarchists, SRs and Mensheviks. Some hundreds, or perhaps thousands, of anarchists had been arrested since 1918, and detained for longer or shorter periods, but never constituted a coherent group. The remaining SRs were rounded up during the trial of 1922. By this time, the Menshevik leaders had almost all left the country.[3] Several scores or hundreds of Mensheviks who remained, and did not

[1] According to F. Dan, *Dva Goda Skitanii* (Berlin, 1922), pp. 136-137, a proposal was made to shoot leading Mensheviks as " hostages for Kronstadt ", but was vetoed by the party central committee. Lenin is alleged to have said at the tenth party congress that " Mensheviks and SRs should be carefully isolated in places of confinement " (Yu. Martov, *Geschichte der Russischen Sozialdemokratie* (1926), p. 319). Lenin's alleged remark does not appear to be on record, but a resolution of the tenth party congress of March 1921 drafted by Lenin accused the Mensheviks of " utilizing differences of opinion within the RKP in order effectively to incite and support the Kronstadt mutineers, SRs and white guardists " (*VKP(B) v Rezolyutsiyakh* (1941), i, 365 ; Lenin, *Sochineniya*, xxvi, 260).

[2] The Menshevik leader Martov had denounced the Bolsheviks at the Halle congress of the USPD in October 1920 ; and since 1921 a Menshevik organization in Berlin had published an influential and often well-informed anti-Soviet journal *Sotsialisticheskii Vestnik*. Anarchist organizations had also been active in anti-Soviet propaganda abroad, especially since the death of Kropotkin in 1921.

[3] F. Dan, *Dva Goda Skitanii* (Berlin, 1922), pp. 231-267, gives a detailed account of negotiations with arrested Menshevik leaders who, having threatened a hunger-strike, were at length permitted to go abroad.

make the transition to Bolshevism, were now arrested. In accordance with the newly established procedure of administrative exile, some of those arrested were merely deprived of the right to live in the principal cities, but some were sent to two new camps for political offenders, one at Suzdal, the other in the Solovetsky islands in the White Sea, some 300 miles from Archangel, the site of a former monastery.[1]

Conditions of imprisonment at Suzdal, where the settlement seems to have been originally established to receive Georgian Mensheviks arrested after the troubles of 1921, were relatively mild. In Solovki[2] climatic and other conditions were rigorous in the extreme. Communications in summer were by a rare steamer from Kemi on the Murmansk railway ; throughout the arctic winter the settlement was entirely isolated. In December 1923 a tragic event occurred in the island. A new regulation was issued curtailing the freedom of movement of inmates of the camp after nightfall. This was a period when political prisoners regarded themselves, and were to some extent still regarded by the authorities, as enjoying " rights " which could not be lightly infringed. The prisoners staged a mass demonstration in defiance of the new regulation. The camp authorities were seized with panic, or deliberately decided on an exhibition of ruthlessness. Troops were called out and fired, apparently several times, on the demonstrators, of whom at least five were killed and three seriously wounded. A vehement protest from the prisoners and a report from the authorities were transmitted to Moscow, where it was decided to set up a commission consisting of representatives of TsIK, of the central control commission of the party and of the People's Commissariat of Justice to investigate the incident. The SR, Left SR and Menshevik groups in the camp were

[1] An article in *Internationale Presse-Korrespondenz*, No. 137, October 21, 1924, pp. 1815–1816, gave the total number of political offenders as 1500, of whom 500 were in custody, the remainder being merely debarred from residence in Moscow or Leningrad : this may have been after a release of 350 from the Solovetsky camp reported *ibid.* No. 140, October 28, 1924, pp. 1859–1862. But the numbers are probably understated. According to an eye-witness account in D. Dallin and B. Nicolaevsky, *Forced Labour in Soviet Russia* (1948), p. 171, there were " about 4000 prisoners " in the Solovetsky camp in 1923 ; but not all of these were political.

[2] Solovki, the name of the principal island, was commonly used for the whole group.

invited to send delegates to give evidence to the commission.
The invitation was refused on the ground that this was merely " a
bureaucratic commission" not sitting in public. These exchanges
are symptomatic of the status accorded to political prisoners at
this time, and of the attitude adopted by them.[1]

Only when news of this disaster reached the outside world,
and penetrated to foreign countries, in the summer of 1924, did
it become widely known that a number of SRs, Mensheviks
and anarchists had been subjected by the Soviet Government to
conditions as hard as any formerly imposed by the Tsars on
political offenders. The shock of this discovery was considerable.
A protest against what had happened, combined with an appeal
for humane treatment of political prisoners, was drawn up in
June 1924 by representatives of the SR, Left SR, and Menshevik
groups in the camp, and obtained extensive publicity in foreign
countries.[2] The Soviet press for the first time took cognizance of
the affair, and articles began to appear in which an apologetic
note could be clearly detected. The disturbances of December
1923 were attributed to deliberate provocation by political
prisoners ; and persons detained there and at Suzdal were
induced to testify to the humane conditions prevailing in the
settlements.[3] In September 1924 Krasikov, the procurator of
the Supreme Court of the USSR, was sent to Solovki to report
on conditions. The report was, not unnaturally, of the white-
washing kind. The visitor found that conditions of work and
living had much improved during the year (a tacit admission of
earlier defects), that 350 persons, including 16 sailors who had
taken part in the Kronstadt rising, had been recently released,

---

[1] The most complete account of these events is in the SR journal published
in Prague ; it is naturally written from the standpoint of the prisoners,
but reproduces the principal documents (*Revolyutsionnaya Rossiya*, No. 39-
40, November 1924, pp. 2-20). An eye-witness account is quoted in
D. Dallin and B. Nicolaevsky, *Forced Labour in Soviet Russia* (1948), pp.
177-181.

[2] For the text see *Die Tragödie auf den Solowetzinseln* (1925), pp. 4-10 :
this document is not in the issue of *Revolyutsionnaya Rossiya* quoted in the
preceding note.

[3] *Izvestiya*, September 30, 1924 ; *Internationale Presse-Korrespondenz*, No.
117, September 9, 1924, pp. 1537-1538 ; No. 137, October 21, 1924, pp. 1815-
1816 (these articles, like almost everything that appeared in *Inprekorr*, were
certainly translated from the Soviet press, though the originals have not been
traced).

and that the prisoners themselves had been guilty of exaggerated demands and unruly behaviour.[1] Notwithstanding this verdict, however, a decree was issued in the summer of 1925 terminating the use of " the Solovetsky concentration camp " for the imprisonment of " members of anti-Soviet parties (Right SRs, Left SRs, Mensheviks and anarchists) ", and providing for their transfer to " places of confinement on the mainland under the jurisdiction of the OGPU ".[2] The tradition that political opponents whom it was necessary to detain in the interests of public security should none the less not be subject to unduly harsh conditions of confinement was still not dead.

Another episode of this period illustrated the state of relations between the authorities and political prisoners. The SRs who had been condemned to death in 1922 and then reprieved [3] had since been kept in confinement in or near Moscow.[4] At the beginning of 1925, two of them, Artemiev and Ratner, were informed that they were to be released from confinement and deported to Narym in the far north of Siberia ; and the others learned that similar destinations awaited them. This led to the declaration on January 28, 1925, of a hunger-strike. In the name of the whole group Gotz told the OGPU agent who came to remonstrate with them " that they would not go to Narym ". An offer by the OGPU to substitute the less distant but equally arctic Ust-Tsylma, on the Pechersky coast, for Narym, was also refused. The SRs demanded that their place of exile should be a town of not less than 20,000 inhabitants and situated on a railway, where they could find some means of livelihood. After further negotiations it was agreed that Artemiev should be sent to Temir-Khan-Shura and Ratner to Kislovodsk, both in the Caucasus ; and the hunger-strike came to an end on its ninth

[1] *Internationale Presse-Korrespondenz*, No. 140, October 28, 1924, pp. 1859-1862.
[2] *Sobranie Zakonov, 1925*, No. 38, art. 287. According to *Sotsialisticheskii Vestnik* (Berlin), No. 23-24 (117-118), December 21, 1925, pp. 11-13, they were transferred to Verkhne-Udinsk and Tobolsk ; another isolator was established at Sverdlovsk. A hunger-strike a few months later in Tobolsk was reported *ibid.* No. 9 (127), May 12, 1926, p. 10.
[3] See *The Bolshevik Revolution, 1917–1923*, Vol. 1, pp. 182-183.
[4] According to an interview with Kursky in *Izvestiya*, October 9, 1924, the SR leaders were then living on the outskirts of Moscow in a *dacha* on the Kaluga road.

day.[1] Where the rest were sent does not appear to be recorded. But Gotz, after deportation, rearrest and another hunger-strike, was living at the end of 1925 " under house arrest " in Ulyanovsk (the former Simbirsk).[2] The SRs continued to enjoy a certain measure of respect and indulgence at this time, partly as old revolutionaries, and partly owing to the support and publicity which they received from socialist opinion abroad. But as the struggle within the party became more intense, wider use was made, on all sides, of measures of repression and the power of the OGPU increased ; and this in turn was reflected in the growing severity of the penal system for political offences. When the political prisoners were transferred from Solovki in the summer of 1925, non-political prisoners remained. Very soon the settlement was again in use for political prisoners ; Georgian Mensheviks who had been arrested after the rising of August 1924 were said to have been deported there in the autumn of 1925.[3]

In the summer of 1924 the Soviet security organs scored a remarkable success in the arrest, public trial, condemnation and reprieve of the notorious terrorist, Boris Savinkov. In his youth Savinkov had participated actively in the SR terrorist organization, and had written two revolutionary novels of distinction, *The Pale Horse* and *That Which Was Not*. Since about 1907 he had broken with the SRs, and, after the revolution, established an independent anti-Bolshevik terrorist organization which he called " the league for the defence of the fatherland and of liberty ". During the civil war he had been in contact with French, British and Polish politicians hostile to Soviet Russia, including Tardieu, Winston Churchill and Piłudski, and with French and British agents engaged in anti-Soviet activity. Later he appealed in vain to Mussolini for subsidies. Exactly how much help he received, or how much he achieved, will probably never be known : little

[1] These proceedings are described in detail in *Sotsialisticheskii Vestnik* (Berlin), No. 3 (97), February 18, 1925, p. 14 ; No. 4 (98), March 5, 1925, p. 12 ; the assumption was apparently maintained that the consent of the prisoners to their deportation was required, with the hunger-strike functioning as an effective weapon or threat.

[2] *Ibid.* No. 20 (114), October 29, 1925, p. 11 ; No. 23-24 (117-118), December 21, 1925, p. 15.

[3] *Ibid.* No. 2-3 (120-121), February 11, 1926 ; that Solovki was again being used for political prisoners was implied in an article in *Pravda*, April 2, 1926, stressing the humane conditions now prevailing there.

evidence exists except his own assertions. But by 1923 he had become thoroughly disillusioned. A sketch published in Paris in that year, *The Black Horse*, bore witness to his flagging convictions. In August 1924 he crossed the frontier in disguise with a false passport, allegedly in order to visit his agents and to study the prospects of future work in Soviet territory. On August 18, 1924, he was arrested in Minsk and his identity revealed. On August 21 he wrote a statement fully admitting his past activities, confessing his error in having treated the Soviet Government as unrepresentative of the Russian people and of Russian national interests, and claiming to be regarded as a " prisoner of war " rather than a criminal. The indictment was handed to him on August 23, and the trial took place on August 27 and 28. Savinkov made no attempt to deny the charges against him : they were indeed based directly on his own deposition. He described in full his contacts with foreign countries. It may be presumed that he also disclosed in private his agents and contacts in the Soviet Union. But these were not named in his statement, and no questions were asked about them at the trial. Savinkov repeated that he had undergone a change of heart and repented of his past activities against the Soviet régime. The sentence of death was pronounced, but accompanied by a recommendation to mercy in the light of the penitent attitude of the accused. A decree of VTsIK was at once issued commuting the sentence to one of imprisonment for ten years.[1] On May 12, 1925, it was announced in the press that Savinkov had died in prison a few days earlier. He was understood to have committed suicide ; but no details were divulged of the manner of his death.

Savinkov's surrender and recantation symbolized the end of a period. Savinkov was the last important " white " Russian engaged, with intermittent foreign backing, in organized terrorist

---

[1] Savinkov's arrest was not announced in the press till August 29, 1924, when communiqués reporting the arrest, trial and sentence appeared in all the principal newspapers. The trial proceedings were fully reported in *Pravda* and *Izvestiya*, August 31, 1924, and long translated extracts appeared in *Internationale Presse-Korrespondenz*, No. 116, September 5, 1924, pp. 1516-1519 ; No. 117, September 9, 1924, pp. 1532-1533. The indictment, Savinkov's statement of August 21, a full record of the trial, and the decree of TsIK were published in *Boris Savinkov pered Voennoi Kollegiei Verkhovnogo Suda SSSR* (1924) ; facsimiles of notes and letters written by him in prison in September–October 1924 appeared in an appendix.

activities against the Soviet régime ; and, with the disbandment of all Left opposition parties, organized opposition to the Soviet régime might be said to have come to an end. Throughout the nineteen-twenties nearly all the numerous Russian parties opposed to the Bolsheviks continued to maintain, though with increasing difficulty, some form of organization in Paris, Berlin or Prague. A daily Kadet newspaper *Poslednie Novosti* flourished in Paris under the editorship of Milyukov. The Menshevik journal *Sotsialisticheskii Vestnik*, the best written and best informed of the *émigré* publications (since the Menshevik group contained by far the highest quota of intellectuals), appeared twice monthly, with occasional gaps, in Berlin, the SR *Revolyutsionnaya Rossiya*, less regularly, in Prague. A Left SR journal *Znamya Bor'by* and a Right-wing Kadet sheet *Rul'* came out intermittently in Berlin. But none of these groups now had any serious contacts with the Soviet Union or exercised any influence there. From 1925 onwards opposition in the Soviet Union took on the different character of dissent within the party. This, apart from the remoter and occasional bogy of foreign intervention, was all that the régime now had to fear. Security no longer meant the defence of the Soviets against the champions of the *ancien régime* ; it no longer meant, within the Soviets, the defence of Bolshevik revolution against the challenge of dissident parties of the Left ; it meant, within the Bolshevik party, the defence of a specific ruling group or order. And this in turn involved a conspicuous change in the character and functions of the security organs. The repressive powers of the OGPU were henceforth directed primarily against opposition in the party, which was the only effective form of opposition in the state.

NOTE A

LOCAL FINANCE

In the policies aiming at the revitalization of the Soviets and the creation of an efficient machinery of local government, the establishment of local financial autonomy played a subsidiary, but important, part. Under the régime of war communism the financial arrangements of both central and local authorities had been chaotic : in theory, all revenues and expenditure had been directly controlled by Narkomfin, local organs having no recognized financial powers. In this respect, as in others, the introduction of NEP brought a return to more familiar procedures. The restoration of the financial autonomy of local — meaning, in the first instance, provincial — authorities had been decided in principle in the autumn of 1921.[1] During the next two years the size and importance of provincial budgets had been gradually increased by the haphazard method of imposing on the provincial authorities fresh obligations and assigning to them fresh sources of revenue,[2] though, since the latter never fully balanced the former, direct state aid to the provincial budgets continued to be necessary. Financial autonomy and independent budgets were also gradually restored to the counties, though as late as 1923 many county budgets were said to be still simply drafted in the financial department of the province.[3] In September 1923 Sokolnikov announced that the time had come to establish independent budgets for the rural districts ;[4] and in November 1923 TsIK adopted a " temporary decree on local finances " which, together with a decree " on state property of local importance ", constituted a first attempt to bring order into the whole system, and was commended by Sokolnikov as a salutary retreat from " the system of extreme centralization " practised between 1918 and 1921 to " a system of financial decentralization ".[5] But no real independence was contemplated, since no local taxes or levies might be

---

[1] See *The Bolshevik Revolution, 1917–1923*, Vol. 2, pp. 347-348.
[2] Relevant decrees are listed in R. W. Davies, *The Soviet Budgetary System* (1958), p. 75.   [3] *Vestnik Finansov*, No. 1, January 1924, pp. 132-136.
[4] G. Sokolnikov, *Finansovaya Politika Revolyutsii*, ii (1926), 133-139.
[5] *Tret'ya Sessiya Tsentral'nogo Ispolnitel'nogo Komiteta SSSR* (1923), p. 75 ; the decree is in *Postanovleniya Tret'ei Sessii Tsentral'nogo Ispolnitel'nogo Komiteta SSSR* (1923), pp. 80-128, and in *Sobranie Uzakonenii, 1923*, No. 111-112, art. 1045.

raised without the sanction in each case of the government of the republic concerned.[1] It is not surprising that, with this limitation, the development of local budgets at this time was halting and unsystematic, and (except in the Ukraine, where rural district budgets were general by the summer of 1924 [2]) did not go below the county level.[3] At the session of TsIK in October 1924, Sokolnikov devoted a substantial section of his budget speech to local budgets, complaining that some people had not yet learned to distinguish these from the budgets of the union republics and autonomous republics which formed part of the global budget of the USSR. He estimated that the total of local budgets would increase from 522 million rubles in 1923–1924 to 705 millions in 1924–1925; objected to the system of direct grants from the state budget on the ground that it deprived the local authorities of any incentive to balance their budgets; and recognized " the fundamental question of the possibility of really drawing the peasantry into Soviet public life " as closely bound up with the financial problem. A new and more elaborate decree on the finances of provinces, counties and rural districts was drawn up to replace the temporary order of the previous year.[4] Its most important provision was the substitution, for the existing system of grants from the state budget, of a system of subventions under which the state budget would undertake the payment of a certain proportion of expenses falling on the local budgets for specific purposes. On the other hand, the administrative expenses of local congresses of Soviets and executive committees as well as of local health, social insurance and educational institutions were transferred to the local budgets.[5] An essential feature of the system was that local budgets, unlike the budgets of the republics, were excluded from the

---

[1] The eleventh All-Russian Congress of Soviets in January 1924, while admitting that the institution of rural district budgets would " assist the organizational strengthening of the primary organs of Soviet power in the countryside ", emphatically reaffirmed " the complete inadmissibility of self-imposed taxes or the practice of self-taxation " on the part of local authorities (S"ezdy Sovetov v Dokumentakh, iv, i (1962), 23 ; Sobranie Uzakonenii, 1924, No. 27, art. 260).

[2] V. Dyachenko, Sovetskie Finansy v Pervoi Faze Razvitiya Sovetskogo Gosudarstva, i (1947), 444 ; this was apparently a legacy of the Tsarist period, when local government had been more advanced in the Ukraine than elsewhere.

[3] For some figures of local budgets in these years see R. W. Davies, The Soviet Budgetary System (1958), p. 76.

[4] SSSR: Tsentral'nyi Ispolnitel'nyi Komitet 2 Sozyva : 2 Sessiya (1924), pp. 158-162 ; id. : Postanovleniya (1924), pp. 43-88 (also in Sobranie Zakonov, 1924, No. 22, art. 199).

[5] A year later another decree listed the purposes for which subventions would be forthcoming : these included salaries of teachers, doctors, people's judges, rural district or district officials, and the building of roads, schools and hospitals (Sobranie Zakonov, 1925, No. 56, art. 419).

unified state budget of the USSR — except, of course, in so far as they were dependent on subsidies from it. Kalinin was already behind the times when in April 1925 he spoke of the need to split " our present unified budget " into " state and local budgets ". But he was on more practical ground when he added that " local budgets must be handed over completely to the management of local organs ", and looked forward to the day when the single agricultural tax would cease to be a state tax and become a local tax.[1]

While, however, order was gradually being brought into the system of provincial and county finance, the establishment of rural district budgets was delayed both by the vested interests of the county authorities and by inability to provide a sufficient number of trained officials at the rural district level ; and it proved the most contentious issue in the policy of local finance during this period. The "temporary decree " of November 1923 had been accompanied by a special decree ordering that rural district budgets should be established " everywhere, with the exception of those republics which do not have territorial divisions corresponding to the rural district ", as from January 1, 1924. The rural district authorities were to become responsible for maintaining the machinery of administration of the rural districts and the villages and for certain social services ; their revenue was to be derived from profits from small local enterprises and from a one-tenth share in the supplement levied for local revenues on the single agricultural tax.[2] Six months later, the political importance of rural district budgets was stressed by the thirteenth party congress of May 1924 : they would help to create " new possibilities . . . of developing the economic and cultural work of rural district and village Soviet organs, and of drawing the whole mass of middle and poor peasants into their work ".[3] Progress was, however, extremely slow. Out of a sample of 31 rural districts in the RSFSR investigated by Rabkrin only six had budgets for the full financial year 1923–1924 ; 16 more introduced them in the course of the year. But examination showed that these were not real budgets of the rural district authorities, but had been drawn up in the county finance department.[4]

The " Face to the countryside " policy had by this time been set in

---

[1] *Soveshchanie po Voprosam Sovetskogo Stroitel'stva 1925 g. : Aprel'* (1925), p. 164. The idea that the agricultural tax, being levied on the peasant, should be spent on local needs was fashionable at this time ; Kamenev propounded it at the ninth Ukrainian Congress of Soviets in May 1925 (L. Kamenev, *Stat'i i Rechi*, xii (1926), 197-198).

[2] *Sobranie Uzakonenii, 1923*, No. 113, art. 1047.

[3] *VKP(B) v Rezolyutsiyakh* (1941), i, 595.

[4] *Soveshchanie po Voprosam Sovetskogo Stroitel'stva 1925 g. : Aprel'* (1925), p. 113.

motion. At the beginning of October 1924 the Orgburo sent out a letter
to local party committees signed by Molotov, instancing the failure
in many provinces to establish rural district budgets as an example of
the lack of attention paid to the needs of the countryside in comparison
with those of the towns : it was essential at the earliest possible moment
to make the rural district " a financial and economic unit ".[1] *Pravda*
published an article demanding " the creation of rural district budgets
with the active participation of the peasant masses ".[2] Zinoviev's
article of October 11, 1924, launching the campaign for the revitalization of the Soviets demanded that reform should be carried down to the
level of the rural district and the village.[3] The session of the TsIK of
the RSFSR in October 1924, which drew up the statute for rural
districts,[4] also adopted a special decree on rural district budgets which,
in the words of the *rapporteur*, " broadens the scope of the rural district
budget and transforms it from a budget spending 63 per cent of its
revenues on administrative apparatus into a budget embracing all the
basic needs of the countryside and, first and foremost, its cultural
needs ".[5] The decree of TsIK, on local finance, issued in the same
month,[6] applied equally to provincial, county and rural district budgets.
But it was easier to pass decrees than to create the necessary conditions
on the spot. Apart from the Ukraine, the regions which advanced most
rapidly towards financial autonomy were the newly created Ural and
North Caucasian regions : here district budgets were said to have been
established on an extensive scale in 1924–1925.[7] But elsewhere
scepticism continued to prevail about the practicability of independent
rural district budgets ; both sources of local revenue and the supply
of local officials were hopelessly inadequate.[8] It seemed a counsel of
perfection when a conference of financial officials in January 1925
looked forward to " independent and stable sources of revenue " for
rural districts (and the corresponding new " districts " under the

---

[1] *Pravda*, October 4, 1924 ; the letter was republished in *Izvestiya Tsentral'-
nogo Komiteta Rossiiskoi Kommunisticheskoi Partii (Bol'shevikov)*, No. 2 (7),
October 13, 1924, without Molotov's signature and described as a letter of the
party central committee. A calculation was current at this time that 20 times
as much was spent from public funds on the inhabitant of a provincial capital,
and 15 times as much on the inhabitant of a county town, as on the inhabitant
of the countryside (*Soveshchanie po Voprosam Sovetskogo Stroitel'stva 1925 g. :
Aprel'* (1925), p. 109).

[2] *Pravda*, October 5, 1924 ; a leading article in the same sense and in even
stronger terms appeared on the same date in *Leningradskaya Pravda*.

[3] See pp. 320–321 above.   [4] See pp. 321–322 above.

[5] *Vserossiiskii Tsentral'nyi Ispolnitel'nyi Komitet XI Sozyva : Vtoraya
Sessiya* (1924), p. 200 ; the decree is in *Sobranie Uzakonenii, 1924*, No. 87,
art. 878.   [6] See p. 456 above.

[7] *Raionirovanie SSSR*, ed. K. Egorov (1925), p. 272.

[8] See, for example, articles in *Pravda*, December 10, 1924, January 6, 1925.

regionalization scheme).[1] In the following month a decree was issued
standardizing the salaries of rural district officials. The president of a
rural district executive committee was to receive from 54 to 38 rubles
a month, and the secretary from 42 to 29 rubles a month, according to
zones laid down in the decree ; a rural district people's judge was to
receive from 48 to 33 rubles.[2] But the salaries of rural district officials
were at this time, subject to a subvention of from 40 to 25 per cent
from the central budget, still borne on the provincial or county budgets.
The campaign to make the rural districts financially autonomous
now began, however, to gather weight. At its session in March 1925
TsIK voted to " extend and strengthen the rural district (or district)
budget ".[3] An article in the party journal *Bol'shevik* concluded that
the institution of rural district budgets was a necessary condition of
creating " a lower Soviet apparatus which is humane and sensitive to
the needs of the peasantry " ; [4] and Stalin in April 1925 described the
organization of local budgets as providing, together with the agricultural
tax, the chief tasks for party workers in the countryside. The problem
was " how to spend the money in the local budget and for what purposes ", and " how to make sure that abuses in this field will be brought
to light and eradicated ".[5] The question of rural district budgets was
a prominent item on the agenda of the April session of the conference
on the revitalization of the Soviets. It was, said Kaganovich in his
opening speech, " in substance the question of the transfer of certain
functions from the county to the rural district executive committee
and the revitalization of the activity of the rural district executive committee " ; [6] as another delegate put it, the Soviets could not be brought
to life so long as they had " empty hands ".[7] A detailed resolution
was adopted on ways and means of making the rural district an effective
budgetary and administrative unit. The rural district was to become
responsible for ministering to the " cultural-economic " needs of the
population ; for this purpose " property, institutions and enterprises
of local importance ", including mills (the main form of local economic
enterprise), kitchens, schools and hospitals were to be placed under the
management of the rural district executive committee. Rural districts
would be allowed to retain profits from local enterprises and to raise
independent taxes, but would be financed in the main by a guaranteed

    [1] *Vestnik Finansov*, No. 1, January 1925, pp. 99-100.
    [2] *Sobranie Zakonov, 1925*, No. 9, art. 86.
    [3] SSSR : *Tsentral'nyi Ispolnitel'nyi Komitet 2 Sozyva : 2 Sessiya : Postano-
vleniya* (1925), p. 18.
    [4] *Bol'shevik*, No. 5-6 (21-22), March 25, 1925, pp. 38-43.
    [5] Stalin, *Sochineniya*, vii, 80-81.
    [6] *Soveshchanie po Voprosam Sovetskogo Stroitel'stva 1925 g. : Aprel'* (1925),
p. 16.   [7] *Ibid.* p. 102.

share in general revenues set apart for local needs. An ingenious plan was proposed by which rural districts would retain 70 per cent of the supplement to the agricultural tax [1] collected in their territory, the balance of 30 per cent being administered by the county as a fund to aid the poorer rural districts.[2] It was under these multiplied pressures that the TsIK of the RSFSR issued in April 1925 two decrees on the rural districts (or districts), the first attempting to define and delimit their functions, the second according to them certain restricted borrowing powers.[3]

The crucial moment in the development of rural district budgets was probably the decision of the fourteenth party conference at the end of April 1925 that the 100 million rubles, deducted for local needs from the single agricultural tax, should be allocated " to rural district budgets for the purpose of strengthening these and assisting the political and economic development of the rural district ".[4] The twelfth All-Russian Congress of Soviets in May 1925 voted for " a further improvement of the rural district budget and an increase in its volume ", and for the transfer to it of " enterprises and property of rural district significance ".[5] A delegate at the third Union Congress of Soviets in the same month noted with satisfaction that the estimates of local revenue and expenditure for 1924–1925 included for the first time an item of 150 million rubles covering rural district budgets, and expressly connected this innovation with the policy of revitalizing the Soviets.[6] A resolution of the congress recommended an increase of rural district budgets to 300 million rubles in 1925–1926 ; [7] and, under an instruction of June 2, 1925, from the Sovnarkom of the USSR to the Sovnarkoms of the union republics, the increase was to be financed in the main by a percentage deduction from the gross receipts of the agricultural tax in each republic for the benefit of rural district or district budgets.[8]

---

[1] For this supplement see Vol. 1, p. 253 ; after 1925 it took the form of a deduction instead of a supplement.

[2] *Soveshchanie po Voprosam Sovetskogo Stroitel'stva 1925 g. : Aprel'* (1925), pp. 182-185 ; effect was given to this recommendation in a decree of the RSFSR of December 1925 establishing regional, provincial, department and county " regulating funds ", designed to give support to the poorer units at each level (*Sobranie Uzakonenii, 1925*, No. 92, art. 668).

[3] *Ibid.* No. 24, art. 170 ; No. 27, art. 192.

[4] *VKP(B) v Rezolyutsiyakh* (1941), ii, 23.

[5] *S"ezdy Sovetov RSFSR v Postanovleniyakh* (1939), pp. 329-330.

[6] *Tretii S"ezd Sovetov SSSR* (1925), p. 430 ; an analysis of rural district budgets in the four constituent republics of the USSR for 1924–1925 gave totals of 99·4 million rubles for the RSFSR, 39·9 millions for the Ukraine, 4·8 millions for White Russia and 3·3 millions for the Transcaucasian SFSR (*Soveshchanie po Voprosam Sovetskogo Stroitel'stva 1925 g. : Aprel'* (1925), pp. 82-83).   [7] *Tretii S"ezd Sovetov SSSR : Postanovleniya* (1925), p. 32·

[8] *Sobranie Zakonov, 1925*, No. 37, art. 279.

These official measures were backed up by an instruction of the party central committee of June 18, 1925, to local party organizations, which received wide publicity. It issued a warning against the " sceptical attitude towards the consolidation of the rural district as a financial-economic unit " prevalent in many localities, and insisted on the urgent need to introduce rural district or district budgets and to train local officials capable of drawing them up and managing them.[1] Finally, rural district or district budgets were placed on a firm basis by a decree of TsIK of August 14, 1925. Local administrative, social and cultural institutions were henceforth to be carried on the rural district budget ; revenues were to include receipts from small local enterprises, from the agricultural tax and from percentage shares in other state levies and revenues derived from the district.[2] Statistics for all local budgets in the USSR showed that in the year 1924–1925, 34·7 per cent of expenditure was devoted to cultural and social purposes, 29·2 to economic enterprises, 20·6 to administration (including judicial administration) and 15·5 per cent to unclassified headings.[3] Of the rural district budgets of 1924–1925 in the RSFSR, 39 per cent was spent on administration, 34·5 per cent on education, 5 per cent on medical services, the rest on roads, agricultural aid and fire and other minor public services.[4] Medical services were primitive ; many rural districts did not have a single hospital. For the same year more than 70 per cent of local revenues in the RSFSR, the Ukrainian SSR, the Transcaucasian SFSR and the Uzbek SSR came from what were classified as local sources. But more than half of the amount came from economic enterprises under local management (in the other two union republics, where such enterprises were fewer, the proportion of local receipts to total revenue was also lower), and most of the remainder from supplements to union taxes. The proportion derived from local taxes remained insignificant.[5]

Once rural district budgets had become a reality, the logical next step was the creation of village budgets. The same argument was heard that the village Soviet could never be effective without financial

---

[1] *Izvestiya Tsentral'nogo Komiteta Rossiiskoi Kommunisticheskoi Partii (Bol'-shevikov)*, No. 22-23 (97-98), June 22, 1925, p. 14 ; *Pravda*, June 23, 1925.

[2] *Sobranie Zakonov, 1925*, No. 53, art. 400.

[3] See the table in V. Dyachenko, *Sovetskie Finansy v Pervoi Faze Razvitiya Sovetskogo Gosudarstva*, i (1947), 438. In an increasing total budget the percentages were fairly constant from year to year, but interesting divergencies were shown in the percentages for the different republics.

[4] *Vestnik Finansov*, No. 6, June 1925, pp. 123-124 ; *Soveshchanie po Voprosam Sovetskogo Stroitel'stva 1925 g. : Aprel'* (1925), pp. 108-110.

[5] See the table in V. Dyachenko, *Sovetskie Finansy v Pervoi Faze Razvitiya Sovetskogo Gosudarstva*, i (1947), 443 ; the percentages did not vary significantly in the following year.

powers ; and the same practical objections presented themselves in even stronger form. In August 1924 a decree of the USSR recognized the right of local Soviets to vote voluntary contributions for local needs.[1] But, since it was made clear that these were obligatory only for those voting for them, and since the consent of the rural district executive committee was required in each case, it did little to strengthen the authority of the village Soviets. The statute for village Soviets adopted by the TsIK of the RSFSR in October 1924 [2] prescribed that village revenues and expenditures formed part of the rural district budget. The village Soviet was "responsible to its electors and to the rural district executive committee " for sums placed at its disposal ; but these were petty grants for specific purposes. The average annual " budget " (in this sense of the word) of the village Soviet in the RSFSR was not more than 200 or 300 rubles ; in the province of Kharkov in the Ukraine, where villages tended to be larger and local administration more developed, it reached 900 rubles.[3] Conditions were, however, not uniform, and practice probably outran theory.

> In one form or another, [wrote a commentator at this time], whether in the form of voluntary self-taxation or of services in kind, the village draws up its estimates and has its budget.[4]

The statute of October 1924 admitted that in exceptional cases, and with the special authority of the provincial executive committee, " enlarged " village Soviets might acquire budgetary rights. In the same month the Volga German autonomous republic, where the peasant population was far more advanced, economically and culturally, than anywhere else in the Soviet Union, instituted village Soviet budgets ; the village Soviets were to receive revenue from local enterprises and from a share in local dues and taxes, and were responsible for the upkeep of elementary schools, local roads and the fire service.[5] But this appears to have been unique at the time. A decree of the TsIK of the RSFSR of December 8, 1924, recalled previous prohibitions on the levying of taxes by local authorities, declared that these prohibitions had been infringed, and threatened penalties for future infractions.[6]

---

[1] *Sobranie Zakonov, 1924*, No. 6, art. 69.   [2] See p. 322 above.
[3] *Soveshchanie po Voprosam Sovetskogo Stroitel'stva 1925 g. : Aprel'* (1925), pp. 66-67.   [4] *Raionirovanie SSSR*, ed. K. Egorov (1925), p. 274.
[5] For this development see *Planovoe Khozyaistvo*, No. 6, 1925, pp. 216-217 ; this article contains a detailed discussion of the question of village budgets. Figures for the village budgets of the Volga German republic for 1924–1925 are given in *Raionirovanie SSSR*, ed. K. Egorov (1925), pp. 276-277.
[6] *Sobranie Uzakonenii, 1925*, No. 1, art. 4 ; for earlier prohibitions see p. 456, note 1 above.

The campaign for the revitalization of the Soviets and the insistence on the importance of rural district budgets led at the beginning of 1925 to a movement in party circles for budgets for village Soviets. On April 1, 1925, on the eve of the second session of the conference on revitalization, *Pravda* featured a letter from a peasant voicing the demand ; and at the conference itself Kalinin repeated the argument that, " if we want the local Soviets really to become organs of the sovereign people, this cannot of course be achieved without a financial basis ".[1] No formal proposals were made, but several delegates declared that the village Soviets could not exist without exacting both service in kind and contributions, and complained of inability to enforce payment against the " 2 or 3 per cent " who held aloof. The representative of Narkomfin, while adamant against village budgets, was sympathetic to service in kind. His reply to one of the advocates of budgets did not lack cogency :

> When comrade Konovalov says that service in kind is the worst form of self-taxation, and that this involves some sort of contradiction in our proposal, he is profoundly mistaken. He does not reckon with the political and economic circumstances in which we are living. If we take into account the excess of labour power in the countryside, the less than full use of working animals, and the absence of opportunity to apply this labour power for the purpose of receiving a monetary equivalent, it is, I think, absolutely inappropriate from the political and economic point of view to speak of monetary self-taxation in NEP conditions.
>
> We say : so long as the necessity exists to repair bridges and roads, to maintain fire protection, post-horses, cartage of wood etc., and these requirements are not catered for in the rural district budget, . . . it is essential to resort to one form or another of service in kind.

The most that could be done would be to allow individual peasants to buy exemption from service in kind by a monetary payment.[2] It was a thorny subject. The primitive standard of living and efficiency in the Soviet village impeded even the introduction of a monetary economy. The resolution of the conference, in an attempt to appease the champions of village Soviet budgets, admitted that the accounts of village Soviets might be drawn up separately within the rural district budget, and added a grudging footnote :

> In particular cases, in the largest village Soviets, the creation of a village budget with the permission of the provincial executive committee is recognized as possible.

[1] *Soveshchanie po Voprosam Sovetskogo Stroitel'stva 1925 g. : Aprel'* (1925), pp. 164-165.   [2] *Ibid.* pp. 103, 107, 119.

A special enquiry was recommended into " the economic and political desirability of retaining certain forms of service in kind ".[1]

The conference as a whole gave little encouragement to proposals to revitalize the village Soviet by making it a financial and budgetary unit. The twelfth All-Russian Congress of Soviets in the following month demanded that " attention should be given to the greatest possible cover for the needs of village Soviets ", but only by way of allocations from the increased rural district budget.[2] Narkomfin remained unalterably opposed to schemes for village Soviet budgets on the ground that not enough trained officials were available even to run the rural district budgets.[3] A few localities seem to have experimented spasmodically with village budgets; a project was announced to introduce them in the North Caucasian region on October 1, 1925.[4] About the same time attempts were made to extend village budgets to the larger villages in the Ukraine, the size of which had recently been increased in the process of regionalization, but without much success.[5] Everywhere the primitive level of the village Soviet continued to impede any serious progress towards its financial autonomy. Nor does any general enquiry appear to have been made into the imposition of service in kind by village Soviets. This was perhaps a matter more easily settled by customary prescription than by official regulation.

The last enactment on local finance in this period was a detailed decree adopted by TsIK at its session of April 1926 to replace the decree of October 1924.[6] Its main purpose was to carry the process of decentralization down from the department and the county to the city, the rural district and the district. City and rural district budgets, explained the rapporteur, were to become the " fundamental cells " of the system of local taxation. While, however, he linked village budgets with city and rural district budgets as a means of contact with the masses, he was less encouraging about their prospects : it would be necessary in the first instance to study the experiment of village budgets in the few villages where they had been introduced.

[1] Soveshchanie po Voprosam Sovetskogo Stroitel'stva 1925 g. : Aprel' (1925), pp. 184-185.

[2] For this resolution see p. 460, note 5 above.

[3] Vestnik Finansov, No. 7, July 1925, p. 252.

[4] Planovoe Khozyaistvo, No. 6, 1925, p. 216 ; for an experiment with village budgets in the Ural region see Raionirovanie SSSR, ed. K. Egorov (1925), p. 275.

[5] SSSR : Tsentral'nyi Ispolnitel'nyi Komitet 3 Sozyva : 2 Sessiya (1926), p. 441 ; for the concentration of " villages " see p. 298 above.

[6] SSSR : Tsentral'nyi Ispolnitel'nyi Komitet 3 Sozyva : 2 Sessiya : Postanovleniya (1926), p. 76 ; the decree is also in Sobranie Zakonov, 1926, No. 31, art. 199. For the decree of October 1924 see p. 456 above.

Nor should it be supposed that decentralization implied any weakening of control by the central authorities ; such control was required by the principle of planning and by the necessity of subventions. But, subject to this limitation, direct control was to be transferred from the union to the republican governments.   In reply to questions the *rapporteur* agreed that villages might exercise a right of " self-taxation " in the form of service in kind for road building ; but the consent of the rural district executive committee should be required.[1] The decree declared the district, rural district and city budgets to be the " fundamental local budgets ", the budgets of the higher local authorities being " regulating budgets in relation to the lower budgets ". This measure of devolution, designed to bring financial administration into closer contact with the population, appears to have been its main significance.

[1] For the *rapporteur's* speech and concluding remarks see *SSSR : Tsentral'-nyi Ispolnitel'nyi Komitet 3 Sozyva : 2 Sessiya* (1926), pp. 882-916, 1024-1035.

NOTE B

PEASANT COMMITTEES OF MUTUAL AID

THE peasant committees of mutual aid (krestkomy), which had been a subject of dissension at the thirteenth party congress in May 1924,[1] were among the institutions called on to play their part in the general policy of strengthening relations with the countryside. An attempt to breathe new life into them was made in a decree of the RSFSR of September 1924. This defined their functions as the rendering of aid to families of soldiers and war veterans and, in general, to the poorest parts of the population, the struggle with the problems of homeless children, prostitution and drunkenness, and the organization of co-operatives and other forms of collective enterprise : this last measure was apparently expected to provide funds for the krestkomy, which were otherwise dependent solely on the contributions of members. The only recognition in the decree of the class character which some had wished to impart to the krestkomy was the inclusion among their functions of the provision of legal aid, especially to those seeking dissolution of oppressive labour contracts.[2] The decree settled nothing. While some continued to hope, and some to fear, that the krestkomy would emulate the rôle of the committees of poor peasants of 1918 by leading a new campaign against the *kulak*, others drew attention to the apparently more immediate danger that they would fall under the domination of the *kulaks*.[3] Kalinin, the strongest official champion of the krestkomy, admitted that many regarded them with doubt and dissatisfaction, and was reduced to the argument that, since the Soviet Government was faced with " the exceptionally difficult task of organizing the millions of peasants in a country where habits of organization are particularly weak ", it could not afford to neglect the help which even the krestkomy could render.[4]

In one respect the krestkomy repeated the history of the kombedy : they, too, were potential rivals of the village Soviets and excited opposition on that score. The conference on the revitalization of the Soviets

[1] See *The Interregnum, 1923–1924*, pp. 148-149.
[2] *Sobranie Uzakonenii, 1924*, No. 81, art. 813.
[3] *Bol'shevik*, No. 12-13, October 20, 1924, p. 85 ; the opposite complaint was also heard that provincial and county party committees sometimes interfered in the affairs of the local krestkomy, claiming to nominate their presidiums and dispose of their funds (*Pravda*, October 3, 1924).
[4] *Leningradskaya Pravda*, October 6, 1924.

which met in January and April 1925 was on the whole unfavourable
to the krestkomy. Kiselev, an official spokesman, thought that the
rural district executive committees should "direct to some extent the
activity of the krestkomy", and launched a violent attack on the corruption of krestkomy officials. In some cases the payments made to
them swallowed up more than 80 per cent of the revenue of the committee ; in others the officials had broken up and sold for timber
buildings placed at the disposal of the committee. Some krestkomy
ran efficient enterprises and made profits. But this was at the expense
of the village or rural district Soviet organs for whose benefit the
enterprises could otherwise be run.[1] Other critics alleged that " mutual
aid " was absent from everything but the name of the committees. At
best they administered " direct aid " on social security principles ; at
worst, they persuaded the middle peasant to lend his horse to the poor
peasant in return for an undertaking by the poor peasant to scythe
and reap and thresh for him, thus organizing a form of " concealed
exploitation ". Another speaker excused the faults of the krestkomy
on the ground that they were " utilized by *kulaks* ".[2] A more popular
criticism was directed against the " multiplicity of organizations " in
the village — the village meeting, the *mir*, the village Soviet, the peasant
committee of mutual aid ; the krestkomy were not only " lifeless ",
but " put a brake on the work of the village Soviets ".[3] Only one
delegate had a point to make in their favour :

> The peasants say : " The committee of mutual aid is ours, it
> works for us ; the village Soviet is not ours, it oppresses us ".[4]

Molotov at the fourteenth party congress in December 1925 mentioned
the committees without enthusiasm, and noted with approval a reduction in their number due to the elimination of " many paper
krestkomy ".[5] Three months later a party report admitted that the
" mistrustful " attitude of the peasants to the krestkomy was shared
by many lower party workers.[6] The committees continued to exist
for several years, but never attained social or political importance.
A detached observer, summing up their record in 1927, thought
that they fell between two stools, being neither genuine charitable
organizations nor genuine cooperatives, and called them " a still-born
institution ".[7]

---

[1] *Soveshchanie po Voprosam Sovetskogo Stroitel'stva 1925 g. : Aprel'* (1925),
pp. 23-24. [2] *Ibid.* pp. 34, 35, 52. [3] *Ibid.* pp. 44, 64.
[4] *Ibid.* p. 51.
[5] *XIV S"ezd Vsesoyuznoi Kommunisticheskoi Partii (B)* (1926), p. 70.
[6] *Izvestiya Tsentral'nogo Komiteta Vsesoyuznoi Kommunisticheskoi Partii (B)*
No. 8 (129), March 1, 1926, p. 1.
[7] A. M. Bolshakov, *Sovetskaya Derevnya, 1917–1927* (1927), p. 149.

NOTE C

REVOLUTIONARY LEGALITY

THE elusive concept of " revolutionary legality " continued to play an important rôle in the discussion of legal and administrative questions in the middle nineteen-twenties. It had first arisen in the period 1921–1922 when it had served to provide an ideological basis both for the system of regular civil-law relations required by NEP, and for a system of uniform administration under legal guarantees to replace the uninhibited initiative of revolutionary caprice. In the latter capacity it was closely associated with the office of the procurator who became the supreme custodian of revolutionary legality.[1] The qualifying epithet " revolutionary " was at this time commonly forgotten ; and the concept appeared to represent the principles of security and uniformity as against the principles of revolution and class warfare.

It was no accident that the " Face to the countryside " policy adopted in the autumn of 1924, followed by the turn towards the well-to-do peasant and the campaign for the revitalization of the Soviets, should have inspired a renewal of the cult of " revolutionary legality ". Bukharin commended it in November 1924 as a " forced ' normalization ' of the Soviet regime " in the interest of the peasant, and declared that " the peasant must have before him Soviet *order*, Soviet *right*, Soviet *law* ".[2] The days when the peasantry was interested in the forcible acquisition of landowners' land, or when the poor peasant was incited to seize the stocks of the *kulak*, were as far away as the days when the Bolsheviks were concerned to overthrow legally constituted authority. The government now wanted only to govern, the well-to-do peasant to possess and to cultivate : both needed the stability of law. Molotov explained apologetically that Lenin's famous phrase " Loot what has been looted from you " had been uttered " in the most heated period of October ", and had been intended merely as a paraphrase in plain Russian of " the expropriation of the expropriators ".[3] Semashko, the People's Commissar for Health, offered a more homely illustration of the function of law :

[1] See Vol. 1, pp. 74-75, 81-85.
[2] *Bol'shevik*, No. 14, November 5, 1924, p. 34.
[3] *Pravda*, December 9, 1924 ; for the phrase see *The Bolshevik Revolution, 1917-1923*, Vol. 2, p. 94.

Once a citizen has by our laws the right to possess a complete suit of clothes, nobody has the right to strip him on the principle of equality simply because he happens to meet on the street a man without a suit of clothes.[1]

Revolutionary legality seemed in this context the very expression of the policy which Bukharin attempted to crystallize in the unfortunate slogan " Enrich yourselves ".

But the other special connotation of revolutionary legality — the rule of law in administration — was also important, and typical of a time when the establishment of an orderly and efficient Soviet system in the countryside had become a major objective. The discussion on revolutionary legality at the conference on the revitalization of the Soviets in January 1925 [2] was a direct contribution to this purpose. Kaganovich expressly commended it on the ground of its appeal to the peasant :

We must and can here and now make the peasant feel that we are striving, not in word but in deed, to combat cases of caprice, bureaucratism, corruption and all kinds of irregularities such as we have at present.[3]

Kalinin in turn explained that revolutionary legality " signifies that it is indispensable to resort as little as possible to administrative orders — one might say, to administrative caprice, even if this caprice pursues the most excellent ends — and that it is indispensable to introduce scrupulous regularity in the sphere of administration " ; and the conference readily passed a resolution " On Strengthening the Principles of Revolutionary Legality ".[4] The question was pursued at the fourteenth party conference three months later, where revolutionary legality appeared for the first time as an item on the party agenda. On the eve of the conference *Pravda* published the text of Lenin's confidential letter of May 1922 complaining of the " sea of lawlessness " in which Soviet affairs were immersed, and of " local influence " as the great enemy of legality.[5] The conference took the hint, adding to its resolution in support of revolutionary legality the qualification " especially in the lower organs of government ".[6] A resolution of the third Congress of Soviets of the USSR in the following month once more identified

---

[1] *Pravda*, December 30, 1924.   [2] See p. 326 above.

[3] *Soveshchanie po Voprosam Sovetskogo Stroitel'stva 1925 g. : Yanvar'* (1925), p. 115 ; at the session of the conference in April 1925 one delegate alleged that " local militia men freely arrest peasants at any time — you can settle with them later ", and that this happened " almost everywhere and on almost every question " (*id. : Aprel'* (1925), p. 164).

[4] *Id. : Yanvar'* (1925), pp. 210, 219-221.

[5] *Pravda*, April 23, 1925 ; for the letter see Vol. i, pp. 81-82.

[6] *VKP(B) v Rezolyutsiyakh* (1941), ii, 25.

revolutionary legality with the struggle against " administrative caprice, bribe-taking, rude and inconsiderate treatment of citizens and in general examples of abuse of power of every kind ".[1] Bukharin explained that " revolutionary legality should *replace all remnants of administrative caprice, even if that should be revolutionary* ".[2] The cult of legality, while it registered the victory of the new phase of the revolution which had set in with NEP, was specifically directed to the practical task of improving the administration, and continued to be associated with the policy of revitalizing the local Soviets.

The strengthening of revolutionary legality brought enhanced authority and prestige to the Procurator of the Supreme Court. Among the concrete recommendations of the conference on the revitalization of the Soviets was one that representatives of the procurator's department should tour the villages to inspect the administration, and to receive and examine " complaints of the population against bureaucratism, administrative caprice and similar breaches of the law ".[3] During the next year this part of the procurator's functions multiplied rapidly.[4] The work ran parallel to that of Rabkrin, the procurator being concerned with legality, Rabkrin with efficiency ; and an attempt was made, no doubt in default of other personnel, to draw the *rabkors* and *sel'kors* into it. At the fourteenth party conference in April 1925 Solts eulogized them as " defenders of revolutionary legality " against administrative abuses.[5] The journal of Narkomvnudel described the procurator and the *rabkors* and *sel'kors* as " blood brothers ", and gave an account of the large number of reports on offences of all kinds sent by *rabkors* and *sel'kors* to the office of the Moscow provincial procurator.[6]

[1] *Sobranie Zakonov*, 1925, No. 35, art. 247.
[2] N. Bukharin, *Put' k Sotsializmu i Rabochii-Krest'yanskii Soyuz* (1925), p. 79.
[3] According to a report of Skrypnik from the Ukraine, representatives of the procurator first appeared in the districts and villages in 1924 ; at the outset this caused friction with party workers, but later it was recognized that they had done good work in checking administrative abuses (*Radyan'ska Ukraina*, No. 13 (19), April 1926, pp. 9-20). Initial friction with the party is confirmed in *Bol'shevik*, No. 1, January 15, 1926, p. 43, and *Sovetskoe Stroitel'stvo : Sbornik*, iv-v (1926), 68-69.
[4] *Vlast' Sovetov*, No. 44, November 1, 1925, pp. 4-6, under the title *The Struggle for Revolutionary Legality* reviewed the complaints received by provincial offices of the procuratorship in the first half of 1925 — 14,000 in all ; in the first half of 1926 the procurator's department is said to have received 166,000 complaints (*Sovetskoe Stroitel'stvo : Sbornik*, iv-v (1926), 63). But it is not clear that the figures are comparable.
[5] *Chetyrnadtsataya Konferentsiya Rossiiskoi Kommunisticheskoi Partii (Bol'-shevikov)* (1925), pp. 248, 251-252.
[6] *Vlast' Sovetov*, No. 30, July 26, 1925, pp. 18-19. Their activities as informers can hardly have increased their popularity locally : " *kulaks* and simply criminal elements " were said to be carrying on a campaign to bring

A circular of the central control commission instructed local organs of Rabkrin to keep in touch with the *rabkors* and *sel'kors* in their regions and draw them into the work of Rabkrin and of the control commissions.[1]

At a later period, when agrarian policy had moved towards the Left, and when it was desired to discredit Bukharin, attention was once more drawn to the epithet " revolutionary " applied to legality, and the undue emphasis placed at this time on legality pure and simple was treated as a deviation.

against the *rabkor* and *sel'kor* " charges that discredit him " (*ibid*. No. 5, January 31, 1926, p. 4).   Later they were commonly believed to act as informers for the OGPU.

    [1] *Spravochnik Partiinogo Rabotnika*, v, 1925 (1926), pp. 506-507.

LIST OF ABBREVIATIONS

(Supplementary to List in Vol. I, pp. 537-539)

Glavpolitprosvet = Glavnyi Politiko-Prosvetitel'nyi Komitet (Chief Committee for Political Education).

Istpart = Komitet po Istorii Oktyabr'skoi Revolyutsii Vsesoyuznoi Kommunisticheskoi Partii (Committee of the All-Union Communist Party for the History of the October Revolution).

Komvuz = Kommunisticheskoe Vysshee Uchebnoe Zavedenie (Communist Higher Education Establishment).

MAPP = Moskovskaya Assotsiatsiya Proletarskikh Pisatelei (Moscow Association of Proletarian Writers).

Narkomyust = Narodnyi Komissariat Yustitsii (People's Commissariat of Justice).

Orgraspred = Organizatsionno-Raspredelitel'nyi Otdel (Organization and Distribution Section).

Politprosvet = Politiko-Prosvetitel'nyi Komitet (Committee for Political Education).

PUR = Politicheskoe Upravlenie Revvoensoveta (Political Administration of the Revolutionary Military Council).

RAPP = Russkaya Assotsiatsiya Proletarskikh Pisatelei (Russian Association of Proletarian Writers).

Sovnarkhoz = Sovet Narodnogo Khozyaistva (Council of National Economy).

Uchraspred = Uchetno-Raspredelitel'nyi Otdel (Account and Distribution Section).

VLKSM = Vsesoyuznyi Leninskii Kommunisticheskii Soyuz Molodezhi (All-Union Leninist Communist League of Youth).

Vsevobuch = Glavnoe Upravlenie Vseobshchego Voennogo Obucheniya (Chief Administration of Universal Military Training).

ZSFSR = Zakavkazskaya Sotsialisticheskaya Federativnaya Sovetskaya Respublika (Transcaucasian Socialist Federal Soviet Republic).

INDEX

196-199, 201 ; and party appointments, 198, 201-214 ; and "platform of the 46", 199, 204, 209-210, 217-219, 395-396 ; and the "apparatus", 199-201, 210-211, 223, 369 n. ; and party officials, 199-201, 205, 209, 214, 216, 314-317, 320, 369 n. ; and bureaucracy, 200-201, 210 ; and Uchraspred, 202-204, 206-207, 209, 211 ; and "mass mobilizations", 202, 204 ; and promotion, 203-204, 207 ; and Orgraspred, 204, 206, 209, 211-212, 218, 221 ; and dictatorship of the proletariat, 205 ; and election to posts, 205-206, 208-209, 211-213, 224 ; and Moscow provincial party committee, 205-206 ; and nomination to posts, 206-212 ; and school for county party secretaries, 209 ; reprisals in, 210-211, 213-214, 216, 218-220 ; and dissenters, 211, 214, 216, 219-220, 222-224, 454 ; and regionalization, 212-213, 274-275, 279-280, 288, 292-293, 351 ; and power of dismissal and transfer, 213-214 ; and party orthodoxy, 213-214, 216-217, 219, 222, 224, 448 ; and criticism, 215 ; and Rabkrin, 215, 217 n. ; ethical code of, 216-217 ; expulsions from, 216, 218-219, 223, 224 n., 311 ; suicides in, 218 ; and "Pililenko affair", 218-220 ; and democratic centralists, 218-219, 367 n., 375 ; and loyalty to party and state, 219-220 ; and new criminal code, 220 ; and Cheka, 220-221 ; and OGPU, 221, 454 ; recantations in, 221-222 ; and "monolithism", 222-224 ; and personal dictatorship, 224, 226-227 ; headquarters of, moved to Moscow, 224-225 ; and party bosses, 225-226 ; and system of "principalities" 225-226 ; national units of, 252 ; and Soviets, 305-306, 311-321, 323-327, 331-332, 334-335, 337-341, 345-346, 348-351, 354, 360, 362-364, 367-371, 457-458, 460-462, 469, 470 n. ; and administrative decentralization, 319-320 ; and peasant committees of mutual aid, 320, 466-467 ; and anti-religious propaganda, 324, 344 ; and alliance with middle peasants, 346 ; and

bourgeoisie, 363, 367 ; and "military opposition", 375-378 ; and Red Fleet, 416-417, 419 ; and Kronstadt rising, 416, 448 ; and penal policy, 421-422, 428 n., 436-438, 440, 444, 447-449, 452 ; and revolutionary legality, 438-439, 444, 469-470 ; and revolutionary expediency, 444-445. *See also* Bolshevism, Bolsheviks ; Menshevism, Mensheviks

All - Union Leninist Communist League of Youth (Komsomol) [*formerly* Russian Leninist Communist League of Youth, *previously* Russian Communist League of Youth] : sixth congress, 1924, 3, 94 ; change of name, 3, 161 ; and Communist Youth International, 18, 92 ; and Trotsky, 23, 53, 89, 91-97, 101 ; and struggle between Leningrad and Moscow, 53, 95-98, 102, 104-106, 113 n., 129 ; and *Molodaya Gvardiya*, 76, 96 n. ; and literature, 76-77 ; founded, 88 ; first congress, 1918, 88, 94, 97 ; and party, 88-107, 147, 149, 157 n., 160-162, 178, 214, 221, 341-342 ; finances of, 89, 107 ; second congress, 1919, 89, 91 ; and Narkompros, 89 n. ; and military crisis of 1919, 89 ; and trade unions, 89-90 ; third congress, 1920, 89-91 ; disputes in, 89-106 ; and Soviets, 90, 317-318, 326, 331, 334, 359 ; and "workers' opposition", 90 ; and *klassoviki*, 90 ; proletarian character of, 90-91, 97-98, 101-104, 106 ; and freedom of discussion, 90 ; and students, 91-92, 102, 188 ; and intellectuals, 91, 99 ; membership of, 91-92, 94-95, 99-104, 106, 179, 186, 188 ; concentration of power within, 91 ; purge of, 1921, 91, 99 ; as focus of opposition, 91-96, 107, 160-162 ; and "platform of the 46", 91 ; fourth congress, 1921, 91, 99 ; fifth congress, 1922, 91 ; conference of, 1923, 91 ; and political neutrality, 93, 106-107 ; and NEP, 94 ; and Lenin enrolment, 94 ; and *Lessons of October*, 95 ; seventh congress, 1926, 96 n., 103 n. 104, 161, 214, 221 ; and "socialism in one country", 96 n. ; purge of, 1925, 98 ; social composition of,

THE END